CONTENTS

2   CYBER-ASSURANCE THROUGH EMBEDDED SECURITY FOR THE INTERNET OF THINGS   101

Tyson T. Brooks and Joon Park

3   A SECURE UPDATE MECHANISM FOR INTERNET OF THINGS DEVICES   129

Martin Goldberg

PART II TRUST IMPACT   137

PART III WEARABLE AUTOMATION PROVENANCE   175

10   AN ARTIFICIAL INTELLIGENCE PERSPECTIVE ON ENSURING CYBER-ASSURANCE FOR THE INTERNET OF THINGS   249

Utku Köse

11   PERCEIVED THREAT MODELING FOR CYBER-PHYSICAL SYSTEMS   257

Christopher Leberknight

APPENDICES

A   LIST OF IEEE INTERNET OF THINGS STANDARDS   283

B   GLOSSARY   319

LIST OF FIGURES

LIST OF TABLES

FOREWORD

Effective Cyber-Assurance Will be Essential for the Internet of Things

ZEAL ZIRING
Information Assurance Technical Director, National Security Agency,
Fort Meade, MD, USA

Our society has become substantially dependent upon the Internet, on the ability to access and use cyberspace, in a wide variety of ways. The Internet has given us amazing capabilities to exchange information, conduct commerce, enlighten, and entertain. But for all of the development and growth of the Internet, the virtual world and the physical world were at most lightly connected, often through the actions of people. The domain of packets and protocols was always separate from the world of fields, roads, and buildings. No longer the virtual world and the physical are becoming increasingly intertwined. The interposition has profound potential for benefits and for harm. This revolution-in-progress has been dubbed the Internet of Things (IoT), and cyber-physical systems (CPS), and various other names. It is a complex trend, founded on technology advances, but with economic and social drivers. It is already well underway, though we are feeling only modest effects so far.

As IoT technologies and capabilities become more prevalent, and eventually ubiquitous, many aspects of the physical world will become more visible from cyberspace. In some cases, processes in cyberspace will influence or control physical objects and environments. Points of contact between the physical world and the virtual will proliferate. There have been many estimates of how many connected "things" will be dispersed through our physical environment during the growth of IoT, from 10 to 50, to even 200 billion. As a result of the greatly increased integration between physical and virtual worlds, our dependence upon the Internet and associated technologies will increase.

There have been many books and articles written about the technologies driving the IoT, and the wonderful benefits we will realize from it. But those benefits are not certain. As the physical world becomes more dependent on the virtual, threats that are today confined to cyberspace will expand and transform. The benefits we hope to enjoy will be at risk, subject to attacks mediated and scaled by cyberspace. This book is about understanding those risks: why they arise, how they differ from cyber risks that we face today, and especially how to address them.

SOME HISTORY

There have been many histories written about the Internet, focused on technology or people or other factors. One way of looking at the Internet is how it grew from convergence of previously independent systems and domains. This is relevant to understanding the IoT and the importance of its cyber-assurance, because it represents the biggest convergence yet.

From the beginnings of telephony and radio, military and civilian communications were distinct and separated. From the time of World War II, they used different technologies and different means of protection. Military communications were usually encrypted, used different frequency bands protocols, and infrastructure from their civilian counterparts. Since its creation in 1952, the National Security Agency (NSA) designed and codified the security necessary for national security communications, including military. Working there, it became clear around 1990 that convergence was inevitable. Over the course of two decades, from the mid-1990s to today, military and civilian (commercial) communications have become much closer: common technologies, protocols, infrastructure, and standards underpin both. Levels of cryptographic strength that were first envisioned for safeguarding national security are now used to protect both strategic intelligence and social media. Tactical military operations still use specialized radios, but they also use commercial smartphones and cellular standards. From the military side, convergence has been driven mainly by the greater functionality and capability available from the commercial products. From the commercial side, adoption of security mechanisms formerly confined to national security applications has been driven by the need for assurance and privacy for business conducted online.

Another convergence is still underway, though nearly complete: convergence of voice telephony and data networks. Voice telephony networks came first, of course, and by the time computing began to grow in the 1960s, national and international telephone networks were already well-established. In fact, the telephone network was so large and reliable that early digital communications used it as an infrastructure, converting digital data from serial lines into modulated audio signals, transferring them over the telephone networks, and then converting them back into bits at the other end. But over the course of the 1970s and 1980s, the telephone network itself became digital, and the same switching networks were used to carry voice calls and dedicated digital links (so-called "leased lines"). Some of the earliest wide-area data exchanges, such as bulletin boards and Usenet, employed these technologies. But at the same time, the foundations of packet networking were being created in universities and companies and the U.S. Department of Defense (DoD).

By the early 1980s, many of the key technologies were in place for the Internet to begin exponential growth. But the telephony network was still built around static trunks lines and circuit switching. Over the course of the 1990s and 2000s, the core technologies of packet switching and Internet protocols were integrated into global telephony networks, and voice became just another kind of digital traffic on packet networks. Today, the global network fabric is entirely packet-based, and the distinction between voice service and data service is visible mainly for cellular systems. But the convergence of formerly independent voice and data networks has had security consequences. Voice telephony services can be attacked over data networks, but assurances built into modern networks can help protect both voice and data services.

One more convergence is also underway, and is especially relevant here: the convergence of industrial networks and public data networks. Computer control of industrial systems began in the 1960s with direct digital control (DDC) systems. The first programmable logic controller (PLC) system was built in 1968. By the late 1970s, PLCs were being connected using modems, serial links, and proprietary protocols. Standards for interoperability and transport of industrial control protocols over Transmission Control Protocol/Internet Protocol (TCP/IP) emerged in the early 1990s, but control systems were still connected and managed over dedicated links or leased lines. But since about 2000, controlling industrial systems over the Internet has been growing rapidly. There are several drivers for this convergence: reduced cost, greater operational flexibility, and especially integration of industrial control and monitoring systems with business systems. The benefits are substantial, but exposing industrial systems to direct or indirect access from the Internet imposes substantial risks. Control system components are generally designed for reliability, simplicity, and economy. Repeated tests by government, academic, and commercial labs have identified numerous vulnerabilities, consistently across the industry, for well over a decade. The trend toward connecting industrial control systems to the Internet, and integrating them with other Internet systems, is sometimes called "the industrial Internet," as if it were a separate network – it is not.

Along with the convergence history sketched above, there is a parallel history of malicious activities directed at computers and data networks. That history is documented in multiple books and papers, only a few highlights are necessary to illustrate the growth of the threat. In the pre-Internet years, computers and networks were certainly subject to malicious acts, but they were relatively narrow in scope. Some early personal computer (PC) viruses propagated fairly widely, but were confined to a very narrow range of operating systems and applications. Military networks were subject to passive collection by nation-state actors, but that was expected and the risks posed were manageable – risks from passive collection can be managed with effective encryption.

In the early years of the global Internet, there were many large-scale malicious events, beginning with the Morris Worm in 1988, and continuing through the 1990s and into the early 2000s. While these infections garnered headlines, there was also a quiet growth of more sophisticated malware and capabilities for espionage. Also, with the growth of the World Wide Web (www), there was a corresponding growth in web defacement attacks. During much of this period, the value of information stored and business conducted on the Internet was modest. Many malicious actors were motivated by notoriety: releasing a virus that spread worldwide garnered acclaim from peers. Web sites were important to the image of a company or government agency, and thus web defacers attacked the element of value that was most accessible to them. The primary suppliers of computer and network technology also began to take security much more seriously during this period. As an example, in 1992, Microsoft's flagship product was Windows 3.1, which shipped with effectively no security; by 2000, their flagship Windows 2000 product included a broad array of security features.

In the most recent decade, convergence has driven large portions of our economy, government, and society onto the Internet. The increase of value and diversity of connected systems and services has driven a corresponding growth and diversification of malicious activities. For example, greater use of Internet services for banking was quickly followed by Internet crime targeting bank accounts and transactions. Similarly, as national governments and economies became more dependent on the Internet, governments around the world have increased their use of the Internet as a domain for collecting intelligence and pressuring rivals. Many nations, including the United States, have incorporated cyberspace operations into their military doctrine.

We have also seen the first Internet-borne attacks where effects have extended beyond cyberspace into the physical world. Most of the early ones were accidental, denials of service by PC malware infecting PCs used to manage industrial controls. But by 2008, it was clear that some actors were deliberately targeting power utilities to conduct extortion. In 2010, the Stuxnet worm was discovered; it appeared to have been targeted at a particular industrial installation, propagated over the Internet and other networks, and caused physical damage to that installation (as well as disruption elsewhere).

The clear message from history is this: attacks follow value. The more value and dependence we place on the Internet, the greater motivation malicious actors, criminals, and hostile regimes will have to operate there. We are in the early stages of the biggest convergence yet, and the assurance we will require with be commensurately great.

THE BREADTH AND DIVERSITY OF THE INTERNET OF THINGS

The IoT is a very broad phenomenon, ranging across nearly every sector of industry, many different technology standards, and geographic scales. It encompasses both the connected "things" and the various data analysis, management, and infrastructure services with which they interact. The data and interaction are the foundation for the benefits we expect to gain – a single car with an Internet connection might help one driver navigate to their destination, but when a majority of cars are connected, analytics and active management will keep traffic flowing efficiently across a city. Innovative companies are devising new models for analyzing data and acting on it in sectors like housing, transportation, manufacturing, healthcare, public safety, energy, retail, and more.

The standards landscape for IoT is complicated, and in many areas, standards are still emerging or evolving rapidly. Standards are essential for IoT because they foster interoperability, stability, and innovation. There are many areas where standards will be essential, but four are particularly relevant to IoT cyber-security.

- Cellular communication – the radio spectrum is a finite, precious resource. As more devices join the Internet, managing the availability of that resource for all of them will be critical.
- Personal Area Networks (PAN) – standards for very short-range data exchange among wearable and nearby devices are still evolving to support all the capabilities and assurances we will need.
- Security and cryptography – most existing secure protocols, credential schemes, and other standards were designed for the world of desktop computers and enterprise servers. Standards will be needed to provide basic security services to large numbers of small, constrained devices. These services include identity and credential management, authorization, data protection, and more. As discussed below, IoT will impose new requirements in provisioning, efficiency, and scale.
- Sensing and data management – some of IoT's greatest benefits will flow from sensing aspects of the physical world, and exposing that data for analysis and fusion in cyberspace. Standards will be needed for representing and managing vast amounts of sensor data.

IoT devices will use a variety of modalities in connecting to the Internet. Some will be accessible only when activated by something else, such as a radio frequency identification (RFID) tag reader. Others will have periodic interaction, delivering data or accepting commands, but otherwise quiet (e.g., an implanted medical device, a weather sensor). Many devices will expect continuous connectivity to deliver data or allow remote entities to exert real-time control (e.g., a smart TV, an electrical substation monitor) and still others will act as local gateways, supporting local interaction and providing Internet connectivity for other devices within their scope (e.g., a smart car, bus, or train).

As described above, IoT will offer us enormous benefits, but most of those benefits will depend on some form of trust. We will need confidence enough in the operation of IoT devices and supporting services to entrust them with control of physical systems and environments. We will need confidence that the data delivered from sensors is accurate in order to rely on them when making personal, business, and even military decisions. Establishing and maintaining necessary trust will be challenging in many ways. Complete and comprehensive trust is not usually possible, even for narrowly scoped traditional computers. Instead, we will need to build systems that can deliver specific kinds of trust. We will need trust management and associated assurances at several levels for IoT systems: individual devices, populations of devices, users, services, and infrastructure.

WHAT IS CYBER-ASSURANCE FOR THE INTERNET OF THINGS, AND WHY DOES IT MATTER?

At the highest level, assurance for the IoT is just like assurance for other elements of cyberspace. But the scale and constraints of IoT, and the potential impacts of assurance failures, will mean that current strategies for achieving assurance will not be sufficient.

The five basic assurance properties are:

1. Authenticity – assurance that an entity claiming an identity does possess the right to use it. Assigning and authenticating identities will be challenging for IoT.
2. Integrity – assurance that information is created, modified, and deleted only by entities with the rights to do so.
3. Confidentiality – assurance that information is accessible or readable only by entities with requisite rights.
4. Availability – assurance that information or services are available or accessible under all conditions that it is supposed to be.
5. Non-repudiation – assurance that an action can be irrefutably bound to an accountable entity.

These assurances are primitives. By using and combining them, systems can offer higher order properties, such as privacy, legal compliance, or resilience. All of them will be important to the secure operation of IoT devices and the services they will support.

In addition to direct security risks to devices, IoT will have profound effects on the risk posture of traditional systems and networks to which they are attached. Connecting a broad range of IoT devices to conventional networks will expand the attack surface for those networks. To support the devices, conventional networks will have to support a broader set of protocols and data formats, adding new potential for exploitable vulnerabilities. Finally, many IoT use cases bridge traditional trust boundaries, or require system owners to establish new trust relationships. Build assurance into IoT devices and systems will be essential for managing these risks too.

Achieving the basic assurance properties for conventional networks has proven extremely difficult – recent security incidents have shown us that our technical measures and practices are not sufficient to prevent adverse impacts from cyber-attacks. Achieving the basic properties will be even more difficult for IoT systems. Why? First, the scale and diversity of IoT will require approaches and standards that span a very wide range. Device capabilities vary along several axes, such as computation speed, data storage, and communication bandwidth. For connected devices, some of these capabilities will vary over six orders of magnitude or more, from tiny tags and sensors to smart vehicles and buildings.

Another challenge for supporting assurance for connected devices and service is their diversity of security needs. Some devices will need very tight security rights – for example, an implanted medical device will have very high integrity requirements, and should deliver data only to the patient and authorized doctors; in contrast, a weather sensor might offer data to any requester. Longevity will also present a challenge for assuring some IoT devices. Some devices will have the power and bandwidth to accept frequent security updates, but others will not. Some types of sensors, for example, will have to operate for years, and cannot be expected to receive any software updates or trust anchor updates in that time. This means that the security mechanisms built into such devices will need to be exceptionally simple and robust.

Finally, there will be many assurance challenges for IoT based on the relative immaturity of the law, policy, and practices for assuring IoT device data and access. Consider a smart building – what parties should be authorized to read the sensor data from the building's systems? The building owner? The tenants? The local fire department? Maintenance workers, such as plumbers or electricians? Each of these stakeholders has a good rationale for accessing portions of the building's data or adjusting aspects of the building's operation. But neither the technical controls, legal precedents, nor accepted practices are ready to support them.

The IoT will let us use the flexibility and power of information technology to sense, understand, manage, and optimize many aspects of the physical world, from wearables on a single person, to a retail store, to a highway system. We can only depend on IoT to do these things for us, and enjoy the corresponding benefits, if we have certain essential assurances. The list below is based on the fundamental properties, but is tuned to be actionable for designers and builder of IoT systems:

- Assurance that collected data are valid (i.e., values reported are values sensed).
- Assurance that access to collected data is appropriately constrained.
- Assurance that control over devices is exercised only by authorized parties, and that those parties can be held accountable.
- Assurance that applicable laws, regulations, and policies are enforced.
- Assurance that the interactions between IoT systems and other cyber systems can be monitored and controlled.
- Assurance that overall security properties continue to hold as individual devices or components are updated or replaced.

The most important security properties for IoT will be system properties, assurances that are offered by, qualified over, and dependent upon multiple layers of hardware and software, service providers, data aggregation middleware, and presentation systems.

EXAMPLES

The examples below examine the assurance challenges for four different IoT scenarios.

Example 1 – A medical implant with connection to the Internet can offer faster detection of health problems, more nuanced responses, and better overall health monitoring. The devices themselves are subject to serious limitations on size, power consumption, and connectivity. There are immediate risks to use of such a device – a cyber-attack against it might pose direct threat to the user's health and safety. But an attack that alters data reported by a device may also pose such a threat, because medical treatment might be based on it. There are also strong privacy concerns around the collected data. Assurance for data access will be complex, because there are multiple stakeholders: the patient, their doctors, hospitals, first responders, insurance companies, the device manufacturer, etc. Also, medical devices and health data are subject to a complex regulatory regime that is still adapting to cyber threats.

Example 2 – A connected car will support a wide variety of use cases, from simple collision avoidance to entertainment to maintenance to full autonomous operation. There are large potential benefits for transportation safety and efficiency. Such a complex system will also have a complicated authorization model, with different rights for the driver, the mechanic, the manufacturer, highway systems, and network infrastructure. Some operations will be subject to hard real-time constraints, while others involve communication with the global Internet. Interactions between vehicles and smart highway systems are still being defined, but imply a very close trust relationship. Recent vulnerability demonstrations from researchers have shown that current vehicle telematics systems do not enforce trust boundaries effectively, that will have to change. Lastly, connected cars will connect to a wide variety of other networks, in owner's homes, at maintenance facilities, and while on the highway. There will need to be very specific and bounded trust relationships between each car and these networks.

Example 3 – Smart buildings will contain a wide variety of sensors, actuators, and control systems for a wide variety of purposes: lighting, safety, heating and cooling, entry control, and more. Many of these systems are installed to improve the cost efficiency of a building, or make it more hospitable to users. There will be some privacy or confidentiality concerns for the collected data. But the primary risks will be based on control: abuse of the control systems within a building can make it uninhabitable or even damage it. Control integrity and authorization will be key assurance concerns for smart buildings, but as noted above, the set of authorized users for such buildings will be large and diverse. In addition to the exposure from connection to the Internet, many building automation technologies employ wireless networks, using standards such as Wi-Fi, ZigBee, and Bluetooth. These can leave the network of a building exposed to anyone with physical proximity.

Example 4 – Sensor networks offer the potential from monitoring physical conditions across many different environments and locales. An ocean sensor network, for example, might be composed of sensor buoys, communication relays, and other floating and anchored elements. The components of the network will be widely distributed and subject to harsh conditions and uncertain connectivity.

The components may be power-constrained, expected to operate for long periods on stored power. The data collected from such sensors may be public, but its integrity may be critical for ocean navigation and weather prediction. Data from the sensor network will be fused with other sources in analytic systems, where there is likely to be much greater value to attract threat actors. This implies a need to manage the trust between the sensor network and the analysis systems, to prevent compromise of a sensor propagating upward.

These four examples show several common elements. First, integrity is a crucial concern for most IoT use cases – integrity of reported data, and integrity of control. Second, many of the suppliers that produce components for various IoT sectors have not, historically, had to worry about cyber-assurance for their products – it is only now that their products are exposed to such threats. Third, there is no simple model or universal model for trust relationships in these use cases. Each of them includes a variety of stakeholders with different roles and rights. Finally, none of the connected devices in these use cases operate independently, they all interact with other infrastructures and systems, and both inherit risks from and impose risks on those systems.

KEY ELEMENTS OF CYBER-ASSURANCE FOR IoT

Researchers, academics, professionals, and science-practitioners have a lot of work ahead to create an assured and trustworthy IoT. Research is already underway and needs to continue. Standards bodies and consortia have taken up the challenge of building security into many of the standards required. The next step is for the broader community, manufacturers, service providers, data aggregators, to build assurance into their offerings, and for users to demand it. We do not yet know all the assurances and security features that IoT will require, but we know some that will be essential. That kind of partial knowledge, and learning while building, had been a feature of every major convergence leading to today's Internet environment. We can learn as we build, but we must build in the essentials at every step. Some of those essentials are listed below, and explored more fully in the chapters of this book.

Basic security properties, the fundamentals, must be designed in to IoT devices, infrastructures, and back-end analysis systems. The security designs must reflect IoT requirements and constraints, and must enable high-level assurance as end-to-end guarantees. Chapters 1 and 2 explore general facets of designing cyber-assurance for IoT. Provisioning identities for IoT devices and services, and managing credentials, attributes, and rights associated with those identities, will be critical for supporting high-level assurance properties like privacy and access control. Several chapters touch on this area. IoT devices must be able to integrate securely into existing network services and enterprise IT environments – this will require certain security features in the devices themselves and substantial evolution in the way enterprises handle trust boundaries in which Chapter 3 explores this very challenging area. Establishing and maintaining assurance for IoT systems will depend on trust management services, which will have to extend from individual devices to high-level data analysis services which Chapters 4 and 5 examine. Chapter 6 reviews the privacy and security concerns of wearable computing while Chapter 7 focuses on the vulnerabilities of industrial control systems. Chapter 8 approaches to leverage Big Data techniques to enhance IoT provenance, which is itself only one of multiple measures needed to improve cyber-assurance. Assurance is not something that can be established once and then forgotten – it must be actively managed, measured, and maintained and Chapter 9 explores the more general challenge of assessing security mechanisms. Chapter 10 researches the future artificial intelligence aspect of cyber-assurance and Chapter 11 explores the threats toward cyber physical systems for the IoT.

To ensure that the essential assurance elements are built into the devices and systems that will comprise the Internet of Things, it is necessary to raise awareness about the challenges and possible solutions. This book is one step in that direction. By raising tough issues, and presenting potential solutions, it will encourage discussion and debate, expose engineers and designers to new strategies and emerging standards, and promote active development of cyber-assurance. With those assurances, we will be able to take full advantage of the potential benefits of the IoT.

PREFACE

The Internet of Things (IoT) has resulted in the widespread deployment of a relatively immature technology. There are, however, many significant challenges faced by the programmers, designers, and implementers of IoT technologies in ensuring that the level of security afforded is appropriate. As innovative technologies using the IoT will focus more on wireless technologies, there are numerous complex considerations which must be taken into account when deploying wireless infrastructures and without adequate forethought their use may be ill-advised. Researchers and commercial organizations are predicting that there will be 50 billion devices connected to the Internet by 2020[1] and the potential economic impact – including consumer surplus – of as much as $11.1 trillion per year in 2025 for IoT applications.[2] IoT networks will become popular because they can be deployed quickly with very little equipment infrastructures. These networks also lend themselves well to environments with populations of transient users. The possible applications of the IoT are almost limitless and organizations throughout the world have been quick to realize its potential.

The heavy utilization of wireless equipment and technologies renders the IoT operation very complicated. At the same time, the pace of data-in-transit and data-in-storage processing is significantly accelerated with the focus of how the data are delivered to the IoT systems, whereas the quick shifting of the focus will inevitably bring about swift and constant changes in the tactics of information security. Under such a highly complex and ever-changing environment, organizations must pay attention to the use of information security tools and techniques with a view to defeating

[1] http://blogs.cisco.com/news/cisco-connections-counter
[2] http://www.mckinsey.de/sites/mck_files/files/unlocking_the_potential_of_the_internet_of_things_full_report.pdf

cyber-attacks within this new environment. The future platform for the IoT will have to operate in a very harsh environment where there are serious advance persistent threats (APTs) to the safety of the information being processed. These APTs to the safety of the data being processed include the IoT network security, information security, and physical security, and its necessity to adopt appropriate countermeasures against these APTs to secure the initiative in confronting cyber-attacks. The primary measures to be taken include: using different kinds of technical defense measures, strengthening the security design of the IoT networks and devices, and undertaking research and production of these networks and devices.

This book presents the concept of a cyber-assurance approach to the IoT. This book presents the concept of a cyber-assurance approach to the IoT. This book is needed to understand the variety of cyber-assurance techniques and technologies supporting the task of seeking out defects that have the potential to be successfully targeted as exploitable vulnerabilities by a cyber-attacker. Furthermore, this book will support information security, assurance, and IoT industry practitioners' understanding of how to design and build cyber-assurance into the IoT. The target audience of this book will be those researchers, professionals, and students working in the field of wireless technologies, information system theory, systems engineering, information security architecture, and security system design along with university professors and researchers involved in cyber-assurance and IoT-related networking.

Through a collection of edited essays from cyber-assurance, information assurance, information security, and IoT industry practitioners and experts, this book is written for graduate students, researchers, and academics who want to improve their understanding of the latest developments of cyber-assurance for the IoT. Since these IoT networks present unique information assurance (IA) challenges, there will be a heavy reliance on the secure communication of urgent and time-sensitive information over these IoT networks.

Chapter 1: provides an approach intended to design security in the categories of (1) IoT secure-by-design systems and (2) processes and procedures that minimize human error and vulnerability introduction through the building of hardware and software components.

Chapter 2: provides the concept of automatically securing Internet of Things networks and devices through an embedded sensor which identifies cyber-attacks and mitigates any threats to the device and network before continuing to process the data.

Chapter 3: discusses a potential set of uniform methods for securely updating IoT devices, which could be applied to devices of any form factor or function by categorizing an IoT device based on its crypto processing ability, available storage, and how it achieves network connectivity.

Chapter 4: explains vulnerabilities in *ad hoc* and sensor networks and design attributes for trust management schemes are elucidated with their respective design metrics and analysis.

Chapter 5: discusses the two sides to the trust boundary discussion: how an approved IoT device affects the security posture when accepted into the trust boundary of a network and how an unapproved IoT device affects the security posture when interacting with devices that fall within the trust boundary of a network.

Chapter 6: reviews a Fitbit wearable device experiment and its relations to privacy/security concerns about wearable IoT devices.

Chapter 7: deals with a specific area where IoT sensor devices are applied, feedback loops in the consumer environment, highlighting vulnerabilities in areas such as automatic control theory, control systems engineering, information technology, data science, technical standards, and many others.

Chapter 8: reviews the systematic exploitation of two broad trends in computing, complex event processing and Big Data, present opportunities for enhancing provenance and related aspects of IoT security.

Chapter 9: identifies a framework that simplifies and aggregates the functionality of security-critical things (e.g., embedded devices, tags, actuators, smart objects) in a cloud-of-things architecture.

Chapter 10: discusses an artificial intelligence approach toward ensuring cyber-assurance for the IoT.

Chapter 11: evaluates a proposed cyber physical systems to help derive a set of input requirements and provide a mechanism for an automated approach for threat detection and assessment for the IoT.

TYSON T. BROOKS

ACKNOWLEDGMENTS

I would first like to give honor to my Lord and Savior Jesus Christ whom all my blessing come from. To my parents, my dad [the late] F. Burrell Brooks and my mom, W. Michelle Brooks and my entire family for all their love and encouragement. An extra special thanks to my lovely wife Lisa and children, Tyson Jr. and Taylor, for always supporting and loving me in whatever initiative "keeps me on the computer."

I would also like to thank IEEE, U.S. Department of Defense and the faculty and staff of Syracuse University's Center for Information and Systems Assurance and Trust (CISAT) and the School of Information Studies (iSchool) for all the guidance, direction, support, and encouragement in assisting me pursue my passion for research over the years.

TYSON T. BROOKS

CONTRIBUTORS

M. BALA KRISHNA received B.E. in Computer Engineering from Delhi Institute of Technology (presently Netaji Subhash Institute of Technology), University of Delhi, Delhi, India, and M.Tech. in Information Technology from University School of Information Technology (presently University School of Information and Communication Technology), Guru Gobind Singh Indraprastha University, New Delhi, India. Dr. Krishna received his Ph.D. in Computer Engineering from JMI Central University, New Delhi, India. Dr. Krishna had earlier worked as Senior Research Associate and Project Associate in Indian Institute of Technology, Delhi, India, in the areas of digital systems and embedded systems. Dr. Krishna had worked as faculty member and had handled projects related to networking and communication. Dr. Krishna is presently working as Assistant Professor in University School of Information and Communication Technology, Guru Gobind Singh Indraprastha University. Dr. Krishna's areas of interest include computer networks, wireless networking and communications, mobile and ubiquitous computing, and embedded system design. Dr. Krishna has publications in international journals, conferences, and book chapters. Dr. Krishna's teaching areas include wireless networks, mobile computing, data and computer communications, embedded systems, programming languages, etc. Dr. Krishna's current research work includes wireless *ad hoc* and sensor networks, green networking and communications, cognitive networks, and advances in mobile computing and communications. Dr. Krishna is a member of various IEEE and ACM technical societies and international conferences.

TYSON T. BROOKS is an information security technologist, science-practitioner, and an adjunct professor in the School of Information Studies (iSchool) at Syracuse University, Syracuse, NY, and also works with the Center for Information and

Systems Assurance and Trust (CISAT) at Syracuse University. Dr. Brooks has over 20 years of professional experience in the design, development, and production of complex information systems, as well as leading the effort to develop secure information systems architectures. Dr. Brooks's expertise includes work in the areas of information assurance, cyber-security, enterprise architecture, and network-based intrusion analysis in both the public and private sector. Dr. Brooks is the Founder/Editor-in-Chief of the *International Journal of Internet of Things and Cyber-Assurance* (IJITCA), an Associate Editor for *IEEE Access*, the *Journal of Enterprise Architecture* (JEA), the *International Journal of Cloud Computing and Services Science* (IJ-CLOSER), and the *International Journal of Information and Network Security* (IJINS), and is also a reviewer for the *IEEE Internet of Things Journal*. Dr. Brooks received his doctorate in Information Management from Syracuse University and holds master's degree in Information and Telecommunications Systems from Johns Hopkins University, a master's degree in Business Administration from Thomas More College, and a bachelor's degree in Business Administration/Management from Kentucky State University. Dr. Brooks is also a senior member of the Institute of Electrical and Electronics Engineers (IEEE) and a member of the Project Management Institute (PMI) and the Association of Enterprise Architects (AEA).

SHIU-KAI CHIN is a Professor in the Department of Electrical Engineering and Computer Science and a Provost Faculty Fellow focused on strategic planning at Syracuse University, Syracuse, NY. Dr. Chin is Co-director of the Center for Information and Systems Assurance and Trust (CISAT) and is affiliated with the Institute for National Security and Counterterrorism. Dr. Chin's research applies mathematical logic to the engineering of trustworthy systems and supports the research program of the Air Force Research Laboratory's Information Directorate in trustworthy systems and hardware-based computer security. Dr. Chin's research focus is on access control and policy-based design and verification. With JP Morgan Chase, Dr. Chin applies his research to reasoning about credentials and entitlements in large-value commercial transactions. Dr. Chin is co-author, with Dr. Susan Older, of the textbook *Access Control, Security, and Trust: A Logical Approach*, CRC Press, 2010. Dr. Chin served as the Interim Dean of the L.C. Smith College of Engineering and Computer Science from 2006 to 2008. From 1998 until 2006, he was Director of the Center for Advanced Systems Engineering (CASE) at Syracuse University – a New York State Center of Advanced Technology funded by the New York State Foundation for Science, Technology, and Innovation (NYSTAR).

MARTIN GOLDBERG graduated from Baruch College – City University of New York (CUNY) with BBA in Computer Information Systems and proceeded to work in private industry for 8 years. Following that, Mr. Goldberg took part in the National Science Foundation's (NSF) Scholarship for Service (SFS) program where he graduated from Polytechnic Institute of New York University (NYU Poly) with M.S. in Computer Science. Upon graduating from NYU Poly in 2005, Mr. Goldberg joined the U.S. Department of Defense, Fort Meade, MD.

UTKU KÖSE received B.S. in Computer Education from Gazi University, Turkey, M.S. in Computer Science from Afyon Kocatepe University, Turkey, and D.S./Ph.D. in Computer Engineering from Selcuk University, Turkey. Between 2009 and 2011, Dr. Köse has worked as a Research Assistant in Afyon Kocatepe University. Dr. Köse has also worked as Lecturer and Vocational School Vice Director in Afyon Kocatepe University between 2011 and 2012. Currently, Dr. Köse is Lecturer in Usak University, Usak, Turkey, and also Director of the Computer Sciences Application and Research Center at Usak University. Dr. Utku Köse's research interest includes artificial intelligence, the chaos theory, distance education, e-learning, computer education, and computer science.

CHRISTOPHER LEBERKNIGHT received B.A. in Computer Science from Rutgers University, New Brunswick, NJ, M.S. in Computer Science, and Ph.D. in Information Systems from the New Jersey Institute of Technology (NJIT), Newark, NJ. Dr. Leberknight began his academic career as a Postdoctoral Research Associate in the Department of Electrical Engineering at Princeton University, followed by an appointment as an Assistant Professor in the Computer Science Department at William Paterson University. Dr. Leberknight's primary research interests are networking and social computing and his research has been published in top tier journals as well as national and international conferences. In addition to his academic experience, Dr. Leberknight has over 10 years of professional experience in the computer and telecommunication industries and served as the CEO for two start-up companies. Dr. Leberknight also has experience with decision support and location aware systems (Patent no. 7,406,448). Dr. Leberknight is a member of the Institute of Electronic and Electrical Engineers (IEEE), Association of Computing Machinery (ACM), and the Association for Information Systems (AIS). Dr. Leberknight also serves on the Editorial Board for the *Journal of Privacy and Information Security*, *International Journal of Internet of Things and Cyber-Assurance*, and the *International Journal of E-Politics*.

MARTHA LERSKI, a graduate of the University of Pennsylvania, is an instructor and business librarian at Lehman College, CUNY, Bronx, NY. Ms. Lerski's early career work in currencies in the Finance Division of Swiss Bank supports her continued interest in global information flows, including arts metadata. Ms. Lerski studied Digital Libraries at Syracuse University, Syracuse, NY, and holds MLS from Queens College.

ROBERT MCCLOUD is Distinguished Global Professor and Associate Professor of Computer Science at Sacred Heart University, Fairfield, CT. In his 16 years as a faculty member, he has published one e-book and three print books in addition to many research articles. Dr. McCloud has also been awarded five international fellowships, including two Fulbrights and a World Bank research grant.

LEE MCKNIGHT is Kauffman Professor of Entrepreneurship and Innovation and Associate Professor in the iSchool (The School of Information Studies), Syracuse University, Syracuse, NY. Dr. McKnight was Principal Investigator of the National Science Foundation Partnerships for Wireless Grids Innovation Testbed

(WiGiT) project 2009–2014, which was the recipient of the 2011 TACNY Award for Technology Project of the Year. Dr. McKnight is the inventor of Edgeware, a new class of software for creating secure *ad hoc* overlay cloud to edge applications, known as Gridlets and Wiglets. Dr. McKnight's research focuses on cloud to edge services and policy, virtual markets and wireless grids, the global information economy, national and international technology policy, and Internet governance. Dr. McKnight was an Associate Professor of International Information and Communication and Director of the Edward R. Murrow Center at the Fletcher School of Law and Diplomacy, Tufts University; Principal Research Associate and Lecturer at MIT; and founder of the Internet Telephony Consortium, also at MIT. Lee served on the Enterprise Cloud Leadership Council of TM Forum; and as a member of IEEE P2030.4 smart grid interoperability task force. Lee is founder and was a member of the Board of Directors of Wireless Grids Corporation, 2004–2014. Dr. McKnight was a founding member of the Board of Directors of Summerhill Biomass Systems, 2007–2013. Dr. McKnight received his doctorate in 1989 from MIT; an M.A. from the School of Advanced International Studies, Johns Hopkins University, in 1981; and a B.A. *magna cum laude* from Tufts University in 1978.

MARTIN MURILLO works as Data Scientist with the University of Notre Dame, South Bend, IN. Dr. Murillo has Ph.D. in Optimal Control Systems and M.S. in Measurement and Control Systems. Dr. Murillo has authored various papers in control systems theory and applications and has also focused on other topics that bridge technology, policy, and governance. Currently, Dr. Murillo focuses on the study of vulnerability of political and administrative entities in the context of climate change and the emergence of smart cities and already existing vulnerable cyber-physical infrastructure. Dr. Murillo has worked in industry leading the design and implementation of security and control modules for dedicated short-range communications applications for vehicles and road structures. Dr. Murillo has served in various leadership positions in the IEEE, including managing several humanitarian initiatives.

NICOLE NEWMEYER is the Mission Director for the Mission Software Services Office within the Information Assurance Operations Deputy Directorate at the National Security Agency (NSA), U.S. Department of Defense, Fort Meade, MD. As Mission Director, Ms. Newmeyer is responsible for guiding short term and strategic Information providing technical leadership to capability development teams, and providing technical guidance to leadership. Ms. Newmeyer is currently in the Agency's Senior Technical Development Program, focused on the Internet of Things. Ms. Newmeyer has held technical leadership positions in both the signals intelligence and information assurance missions at NSA. She holds B.S. in Computer Science from the University of Maryland, Baltimore County, and is currently working toward M.S. in Technology Intelligence at the National Intelligence University.

JOON PARK is Professor at the School of Information Studies (iSchool), Syracuse University, Syracuse, NY. Over the past decades, Prof. Park has been involved with theoretical/practical research, education, and services in information and systems security. Dr. Park served as the founding director of the Certificate of Advanced Study (CAS) in Information Security Management (ISM) at the Syracuse iSchool (2003–2013). Dr. Park is Syracuse University's point of contact (PoC) at the Center of Academic Excellence (CAE) in Information Assurance/Cyber Defense programs, which are designated by the National Security Agency (NSA) and the Department of Homeland Security (DHS).

MARK UNDERWOOD is the President and CEO of Krypton Brothers LLC, a consultancy specializing in Big Data security, rapid intranet exploitation, digital forensics, software quality, and domain-specific frameworks. Mr. Underwood is an advocate for patient-managed health information, including access to automated decision support and complex event processing resources. Founder/co-founder of five technology startups, Mr. Underwood co-designed one of the earliest ambulatory care health information systems (IATROS). Mr. Underwood has served as lead engineer or principal investigator on artificial intelligence projects for DARPA and for U.S. Army and Air Force research laboratories. Currently, Mr. Underwood is working with standards organizations to foster information assurance and provenance transparency. Mr. Underwood is co-chair of the NIST Big Data Public Working Group's Security and Privacy subgroup, and was co-chair of the 2015 Ontology Summit, which focused on the Internet of Things. In 2014, Mr. Underwood served on the workshop committee for the IEEE Big Data Conference and moderated several panels. Mr. Underwood is an ASQ Certified Software Quality Engineer and holds a US secret clearance.

ACRONYMS

3D	three-dimensional
6LoWPAN	IPv6 over low power wireless personal area network
AE	action engine
AES	Advanced Encryption Standard
AFRL	Air Force Research Laboratory
A.I.	artificial intelligence
AIoT	advanced Internet of Things
ANSI	American National Standards Institute
AONS	Advanced Object Naming Service
AP	access point
API	application programmatic interface
APT	advanced persistent threats
ARM	advanced RISC machines
ASI	AIoT standard interface
AV	autonomous vehicles
BS	Bachelor of Science
BVCC	boosted power supply voltage
BYOB	bring your own device
C2	command-and-control
CA	certificate authority
CAD	computer-aided design
CAN	controller area network
CAR	computer-assisted reasoning
CC	cloud computing
CCP	custom cryptographic processor
CCS	calculus of communicating systems

CCSA	China Communications Standards Association
CEKM	crypto engine for key management
CEP	complex event processing
CH	cluster head node
CIP	Common Industrial Protocol
CIPS	central information processing system
CMS	cryptographic message syntax
CoAP	Constrained Application Protocol
CONOPS	concept of operations
CoRE	Constrained RESTful Environments
CoT	Cloud of Things
CPNS	cyber-physical networking systems
CPS	cyber-physical system
CPU	central processing unit
CRL	certificate revocation lists
CSBD	certified security by design
CSP	communicating sequential processes
CSO	chief security officers
CT	cipher text
D2D	device-to-device
DAG	directed acyclic graph
DDS	direct digital control
DDoS	distributed denial of service
DICE	DTLS in constrained environments
DoD	Department of Defense
DoS	denial of service
DPWSec	devices profile for web services security
DSL	digital subscriber line
DSS	Digital Signature Standard
DTLS	Datagram Transport Layer Security
DTN	delay tolerant networks
EAP	Extensible Authentication Protocol
EAS	electronic article surveillance
ECC	elliptic curve surveillance
ECAC	error checking and correction
ECC	elliptic curve cryptography
ECDH	elliptic curve Diffie-Hellman
ECDSA	Elliptic Curve Digital Signature Algorithm
ECQV	elliptic curve QuVanstone
EDA	electronic design automation
EDAS	event-driven adaptive security
e.g.	*exempla grata* (Latin term meaning "given as an example")
ELF	extremely low frequency
EMI	electromagnetic interface
EPC	Electronic Product Code

ERP	enterprise resource planning
ES	embedded systems
et al.	*et alii, et aliae, et alia* (Latin term meaning "and all of them")
ETL	extracted, transformed, and loaded
FAA	Federal Aviation Administration
FGTM	Front-End-Loaded Grounded Theory Method
FPGA	field-programmable gate array
FRiMA	faster risk malicious assessment
FTPS	fire, theft prevention system
GPS	global positioning system
H AFIX	hardware-assisted flow integrity extension
HCI	Human Computer Interaction
HF	high frequency
HIPPA	Health Insurance Portability and Accountability Act
HOL	high order logic
HTML	HyperText Markup Language
HTTP	HyperText Transmission Protocol
HVAC	heating, ventilating and air conditioning
IA	information assurance
IaaS	infrastructure-as-a-service
ICD	internet-connected device
ICs	integrated circuits
ICT	information and communication technology
ID3	Iterative Dischotomiser 3
i.e.	*id est* (Latin term meaning "that is")
INFOSEC	information security
I/O	input/output
IIoT	industrial Internet of Things
IoT	Internet of Things
IoTTMP	Internet of Things Trust Management Protocols
IP	Internet Protocol
IPv4	Internet Protocol Version 4
IPv6	Internet Protocol Version 6
IT	information technology
ITIL	information technology infrastructure library
KBPS	kilobits per second
KDC	key distribution center
KDD	knowledge discovery in databases
LAN	local area network
LCG	linear congruential generator
LLN	low-power and lossy networks
M	meters
mA	milliamps
MAC	media access control
mAh	milliampere-hour

MANETS	mobile *ad hoc* networks
MCU	microcontrollers
MEs	mobile elements
M2M	machine-to-machine
MoA	memoranda of agreement
MoU	memoranda of understanding
NBD-PWG	NIST Big Data public working group
NERC	North American Electric Reliability Corporation
NFC	near-field communication
NGN	next-generation network
NIST	National Institute of Standards and Technologies
NSA	National Security Agency
OAuth	open authorization
OS	operating system
OSI	open systems interconnection
PaaS	platform-as-a-service
PAN	personal area network
PC	personal computer
PDA	personal digital assistant
PhD	Doctor of Philosophy
PII	personally identifiable information
PLC	programmable logic controller
PMS	property management system
PSS	physical security system
PT	plain text
QoS	quality of service
QR	quick response
RAM	random access memory
RDSA	RSA Digital Signature Algorithm
REST	representational state transfer
RF	radio frequency
RFID	radio frequency identification
RISC	reduced instruction set computing
ROM	read-only memory
ROP	return-oriented programming
RTU	remote terminal units
SaaS	software-as-a-service
SAM	secure access modules
SCADA	supervisory control and data acquisition
SCP	secure control processor
SDN	software-defined network
SHS	Secure Hash Standard
S-HTTP	Secure Hypertext Transfer Protocol
SID	Standard Identity
SIEM	security information and event management

SOA	service-oriented architecture
SOM	self-organizing map
SPD	security privacy dependability
SPM	secure packet mechanism
SSD	service supplier domain
SSM	secure state machine
SSN	secure state machines
SSS	surrounding security subsystem
SW-ARQ	stop and wait automatic repeat request
SYN	synchronization
TBSS	trust-based security solution
TCP/IP	Transmission Control Protocol/Internet Protocol
TLS	transport layer security
UHF	ultra-high frequency
UII	unique item identifier
UODL	Unified Object Description Language
UPC	Universal Product Code
URL	uniform resource locator
uRPF	unicast reverse path forwarding
US	United States
Vcc	positive-voltage supply
VLAN	virtual local area network
VLSI	very large scale integrated
VM	virtual machine
VMM	virtual machine monitors
VMS	vehicle management subsystem
VoIP	Voice-over-Internet Protocol
VPN	virtual private network
VTC	video teleconferencing
VW	Volkswagen
WAN	wide area network
WID	wireless intrusion detection
Wi-Fi	wireless frequency
WiMAX	worldwide interoperability for microwave access
WIPS	wireless intrusion prevention systems
WLAN	wireless local area network
WMAN	wireless metropolitan area network
WoT	Web of Things
WPAN	wireless personal area network
WS	Web service
WSN	wireless sensor network
WWW	World Wide Web
XML	eXtensible Markup Language

INTRODUCTION

TYSON T. BROOKS

School of Information Studies, Syracuse University, Syracuse, NY, USA

The Internet of Things (IoT) has provided a promising opportunity to build powerful systems and applications by leveraging the growing ubiquity of radio frequency identification (RFID), wireless, mobile and sensor devices (Xu et al. 2014). While wireless devices can be subject to the same abuse as fixed local area and wide area networks, the mobile nature of wireless networks adds greater susceptibility of vulnerability exploitation. If IoT applications are to be extended from the current insolated intranet or extranet environments to the wide area as well as global Internet landscape, some fundamental changes in the networking systems have to be considered in a converged next-generation network (NGN) setting (Zhou 2012). For this reason, the IoT network may not be well protected, leaving it open to malicious activity. IoT traffic will require more virtual network switching and roaming on other networks, which complicates tracking and billing of customers and enforcement of interconnection agreements. Mobile personal satellite services may have users around the world relying on honest distributors to reach their customers. The absence of fixed customer residences will make subscription vulnerabilities easier to perpetrate. Finally, the IoT wireless smart devices will be constantly at risk of being lost or stolen. While many of these concerns are still being addressed, the intense focus on information assurance (IA) and the pattern of regular security enhancements continue.

IoT infrastructures will allow combinations of smart objects, sensor network technologies, and human beings using different but interoperable communication protocols and realizes a strategic and dynamic multimodal/heterogeneous network that can be deployed also in inaccessible, or remote spaces (e.g., oil platforms, mines, forests, tunnels, pipes, etc.) or in cases of emergencies or hazardous situations (e.g., earthquakes, fire, floods, radiation areas, etc.) (Clark et al. 2002). Network management platforms are a necessity in today's telecom networks primarily for fault and configuration management and detection and intrusion resolution on circuits and equipment but they are also there to protect the network from malicious activity through secure measures (Cordesman & Cordesman 2002). The security measures implemented into a network management platform are usually an overlay network via a software solution or an additional piece of hardware equipment or possibly both. In case of the IoT network, numerous applications, devices, software, etc. must provide the security implemented on the IoT network platform for secure data communications.

While the Internet has enabled computer users to share information, it has also brought about negative phenomena, such as computer viruses, pornographic information, illegal access attempts, theft of confidential information, and corruption of internal information (Clark et al. 2002). Computer "hackers" today not only possess a full range of attack instruments but have mastered very complicated stealth and evading techniques so sophisticated that they enjoy almost full freedom on the Internet (Sanders 2003). With the trend of integrating complex systems with advance computer and communication technologies, this has introduced serious cyber-security concerns, especially toward IoT architecture environments, where the architecture may no longer be regarded as reliable to support communications as before. Due to the important role of mobile smart devices, wireless networks and the smart grid as the key energy infrastructure, the IoT will need to support the middleware of providing the dynamic *ad hoc* sharing of heterogonous devices. Protecting data in these IoT environments is an extremely important task which significantly contributes to information security issues given the threats of cyber-attacks.

Cyber-attacks will directly cause IoT architecture failures and crashes. Cyber-attacks or the failures of key smart devices (e.g., control server or main router), will downgrade the performance of these architectures. Since these IoT systems will rely on devices for sensing, communication, and information processing, the performance degradation of the architecture will disturb the control process of the system and potentially lead to the instability of the environment. This instability can cause the cascading failures of its components (e.g., smart grid generators or transmission lines) or potentially lead to the continuous collapse of the overall environment. Due to the its heavy reliance on the cyber-infrastructure for sensing and control, the IoT will be exposed to new risk from computer network vulnerabilities as well as inherit existing risks from physical vulnerabilities within existing systems (Bizeul 2007). Consequently, these IoT systems and infrastructures, and the way people use them, are inherently vulnerable to malicious activity by hackers – individuals who breaks into computers and computer networks to cause harm (Thomas 2002). This malicious activity can take one of two forms, one destructive in nature (attack) and the other non-destructive (exploitation) (Luiijf 2012). While a cyber-attack refers to deliberate actions to harm or render useless a victim's computer system and network, exploitation refers to the use of techniques, usually clandestine, to gain unauthorized access, typically to steal information resident on a network (Luiijf 2012). This dichotomy has been a problem to security professionals since the invention of computers and creates opportunities for hackers toward the IoT.

TRANSITING INFORMATION ASSURANCE TOWARD CYBER-ASSURANCE FOR THE IoT

Services will be able to interact with these smart devices using standard interfaces that will provide the necessary link via the Internet, to query and change their state and retrieve any information associated with them, taking into account security and privacy issues (Clark et al. 2002). Internet-connected devices (ICD) can only become context-aware, sense, communicate, interact, exchange data, information, and knowledge if they are suitably equipped with appropriate object-connected technologies unless of course they are human "things" or other entities with these intrinsic capabilities (Clark et al. 2002). In this vision, through the use of intelligent decision-making algorithms in software applications, appropriate rapid responses can be given to physical phenomena, based on the very latest information collected about physical entities and consideration of patterns in the historical data, either for the same entity or for similar entities (Clark et al. 2002). The failures of these algorithmic components can cause disturbances to the system and consequently threaten its security. In the IoT networks, IA will have increasing importance of ensuring the confidentially, integrity, and availability, since the IoT networks can only fulfill its functions with the support of the cyber-infrastructure.

These new IoT networks are considered new types of communication systems that overlay existing IT infrastructures. By enabling flexible, high-speed data transmissions with a minimum of transmission errors, IoT networks will provide the connection to other networks via the Internet. Hypothetically, before an ICD can send data, it must register with the IoT network. It sends the data communication request to the network and it also executes subscriber authentication on the basis of information it receives from the ICD. One important aspect is that if authentication is approved, the IoT network establishes a line connection to the ICD and starts communications. The IoT network intakes the transmission and reception of data by sending a data packet communications registration response to the ICD. If the data packets are being sent to another ICD, data are sent from the network to the destination ICD. The destination ICD then conducts a data communication registration in order to accept the incoming data packets. To stop the progress of packet communication, the ICD first transmits a packet communication release request to the IoT. The IoT then releases the packet communications status at the IoT network. The release of packet communications is completed when the packet communications registration release confirmation from the ICD and the IoT network is disconnected. This disconnection will usually come in the form a cyber-attack.

In order to defend against future hacking threats and cyber-attacks, it is necessary to adopt the concept of cyber-assurance. Cyber-assurance is the justified confidence that networked systems are adequately secure to meet operational needs, even in the presence of attacks, failures, accidents, and unexpected events (Alberts et al. 2009). Existing IA assurance approaches are primarily single system and single organization focused; with the highly interconnected, complex environments in use today, effective cyber-assurance must be addressed across multi-program acquisitions, through the supply chains, and among operational environments that span multiple organizations

(Alberts et al. 2009). Furthermore, cyber-assurance encompasses the concept of recognition, fortification, reestablishment, and survivability capabilities in order to defend IoT systems and networks against cyber-attacks. Recognition includes the identification of a cyber-attack being performed leading to the fortification of smart IoT devices, networks and systems. Fortification means to apply embedded network security techniques in IoT devices for protecting IoT networks and systems during a cyber-attack. Reestablishment means to return the IoT ICDs, networks and systems to its operational condition before the cyber-attack. Survivability entails the capability of an IoT device to continue processing even in the presence of cyber-attacks, internal failures, or accidents.

Cyber-assurance provides a way to determine whether individual IoT components (e.g., software, hardware) as well as the whole IoT systems operate to circumvent intentional attempts to compromise their correct operation. In order to make this determination, cyber-assurance applies a variety of techniques and technologies to the task of seeking out defects that have the potential to be successfully targeted as exploitable vulnerabilities by an attacker. However, achieving these dynamic capabilities within the IoT will be difficult because this future technology may be surprisingly fragile. IoT network protocols must allow smart devices to run multiple copies of networks, manipulate their processing speed, and retain control over their data execution. This new network logic is tightly coupled with the physical network equipment of the IoT. Therefore, cyber-assurance can be said to provide embedded solutions to avoid or withstand cyber-attacks.

Innovative cyber-assurance techniques are needed to secure the IoT and its operating environment. This is due to several factors, which include: the extensive spread of the Internet and an increase in wireless smart devices. Changes in the nature and use of innovative technologies (e.g., cloud computing, virtualization) must ensure that the systems using IoT technology actually meet their performance and reliability objectives as well as the added security requirements needed. Historically, organizations could secure vital information and functions by inhibiting access to and encrypting communications between high assurance enclaves (e.g., segments of internal networks). However, in the IoT network age, the contested terrain is far more complex and fluid. IoT systems are distributed and users are dispersed, secure connectivity is a necessity and the technology must be ubiquitous. Vulnerabilities are many and subtle and shift as these systems operate and evolve. Opportunities to bypass or co-opt traditional protective measures abound. Therefore, cyber-assurance should be practiced in automatically preventing and mitigate threats toward IoT network and systems.

The goal of this book is to increase the visibility of current research and emergent trends in cyber-assurance theory, application, architecture, and information security in the IoT based on theoretical aspects and studies of practical applications. This book will cover fundamental to advanced concepts necessary to grasp IoT current cyber-assurance issues, challenges, and solutions as well as future trends in IoT infrastructures, architectures, and applications. In addition, the educational value of this book is to serve as an effective bridge between academic research on theory, and science-practitioners work with IoT technology. It is anticipated that this work will be a primary source of reading for students wishing to become involved in cyber-assurance for IoT research. Additionally, the book is to gather the knowledge and experience of expert cyber-assurance and IoT researchers who work in the area of wireless networks, cloud computing, information security architecture, and IoT, and elicit their knowledge in a collaborative effort that leads to an edited book which will be one of the first of its kind. The consecutive chapters of this book will present topics related to the actual cyber-assurance IoT research that work together to carry out coordinated functions. The chapters will also present new information security theory and applications devoted to the improvement and development of cyber-assurance IoT research.

REFERENCES

Alberts, C., Ellison, R.J., & Woody, C. 2009. Cyber assurance. 2009 CERT Research Report. Software Engineering Institute, Carnegie Mellon University. Available at http://resources .sei.cmu.edu/library/asset-view.cfm?assetid=77638.

Bizeul, D. 2007. Russian business network study. Unpublished paper, November 20, 2007.

Clark, D.D., Wroclawski, J., Sollins, K.R., & Braden, R. 2002. Tussle in cyberspace: defining tomorrow's internet. *ACM SIGCOMM Computer Communication Review*, 32(4), pp. 347–356.

Cordesman, A.H., & Cordesman, J.G. 2002. *Cyber-Threats, Information Warfare, and Critical Infrastructure Protection: Defending the US Homeland*. Greenwood Publishing Group.

Da Xu, L., He, W., & Li, S. 2014. Internet of things in industries: a survey. *IEEE Transactions on Industrial Informatics*, 10(4), pp. 2233–2243.

Luiijf, E. 2012. *Understanding Cyber Threats and Vulnerabilities*. Springer, Berlin/Heidelberg, pp. 52–67.

Sanders, A.D. 2003. Teaching tip: utilizing simple hacking techniques to teach system security and hacker identification. *Journal of Information Systems Education*, 14(1), p. 5.

Thomas, D. 2002. *Hacker Culture*. University of Minnesota Press.

Zhou, H., 2012. *The Internet of Things in the Cloud: A Middleware Perspective*. CRC Press.

PART I

EMBEDDED DESIGN SECURITY

CHAPTER 1

CERTIFIED SECURITY BY DESIGN FOR THE INTERNET OF THINGS

SHIU-KAI CHIN

Department of Electrical Engineering and Computer Science, Syracuse University, Syracuse, NY, USA

1.1 INTRODUCTION

Incorporating security into the design of components used in the Internet of Things (IoT) is essential for securing the operations of the IoT and the cyber-physical infrastructure upon which society depends. The pervasiveness of the IoT and its part in critical infrastructure requires incorporating security into the design of components from the start. There are several challenges to incorporating security into the design of IoT components from the start. These challenges include (1) precisely describing confidentiality and integrity policies in ways that are amenable to formal reasoning, (2) maintaining logical consistency among confidentiality and integrity policies and implementation at all levels of abstraction, from high-level behavioral descriptions at the user level, down to implementations at the level of state machines and transition systems, and (3) providing compelling evidence of security that is quickly and easily reproducible by certifiers.

This is not the first time the electrical and computer engineering profession has faced these challenges. In fact, the IoT is compelling evidence of successfully meeting the challenges of design, accountability, consistency, and verifiability across multiple levels of abstraction. To learn and draw inspiration from the past, we need only look back to the 1970s and 1980s when the challenges of designing and implementing very large-scale integrated (VLSI) circuits were encountered and overcome.

1.2 LESSONS FROM THE MICROELECTRONICS REVOLUTION

In the 1970s, it was inconceivable that designers of algorithms and instruction-set architectures could fashion specialized integrated circuits down to the level of physical

Cyber-Assurance for the Internet of Things, First Edition. Edited by Tyson T. Brooks.
© 2017 by The Institute of Electrical and Electronic Engineers, Inc. Published 2017 by John Wiley & Sons, Inc.

layouts. Each level of design had its collection of design detail, for example, transistor models at the circuit design level, and minimum separation distances among metal and polysilicon features at the layout level.

The union of all design concepts spanning algorithm design down to layouts was too much for a single designer to grasp conceptually. The prospect of a single designer accounting for all design details spanning algorithm to layout design was even more daunting. Conway's key insight that made VLSI design possible was:

> *"... to sidestep tons of accumulated vestigial practices in system architecture, logic design, circuit design and circuit layout, and replace them with a coherent but minimalist set of methods." (Conway, L 2012)*

Specifically, the minimalist set of methods made use of:

- parameterization, that is, specifying λ as the biggest of all the required minimum feature sizes.
- idealized transistor behavior as switch behavior,
- consistent interpretations of voltages, transistor state, truth values,
- interpretations linking models at multiple levels, spanning layouts to transition systems, and
- computer-aided design (CAD) tools.

Computer hardware design is often called logic design for good reason. Propositional logic pervades all levels of abstraction in VLSI design. Transistor circuits and layouts are related to logic operators such as *negation*, *nand*, and *nor*. Networks of logic gates implement arithmetic logic units, multiplexers, flip-flops, and registers that are the components of datapaths. Base 2 arithmetic is used precisely because operations on binary numbers conveniently map to logic operations. Timing and control is achieved using finite-state machines. Finite-state machines are parameterized by next-state and output functions described by propositional logic formulas and implemented by combinational logic components. Instruction-set architectures are implemented by a combination of data and control paths, whose operations are controlled and sequenced by finite-state machines. The VLSI-inspired vision for securing the integrity of the IoT is this: harmonize multiple levels of abstraction by using the same logic at all levels to describe behavior at each level. This enables designs at each level of abstraction to be related to behavior at other levels. This provides the means for a continuous thread of logical consistency and a foundation for formally verified assurances of security and integrity.

The aspects of security and integrity of the IoT upon which we focus revolve around answering the question, *when given a request to execute a command within a security context of policies, authorizations, and trust assumptions, should we execute the command or not?* This question, and others like it, falls squarely within the realm of access control. Access control is a central concept behind firewalls, reference monitors, security kernels, and hypervisors. What is needed is an access-control logic that describes our security and integrity concerns in much the same way that propositional logic describes functional behavior.

For pragmatic reasons, an access-control logic, and the methodologies built upon it, must integrate well with the propositional logic, models, and design methods of computer hardware designers. As is often the case, simplicity brings the benefits of wide applicability, broad utility, and durability, as illustrated by propositional logic in hardware design. The access-control logic we use in this chapter is a form of propositional modal logic, that is, a logic that incorporates modes (e.g., states, worlds, configurations, or possibilities) into determining the truth value of logical propositions. This is an incremental step above the propositional logic of conventional hardware design and enables us to blend access control into machine design and verification.

Before delving into the details of a particular access-control logic, we describe the objectives of what we call certified security by design (CSBD), provide a simple motivating application as context, and state the critical requirements that must be satisfied to make CSBD a reality.

1.3 CERTIFIED SECURITY BY DESIGN

CSBD is an approach intended to design security into systems from the start and provide credible evidence that security claims are true. The goals of CSBD are:

- Complete mediation – authenticating and authorizing – all commands at all levels from high-level concepts of operations down to transition systems realized as state machines in hardware, and
- Formal proofs of integrity and security that are easily and rapidly verified by third parties, similar to the way VLSI circuits are described and verified using an array of electronic design automation (EDA) tools.

1.3.1 Concepts of Operations

Users of systems, where systems are machines, software applications, protocols, or processes coordinating the work among human organizations, typically have behavioral models of the systems they use. These models are concepts of operations (CONOPS). As defined by IEEE Standard 1362 (1998), a CONOPS expresses the "characteristics for a proposed system from a user's perspective. A CONOPS also describes the user organization, mission, and objectives from an integrated systems point of view." The US military has a similar definition of CONOPS in the Joint Publication 5-0, *Joint Operational Planning* (2011). For military leaders planning a mission, a CONOPS describes "how the actions of components and organizations are integrated, synchronized, and phased to accomplish the mission." Put plainly, a CONOPS describes the who, what, when, and why. When we explicitly address security and integrity concerns, we state how we know with whom we are dealing and what authority they have, that is, how we authenticate and authorize people,

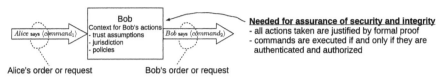

FIGURE 1.1 Flow of command and control (C2) for a simple CONOPS. Reproduced with permission of IEEE.

processes, statements, and commands. Figure 1.1 shows a diagram of a simple CONOPS along with its interpretation:

1. The flow of command and control in this figure is from left to right. Alice issues a command by some means (speaking, writing, electronically, telepathy, etc.). This is symbolized by:

$$Alice\ says\ <command1> \tag{1.1}$$

2. The box in the center labeled **Bob** shows Bob receiving Alice's command on the left. Inside the box are the things Bob "knows," that is, the context within which he attempts to justify acting on Alice's command. The context might include a policy that if Bob receives a particular command, such as *go*, then he is to issue another command, such as *launch*. Typically, before Bob acts on Alice's command, his operational context includes statements or assumptions such as Alice has the authority, jurisdiction, or is believed on matters related to the command she has made.

3. The arrow coming from the right-hand side of the box shows Bob's statement or command, which is symbolized by:

$$Bob\ says\ <command2> \tag{1.2}$$

4. What Figure 1.1 shows is one C2 sequence starting from left to right. Bob gets an order from Alice. Bob decides based on Alice's order and what he knows (the statements inside the box), that it is a good idea to issue *command2*. This is symbolized by:

$$Bob\ says\ <command2> \tag{1.3}$$

Regarding the comment in Figure 1.1, for assurance what we want is a logical justification of the actions Bob takes, given the order he receives and the context within which he is operating. For us, logical justifications are proofs in mathematical logic.

Security vulnerabilities often result from inconsistencies among CONOPS at various levels of abstraction. Military commanders might assume that only authorized operators are able to launch an application, whereas the application itself might incorrectly trust that all orders it receives are from authorized operators and never authenticate the inputs it receives. Any design for assurance methodology must address authentication and authorization in order to avoid vulnerabilities due to unauthorized access or control. Rigorous assurance requires mathematical models and proofs. Our intent is to illustrate a structured way to achieve security by design.

To illustrate the above concepts, throughout this chapter we apply them within the context of securing the integrity of a networked thermostat. We picked this example because (1) its function and purpose are easily understood, and (2) in a distributed control environment, its security and integrity concerns are representative of many other C2 applications.

1.3.2 A Networked Thermostat as a Motivating Example

Figure 1.2 shows a networked thermostat and its operating environment. The thermostat has a keyboard and a network interface. Commands received by the thermostat from its keyboard are assumed to originate from the thermostat's *Owner*. The *Owner* has the authority to execute any command.

The thermostat also receives commands via a network interface to a remote *Server*. The *Server* relays commands from the *Owner* via the *Owner's* account on the *Server*. The *Server* relays commands from the *Utility* supplying energy to the *Owner*. The *Utility* has authority over the thermostat's operation, if granted that authority by the *Owner*.

The reasons for granting authority to the *Utility* include reducing electrical loads on the grid during peak usage times. The benefits to the *Owner* are reduced electricity costs if cooling during the day can be deferred while the *Owner* is at work or away. The benefits to the *Utility* include deferred use of expensive generators as well as reduced strain on distribution systems.

Upon request, the thermostat reports its status back to the *Owner* and the *Utility* via the *Server* or using the physical display on the thermostat itself. The status of the thermostat is given by its state. Informally, the state of the thermostat is its operating mode and its temperature setting.

We consider three use cases with respect to Figure 1.2:

1. The *Owner* issues commands via the thermostat's keyboard.
2. The *Owner* issues commands to the thermostat via the *Owner's* account on the *Server*.
3. The *Utility* issues commands to the thermostat via the *Server*.

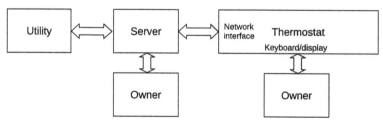

FIGURE 1.2 A networked thermostat and its operating environment. Reproduced with permission of IEEE.

At a high level, the thermostat commands are as follows.

1. **Setting** the temperature *value*. This command has security considerations as losing control over the temperature potentially is a threat to the safety of lives and property.
2. **Enabling** the *Utility* to exercise control over setting the temperature. This command has security considerations as *Owners* want to make sure they have the ultimate authority over their thermostat.
3. **Disabling** the *Utility* to exercise control over setting the temperature. This command has similar security considerations as the command used to enable the *Utility* to alter the thermostat's temperature setting.
4. **Reporting** the **Status** of the thermostat, which is displayed on the thermostat and sent to the *Server*. This command does not alter the thermostat's temperature setting or operating mode. As such, there are no security sensitivities with respect to reporting status. For our illustration, we assume there are no privacy concerns. If needed, privacy is handled in the usual ways including multi-level security, role-based access control, access-control lists (Bell & La Padula 1973, 1976; Biba 1977; Ferraiolo & Kuhn 1992; Sandhu et al. 1996), etc.

At this point in conceptualizing the networked thermostat, we need to consider the concepts we use to secure integrity of the thermostat's operations. We incorporate the following concepts into our design:

- Authenticating principals issuing commands using mechanisms such as (1) userids and passwords associated with *Owner* accounts on the *Server*, and (2) cryptographically signed messages from the *Server* to the thermostat and from the *Utility* to the *Server*,
- Authorizing principals issuing commands by making explicit the context in which authorization is done, that is, public-key certificates, root trust assumptions on keys and jurisdiction, and policies stating what actions are taken in particular circumstances, and
- Executing or trapping commands based on a principal's authority and the security sensitivity of the command they are attempting to execute.

The description of the networked thermostat example and the goals of CSBD lead us to the following requirements to realize the goals of CSBD:

- A C2 calculus used to reason about access-control decisions. The calculus we used is fully described in Chin and Older (2010) and is an extension and modification of an access-control logic for distributed systems (Abadi et al. 1993).
- Computer-assisted reasoning (CAR) tools to (1) formally verify all proofs and assurance claims, and (2) enable rapid reproduction of all results by third parties

and certifiers. We use the Cambridge University HOL-4 (higher-order logic) theorem prover (Gordon & Melham 1993). It is freely available and has been in use since 1987.

- A model of idealized cryptographic operations and their properties implemented in HOL.
- Models of state machine transition systems incorporating authentication, authorization, next-state functions, and output functions as parameters in support of security and to avoid state explosion. Our networked thermostat illustration build upon the foundations of virtual machines, in particular (Popek & Goldberg 1974).

1.4 CHAPTER OUTLINE

The remainder of this chapter is organized as follows:

- Section 1.5 defines the syntax, semantics, and inference rules for an access-control logic used to reason about command and control (C2).
- Section 1.6 gives an overview of the Higher-Order Logic (HOL) theorem prover we use as a computer-assisted reasoning (CAR) tool. The access-control logic is implemented as a conservative extension to HOL. The full access-control logic report is located in Appendix D.
- Section 1.7 describes the HOL implementation of the access-control logic and the C2 calculus.
- Section 1.8 describes algebraic models of ideal cryptographic operations such as hashing, symmetric and asymmetric encryption, and cryptographic signing and verification. These algebraic models are implemented in HOL.
- Section 1.12 shows how security is built into state machines by labeled-transition descriptions incorporating security policies described in the access-control logic.
- Section 1.13 is a detailed example showing how security is designed into a networked thermostat.
- Section 1.19 contains our conclusion.

1.5 AN ACCESS-CONTROL LOGIC

This section describes an access-control logic that is our C2 calculus. Our description is brief for space considerations and a full account appears in Chin and Older (2010). We present the syntax, semantics, and inference rules in the following sections.

To follow the thermostat example, readers will need to comprehend the syntax and inference rules of the C2 calculus. Justifying the logical soundness of the C2 logic requires understanding the semantics of the logic. However, the semantics may be skipped if the primary purpose is to follow the thermostat example. Of course, the syntax, semantics, and inference rules are fully implemented and verified in HOL.

1.5.1 Syntax

The syntax of the logic has two major components:

1. The syntax of *principals*, where principals are informally thought of as the actors making statements, for example, people, cryptographic keys, userids and passwords associated with accounts, etc.
2. The syntax of logical formulas.

The syntax of principal expressions *Princ* is defined as follows:

$$\textbf{Princ ::= PName / Princ \& Princ / Princ | Princ} \tag{1.4}$$

"&" is pronounced "with"; " | " is pronounced "quoting." The type of principal expressions is composed of principal names, for example, Alice, cryptographic keys, and userid with passwords. Compound expressions are created with & and |. Examples of principal expressions include

$$Alice \quad K_{Alice} \quad Alice \ \& \ Bob \quad Alice|Bob \tag{1.5}$$

Informally, *Alice* is Alice, K_{Alice} is Alice's cryptographic key, *Alice & Bob* is Alice and Bob together, *Alice | Bob* is Alice quoting Bob (relaying his statements). The syntax of logical formulas *Form* consists of propositional variables, expressions using the usual propositional operators corresponding to modal versions of negation, conjunction, disjunction, implication, and equivalence, coupled with operators $\Rightarrow$ (pronounced "speaks for"), *says*, *controls*, and *reps*.

In this presentation of the C2 calculus, we use the same propositional logic symbols for negation, conjunction, disjunction, implication, and equivalence. In the HOL implementation of the access-control logic, negation, conjunction, disjunction, implication, and equivalence in the access-control logic are represented using different symbols to clearly distinguish between access-control logic formulas and propositional logic formulas:

$$
\begin{aligned}
\textbf{Form ::=}\ & \textbf{PropVar}/\neg\textbf{Form}/ \\
& \textbf{(Form} \lor \textbf{Form})/\textbf{(Form} \land \textbf{Form})/ \\
& \textbf{(Form} \supset \textbf{Form})/\textbf{(Form} \equiv \textbf{Form})/ \\
& \textbf{(Princ} \Rightarrow \textbf{Princ})/\textbf{(Princ says Form)}/ \\
& \textbf{(Princ controls Form)}/\textbf{Princ reps Princ on Form}
\end{aligned}
\tag{1.6}
$$

TABLE 1.1   CONOPS Statements and Their Representation in the C2 Calculus. Reproduced with permission of IEEE

C2 Statement	Formula
If $\varphi1$ is true then $\varphi2$ is true (typical of policy statements)	$\varphi1 \supset \varphi2$
Key associated with Alice	Ka $\Rightarrow$ Alice
Bob has jurisdiction (controls or is believed) over statement φ	Bob controls φ
Alice and Bob together say φ	(Alice & Bob) says φ
Alice quotes Bob as saying φ	(Alice I Bob) says φ
Bob is Alice's delegate on statement φ	Bob reps Alice on φ
Carol is authorized in Role on statement φ	Carol reps Role on φ
Carol acting in Role makes statement φ	(Carol I Role) says φ

Table 1.1 is a table of typical C2 statements and their representation as formulas in the C2 calculus.

1.5.2 Semantics

The semantics of the access-control logic uses Kripke structures. A Kripke structure M is a three-tuple (W, I, J), where:

- W is a nonempty set, whose elements are called worlds.
- I: **PropVar** $\rightarrow P(W)$ is an interpretation function that maps each propositional variable p to a set of worlds.
- J: **PName** $\rightarrow P(W \times W)$ is a function that maps each principal name A into a relation on worlds (i.e., a subset of $W \times W$).

The semantics of principal expressions $Princ$ involves J and its extension $\hat{J}$. We define the extended function $\hat{J}$: **Princ** $\rightarrow P(W \times W)$ inductively on the structure of principal expressions, where A $\in$ **PName**.

$$\begin{align}
\hat{J}(A) &= J(A) \\
\hat{J}(P \& Q) &= \hat{J}(P) \cup \hat{J}(Q) \\
\hat{J}(P \mid Q) &= \hat{J}(P) \circ \hat{J}(Q)
\end{align} \tag{1.7}$$

Note: $R_1 \circ R_2 = \{(x,z) \mid \exists y.(x, y) \in R_1 \text{ and } (y, z) \in R_2\}$.
Each Kripke structure $M = (W, I, J)$ gives rise to a **semantic function:**

$$E_M[[-]] : \textbf{Form} \rightarrow P(W), \tag{1.8}$$

where: $E_M[[\varphi]]$ is the set of worlds in which φ is considered true.

E_M [[φ]] is defined inductively on the structure of φ, as shown in function (1.9). (*Note*: In the definition of E_M [[P says φ]], that $\hat{J}(P)(w)$ is simply the image of world w under the relation $\hat{J}(P)$.)

$$
\begin{aligned}
\mathcal{E}_{\mathcal{M}}[\![p]\!] &= I(p) \\
\mathcal{E}_{\mathcal{M}}[\![\neg\varphi]\!] &= W - \mathcal{E}_{\mathcal{M}}[\![\varphi]\!] \\
\mathcal{E}_{\mathcal{M}}[\![\varphi_1 \wedge \varphi_2]\!] &= \mathcal{E}_{\mathcal{M}}[\![\varphi_1]\!] \cap \mathcal{E}_{\mathcal{M}}[\![\varphi_2]\!] \\
\mathcal{E}_{\mathcal{M}}[\![\varphi_1 \vee \varphi_2]\!] &= \mathcal{E}_{\mathcal{M}}[\![\varphi_1]\!] \cup \mathcal{E}_{\mathcal{M}}[\![\varphi_2]\!] \\
\mathcal{E}_{\mathcal{M}}[\![\varphi_1 \supset \varphi_2]\!] &= (W - \mathcal{E}_{\mathcal{M}}[\![\varphi_1]\!]) \cup \mathcal{E}_{\mathcal{M}}[\![\varphi_2]\!] \\
\mathcal{E}_{\mathcal{M}}[\![\varphi_1 \equiv \varphi_2]\!] &= \mathcal{E}_{\mathcal{M}}[\![\varphi_1 \supset \varphi_2]\!] \cap \mathcal{E}_{\mathcal{M}}[\![\varphi_2 \supset \varphi_1]\!] \\
\mathcal{E}_{\mathcal{M}}[\![P \Rightarrow Q]\!] &= \begin{cases} W, & \text{if } \hat{J}(Q) \subseteq \hat{J}(P) \\ \varnothing, & \text{otherwise} \end{cases} \\
\mathcal{E}_{\mathcal{M}}[\![P \text{ says } \varphi]\!] &= \{w \mid \hat{J}(P)(w) \subseteq \mathcal{E}_{\mathcal{M}}[\![\varphi]\!]\} \\
\mathcal{E}_{\mathcal{M}}[\![P \text{ controls } \varphi]\!] &= \mathcal{E}_{\mathcal{M}}[\![(P \text{ says } \varphi) \supset \varphi]\!] \\
\mathcal{E}_{\mathcal{M}}[\![P \text{ reps } Q \text{ on } \varphi]\!] &= \mathcal{E}_{\mathcal{M}}[\![(P \mid Q \text{ says } \varphi) \supset Q \text{ says } \varphi]\!]
\end{aligned}
\tag{1.9}
$$

1.5.3 Inference Rules

Our use of the access-control logic as a C2 calculus rarely, if ever, uses Kripke structures explicitly. Instead, we rely upon inference rules to derive expressions soundly. An inference rule in the C2 calculus has the form:

$$
\frac{H_1 \ \ldots \ H_k}{C,}
\tag{1.10}
$$

where $H_1 \ \ldots \ H_k$ is a (possibly empty) set of hypotheses expressed as access-control logic formulas, and C is the conclusion, also expressed as an access-control logic formula. Whenever all of the hypotheses in an inference rule are present in a proof, then the rule states it is permissible to include the conclusion in the proof, too.

The meaning of *sound* depends on the definition of *satisfies* in the access-control logic. A Kripke structure M **satisfies** a formula φ when E_M [[φ]] = W, that is, φ is true in all worlds W of M. We denote M satisfies φ by $M \vDash \varphi$.

A C2 calculus inference rule is **sound** if, for all Kripke structures M, whenever M satisfies all the hypotheses $H_1 \ \ldots \ H_k$, then M also satisfies C, that is, if for all M: $M \vDash H_i$ for $1 \leq i \leq k$, then it must be the case that $M \vDash C$. All inference rules presented here and in Chin and Older (2010) are proved to be logically sound. Rule (1.11) shows the core inference rules of the access of the access-control logic.

$$P \text{ controls } \varphi \stackrel{\text{def}}{=} (P \text{ says } \varphi) \supset \varphi \qquad P \text{ reps } Q \text{ on } \varphi \stackrel{\text{def}}{=} P \mid Q \text{ says } \varphi \supset Q \text{ says } \varphi$$

$$\textit{Modus Ponens} \quad \frac{\varphi \quad \varphi \supset \varphi'}{\varphi'} \qquad \textit{Says} \quad \frac{\varphi}{P \text{ says } \varphi} \qquad \textit{Controls} \quad \frac{P \text{ controls } \varphi \quad P \text{ says } \varphi}{\varphi}$$

$$\textit{Derived Speaks For} \quad \frac{P \Rightarrow Q \quad P \text{ says } \varphi}{Q \text{ says } \varphi} \qquad \textit{Reps} \quad \frac{Q \text{ controls } \varphi \quad P \text{ reps } Q \text{ on } \varphi \quad P \mid Q \text{ says } \varphi}{\varphi}$$

$$\textit{\& Says (1)} \quad \frac{P \& Q \text{ says } \varphi}{P \text{ says } \varphi \wedge Q \text{ says } \varphi} \qquad \textit{\& Says (2)} \quad \frac{P \text{ says } \varphi \wedge Q \text{ says } \varphi}{P \& Q \text{ says } \varphi}$$

$$\textit{Quoting (1)} \quad \frac{P \mid Q \text{ says } \varphi}{P \text{ says } Q \text{ says } \varphi} \qquad \textit{Quoting (2)} \quad \frac{P \text{ says } Q \text{ says } \varphi}{P \mid Q \text{ says } \varphi}$$

$$\textit{Idempotency of} \Rightarrow \quad \frac{}{P \Rightarrow P} \qquad \textit{Monotonicity of} \Rightarrow \quad \frac{P' \Rightarrow P \quad Q' \Rightarrow Q}{P' \mid Q' \Rightarrow P \mid Q}$$

$$(1.11)$$

1.5.4 Describing Access-Control Concepts in the C2 Calculus

To illustrate how the C2 calculus is used to reason about authentication and authorization, we consider the following use case.

Example 1.1 Bob guards access to sensitive files. He receives requests electronically and says yes or no to each request. Specifically, the requests he receives are digitally signed by a cryptographic key. Keys are associated with people, for example, Alice. If the person, say Alice, who owns the key has permission to access the file, then Bob says yes.

Suppose Bob receives an access request signed by Alice's key K_A, and that Alice is permitted to access the files. We represent the request, the link between Alice and her key K_A, and her permission to access the files by the following statements in the access-control logic:

1. Digitally signed request received by Bob: K_A says *<access files>*.
2. K_A is Alice's key: $K_A \Rightarrow Alice$.
3. Alice has permission to access the files: *Alice* controls *<access files>*

Using the inference rules of the C2 calculus, Bob justifies his decision to grant Alice's request by the following proof, where lines 1–3 are the assumptions, and everything that follows is derived using the inference rules of the C2 calculus.

1.	K_A says *<access files>*	Digitally signed request
2.	$K_A \Rightarrow Alice$	Key associated with Alice
3.	*Alice* controls *<access files>*	Alice's capability to access files
4.	*Alice* says *<access files>*	2, 1 Derived speaks for
5.	*<access files>*	3, 4 Controls

Line 4 amounts to authenticating that Alice is the originator of the access request within the context established by lines 1 through 3. Line 3 establishes Alice's authority to access the files. Line 5 is Bob's deduction that granting Alice access is justified.

As a result of the proof, Bob has a derived inference rule, which he knows is sound because he derived it using the inference rules in (1.11). The derived inference rule is:

$$\frac{K_A \text{ says } \langle access\ files \rangle \quad K_A \Rightarrow Alice \quad Alice \text{ controls } \langle access\ files \rangle}{\langle access\ files \rangle} \tag{1.12}$$

The inference rule amounts to a checklist. If he (1) gets a message cryptographically signed with K_A, (2) K_A is Alice's key, and (3) Alice has permission to access the files, then granting access to Alice is justified.

Looking back at Figure 1.1, the inference rule is a logically sound description of what Bob does in the top-level CONOPS. The inference rule makes explicit the policies and trust assumptions and how they combine to justify Bob's actions.   □

Delegation is widely used. Our definition of delegation is given by the definition of *reps* and the *Reps* inference rule:

$$P \text{ reps } Q \text{ on } \varphi \stackrel{\text{def}}{=} P \mid Q \text{ says } \varphi \supset Q \text{ says } \varphi$$

$$Reps \quad \frac{Q \text{ controls } \varphi \quad P \text{ reps } Q \text{ on } \varphi \quad P \mid Q \text{ says } \varphi}{\varphi} \tag{1.13}$$

The consequence of the definition of *reps* in the first formula shows this: if you believe *Alice* reps *Bob* on φ is true, then if Alice says Bob says φ you will conclude that Bob says φ. In other words, Alice is trusted when she says Bob says φ.

In a command and control application, if you believe (1) Bob is authorized on command φ, (2) Alice is Bob's delegate or representative on a command φ, and (3) Alice says Bob says command φ, then you are justified to conclude the command φ is legitimate. This is the *Reps* inference rule.

Reps is particularly useful for delegating limited authority to delegates. Unlike $\Rightarrow$, where all statements of one principal are attributable to another, *Reps* specifies which statements made by a delegate are attributable to another.

Reps is used when people are acting in defined roles, for example, the roles of *Commander* and *Operator*. The following example shows the use of *reps* in the context of roles.

Example 1.2   Suppose we have two roles, two people, and two commands. The roles are *Commander* and *Operator;* the people are Alice and Bob; the two commands are *go* and *launch*. A *Commander* has the authority to issue a *go* command. An *Operator* has the authority to issue a *launch* command whenever a *go* command is received from a *Commander*. *Commanders* are not authorized to *launch*. *Operators* are not authorized to *launch* unless they receive a *go* command.

In this scenario, *Alice* is the *Commander* and *Bob* is an *Operator*. Notice that this scenario is captured by Figure 1.1.

We represent the notion that *Alice* and *Bob* are acting in their assigned roles of *Commander* and *Operator* using quotation and delegation. With Figure 1.1 in mind, we do the following analysis from Bob's perspective:

1. Message Bob receives signed by Alice's key:

$$K_A | Commander \text{ says } < go > \tag{1.14}$$

2. Bob's belief that *KA* is Alice's key:

$$K_A \Rightarrow Alice \tag{1.15}$$

3. Bob's recognition that Alice is acting as *Commander* when issuing a *go* command:

$$Alice \text{ reps } Commander \text{ on } < go > \tag{1.16}$$

4. Bob's belief that *Commanders* have authority to issue *go* commands:

$$Commander \text{ controls } < go > \tag{1.17}$$

5. The policy guiding Bob's actions, when he authenticates and authorizes a *go* command, then he is to issue a *launch* command:

$$< go > \supset < launch > \tag{1.18}$$

The input in line 1 with the other 4 assumptions as security context for Bob's decision is sufficient for Bob to issue the command $K_B | Operator$ says *<launch>*.

The proof is as follows using the inference rules in (1.11):

1.	$K_A \vert Commander$ says $< go >$	Input signed by K_A
2.	$K_A \Rightarrow Alice$	Trust assumption $- K_A$ is Alice's key
3.	$Alice$ reps $Commander$ on $< go >$	Trust assumption $-$ Alice is acting as a Commander when issuing a go command
4.	$Commander$ controls $< go >$	Trust assumption $-$ Commanders have authority to issue a go command
5.	$< go > \supset < launch >$	Policy assumption $-$ if go is true then so is $launch$
6.	$Commander \Rightarrow Commander$	Idempotency of $\Rightarrow$
7.	$K_A \vert Commander \Rightarrow Alice \vert Commander$	2, 6 Monotonicity of $\Rightarrow$
8.	$Alice \vert Commander$ says $< go >$	7, 1 Derived Speaks for
9.	$< go >$	4, 3, 8 Reps
10.	$< launch >$	9, 5 Modus Ponens
11.	$K_B \vert Operator$ says $< launch >$	10 Says

$$(1.19)$$

The above proof justifies a derived inference rule showing the soundness of Bob's actions:

$$\frac{\begin{array}{c} K_A \mid Commander \text{ says } \langle go \rangle \\ K_A \Rightarrow Alice \quad Alice \text{ reps } Commander \text{ on } \langle go \rangle \\ Commander \text{ controls } \langle go \rangle \quad \langle go \rangle \supset \langle launch \rangle \end{array}}{K_B \mid Operator \text{ says } \langle launch \rangle} \qquad (1.20)$$

The derived inference rule is a logical checklist. If (1) *Bob* receives a cryptographically signed message using key K_A issuing a *go* order while quoting a *Commander* role, (2) K_A is *Alice's* key, (3) *Alice* is authorized to issue a *go* command as a *Commander*, (4) *Commanders* have the authority to issue a *go* command, and (5) the policy is when *go* is true the *launch* is true, then issuing $K_B \mid Operator$ says *<launch>* is justified, where K_B is Bob's key.   □

We now turn our attention to automated support for reasoning using the HOL theorem prover for the C2 calculus in Section 1.6, and cryptographic operations and for state-transition systems in subsequent sections.

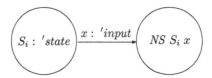

FIGURE 1.3   Parameterized state-transition relation. Reproduced with permission of IEEE.

1.6 AN INTRODUCTION TO HOL

Automated tools are essential for any realistic design and verification methodology. In this section, we introduce our use of the HOL theorem prover (10). A detailed description is infeasible, given space limitations, and is beyond the scope of this chapter. Instead, we present an introduction to how proofs are done in HOL with enough detail to enable a reading level of comprehension. The HOL system is equipped with several tutorials, user guides, and encyclopedic manuals. HOL and its documentation are available freely from online sources.[1]

The advantages of using CAR tools in general and HOL specifically include:

- Formal verification of assurance claims,
- Automated support to manage large and complicated formulas and proofs; access to vast and comprehensive libraries of verified theories containing definitions and theorems spanning mathematical logic, programming languages, instruction sets, and microprocessors, allowing designers to easily build upon a logically sound foundation of previous work,
- LaTeX macros of definitions, theorems, and formulas automatically generated by HOL, thus reducing or eliminating the burden of manually typesetting formulas and introducing typographical errors, while enabling easy updates to documentation when theories are modified, and,
- rapid and easy reproduction by third parties of all verification results.

All of the above factors combine to produce precision, accuracy, and confidence in assurance results. Results verified in HOL enable (1) system designers and verifiers to have confidence in their own work, and (2) others with more technical sophistication and experience, to reproduce and have confidence in results produced by those with comparatively less experience and sophistication.

In the following three examples, we define two parameterized theories of state machines and show they are equivalent. In section 1.7, Example 1.3, we show the syntax, semantics, and HOL theorems that define the access-control logic in HOL.

Example 1.3   Suppose we wish to define state machines parametrically in terms of their state, input, and next-state transition functions, as shown in Figure 1.3. States

---

[1] Readers who are interested in using HOL are able to download its sources and executable images from sites easily found by common search engines.

and inputs are envisioned to be any type and each may have an infinite number of elements. The notation in Figure 1.3 is used in HOL. Terms and their types are represented in HOL by *hol_term: hol_type*, that is, HOL terms followed by their types separated by a colon. For example, 1: *num*, states that 1 is of type *num* in HOL.

HOL supports polymorphism by using *type variables*. Type variables in HOL all have a leading prime symbol, '. Figure 1.3 shows state S_i with type variable '*state*, symbolized by S_i: '*state*. The expression x: '*input* says x is polymorphic with type variable '*input*, which also can be any type. As '*state* and '*input* are different type variables, the types of S_i and x need not be (and typically are not) the same.

The state-transition behavior of a deterministic state-machine is defined by its next-state function. In Figure 1.3 this is the function *NS*. What the figure shows is that if the machine is in state S_i, then the next state of the machine is *NS* S_i x, where the type signature of *NS* is '*state* $\rightarrow$'*input* $\rightarrow$'*state*.

The arrow labeled with x: '*input* from state S_i to state *NS* S_i x is modeled as an *inductively defined relation* in HOL. Inductive relations are used to define familiar sets of objects, for example, the set of *even* numbers. The set of even numbers is specified by the following rules:

1. 0 is **even**.
2. If n is **even** then $n + 2$ is **even**.
3. The set **even** is the *smallest set* satisfying rules (1) and (2).

HOL has an extensive library of theories and functions, including functions for inductive definitions. The code snippet below illustrates the use *Hol_reln to define inductively* the predicate *even* on the natural numbers. The function *Hol_reln* when applied to its arguments corresponding to rules (1) and (2) above, returns three theorems, which are assigned to names *even rules*, *even induction*, and *even cases* (see Figure 1.4). In HOL, *val* is used for assigning values to names. HOL supports pattern matching, so we can assign names to the 3-tuple of theorems returned by *Hol_reln*. (*Note*: HOL uses ASCII symbols; ! is the universal quantifier $\forall$; ==>is logical implication $\Rightarrow$; and /\ is logical conjunction $\wedge$.

```
val (even_rules, even induction, even_cases) =
Hol_reln
 'even 0/ \
 (!n. even n ⇒ even (n + 2))' ;
```

FIGURE 1.4   Hol_reln function.

The HOL code above in Figure 1.4 produces three theorems, which are pretty-printed below in formulas 1.21, using HOL-generated LaTeX macros. HOL uses *sequents* to represent theorems. Sequents have the form $\Gamma \vdash t$, where t is a term in predicate logic and Γ is a set of predicate logic terms. What $\Gamma \vdash t$ states is when all the terms in Γ are true, then t must be true, too. If Γ is empty, then we write $\vdash t$. In each of the following three theorems in 1.21, Γ is empty:

[even_rules]
$\vdash$ even $0 \wedge \forall n.$ even $n \Rightarrow$ even $(n + 2)$

[even_induction]
$\vdash \forall even'.$
$\qquad even'\ 0\ \wedge\ (\forall n.\ even'\ n \Rightarrow even'\ (n + 2))\ \Rightarrow$ (1.21)
$\qquad \forall a_0.$ even $a_0 \Rightarrow even'\ a_0$

[even_cases]
$\vdash \forall a_0.$ even $a_0 \iff (a_0 = 0) \vee \exists n.\ (a_0 = n + 2) \wedge$ even n

The first theorem *even_rules* is a commonly used description of even numbers: 0 is even, and if n is even then so is $n + 2$. The second theorem *even_induction* is an induction principle using the fact that the inductive definition of *even* is the *smallest set of numbers satisfying the even rules*. In other words, if a relation *even'* satisfies the same rules as *even*, then when *even* is true *even'* must be true, too. Finally, the third theorem *even_cases* states that if a_0 is even, then a_0 is either 0 or there is an even number n such that $a_0 = n + 2$.

Returning to formalizing what is expressed graphically in Figure 1.3 by $\underset{\sim}{x}$, i.e., arrow labeled by x. We define a labeled transition relation *Trans x*, in words as follows:

1. For all next-state functions *NS*, inputs x, and states s, the predicate *Trans x* is true for states s and *NS s x*.
2. The set defining *Trans x* is the smallest set satisfying rule (1).

The following code snippet in Figure 1.5 defines the transition relation *Trans* labeled with input *x:*

```
val (Trans_rules, Trans_ind, Trans_cases) =
Hol_reln
  '!NS (s:' state) (x:' input).
  Trans x s ((NS:' state -> 'input -> 'state ) s x) '
```

FIGURE 1.5   The transition relation *Trans*.

Hol_reln returns three theorems, *Trans_rules*, *Trans_ind*, and *Trans_cases* shown below:

[Trans_rules]
$\vdash \forall NS\ s\ x.\ \text{Trans}\ x\ s\ (NS\ s\ x)$

[Trans_ind]
$\vdash \forall \textit{Trans}'.$

$\qquad (\forall NS\ s\ x.\ \textit{Trans}'\ x\ s\ (NS\ s\ x))\ \Rightarrow$ (1.22)
$\qquad \forall a_0\ a_1\ a_2.\ \text{Trans}\ a_0\ a_1\ a_2\ \Rightarrow\ \textit{Trans}'\ a_0\ a_1\ a_2$

[Trans_cases]
$\vdash \forall a_0\ a_1\ a_2.\ \text{Trans}\ a_0\ a_1\ a_2\ \Longleftrightarrow\ \exists NS.\ a_2 = NS\ a_1\ a_0$

The first theorem *Trans_rules* is a formalization of rule (1). The second theorem *Trans_ind* is a consequence of *Trans x* being the small set satisfying rule (1). *Trans_cases* state that for all inputs a_0 and states a_1 and a_2, there is always some next-state function *NS* such that a_2 is the next state of a_1 for a given input a_0.

While the above example is simple, it shows some of the advantages of higher order logic in general, and CAR tools, such as HOL, in particular. The higher-order nature of the logic allows us to parameterize over functions, for example, the next-state function *NS*. HOL's extensive library of theories and functions supports the creation of logically sound extensions by engineers. □

Example 1.4 In this example we define another way of looking at the behavior of state machines. Figure 1.6 shows a state machine with both an input stream and an output stream. Both streams are modeled by lists of inputs and outputs. The state machine is described parametrically by a next-state function *NS*.

We can define a transition relation *TR x* similar to the relation *Trans x* in Example 1.3, except this relation is over *state-machine configurations* that incorporate input streams, state, and output streams. We define a *configuration* algebraic type in HOL using the code snippet in Figure 1.7 below:

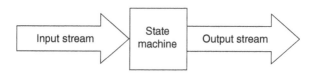

FIGURE 1.6   State machine behavior with input and output streams.

```
val _ =
Hol_datatype
 'configuration =
 CFG of 'input list ⇒ 'state ⇒ 'output list '
```

FIGURE 1.7   A configuration algebraic type in HOL. Reproduced with permission of IEEE.

The HOL function *Hol_datatype* introduces new type definition into HOL. In this case, the datatype *configuration* is defined as having a type constructor CFG and takes as inputs three arguments whose types are *'input list, 'state*, and *'output list*. These arguments are polymorphic, as indicated by their respective type variables, and correspond to input streams, states, and output streams. The pretty-printed result of executing the above code snippet is the introduction of *configuration* as an algebraic type:

$$\textit{configuration} = \text{CFG (}'\texttt{input list)}\ '\texttt{state (}'\texttt{output list)} \quad (1.23)$$

Conveniently, HOL provides extensive support for reasoning about algebraic types. In particular, we use the HOL function *one_one_of* to prove a theorem stating that two configurations are equal if and only if their components are equal. The code snippet is shown below in Figure 1.8 along with the pretty-printed theorem *configuration_one_one*:

```
val
 configuration_one_one =
 one_one_of ' ':( ' input, 'state, 'output) configuration ' '
```

FIGURE 1.8   HOL Configuration_one_one code snippet. Reproduced with permission of IEEE.

$$
\begin{aligned}
&[\texttt{configuration\_one\_one}] \\
&\vdash \forall a_0\ a_1\ a_2\ a'_0\ a'_1\ a'_2. \\
&\qquad (\text{CFG }a_0\ a_1\ a_2 = \text{CFG }a'_0\ a'_1\ a'_2) \iff \\
&\qquad (a_0 = a'_0) \wedge (a_1 = a'_1) \wedge (a_2 = a'_2)
\end{aligned}
\quad (1.24)
$$

With the algebraic type *configuration* defined in HOL, we define the relation *TR* *x* on a starting configuration whose input stream is *x::ins*, state *s*, and output stream *outs*, with next-state transition function *NS* and output function *Out*.

1. For all next-state functions *NS*, output functions *Out*, inputs *x*, input streams *ins*, states *s*, and output streams *outs*, the predicate *TR x* is true for configurations (*CFG (x::ins) s outs*) and (*CFG ins (NS s x) (Out s x::outs)*).

2. The set defining *TR x* is the smallest set satisfying rule (1).

The code snippet below in Figure 1.9 defines the transition relation *TR x* on configurations with input *x*.

```
val (TR_rules, TR_ind, TR_cases) =
Hol_reln
'!NS Out (s : ' state) (x : ' input) (ins : ' input list)
  (outs : ' output list).
  TR x
  (CFG (x : : ins) s outs)
  (CFG ins (NS s x) ((Out s x) : : outs))'
```

FIGURE 1.9   Transition relation *TR x* on configurations with input *x*.

Hol_reln returns three theorems, *TR_rules*, *TR_ind*, and *TR_cases* shown below:

```
[TR_rules]
```
$$\vdash \forall NS \ Out \ s \ x \ ins \ outs.$$
$$TR \ x \ (CFG \ (x::ins) \ s \ outs)$$
$$(CFG \ ins \ (NS \ s \ x) \ (Out \ s \ x::outs))$$

```
[TR_ind]
```
$$\vdash \forall TR'.$$
$$(\forall NS \ Out \ s \ x \ ins \ outs.$$
$$TR' \ x \ (CFG \ (x::ins) \ s \ outs)$$
$$(CFG \ ins \ (NS \ s \ x) \ (Out \ s \ x::outs))) \ \Rightarrow \quad (1.25)$$
$$\forall a_0 \ a_1 \ a_2. \ TR \ a_0 \ a_1 \ a_2 \Rightarrow TR' \ a_0 \ a_1 \ a_2$$

```
[TR_cases]
```
$$\vdash \forall a_0 \ a_1 \ a_2.$$
$$TR \ a_0 \ a_1 \ a_2 \iff$$
$$\exists NS \ Out \ s \ ins \ outs.$$
$$(a_1 = CFG \ (a_0::ins) \ s \ outs) \ \wedge$$
$$(a_2 = CFG \ ins \ (NS \ s \ a_0) \ (Out \ s \ a_0::outs))$$

As with similar definitions, *TR_rules* is the formalization of rule (1), *TR_ind* is a result of *TR x* being the smallest set satisfying rule (1), and *TR cases* relates the components of the second configuration to the components of the first configuration in conjunction with the next-state and output functions *NS* and *Out*, respectively.   □

Example 1.5 With two definitions of transition relations on state machines, we can prove they are logically equivalent. In this example, we give a brief illustration of goal-oriented proof in HOL. The theorem we prove as an illustration states that if *Trans x s (NS s x)* is true, then so is *TR x (CFG (x::ins) s outs) (CFG ins (NS s x) (Out s x::outs))*. The theorem below, *Trans_TR_lemma* states this fact.

[Trans_TR_lemma]

$$\vdash \text{Trans } x\, s\ (NS\ s\ x) \Rightarrow \tag{1.26}$$
$$\text{TR } x\ (CFG\ (x\!::\!ins)\ s\ outs)\ (CFG\ ins\ (NS\ s\ x)\ (Out\ s\ x\!::\!outs))$$

In HOL, goal-oriented proofs work by stating the desired goal with the same components as a sequent corresponding to ultimate theorem: we provide a pair consisting of a list of assumptions and the conclusion. This is done by the HOL function *set_goal*. As displayed in Figure 1.10 below, *set_goal* is applied to *([]*, *''(Trans (x:'input) (s:'state) (NS s x))''*, that is, the goal of proving Trans x implies *TR x*, with no assumptions.

```
– set_goal ( [] , ' ' (Trans (x:' input) (s:' state) (NS s x))  ⇒
(TR x (CFG (x : : ins) s (outs:' output list)) (CFG ins (NS s x) ((Out s x) : : outs)))) ' ');
> val it =
  Proof manager status: 1 proof.
  1. Incomplete goalstack:
       Initial goal:

       Trans x s (NS s x)  ⇒
       TR x (CFG (x : : ins) s outs) (CFG ins (NS s x) (Out s x : : outs))
```

FIGURE 1.10 Goal *Trans x* implies *TR x* with no assumptions. Reproduced with permission of IEEE.

Our next proof step is to simplify the assumptions as much as possible by moving all antecedents of implications into the assumption list. This is done by executing *STRIP_TAC* as displayed in Figure 1.11:

```
– e (STRIP_TAC);
OK..
1 subgoal:
> val it =

    TR x (CFG (x::ins) s outs) (CFG ins (NS s x) (Out s x: :outs))
    ------------------------------
         Trans x s (NS s x)
         : proof
```

FIGURE 1.11 *STRIP_TAC* step. Reproduced with permission of IEEE.

We recognize that the goal corresponds to the theorem *TR_rules*. We supply *TR_rules* to a high-level decision procedure in HOL name *PROVE_TAC*. The results and completed proof are displayed in Figure 1.12 below:

```
- e (PROVE_TAC [TR_rules]);
OK..
Meson search level: . .

Goal proved.
  [.] I- TR x (CFG (x: :ins) s outs) (CFG ins (NS s x) (Out s x: :outs))
> val it =
    Initial goal proved.
    I- Trans x s (NS s x) ⇒
        TR x (CFG (x: :ins) s outs) (CFG ins (NS s x) (Out s x: :outs))
    : proof
```

FIGURE 1.12 PROVE_TAC step. Reproduced with permission of IEEE.

In a similar fashion, we prove the converse of Trans_TR_lemma. The theorem is shown below as *TR Trans_lemma*.

$$[\text{TR\_Trans\_lemma}]$$

$$\vdash \text{TR } x \ (\text{CFG } (x::ins) \ s \ outs) \qquad (1.27)$$
$$(\text{CFG } ins \ (NS \ s \ x) \ (Out \ s \ x::outs)) \Rightarrow$$
$$\text{Trans } x \ s \ (NS \ s \ x)$$

With the two lemmas *Trans_TR_lemma* and *TR_Trans_lemma*, it is straightforward to prove that *Trans* and *TR* are logically equivalent. The following code snippet illustrates how the HOL function TAC_PROOF is used to prove the logical equivalence of *Trans* and *TR* as displayed in Figure 1.13:

```
val (Trans_Equiv_TR =
TAC_PROOF
(([],
' '(TR (X:' input)
    (CFG (x: :ins) (s:' state)(outs:' output list))
    (CFG ins (NS s x)((Out s x): :outs))) =
  (Trans (x:' input) (s:' state) (NS s x)) ' ' ),
PROVE_TAC[TR_Trans_lemma, Trans_TR_lemma])
```

FIGURE 1.13 TAC_PROOF proving *Trans* and *TR*. Reproduced with permission of IEEE.

The results of the proof are shown below:

```
– val Trans_Equiv_TR =
TAC_PROOF (
([],
' ' (TR (x:' input)
    (CFG (x: :ins) (s:' state) (outs:' output list))
    (CFG ins (NS s x) ((Out s x) : : outs))) =
  (Trans (x:' input) (s:' state) (NS s x)) ' ' ),
PROVE_TAC [TR_Trans_lemma, Trans_TR_lemma]);
Meson search level: . . . . . .
> val Trans_Equiv_TR =
    |– TR x (CFG (x: :ins) s outs) (CFG ins (NS s x) (Out s x: :outs)) <=>
        Trans x s (NS s x)
      : thm
```

FIGURE 1.14   Results of TAC_PROOF.   □

The three examples in this section briefly illustrate how definitional extension and proofs are done in HOL. In the remaining sections, we focus on the definitions and theorems, while omitting the details of how the proofs are done in HOL. (*Note*: In everything that follows, all formulas starting with $\vdash$ are theorems in HOL, typeset in LaTeX by HOL, and formally verified in HOL).

1.7 THE ACCESS-CONTROL LOGIC IN HOL

The access-control logic described in Section 1.5 is implemented in HOL by defining its syntax as an algebraic type *Form*, inductively defining the semantic function $E_M[[-]]$ in HOL over the type *Form* of access-control logic formulas, and proving theorems in HOL corresponding to inference rules of the C2 calculus.

The benefits of implementing the access-control logic in HOL include:

1. complete disclosure of all access-control logic and C2 calculus syntax and semantics,
2. formal machine-checked proofs of all properties of the access-control logic,
3. quantification over access-control logic formulas,
4. ability to combine the access-control logic with other logical descriptions, and,
5. rapid and easy reproduction of all results by third parties.

Sections 1.7.1, 1.7.2, and 1.7.3 describe the syntax, semantics, and theorems corresponding to the inference rules of the access-control logic and C2 calculus, respectively.

1.7.1 Syntax of the Access-Control Logic in HOL

The access-control logic is implemented as a conservative extension to the HOL system. What this means is that the HOL logic is extended by defining the *Form* algebraic type corresponding to access-control logic formulas, the algebraic type *Princ* corresponding to principal expressions, and the algebraic type *Kripke* corresponding to *Kripke* structures. The semantics of *Form* and *Princ* are defined using *Kripke* and existing HOL operators. The properties of the access-control logic are proved as theorems in HOL.

Theorem (1.28) shows the HOL type *Form* corresponding to access-control logic formulas in HOL. Notice that the HOL implementation uses *notf, andf, orf, impf,* and *eqf* to represent negation, conjunction, disjunction, implication, and equivalence in the access-control logic. Their semantics is defined in terms of sets of worlds from the universe of worlds that is part of a Kripke structure *M*. This is different than the semantics of the corresponding operators in propositional logic. The propositional logic operators are defined in terms of truth values instead of sets of worlds.

```
Form =
    TT
  | FF
  | prop 'aavar
  | notf (('aavar, 'apn, 'il, 'sl) Form)
  | (andf) (('aavar, 'apn, 'il, 'sl) Form)
           (('aavar, 'apn, 'il, 'sl) Form)
  | (orf) (('aavar, 'apn, 'il, 'sl) Form)
          (('aavar, 'apn, 'il, 'sl) Form)
  | (impf) (('aavar, 'apn, 'il, 'sl) Form)
           (('aavar, 'apn, 'il, 'sl) Form)
  | (eqf) (('aavar, 'apn, 'il, 'sl) Form)
          (('aavar, 'apn, 'il, 'sl) Form)
  | (says) ('apn Princ) (('aavar, 'apn, 'il, 'sl) Form)
  | (speaks_for) ('apn Princ) ('apn Princ)
  | (controls) ('apn Princ) (('aavar, 'apn, 'il, 'sl) Form)
  | reps ('apn Princ) ('apn Princ)
         (('aavar, 'apn, 'il, 'sl) Form)
  | (domi) (('apn, 'il) IntLevel) (('apn, 'il) IntLevel)
  | (eqi) (('apn, 'il) IntLevel) (('apn, 'il) IntLevel)
  | (doms) (('apn, 'sl) SecLevel) (('apn, 'sl) SecLevel)
  | (eqs) (('apn, 'sl) SecLevel) (('apn, 'sl) SecLevel)
  | (eqn) num num
  | (lte) num num
  | (lt) num num
```

$$(1.28)$$

The type definition in theorem (1.28) is polymorphic, that is, allows for type substitution into type variables. Recall that type variables in HOL start with the backquote symbol ′. For example, atomic propositions in the access-control logic in HOL start with the type constructor *prop* and are applied to any type, as represented by ′*aavar*. For example, *prop command* takes elements of the type *command* and maps them to propositions in the access-control logic in HOL.

Theorem (1.29) shows the syntax of principal expressions, integrity and security labels, and Kripke structures in HOL. The HOL implementation parameterizes security labels, integrity labels, and their partial orders. As our thermostat example does not rely upon security or integrity labels, we will not discuss their use further. Examples using security and integrity labels are in Chin & Older 2010.

```
Princ =
    Name 'apn
  | (meet) ('apn Princ) ('apn Princ)
  | (quoting) ('apn Princ) ('apn Princ) ;

IntLevel = iLab 'il | il 'apn ;

SecLevel = sLab 'sl | sl 'apn


Kripke =
    KS ('aavar -> 'aaworld -> bool)
        ('apn -> 'aaworld -> 'aaworld -> bool) ('apn -> 'il)
        ('apn -> 'sl)
```

$$(1.29)$$

The type constructor *Name* is polymorphic as seen in the type definition of *Princ*, where it is applied to the type variable *'apn*. The infix type constructor *meet* corresponds to &. The infix type constructor *quoting* corresponds to |.

Table 1.2 shows how formulas in the C2 calculus are written in HOL implementation of the access-control logic. The proposition *<jump>* is written as *prop jump*

TABLE 1.2   C2 Formulas and Their Representation in HOL. Reproduced with permission of IEEE

C2 Formula	HOL Syntax
<jump>	prop jump
¬*<jump>*	notf (prop jump)
<run> ∧ *<jump>*	prop run andf prop jump
<run> ∨ *<stop>*	prop run orf prop stop
<run> ⊃ *<jump>*	prop run impf prop jump
<walk> ≡ *<stop>*	prop walk eqf prop stop
Alice says *<jump>*	Name Alice says prop jump
Alice & Bob says *<stop>*	Name Alice meet Name Bob says prop stop
*Bob	Carol* says *<run>*	Name Bob quoting Name Carol says prop run
Bob controls *<walk>*	Name Bob controls prop walk
Bob reps *Alice* on *<jump>*	reps (Name Bob) (Name Alice) (prop jump)
Carol ⇒ *Bob*	Name Carol speaks_for Name Bob

in HOL. Negation of a C2 formula, such as ¬ *<jump>* is written as *notf (prop jump)* in HOL. *Alice* says *<jump>* is written as *Name Alice says prop jump*, etc.

1.7.2 Semantics of the Access-Control Logic in HOL

With the introduction of logical expressions, principal expressions, and Kripke structures as datatypes into HOL, we can define the HOL function *Efn* corresponding to the function $E_M[[-]]$ in theorem (1.9), which defines the Kripke semantics of the access-control logic. The definition of *Efn* is in Appendix 1.A.2. The definitions of $E_M[[-]]$ and *Efn* closely correspond to one another syntactically.

Of course, the question is how do we know that the implementation in HOL corresponds to the logic described in theorem (1.9) and as described in Chin & Older 2010? The answer is if we can prove theorems in HOL about the HOL implementation that correspond to the inference rules in Chin & Older 2010, then we are satisfied.

1.7.3 C2 Inference Rules in HOL

Recall in Section 1.5.3 that $M \vDash \varphi$ denoted $E_M[[\varphi]] = W$, that is, φ is true for all worlds in M. Inference rules in the C2 calculus are sound because whenever M satisfies all the hypotheses $H_1 \ldots H_k$, then M satisfies conclusion C as well.

In our HOL implementation, we say Kripke structure M with partial orders O_i and O_s on integrity and security labels, respectively, satisfies an access-control logic formula f whenever the HOL semantic function *Efn*, whose definition appears in Appendix 1.A.2, applied to M, O_i, O_s, and f equals the universe of worlds in M. The definition of *sat* in HOL is as follows.

```
[sat_def]
 ⊢ ∀M Oi Os f. (M,Oi,Os) sat f ⟺ (Efn Oi Os M f = 𝒰(:'world))
```
$$(1.30)$$

An inference rule in the C2 calculus of the form:

$$\frac{H_1 \ldots H_k}{C} \tag{1.31}$$

has a corresponding theorem in HOL:

$$\vdash \forall M\ O_i\ O_s.(M,O_i,O_s)\ sat\ H_1 \Rightarrow \cdots \Rightarrow (M,O_i,O_s)\ sat\ H_k \Rightarrow (M,O_i,O_s)\ sat\ C$$
$$(1.32)$$

where $\Rightarrow$ corresponds to logical implication in HOL. Rules (1.33) and (1.34) show the HOL theorems corresponding to the C2 inference rules in (1.11).

```
[Controls_Eq]
⊢ ∀M Oi Os P f.
    (M,Oi,Os) sat P controls f ⟺ (M,Oi,Os) sat P says f impf f
[Reps_Eq]
⊢ ∀M Oi Os P Q f.
    (M,Oi,Os) sat reps P Q f ⟺
    (M,Oi,Os) sat P quoting Q says f impf Q says f
[Modus Ponens]
⊢ ∀M Oi Os f₁ f₂.
    (M,Oi,Os) sat f₁ ⇒
    (M,Oi,Os) sat f₁ impf f₂ ⇒
    (M,Oi,Os) sat f₂
[Says]
⊢ ∀M Oi Os P f. (M,Oi,Os) sat f ⇒ (M,Oi,Os) sat P says f
[Controls]
⊢ ∀M Oi Os P f.
    (M,Oi,Os) sat P says f ⇒
    (M,Oi,Os) sat P controls f ⇒
    (M,Oi,Os) sat f
[Derived_Speaks_For]
⊢ ∀M Oi Os P Q f.
    (M,Oi,Os) sat P speaks_for Q ⇒
    (M,Oi,Os) sat P says f ⇒
    (M,Oi,Os) sat Q says f
```

$$(1.33)$$

```
[Reps]
⊢ ∀M Oi Os P Q f.
    (M,Oi,Os) sat reps P Q f ⇒
    (M,Oi,Os) sat P quoting Q says f ⇒
    (M,Oi,Os) sat Q controls f ⇒
    (M,Oi,Os) sat f
[And_Says_Eq]
⊢ (M,Oi,Os) sat P meet Q says f ⟺
   (M,Oi,Os) sat P says f andf Q says f
[Quoting_Eq]
⊢ ∀M Oi Os P Q f.
    (M,Oi,Os) sat P quoting Q says f ⟺
    (M,Oi,Os) sat P says Q says f
[Idemp_Speaks_For]
⊢ ∀M Oi Os P. (M,Oi,Os) sat P speaks_for P
[Mono_Speaks_For]
⊢ ∀M Oi Os P P' Q Q'.
    (M,Oi,Os) sat P speaks_for P' ⇒
    (M,Oi,Os) sat Q speaks_for Q' ⇒
    (M,Oi,Os) sat P quoting Q speaks_for P' quoting Q'
```

$$(1.34)$$

1.8 CRYPTOGRAPHIC COMPONENTS AND THEIR MODELS IN HIGHER-ORDER LOGIC

Cryptographic operations are an integral part of protecting integrity and confidentiality. In this section, we provide algebraic models in higher-order logic and HOL of idealized cryptographic operations. Missing is any notion of cryptographic strength and a particular algorithm's ability to withstand cryptanalysis.

Our descriptions of ideal cryptographic behavior are similar to Conway's (2012) description of ideal transistors as switches. Her design approach focused on how transistors are used and the accompanying expectations as a binary device, as opposed to giving details of its amplification performance as an analog device.

In what follows, the models of crypto operations, combined with the access-control logic, enable us to reason about systems using cryptographic-based authentication and authorization. In the following sections on symmetric-key and asymmetric-key encryption and decryption, cryptographic hash functions, and digital signatures, we describe the operation, how it is used, and the ideal behavior we model in HOL.

1.8.1 Symmetric-Key Cryptography

Figure 1.15 is a schematic of symmetric-key encryption and decryption. Suppose Bob wishes to send a message to Alice that only he and Alice can read. Also suppose that Bob and Alice share the same secret key, which is also known as a symmetric key. Here are the steps that Bob and Alice take to communicate confidentially:

1. Bob *encrypts* his message in plaintext with the secret key k he shares with Alice. He forwards to encrypted message, that is, the ciphertext, to Alice.
2. Alice uses symmetric key k to decrypt the ciphertext to retrieve the plaintext message.

1.8.1.1 Idealized Behavior Symmetric-key cryptography is used with the following expectations: (1) the same key is the only means to decrypt what is encrypted,

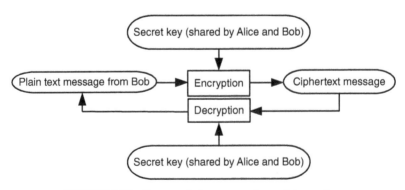

FIGURE 1.15 Symmetric-key encryption and decryption.

(2) if something useful and recognizable is decrypted, then it must mean that the decrypted text and the decryption key are identical to the original text and encryption key, and (3) using anything other than the original encryption key to decrypt will result in an unusable result. We capture these expectations semiformally by the following statements:

1. Whatever is encrypted with key k is retrieved unchanged by decrypting with the same key k.
2. If key k_1 encrypted any plaintext, and key k_2 decrypted the resulting ciphertext and retrieved the original text, then $k_1 = k_2$.
3. If plaintext is encrypted with key k_1, decrypted with key k_2, and nothing useful results, then $k_1 \neq k_2$.
4. If nothing useful is encrypted using any key, then nothing useful is decrypted using any key.

1.8.1.2 *Modeling Idealized Behavior in HOL*
Adding "nothing useful" as a value is one aspect we must model. We add "nothing useful" as a value or result by using *option* theory in HOL. Figure 1.35 shows the type definition of *option* and the properties of *option* types in HOL in the theorem *option_CLAUSES*.

The *option* type is polymorphic. *Option* types are created from other types using the type constructor *SOME*. For example, when *SOME* is applied to the natural number 1, that is, *SOME 1*, the resulting value is of type *num* option. The *num* option type has all the values of *SOME n*, where n is a natural number in HOL, with one added value: *NONE*. We use *NONE* when we want to return a value other than a natural number, for example, in the case where we return a result of dividing by zero.

```
option = NONE | SOME 'a
[option_CLAUSES]
⊢ (∀x y. (SOME x = SOME y) ⟺ (x = y)) ∧
  (∀x. THE (SOME x) = x) ∧ (∀x. NONE ≠ SOME x) ∧
  (∀x. SOME x ≠ NONE) ∧ (∀x. IS_SOME (SOME x) ⟺ T) ∧
  (IS_SOME NONE ⟺ F) ∧ (∀x. IS_NONE x ⟺ (x = NONE)) ∧
  (∀x. ¬IS_SOME x ⟺ (x = NONE)) ∧
  (∀x. IS_SOME x ⟹ (SOME (THE x) = x)) ∧
  (∀x. option_CASE x NONE SOME = x) ∧
  (∀x. option_CASE x x SOME = x) ∧
  (∀x. IS_NONE x ⟹ (option_CASE x e f = e)) ∧
  (∀x. IS_SOME x ⟹ (option_CASE x e f = f (THE x))) ∧
  (∀x. IS_SOME x ⟹ (option_CASE x e SOME = x)) ∧
  (∀v f. option_CASE NONE v f = v) ∧
  (∀x v f. option_CASE (SOME x) v f = f x) ∧
  (∀f x. OPTION_MAP f (SOME x) = SOME (f x)) ∧
  (∀f. OPTION_MAP f NONE = NONE) ∧ (OPTION_JOIN NONE = NONE) ∧
  ∀x. OPTION_JOIN (SOME x) = x
```

$$(1.35)$$

In the case of modeling encryption and decryption, we use option types to add the value *NONE* to whatever we are encrypting or decrypting. Doing so allows us to handle cases such as what value to return if the wrong key is used to decrypt an encrypted message.

Finally, the accessor function *THE* is used to retrieve the value to which *SOME* is applied. For example, *THE(SOME x) = x*, as shown in *option CLAUSES*.

1.8.1.3 Symmetric Keys, Encryption, Decryption, and their Properties

Rule (1.36) shows the definitions and properties of symmetric-key encryption and decryption. The following is a list of key definitions and properties.

- Symmetric keys are modeled by the algebraic type *symKey*. The type constructor is *sym*. For example, *sym 1234* is a symmetric key. Abstractly, *sym 1234* is the symmetric key which is identified by number 1234.

- Two symmetric keys are identical if they have the same number to which *sym* is applied. This is shown in theorem *symKey_one_one*.

- Symmetrically encrypted messages are modeled by the algebraic type *symMsg*, whose type constructor is *Es*. Symmetrically encrypted messages have two arguments: (1) a *symKey*, and (2) a *'message option*. For example, *Es (sym 1234) (SOME "This is a string")* is a symmetrically encrypted message using: (1) the symmetric key *sym 1234*, and (2) the *string option* value *SOME "This is a string."* Abstractly, the type constructor *Es* stands for any symmetric-key encryption algorithm, for example, Data Encryption Standard (DES) or Advanced Encryption Standard (AES).

```
symKey = sym num
[symKey_one_one]
 ⊢ ∀a a'. (sym a = sym a')  ⟺  (a = a')
symMsg = Es symKey ('message option)
[symMsg_one_one]
 ⊢ ∀a₀ a₁ a'₀ a'₁.
      (Es a₀ a₁ = Es a'₀ a'₁)  ⟺  (a₀ = a'₀) ∧ (a₁ = a'₁)
[deciphS_def]
 ⊢ (deciphS k₁ (Es k₂ (SOME x)) =
    if k₁ = k₂ then SOME x else NONE) ∧
    (deciphS k₁ (Es k₂ NONE) = NONE)
[deciphS_clauses]
 ⊢ (∀k text. deciphS k (Es k (SOME text)) = SOME text) ∧
    (∀k₁ k₂ text.
        (deciphS k₁ (Es k₂ (SOME text)) = SOME text)  ⟺
        (k₁ = k₂)) ∧
    (∀k₁ k₂ text.
        (deciphS k₁ (Es k₂ (SOME text)) = NONE)  ⟺  k₁ ≠ k₂) ∧
    ∀k₁ k₂. deciphS k₁ (Es k₂ NONE) = NONE
[deciphS_one_one]
 ⊢ (∀k₁ k₂ text₁ text₂.
        (deciphS k₁ (Es k₂ (SOME text₂))) = SOME text₁)  ⟺
        (k₁ = k₂) ∧ (text₁ = text₂)) ∧
    ∀enMsg text key.
      (deciphS key enMsg = SOME text)  ⟺
      (enMsg = Es key (SOME text))
```

$$(1.36)$$

- Two *symMsg* values are identical if their corresponding components are identical. This is shown in theorem *symMsg_one_one*.
- Symmetric-key decryption of *symMsgs* is defined by *deciphS_def*. If the same *symKey* is used to decipher an encrypted *SOME x*, then *SOME x* is returned. Otherwise, *NONE* is returned. If nothing useful is encrypted, then nothing useful is decrypted. Abstractly, *deciphS* represents any symmetric-key decryption algorithm.
- Finally, deciphS_clauses states the properties of deciphS: (1) the same key when used for encryption and decryption returns the original message, (2) if the original message was retrieved, identical keys were used, (3) if a different key is used to decrypt ciphertext, then nothing useful is returned, and (4) garbage in and garbage out holds true.

1.9 CRYPTOGRAPHIC HASH FUNCTIONS

Cryptographic hash functions are used to map inputs of any size into a fixed number of bits. Cryptographic hash functions are one-way functions, (1) the output is easy to compute from the input, and (2) it is computationally infeasible to determine an input when given only a hash value. Hash values are also known as digests.

Rule (1.37) shows the type definition of digest and their properties. The following describes the type definition and its properties.

$$
\begin{aligned}
&digest \; = \; \texttt{hash} \; (\texttt{'message option}) \\
&\texttt{[digest\_one\_one]} \\
&\vdash \forall a \; a'. \; (\texttt{hash} \; a = \texttt{hash} \; a') \iff (a = a')
\end{aligned}
\tag{1.37}
$$

- Digests or hashes are modeled by the algebraic type *digest*. The type constructor is *hash* and is meant to represent any hash algorithm, for example, SHA1 and SHA2. Notice that the hash is applied to polymorphic arguments of type *'message option*, for example, *hash (SOME "A string message")*.
- The key property of ideal digests is they are one-to-one, as shown by the theorem *digest_one_one*. In reality, hashes cannot be one-to-one due to their fixed-length output. Modeling digests in this way is analogous to modeling the electrical behavior of transistors as perfect switches.

1.10 ASYMMETRIC-KEY CRYPTOGRAPHY

Figure 1.16 is a schematic of asymmetric-key encryption and decryption. The asymmetric nature of asymmetric-key, or public-key cryptography, is that two different keys are used instead of the same key. One key, known as a public key, may be freely disclosed. The other key, known as a private key, must be known only by one principal.

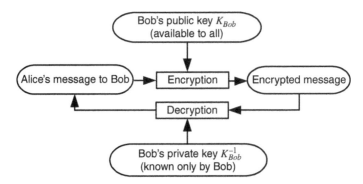

FIGURE 1.16   Asymmetric-key encryption and decryption.

Suppose Alice wishes to send a message to Bob that only Bob can read. Alice encrypts the message to Bob using his public key K_{Bob}. Only Bob, who alone possesses the private key $K^{-1}{}_{Bob}$, is able to decrypt the message encrypted with his public key K_{Bob}.

Asymmetric-key cryptography is used with the following expectations: (1) plaintext that is encrypted with a private key can be retrieved only with the corresponding public key, (2) plaintext that is encrypted with a public key can be retrieved only with the corresponding private key, (3) if plaintext was retrieved that was encrypted with a private key, then the corresponding public key was used to decrypt the ciphertext, (4) if plaintext was retrieved that was encrypted with a public key, then the corresponding private key was used to decrypt the ciphertext, and (5) nothing useful results if decryption uses anything but the corresponding public or private key used in encryption.

Rule (1.38) shows the type definitions for asymmetric keys *pKey*, that is, public and private keys, and asymmetrically encrypted messages *asymMsg*. (1.38) also shows properties of *pKey* and *asymMsg*.

pKey = pubK 'princ | privK 'princ
[pKey_distinct_clauses]
$\vdash$ ($\forall a'$ a. pubK $a \neq$ privK a') $\wedge$ $\forall a'$ a. privK $a' \neq$ pubK a
[pKey_one_one]
$\vdash$ ($\forall a$ a'. (pubK a = pubK a') $\Longleftrightarrow$ (a = a')) $\wedge$
    $\forall a$ a'. (privK a = privK a') $\Longleftrightarrow$ (a = a')
asymMsg = Ea ('princ pKey) ('message option)
[asymMsg_one_one]
$\vdash$ $\forall a_0$ a_1 a'_0 a'_1.
        (Ea a_0 a_1 = Ea a'_0 a'_1) $\Longleftrightarrow$ (a_0 = a'_0) $\wedge$ (a_1 = a'_1)

$$(1.38)$$

- The type *pKey* has two forms, *pubK P* and *privK P*, public and private, respectively. Asymmetric keys are polymorphic and intended to be associated with principals *P* with variable type $'princ$.
- The private and public keys of any principal are not the same.
- Public and private keys are the same if they have the same parameters.
- The type *asymMsg* represents asymmetrically encrypted messages. The parameters of type constructor *Ea* are a *pKey* and a $'message$ *option*. Abstractly, the type constructor *Ea* stands for any asymmetric-key algorithm, for example, RSA.
- Two asymMsgs are the same if they have the same pKey and $'message$ option values.

Rule (1.39) shows the definition and properties of *deciphP*, which models the decryption of asymmetrically encrypted messages. Similar to symmetric-key encryption, to retrieve the plaintext *SOME x* requires use of the correct key, in this case *privK P* if the message was encrypted using *pubK P*, or *pubK P* if the message was encrypted with *privK P*. As before, garbage in produces garbage out.

```
[deciphP_def]
 ⊢ (deciphP key (Ea (privK P) (SOME x)) =
     if key = pubK P then SOME x else NONE) ∧
    (deciphP key (Ea (pubK P) (SOME x)) =
     if key = privK P then SOME x else NONE) ∧
    (deciphP k₁ (Ea k₂ NONE) = NONE)
[deciphP_clauses]
 ⊢ (∀P text.
        (deciphP (pubK P) (Ea (privK P) (SOME text)) =
        SOME text) ∧
        (deciphP (privK P) (Ea (pubK P) (SOME text)) =
        SOME text)) ∧
    (∀k P text.
        (deciphP k (Ea (privK P) (SOME text)) = SOME text ⟺
        (k = pubK P)) ∧
    (∀k P text.
        (deciphP k (Ea (pubK P) (SOME text)) = SOME text ⟺
        (k = privK P)) ∧
    (∀x k₂ k₁ P₂ P₁.
        (deciphP (pubK P₁) (Ea (pubK P₂) (SOME x)) = NONE) ∧
        (deciphP k₁ (Ea k₂ NONE) = NONE)) ∧
    ∀x P₂ P₁. deciphP (privK P₁) (Ea (privK P₂) (SOME x)) = NONE
```
$$(1.39)$$

The properties of *deciphP* are shown in rules (1.39) and (1.40) by theorems *deciphP_clauses* and *deciphP_one_one*. Together, they show the circumstances under which the original plaintext is decrypted, when nothing useful is decrypted, and the conditions that ensure that the expected keys and plaintext messages were in fact, used.

```
[deciphP_one_one]
```
$\vdash$ $(\forall P_1\ P_2\ \textit{text}_1\ \textit{text}_2.$
          $(\texttt{deciphP}\ (\texttt{pubK}\ P_1)\ (\texttt{Ea}\ (\texttt{privK}\ P_2)\ (\texttt{SOME}\ \textit{text}_2))$ =
          $\texttt{SOME}\ \textit{text}_1)\ \Longleftrightarrow\ (P_1\ =\ P_2)\ \wedge\ (\textit{text}_1\ =\ \textit{text}_2))\ \wedge$
$(\forall P_1\ P_2\ \textit{text}_1\ \textit{text}_2.$
          $(\texttt{deciphP}\ (\texttt{privK}\ P_1)\ (\texttt{Ea}\ (\texttt{pubK}\ P_2)\ (\texttt{SOME}\ \textit{text}_2))$ =
          $\texttt{SOME}\ \textit{text}_1)\ \Longleftrightarrow\ (P_1\ =\ P_2)\ \wedge\ (\textit{text}_1\ =\ \textit{text}_2))\ \wedge$
$(\forall p\ c\ P\ \textit{msg}.$
          $(\texttt{deciphP}\ (\texttt{pubK}\ P)\ (\texttt{Ea}\ p\ c)\ =\ \texttt{SOME}\ \textit{msg})\ \Longleftrightarrow$
          $(p\ =\ \texttt{privK}\ P)\ \wedge\ (c\ =\ \texttt{SOME}\ \textit{msg}))\ \wedge$
$(\forall \textit{enMsg}\ P\ \textit{msg}.$
          $(\texttt{deciphP}\ (\texttt{pubK}\ P)\ \textit{enMsg}\ =\ \texttt{SOME}\ \textit{msg})\ \Longleftrightarrow$
          $(\textit{enMsg}\ =\ \texttt{Ea}\ (\texttt{privK}\ P)\ (\texttt{SOME}\ \textit{msg})))\ \wedge$
$(\forall p\ c\ P\ \textit{msg}.$
          $(\texttt{deciphP}\ (\texttt{privK}\ P)\ (\texttt{Ea}\ p\ c)\ =\ \texttt{SOME}\ \textit{msg})\ \Longleftrightarrow$
          $(p\ =\ \texttt{pubK}\ P)\ \wedge\ (c\ =\ \texttt{SOME}\ \textit{msg}))\ \wedge$
$\forall \textit{enMsg}\ P\ \textit{msg}.$
          $(\texttt{deciphP}\ (\texttt{privK}\ P)\ \textit{enMsg}\ =\ \texttt{SOME}\ \textit{msg})\ \Longleftrightarrow$
          $(\textit{enMsg}\ =\ \texttt{Ea}\ (\texttt{pubK}\ P)\ (\texttt{SOME}\ \textit{msg}))$

$$(1.40)$$

1.11 DIGITAL SIGNATURES

Digitally signed messages are often a combination of cryptographic hashes of messages encrypted using the *private key* of the sender. This is shown in Figure 1.17,
which depicts signature generation as the following sequence of operations:

1. A message is hashed, then,
2. The message hash is encrypted using the private key of the sender.

The intuition behind signatures is this: (1) the cryptographic hash is a unique
pointer to the message (and potentially much smaller than the message), and (2)
encrypting using the sender's private key (which is reversible by the sender's public
key) is a unique pointer to the sender.

Figure 1.18 shows how decrypted messages are checked for integrity using digital
signatures. The top-most sequence from left to right shows how the decrypted hash
value is retrieved from the received digital signature. The digital signature is decrypted
using the sender's public key to retrieve the hash or digest of the original message.
The retrieved hash is compared to the hash of the decrypted message. If the two hash

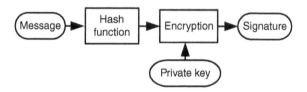

FIGURE 1.17   Digital signature generation.

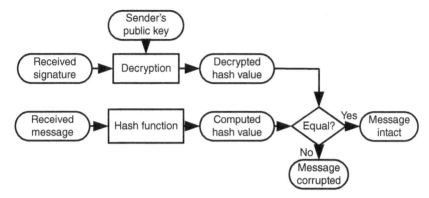

FIGURE 1.18   Digital signature verification.

values are the same, then the received message is judged to have arrived unchanged from the original.

Rule (1.41) shows the function definitions in HOL of *sign* and *signVerify*. *sign* takes as inputs a *pKey* and a digest and returns an asymmetrically encrypted digest using the asymmetric *pKey*. *signVerify* takes as input a *Key*, digital signature, and a received message and compares the decrypted hash in the signature with the hash of the received message. The properties of *signVerify* and *sign* are in theorems *signVerifyOK* and *signVerify_one_one*:

- *signVerify* is always true for signatures generated as shown in Figure 1.17.

- *signVerify* and *sign* combine to have the desired properties that the plaintext must match and the corresponding keys must match.

```
[sign_def]
⊢ ∀pubKey dgst. sign pubKey dgst = Ea pubKey (SOME dgst)
[signVerify_def]
⊢ ∀pubKey signature msgContents.
      signVerify pubKey signature msgContents  ⟺
      (SOME (hash msgContents) = deciphP pubKey signature)
[signVerifyOK]
⊢ ∀P msg.
      signVerify (pubK P) (sign (privK P) (hash (SOME msg)))
        (SOME msg)
[signVerify_one_one]
⊢ (∀P m₁ m₂.
      signVerify (pubK P) (Ea (privK P) (SOME (hash (SOME m₁)))))
        (SOME m₂)  ⟺  (m₁ = m₂)) ∧
   (∀signature P text.
      signVerify (pubK P) signature (SOME text)  ⟺
      (signature = sign (privK P) (hash (SOME text)))) ∧
   ∀text₂ text₁ P₂ P₁.
      signVerify (pubK P₁) (sign (privK P₂) (hash (SOME text₂)))
        (SOME text₁)  ⟺  (P₁ = P₂) ∧ (text₁ = text₂)
```
$$(1.41)$$

1.12   ADDING SECURITY TO STATE MACHINES

In this section, we use the infrastructure we have described in previous sections to add authentication and authorization to the description of state machines. Traditionally, this authentication and authorization was a function of virtual machine monitors (VMMs) or hypervisors. Our approach is to combine VMM functions into the description of state machines. We call these machines secure-state machines (SSMs).

At this point, we now have the following logical infrastructure:

1. An access-control logic and a C2 calculus in the form of inference rules implemented and verified as sound within the HOL theorem prover.
2. A means to represent CONOPS in the access-control logic where each action taken in the CONOPS is a derived inference rule, that is, logically sound.
3. Algebraic models in HOL of cryptographic operations including symmetric and asymmetric encryption and decryption, cryptographic hashes, and digital signature generation and verification.
4. Parameterized state machines of arbitrary size described in HOL using labeled transition relations defined inductively in HOL.

Using the above infrastructure, we combine the above elements to extend the parameterized state-machine description in Section 1.6 to account for authentication and authorization and we do so at two levels:

1. State-machine transition behavior at a purely logical level where inputs and the security context are described in the access-control logic, and
2. State-machine transition behavior at a concrete level using (1) message and certificate data structures, and (2) interpretations in the access-control logic of messages and certificates.

There are many policies that define secure behavior, for example, the classic military confidentiality policies of Bell and La Padula (1973, 1976), the integrity policies of Biba (1977), and role-based access control (Ferraiolo & Kuhn 1992; Chin & Older 2010). For illustrative purposes, the security policy we use is based on Popek and Goldberg's (1974) virtualization policies. We chose virtualization because it lends itself to state-machine descriptions and it supports specifications where authorization and authentication are parameters.

The high-level policy followed by SSMs is as follows:

1. If an input to the machine fails to pass the supplied integrity check used by the machine, the input is discarded.
2. Inputs that are authenticated and deemed intact are checked for authorization within the context of a state-interpretation function and list of certificates. An example of a security-interpretation of a state is when a mode bit is used to indicate if the machine is operating in privileged mode or user mode. An

example of a certificate used for authorization is a ticket granting permission to access or use an object or service.

    a. Authorized commands are executed.

    b. Unauthorized commands are trapped.

3. Within the context of a specific application, commands are divided into two groups:

    a. Security-sensitive commands, that is, commands that if misused, compromise the integrity or confidentiality of operations, for example, compromising process isolation, or,

    b. Innocuous commands, that is, commands that do not compromise integrity or confidentiality.

4. In keeping with the requirements for virtualizability as defined in Popek and Goldberg (1974), all security-sensitive commands are privileged commands, that is, executable only by authorized principals. Attempts by unauthorized principals to execute privileged commands are trapped.

In keeping with making our SSM theories as reusable as possible, we fully parameterize them in terms of:

- authentication functions,
- authorization context given by lists of certificates and credentials, which have meaning in the access-control logic,
- functions for defining the meaning of inputs, certificates, and states, in the access-control logic,
- next-state functions,
- output functions, and
- type variables for inputs, outputs, and states in support of polymorphism.

We develop two levels of SSM description:

1. high-level logical description relying on access-control logic formulas for inputs and certificates, and
2. lower-level description using type variables and interpretation functions for inputs, states, and certificates.

This lower-level description is a refinement of the high-level description of behavior.

1.12.1 Instructions and Transition Types

Rule 1.42 shows the definition and properties of SSM instructions *inst* and state-transition types *trType*. The *inst* type is polymorphic, and is constructed with the type variable *'command and the type constructor CMD*. One additional instruction, *TRAP*, is added to all the commands that are in *'command*. The theorems *inst_distinct clauses* and *trType_distinct_clauses* are the usual theorems stating that each form of *inst* or *trType* is distinct from the other.

```
inst = CMD 'command | TRAP
[inst_distinct_clauses]
⊢ (∀a. CMD a ≠ TRAP) ∧ ∀a. TRAP ≠ CMD a
trType = discard | trap 'inst | exec 'inst
[trType_distinct_clauses]
⊢ (∀a. discard ≠ trap a) ∧ (∀a. discard ≠ exec a) ∧
  (∀a' a. trap a ≠ exec a') ∧ (∀a. trap a ≠ discard) ∧
  (∀a. exec a ≠ discard) ∧ ∀a' a. exec a' ≠ trap a
```

$$(1.42)$$

There are two points regarding *inst*:

1. The purpose of *inst* is to add *TRAP* to the set of commands. Doing so facilitates writing policies in the access-control logic specifying when *TRAPs* should occur.
2. We can achieve the same effect by using option types, that is, using *SOME* and *NONE*. To enhance readability, we use *CMD* and *TRAP* instead.

1.12.2 High-Level Secure-State Machine Description

Rule (1.43) shows the definition of high-level SSM configurations and their properties. Configurations have six components:

```
configuration =
    CFG (('command inst, 'principal, 'd, 'e) Form -> bool)
        ('state -> ('command inst, 'principal, 'd, 'e) Form)
        (('command inst, 'principal, 'd, 'e) Form list)
        (('command inst, 'principal, 'd, 'e) Form list) 'state
        ('output list)
[configuration_11]
⊢ ∀a₀ a₁ a₂ a₃ a₄ a₅ a'₀ a'₁ a'₂ a'₃ a'₄ a'₅.
    (CFG a₀ a₁ a₂ a₃ a₄ a₅ = CFG a'₀ a'₁ a'₂ a'₃ a'₄ a'₅) ⟺
    (a₀ = a'₀) ∧ (a₁ = a'₁) ∧ (a₂ = a'₂) ∧ (a₃ = a'₃) ∧
    (a₄ = a'₄) ∧ (a₅ = a'₅)
```

$$(1.43)$$

1. An authentication function with type *('command inst, 'principal, 'd, 'e) Form -> bool* that returns *true* or *false* when applied to inputs expressed as access-control logic formulas. This function determines whether or not commands originate from known and approved sources.

2. A state interpretation function with type *'state* -> (*'command inst, 'principal,'d, 'e*) *Form* that maps a state into an access-control logic formula. The interpretation function and state are part of the security context informing the decision on whether or not an authenticated request is authorized.

3. A list of access-control logic formulas (*'command inst, 'principal, 'd, 'e*) *Form list* that represent the security context, with security interpretation of the current state, in which authenticated requests are authorized or not. The list elements correspond to the meaning of certification, polices, trust assumptions, and authorizations in the access-control logic.

4. An input stream of access-control logic formulas (*'command inst, 'principal,'d, 'e*) *Form* list.

5. The current state *'state*.

6. An output stream *'output list*.

The theorem *configuration_11* is the typical property stating that two configurations are identical if and only if all their components are identical.

1.12.3 Semantics of Lists of Access-Control Logic Formulas Defined

To assist in the interpretation of configurations, we define the function *satList*, whose purpose is to give meaning to a list of access-control logic formulas, for example, [*f1; f2; …; fn*]. Rule (1.44) defines *satList* and its properties. The net effect of the *satList* definition and theorems is *satList* applied to a Kripke structure M, partial orders O_i and O_s, and a list of access-control logic formulas [*f1; f2; …; f_n*], is that *satList* is the *and reduction* of (M, O_i, O_s) *sat* mapped over each formula f_i. For example, (M, O_i, O_s) *satList* [$f_1; f_2; …; f_n$] = (M, O_i, O_s) *sat* $f_1 \wedge … \wedge$ (M, O_i, O_s) *sat* f_n:

```
[satList_def]
 ⊢ ∀M Oi Os formList.
      (M,Oi,Os) satList formList ⟺
      FOLDR (λx y. x ∧ y) T (MAP (λf. (M,Oi,Os) sat f) formList)
[satList_nil]
 ⊢ (M,Oi,Os) satList []
[satList_CONS]
 ⊢ ∀h t M Oi Os.
      (M,Oi,Os) satList (h::t) ⟺
      (M,Oi,Os) sat h ∧ (M,Oi,Os) satList t
[satList_conj]
 ⊢ ∀l₁ l₂ M Oi Os.
      (M,Oi,Os) satList l₁ ∧ (M,Oi,Os) satList l₂ ⟺
      (M,Oi,Os) satList (l₁ ++ l₂)
```

$$(1.44)$$

Rule (1.45) shows the definition *CFGInterpret_def*, which defines the meaning of configurations in the access-control logic. Simply put, the security interpretation of a configuration is the conjunction of formulas (M, O_i, O_s) *sat* f_i, where f_i corresponds to the formulas in the list *context*, the meaning of input x, and the interpretation of state.

```
[CFGInterpret_def]
 ⊢ CFGInterpret (M, Oi, Os)
       (CFG inputTest stateInterp context (x::ins) state
           outStream)   ⟺
     (M, Oi, Os) satList context ∧ (M, Oi, Os) sat x ∧
     (M, Oi, Os) sat stateInterp state
```
(1.45)

We define inductively the transition relation *TR* on configurations using the same techniques as shown in Example 1.4 on pg. 20. This time, we account for the security interpretation of configurations. Appendix 1.A.3 gives the HOL source code for defining *TR*. Appendix 1.A.3.2 shows the three defining properties of *TR* in HOL resulting from the inductive definition.

These properties are *TR_rules*, *TR_ind*, and *TR_cases*, which give the transition rules, induction property, and cases theorem, respectively. Looking at *TR_rules*, we see there are three clauses, one each for the three *trTypes* labeling the transition relation *TR* (M, O_i, O_s):

1. *TR* (M, Oi, O_s) (*exec* (*CMD cmd*)): the rule specifying when a command *cmd* is executed. The conditions are:
   a. the input *P says prop* (*CMD cmd*) must be authenticated by *inputTest*, and
   b. the security interpretation of the current configuration is given by *CFGInterpret*.
2. *TR* (M, O_i, O_s) (*trap* (*CMD cmd*)): the rule specifying when a command *cmd* is trapped. The conditions are:
   a. the input *P says prop* (*CMD cmd*) must be authenticated by *inputTest*, and
   b. the security interpretation of the current configuration is given by *CFGInterpret*.
3. *TR* (M, O_i, O_s) *discard*: the rule specifying when an input x is discarded. The rule states when x fails to be authenticated by *inputTest*, x is discarded from the input stream.

Based on the definitions of *TR*, *satList*, and *CFGInterpret*, and their properties, we can prove three equality properties related to each of the transition types *trType*. The following three equality rules are parameterizable, convenient, and essential for easily certifying the security properties of devices such as the networked thermostat. The equality theorems are:

1. *TR_discard_cmd* rule as shown in rule (1.46). It states that a discard transition occurs for an input x if and only if x fails to be authenticated, that is, $\neg inputTest$ x is true.

```
[TR_discard_cmd_rule]
⊢ TR (M,Oi,Os) discard
      (CFG inputTest stateInterp certs (x::ins) s outs)
      (CFG inputTest stateInterp certs ins (NS s discard)
        (Out s discard::outs)) ⟺ ¬inputTest x
```
(1.46)

2. *TR_exec_cmd_rule* as shown in (1.47). It states that *if* (M, O_i, O_s) *sat prop* (*CMD cmd*) is justified, that is, implied by the security interpretation of the current configuration, as specified by *CFGInterpret*, then *cmd* is executed if and only if (a) the input is authenticated, (b) *CFGInterpret* is the security interpretation, and (c) (M, O_i, O_s) *sat prop* (*CMD cmd*) is true.

```
[TR_exec_cmd_rule]
⊢ ∀inputTest certs stateInterp P cmd ins s outs.
    (∀M Oi Os.
       CFGInterpret (M,Oi,Os)
         (CFG inputTest stateInterp certs
             (P says prop (CMD cmd)::ins) s outs) ⇒
         (M,Oi,Os) sat prop (CMD cmd)) ⇒
    ∀NS Out M Oi Os.
      TR (M,Oi,Os) (exec (CMD cmd))
        (CFG inputTest stateInterp certs
            (P says prop (CMD cmd)::ins) s outs)
        (CFG inputTest stateInterp certs ins
            (NS s (exec (CMD cmd)))
            (Out s (exec (CMD cmd))::outs)) ⟺
      inputTest (P says prop (CMD cmd)) ∧
      CFGInterpret (M,Oi,Os)
        (CFG inputTest stateInterp certs
            (P says prop (CMD cmd)::ins) s outs) ∧
      (M,Oi,Os) sat prop (CMD cmd)
```
(1.47)

3. *TR_trap_cmd* as shown in rule (1.48). It states that if (M, O_i, O_s) *sat prop* *TRAP* is justified, that is, implied by the security interpretation of the current configuration, as specified by *CFGInterpret*, then *cmd* is trapped if and only if (a) the input is authenticated, (b) *CFGInterpret* is the security interpretation, and (c) (M, O_i, O_s) *sat prop TRAP* is true.

```
[TR_trap_cmd_rule]
```
$\vdash \forall inputTest\ stateInterp\ certs\ P\ cmd\ ins\ s\ outs.$
$(\forall M\ Oi\ Os.$
    ```
    CFGInterpret (M, Oi, Os)
    ```
        $(CFG\ inputTest\ stateInterp\ certs$
            ```
            (P says prop (CMD cmd)::ins) s outs) ⇒
            (M, Oi, Os) sat prop TRAP) ⇒
            ```
    $\forall NS\ Out\ M\ Oi\ Os.$
        ```
        TR (M, Oi, Os) (trap (CMD cmd))
        ```
            $(CFG\ inputTest\ stateInterp\ certs$
                ```
                (P says prop (CMD cmd)::ins) s outs)
                ```
            $(CFG\ inputTest\ stateInterp\ certs\ ins$
                ```
                (NS s (trap (CMD cmd)))
                (Out s (trap (CMD cmd)))::outs)) ⟺
                ```
    $inputTest$ ```(P says prop (CMD cmd))``` $\wedge$
    ```
    CFGInterpret (M, Oi, Os)
    ```
        $(CFG\ inputTest\ stateInterp\ certs$
            ```
            (P says prop (CMD cmd)::ins) s outs) ∧
            (M, Oi, Os) sat prop TRAP
            ```

(1.48)

Note that in the above three theorems, the following functions and types are parameterized, making the theorems applicable to state machines in general using the concepts of discarding, trapping, and executing commands. The specific parameters are:

1. *inputTest*: the authentication function,
2. *stateInterp*: the state interpretation function,
3. *certs*: the credentials, trust assumptions, delegations, and authorizations informing authorization decisions,
4. *commands*: commands are polymorphic,
5. *states*: states are polymorphic,
6. *outputs*: outputs are polymorphic,
7. *NS*: the next-state function, and
8. *Out*: the output function.

The three theorems in (1.46), (1.47) and (1.48), provide a parameterized framework at the logic design level of state machines. We use this framework in specific applications, such as the networked thermostat, by specifying each of the eight parameters listed above.

Where is assurance of security accounted for in these theorems?

1. In *TR_discard_cmd_rule* the authentication function *inputTest* eliminates all unauthenticated commands.
2. In *TR_exec_cmd_rule*, the condition:

$\forall M\ Oi\ Os.$
CFGInterpret (M,Oi,Os)
(CFG *inputTest stateInterp certs* $(P$ says prop (CMD *cmd*)::*ins*) *s outs*) $\Rightarrow$
(M,Oi,Os) sat prop (CMD *cmd*)

$$(1.49)$$

corresponds to a *derived inference rule* in the C2 calculus. In effect, the theorem states that if the above is proved to be a theorem in the C2 calculus, then the remaining if and only if clause of the theorem holds.

3. In *TR_trap_cmd_rule*, similar to *TR_exec_cmd_rule*, the condition:

$\forall M\ Oi\ Os.$
CFGInterpret (M,Oi,Os)
(CFG *inputTest stateInterp certs* $(P$ says prop (CMD *cmd*)::*ins*) *s outs*) $\Rightarrow$
(M,Oi,Os) sat prop TRAP

$$(1.50)$$

corresponds to a *derived inference* rule in the C2 calculus. In effect, the theorem states that if the above is proved to be a theorem in the C2 calculus, then the remaining if and only if clause of the theorem holds.

1.12.4 Secure-State Machines Using Message and Certificate Structures

The previous high-level state-machine descriptions relied on access-control logic formulas only. To illustrate how details such as message and certificate structures are introduced, we develop an SSM description using polymorphic messages and certificates, and corresponding interpretation functions. We show that the transition relations *TR* and *TR2* are logically equivalent when they are applied to their corresponding configurations.

Theorem (1.51) shows the type definition of *configuration2* and its interpretation function *CFG2Interpret*. The refined configuration *configuration2* has eight components:

```
configuration₂ =
    CFG2 ('input -> ('command inst, 'principal, 'd, 'e) Form)
         ('cert -> ('command inst, 'principal, 'd, 'e) Form)
         (('command inst, 'principal, 'd, 'e) Form -> bool)
         ('cert list)
         ('state -> ('command inst, 'principal, 'd, 'e) Form)
         ('input list) 'state ('output list)
[CFG2Interpret_def]
⊢ CFG2Interpret (M, Oi, Os)
      (CFG2 inputInterpret certInterpret inputTest certs
          stateInterpret (x::ins) state outStream)  ⟺
      (M, Oi, Os) satList MAP certInterpret certs ∧
      (M, Oi, Os) sat inputInterpret x ∧
      (M, Oi, Os) sat stateInterpret state
```

$$(1.51)$$

1. An input interpretation function with type *'input* -> *('command inst, 'principal, 'd,'e) Form*. This function gives meaning to inputs in the access-control logic.

2. A certificate interpretation function with type *'cert* -> *('command inst, 'principal, 'd,'e) Form*. This function gives meaning to certificates in the access-control logic.

3. An authentication function with type *('command inst, 'principal, 'd, 'e) Form* -> *bool* that returns *true* or *false* when applied to inputs expressed as access-control logic formulas. This function determines whether or not commands originate from known and approved sources.

4. A list of certificates with type *'cert list* that represent the security context, with security interpretation of the current state, in which authenticated requests are authorized or not.

5. A state interpretation function with type *'state* -> *('command inst, 'principal, 'd, 'e) Form* that maps a state into an access-control logic formula. The interpretation function and state are part of the security context informing the decision on whether or not an authenticated request is authorized.

6. An input stream of access-control logic formulas *'input list*.

7. The current state *'state*.

8. An output stream *'output list*.

We define inductively the transition relation *TR2* in an analogous way to the definition of *TR*. Appendix 1.A.4.1 gives the HOL source code for defining *TR2*. Appendix 1.A.4.2 shows the three defining properties of *TR2* in HOL resulting from the inductive definition. These properties are *TR2_rules*, *TR2_ind*, and *TR2_cases*, which are the transition rules, induction property, and cases theorem, respectively.

Based on the defining properties of *TR2* and *CFG2Interpret*, similar to *TR*, we prove three equality properties for the three transition types, *discard*, *exec* (*CMD cmd*), and *trap* (*CMD cmd*).

Note that in the referenced theorems (1.52), (1.53) and (1.54), the following functions and types are parameterized, making the theorems applicable to state machines in general using the concepts of discarding, trapping, and executing commands. The specific parameters are:

1. *inputInterpret* : the input interpretation function,

2. *certInterpret* : the interpretation function for certificates,

3. *inputTest* : the authentication function,

4. *stateInterp*: the state interpretation function,

5. *certs*: the credentials, trust assumptions, delegations, and authorizations informing authorization decisions,

6. *commands*: commands are polymorphic,

7. *states*: states are polymorphic,

8. *outputs*: outputs are polymorphic,

9. *NS*: the next-state function, and

10. *Out*: the output function.

The three theorems in (1.52), (1.53), and (1.54) provide a parameterized framework for state machines with specific formats for inputs and certificates. We use this framework in specific applications, such as the networked thermostat, by specifying each of the eight parameters listed above.

$$
\begin{aligned}
&\texttt{[TR2\_discard\_cmd\_rule]} \\
&\vdash \texttt{TR2}\ (M, Oi, Os)\ \texttt{discard} \\
&\qquad (\texttt{CFG2}\ inputInterpret\ certInterpret\ inputTest\ certs \\
&\qquad\qquad stateInterpret\ (x::ins)\ state\ outStream) \\
&\qquad (\texttt{CFG2}\ inputInterpret\ certInterpret\ inputTest\ certs \\
&\qquad\qquad stateInterpret\ ins\ (NS\ state\ \texttt{discard}) \\
&\qquad\qquad (Out\ state\ \texttt{discard}::outStream))\ \Longleftrightarrow \\
&\qquad \neg inputTest\ (inputInterpret\ x)
\end{aligned}
\tag{1.52}
$$

$$
\begin{aligned}
&\texttt{[TR2\_exec\_cmd\_rule]} \\
&\vdash \forall inputInterpret\ certInterpret\ inputTest\ certs\ stateInterpret \\
&\qquad x\ cmd\ ins\ state\ outStream. \\
&\quad (\forall M\ Oi\ Os. \\
&\qquad \texttt{CFG2Interpret}\ (M, Oi, Os) \\
&\qquad\quad (\texttt{CFG2}\ inputInterpret\ certInterpret\ inputTest\ certs \\
&\qquad\qquad stateInterpret\ (x::ins)\ state\ outStream)\ \Rightarrow \\
&\qquad (M, Oi, Os)\ \texttt{sat prop}\ (\texttt{CMD}\ cmd))\ \Rightarrow \\
&\quad \forall NS\ Out\ M\ Oi\ Os. \\
&\qquad \texttt{TR2}\ (M, Oi, Os)\ (\texttt{exec}\ (\texttt{CMD}\ cmd)) \\
&\qquad\quad (\texttt{CFG2}\ inputInterpret\ certInterpret\ inputTest\ certs \\
&\qquad\qquad stateInterpret\ (x::ins)\ state\ outStream) \\
&\qquad\quad (\texttt{CFG2}\ inputInterpret\ certInterpret\ inputTest\ certs \\
&\qquad\qquad stateInterpret\ ins\ (NS\ state\ (\texttt{exec}\ (\texttt{CMD}\ cmd)))) \\
&\qquad\qquad (Out\ state\ (\texttt{exec}\ (\texttt{CMD}\ cmd))::outStream))\ \Longleftrightarrow \\
&\quad inputTest\ (inputInterpret\ x)\ \wedge \\
&\quad \texttt{CFG2Interpret}\ (M, Oi, Os) \\
&\qquad (\texttt{CFG2}\ inputInterpret\ certInterpret\ inputTest\ certs \\
&\qquad\quad stateInterpret\ (x::ins)\ state\ outStream)\ \wedge \\
&\quad (M, Oi, Os)\ \texttt{sat prop}\ (\texttt{CMD}\ cmd)
\end{aligned}
\tag{1.53}
$$

```
[TR2_trap_cmd_rule]
```
$\vdash \forall inputInterpret\ certInterpret\ inputTest\ certs\ stateInterpret$
$\quad x\ cmd\ ins\ state\ outStream.$
$\quad (\forall M\ Oi\ Os.$
$\qquad \text{CFG2Interpret}\ (M, Oi, Os)$
$\qquad\quad (\text{CFG2}\ inputInterpret\ certInterpret\ inputTest\ certs$
$\qquad\qquad stateInterpret\ (x::ins)\ state\ outStream) \Rightarrow$
$\qquad (M, Oi, Os)\ \texttt{sat prop TRAP}) \Rightarrow$
$\quad \forall NS\ Out\ M\ Oi\ Os.$
$\qquad \text{TR2}\ (M, Oi, Os)\ (\texttt{trap}\ (\texttt{CMD}\ cmd))$ $\qquad\qquad (1.54)$
$\qquad\quad (\text{CFG2}\ inputInterpret\ certInterpret\ inputTest\ certs$
$\qquad\qquad stateInterpret\ (x::ins)\ state\ outStream)$
$\qquad\quad (\text{CFG2}\ inputInterpret\ certInterpret\ inputTest\ certs$
$\qquad\qquad stateInterpret\ ins\ (NS\ state\ (\texttt{trap}\ (\texttt{CMD}\ cmd)))$
$\qquad\qquad (Out\ state\ (\texttt{trap}\ (\texttt{CMD}\ cmd))::outStream)) \iff$
$\qquad inputTest\ (inputInterpret\ x) \wedge$
$\qquad \text{CFG2Interpret}\ (M, Oi, Os)$
$\qquad\quad (\text{CFG2}\ inputInterpret\ certInterpret\ inputTest\ certs$
$\qquad\qquad stateInterpret\ (x::ins)\ state\ outStream) \wedge$
$\qquad (M, Oi, Os)\ \texttt{sat prop TRAP}$

In exactly the same way for *TR*, assurance of security is accounted for in *TR2* as follows:

1. In *TR2_discard_cmd_rule* the authentication function *inputTest* eliminates all unauthenticated commands.

2. In *TR2_exec_cmd_rule*, the condition:

$\quad \forall M\ Oi\ Os.$
$\quad\ \text{CFG2Interpret}\ (M, Oi, Os)$
$\qquad (\text{CFG2}\ inputInterpret\ certInterpret\ inputTest\ certs$ $\qquad (1.55)$
$\qquad\quad stateInterpret\ (x::ins)\ state\ outStream) \Rightarrow$
$\qquad (M, Oi, Os)\ \texttt{sat prop}\ (\texttt{CMD}\ cmd)$

corresponds to a *derived inference rule* in the C2 calculus. In effect, the theorem states that if the above is proved to be a theorem in the C2 calculus, then the remaining if and only if clause of the theorem holds.

3. In *TR2_trap_cmd_rule*, similar to *TR_exec_cmd_rule*, the condition:

$\quad \forall M\ Oi\ Os.$
$\quad\ \text{CFG2Interpret}\ (M, Oi, Os)$
$\qquad (\text{CFG2}\ inputInterpret\ certInterpret\ inputTest\ certs$ $\qquad (1.56)$
$\qquad\quad stateInterpret\ (x::ins)\ state\ outStream) \Rightarrow$
$\qquad (M, Oi, Os)\ \texttt{sat prop TRAP}$

corresponds to a derived inference rule in the C2 calculus. In effect, the theorem states that if the above is proved to be a theorem in the C2 calculus, then the remaining if and only if clause of the theorem holds.

1.13   A NETWORKED THERMOSTAT CERTIFIED SECURE BY DESIGN

Based on the all of the previous sections, we develop a networked thermostat that is certified secure by design. We pick up where we left off in Section 1.3.2, which gave the top-level CONOPS of a networked thermostat. In the descriptions that follow, we start from a top-level CONOPS and end with two SSM descriptions of the thermostat. The first SSM is a high-level logical description. The second SSM is a refinement of the first.

The tasks we need to do are:

1. Enumerate all commands and segregate them into two classes: privileged and non-privileged.
2. Enumerate all principals and their associated privileges within the envisioned thermostat operating modes.
3. Enumerate all thermostat use cases.
4. Specify the certificates needed to support authentication and authorization of all the use cases.
5. Devise the top-level SSM description by specializing *configurations* with definitions of:
   a. an authentication function,
   b. a set of certificates described as formulas in the access-control logic,
   c. a type for thermostat states,
   d. a state-interpretation function,
   e. a next-state function, and
   f. an output function.
6. Formally define what is meant by the term "security" by defining a *security property* that is preserved by all thermostat SSM descriptions. Prove that all SSM descriptions satisfy the defined security property.
7. Refine the top-level SSM description into a second more detailed SSM description by augmenting the top-level SSM description with definitions of:
   a. an input message datatype,
   b. an input message interpretation function,
   c. a certificate datatype, and
   d. a certificate interpretation function.
8. Prove the top-level and refined SSM descriptions are equivalent.

1.13.1 Thermostat Commands: Privileged and Non-Privileged

In Section 1.3.2, we gave a high-level description of the commands, which we summarize as follows:

1. Setting the temperature value.
2. Enabling the *Utility* to exercise control over setting the temperature.
3. Disabling the *Utility* to exercise control over setting the temperature.
4. Reporting the Status of the thermostat, which is displayed on the thermostat and sent to the *Server*.

Besides introducing the functionality of commands in Section 1.3.2, we also included an assessment of security sensitivity. Temperature setting, enabling, and disabling the *Utility's* ability to exercise control over the thermostat are viewed as security-sensitive commands, as they can change the temperature setting and operating mode of the thermostat. In contrast, the *Status* command is viewed as innocuous, that is, not security-sensitive, because reporting the thermostat's temperature setting and operating mode changes nothing.

The above partitioning of commands into two types (sensitive and non-sensitive) and why, is vital to incorporating security into designs from the beginning. In the case of the thermostat, the underlying basis for declaring a command to be security sensitive or not is whether or not the command in question can change either the temperature setting or operating mode.

Rule (1.57) shows the definitions of thermostat commands as types in HOL and their properties. These definitions incorporate the distinctions between security-sensitive and innocuous commands. The *privcmd* type has three thermostat commands, each of which are security sensitive and require *Owner* level privileges to execute.

$$
\begin{aligned}
&\textit{privcmd} \;=\; \texttt{Set}\ \texttt{num}\ \mid\ \texttt{EU}\ \mid\ \texttt{DU} \\
&\textit{npriv}\;=\;\texttt{Status} \\
&\textit{command}\;=\;\texttt{PR}\ \textit{privcmd}\ \mid\ \texttt{NP}\ \textit{npriv} \\
&[\texttt{privcmd\_distinct\_thm}] \\
&\quad \vdash\ (\forall a.\ \texttt{Set}\ a \neq \texttt{EU})\ \wedge\ (\forall a.\ \texttt{Set}\ a \neq \texttt{DU})\ \wedge\ \texttt{EU} \neq \texttt{DU} \\
&[\texttt{privcmd\_nchotomy\_thm}] \\
&\quad \vdash\ \forall pp.\ (\exists n.\ pp = \texttt{Set}\ n)\ \vee\ (pp = \texttt{EU})\ \vee\ (pp = \texttt{DU}) \\
&[\texttt{set\_privcmd\_11}] \\
&\quad \vdash\ \forall a\ a'.\ (\texttt{Set}\ a = \texttt{Set}\ a')\ \Longleftrightarrow\ (a = a') \\
&[\texttt{npriv\_nchotomy\_thm}] \\
&\quad \vdash\ \forall a.\ a = \texttt{Status} \\
&[\texttt{command\_distinct\_thm}] \\
&\quad \vdash\ \forall a'\ a.\ \texttt{PR}\ a \neq \texttt{NP}\ a' \\
&[\texttt{command\_nchotomy\_thm}] \\
&\quad \vdash\ \forall cc.\ (\exists p.\ cc = \texttt{PR}\ p)\ \vee\ \exists n.\ cc = \texttt{NP}\ n \\
&[\texttt{set\_command\_11}] \\
&\quad \vdash\ (\forall a\ a'.\ (\texttt{PR}\ a = \texttt{PR}\ a')\ \Longleftrightarrow\ (a = a'))\ \wedge \\
&\qquad\quad \forall a\ a'.\ (\texttt{NP}\ a = \texttt{NP}\ a')\ \Longleftrightarrow\ (a = a')
\end{aligned}
\tag{1.57}
$$

1. *Set num*, which sets the temperature setting to the number supplied,
2. *EU*, which enables the *Utility* to control the thermostat, and
3. *DU*, which disables the *Utility* from controlling the thermostat.

The type *npriv* has a single thermostat command *Status*, which is innocuous and does not require *Owner* level privileges to execute. The type *command* defines all the thermostat commands into a single type using the type constructor *PR* for privileged commands *privcmd*, and the type constructor *NP* for *npriv* commands.

Rule (1.57) has seven theorems describing the properties of commands. The *distinct* theorems state that each command is different than all the others in its type. The *nchotomy* theorems completely enumerate the values or forms of a member of the particular type can have. The "_11" theorems, for example, *set_privcmd_11*, state (where applicable) that identical values have identical components.

1.13.2 Thermostat Principals and Their Privileges

Recall Figure 1.2 in Section 1.3.2, which shows a networked thermostat receiving commands from two sources: (1) a *Keyboard* directly connected to it, and (2) the *Server* using a network interface. The operating assumptions are (1) all commands received from the *Keyboard* are from the *Owner*, and (2) the *Server* is relaying commands from the *Owner* or a *Utility*. *Owners* and *Utilities* have a unique ID number, where ID numbers are modeled as natural numbers.

1.13.2.1 Principals Equation (1.58) shows the type definitions of the principals that interact with the thermostat:

$$
\begin{aligned}
keyPrinc\ =\ & \text{CA | Server | Utility num} \\
principal\ =\ & \\
& \text{Role keyPrinc} \\
| & \text{ Key (keyPrinc pKey)} \\
| & \text{ Keyboard} \\
| & \text{ Owner num} \\
| & \text{ Account num num}
\end{aligned}
\tag{1.58}
$$

The *keyPrinc* type defined principals that will have asymmetric cryptographic keys. These principals are

1. *CA*: the Certificate Authority issuing public-key certificates.
2. *Server*: the *Server* relaying messages from the *Owner* or *Utility* to the thermostat.
3. *Utility*: the *Utility* with a numerical identifier to distinguish among the various utilities.

TABLE 1.3   **Principals and Their Associated Privileges.**

Principal	Innocuous Commands	Privileged Commands
Owner	Yes	Yes
Keyboard	*Owner*	Yes	Yes
Server	*Owner*	Yes	Yes
Server	*Utility*	Yes	Yes, when *Utility* is *enabled* for control. No, otherwise.
Public keys	No	No
CA	No	No
Owner accounts	No	No

The *principal* type has five kinds of principals.

1. Principals that are *keyPrincs*, for example, CA, *Server*, or *Utility* utilityID.
2. Public keys of *keyPrincs*, for example, Key (pubK CA) – the public-key of the certificate authority *CA*.
3. A *Keyboard* attached to a thermostat.
4. An *Owner* with a unique numerical identifier to distinguish a thermostat and its owner from all other thermostats.
5. An *Account* on the *Server* with two numerical identifiers, one corresponding to the *Owner* and the second corresponding to a PIN or password.

1.13.2.2 *Privileges*   Principals and their associated privileges are shown in Table 1.3. Any command involving *Owners* is authorized. *Utilities* are authorized on innocuous (non-security sensitive) commands. *Utilities* execute privileged commands only if the thermostat's operating mode is in a state that gives utilities authorization. All other listed principals have no authorization to execute any command, innocuous or otherwise.

1.14 THERMOSTAT USE CASES

1.14.1 Manual Operation

The thermostat is operated manually whenever the physical controls on the thermostat are used. The presumption is if the thermostat is operated manually then the *Owner* is behind the commands. This use case is illustrated, with the security context of the thermostat, in Figure 1.19.

When commands come from the keyboard, the interpretation of what is received is *Keyboard* | *Owner* says <*command*>. The thermostat's security context is:

1. The *Owner* has full authority over all commands, that is, *Owner* controls <*command*>.

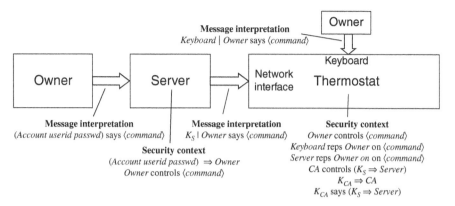

FIGURE 1.19 Owner control: manually and via the server.

2. The *Keyboard* is the *Owner's* delegate on *<command>*. This is represented as *Keyboard* reps *Owner* on *<command>*.

1.14.2 User Control via the Server

The thermostat is also controlled by the *Owner* through the *Owner's* Account on the *Server*. Figure 1.19 illustrates the messages and security context of the *Server* and thermostat. The *Server* and thermostat assume that the *Owner* has complete authority over all commands executed by the thermostat.

The *Server* identifies the *Owner* by the *Account userid passwd* associated with the *Owner*. After the *Server* authenticates the command from the *Owner*, it relays the command to the thermostat in a message that is cryptographically signed using its private key K_S^{-1}. If the cryptographically signed message passes the integrity check using the *Server's* public key K_S, then the message is interpreted to be $K_S \mid Owner$ says *<command>* by the thermostat.

The thermostat's security context assumes:

1. The Owner has full authority over all commands, *Owner* controls *<command>*.
2. The *Server* is the *Owner's* delegate on *<command>*. This is *Server* reps *Owner* on *<command>*.
3. The public key of the certificate authority CA is K_{CA}, that is, $K_{CA} \Rightarrow CA$.
4. CA is trusted on public keys, that is, *CA* controls ($K_S \Rightarrow Server$).

1.14.3 Utility Control via the Server

When the *Utility* wishes to take control of the *Owner's* thermostat, for example, to reduce air conditioning loads during peak power periods during the work day, the *Utility* will send the *Server* a command cryptographically signed by its private key K_U^{-1}. If the cryptographically signed message passes the integrity check using the *Utility's* public key K_U, then the message is interpreted to be $K_U \mid Owner$ says *<priv cmd>*.

The *Server* has the content to authenticate the *Utility's* message by verifying the cryptographic signature. The part of the security context of the *Server* dealing with *Utility* authentication is:

1. *CA* controls ($K_U \Rightarrow$ *Utility*), that is, the *Server* trusts *CA* on public keys.
2. K_{CA} says ($K_U \Rightarrow$ *Utility*). This is the public-key certificate for K_U cryptographically signed by K_{CA}.
3. $K_{CA} \Rightarrow CA$. This is a root trust assumption of the *Server that K_{CA}* is indeed *CA's* public key.

The remaining formulas in the *Server's* security context all deal with establishing the conditions under which the *Server* passes on the *Utility's* privileged command (*priv cmd*). Specifically, the following three formulas set the context for the *Owner* authorizing the *Server* to forward commands to the *Owner's* thermostat. The first formula states that the *Owner* has authority to authorize the *Server* to forward the request. The second formula is the actual authorization by *Account userid passwd*, the *Owner's* account. The third formula associates *Account userid passwd* with the *Owner*.

1. *Owner* controls (*Utility | Owner* says *<priv cmd>* ⊃ *Utility* says *<priv cmd>*)
2. (*Account userid passwd*) says (*Utility | Owner* says *<priv cmd>* ⊃ *Utility* says *<priv cmd>*)
3. (*Account userid passwd*) ⇒ *Owner*

The Figures 1.20 and 1.21 illustrate the security context of the thermostat. Figure 1.20 shows the security context for authorizing the *Utility* to execute privileged commands, for example, changing the temperature setting on the thermostat. Figure 1.2.1 shows the case when the thermostat has not authorized the *Utility* to execute privileged commands. If the *Utility* attempts to execute a privileged command, then it is trapped.

Both use cases share the same security context stating that the *Owner* has authority on privileged commands, the *Server* is the *Owner's* delegate, and the statements related to public-key certificates, the CA's authority, and the root trust assumption on the CA's public key. The last statement says that the *Server* is the *Utility's* delegate on privileged commands.

1. *Owner* controls *<priv cmd>*
2. *Server* reps *Owner* on *<priv cmd>*
3. *CA* controls ($K_S \Rightarrow$ *Server*)
4. $K_{CA} \Rightarrow CA$
5. K_{CA} says ($K_S \Rightarrow$ *Server*)
6. *Server* reps *Utility* on *<priv cmd>*

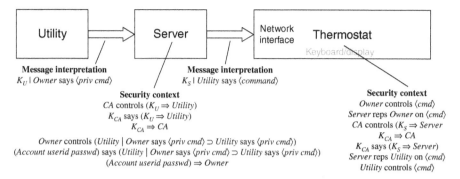

FIGURE 1.20   Utility control via the server – utility is authorized. Reproduced with permission of IEEE.

Figure 1.20 illustrates the use case where the *Utility* is authorized by the *Owner* to exercise privileged commands, such as changing the temperature setting of the thermostat.

The additional statements:

$$Utility \text{ controls } < NP \text{ } npriv >$$
$$Utility \text{ controls } < PR \text{ } privcm >$$

authorize the Utility to execute all (privileged and non-privileged) commands.

Figure 1.21 illustrates the use case where the *Utility* is not authorized by the *Owner* to exercise privileged commands, such as changing the temperature setting of the thermostat, but is authorized to execute non-privileged (innocuous) commands:

The additional statements force privileged commands issued by the Utility to be trapped:

$$Utility \text{ controls } < NP \text{ } npriv >$$
$$Utility \text{ says } < PR \text{ } privcm > \supset (trap < PR \text{ } privcmd >)$$

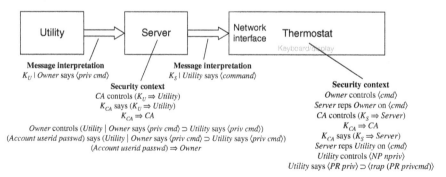

FIGURE 1.21   Utility control is not authorized on privileged commands.

1.15 SECURITY CONTEXTS FOR THE SERVER AND THERMOSTAT

1.15.1 Server Security Context

The combined security context covering all the use cases is as follows. An explanation of the intent of each formula follows the formulas below:

1. *Owner* controls *<cmd>*
2. (*Account userid passwd*) $\Rightarrow$ *Owner*
3. *CA* controls ($K_U \Rightarrow$ *Utility*)
4. K_{CA} says ($K_U \Rightarrow$ *Utility*)
5. $K_{CA} \Rightarrow CA$
6. *Owner* controls (*Utility* | *Owner* says *<cmd>* ⊃ *Utility* says *<cmd>*)
7. (*Account userid passwd*) says (*Utility* | *Owner* says *<cmd>* ⊃ *Utility* says *<cmd>*)

Formula 1 states the *Owner's* authority to execute any command on her thermostat. Formula 2 states the association between the *Owner* and her account *Account userid passwd* on the *Server*. Formulas 3 through 5 deal with certificate authorities, root *CA* public keys, and public-key certificates. The third formula recognizes *CA's* is trusted on distributing the public key of the *Server*. The fourth formula corresponds to the public-key certificate of the *Utility* digitally signed by *CA's* private key. The fifth formula is a root trust assumption stating that K_{CA} *is CA's* public key. Formulas 6 and 7 state the *Owner's* authority and statement to authorize the *Server* to pass on commands from the *Utility* to the *Owner's* thermostat.

1.15.2 Thermostat Security Context

The thermostat has two mutually exclusive operating modes, (1) the *Utility* is authorized to execute privileged security-sensitive commands, which the thermostat will execute when received from the *Utility* relayed by the *Server*, or (2) the *Utility* is unauthorized on privileged commands and will trap any attempt by the *Utility* to execute a privileged command received from the *Utility* relayed by the *Server*. As a preview to our next Section, we handle mutually exclusive operating modes by *changing thermostat configurations*. These mode or configuration changes switch security contexts and the commands to switch from one context to another are privileged and regarded as security sensitive. Such configuration changes are described by labeled transitions generally, for example, high-level state machine descriptions, and by inductively defined relations in HOL.

The common security context shared in both operating contexts is shown below. The intent of each formula follows the formulas below.

1. *Owner* controls *<cmd>*
2. *Keyboard* reps *Owner* on *<cmd>*
3. *Server* reps *Owner* on *<cmd>*
4. *CA* controls ($K_S \Rightarrow$ *Server*)
5. $K_{CA} \Rightarrow CA$

6. K_{CA} says ($K_S \Rightarrow$ *Server*)
7. *Server* reps *Utility* on *<NP npriv>*
8. *Server* reps *Utility* on *<PR privcmd>*
9. *Utility* controls *<NP npriv>*

The first formula states the *Owner's* authority to execute any command *<cmd>*. The second formula states the *Keyboard* is the *Owner's* delegate. In later refinements of the thermostat, we will interpret anything typed on the *Keyboard* as *Keyboard | Owner*. The third formula states that the *Server* is trusted to be the *Owner's* delegate when the *Server* quotes the *Owner*. (*Note*: This points to a risk with networked devices – the devices must trust the integrity of their servers.) The fourth, fifth, and sixth formulas deal with certificate authorities, root *CA* public keys, and public-key certificates. The fourth formula recognizes *CA* as trusted on distributing the public key of the *Server*. The fifth formula corresponds to the public-key certificate of the *Server* digitally signed by *CA's* private key. The sixth formula is a root trust assumption stating that K_{CA} is *CA's* public key.

The seventh and eighth formulas state that the *Server* is trusted to be the *Utility's* delegate when the *Server* quotes the *Utility* on both non-privileged and privileged commands. The ninth and final formula states that the *Utility* is authorized to execute non-privileged commands on the thermostat, for example, query the status of the thermostat. (Note: The thermostat is relying again upon the integrity of the *Server* to quote the correct originating principal behind a command.) If the *Server* quotes the wrong principal, for example, quotes the *Owner* instead of the *Utility*, then the thermostat potentially is duped into executing an unauthorized privileged instruction.

Rule (1.59) shows the definition of *certs* in HOL. The definition of *certs* is a list of access-control logic formulas in HOL corresponding to Formulas 1 through 9 above:

```
[certs_def]
 ⊢ ∀ownerID utilityID cmd npriv privcmd.
     certs ownerID utilityID cmd npriv privcmd =
     [Name (Owner ownerID) controls prop (CMD cmd);
      reps (Name Keyboard) (Name (Owner ownerID))
        (prop (CMD cmd));
      reps (Name (Role Server)) (Name (Owner ownerID))
        (prop (CMD cmd));
      Name (Role CA) controls
      Name (Key (pubK Server)) speaks_for Name (Role Server);
      Name (Key (pubK CA)) speaks_for Name (Role CA);
      Name (Key (pubK CA)) says
      Name (Key (pubK Server)) speaks_for Name (Role Server);
      reps (Name (Role Server))
        (Name (Role (Utility utilityID)))
        (prop (CMD (NP npriv)));
      reps (Name (Role Server))
        (Name (Role (Utility utilityID)))
        (prop (CMD (PR privcmd)));
      Name (Role (Utility utilityID)) controls
      prop (CMD (NP npriv))]
```

(1.59)

1.16 TOP-LEVEL THERMOSTAT SECURE-STATE MACHINE

The top-level thermostat SSM description is an instantiation of the high-level SSM description in Section 1.12.2. The top-level thermostat SSM specializes the general high-level SSM with the following instantiations:

1. The type variable *'command* is instantiated with type *command*, as defined in (1.57).
2. The type variable *'state* is instantiated with type *state* defined below.
3. The state interpretation function in *configuration* is instantiated with *thermoStateInterp* defined later.
4. The type variable *'output* is instantiated with type *output* defined below.
5. The next-state function *NS* is instantiated with *thermo1NS* defined below.
6. The output function *Out* is instantiated with *thermo1Out* defined below.
7. The certificate list in *configuration* is instantiated with the high-level certificate list *certs*, as defined in rule (1.59).
8. The authentication function in *configuration* is instantiated with *isAuthenticated* defined below.

In the subsections immediately below, we describe each of the instantiations that have not yet been defined. We then present theorems corresponding to each of the three transition types, *discard, exec,* and *trap*, specialized to the thermostat.

1.16.1 States and Operating Modes

The thermostat has two operating modes: (1) the *Utility* is *enabled* to execute privileged instructions, or (2) the *Utility* is *disabled* from executing privileged instructions. This is defined in HOL by the datatype *mode*.

We define the thermostat's *state* as its operating mode and its temperature setting, which we model as a natural number *num* in HOL. The type definitions of *mode* and *state* are:

$$mode = \text{enabled}|\text{disabled}$$
$$state = \text{State mode num}$$

1.16.2 State Interpretation Function

The interpretation function for thermostat states is given by *thermoStateInterp_def* in (1.60). The definition covers both operating modes:

```
[thermoStateInterp_def]
⊢ (thermoStateInterp utilityID privcmd (State enabled temp) =
   Name (Role (Utility utilityID)) controls
   prop (CMD (PR privcmd))) ∧
  (thermoStateInterp utilityID privcmd (State disabled temp) =
   Name (Role (Utility utilityID)) says
   prop (CMD (PR privcmd)) impf prop TRAP)
```
$$(1.60)$$

1. When the operating mode is *enabled*, then the *Utility* has authority to execute privileged commands.

> *thermoStateInterp utilityID privcmd (State enabled temp)* =
> *Name (Role (Utility utilityID)) controls prop (CMD (PR*
> *privcmd))*

2. When the operating mode is *disabled*, then the *Utility's* attempt to execute any privileged instruction is trapped.

> *thermoStateInterp utilityID privcmd (State disabled temp)* =
> *Name (Role (Utility utilityID)) says prop (CMD (PR*
> *privcmd)) impf prop TRAP*

The combination of *thermoStateInterp* with the nine access-control logic formulas in *cert*, defined in rule (1.59), gives the overall security context for the thermostat's SSM to authorize authenticated commands.

1.16.3 Next-State Function

The next-state transition function for the thermostat can be viewed from the stand-points of the *Owner* and *Utility*. Figures 1.22 and 1.23 are the state-transition

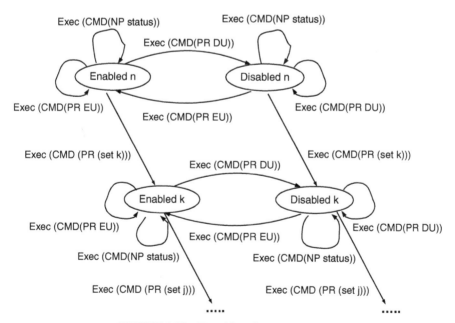

FIGURE 1.22 Transition diagram for owner.

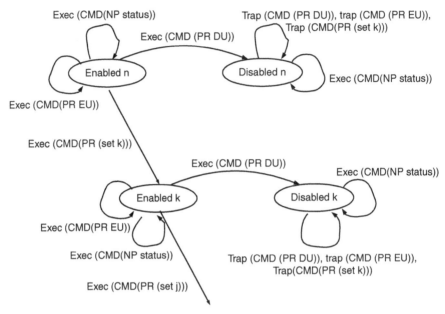

FIGURE 1.23 Transition diagram for utility. Reproduced with permission of IEEE.

diagrams for *Owner* and *Utility* originated commands, respectively. Figure 1.22 shows that *Owners* are authorized to execute any command in any state. In particular, they can change the temperature settings and enable or disable the authority of utilities to execute privileged commands. Figure 1.23 shows that Utilities can execute privileged commands only if their authority is enabled, that is, the state mode is enabled. If utilities attempt to execute a privileged command in a disabled mode, the attempt is trapped. As privileged commands are commands that can change the thermostat's state, that is, changing either a temperature or mode value, trapped commands result in no state change.

Rule (1.61) shows the definition of *thermo1NS*, the next-state function for the thermostat. If the input is an *exec* (*CMD cmd*), then the command results in the appropriate state change or status report. If the input is *trap* (*CMD cmd*), then no state change occurs. Rule (1.62) shows shows two theorems *npriv_Safe* and *privcmd_Security_Sensitive*. The first theorem states that the next-state function *thermo1NS* has the property that all non-privileged commands *NP npriv* result in no state change. The second theorem states that for all privileged commands *PR privcmd* that a state change is possible when executing the privileged command. These two theorems prove the non-privileged commands are safe, when safety is defined as no change in temperature or operating mode, and that the privileged commands have the capability to change either mode or temperature.

```
[thermo1NS_def]
⊢ (thermo1NS (State opMode temp) discard = State opMode temp) ∧
  (thermo1NS (State opMode temp)
     (exec (CMD (PR (Set newTemp))))) =
  State opMode newTemp) ∧
  (thermo1NS (State opMode temp) (exec (CMD (PR EU))) =
  State enabled temp) ∧
  (thermo1NS (State opMode temp) (exec (CMD (PR DU))) =
  State disabled temp) ∧
  (thermo1NS (State opMode temp) (exec (CMD (NP Status))) =
  State opMode temp) ∧
  (thermo1NS (State opMode temp)
     (trap (CMD (PR (Set newTemp))))) =
  State opMode temp) ∧
  (thermo1NS (State opMode temp) (trap (CMD (PR EU))) =
  State opMode temp) ∧
  (thermo1NS (State opMode temp) (trap (CMD (PR DU))) =
  State opMode temp)
```

$$(1.61)$$

```
[npriv_Safe]
⊢ ∀npriv state. thermo1NS state (exec (CMD (NP npriv))) = state
[privcmd_Security_Sensitive]
⊢ ∀privcmd.
     ∃state. thermo1NS state (exec (CMD (PR privcmd))) ≠ state
```

$$(1.62)$$

1.16.4 Input Authentication Function

The input authentication function for the top-level thermostat SSM, *isAuthenticated*, is defined by the HOL source code in Figure 1.24. Recall, the top-level SSM uses only access-control logic formulas for inputs and certificates. Given the use cases, there are only three forms of access-control logic formulas that are authenticated:

1. *Keyboard | Owner* says *<inst>*, that is, instructions entered in on the attached keyboard,
2. *Server | Owner* says *<inst>*, that is, the *Server* relaying instructions from the Owner, and
3. *Server | Utility* says *<inst>*, that is, the *Server* relaying instructions from the Utility.

All other forms of access-control logic formulas are not authenticated. The three cases above correspond to the first three clauses in the definition in Figure 1.24. The last clause of the definition containing *isAuthenticated* = F is interpreted by HOL as

```
val isAuthenticated_def =
Define
'(isAuthenticated
 ((((Name Keyboard) quoting (Name (Owner ownerID))) says
 (prop (CMD (cmd:command))))):(command inst, principal, 'd, 'e)Form) = T) /\
(isAuthenticated
 ((((Name (Key (pubK Server))) quoting (Name (Owner ownerID))) says
 (prop (CMD (cmd:command))))):(command inst, principal, 'd, 'e)Form) = T) /\
(isAuthenticated
 ((((Name (Key (pubK Server))) quoting (Name ((role (Utility utilityID )))))) says
 (prop (CMD (cmd:command))))):(command inst, principal, 'd, 'e)Form) = T) /\
(isAuthenticated_ = F) '
```

FIGURE 1.24   HOL source code defining *isAuthenticated*.

all other forms as input produce F as an output. The resulting defining theorem is quite long and appears in Appendix 1.A.4.3.

1.16.5   Output Type and Output Function

Theorem (1.63) shows the definitions of the thermostat output type output and the output function *thermo1Out*. There are three kinds of outputs:

1. reporting a state,
2. flagging a command, and
3. null.

Whenever a command is executed, then the new state is reported as output. If a command is trapped, then the command is flagged. If an input is discarded, the *null* is output:

```
output = report state | flag command | null
[thermo1Out_def]
 ⊢ (thermo1Out (State enabled temp)
     (exec (CMD (PR (Set newTemp))))) =
   report (State enabled newTemp)) /\
   (thermo1Out (State disabled temp)
     (exec (CMD (PR (Set newTemp))))) =
   report (State disabled newTemp)) /\
   (thermo1Out (State enabled temp) (exec (CMD (PR EU))) =
   report (State enabled temp)) /\
   (thermo1Out (State disabled temp) (exec (CMD (PR EU))) =
   report (State enabled temp)) /\
   (thermo1Out (State enabled temp) (exec (CMD (PR DU))) =
   report (State disabled temp)) /\
   (thermo1Out (State disabled temp) (exec (CMD (PR DU))) =
   report (State disabled temp)) /\
```

```
(thermolOut (State enabled temp) (exec (CMD (NP Status))) =
 report (State enabled temp)) ∧
(thermolOut (State disabled temp) (exec (CMD (NP Status))) =
 report (State disabled temp)) ∧
(thermolOut (State enabled temp)
   (trap (CMD (PR (Set newTemp))))) =
 flag (PR (Set newTemp))) ∧
(thermolOut (State disabled temp)
   (trap (CMD (PR (Set newTemp))))) =
 flag (PR (Set newTemp))) ∧
(thermolOut (State enabled temp) (trap (CMD (PR EU))) =
 flag (PR EU)) ∧
(thermolOut (State disabled temp) (trap (CMD (PR EU))) =
 flag (PR EU)) ∧
(thermolOut (State enabled temp) (trap (CMD (PR DU))) =
 flag (PR DU)) ∧
(thermolOut (State disabled temp) (trap (CMD (PR DU))) =
 flag (PR DU)) ∧
(thermolOut (State enabled temp) discard = null) ∧
(thermolOut (State disabled temp) discard = null)
```

$$(1.63)$$

1.16.6 Transition Theorems

We present five configuration theorems and five transition theorems that characterize the behavior of the thermostat. All justify the properties that state if an SSM transition occurred corresponding to executing or trapping an instruction, then it was justified by the security interpretation of the starting configuration.

Theorems 1.64–1.68 show that executing or trapping an instruction is derivable from the security interpretation provided by *CFGInterpret* applied to the starting configuration. These theorems show that the certificates, state interpretation, and input, do in fact justify executing or trapping an instruction. In other words, that the SSM's actions correspond to sound inference rules.

```
[CFGInterpret_Owner_Keyboard_thm]
⊢ ∀M Oi Os.
    CFGInterpret (M, Oi, Os)
      (CFG isAuthenticated
        (thermoStateInterp utilityID privcmd)
        (certs ownerID utilityID cmd npriv privcmd)
        (Name Keyboard quoting Name (Owner ownerID) says
          prop (CMD cmd)::ins) s outs) ⇒
    (M, Oi, Os) sat prop (CMD cmd)
```

$$(1.64)$$

```
[CFGInterpret_Owner_KServer_thm]
⊢ ∀M Oi Os.
     CFGInterpret (M, Oi, Os)
        (CFG isAuthenticated
            (thermoStateInterp utilityID privcmd)
            (certs ownerID utilityID cmd npriv privcmd)
            (Name (Key (pubK Server)) quoting
             Name (Owner ownerID) says prop (CMD cmd)::ins) s
            outs) ⇒
        (M, Oi, Os) sat prop (CMD cmd)
```

$$(1.65)$$

```
[CFGInterpret_Utility_KServer_npriv_thm]
⊢ ∀M Oi Os.
     CFGInterpret (M, Oi, Os)
        (CFG isAuthenticated
            (thermoStateInterp utilityID privcmd)
            (certs ownerID utilityID cmd npriv privcmd)
            (Name (Key (pubK Server)) quoting
             Name (Role (Utility utilityID)) says
             prop (CMD (NP npriv))::ins) s outs) ⇒
        (M, Oi, Os) sat prop (CMD (NP npriv))
```

$$(1.66)$$

```
[CFGInterpret_Utility_KServer_privcmd_thm]
⊢ ∀M Oi Os.
     CFGInterpret (M, Oi, Os)
        (CFG isAuthenticated
            (thermoStateInterp utilityID privcmd)
            (certs ownerID utilityID cmd npriv privcmd)
            (Name (Key (pubK Server)) quoting
             Name (Role (Utility utilityID)) says
             prop (CMD (PR privcmd))::ins)
            (State enabled temperature) outs) ⇒
        (M, Oi, Os) sat prop (CMD (PR privcmd))
```

$$(1.67)$$

```
[CFGInterpret_Utility_KServer_trap_thm]
```
$\vdash \forall M\ Oi\ Os.$

    `CFGInterpret` (M, Oi, Os)

      `(CFG isAuthenticated`

        `(thermoStateInterp` *utilityID privcmd*`)`

        `(certs` *ownerID utilityID cmd npriv privcmd*`)`   (1.68)

        `(Name (Key (pubK Server)) quoting`

        `Name (Role (Utility` *utilityID*`)) says`

        `prop (CMD (PR` *privcmd*`)) ::` *ins*`)`

        `(State disabled` *temperature*`) outs)` $\Rightarrow$

    (M, Oi, Os) `sat prop TRAP`

For example, the theorem *CFGInterpret_Utility_KServer_privcmd_thm* in rule (1.67) states that the security interpretation of the starting configuration justifies executing the privileged command requested by the *Utility* via the *Server*. Specifically, (M, O_i, O_s) sat prop (CMD (PR *privcmd*)) is derivable from the interpretation *CFGInterpret* applied to the configuration shown in Theorem 1.69 below:

```
[CFGInterpret_Utility_KServer_privcmd_thm]
```

$\vdash \forall M\ Oi\ Os.$

    `CFGInterpret` (M, Oi, Os)

      `(CFG isAuthenticated`

        `(thermoStateInterp` *utilityID privcmd*`)`

        `(certs` *ownerID utilityID cmd npriv privcmd*`)`   (1.69)

        `(Name (Key (pubK Server)) quoting`

        `Name (Role (Utility` *utilityID*`)) says`

        `prop (CMD (PR` *privcmd*`)) ::` *ins*`)`

        `(State enabled` *temperature*`) outs)` $\Rightarrow$

    (M, Oi, Os) `sat prop (CMD (PR` *privcmd*`))`

Theorems 1.64–1.68 above in conjunction with the *TR_exec_cmd_rule* theorem, previously proved in (1.47), give rise to the execution and trap Theorems (1.70)–(1.74) identified below:

[exec_Keyboard_Owner_cmd_Justified]
$\vdash \forall NS$ *Out outs s ins npriv privcmd cmd ownerID utilityID M Oi*
    Os .
    TR (M, Oi, Os) (exec (CMD *cmd*))
      (CFG isAuthenticated
        (thermoStateInterp *utilityID privcmd*)
        (certs *ownerID utilityID cmd npriv privcmd*)
        (Name Keyboard quoting Name (Owner *ownerID*) says
         prop (CMD *cmd*) :: *ins*) *s outs*)
      (CFG isAuthenticated
        (thermoStateInterp *utilityID privcmd*)
        (certs *ownerID utilityID cmd npriv privcmd*) *ins*
        (*NS s* (exec (CMD *cmd*)))
        (*Out s* (exec (CMD *cmd*)) :: *outs*)) $\Rightarrow$
    (M, Oi, Os) sat prop (CMD *cmd*)

(1.70)

[exec_KServer_Owner_cmd_Justified]
$\vdash \forall NS$ *Out outs s ins npriv privcmd cmd ownerID utilityID M Oi*
    Os .
    TR (M, Oi, Os) (exec (CMD *cmd*))
      (CFG isAuthenticated
        (thermoStateInterp *utilityID privcmd*)
        (certs *ownerID utilityID cmd npriv privcmd*)
        (Name (Key (pubK Server)) quoting
         Name (Owner *ownerID*) says prop (CMD *cmd*) :: *ins*) *s*
        outs)
      (CFG isAuthenticated
        (thermoStateInterp *utilityID privcmd*)
        (certs *ownerID utilityID cmd npriv privcmd*) *ins*
        (*NS s* (exec (CMD *cmd*)))
        (*Out s* (exec (CMD *cmd*)) :: *outs*)) $\Rightarrow$
    (M, Oi, Os) sat prop (CMD *cmd*)

(1.71)

[exec_KServer_Utility_npriv_Justified]
$\vdash \forall NS$ *Out outs s ins npriv privcmd cmd ownerID utilityID M Oi*
    Os .
    TR (M, Oi, Os) (exec (CMD (NP *npriv*)))
      (CFG isAuthenticated
        (thermoStateInterp *utilityID privcmd*)
        (certs *ownerID utilityID cmd npriv privcmd*)
        (Name (Key (pubK Server)) quoting
         Name (Role (Utility *utilityID*)) says
         prop (CMD (NP *npriv*)) :: *ins*) *s outs*)
      (CFG isAuthenticated
        (thermoStateInterp *utilityID privcmd*)
        (certs *ownerID utilityID cmd npriv privcmd*) *ins*
        (*NS s* (exec (CMD (NP *npriv*))))
        (*Out s* (exec (CMD (NP *npriv*))) :: *outs*)) $\Rightarrow$
    (M, Oi, Os) sat prop (CMD (NP *npriv*))

(1.72)

```
[exec_KServer_Utility_privcmd_Justified]
```
⊢ ∀*NS Out outs temperature ins npriv privcmd cmd ownerID*
  utilityID M Oi Os .
  TR (*M,Oi,Os*) (exec (CMD (PR *privcmd*)))
    (CFG isAuthenticated
      (thermoStateInterp *utilityID privcmd*)
      (certs *ownerID utilityID cmd npriv privcmd*)
      (Name (Key (pubK Server)) quoting
       Name (Role (Utility *utilityID*)) says
       prop (CMD (PR *privcmd*))::*ins*)   (1.73)
      (State enabled *temperature*) *outs*)
    (CFG isAuthenticated
      (thermoStateInterp *utilityID privcmd*)
      (certs *ownerID utilityID cmd npriv privcmd*) *ins*
      (*NS* (State enabled *temperature*)
        (exec (CMD (PR *privcmd*))))
      (*Out* (State enabled *temperature*)
        (exec (CMD (PR *privcmd*))))::*outs*)) ⇒
  (*M,Oi,Os*) sat prop (CMD (PR *privcmd*))

```
[trap_KServer_Utility_privcmd_Justified]
```
⊢ ∀*NS Out outs temperature ins npriv privcmd cmd ownerID*
  utilityID M Oi Os .
  TR (*M,Oi,Os*) (trap (CMD (PR *privcmd*)))
    (CFG isAuthenticated
      (thermoStateInterp *utilityID privcmd*)
      (certs *ownerID utilityID cmd npriv privcmd*)
      (Name (Key (pubK Server)) quoting
       Name (Role (Utility *utilityID*)) says
       prop (CMD (PR *privcmd*))::*ins*)   (1.74)
      (State disabled *temperature*) *outs*)
    (CFG isAuthenticated
      (thermoStateInterp *utilityID privcmd*)
      (certs *ownerID utilityID cmd npriv privcmd*) *ins*
      (*NS* (State disabled *temperature*)
        (trap (CMD (PR *privcmd*))))
      (*Out* (State disabled *temperature*)
        (trap (CMD (PR *privcmd*))))::*outs*)) ⇒
  (*M,Oi,Os*) sat prop TRAP
```

As an example, consider the *CFGInterpret_Utility_KServer_privcmd_thm* and *exec_KServer_Utility_privcmd_Justified* theorems shown in theorems (1.69) and (1.73). The theorems state that if a *TR* transition occurs corresponding to executing a privileged instruction, that is, (exec (CMD (PR *privcmd*))), then executing command was necessarily authorized.

## 1.17 REFINED THERMOSTAT SECURE-STATE MACHINE

The refined thermostat SSM is an instantiation of the refined SSM description in Section 1.12.4. In addition to the instantiations for the top-level thermostat SSM
```

description in Section 1.16, we refine the top-level description by instantiating the following:

1. algebraic types for orders (commands with principals) and messages (orders sent with digital signatures over the network or from the keyboard),
2. an integrity-checking function *checkmsg*,
3. a message interpretation function *msgInterpret*,
4. algebraic types for certificates used to specify the security context,
5. a message integrity-checking function *checkmsg*, which checks digital signatures, and
6. an interpretation function *cert2Interpret*.

1.17.1 Thermostat Orders and Messages

Continuing the development of a secure networked thermostat, we add the definition of an order to the definitions and properties of commands and principals. The purpose of the *order* type is to add authentication and authorization to commands received via the network. This is done by including information on the principals sending commands to thermostats and on whose behalf the senders are acting. (1.75) shows that an order has three components:

1. A *keyPrinc* that is sending the message.
2. A *principal* on whose behalf the *keyPrinc* is acting.
3. A *command* issued to the thermostat, for example, ORD Server (Role (Utility *utilityID*)) (PR (Set *temperature*)) – the *Server* passing on a *Set temperature* command from *Utility utilityID*.

$$
\begin{aligned}
&order = \text{ORD keyPrinc principal command} \\
&\text{[order\_one\_one]} \\
&\vdash \forall a_0\ a_1\ a_2\ a_0'\ a_1'\ a_2'. \\
&\qquad (\text{ORD}\ a_0\ a_1\ a_2 = \text{ORD}\ a_0'\ a_1'\ a_2') \iff \\
&\qquad (a_0 = a_0') \land (a_1 = a_1') \land (a_2 = a_2') \\
&msg = \\
&\qquad \text{KB num command} \\
&\quad | \ \text{MSG keyPrinc principal order} \\
&\qquad\qquad ((\text{order digest, keyPrinc}) \text{ asymMsg}) \\
&\text{[msg\_distinct\_thm]} \\
&\vdash \forall a_3\ a_2\ a_1'\ a_1\ a_0'\ a_0. \ \text{KB}\ a_0\ a_1 \neq \text{MSG}\ a_0'\ a_1'\ a_2\ a_3 \\
&\text{[msg\_one\_one]} \\
&\vdash (\forall a_0\ a_1\ a_0'\ a_1'. \\
&\qquad (\text{KB}\ a_0\ a_1 = \text{KB}\ a_0'\ a_1') \iff (a_0 = a_0') \land (a_1 = a_1')) \land \\
&\quad \forall a_0\ a_1\ a_2\ a_3\ a_0'\ a_1'\ a_2'\ a_3'. \\
&\qquad (\text{MSG}\ a_0\ a_1\ a_2\ a_3 = \text{MSG}\ a_0'\ a_1'\ a_2'\ a_3') \iff \\
&\qquad (a_0 = a_0') \land (a_1 = a_1') \land (a_2 = a_2') \land (a_3 = a_3')
\end{aligned}
$$

(1.75)

The theorem *order_one_one* states that two orders are the same if and only if their components are the same.

We finally define the type *msg* as shown in (1.75).

A message received by a thermostat has two sources:

1. the attached *keyboard* from a thermostat associated with an *ownerID* number, for example, KB *userID* (NP Status), and

2. the *Server* sending commands from the *Owner* or *Utility* using the network, for example,

> *MSG Server* (*Role*(*Utility utilityID*))
>   (*ORD Server* (*Role*(*Utility utilityID*))(*NP Status*)) *signature*

where *signature* is obtained by signing the hash of the order using the *Server's* private key, that is,

> *sign*
>   (*privK Server*) (*hash*
>   (*SOME*
>   (*ORD Server* (*Role*(*Utility utilityID*)) (*NP Status*))))

The theorems *order_one_one*, *msg_distinct_thm*, and *msg_one_one* are similar to their counterparts for other types. The *distinct* theorem states that network messages are distinct from keyboard messages. The *one_one* theorems state that two orders or messages are the same if and only if their corresponding components are the same.

1.17.2   Authenticating and Checking the Integrity of Messages

Now that the format and contents of messages received by the thermostat are formally defined, we are able to define how messages, orders, and commands are authenticated and checked for integrity. Theorem (1.76) shows the definition of *checkmsg* and the theorem *checkmsg_OK*, where *checkmsg_OK* shows that *checkmsg* has the properties we expect.

```
[checkmsg_def]
 ⊢ (checkmsg
        (MSG sender recipient (ORD originator role cmd)
            signature)  ⟺
     signVerify (pubK sender) signature
        (SOME (ORD originator role cmd)) ∧
     (sender = originator)) ∧ (checkmsg (KB ownerID cmd)  ⟺  T)
[checkmsg_OK]
 ⊢ ((∀ownerID sender recipient originator role cmd.
        (sender = originator)  ⟹
        checkmsg
            (MSG sender recipient (ORD originator role cmd)
                (sign (privK sender)
                    (hash (SOME (ORD originator role cmd)))))) ∧
    ∀ownerID sender recipient originator role cmd.
        sender ≠ originator  ⟹
        ¬checkmsg
            (MSG sender recipient (ORD originator role cmd)
                (sign (privK sender)
                    (hash (SOME (ORD originator role cmd)))))) ∧
    ∀ownerID cmd. checkmsg (KB ownerID cmd)
```

$$(1.76)$$

Looking at the definition of *checkmsg*, we see three things:

1. *checkmsg* applied to orders sent over the network via the *Server* is checked using cryptographic-based digital signatures. Specifically, the digest of the received order is compared against the digest of the original order encrypted using the private key of the sender. This comparison is done using the previously defined cryptographic operation *signVerify*.

2. *checkmsg* as defined requires the *sender* value in the message to match the *originator* value in the order. Of course, there are other definitions of integrity where this might not be the case. We take this approach only as one example out of many.

3. *checkmsg* applied to commands originating from the attached keyboard is assumed to be authentic, that is, only the *Owner* or people with the *Owner's* permission are able to enter commands in manually. Hence, the value of *checkmsg* applied to keyboard-mediated commands is always true. This is only one possible approach. There are many possible approaches including biometric-based authentication. For reasons of simplicity and brevity, we assume only *Owners* or their delegates have physical access to a thermostat's keyboard.

The theorem *checkmsg_OK* reflects the design decisions on integrity-checking policy and assumptions contained in *checkmsg*.

1. When the *sender* and *originator* match on messages received over the network from the *Server*, and the digital signature is generated as expected using the

previously defined cryptographic operation *sign*, then *checkmsg* will be true, indicating the received message is intact and authenticated.

2. When the *sender* and *originator* do not match, even when the digital signature is generated as expected, *checkmsg* will be false, indicating the message is not authenticated.

3. Any well-formed keyboard input is regarded as authentic. This reflects the assumption that only the *Owner* or the *Owner's* delegates have physical access to the thermostat's keyboard.

Section 1.17.3, which follows below, defines the meaning of authenticated messages in the access-control logic. A precise definition of the semantics of messages is essential for assuring a unified view of security among all levels of abstraction.

1.17.3 Interpreting Messages

The formal infrastructure of the access-control logic and algebraic models of idealized cryptographic operations accounts for authentication and authorization within the defined interpretation of messages. Theorem (1.77) shows the theorem *msgInterpret_def*, which defines the interpretation or meaning of messages thermostats receive either from the network or from their keyboards.

```
[msgInterpret_def]
⊢ (msgInterpret
      (MSG sender recipient (ORD originator role cmd)
          signature) =
    if
      checkmsg
        (MSG sender recipient (ORD originator role cmd)
            signature)
    then
      Name (Key (pubK sender)) quoting Name role says
      prop (CMD cmd)
    else TT) ∧
  (msgInterpret (KB ownerID cmd) =
   if checkmsg (KB ownerID cmd) then
      Name Keyboard quoting Name (Owner ownerID) says
      prop (CMD cmd)
   else TT)
```
$$(1.77)$$

The function *msgInterpret* is defined over the two forms of type *msg*:

1. *MSG sender recipient (ORD originator role cmd) signature)*, that is, messages from the network, which are expected to be cryptographically signed, and

2. *KB ownerID cmd,* that is, messages coming directly from a thermostat's keyboard.

In either MSG or KB messages, first, the incoming message is checked using *checkmsg*, and if the message passes the integrity check, the message's non-trivial meaning in the access-control logic is given. If the message fails *checkmsg*, then the assigned meaning is the trivial assumption TT in the access-control logic. Recall KB messages that are well-formed are always authenticated. MSG messages are authenticated using their digital signatures and verify that the sender and originator are the same. Theorem (1.78) gives the value of msgInterpret for various cases.

```
[msgInterpretKB]
 ⊢ (M, Oi, Os) sat msgInterpret (KB ownerID cmd) ⟺
   (M, Oi, Os) sat
   Name Keyboard quoting Name (Owner ownerID) says
   prop (CMD cmd)
[msgInterpretMSG_sender_originator_match]
 ⊢ msgInterpret
     (MSG sender recipient (ORD sender role cmd)
         (sign (privK sender)
             (hash (SOME (ORD sender role cmd)))))) =
   Name (Key (pubK sender)) quoting Name role says
   prop (CMD cmd)
[msgInterpretMSG_denied]
 ⊢ sender ≠ originator ⇒
   (msgInterpret
     (MSG sender recipient (ORD originator role cmd)
         (sign (privK sender)
             (hash (SOME (ORD originator role cmd)))))) =
     TT)
```

$$(1.78)$$

If a MSG message is authenticated, then its interpretation is:

Name (Key (pubK sender)) quoting Name role says prop (CMD cmd)

If a KB message is authenticated, then its interpretation is:

Name Keyboard quoting Name(Owner ownerID says prop(CMD cmd)

1.17.4 Thermostat Certificates

All commands to the thermostat, which are packaged within MSG or KB messages of type *msg*, are evaluated within a security context specified by two kinds of statements:

1. *root* certificates, that is, root trust assumptions corresponding to access-control logic statements, which are *unsigned* because there is no higher authority than *root*, and

2. *digitally signed* certificates, that is, statements that have meaning in the access-control logic that are signed using the private-key of an authority, presumably recognized by thermostat.

In a way that is exactly analogous to MSG messages, digitally signed certificates are authenticated using their digital signatures. Similar to KB messages, which do not have associated signatures, root certificates are taken at face value. In our thermostat example, we have four root certificates and one signed certificate.

1. Root Certificates
   a. Command authority, *RCtrCert P cmd*, interpreted as:

$$\text{Name } P \text{ controls prop (CMD } cmd)$$

   b. Delegation certificate, *RRepsCert P Q cmd*, interpreted as:

$$\text{reps (Name } P) \text{ (Name } Q) \text{ (prop (CMD } cmd))$$

   c. Key authority, *RCtrKCert ca keyKpr keyPpr*, interpreted as

$$\text{Name (Role } ca) \text{ controls Name (Key (pubK } keyKpr))$$
$$\text{speaks\_for Name (Role } keyPpr)$$

   d. Root key certificate, *RKeyCert kppr ca*, interpreted as:

$$\text{Name (Key (pubK } kppr)) \text{ speaks\_for Name (Role } ca)$$

2. Signed public-key certificate, KeyCert *ca keyPpr* (pubK *keyRpr*) *signature*, if authenticated is interpreted as:

$$\textit{Name (Key (pubK ca)) says Name (Key (pubK keyRpr))}$$
$$\text{speaks for Name (Role } keyPpr)$$

Theorem (1.79) defines the type *cert2* of thermostat certificates described earlier. The theorem *checkcert2_def* in (1.79) defines the integrity-checking function for *cert2* certificates. The four root certificates are taken at face value. Signed key certificates are checked using their digital signatures in exactly the same way as MSG messages using the previously defined crypto-function *signVerify*.

cert₂ =

```
   RCtrCert principal command
 | RRepsCert principal principal command
 | RCtrKCert keyPrinc keyPrinc keyPrinc
 | RKeyCert keyPrinc keyPrinc
 | KeyCert keyPrinc keyPrinc (keyPrinc pKey)
            (((keyPrinc × keyPrinc pKey) digest, keyPrinc)
             asymMsg)
```
(1.79)
```
[checkcert2_def]
⊢ (checkcert2 (RCtrCert P cmd)  ⟺  T) ∧
  (checkcert2 (RRepsCert P Q cmd)  ⟺  T) ∧
  (checkcert2 (RCtrKCert keyPpr Kq keyQpr)  ⟺  T) ∧
  (checkcert2 (RKeyCert kp keyPpr)  ⟺  T) ∧
  (checkcert2 (KeyCert CApr Ppr (pubK Rpr) signature)  ⟺
   signVerify (pubK CApr) signature (SOME (Ppr,pubK Rpr)))
```

1.17.5 Certificate Interpretation Function

Theorem (1.80) shows the formal definition in HOL of *cert2Interpret_def*, the theorem defining the mapping of *cert2* certificates in the access-control logic formulas

```
[cert2Interpret_def]
⊢ (cert2Interpret (RCtrCert P cmd) =
   if checkcert2 (RCtrCert P cmd) then
     Name P controls prop (CMD cmd)
   else TT) ∧
  (cert2Interpret (RRepsCert P Q cmd) =
   if checkcert2 (RRepsCert P Q cmd) then
     reps (Name P) (Name Q) (prop (CMD cmd))
   else TT) ∧
  (cert2Interpret (RCtrKCert ca keyKpr keyPpr) =
   if checkcert2 (RCtrKCert ca keyKpr keyPpr) then
     Name (Role ca) controls
     Name (Key (pubK keyKpr)) speaks_for Name (Role keyPpr)
   else TT) ∧
  (cert2Interpret (RKeyCert kppr ca) =
   if checkcert2 (RKeyCert kppr ca) then
     Name (Key (pubK kppr)) speaks_for Name (Role ca)
   else TT) ∧
  (cert2Interpret (KeyCert ca keyPpr (pubK keyRpr) signature) =
   if
     checkcert2 (KeyCert ca keyPpr (pubK keyRpr) signature)
   then
     Name (Key (pubK ca)) says
     Name (Key (pubK keyRpr)) speaks_for Name (Role keyPpr)
   else TT)
```
(1.80)

Theorem (1.81) shows the corresponding meaning of each certificate in terms of Kripke structures satisfying the access-control logic interpretation of each of the five certificate forms.

```
[cert2InterpretRCtrCert]
⊢ (M, Oi, Os) sat cert2Interpret (RCtrCert (Role P) cmd) ⟺
  (M, Oi, Os) sat Name (Role P) controls prop (CMD cmd)
[cert2InterpretRRepsCert]
⊢ (M, Oi, Os) sat
    cert2Interpret (RRepsCert (Role P) (Role Q) cmd) ⟺
    (M, Oi, Os) sat
    reps (Name (Role P)) (Name (Role Q)) (prop (CMD cmd))
[cert2InterpretRCtrKCert]
⊢ (M, Oi, Os) sat cert2Interpret (RCtrKCert P Q Q) ⟺
  (M, Oi, Os) sat
  Name (Role P) controls
  Name (Key (pubK Q)) speaks_for Name (Role Q)
[cert2InterpretRKeyCert]
⊢ (M, Oi, Os) sat cert2Interpret (RKeyCert P P) ⟺
  (M, Oi, Os) sat Name (Key (pubK P)) speaks_for Name (Role P)
[cert2InterpretKeyCert]
⊢ (M, Oi, Os) sat
  cert2Interpret
    (KeyCert ca P (pubK P)
       (sign (privK ca) (hash (SOME (P, pubK P))))) ⟺
  (M, Oi, Os) sat
  Name (Key (pubK ca)) says
  Name (Key (pubK P)) speaks_for Name (Role P)
```

$$(1.81)$$

Note that a certificate's interpretation in the access-control logic is the trivial assumption TT, if it fails its integrity check. Root certificates are not digitally signed, as there is no higher level authority to certify them. These are interpreted at face value, with the assumption that root certificates are loaded into the thermostat under controlled and secure circumstances. Certificates with a digital signature, for example, *KeyCerts*, have their signatures checked using *signVerify*. This is shown below by *checkcert2_def* in rule (1.82):

```
[checkcert2_def]


⊢ (checkcert2 (RCtrCert P cmd) ⟺ T) ∧
  (checkcert2 (RRepsCert P Q cmd) ⟺ T) ∧
  (checkcert2 (RCtrKCert keyPpr Kq keyQpr) ⟺ T) ∧
  (checkcert2 (RKeyCert kp keyPpr) ⟺ T) ∧
  (checkcert2 (KeyCert CApr Ppr (pubK Rpr) signature) ⟺
   signVerify (pubK CApr) signature (SOME (Ppr, pubK Rpr)))
```

$$(1.82)$$

For example, the interpretation of a root key certificate *RKeyCert* is as follows in rule (1.83):

```
[cert2InterpretRKeyCert]
```

$$\vdash (M, Oi, Os) \text{ sat cert2Interpret (RKeyCert } P \text{ } P) \iff$$
$$(M, Oi, Os) \text{ sat Name (Key (pubK } P)) \text{ speaks\_for Name (Role } P)$$

(1.83)

For digitally signed *KeyCerts*, theorem *cert2InterpretKeyCert* shows that key certificates signed as expected are interpreted as expected as shown in rule (1.84):

```
[cert2InterpretKeyCert]
```

$$\vdash (M, Oi, Os) \text{ sat}$$
$$\text{cert2Interpret}$$
$$(\text{KeyCert } ca \text{ } P \text{ (pubK } P)$$
$$(\text{sign (privK } ca) \text{ (hash (SOME } (P, \text{pubK } P))))) \iff$$
$$(M, Oi, Os) \text{ sat}$$
$$\text{Name (Key (pubK } ca)) \text{ says}$$
$$\text{Name (Key (pubK } P)) \text{ speaks\_for Name (Role } P)$$

(1.84)

1.17.6 Transition Theorems

The refined thermostat SSM description has 10 theorems characterizing its behavior corresponding to the 10 theorems for the top-level SSM. Five of the theorems show that the security interpretation of *configuration2* justifies executing or trapping the particular instructions shown. These theorems are derived inference rules in C2 calculus. The five *configuration2* theorems are shown in (1.85)–(1.89) below:

```
[CFG2Interpret_Owner_Keyboard_thm]
```
$$\vdash \forall M \text{ } Oi \text{ } Os.$$
$$\text{CFG2Interpret } (M, Oi, Os)$$
$$(\text{CFG2 msgInterpret cert2Interpret isAuthenticated}$$
$$(\text{certs2 } ownerID \text{ } utilityID \text{ } cmd \text{ } npriv \text{ } privcmd)$$
$$(\text{thermoStateInterp } utilityID \text{ } privcmd)$$
$$(\text{KB } ownerID \text{ } cmd::ins) \text{ } state \text{ } outStream) \Rightarrow$$
$$(M, Oi, Os) \text{ sat prop (CMD } cmd)$$

(1.85)

```
[CFG2Interpret_Owner_KServer_thm]
⊢ ∀M Oi Os.
    CFG2Interpret (M, Oi, Os)
      (CFG2 msgInterpret cert2Interpret isAuthenticated
          (certs2 ownerID utilityID cmd npriv privcmd)
          (thermoStateInterp utilityID privcmd)
          (MSG Server (Owner ownerID)
              (ORD Server (Owner ownerID) cmd)
              (sign (privK Server)
                  (hash
                      (SOME (ORD Server (Owner ownerID) cmd)))))::
                  ins) state outStream) ⇒
      (M, Oi, Os) sat prop (CMD cmd)
```

$$(1.86)$$

```
[CFG2Interpret_Utility_KServer_npriv_thm]
⊢ ∀M Oi Os.
    CFG2Interpret (M, Oi, Os)
      (CFG2 msgInterpret cert2Interpret isAuthenticated
          (certs2 ownerID utilityID cmd npriv privcmd)
          (thermoStateInterp utilityID privcmd)
          (MSG Server (Role (Utility utilityID))
              (ORD Server (Role (Utility utilityID)) (NP npriv))
              (sign (privK Server)
                  (hash
                      (SOME
                          (ORD Server (Role (Utility utilityID))
                              (NP npriv)))))::ins) state outStream) ⇒
          (M, Oi, Os) sat prop (CMD (NP npriv))
```

$$(1.87)$$

```
[CFG2Interpret_Utility_KServer_privcmd_thm]
⊢ ∀M Oi Os.
    CFG2Interpret (M, Oi, Os)
      (CFG2 msgInterpret cert2Interpret isAuthenticated
          (certs2 ownerID utilityID cmd npriv privcmd)
          (thermoStateInterp utilityID privcmd)
          (MSG Server (Role (Utility utilityID))
              (ORD Server (Role (Utility utilityID))
                  (PR privcmd))
              (sign (privK Server)
                  (hash
                      (SOME
                          (ORD Server (Role (Utility utilityID))
                              (PR privcmd)))))::ins)
          (State enabled temperature) outStream) ⇒
      (M, Oi, Os) sat prop (CMD (PR privcmd))
```

$$(1.88)$$

```
[CFG2Interpret_trap_Utility_KServer_trap_thm]
⊢ ∀M Oi Os.
     CFG2Interpret (M,Oi,Os)
       (CFG2 msgInterpret cert2Interpret isAuthenticated
          (certs2 ownerID utilityID cmd npriv privcmd)
          (thermoStateInterp utilityID privcmd)
          (MSG Server (Role (Utility utilityID))
             (ORD Server (Role (Utility utilityID))
                (PR privcmd))
             (sign (privK Server)
                (hash
                   (SOME
                      (ORD Server (Role (Utility utilityID))
                          (PR privcmd))))) ::ins)
          (State disabled temperature) outStream) ⇒
     (M,Oi,Os) sat prop TRAP
```

$$(1.89)$$

For example, theorem 1.88 shows that executing a privileged command at the request of the *Utility* is derivable from the configuration shown in the theorem 1.90. This corresponds exactly to the top-level SSM description, except that the access-control logic formulas corresponding to inputs and certificates are now replaced by input and certificate data structures, and their interpretations:

```
[CFG2Interpret_Utility_KServer_privcmd_thm]

⊢ ∀M Oi Os.
     CFG2Interpret (M,Oi,Os)
       (CFG2 msgInterpret cert2Interpret isAuthenticated
          (certs2 ownerID utilityID cmd npriv privcmd)
          (thermoStateInterp utilityID privcmd)
          (MSG Server (Role (Utility utilityID))
             (ORD Server (Role (Utility utilityID))
                (PR privcmd))
             (sign (privK Server)

          (hash
             (SOME
                (ORD Server (Role (Utility utilityID))
                    (PR privcmd))))) ::ins)
          (State enabled temperature) outStream) ⇒
     (M,Oi,Os) sat prop (CMD (PR privcmd))
```

$$(1.90)$$

The refined execution theorems corresponding to the top-level SSM execution theorems are in (1.91)–(1.95) as shown below:

[exec2_Keyboard_Owner_cmd_Justified]

⊢ ∀*NS Out M Oi Os.*

    TR2 (*M,Oi,Os*) (exec (CMD *cmd*))

        (CFG2 msgInterpret cert2Interpret isAuthenticated

            (certs2 *ownerID utilityID cmd npriv privcmd*)

            (thermoStateInterp *utilityID privcmd*)

            (KB *ownerID cmd::ins*) *state outStream*)   (1.91)

        (CFG2 msgInterpret cert2Interpret isAuthenticated

            (certs2 *ownerID utilityID cmd npriv privcmd*)

            (thermoStateInterp *utilityID privcmd*) *ins*

            (*NS state* (exec (CMD *cmd*)))

            (*Out state* (exec (CMD *cmd*))*::outStream*)) ⇒

      (*M,Oi,Os*) sat prop (CMD *cmd*)

[exec2_KServer_Owner_cmd_Justified]

⊢ ∀*NS Out M Oi Os.*

    TR2 (*M,Oi,Os*) (exec (CMD *cmd*))

        (CFG2 msgInterpret cert2Interpret isAuthenticated

            (certs2 *ownerID utilityID cmd npriv privcmd*)

            (thermoStateInterp *utilityID privcmd*)

            (MSG Server (Owner *ownerID*)

               (ORD Server (Owner *ownerID*) *cmd*)

               (sign (privK Server)

                  (hash   (1.92)

                    (SOME (ORD Server (Owner *ownerID*) *cmd*))))::

               ins) *state outStream*)

        (CFG2 msgInterpret cert2Interpret isAuthenticated

            (certs2 *ownerID utilityID cmd npriv privcmd*)

            (thermoStateInterp *utilityID privcmd*) *ins*

            (*NS state* (exec (CMD *cmd*)))

            (*Out state* (exec (CMD *cmd*))*::outStream*)) ⇒

      (*M,Oi,Os*) sat prop (CMD *cmd*)

[exec2_KServer_Utility_npriv_Justified]

⊢ ∀*NS Out outStream state ins npriv privcmd cmd ownerID*

      utilityID M Oi Os.

    TR2 (*M,Oi,Os*) (exec (CMD (NP *npriv*)))

        (CFG2 msgInterpret cert2Interpret isAuthenticated

            (certs2 *ownerID utilityID cmd npriv privcmd*)

            (thermoStateInterp *utilityID privcmd*)

            (MSG Server (Role (Utility *utilityID*))

               (ORD Server (Role (Utility *utilityID*)) (NP *npriv*))

               (sign (privK Server)

                 (hash   (1.93)

                   (SOME

                     (ORD Server (Role (Utility *utilityID*))

                       (NP *npriv*)))))::*ins*) *state outStream*)

        (CFG2 msgInterpret cert2Interpret isAuthenticated

            (certs2 *ownerID utilityID cmd npriv privcmd*)

            (thermoStateInterp *utilityID privcmd*) *ins*

            (*NS state* (exec (CMD (NP *npriv*))))

            (*Out state* (exec (CMD (NP *npriv*)))*::outStream*)) ⇒

      (*M,Oi,Os*) sat prop (CMD (NP *npriv*))

```
[exec2_KServer_Utility_privcmd_Justified]
⊢ ∀NS Out outStream temperature ins npriv privcmd cmd ownerID
      utilityID M Oi Os.
    TR2 (M, Oi, Os) (exec (CMD (PR privcmd)))
      (CFG2 msgInterpret cert2Interpret isAuthenticated
        (certs2 ownerID utilityID cmd npriv privcmd)
        (thermoStateInterp utilityID privcmd)
        (MSG Server (Role (Utility utilityID))
          (ORD Server (Role (Utility utilityID))
            (PR privcmd))
          (sign (privK Server)
            (hash
              (SOME
                (ORD Server (Role (Utility utilityID))
                  (PR privcmd)))))::ins)
        (State enabled temperature) outStream)
      (CFG2 msgInterpret cert2Interpret isAuthenticated
        (certs2 ownerID utilityID cmd npriv privcmd)
        (thermoStateInterp utilityID privcmd) ins
        (NS (State enabled temperature)
          (exec (CMD (PR privcmd))))
        (Out (State enabled temperature)
          (exec (CMD (PR privcmd)))::outStream)) ⇒
    (M, Oi, Os) sat prop (CMD (PR privcmd))
```

$$(1.94)$$

```
[trap2_KServer_Utility_privcmd_Justified]
⊢ ∀NS Out outStream temperature ins npriv privcmd cmd ownerID
      utilityID M Oi Os.
    TR2 (M, Oi, Os) (trap (CMD (PR privcmd)))
      (CFG2 msgInterpret cert2Interpret isAuthenticated
        (certs2 ownerID utilityID cmd npriv privcmd)
        (thermoStateInterp utilityID privcmd)
        (MSG Server (Role (Utility utilityID))
          (ORD Server (Role (Utility utilityID))
            (PR privcmd))
          (sign (privK Server)
            (hash
              (SOME
                (ORD Server (Role (Utility utilityID))
                  (PR privcmd)))))::ins)
        (State disabled temperature) outStream)
      (CFG2 msgInterpret cert2Interpret isAuthenticated
        (certs2 ownerID utilityID cmd npriv privcmd)
        (thermoStateInterp utilityID privcmd) ins
        (NS (State disabled temperature)
          (trap (CMD (PR privcmd))))
        (Out (State disabled temperature)
          (trap (CMD (PR privcmd)))::outStream)) ⇒
    (M, Oi, Os) sat prop TRAP
```

$$(1.95)$$

As an example, the *exec2_KServer_Utility_privcmd_Justified* is shown in theorem (1.94). Similar to its counterpart in the top-level SSM description, the theorem states that if a transition occurred corresponding to executing a privileged command from the *Utility*, then the execution was justified.

1.18 EQUIVALENCE OF TOP-LEVEL AND REFINED SECURE-STATE MACHINES

The last group of theorems for the networked thermostat are five equivalence theorems. For the cases of (1) executing keyboarded commands by the *Owner*, (2) executing *Owner* commands via the *Server*, (3) executing non-privileged *Utility* commands via the *Server*, (4) executing privileged *Utility* commands via the *Server*, and (5) trapping privileged commands via the *Server*, the theorems state that the top-level and refined SSM transitions are equivalent. The five theorems are theorems (1.96)–(1.100):

```
[TR2_iff_TR_Keyboard_Owner_cmd]
```
$\vdash \forall M$ *Oi Os ownerID utilityID ins ins$_2$ outStream NS Out state*
$\quad$ *npriv privcmd cmd.*
$\quad$ TR2 (M, Oi, Os) (exec (CMD *cmd*))
$\quad\quad$ (CFG2 msgInterpret cert2Interpret isAuthenticated
$\quad\quad\quad$ (certs2 *ownerID utilityID cmd npriv privcmd*)
$\quad\quad\quad$ (thermoStateInterp *utilityID privcmd*)
$\quad\quad\quad$ (KB *ownerID cmd*::*ins$_2$*) *state outStream*)
$\quad\quad$ (CFG2 msgInterpret cert2Interpret isAuthenticated
$\quad\quad\quad$ (certs2 *ownerID utilityID cmd npriv privcmd*)
$\quad\quad\quad$ (thermoStateInterp *utilityID privcmd*) *ins$_2$*
$\quad\quad\quad$ (*NS state* (exec (CMD *cmd*)))
$\quad\quad\quad$ (*Out state* (exec (CMD *cmd*))::*outStream*)) $\Longleftrightarrow$ (1.96)
$\quad$ TR (M, Oi, Os) (exec (CMD *cmd*))
$\quad\quad$ (CFG isAuthenticated
$\quad\quad\quad$ (thermoStateInterp *utilityID privcmd*)
$\quad\quad\quad$ (certs *ownerID utilityID cmd npriv privcmd*)
$\quad\quad\quad$ (Name Keyboard quoting Name (Owner *ownerID*) says
$\quad\quad\quad\quad$ prop (CMD *cmd*)::*ins*) *state outStream*)
$\quad\quad$ (CFG isAuthenticated
$\quad\quad\quad$ (thermoStateInterp *utilityID privcmd*)
$\quad\quad\quad$ (certs *ownerID utilityID cmd npriv privcmd*) *ins*
$\quad\quad\quad$ (*NS state* (exec (CMD *cmd*)))
$\quad\quad\quad$ (*Out state* (exec (CMD *cmd*)))::*outStream*))

```
[TR2_iff_TR_KServer_Owner_cmd]
⊢ ∀M Oi Os ownerID utilityID ins ins₂ outStream NS Out state
    npriv privcmd cmd.
  TR2 (M, Oi, Os) (exec (CMD cmd))
     (CFG2 msgInterpret cert2Interpret isAuthenticated
        (certs2 ownerID utilityID cmd npriv privcmd)
        (thermoStateInterp utilityID privcmd)
        (MSG Server (Owner ownerID)
           (ORD Server (Owner ownerID) cmd)
           (sign (privK Server)
              (hash
                 (SOME (ORD Server (Owner ownerID) cmd)))))::
              ins₂) state outStream)
     (CFG2 msgInterpret cert2Interpret isAuthenticated
        (certs2 ownerID utilityID cmd npriv privcmd)
        (thermoStateInterp utilityID privcmd) ins₂
        (NS state (exec (CMD cmd)))
        (Out state (exec (CMD cmd))::outStream)) ⟺
    TR (M, Oi, Os) (exec (CMD cmd))
       (CFG isAuthenticated
          (thermoStateInterp utilityID privcmd)
          (certs ownerID utilityID cmd npriv privcmd)
          (Name (Key (pubK Server)) quoting
           Name (Owner ownerID) says prop (CMD cmd)::ins) state
          outStream)
       (CFG isAuthenticated
          (thermoStateInterp utilityID privcmd)
          (certs ownerID utilityID cmd npriv privcmd) ins
          (NS state (exec (CMD cmd)))
          (Out state (exec (CMD cmd))::outStream))
```

(1.97)

```
[TR2_iff_TR_KServer_Utility_npriv]
⊢ ∀M Oi Os ownerID utilityID ins ins₂ outStream NS Out state
    npriv privcmd cmd.
  TR2 (M, Oi, Os) (exec (CMD (NP npriv)))
     (CFG2 msgInterpret cert2Interpret isAuthenticated
        (certs2 ownerID utilityID cmd npriv privcmd)
        (thermoStateInterp utilityID privcmd)
        (MSG Server (Role (Utility utilityID))
           (ORD Server (Role (Utility utilityID)) (NP npriv))
           (sign (privK Server)
              (hash
                 (SOME
                    (ORD Server (Role (Utility utilityID))
                       (NP npriv)))))::ins₂) state outStream)
     (CFG2 msgInterpret cert2Interpret isAuthenticated
        (certs2 ownerID utilityID cmd npriv privcmd)
        (thermoStateInterp utilityID privcmd) ins₂
        (NS state (exec (CMD (NP npriv)))
        (Out state (exec (CMD (NP npriv)))::outStream)) ⟺
    TR (M, Oi, Os) (exec (CMD (NP npriv)))
       (CFG isAuthenticated
          (thermoStateInterp utilityID privcmd)
          (certs ownerID utilityID cmd npriv privcmd)
          (Name (Key (pubK Server)) quoting
           Name (Role (Utility utilityID)) says
           prop (CMD (NP npriv))::ins) state outStream)
       (CFG isAuthenticated
          (thermoStateInterp utilityID privcmd)
          (certs ownerID utilityID cmd npriv privcmd) ins
          (NS state (exec (CMD (NP npriv))))
          (Out state (exec (CMD (NP npriv)))::outStream))
```

(1.98)

[TR2_iff_TR_KServer_Utility_privcmd]

⊢ ∀ M Oi Os $ownerID$ $utilityID$ ins ins_2 $temperature$ $outStream$ NS
   Out $npriv$ $privcmd$ cmd.
  TR2 (M,Oi,Os) (exec (CMD (PR $privcmd$)))
    (CFG2 msgInterpret cert2Interpret isAuthenticated
      (certs2 $ownerID$ $utilityID$ cmd $npriv$ $privcmd$)
      (thermoStateInterp $utilityID$ $privcmd$)
      (MSG Server (Role (Utility $utilityID$))
        (ORD Server (Role (Utility $utilityID$))
          (PR $privcmd$))
        (sign (privK Server)
          (hash
            (SOME
              (ORD Server (Role (Utility $utilityID$))
                (PR $privcmd$)))))::ins_2)
      (State enabled $temperature$) $outStream$)
    (CFG2 msgInterpret cert2Interpret isAuthenticated
      (certs2 $ownerID$ $utilityID$ cmd $npriv$ $privcmd$)
      (thermoStateInterp $utilityID$ $privcmd$) ins_2
      (NS (State enabled $temperature$)
        (exec (CMD (PR $privcmd$))))
      (Out (State enabled $temperature$)
        (exec (CMD (PR $privcmd$)))::$outStream$)) ⟺
  TR (M,Oi,Os) (exec (CMD (PR $privcmd$)))
    (CFG isAuthenticated
      (thermoStateInterp $utilityID$ $privcmd$)
      (certs $ownerID$ $utilityID$ cmd $npriv$ $privcmd$)
      (Name (Key (pubK Server)) quoting
       Name (Role (Utility $utilityID$)) says
       prop (CMD (PR $privcmd$))::ins)
      (State enabled $temperature$) $outStream$)
    (CFG isAuthenticated
      (thermoStateInterp $utilityID$ $privcmd$)
      (certs $ownerID$ $utilityID$ cmd $npriv$ $privcmd$) ins
      (NS (State enabled $temperature$)
        (exec (CMD (PR $privcmd$))))
      (Out (State enabled $temperature$)
        (exec (CMD (PR $privcmd$)))::$outStream$))

$$(1.99)$$

```
[TR2_iff_TR_KServer_Utility_trap]
⊢ ∀M Oi Os ownerID utilityID ins ins₂ temperature outStream NS
    Out npriv privcmd cmd.
      TR2 (M,Oi,Os) (trap (CMD (PR privcmd)))
        (CFG2 msgInterpret cert2Interpret isAuthenticated
            (certs2 ownerID utilityID cmd npriv privcmd)
            (thermoStateInterp utilityID privcmd)
            (MSG Server (Role (Utility utilityID))
                (ORD Server (Role (Utility utilityID))
                    (PR privcmd))
                (sign (privK Server)
                    (hash
                        (SOME
                            (ORD Server (Role (Utility utilityID))
                                (PR privcmd)))))::ins₂)
            (State disabled temperature) outStream)
        (CFG2 msgInterpret cert2Interpret isAuthenticated
            (certs2 ownerID utilityID cmd npriv privcmd)
            (thermoStateInterp utilityID privcmd) ins₂
            (NS (State disabled temperature)
                (trap (CMD (PR privcmd))))
            (Out (State disabled temperature)
                (trap (CMD (PR privcmd)))::outStream))  ⟺
      TR (M,Oi,Os) (trap (CMD (PR privcmd)))
        (CFG isAuthenticated
            (thermoStateInterp utilityID privcmd)
            (certs ownerID utilityID cmd npriv privcmd)
            (Name (Key (pubK Server)) quoting
             Name (Role (Utility utilityID))) says
             prop (CMD (PR privcmd))::ins)
            (State disabled temperature) outStream)
        (CFG isAuthenticated
            (thermoStateInterp utilityID privcmd)
            (certs ownerID utilityID cmd npriv privcmd) ins
            (NS (State disabled temperature)
                (trap (CMD (PR privcmd))))
            (Out (State disabled temperature)
                (trap (CMD (PR privcmd)))::outStream))
```

$$(1.100)$$

1.19 CONCLUSIONS

The objectives of CSBD are to:

1. give formally verified assurances that all commands are executed if and only if they are authenticated and authorized,
2. assure a consistent and unified view of security across all levels of abstraction from high-level CONOPS down to implementations, and

3. enable third parties to rapidly and easily reproduce all formally verified assurance results.

In this chapter, we have provided a detailed outline and description of how to do this within a reusable and parameterized design and verification infrastructure consisting of:

1. An access-control logic and C2 calculus based on a multi-agent propositional modal logic with Kripke semantics,
2. An algebraic model of cryptographic operations,
3. SSM models integrating authentication, authorization, security interpretation, next-state, and output functions as parameters in transition relations, and
4. Implementations of all of the above as formally verified machine-checked theories in the HOL-4 theorem prover.

As an illustration, we developed a networked thermostat that incorporated security into all design levels from high-level models down to SSMs using specialized message and certificate structures (the complete theromostat report is located in the back of this book in Appendix C). What is notable is that most of the formal infrastructure is parameterized and reusable. As high-order logic is at the foundation of our methods, we are able to achieve generality by parameterizing over functions such as next-state, output, authentication, authorization, and interpretation functions. All of this leads to the conclusion that formal assurance of command-and-control functions in the IoT is feasible.

APPENDIX

1.A.1   The Definition of ACL Formulas, Kripke Structures, Principals, Integrity Levels, and Security Levels in HOL

```
Form =
     TT
   | FF
   | prop 'aavar
   | notf (('aavar, 'apn, 'il, 'sl) Form)
   | (andf) (('aavar, 'apn, 'il, 'sl) Form)
            (('aavar, 'apn, 'il, 'sl) Form)
   | (orf) (('aavar, 'apn, 'il, 'sl) Form)
           (('aavar, 'apn, 'il, 'sl) Form)
   | (impf) (('aavar, 'apn, 'il, 'sl) Form)
            (('aavar, 'apn, 'il, 'sl) Form)
   | (eqf) (('aavar, 'apn, 'il, 'sl) Form)
           (('aavar, 'apn, 'il, 'sl) Form)
   | (says) ('apn Princ) (('aavar, 'apn, 'il, 'sl) Form)
   | (speaks_for) ('apn Princ) ('apn Princ)
   | (controls) ('apn Princ) (('aavar, 'apn, 'il, 'sl) Form)
   | reps ('apn Princ) ('apn Princ)
         (('aavar, 'apn, 'il, 'sl) Form)
   | (domi) (('apn, 'il) IntLevel) (('apn, 'il) IntLevel)
   | (eqi) (('apn, 'il) IntLevel) (('apn, 'il) IntLevel)
   | (doms) (('apn, 'sl) SecLevel) (('apn, 'sl) SecLevel)
   | (eqs) (('apn, 'sl) SecLevel) (('apn, 'sl) SecLevel)
   | (eqn) num num
   | (lte) num num
   | (lt) num num


Kripke =
     KS ('aavar -> 'aaworld -> bool)
        ('apn -> 'aaworld -> 'aaworld -> bool) ('apn -> 'il)
        ('apn -> 'sl)


Princ =
     Name 'apn
   | (meet) ('apn Princ) ('apn Princ)
   | (quoting) ('apn Princ) ('apn Princ) ;

IntLevel = iLab 'il | il 'apn ;

SecLevel = sLab 'sl | sl 'apn
```

1.A.2   The Definition of the Evaluation Function $E_M[[-]]$ in HOL

The semantics or values of well-formed access-control logic formulas in HOL, are defined by *Efn*. The values of well-formed, access-control logic formulas are sets of worlds that are members of the universe of worlds, for a given Kripke structure *M*.

```
[Efn_def]
⊢ (∀Oi Os M. Efn Oi Os M TT = 𝒰(:'v)) ∧
  (∀Oi Os M. Efn Oi Os M FF = { }) ∧
  (∀Oi Os M p. Efn Oi Os M (prop p) = intpKS M p) ∧
  (∀Oi Os M f.
     Efn Oi Os M (notf f) = 𝒰(:'v) DIFF Efn Oi Os M f) ∧
  (∀Oi Os M f₁ f₂.
     Efn Oi Os M (f₁ andf f₂) =
     Efn Oi Os M f₁ ∩ Efn Oi Os M f₂) ∧
  (∀Oi Os M f₁ f₂.
     Efn Oi Os M (f₁ orf f₂) =
     Efn Oi Os M f₁ ∪ Efn Oi Os M f₂) ∧
  (∀Oi Os M f₁ f₂.
     Efn Oi Os M (f₁ impf f₂) =
     𝒰(:'v) DIFF Efn Oi Os M f₁ ∪ Efn Oi Os M f₂) ∧
  (∀Oi Os M f₁ f₂.
     Efn Oi Os M (f₁ eqf f₂) =
     (𝒰(:'v) DIFF Efn Oi Os M f₁ ∪ Efn Oi Os M f₂) ∩
     (𝒰(:'v) DIFF Efn Oi Os M f₂ ∪ Efn Oi Os M f₁)) ∧
  (∀Oi Os M P f.
     Efn Oi Os M (P says f) =
     {w | Jext (jKS M) P w ⊆ Efn Oi Os M f}) ∧
  (∀Oi Os M P Q.
     Efn Oi Os M (P speaks_for Q) =
     if Jext (jKS M) Q RSUBSET Jext (jKS M) P then 𝒰(:'v)
     else { }) ∧
  (∀Oi Os M P f.
     Efn Oi Os M (P controls f) =
     𝒰(:'v) DIFF {w | Jext (jKS M) P w ⊆ Efn Oi Os M f} ∪
     Efn Oi Os M f) ∧
  (∀Oi Os M P Q f.
     Efn Oi Os M (reps P Q f) =
     𝒰(:'v) DIFF
     {w | Jext (jKS M) (P quoting Q) w ⊆ Efn Oi Os M f} ∪
     {w | Jext (jKS M) Q w ⊆ Efn Oi Os M f}) ∧
  (∀Oi Os M intl₁ intl₂.
     Efn Oi Os M (intl₁ domi intl₂) =
     if repPO Oi (Lifn M intl₂) (Lifn M intl₁) then 𝒰(:'v)
     else { }) ∧
  (∀Oi Os M intl₂ intl₁.
     Efn Oi Os M (intl₂ eqi intl₁) =
     (if repPO Oi (Lifn M intl₂) (Lifn M intl₁) then 𝒰(:'v)
      else { }) ∩
```

if repPO Oi (Lifn M $intl_1$) (Lifn M $intl_2$) **then** $\mathcal{U}$(:'v)
else { }) $\wedge$

($\forall Oi$ Os M $secl_1$ $secl_2$.
    Efn Oi Os M ($secl_1$ doms $secl_2$) =
if repPO Os (Lsfn M $secl_2$) (Lsfn M $secl_1$) **then** $\mathcal{U}$(:'v)
else { }) $\wedge$

($\forall Oi$ Os M $secl_2$ $secl_1$.
    Efn Oi Os M ($secl_2$ eqs $secl_1$) =
    (**if** repPO Os (Lsfn M $secl_2$) (Lsfn M $secl_1$) **then** $\mathcal{U}$(:'v)
     else { }) $\cap$
if repPO Os (Lsfn M $secl_1$) (Lsfn M $secl_2$) **then** $\mathcal{U}$(:'v)
else { }) $\wedge$

($\forall Oi$ Os M $numExp_1$ $numExp_2$.
    Efn Oi Os M ($numExp_1$ eqn $numExp_2$) =
if $numExp_1$ = $numExp_2$ **then** $\mathcal{U}$(:'v) **else** { }) $\wedge$

($\forall Oi$ Os M $numExp_1$ $numExp_2$.
    Efn Oi Os M ($numExp_1$ lte $numExp_2$) =
if $numExp_1$ $\leq$ $numExp_2$ **then** $\mathcal{U}$(:'v) **else** { }) $\wedge$

$\forall Oi$ Os M $numExp_1$ $numExp_2$.
    Efn Oi Os M ($numExp_1$ lt $numExp_2$) =
if $numExp_1$ < $numExp_2$ **then** $\mathcal{U}$(:'v) **else** { }

1.A.3 Definition of Transition Relation TR

1.A.3.1 HOL Source Code Defining TR

```
val (TR_rules, TR_ind, TR_cases) =
Hol_reln
'(!(inputTest:('command inst,'principal,'d,'e)Form -> bool) (P:'principal Princ)
   (NS: 'state -> 'command inst trType -> 'state) M Oi Os Out (s:'state)
   (certs:('command inst,'principal,'d,'e)Form list)
   (stateInterp:'state -> ('command inst,'principal,'d,'e)Form)
   (cmd:'command)(ins:('command inst,'principal,'d,'e)Form list)
   (outs:'output list).
(inputTest ((P says (prop (CMD cmd))):('command inst,'principal,'d,'e)Form) /\
 (CFGInterpret (M,Oi,Os)
   (CFG inputTest stateInterp certs (((P says (prop (CMD cmd)))
   :('command inst,'principal,'d,'e)Form)::ins) s outs))) ==>
(TR
   ((M:('command inst,'b,'principal,'d,'e)Kripke),Oi:'d po,Os:'e po) (exec(CMD cmd))
   (CFG inputTest stateInterp certs (((P says (prop (CMD cmd)))
   :('command inst,'principal,'d,'e)Form)::ins) s outs)
   (CFG inputTest stateInterp certs ins (NS s (exec(CMD cmd))) ((Out s (exec(CMD cmd)))::outs)))) /\
(!(inputTest:('command inst,'principal,'d,'e)Form -> bool) (P:'principal Princ)
   (NS:'state -> 'command inst trType -> 'state) M Oi Os Out (s:'state)
   (certs:('command inst,'principal,'d,'e)Form list)
   (stateInterp:'state -> ('command inst,'principal,'d,'e)Form)
   (cmd:'command)(ins:('command inst,'principal,'d,'e)Form list)
   (outs:'output list).
(inputTest ((P says (prop (CMD cmd))):('command inst,'principal,'d,'e)Form) /\
 (CFGInterpret (M,Oi,Os)
   (CFG inputTest stateInterp certs (((P says (prop (CMD cmd)))
   :('command inst,'principal,'d,'e)Form)::ins) s outs))) ==>
(TR
   ((M:('command inst,'b,'principal,'d,'e)Kripke),Oi:'d po,Os:'e po) (trap(CMD cmd))
   (CFG inputTest stateInterp certs (((P says (prop (CMD cmd)))
   :('command inst,'principal,'d,'e)Form)::ins) s outs)
   (CFG inputTest stateInterp certs ins (NS s (trap(CMD cmd))) ((Out s (trap(CMD cmd)))::outs)))) /\
(!(inputTest:('command inst,'principal,'d,'e)Form -> bool) (NS:'state -> 'command inst trType -> 'state)
   M Oi Os (Out: 'state -> 'command inst trType -> 'output) (s:'state)
   (certs:('command inst,'principal,'d,'e)Form list)
   (stateInterp:'state -> ('command inst,'principal,'d,'e)Form)
   (cmd:'command)(x:('command inst,'principal,'d,'e)Form)(ins:('command inst,'principal,'d,'e)Form list)
   (outs:'output list).
~inputTest x ==>
(TR
   ((M:('command inst,'b,'principal,'d,'e)Kripke),Oi:'d po,Os:'e po) (discard:'command inst trType)
(CFG inputTest stateInterp certs ((x:('command inst,'principal,'d,'e)Form)::ins) s outs)
(CFG inputTest stateInterp certs ins (NS s discard) ((Out s discard)::outs))))'
```

1.A.3.2 Defining Properties of TR

```
[TR_rules]
```

⊢ ($\forall$*inputTest P NS M Oi Os Out s certs stateInterp cmd ins*
       outs .
       inputTest (P `says` `prop` (`CMD` *cmd*)) $\wedge$
       `CFGInterpret` (M, Oi, Os)
         (`CFG` *inputTest stateInterp certs*
             (P `says` `prop` (`CMD` *cmd*) `::` *ins*) *s outs*) $\Rightarrow$
       `TR` (M, Oi, Os) (`exec` (`CMD` *cmd*))
         (`CFG` *inputTest stateInterp certs*
             (P `says` `prop` (`CMD` *cmd*) `::` *ins*) *s outs*)
         (`CFG` *inputTest stateInterp certs ins*
             (*NS s* (`exec` (`CMD` *cmd*)))
             (*Out s* (`exec` (`CMD` *cmd*)) `::` *outs*))) $\wedge$
    ($\forall$*inputTest P NS M Oi Os Out s certs stateInterp cmd ins*
       outs .
       inputTest (P `says` `prop` (`CMD` *cmd*)) $\wedge$
       `CFGInterpret` (M, Oi, Os)
         (`CFG` *inputTest stateInterp certs*
             (P `says` `prop` (`CMD` *cmd*) `::` *ins*) *s outs*) $\Rightarrow$
       `TR` (M, Oi, Os) (`trap` (`CMD` *cmd*))
         (`CFG` *inputTest stateInterp certs*
             (P `says` `prop` (`CMD` *cmd*) `::` *ins*) *s outs*)
         (`CFG` *inputTest stateInterp certs ins*
             (*NS s* (`trap` (`CMD` *cmd*)))
             (*Out s* (`trap` (`CMD` *cmd*)) `::` *outs*))) $\wedge$
    $\forall$*inputTest NS M Oi Os Out s certs stateInterp cmd x ins outs*
       $\neg$*inputTest x* $\Rightarrow$
       `TR` (M, Oi, Os) `discard`
         (`CFG` *inputTest stateInterp certs* (*x* `::` *ins*) *s outs*)
         (`CFG` *inputTest stateInterp certs ins* (*NS s* `discard`)
             (*Out s* `discard` `::` *outs*))

```
[TR_ind]
```

$\vdash \forall TR'.$

        ($\forall inputTest$ P NS M Oi Os Out s $certs$ $stateInterp$ cmd ins
             $outs$.
        $inputTest$ (P `says prop` (CMD cmd)) $\wedge$
        `CFGInterpret` (M, Oi, Os)
          (CFG $inputTest$ $stateInterp$ $certs$
             (P `says prop` (CMD cmd)`::ins`) s $outs$) $\Rightarrow$
        TR' (M, Oi, Os) (`exec` (CMD cmd))
          (CFG $inputTest$ $stateInterp$ $certs$
             (P `says prop` (CMD cmd)`::ins`) s $outs$)

      (CFG $inputTest$ $stateInterp$ $certs$ ins
        (NS s (`exec` (CMD cmd)))
        (Out s (`exec` (CMD cmd))`::outs`))) $\wedge$
($\forall inputTest$ P NS M Oi Os Out s $certs$ $stateInterp$ cmd ins
     $outs$.
   $inputTest$ (P `says prop` (CMD cmd)) $\wedge$
   `CFGInterpret` (M, Oi, Os)
     (CFG $inputTest$ $stateInterp$ $certs$
        (P `says prop` (CMD cmd)`::ins`) s $outs$) $\Rightarrow$
   TR' (M, Oi, Os) (`trap` (CMD cmd))
     (CFG $inputTest$ $stateInterp$ $certs$
        (P `says prop` (CMD cmd)`::ins`) s $outs$)
     (CFG $inputTest$ $stateInterp$ $certs$ ins
       (NS s (`trap` (CMD cmd)))
       (Out s (`trap` (CMD cmd))`::outs`))) $\wedge$
($\forall inputTest$ NS M Oi Os Out s $certs$ $stateInterp$ cmd x ins
     $outs$.
   $\neg inputTest$ x $\Rightarrow$
   TR' (M, Oi, Os) `discard`
     (CFG $inputTest$ $stateInterp$ $certs$ (x`::ins`) s $outs$)
     (CFG $inputTest$ $stateInterp$ $certs$ ins (NS s `discard`)
      (Out s `discard::outs`))) $\Rightarrow$
$\forall a_0$ a_1 a_2 a_3.   TR a_0 a_1 a_2 a_3 $\Rightarrow$ TR' a_0 a_1 a_2 a_3

```
[TR_cases]
```

$\vdash \forall a_0\ a_1\ a_2\ a_3.$
  TR $a_0\ a_1\ a_2\ a_3$ $\iff$
  ($\exists inputTest$ P NS M Oi Os Out s $certs$ $stateInterp$ cmd ins
   $outs$.
   $(a_0 = (M,Oi,Os)) \wedge (a_1 =$ exec (CMD cmd)) $\wedge$
   $(a_2 =$
   CFG $inputTest$ $stateInterp$ $certs$
    (P says prop (CMD cmd)::ins) s $outs$) $\wedge$
   $(a_3 =$
   CFG $inputTest$ $stateInterp$ $certs$ ins
    (NS s (exec (CMD cmd)))
    (Out s (exec (CMD cmd)))::$outs$)) $\wedge$
   $inputTest$ (P says prop (CMD cmd)) $\wedge$
   CFGInterpret (M,Oi,Os)
    (CFG $inputTest$ $stateInterp$ $certs$
     (P says prop (CMD cmd)::ins) s $outs$)) $\vee$
  ($\exists inputTest$ P NS M Oi Os Out s $certs$ $stateInterp$ cmd ins
   $outs$.
   $(a_0 = (M,Oi,Os)) \wedge (a_1 =$ trap (CMD cmd)) $\wedge$
   $(a_2 =$
   CFG $inputTest$ $stateInterp$ $certs$
    (P says prop (CMD cmd)::ins) s $outs$) $\wedge$
   $(a_3 =$
   CFG $inputTest$ $stateInterp$ $certs$ ins
    (NS s (trap (CMD cmd)))

  (Out s (trap (CMD cmd)))::$outs$)) $\wedge$
 $inputTest$ (P says prop (CMD cmd)) $\wedge$
 CFGInterpret (M,Oi,Os)
  (CFG $inputTest$ $stateInterp$ $certs$
   (P says prop (CMD cmd)::ins) s $outs$)) $\vee$
$\exists inputTest$ NS M Oi Os Out s $certs$ $stateInterp$ cmd x ins
 $outs$.
 $(a_0 = (M,Oi,Os)) \wedge (a_1 =$ discard) $\wedge$
 $(a_2 =$ CFG $inputTest$ $stateInterp$ $certs$ (x::ins) s $outs$) $\wedge$
 $(a_3 =$
 CFG $inputTest$ $stateInterp$ $certs$ ins (NS s discard)
  (Out s discard::$outs$)) $\wedge$ $\neg inputTest$ x

1.A.4 Definition of Transition Relation *TR2*

1.A.4.1 *HOL Source Code Defining* TR2

```
val (TR2_rules, TR2_ind, TR2_cases) =
Hol_reln
'(!(inputInterpret: 'input -> ('command inst,'principal,'d,'e)Form)
 (certInterpret: 'cert -> ('command inst,'principal,'d,'e)Form)
 (inputTest:('command inst,'principal,'d,'e)Form -> bool)
 (x:'input)
 (NS: 'state -> 'command inst trType -> 'state)
 (M:('command inst,'b,'principal,'d,'e)Kripke)
 (Oi:'d po)
 (Os:'e po)
 (Out: 'state -> 'command inst trType -> 'output)
 (state:'state)
 (certs:'cert list)
 (stateInterpret:'state -> ('command inst,'principal,'d,'e)Form)
 (cmd:'command)
 (ins:'input list)
 (outStream:'output list).
 (inputTest(inputInterpret (x:'input))) /\
 (CFG2Interpret
 (M,Oi,Os)
 (CFG2 inputInterpret certInterpret inputTest certs stateInterpret
       (x::ins) state outStream)) ==>
 (TR2 (M,Oi,Os) (exec(CMD cmd))
 (CFG2 inputInterpret certInterpret inputTest certs stateInterpret
       (x::ins) state outStream)
 (CFG2 inputInterpret certInterpret inputTest certs stateInterpret
       ins (NS state (exec(CMD cmd))) ((Out state (exec(CMD cmd)))::outStream))))
/\
 (!(inputInterpret: 'input -> ('command inst,'principal,'d,'e)Form)
 (certInterpret: 'cert -> ('command inst,'principal,'d,'e)Form)
 (inputTest:('command inst,'principal,'d,'e)Form -> bool)
 (x:'input)
 (NS: 'state -> 'command inst trType -> 'state)
 (M:('command inst,'b,'principal,'d,'e)Kripke)
 (Oi:'d po)
 (Os:'e po)
 (Out: 'state -> 'command inst trType -> 'output)
 (state:'state)
 (certs:'cert list)
 (stateInterpret:'state -> ('command inst,'principal,'d,'e)Form)
 (cmd:'command)
 (ins:'input list)
 (outStream:'output list).
 (inputTest(inputInterpret (x:'input))) /\
 (CFG2Interpret
 (M,Oi,Os)
 (CFG2 inputInterpret certInterpret inputTest certs stateInterpret
       (x::ins) state outStream)) ==>
 (TR2 (M,Oi,Os) (trap(CMD cmd))
 (CFG2 inputInterpret certInterpret inputTest certs stateInterpret
       (x::ins) state outStream)
 (CFG2 inputInterpret certInterpret inputTest certs stateInterpret
       ins (NS state (trap(CMD cmd))) ((Out state (trap(CMD cmd)))::outStream))))
     (!(inputInterpret: 'input -> ('command inst,'principal,'d,'e)Form)
     (certInterpret: 'cert -> ('command inst,'principal,'d,'e)Form)
     (inputTest:('command inst,'principal,'d,'e)Form -> bool)
     (x:'input)
```

```
(NS: 'state -> 'command inst trType -> 'state)
(M:('command inst,'b,'principal,'d,'e)Kripke)
(Oi:'d po)
(Os:'e po)
(Out: 'state -> 'command inst trType -> 'output)
(state:'state)
(certs:'cert list)
(stateInterpret:'state -> ('command inst,'principal,'d,'e)Form)
(cmd:'command)
(ins:'input list)
(outStream:'output list).
(inputTest(inputInterpret (x:'input))) =>
TR2 (M,Oi,Os) discard
(CFG2 inputInterpret certInterpret inputTest certs stateInterpret
      (x::ins) state outStream)
(CFG2 inputInterpret certInterpret inputTest certs stateInterpret
      ins (NS state discard) ((Out state discard)::outStream))))'
```

1.A.4.2 Defining Properties of TR2

```
[TR2_rules]
```

$\vdash$ ($\forall inputInterpret$ $certInterpret$ $inputTest$ x NS M Oi Os Out
           $state$ $certs$ $stateInterpret$ cmd ins $outStream$.
           $inputTest$ $(inputInterpret$ $x)$ $\wedge$
           CFG2Interpret (M,Oi,Os)
              (CFG2 $inputInterpret$ $certInterpret$ $inputTest$ $certs$
                  $stateInterpret$ $(x::ins)$ $state$ $outStream$) $\Rightarrow$
           TR2 (M,Oi,Os) (exec (CMD cmd))
              (CFG2 $inputInterpret$ $certInterpret$ $inputTest$ $certs$
                  $stateInterpret$ $(x::ins)$ $state$ $outStream$)
              (CFG2 $inputInterpret$ $certInterpret$ $inputTest$ $certs$
                  $stateInterpret$ ins $(NS$ $state$ (exec (CMD cmd)))
                    $(Out$ $state$ (exec (CMD cmd)))$::outStream$))) $\wedge$
     ($\forall inputInterpret$ $certInterpret$ $inputTest$ x NS M Oi Os Out
           $state$ $certs$ $stateInterpret$ cmd ins $outStream$.
           $inputTest$ $(inputInterpret$ $x)$ $\wedge$
           CFG2Interpret (M,Oi,Os)
              (CFG2 $inputInterpret$ $certInterpret$ $inputTest$ $certs$
                  $stateInterpret$ $(x::ins)$ $state$ $outStream$) $\Rightarrow$
           TR2 (M,Oi,Os) (trap (CMD cmd))
              (CFG2 $inputInterpret$ $certInterpret$ $inputTest$ $certs$
                  $stateInterpret$ $(x::ins)$ $state$ $outStream$)
              (CFG2 $inputInterpret$ $certInterpret$ $inputTest$ $certs$
                  $stateInterpret$ ins $(NS$ $state$ (trap (CMD cmd)))
                    $(Out$ $state$ (trap (CMD cmd)))$::outStream$))) $\wedge$
       $\forall inputInterpret$ $certInterpret$ $inputTest$ x NS M Oi Os Out

      state certs stateInterpret cmd ins outStream.
      ¬*inputTest* (*inputInterpret x*) ⇒
      TR2 (*M*,*Oi*,*Os*) discard
         (CFG2 *inputInterpret certInterpret inputTest certs*
            stateInterpret (*x*::*ins*) *state outStream*)
         (CFG2 *inputInterpret certInterpret inputTest certs*
            stateInterpret ins (*NS state* discard)
            (*Out state* discard::*outStream*))

[TR2_ind]

⊢ ∀*TR*$'_2$.
      (∀*inputInterpret certInterpret inputTest x NS M Oi Os Out*
         state certs stateInterpret cmd ins outStream.
        inputTest (*inputInterpret x*) ∧
        CFG2Interpret (*M*,*Oi*,*Os*)
          (CFG2 *inputInterpret certInterpret inputTest certs*
            stateInterpret (*x*::*ins*) *state outStream*) ⇒
        TR$'_2$ (*M*,*Oi*,*Os*) (exec (CMD *cmd*))
          (CFG2 *inputInterpret certInterpret inputTest certs*
            stateInterpret (*x*::*ins*) *state outStream*)
          (CFG2 *inputInterpret certInterpret inputTest certs*
            stateInterpret ins (*NS state* (exec (CMD *cmd*)))
            (*Out state* (exec (CMD *cmd*))::*outStream*))) ∧
      (∀*inputInterpret certInterpret inputTest x NS M Oi Os Out*
         state certs stateInterpret cmd ins outStream.
        inputTest (*inputInterpret x*) ∧
        CFG2Interpret (*M*,*Oi*,*Os*)
          (CFG2 *inputInterpret certInterpret inputTest certs*
            stateInterpret (*x*::*ins*) *state outStream*) ⇒
        TR$'_2$ (*M*,*Oi*,*Os*) (trap (CMD *cmd*))
          (CFG2 *inputInterpret certInterpret inputTest certs*
            stateInterpret (*x*::*ins*) *state outStream*)
          (CFG2 *inputInterpret certInterpret inputTest certs*
            stateInterpret ins (*NS state* (trap (CMD *cmd*)))
            (*Out state* (trap (CMD *cmd*))::*outStream*))) ∧
      (∀*inputInterpret certInterpret inputTest x NS M Oi Os Out*
         state certs stateInterpret cmd ins outStream.
        ¬*inputTest* (*inputInterpret x*) ⇒

TR'_2 (M, Oi, Os) discard

    (CFG2 *inputInterpret* *certInterpret* *inputTest* *certs*
      stateInterpret $(x::ins)$ *state* *outStream*)

    (CFG2 *inputInterpret* *certInterpret* *inputTest* *certs*
      stateInterpret *ins* (*NS* *state* discard)
      (*Out* *state* discard::*outStream*))) $\Rightarrow$

$\forall a_0\ a_1\ a_2\ a_3.$ TR2 $a_0\ a_1\ a_2\ a_3 \Rightarrow TR'_2\ a_0\ a_1\ a_2\ a_3$
[TR2_cases]

$\vdash \forall a_0\ a_1\ a_2\ a_3.$

    TR2 $a_0\ a_1\ a_2\ a_3 \iff$

    ($\exists inputInterpret$ *certInterpret* *inputTest* x *NS* *M* *Oi* *Os* *Out*
      state *certs* *stateInterpret* *cmd* *ins* *outStream*.

      $(a_0 = (M, Oi, Os)) \wedge (a_1 = $ exec (CMD *cmd*)) $\wedge$
      $(a_2 = $

      CFG2 *inputInterpret* *certInterpret* *inputTest* *certs*
        stateInterpret $(x::ins)$ *state* *outStream*) $\wedge$

      $(a_3 = $

      CFG2 *inputInterpret* *certInterpret* *inputTest* *certs*
        stateInterpret *ins* (*NS* *state* (exec (CMD *cmd*)))
        (*Out* *state* (exec (CMD *cmd*))::*outStream*)) $\wedge$

$inputTest$ $(inputInterpret$ $x)$ $\wedge$
$\texttt{CFG2Interpret}$ (M, Oi, Os)
 $(\texttt{CFG2}$ $inputInterpret$ $certInterpret$ $inputTest$ $certs$
  $stateInterpret$ $(x::ins)$ $state$ $outStream))$ $\vee$
$(\exists inputInterpret$ $certInterpret$ $inputTest$ x NS M Oi Os Out
 $state$ $certs$ $stateInterpret$ cmd ins $outStream$.
 $(a_0$ $=$ $(M, Oi, Os))$ $\wedge$ $(a_1$ $=$ $\texttt{trap}$ $(\texttt{CMD}$ $cmd))$ $\wedge$
 $(a_2$ $=$
  $\texttt{CFG2}$ $inputInterpret$ $certInterpret$ $inputTest$ $certs$
   $stateInterpret$ $(x::ins)$ $state$ $outStream)$ $\wedge$
 $(a_3$ $=$
  $\texttt{CFG2}$ $inputInterpret$ $certInterpret$ $inputTest$ $certs$
   $stateInterpret$ ins $(NS$ $state$ $(\texttt{trap}$ $(\texttt{CMD}$ $cmd)))$
   $(Out$ $state$ $(\texttt{trap}$ $(\texttt{CMD}$ $cmd))::outStream))$ $\wedge$
 $inputTest$ $(inputInterpret$ $x)$ $\wedge$
 $\texttt{CFG2Interpret}$ (M, Oi, Os)
  $(\texttt{CFG2}$ $inputInterpret$ $certInterpret$ $inputTest$ $certs$
   $stateInterpret$ $(x::ins)$ $state$ $outStream))$ $\vee$
$\exists inputInterpret$ $certInterpret$ $inputTest$ x NS M Oi Os Out
 $state$ $certs$ $stateInterpret$ cmd ins $outStream$.
 $(a_0$ $=$ $(M, Oi, Os))$ $\wedge$ $(a_1$ $=$ $\texttt{discard})$ $\wedge$
 $(a_2$ $=$
  $\texttt{CFG2}$ $inputInterpret$ $certInterpret$ $inputTest$ $certs$
   $stateInterpret$ $(x::ins)$ $state$ $outStream)$ $\wedge$
 $(a_3$ $=$
  $\texttt{CFG2}$ $inputInterpret$ $certInterpret$ $inputTest$ $certs$
   $stateInterpret$ ins $(NS$ $state$ $\texttt{discard})$
   $(Out$ $state$ $\texttt{discard}::outStream))$ $\wedge$
 $\neg inputTest$ $(inputInterpret$ $x)$

1.A.4.3   *isAutheticated_def*

```
[isAuthenticated_def]
⊢ (isAuthenticated
     (Name Keyboard quoting Name (Owner ownerID) says
       prop (CMD cmd))  ⟺  T) ∧
   (isAuthenticated
     (Name (Key (pubK Server)) quoting
       Name (Owner ownerID) says prop (CMD cmd))  ⟺  T) ∧
   (isAuthenticated
     (Name (Key (pubK Server)) quoting
       Name (Role (Utility utilityID)) says prop (CMD cmd))  ⟺
   T) ∧ (isAuthenticated TT  ⟺  F) ∧ (isAuthenticated FF  ⟺  F) ∧
   (isAuthenticated (prop v)  ⟺  F) ∧
   (isAuthenticated (notf v₁)  ⟺  F) ∧
   (isAuthenticated (v₂ andf v₃)  ⟺  F) ∧
   (isAuthenticated (v₄ orf v₅)  ⟺  F) ∧
   (isAuthenticated (v₆ impf v₇)  ⟺  F) ∧
   (isAuthenticated (v₈ eqf v₉)  ⟺  F) ∧
   (isAuthenticated (v₁₀ says TT)  ⟺  F) ∧
   (isAuthenticated (v₁₀ says FF)  ⟺  F) ∧
   (isAuthenticated (Name v132 says prop v₆₆)  ⟺  F) ∧
   (isAuthenticated (v133 meet v134 says prop v₆₆)  ⟺  F) ∧
   (isAuthenticated
     (Name (Role v174) quoting Name (Role v164) says
       prop (CMD v142))  ⟺  F) ∧
   (isAuthenticated
     (Name (Key v175) quoting Name (Role CA) says
       prop (CMD v142))  ⟺  F) ∧
   (isAuthenticated
     (Name (Key v175) quoting Name (Role Server) says
       prop (CMD v142))  ⟺  F) ∧
   (isAuthenticated
     (Name (Key (pubK CA)) quoting
       Name (Role (Utility v184)) says prop (CMD v142))  ⟺  F) ∧
   (isAuthenticated
     (Name (Key (pubK (Utility v190))) quoting
       Name (Role (Utility v184)) says prop (CMD v142))  ⟺  F) ∧
   (isAuthenticated
     (Name (Key (privK v187)) quoting
       Name (Role (Utility v184)) says prop (CMD v142))  ⟺  F) ∧
   (isAuthenticated
     (Name Keyboard quoting Name (Role v164) says
       prop (CMD v142))  ⟺  F) ∧
   (isAuthenticated
     (Name (Owner v176) quoting Name (Role v164) says
       prop (CMD v142))  ⟺  F) ∧
```

```
(isAuthenticated
   (Name v154 quoting Name (Key v165) says
   prop (CMD v142)) ⟺ F) ∧
(isAuthenticated
   (Name v154 quoting Name Keyboard says prop (CMD v142)) ⟺
F) ∧
(isAuthenticated
   (Name (Role v192) quoting Name (Owner v166) says
   prop (CMD v142)) ⟺ F) ∧
(isAuthenticated
   (Name (Key (pubK CA)) quoting Name (Owner v166) says
   prop (CMD v142)) ⟺ F) ∧
(isAuthenticated
   (Name (Key (pubK (Utility v206))) quoting
   Name (Owner v166) says prop (CMD v142)) ⟺ F) ∧
(isAuthenticated
   (Name (Key (privK v203)) quoting Name (Owner v166) says
   prop (CMD v142)) ⟺ F) ∧
(isAuthenticated
   (Name (Owner v194) quoting Name (Owner v166) says
   prop (CMD v142)) ⟺ F) ∧
(isAuthenticated
   (Name (Account v195 v196) quoting Name (Owner v166) says
   prop (CMD v142)) ⟺ F) ∧
(isAuthenticated
   (Name v154 quoting Name (Account v167 v168) says
   prop (CMD v142)) ⟺ F) ∧
(isAuthenticated
   (v155 meet v156 quoting Name v144 says prop (CMD v142)) ⟺
F) ∧
(isAuthenticated
   ((v157 quoting v158) quoting Name v144 says
   prop (CMD v142)) ⟺ F) ∧
(isAuthenticated
   (v135 quoting v145 meet v146 says prop (CMD v142)) ⟺ F) ∧
(isAuthenticated
   (v135 quoting v147 quoting v148 says prop (CMD v142)) ⟺
F) ∧
(isAuthenticated (v135 quoting v136 says prop TRAP) ⟺ F) ∧
(isAuthenticated (v10 says notf v67) ⟺ F) ∧
(isAuthenticated (v10 says (v68 andf v69)) ⟺ F) ∧
(isAuthenticated (v10 says (v70 orf v71)) ⟺ F) ∧
(isAuthenticated (v10 says (v72 impf v73)) ⟺ F) ∧
(isAuthenticated (v10 says (v74 eqf v75)) ⟺ F) ∧
(isAuthenticated (v10 says v76 says v77) ⟺ F) ∧
(isAuthenticated (v10 says v78 speaks_for v79) ⟺ F) ∧
(isAuthenticated (v10 says v80 controls v81) ⟺ F) ∧
(isAuthenticated (v10 says reps v82 v83 v84) ⟺ F) ∧
```

```
(isAuthenticated (v₁₀ says v₈₅ domi v₈₆)  ⟺  F) ∧
(isAuthenticated (v₁₀ says v₈₇ eqi v₈₈)  ⟺  F) ∧
(isAuthenticated (v₁₀ says v₈₉ doms v₉₀)  ⟺  F) ∧
(isAuthenticated (v₁₀ says v₉₁ eqs v₉₂)  ⟺  F) ∧
(isAuthenticated (v₁₀ says v₉₃ eqn v₉₄)  ⟺  F) ∧
(isAuthenticated (v₁₀ says v₉₅ lte v₉₆)  ⟺  F) ∧
(isAuthenticated (v₁₀ says v₉₇ lt v₉₈)  ⟺  F) ∧
(isAuthenticated (v₁₂ speaks_for v₁₃)  ⟺  F) ∧
(isAuthenticated (v₁₄ controls v₁₅)  ⟺  F) ∧
(isAuthenticated (reps v₁₆ v₁₇ v₁₈)  ⟺  F) ∧
(isAuthenticated (v₁₉ domi v₂₀)  ⟺  F) ∧
(isAuthenticated (v₂₁ eqi v₂₂)  ⟺  F) ∧
(isAuthenticated (v₂₃ doms v₂₄)  ⟺  F) ∧
(isAuthenticated (v₂₅ eqs v₂₆)  ⟺  F) ∧
(isAuthenticated (v₂₇ eqn v₂₈)  ⟺  F) ∧
(isAuthenticated (v₂₉ lte v₃₀)  ⟺  F) ∧
(isAuthenticated (v₃₁ lt v₃₂)  ⟺  F)
```

REFERENCES

Abadi, M., Burrows, M., Lampson, B., & Plotkin, G. 1993. A calculus for access control in distributed systems. *ACM Transactions on Programming Languages and Systems (TOPLAS)*, 15(4), pp. 706–734.

Bell, D.E., & La Padula, L.J. 1973. Secure computer systems: mathematical foundations. No. MTR-2547-VOL-1. MITRE Corp., Bedford, MA.

Bell, D.E., & La Padula, L.J. 1976. Secure computer system: unified exposition and multics interpretation. No. MTR-2997-REV-1. MITRE Corp., Bedford, MA.

Biba, K.J. 1977. Integrity considerations for secure computer systems. No. MTR-3153-REV-1. MITRE Corp., Bedford, MA.

Chin, S.K., & Older, S.B. 2010. *Access Control, Security, and Trust: A Logical Approach*. CRC press.

Conway, L. 2012. Reminiscences of the VLSI revolution: how a series of failures triggered a paradigm shift in digital design. *IEEE Solid-State Circuits Magazine*, 4(4), pp. 8–31.

Ferraiolo, D., & Kuhn, R. 1992. Role-based access controls. In: 15th NISTNCSC National Computer Security Conference, Baltimore, MD, October 13–16, 1992, pp. 554–563.

Gordon, M.J., & Melham, T.F. 1993. *Introduction to HOL A Theorem Proving Environment for Higher Order Logic*. Cambridge University Press, New York.

IEEE Standards Association. IEEE Guide for Information Technology – System Definition – Concept of Operations (ConOps) Document, IEEE Computer Society, IEEE Std 1362-1998, March 19, 1998.

Joint Publication 5-0. Joint Operation Planning, U.S. Department of Defense, August 11, 2011.

Popek, G.J., & Goldberg, R.P. 1974. Formal requirements for virtualizable third generation architectures. *Communications of the ACM*, 17(7), pp. 412–421.

Sandhu, R.S., Coyne, E.J., Feinstein, H.L., & Youman, C.E. 1996. Role-based access control models. *IEEE Computer*, 29(2), pp. 38–47.

CHAPTER 2

CYBER-ASSURANCE THROUGH EMBEDDED SECURITY FOR THE INTERNET OF THINGS

TYSON T. BROOKS and JOON PARK
School of Information Studies, Syracuse University, Syracuse, NY, USA

2.1 INTRODUCTION

The Internet of Things (IoT) comprises billions of Internet-connected devices (ICD) or "things," each of which can sense, communicate, compute, and potentially actuate and can have intelligence, multimodal interfaces, physical/virtual identities, and attributes (Haller et al. 2008; Wang & Ranjan 2015). ICDs can be sensors, radio-frequency identification (RFID), social media, clickstreams, business transactions, actuators (such as machines/equipment fitted with sensors and deployed for mining, oil exploration, or manufacturing operations), or lab instruments (such as high-energy physics synchrotron and smart consumer appliance, e.g., TV, phone, and so on.) (Wang & Ranjan 2015). The IoT faces several technology challenges including leveraging and integrating existing systems and technologies, achieving interoperability with IPv6 networks, enabling both rapid response to malicious events and broader analysis of accumulated malicious information and minimizing new IoT system deployments.

The foundation of computer security is the mastery of profound information technology (Russell & Gangemi 1991). It requires the implementation of information-processing technology for data integration, data exchange, signal processing, encryption and decryption requiring communication protocols and network technologies (Wu & Irwin 2013). The technical characteristics of the IoT will have to adopt various effective measures to guard against malicious network detection, stealing, cyber-attacks, and guarantee secure transmission of data. Consequently, IoT architectures (composed of wireless sensor networks (WSNs), wireless frequency (Wi-Fi), low-power and lossy networks (LLNs), IPv6 over low power wireless personal area

Cyber-Assurance for the Internet of Things, First Edition. Edited by Tyson T. Brooks.
© 2017 by The Institute of Electrical and Electronic Engineers, Inc. Published 2017 by John Wiley & Sons, Inc.

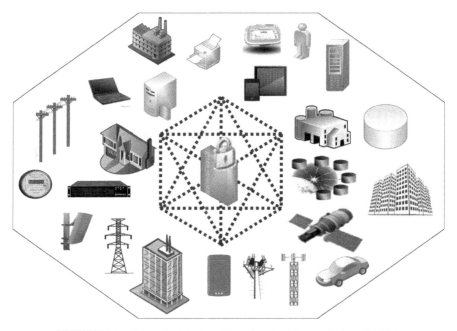

FIGURE 2.1   Internet of Things. Reproduced with permission of IEEE.

networks (6LoWPANs), etc.) allow computers to follow the machine-to-machine (M2M) model instead of client-server or hub-and-spoke, which will be less secure (Yan et al. 2008; Yun & Yuxin 2010). For example, IoT network borders and 6LoW-PAN routers must be capable of receiving and transmitting IPv4 and IPv6 traffic from and to the Internet (in which IPv4 is less secure than IPv6). The IoT, as displayed in Figure 2.1, is transforming the information technology platform by providing an extremely high-bandwidth channel between the cyber-world (represented by clouds, smart grids, smart devices, etc.) and the physical world in which we live (Rabaey 2015; Conovalu & Park 2015; Zhou 2012).

In today's hostile cyber-environment, hackers are continuously evolving their attack methodologies and targets (Brooks et al. 2014). Any communications network is subject to becoming the target of exploitation by criminal hackers looking to gain unauthorized access to an information system (Brooks et al. 2013). In a large-scale IoT computing environment, all trusted relationships/interfaces between IoT ICDs and networks and those between pairs of IoT processes within components need to be examined automatically to ensure that, in the interaction, neither behaves in a way that violates the trust relationship between them. An example of this kind of trust violation would be one IoT process providing erroneous data to another IoT process, or one IoT component attempting to perform an unauthorized operation on another. Even if each individual process or component can be determined to demonstrate its required security properties, the ways in which it interacts with other parties can still represent a source of vulnerabilities. Embedded system software (firmware) is typically purpose-built for an exactly specified hardware (e.g., embedded device) and is an active area of research and other of the promising avenues in the IoT field (Guinard & Trifa 2009; Limin 2010; Kranz et al. 2010; Ukil et al. 2011; Kovacshazy et al. 2013). Embedded devices (e.g., RFID, actuators, WSNs, microcontrollers (MCUs)) running software with a small memory footprint are those smart objects featuring a processor or microcontroller (plus storage capacity) which can be used to process and interpret sensor information, or to give products a "memory" of how they have been used upon network discovery (Asensio et al. 2015). These embedded devices utilizing embedded system software within the IoT will be composed of not only the smart ICD itself, but also the IoT network composed of services and storage components.

Embedded security devices have an intricate role in the IoT (Tseng et al. 2015). The concept of embedded security devices uses physical or logical containers that could include unique processing attributes such as serial numbers, shared secret values, or keys that are used during access control operations to authenticate authorized users (Kocher 2004). Embedded devices employed by IoT organization will require a high-level of assurance when providing authentication of ICDs to determine if they should be granted logical access to information systems and components. Since data will be shared amongst numerous ICDs and IoT networks, the authorized ICD of the data has no knowledge if, when or how the data are maliciously used. Worse yet, the IoT system has no ability to determine if the ICD presenting the data is an authorized ICD or an imposter. To reach a higher-level of assurance during authentication operations, many organizations will have to require the use of embedded security techniques where the authentication data are prevalent.

2.1.1   Related Work in Embedded Security

Cyber-assurance is the justified confidence that networked systems are adequately secure to meet operational needs, even in the presence of attacks, failures, accidents, and unexpected events (Alberts et al. 2009). This form of security is needed for IoT ICDs to perform computational functions embedded in the ICD and IoT network themselves. Embedded security providing security against cyber-attacks is a fundamental concept for the IoT. Xiaojun et al.'s (2015) research presented a self-organizing map (SOM)-based approach to enhance embedded system security by detecting abnormal program behavior. The researchers' proposed method extracts features derived from processor's program counter and cycles per instruction, and then utilizes the features to identify abnormal behavior using the SOM, resulting in the identification of unknown program behaviors (Xiaojun et al. 2015). Davi et al.'s (2015) examination on the Hardware-Assisted Flow Integrity eXtension (HAFIX), a defense against code-reuse attacks like return-oriented programming (ROP), exploited backward edges (returns) on diverse processor architectures. The authors identified the HAFIX as a fine-grained and practical protection an enabling technology for future control-flow integrity instantiations and presents the implementation and evaluation of HAFIX for the Intel® Siskiyou Peak and SPARC-embedded system architectures demonstrating its security and efficiency in code-reuse protection while incurring only 2% performance overhead (Davi et al. 2015).

Kainth et al.'s (2015) research identified a new technique to obfuscate soft microprocessor code which is located outside a field-programmable gate array (FPGA) chip in an unprotected area by providing customizable, data-dependent control-flow modification to make it difficult for attackers to easily understand program behavior. The author's research on the application of the approach identified three benchmarks illustrating a control-flow cyclomatic complexity increase of about 7× with a modest logic overhead for the soft processor (Kainth et al. 2015). Tseng et al. (2015) investigated an Advanced RISC Machines (ARM)-based embedded system dedicated to unattended real-time moving target detections which can be used in a security system and other applications with proper modifications. The authors provide comprehensive procedures in building up an embedded system such as setup environment for cross-compilation, migration of Bootloader, migration of Linux-2.6 kernel, fabrication and migration of root document system and setup of peripheral driving devices, and an algorithm of image background subtraction for moving target detection and tracking technology to transfer the taken invader's pictures to "The Cloud" through Wi-Fi to prevent the pictures being destroyed by the invader (Yuan-Wei et al. 2015).

Bobade and Mankar's (2015) research modified a double point multiplication algorithm and replaced traditional Karatsuba multiplier in an error checking and correction (ECC) processor with a novel modular multiplier. This research design of a modular multiplier follows systolic approach of processing the words instead of processing vector polynomial bit by bit or in parallel using a proposed multiplier recursively processes data as 16-bit words (Bobade & Mankar 2015). Bobade and Mankar's (2015) research of this multiplier when employed in ECC processor reduces drastically the total area utilization and the complete modular multiplier and ECC processor module is synthesized and simulated using Xilinx 14.4 software showing a remarkable improvement in area efficiency, when comparing with other such architecture. Kermani et al.'s (2013) study provides an overview of trends in embedded computing, highlights the researchers' implications on secure embedded system design through examples of hypothetical and real security attacks, and discusses the unique security challenges faced by these systems and some initial efforts toward addressing them. Ukil et al.'s (2011) research provides the requirements of embedded security, the solutions to resist different attacks, and the technology for resisting temper proofing of the embedded devices by the concept of trusted computing based on a secure execution environment for the issue of security for data-at-rest and securing data-in-transit.

Flood and Schukat (2014) researched a new protocol which combines zero-knowledge proofs and key exchange mechanisms to provide secure and authenticated communication in static M2M networks. The author's approach addresses all of the aforementioned issues while also being suitable for devices with limited computational resources and can be deployed in WSNs, while the protocol requires an a priori knowledge about the network setup and structure, guaranteeing perfect forward secrecy (Flood & Schukat 2014). Babar et al.'s (2011) research work highlights the need to provide in-built security in IoT devices to provide a flexible infrastructure for dynamic prevention, detection, diagnosis, isolation, and countermeasures against successful breaches; while defining the security needs taking into account computational time, energy consumption, and memory requirements of the devices proposing an embedded security framework as a feature of software/hardware co-design methodology. Unger and Timmermann (2015) researched a web services (WS) security specification suite for embedded systems which applied to derive the devices profile for web services security (DPWSec) for message level security, authentication and authorization, and the profile for a security architecture. Unger and Timmermann (2015) examined an intelligent rock bolt which is the combination of a traditional rock bolt with an IoT device, that is, a rock bolt with embedded sensors, actuators, processing capabilities, and wireless communication. Eliasson et al. (2014) developed a proposed architecture in which every rock bolt has its own IPv6 address and can establish a wireless mesh network in an *ad hoc* manner by measuring strain and seismic activity and exposing the sensors in the form of services; a number of mining-related activities such as stress on the rock bolt can be detected, falling rocks and the presence of mobile machinery can also be observed.

Ansilla et al.'s (2015) research on smart grid synchronization (SYN) flooding attacks inducing denial-of-service (DoS) attacks proposed a secure web server algorithm embedded in the LPC1768 processor ensures the smart resources are precluded from the attack. Czybik et al. (2013) provided an analysis of algorithms suitable for authenticity protection of data transferred by real-time Ethernet communication systems including an analysis of algorithms and measurement results for a typical embedded system used in industrial Ethernet devices. Ozvural and Kurt (2015) researched low-throughput-embedded IP gateway nodes utilizing both random network coding at low-rate wireless personal area network side and low-overhead Web-Socket protocol for cloud communications. Gope and Hwang (2015) proposed an anonymous authentication scheme, which can ensure some of the notable properties, such as sensor anonymity, sensor untraceability, resistance to replay attacks, cloning attacks, and so on in which the proposed authentication scheme will be useful in many distributed IoT applications (such as RFID-based IoT system, biosensor-based IoT healthcare system, and so on), where the privacy of the sensor movement is greatly desirable. Isa et al. (2014) presented a radio frequency (RF) simulator v1.1 which simulates lightweight security protocols for RF devices communications using Stop and Wait Automatic Repeat Request (SW-ARQ) protocol. The author's research on the RF simulator can be used for a quick trial and debugging for any new cryptography protocol in the simulator before actual implementation or experiment of the protocol in the physical embedded devices (Isa et al. 2014).

Strobel et al. (2014) research on the implementation of sensitive applications on a standard embedded MCUs can lead to severe security problems. Strobel et al. (2014) identified various threats to MCU-based systems, including side-channel analysis and different methods for extracting embedded code allowing an adversary to extract the cryptographic keys which, in turn, leads to a total collapse of the system security. Liu et al.'s (2015) research on WeeRMES, a WS-based e-mail extension for remote monitoring of embedded systems, is used to supplement conventional remote control methods, using e-mails such as sending device instructions, inspecting device status, and gathering data using eXtensible Markup Language (XML) capsulated messages and user interfaces to dynamically achieve by means of XForms generated by Java classes loaded on target devices. Xiang et al.'s (2013) research presents a security mechanism using hardware monitoring to protect the program's execution on embedded system through monitoring: code's basic block checksum, execution time of code's basic block, and the beginning–ending addresses of code's basic block. The researcher's preliminary experimental results show that the designed basic block information extraction tools and the security module can be expected to work properly and additional performance loss and additional requirements of on-chip storage, brought by the security module, were in the acceptable range (Wang et al. 2013).

2.2 CYBER-SECURITY AND CYBER-ASSURANCE

Although similar, cyber-assurance is slightly different than cyber-security. Cyber-security refers to the defense against cyber-attacks for an information technology (IT) infrastructure using people and technologies (i.e., access control technologies, system integrity technologies, cryptography, audit and monitoring tools, configuration management and information assurance) to protect information that is being processed, stored, and transmitted in networked computer systems (GAO 2004; CNSS 2010). By definition, cyber-security protects against advance persistent threats (APTs) using defensive measures, including information assurance, defense computer systems (e.g., intrusion detection systems, intrusion prevention systems, etc.), applications hardening, malware protection, access control, information infrastructure protection, and network security (Agosta & Pelosi 2007). Cyber-security focuses on policies and a collection of defensive technologies (hardware/software), processes, and practices designed to protect networks, computers, programs, and information from attack, damage, or unauthorized access in order to secure systems that are connected to the Internet (Agosta & Pelosi 2007). For example, a network firewall, which is either stateful or stateless, is used to manage and control both network connectivity and network services for traffic entering and leaving the network and preventing unrestricted access to unauthorized users; anti-virus technology is used for promptly detecting and removing viruses in information systems. These defensive measures are some ways to respond to security APTs in cyberspace. Likewise, cyber-security does not just focus on people and technologies, but provides a focus on all information assurance aspects pertaining to processes and polices for confidentiality, integrity, availability, authorization, and non-repudiation in ensuring the sensitivity and criticality of the information processed within these systems (Curts & Campbell 2015).

As previously stated, cyber-assurance is the justified confidence that networked systems are adequately secure to meet operational needs, even in the presence of attacks, failures, accidents, and unexpected events (Alberts et al. 2009). Cyber-assurance means the IoT smart ICDs and networks provide the opportunity of automatically securing themselves against cyber-attacks. The difference is that the concept of cyber-assurance must provide embedded, secure microchips/processors in ICD devices and networks that can continue to operate correctly even when subjected to an attack (Alberts et al. 2009). IoT devices and systems should be able to resist the various security cyber-attacks such as hacking of the IoT network, theft of information, disruption, etc. and be able to continue performing under severe environmental conditions. Through embedded processors and algorithms over the transmitted information (Parameswaran & Wolf 2008), the miscoding and leaking of information during transmission channels has to monitor any loss, miscoding, and leaking of data. Timely adjustments of information with falling quality and automatic switching to the best routing IoT system by making use of multidirectional routing is also warranted. Cyber-assurance will need to provide the principles and technologies to unify these IoT systems to deliver the end-state goal of secure IoT systems for greatly enhanced interoperability, scalability, performance, and agility.

Cyber-assurance tight control over how services utilize IoT devices and networks is essential in the IoT. On the lowest layers of the IoT, sensors and actuators are in contact with the embedding physical environment (Limin 2010; Kovacshazy et al. 2013). This means that each aspect of the IoT at the level of granularity of an individual component, program, or application must be automatically resilient against a cyber-attack. Modern cyber-security techniques are further challenged by the fact that typical security methodologies may use obsolete security abstractions for identifying the legitimacy of potential risks associated with a particular service request. Fortunately, some unique properties of IoT infrastructures may provide the foundation for establishing cyber-assurance. As a new and emerging field, cyber-assurance for the IoT has not yet received the same amount of research attention as cyber-security but is starting to mature. Several related works are, however, directly relevant to this book, in the fields of information assurance (Quain et al. 2010), security architecture (Schoenfield 2015), smart grid security (Goel et al. 2015), and cloud computing security (Krutz & Vines 2010). The monitoring of requests and responses between IoT devices must use a wide-spectrum communications of feasible techniques for an effective approach to detect certain types of attacks (Anderson et al. 2004; Yang et al. 2014; Huang & Zhang 2015; Torrieri 2015). For example, Santamarta (2012) (as identified in Knapp & Samani 2013, pp. 70–71) used a variety of network monitoring and reverse engineering tools to identify Ethernet/Internet protocol (IP) functions to control a Rockwell Automation ControlLogix system and object identifiers for a smart grid supervisory control and data acquisition (SCADA) system which resulted in the disclosure of several of the following attack methods:

- Forcing a system stop: By sending a common industrial protocol (CIP) command to the devices, this attack effectively shuts off the CIP service and renders the device dead; this puts the device into a "major recoverable fault" state,
- Crashing the central processing unit (CPU): This attack crashes the CPU due to a malformed CIP request, which cannot be effectively handled by the CIP stack; again the result is a "major recoverable fault" state,
- Dumping device boot code: This is a CIP function that allows an Ethernet/IP device's boot code to be remotely dumped,
- Reset device: This is a simple misuse of the CIP system reset function; this attack resets the target device,

- Crash device: This attack crashes the target device due to vulnerability in the device's CIP stack and,
- Flash update: CIP, like many industrial protocols, supports writing data to remove devices, including register and rely values, but also files; this attack misuse this capability to write new firmware to the target device.

Note: the flash update attack identified under Project Basecamp loosely mimics the behavior of St****t, which wrote new logic to a Siemens PLC in a similar fashion using the Profinet protocol. Surprisingly, many of these types of attacks are possible across many other ICS protocols, as they represent predefined function codes within the protocol (Knapp & Samani 2013, p. 71).

Cyber-assurance embedded defense mechanisms within ICDs and the IoT network provides a stable and reliable system with strong anti-damage abilities with good defense capabilities. This will include detecting technical loopholes, topographic structures of various IoT networks, discovering and determining technical parameters of wireless communications, discovering irregularities of activities of IoT systems and threat levels while analyzing their strong and weak points and providing intelligence support for organizing and carrying out secure information processing. The basic concept is to guarantee that the IoT network can perform its functions before, during, and even under a cyber-attack (Gao & Ansari 2005). Due to the timing of IoT network attacks, forms of attacks, scope and extent of attacks, cyber-assurance requirements must be implemented at conception to determine the overall IoT strategy. In the cyber-world dominated by information and information technology, ICDs and IoT networks, nodes and information processing are certainly the major targets of reconnaissance and cyber-attacks. Their survival is subject to serious challenge, thus reliability is an important indicator of the IoT system.

However, cyber-security and cyber-assurance do complement each other. Both require the characteristics of being stealth, complicated, and changeable requiring that networks enhance their emergency response capabilities to attacks and making flexible responses to changes. However, with the advent of the IoT, the adversary will certainly carry out more powerful cyber-attacks in these networks in order to lower the efficacy of the overall systems. Cyber-assurance concepts will have to include those embedded security solutions to automatically protect the topographic structure of the IoT, the information stored (data-at-rest) and transmitted (data-in-transit), the location of ICDs and the conditions of their operation activity including signal waveforms, transmission speeds, and other technical parameters within the IoT domain.

2.3 RECOGNITION, FORTIFICATION, RE-ESTABLISHMENT, SURVIVABILITY

The robustness of cyber-assurance to the subversion of the IoT security methods is critical, since the threat of information systems subversion presents a significant risk (Anderson et al. 2004). Information assurance for IoT networks is reliant on the security of its backbone architecture and the smart ICD providing networked services. In order to perform successful cyber-assurance techniques, the process itself that carries it out must be trusted. This requires that the process itself is robust and resistant to the type of cyber-attacks that may be leveled against it. As a result, the level of trust associated with the cyber-assurance process must be evaluated in light of the assumed threat profile, which may be different for each individual ICD and/or IoT network. The detection of any alarm condition should immediately initiate steps to protect all information and resources that are being protected by the ICD. Although the security processor chips do contain hardware devices intended to monitor these indicators and raise an alarm if any out-of-bound condition is detected, this is typically not the case for other ICDs in this type of environment.

Notwithstanding the complexity of features of ICDs and IoT networks, these new types of wireless systems, by their very nature, will continue to have a number of vulnerabilities due to their method of operations. Most known APTs can be classified into impersonation, penetration, side-channel, and brute force attacks. To invade an IoT network, attackers will first try to determine the access parameters for that particular network. Hacking techniques such as media access control (MAC) spoofing may be used to attack IoT networks (Qian et al. 2010). For example, if the underlying network uses MAC-address filtering of clients, all an intruder has to do is to find out the MAC address and the assigned IP address for a particular client. The intruder will wait till that client goes off the network and then start using the network and its resources while appearing as a valid user (Unger & Timmermann 2015). However, it may be impracticable for MAC address filtering within IoT systems due to the millions of possible nodes. MAC filtering mechanisms tend to slow down network traffic when used at a massive scale. Where most IoT systems are intended toward near real-time processing, MAC address filtering could disrupt their intended use.

A hijack attack of abuse of routing protocols to allow eavesdropping on victim out-of-range of an attacker by detouring the traffic through corrupted nodes within the transmission range of both victim and attacker (Kovacshazy et al. 2013). A rogue IoT access point (AP) is one that is installed by an attacker (usually in public areas like shared office spaces, airports, etc.) to accept traffic from wireless clients to whom it appears as a valid authenticator. Packets thus captured can be used to extract sensitive information or for launching further attacks by, for example, modifying the content of the captured packet and re-inserting it into the network (Unger & Timmermann 2015). Authenticating the IEEE 802 48-bit hardware address can, at best, only establish the identity of the physical machine, not its human user; thus an attacker who manages to steal a laptop with a registered MAC address will appear to the network as a legitimate user (Isa et al. 2014). In practical applications this provides no security at all, as the MAC address is easily spoofed on virtually every type of wireless local area network (WLAN) interface card available in the market today (Ozvural & Kurt 2015). Details of commonly available passive and active IoT network analysis and attack tools exploiting these vulnerabilities, either as part of a defensive strategy or to mount attacks, could be performed by using applications such as Kismet, Ethereal, NetStumbler, AirSnort, Airsnarf, Airjack, Aircrack, and WepLab (Engebretson 2013). All of these vulnerabilities are well known and have proven, easily-used and regularly deployed exploits.

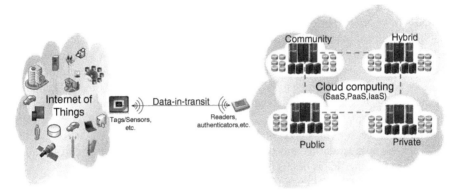

FIGURE 2.2   IoT data-in-transit. Reproduced with permission of IEEE.

Due to the wireless nature of the IoT, ICDs in use will autonomously power-up and participate in data transactions. Some ICDs may (or may not) have an integrated power source but instead rely upon readers, authenticators, etc., between other ICDs or cloud computing environments, using gateway portals to radiate an antenna field that is able to detect the transmission of another ICD, convert it to RFID/electrical current, and store it in a capacitor (Burbridge & Harrison 2009). When the capacitor reaches a threshold level it will discharge thereby powering the ICD and its transmitter to send data to other ICDs or cloud computing environments in IoT networks (Figure 2.2). Upon detecting the ICD, these readers, authenticators, etc., will have to detect valid RFID/electrical currents to perform IoT-defined, shared-secret challenge-response protocols with other ICDs or IoT devices to establish a secure session or tunnel for data communications.

2.3.1 Recognition

Recognition includes the identification of a cyber-attack being performed leading to the fortification of smart ICDs before gaining access to IoT networks and systems. Because of the availability of random access function in the IoT, its devices and networks must possess a function of automatic malicious identity recognition. The ICD design efforts should focus on determining whether and how a given ICD insecure security behaviors can be reconciled with the required security properties and behaviors of the IoT system as a whole. At a more concrete level, ICD design should focus on determining whether the ICD sensor agent (i.e., central embedded microprocessor) has been implemented within the integrated/assembled system with whatever countermeasures (e.g., security wrappers, virtual machines/sandboxes, application-level firewalls) are necessary to protect it from detrimental effects of any insecure standards and technologies used in that ICD sensor agent's development. The ICD sensor agent should automatically recognize and verify the identities of malicious activities (e.g., virus, worms, Trojan horses, attack scripts, logic bombs) that are trying to gain random access to the IoT system through automatic detection techniques and should be able to distinguish whether the information that is trying to

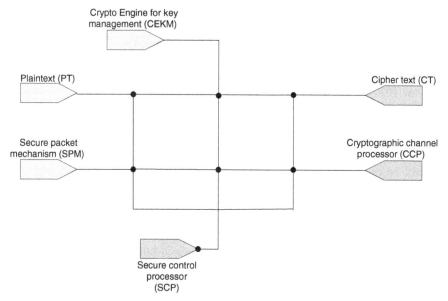

FIGURE 2.3 ICD/IoT-embedded microprocessor/sensor. Reproduced with permission of IEEE.

enter the IoT system is valid or malicious. Through self-monitoring, when an outside attack is threatening the safety of the system, an ICD sensor agent should be able to connect to the corresponding defense fortification process.

To defend against cyber-attacks amongst ICDs and IoT networks, identification of cyber-attacks through an embedded ICD sensor agent, as shown in Figure 2.3, should be installed for operations in ICDs and IoT network environments. These ICD sensor agents could be designed in ICDs and IoT networks consisting of several components that can form resistors and be connected as voltage dividers.

The ICD sensor agent above has a custom cryptographic channel processor (CCP) designed to support high-performance cryptographic algorithms (e.g., elliptic curve cryptography, field programmable gate arrays) for performing operations for cryptographic applications and a bus for connecting each processor to a CPU (Elbe et al. 2003; Carvajal et al. 2005). The algorithms can be implemented using a crypto domain specific language (DSL), a language designed from the development of cryptographic algorithms (Leventis et al. 2003, Agosta & Pelosi 2007). The ICD sensor agent includes a plaintext (PT) and cipher text (CT) interface processors that buffer the input/output (I/O) between the crypto processors. The secure packet mechanism (SPM) initiates countermeasures to confine data and stop processing if malicious activity is found amongst the PT and CT. This malicious data are sent to the control processor and the control processor revokes any attempt to obtain a token since the data are identified as malicious. The crypto engine for key management (CEKM) purpose is the support the key management functions in support of the custom crypto processors (Liu et al. 2005; Porambage et al. 2013; Veltri et al. 2013). The CEKM is a general-purpose processor with a multilevel operating system offering significant assurance of separation between tasks and provides key management functions in support of the custom crypto processors (Ballardie 1996; Du et al. 2005; Liu et al. 2005; Porambage et al. 2013; Veltri et al. 2013). The CEKM runs a secure operation system which provides tasks and object separation and the ICD agent should support at least 1024 simultaneous channels (Du et al. 2005; Liu et al. 2005; Porambage et al. 2013).

The ICD sensor agent provides two kinds of separation between the cryptographic channels (CC). The CC are supported by several processors that form the lower part of the ICD sensor agent. The CC combine to support up to 1024 separate CC. The control processor (CP) ensures that the CCs and the IO processors (PT and CT) perform in a manner that provides channel separation between the active channels flowing through the ICD sensor agent. The CC also supports cryptographic channel separation through its support of fast context switching between the channels. Each channel has a (possibly different) cryptographic algorithm and key. When a channel is swapped out in favor of another channel, the algorithm and key are swapped out of the memory used by the CC1 or CC2. The channel can be swapped out to RAM onboard the ICD sensor agent or to external memory. When it is swapped to external memory, it is stored in encrypted format. The support for context switching ensures that channel algorithms, keys, and state are kept separate even for inactive channels. The SPM initiates countermeasures to confine data and stop processing if malicious activity is found. Data are then sent to the control processor and the control processor revokes any attempt to obtain a token since the data are malicious.

By installing these embedded ICD sensor agent tracers within different ICDs and changing the traces (e.g., configuration) depending on the ICD type, an intrusion could be detected if the traces are broken or shorted together. For example, a three channel circuit can be configured by providing a voltage between node A through D. Nodes B, D, E would each have a voltage of 1/2 positive-voltage supply (Vcc) with respect to ground if all the resistive elements are equal. If a resistor on a single channel is broken, then the node voltage will become Vcc or ground. If both resistors were broken, then the node would float. To detect this, a pull-down resistor is required for each channel. Shorting tow resistors together will change the two node voltages to be either 2/3 Vcc or 1/3 Vcc. Finally, shorting Vcc to Gnd can also be detected since all node voltages would then become 0V. To detect all the possible changes on each node, a circuit will need to be able to determine if the voltage of a node moves outside of an accepted operating window. To accomplish this, each channel requires two comparators, one to detect if the node voltage goes above a reference and one to detect if the node voltage goes below a reference (Razavi & Wooley, 1992). For the three-channel sensor example, six comparators are required and the outputs are wired together as open drain to pull a detection signal low.

A voltage ladder is used to provide the high- and low-reference voltages as displayed in Figure 2.4. For the example above using standard resistor values, Ref_1 would be approximately 60% of boosted power supply voltage (BVCC) and Ref_2 would be 40% of BVCC; since both Ref_1 and Ref_3 are components of the BVCC voltage ladder which manage voltage power to the secure packet mechanism. These

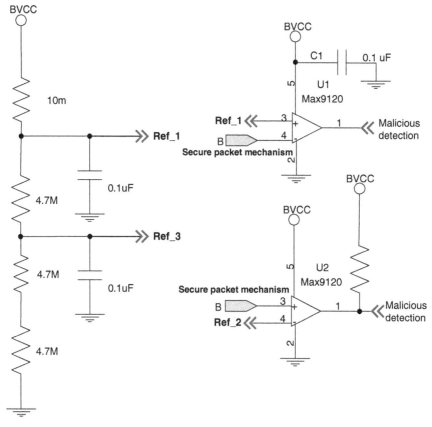

FIGURE 2.4 ICD sensor agent voltage ladder. Reproduced with permission of IEEE.

voltage references can be shared between all three comparators if they have high impedance inputs. The window is wide enough to detect for some drift and noise, but still detect the tamper conditions described previously. Sharing the references and using the open-drain comparators help to minimize component count.

Filtering is required on each channel node to maintain reliable operation. Malfunctions from the power supply of electromagnetic interface (EMI) could cause a false positive. This problem is made worse by the fact that current at each node is very small. Filtering capacitors help to maintain the node and reference voltage. Unfortunately, this filtering causes delays in the response time of the detection signal. If a mesh trace is broken, it will take time for the voltage across the node filtering capacitor to change. This change could take between several seconds to be detected by the comparators. The worst case is if two resistors are broken and a node is left floating, then the time to discharge the filtering cap will be dependent on the pull-down resistance for the node. To minimize current consumption, this resistance is very high. Integrating the tamper circuit into a single ICD will reduce the board component count, power consumption, and cost. The example design uses six Maxim

9120 comparators each drawing 350 milliamps (mA). This pushes the power requirements for the design to over 2 uA not including the pull-down resistors and the voltage dividers created by the sensor. This current consumption is also in addition to any required real-time clocks and battery backed random-access memory (RAM). The actual operating current is closer to 4 uA. Using a 180-milliampere-hour (mAh) battery would yield a 5 years of reliable operation if left unpowered. When active, the sensor circuit is powered from the main supply, by passing the battery.

To detect any malicious tamper, the ICD sensor agent would constantly change the value on the output port. The input port would then be read and if the values match, then the traces are intact. If a trace is broken, then it would be detected when it is pulled high during a sequence. If a trace is shortened, it will be driven by an adjacent trace. The response time of this design depends on the number of signals and how fast a pattern can be applied and detected. In addition, the pattern should be random and hard to predict by an attacker. The main advantage of this design is the integration of the ICD sensor agent MCU with the necessary comparators to monitor the ICD which may be running at all times, it offers a higher degree of integration to reduce component and board count and needs increased performance to run fast enough to detect a malicious condition.

2.3.2 Fortification

The cyber-assurance recognition strategy here is to define only the service-level interfaces and leave out domain-specific implementation details. Once the recognition of a cyber-attack has been identified from the recognition process, the fortification process takes place. Fortification means to apply automatic embedded network protection techniques in ICD devices for protecting IoT devices and networks during a cyber-attack. Fortification includes additional key hardware and chips installed as smart chips with embedded tokens for failure points and covert theft of information with general techniques, all relying on code instrumentation and runtime assertion checking. Specific technical detail varies depending on programming language used for the implementation of the ICD.

Once a cyber-attack has been identified through recognition, the embedded ICD SPM initiates a countermeasure to confine the signal containing the data package and stop processing the data (Figure 2.5).

The malicious data are then sent to the SPM and the ICD sensor agent processor revokes any attempt to obtain a token since the signal was deemed malicious. If an ICD relies on the host operating system to maintain an audit log, and the host operating

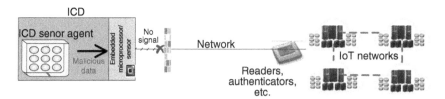

FIGURE 2.5   Fortification. Reproduced with permission of IEEE.

system does satisfy this requirement – by compilation the ICD is considered to have satisfied this requirement. However, if the host operating system does not maintain an audit log – the host operating system is non-compliant and by compilation the ICD is non-compliant as well. For example, Chasaki and Wolf (2010, p. 5) developed a secure pack processor on future instruction options such as opcode, instruction address, instruction address+instruction word, and hash of any of the above and defined those as follows:

- Opcode: The ICD secure sensor packet mechanism can monitor the operations performed on the embedded processor, which indicate the functionality of the executed application. For an attack to become possible, the attacker will have to replace the instruction set, with another malicious set of instructions that use the same opcodes in the exact same sequence.
- Instruction address: Since the memory address used to store the instruction set is unique, the attacker would have to write malicious code that stores the new instructions in the same location in the instruction memory as the original application does. This would also require the malicious code to branch at the same exact points with the legitimate code.
- Instruction address+Instruction word: This kind of streaming pattern combines two pieces of information, and makes it harder for an attacker to come up with attack code that goes undetected. Additionally, by adding the opcode, or control-flow information to the monitoring stream, this could cause a significant increase in the system's resource consumption.
- Hash of any of the above: The embedded processor is streaming a compact hashed value of any of the above combinations. The more bits used to compute the hash, the stronger the monitoring pattern is. However, the number of used bits will affect the memory utilization. After all, it is a tradeoff between available memory on the hardware platform and the strength of security features.

If the IoT signal containing packet data is valid, the ICD sensor agent will invoke its token security services. The token security services should define the interfaces to access the ICD secure packet sensor mechanism which will have to be designed, developed, and built. Compared with existing direct authentication models using asymmetric key exchange specified in Zhou & Chao 2011; Dlamini et al. 2012; and Yang et al. 2013, this method should be performed by removing redundant per-message authentication. The interfaces to access ICD sensor agent tokens can be based on IoT authentication mechanisms, such as those in WSNs like the Elliptic Curve Menezes-Qu-Vanstone (ECMQV) implicit certificate scheme and Elliptic Curve Diffie-Hellman (ECDH) key exchange protocol (Hankerson et al. 2006; SEC4 2011; Porambage et al. 2014). That said, it is the intention of cyber-assurance to keep the authentication/authorization aspect of the process implementation-agnostic, and here to merely define how the decisions would be exchanged. For example, IoT-open authorization (OAuth) is an open protocol, which allows secure authorization in a simple and standardized way from third-party applications accessing online services, based on the representational state transfer (REST) web architecture (Cirani et al.

2015). The OAuth protocol provides an authorization layer for hypertext transfer protocol (HTTP)-based service application programming interfaces (API), typically on top of a secure transport layer, such as HTTP-over-transport layer security (TLS) (i.e., HTTPS) (Dierks & Rescorla 2008; Cirani et al. 2015). IoT- OAuth architecture is meant to be flexible, highly configurable, and easy to integrate with existing services for the IoT by delegating the authorization functionality by: (1) lower processing load with respect to solutions, where access control is implemented on the smart object; (2) fine-grained (remote) customization of access policies; and (3) scalability, without the need to operate directly on the device (Cirani et al. 2015).

To further support fortification, the ICD token will generate a random challenge, send it to the host and the host will sign it and send it back for verification, using a certificate (or a least a public key) signed by a trusted entity. The trusted entity is yet to be determined but its credentials must have been previously loaded on the token so that validation of the host credentials can be anchored to a known trust point. Now it should be noted that there are issues involved in certificated path validation on small microprocessors and the longer the path, the longer this process will take. In addition, access to current certificate revocation lists (CRL) to perform certificate revocation checking should also be problematic. May low assurance systems solve these problems by off-loading this processing to the host. However, the host is not yet trusted until after this authentication has been performed. If the host fails its validation by the token, access to the token should be blocked. No information has been compromised at this point so the token should not be zeroized but at the same time, the token should not be considered available for use.

After the host has been successfully authenticated, the token must be authenticated to the host. The host will generate a random challenge, send it to the token and the token will sign-it, using a per-token key that is signed by a trusted entity and send it back for verification. As in the previous step, the trusted entity is yet to be determined but verification should be much easier for the host since it should have greater access to certificates and CRL. In this case, if the token's signature fails, the host must refuse further communication and log off the token. The occurrence of this condition most likely indicates that a nearly successful impersonation attack has been performed. If it is caught at this point, at least no sensitive data, other than authentication values, have been compromised, but it should be considered an important enough condition that occurrence is reported. As a result, the host should have provision for creating an audit trail and collecting forensic evidence. After both the token and the host have been successfully authenticated to each other, then and only then, should the process be considered completed. At this time, the token can be made available for full use by the ICD.

2.3.3 Re-establishment

Reestablishment is a means to return the ICDs to its operational condition after the cyber-attack through remapping to a different route since the ICD was under attack (see Figure 2.6). To correlate monitored traffic with other data sources, association rule-based approaches are traditionally used. However, the problem is more challenging in this case. Indeed, one of the advantages of IoT systems is their greater

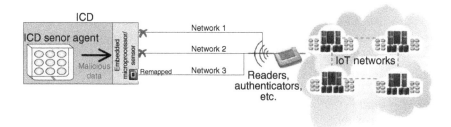

FIGURE 2.6   Remapping ICD to the IoT network. Reproduced with permission of IEEE.

flexibility, but because of the open and loosely coupled nature of such systems, they tend to be subject to a great variety of usage scenarios (even if operated entirely within a single institution). As a consequence, the global behavior of such as system, and therefore a global view of transactions, tends to be difficulty predictable; in extreme cases, the global behavior might be emergent rather than expected and predefined. It is thus correspondingly more difficult to model in terms of association rules. As virtual smart ICDs decouple servers from physical hardware, the IoT network will have to decouple entire networks from physical networks. Once a cyber-attack has been recognized and fortified, the dynamic association of smart ICDs, their IP addresses, and locations will have to transpose back to a stable system. By changing the placement of smart ICD routing information and IP addresses will help defend against cyber-attacks.

Running multiple service instances in parallel is an effective way to survive malicious bugs, detect information leakage, and evaluate infrastructure configurations (Xiang et al. 2013). Once a change is detected, a new configuration is developed and mapped to execution resources based on implementation forms available for the required functionalities (Kovacshazy et al. 2013). Kovacshazy et al. (2013, pp. 3–4) identify some basic priority-based rules which may apply for mapping functionalities to execution resources of the IoT:

- If a functionality is available in a platform-specific native form and can be executed efficiently on a native execution resource, it is mapped to such a resource and executed there.
- If a functionality is available in a portable compiled language code and that can be mapped to an execution resource for which a compiler exists, then the code is compiled specifically for that execution resource and mapped to such a resource and executed there.
- If a functionality is available in a virtual machine based language code and there exists a virtual machine for that language for execution resources, then the functionality can be mapped to such a resource and executed there.
- If the functionality exists only for a specific platform in native form and there is not available execution resource for that platform, platform virtualization is taken as the last option. The functionality is mapped to an execution resource which has emulation capabilities for the specific platform and executed there.

Techniques such as embedded virtualization supporting multiple virtual networks – each consisting of host, links, nodes and switches – on a shared physical infrastructure could be applied (Lin et al. 2011; Nakajima et al. 2011; Kovacshazy et al. 2013; Yuan et al. 2015). Each IoT network may apply its own policies (e.g., for routing, access control, packet scheduling, mobility) for operating but needs to improve resiliency by allowing ICDs to dynamically change a virtual network mapping to the underlying physical hardware. As displayed in Figure 2.6, once authenticated, an ICD sensor agent is granted access control to an IoT network. Since each ICD sensor agent needs a network resource in the IoT physical infrastructure (including servers, wireless nodes, bandwidth links, and virtual switches and routers), the ICD sensor agent runs an embedding system algorithm in the embedded processor to identify whether and where the ICD sensor agents should execute in the IoT network. The IoT will need to keep track of existing ICD allocations and run an optimization embedded algorithm to compute efficiency by allowing a single ICD to span multiple IoT networking paths.

Through path multiplicity, the ICD sensor agent can combine resources from multiple network paths to improve scalability, reliability, and security (Kommareddy et al. 2003). By network redirecting or remapping, an ICD will be useful to transparently recover from physical failures and mitigate adversary attacks. For example, if a physical ICD link is malicious and happens to pass through the recognition and/or fortification processors, the ICD sensor agent can map one or more ICDs to alternate physical paths, shielding the IoT network from processing the malicious packet. The embedded SPM in the ICD sensor agent can completely redirect an ICD onto a different collection of IoT network routers, switches, and nodes, by re-running the embedding algorithm to remap the end hosts through assigning a new IP or MAC address or performing virtual machine migration to move virtual servers to a new physical IoT location, installing additional packet-handling rules in new IoT network locations and moving traffic to the new IoT network without disrupting the IoT traffic. Additionally, API's for specifying the desired frequency of changes to the physical IoT mappings must be dynamically triggered in response to suspected attacks or intrusions.

Shifting the addresses, locations, and IoT network paths for an IoT service requires ICDs to share a secret numeric key with the IoT network. Similar to previous work on frequency hopping in wireless networks, the key modulates the changing of the IP addresses of the service (Seba et al. 2013). The ICD and IoT need to change the server addresses by rewriting packet headers in routers and switches. Using network devices with anti-spoofing functionality, such as unicast reverse path forwarding (uRPF), can reduce network vulnerability conditions (e.g., denial of service), as the ICD verifies the validity of a source IP address and discards the traffic if the source IP address is not valid or is spoofed (Graham et al. 2010). For example, virtual machines (VM) will be migrated from one physical server to another and the remapping of virtual links to IoT network paths through virtual switches and links to different physical location will also take place. Remapping IoT network paths does require coordination with end devices (e.g., cloud severs), allowing the ICD to make these changes frequently to avoid sharing a physical server or link with other virtual networks, including response to suspected attacks. The ICD will trigger changes in VM addresses and locations and the remapping of virtual switches and links will travel over a special management virtual local area networks (VLAN). To ensure fast transitions from one configuration to another, the ICD will establish the new network processing route and iteratively copy server state and switch rules, while discontinuing to operate on the previous network path.

One issue with re-establishment could entail misconstrued information. From past research in the intrusion detection field, log data obtained tends frequently to be incomplete, ambiguous, or otherwise unreliable (Sabahi & Movaghar 2008). This difficulty is increasingly acknowledged by the research community and the problem of log correlation in the presence of incomplete or unreliable data has received research attention (Abad et al. 2003; Li et al. 2004; Lee et al. 2006). In the context of the IoT, this problem is in fact related in certain cases to the emergent behavior problem; since emergent behavior has by nature no definition a priori, it follows that the precise corresponding correlation rules are also unknown or probabilistic, as opposed to discrete (Zhai et al. 2015).

2.3.4 Survivability

When the IoT technologies are used as part of mission critical systems, the IoT services should be survivable in order to support the important missions. Park et al. (2013) define survivability as the capability of an entity to continue its mission even in the presence of cyber-attacks, internal failures, or accidents (Park & Chandramohan 2004; Park et al. 2005; Park et al. 2009). An entity ranges from a single component (object), with its mission in a distributed computing environment, to an information system that consists of many components to support the overall mission. An entity may support multiple missions and it identifies the static and dynamic models.

The static survivability model is based on redundant components (e.g., multiple copies of a critical component), prepared before the operation, to support critical services continuously in a distributed computing environment. Redundant components can be located in the same machine or in different machines in the same domain or even different domains. The same service can be provided by identical components (e.g., copies of the original component) or by diverse components that are implemented in various ways. Isolated redundancy (in different machines or domains) usually provides higher survivability because the replaced component can be running in an unaffected area. For instance, if the redundant components are distributed in different places of the network, the services provided by those components can be recovered in the event of primary network service failures. However, if there is a successful attack to a component, replacing that component with an identical copy is not a fundamental solution, because identical components are vulnerable to the same exploit used in the previously successful attack.

In the dynamic survivability model, unlike the static model, there are no redundant components. The components that have failed or are under the control of malicious codes are replaced by dynamically generated components on-the-fly and deployed in runtime when they are required. Furthermore, this model allows the replacement of the malicious components with immunized components if possible, which enables it to provide more robust services than the static model. If we do not know the exact reason for the failures or types of malicious codes, or if it is hard to recover components against known failures or from the influence of malicious codes, we can simply replace the affected component with a new one – thereby creating in a renewed service. We call this a generic immunization strategy, which can be effective against cyber-attacks. If a component (a machine or a whole domain) is under attack, the generic immunization strategy suggests generating a new copy of the component and deploying it in a new environment that is safe from the attack. Although the generic immunization strategy supports service availability continuously, the new component might still be susceptible to the same failures or attacks.

Technically, it is simpler to implement the static survivability model than the dynamic survivability model because the former basically requires redundant components prepared to be used if necessary, while the latter requires other support mechanisms to deal with the component in runtime. In the static model, the service downtime is relatively short because the system just needs to change the service path with one of the previously prepared redundant components. However, if the initially selected component is running in its normal state, we do not need to use other redundant components. We say that in this situation, the resource efficiency is low. The adaptation capability in this model is based on the reconfiguration among predefined alternatives. On the contrary, the dynamic model can adapt dynamically to the kind of failures or attacks that occur in runtime. Furthermore, if component immunization is possible, it can provide resistance to the same kinds of future failures and attacks. Therefore, the overall robustness in this model is higher than in the static model. However, the dynamic model has an inherent disadvantage in terms of service downtime. The recovery process can range from seconds to a few minutes. This downtime drawback will cause major problems in mission-critical systems because there will be no service provided by the component available during the recovery period.

Therefore, in order to compensate for the weaknesses in the two models and to enhance the overall survivability in a mission-critical system, we incorporate the idea of a hybrid model, which can be implemented by using diverse critical components – components that are functionally equivalent but whose make-ups are diverse.

2.4 CONCLUSION

Cyber-assurance is warranted for the forthcoming IoT. Unlike traditional IT systems, the IoT network presents a much higher degree of risk and instability and a much higher change of being attacked. Hence, it is necessary to consider security as an important indicator to take the appropriate measures right at the initial stages of IoT network design, hardware production, and software development. ICDs and IoT network designers and developers should insist on using physical isolation measures in ICD and IoT network design. Embedded key hardware and chips should prevent our enemy from installing components such as defective chips which will lead to serious security issues such as breakdown of the IoT system, theft of information, and the failure of the chips at critical moments. ICD and IoT developers must persevere security in the development of operating software in order to prevent the adversary in presetting hidden attacks, loopholes, and virus programs thus avoiding grave potential APTs to the IoT system.

Many of the APTs leveled against ICDs and IoT networks involve attacking the mechanisms employed to implement the cyber-assurance process. As a result, the stronger these mechanisms the more resistant the process will be to attack and the higher the degree of trust that can be placed in it. Extensive analysis will have to be performed on different suites of algorithms to determine whether they are strong enough to protect various levels of data processing. These algorithms will only make it possible to protect information to a certain level and whether this level can really be protected will depend very heavily on the actual implementation of the cryptographic processing employed. Even when strong cryptographic algorithms are used, the strength of an implementation can be significantly eroded if insufficient entropy is used in the cyber-assurance generation or if the implementation makes it easy to guess or in some way derive the value of the data being used. In addition, static protection of data stored on a device must be equal to or greater than the strength of the keys being protected. Careful attention must be paid to random number generation, key management, mitigation of side channel attacks, and tamper protection against a variety of penetration attacks

In pursuit of this goal, the IoT faces several technology challenges and requires additional research in the areas of leveraging and integrating existing networks and systems with new microprocessors and sensors, implementing all cryptographic processing algorithms to minimize vulnerabilities, specific hardware countermeasures designed to detect and react to or notify the firmware on board the device when certain types of attacks are detected, achieving integration via interoperability with the broader IoT community, minimizing the IoT systems deployment footprint, and reducing required "human" support in creating a flexible IoT network of systems that can be readily adapted to changing cyber-threat needs. The technology challenge facing the IoT requires a multidisciplined approach to security engineering and it is critical that the cyber-assurance effort address both data for analytics and event-driven systems for rapid response to significant malicious activities. The concept of a cyber-assurance approach provides the principles and concepts to deliver the foundation for greatly enhanced interoperability, scalability, performance, and agility for a secured IoT future. Ultimate success requires steadfast technology leadership to traverse the many obstacles to change that inhibit any transformational initiative.

While the concept of cyber-assurance greatly reduces the overall system complexity through the decomposition of malicious security functions into modular, embedded services, it does call for increased attention to the process of developing, integrating, and testing these services. This is important to monitor the reliability of the implementation of the processes. Since hardware components can degrade and malfunction, and since there can be implementation bugs in the software/firmware running on a device it is important to detect (if not correct) processing errors that occur on the device. When these occur, new and unplanned-for vulnerabilities may present themselves in a device. As a result, detection of any malfunction in the processing of a device should initiate steps to protect all the information and resources that are being protected by the device. The integration lifecycle can no longer be a sequential waterfall process. Because each individual IoT service or IoT service family may have its own development timeline, waiting to start overall security integration until all services to be developed and unit-tested may not be realistic. Rather, the IoT environment will have to incrementally incorporate testing of the services as they become "online," constantly regression-testing the overall IoT system behavior along the way. This will heighten the need for test harnesses, prototypes, and simulators that can act as a surrogate while the true service capabilities are being developed.

REFERENCES

Abad, C., Taylor, J., Sengul, C., Yurcik, W., Zhou, Y., & Rowe, K. 2003. Log correlation for intrusion detection: a proof of concept. In: Computer Security Applications Conference, 2003. Proceedings. 19th Annual, December 2003. pp. 255–264.

Agosta, G., & Pelosi, G. 2007. A domain specific language for cryptography. In: Proceedings of the Forum on specification and Design Languages (FDL), pp. 159–164.

Alberts, C., Ellison, R.J., & Woody, C. 2009. Cyber Assurance. 2009 CERT Research Report. Software Engineering Institute, Carnegie Mellon University. Available at http://resources.sei.cmu.edu/library/asset-view.cfm?assetid=77638.

Anderson, E.A., Irvine, C.E., & Schell, R.R. 2004. Subversion as a threat in information warfare. *Journal of Information Warfare*, 3(2), 52–65.

Ansilla, J.D., Vasudevan, N., JayachandraBensam, J., & Anunciya, J.D. 2015. Data security in smart grid with hardware implementation against DoS attacks. In: IEEE International Conference on Circuit, Power and Computing Technologies (ICCPCT), March 2015, pp. 1–7.

Asensio, Á., Blanco, T., Blasco, R., Marco, Á., & Casas, R. 2015. Managing emergency situations in the smart city: The smart signal. *Sensors*, 15(6), pp. 14370–14396.

Babar, S., Stango, A., Prasad, N., Sen, J., & Prasad, R. 2011. Proposed embedded security framework for Internet of Things (IoT). In: IEEE 2nd International Conference on Wireless Communication, Vehicular Technology, Information Theory and Aerospace & Electronic Systems Technology (Wireless VITAE), February 2011, pp. 1–5.

Ballardie, A. 1996. Scalable multicast key distribution.

Bobade, S.D., & Mankar, V.R. 2015. VLSI architecture for an area efficient Elliptic Curve Cryptographic processor for embedded systems. In: IEEE International Conference on Industrial Instrumentation and Control (ICIC), May 2015, pp. 1038–1043.

Brooks, T., Kaarst-Brown, M., Caicedo, C., Park, J., & McKnight, L. 2013. A failure to communicate: security vulnerabilities in the gridstreamx edgeware application. In: IEEE 8th International Conference for Internet Technology and Secured Transactions (ICITST), December 2013, pp. 516–523.

Brooks, T., Kaarst-Brown, M., Caicedo, C., Park, J., & McKnight, L.W. 2014. Secure the edge? Understanding the risk towards wireless grids Edgeware technology. *International Journal of Internet Technology and Secured Transactions*, 5(3), pp. 191–222.

Burbridge, T., & Harrison, M. 2009. Security considerations in the design and peering of RFIDdiscovery services. In IEEE International Conference on RFID, April 2009. pp. 249–256.

Carvajal, R.G., Ramírez-Angulo, J., López-Martín, A.J., Torralba, A., Galán, J.A.G., Carlosena, A., & Chavero, F.M. 2005. The flipped voltage follower: a useful cell for low-voltage low-power circuit design. *IEEE Transactions on Circuits and Systems I: Regular Papers*, 52(7), pp. 1276–1291.

Chasaki, D., & Wolf, T. 2010. Design of a secure packet processor. In: ACM/IEEE Symposium on Architectures for Networking and Communications Systems (ANCS), October 2010, pp. 1–10.

Cirani, S., Picone, M., Gonizzi, P., Veltri, L., & Ferrari, G. 2015. IoT-OAS: an OAUth-based authorization service architecture for secure services in IoT scenarios. *IEEE Sensors Journal*, 15(2), pp. 1224–1234.

Committee on National Security Systems (CNSS) Instruction, 2010. 4009 National Information Assurance (IA) Glossary.

Conovalu, S., & Park, J. 2015. Cybersecurity strategies for smart grids. In: The International Conference on Information and Network Security, Shanghai, China, July 29–30, 2015.

Curts, R.J., & Campbell, D.E. 2015. Cybersecurity requires a clear systems engineering approach as a basis for its cyberstrategy. *Cybersecurity Policies and Strategies for Cyberwarfare Prevention*, p. 19.

Czybik, B., Hausmann, S., Heiss, S., & Jasperneite, J. 2013. Performance evaluation of MAC algorithms for real-time Ethernet communication systems. In: 11th IEEE International Conference on Industrial Informatics (INDIN), July 2013, pp. 676–681.

Davi, L., Hanreich, M., Paul, D., Sadeghi, A. R., Koeberl, P., Sullivan, D., Arias, O. & Jin, Y. (2015). HAFIX: hardware-assisted flow integrity extension. In Proceedings of the 52nd Annual Design Automation Conference (p. 74–80). ACM.

Dierks, T., & Rescorla, E. 2008. The Transport Layer Security (TLS) Protocol Version 1.2. IETF RFC 5246, 2008. Available at http://www.ietf.org/rfc/rfc5246.txt.

Dlamini, M., Venter, H., Eloff, J., & Mitha, Y. 2012. Authentication in the cloud: a risk-based approach. University of Pretoria. Available at http://www.satnac.org.za/proceedings/2012/papers/8.Data_Centre_Cloud/108.pdf.

Du, W., Deng, J., Han, Y.S., Varshney, P.K., Katz, J., & Khalili, A. 2005. A pairwise key predistribution scheme for wireless sensor networks. *ACM Transactions on Information and System Security (TISSEC)*, 8(2), pp. 228–258.

Elbe, A., Janssen, N., & Sedlak, H. 2003. Cryptographic processor. U.S. Patent Application 10/461,913.

Eliasson, J., Pereira, P.P., Makitaavola, H., Delsing, J., Nilsson, J., & Gebart, J. 2014. A feasibility study of SOA-enabled networked rock bolts. In: Emerging Technology and Factory Automation (ETFA), September 2014, pp. 1–8.

Engebretson, P. 2013. *The Basics of Hacking and Penetration Testing: Ethical Hacking and Penetration Testing Made Easy*. Elsevier.

Flood, P., & Schukat, M. 2014. Peer to peer authentication for small embedded systems: a zero- knowledge-based approach to security for the Internet of Things. In: IEEE 10th International Conference on Digital Technologies (DT), July 2014, pp. 68–72.

Gao, Z., & Ansari, N. 2005. Tracing cyber-attacks from the practical perspective. *IEEE Communications Magazine*, 43(5), pp. 123–131.

U.S. General Accounting Office (GAO)(2004). Technology Assessment: Cybersecurity and critical infrastructure protection. Technical Report GAO-04-321: Published: May 28, 2004, pp. 1–223. Available at http://www.gao.gov/products/GAO-04-321.

Goel, S., Hong, Y., Papakonstantinou, V., & Kloza, D. 2015. *Smart Grid Security*. Springer, London.

Gope, P., & Hwang, T. 2015. Untraceable sensor movement in distributed IoT infrastructure. *IEEE Sensors Journal*, 15(9), pp. 5340–5348.

Graham, J., Olson, R., & Howard, R. (Eds.). 2010. *Cyber Security Essentials*. CRC Press.

Guinard, D., & Trifa, V. 2009. Towards the Web of Things: Web mashups for embedded devices. In: Workshop on Mashups, Enterprise Mashups and Lightweight Composition on the Web (MEM 2009), in proceedings of WWW (International World Wide Web Conferences), Madrid, Spain, April 2009, p. 15.

Haller, S., Karnouskos, S., & Schroth, C. 2008. *The Internet of Things in an Enterprise Context*. Springer, Berlin/Heidelberg, pp. 14–28.

Hankerson, D., Menezes, A.J., & Vanstone, S. 2006. *Guide to Elliptic Curve Cryptography*. Springer Science & Business Media; 2006 Jun 1.

Huang, W., & Zhang, S. 2015. Research and review on novel spread spectrum communication theory. In: *International Conference on Education, Management and Computing Technology (ICEMCT-15)*. Atlantis Press.

Isa, M.A.M., Hashim, H., Ab Manan, J.L., Adnan, S.F.S., & Mahmod, R. 2014. RF simulator for cryptographic protocol. In: 2014 IEEE International Conference on Control System, Computing and Engineering (ICCSCE), November 2014, pp. 518–523.

Kainth, M., Krishnan, L., Narayana, C., Virupaksha, S.G., & Tessier, R. 2015. Hardware assistedcode obfuscation for FPGA soft microprocessors. In: Proceedings of the 2015 Design, Automation & Test in Europe Conference & Exhibition, EDA Consortium, March 2015, pp. 127–132.

Kermani, M.M., Zhang, M., Raghunathan, A., & Jha, N.K. 2013. Emerging frontiers in embedded security. In: IEEE International Conference on VLSI Design and 2013 12th International Conference on Embedded Systems (VLSID), January 26, 2013, pp. 203–208.

Knapp, E.D., & Samani, R. 2013. *Applied Cyber Security and the Smart Grid: Implementing Security Controls into the Modern Power Infrastructure*. Syngress.

Kocher, P., Lee, R., McGraw, G., Raghunathan, A., & Moderator-Ravi, S. 2004. Security as a new dimension in embedded system design. In: Proceedings of the 41st annual Design Automation Conference, ACM, June 2004, pp. 753–760.

Kommareddy, C., Güven, T., Bhattacharjee, B., La, R.J., & Shayman, M.A. 2003. Overlay routing for path multiplicity, vol. 70, Technical Report, UMIACS-TR.

Kovacshazy, T., Wacha, G., Daboczi, T., Erdos, C., & Szarvas, A. 2013. System architecture for Internet of Things with the extensive use of embedded virtualization. In: IEEE 4th International Conference on Cognitive Infocommunications (CogInfoCom), December 2013, pp. 549–554.

Kranz, M., Holleis, P., & Schmidt, A. 2010. Embedded interaction: Interacting with the internet of things. *IEEE Internet Computing*, 14(2), pp. 46–53.

Krutz, R.L., & Vines, R.D. 2010. *Cloud Security: A Comprehensive Guide to Secure Cloud Computing*. John Wiley & Sons.

Lee, S., Chung, B., Kim, H., Lee, Y., Park, C., & Yoon, H. 2006. Real-time analysis of intrusion detection alerts via correlation. *Computers & Security*, 25(3), pp. 169–183.

Leventis, P., Chan, M., Chan, M., Lewis, D., Nouban, B., Powell, G., Vest, B., Wong, M., Xia, R., & Costello, J. 2003. Cyclone™: a low-cost, high-performance FPGA. In: Proceedings of the IEEE Custom Integrated Circuits Conference, November 1999, pp. 49–52.

Li, Z., Taylor, J., Partridge, E., Zhou, Y., Yurcik, W., Abad, C., Barlow, J.J., & Rosendale, J. 2004. *UCLog*: a unified, correlated logging architecture for intrusion detection. In: the 12th International Conference on Telecommunication Systems-Modeling and Analysis (ICTSM).

Limin, H. 2010. Embedded System for Internet of Things. *Microcontrollers & Embedded Systems*, 10, pp. 5–8.

Lin, T.H., Kinebuchi, Y., Courbot, A., Shimada, H., Morita, T., Mitake, H., Lee, C.Y., & Nakajima, T. 2011. Hardware-assisted reliability enhancement for embedded multi-core virtualization design. In: 14th IEEE International Symposium on Object/Component/Service-Oriented Real-Time Distributed Computing (ISORC), March 2011, pp. 241–249.

Liu, D., Ning, P., & Li, R. 2005. Establishing pairwise keys in distributed sensor networks. *ACM Transactions on Information and System Security (TISSEC)*, 8(1), pp. 41–77.

Liu, P., Dai, G., & Fu, T. 2015. A Web Services Based Email Extension for Remote Monitoring of Embedded Systems. Software Engineering, Artificial Intelligence, Networking, and Parallel/Distributed Computing, 2007. SNPD 2007. Eighth ACIS International Conference on, Qingdao, 2007, pp. 412–416.

Nakajima, T., Kinebuchi, Y., Shimada, H., Courbot, A., & Lin, T.H. 2011. Temporal and spatial isolation in a virtualization layer for multi-core processor based information appliances. In Proceedings of the 16th Asia and South Pacific Design Automation Conference (pp. 645–652). IEEE Press.

Ozvural, G., & Kurt, G.K. 2015. Advanced approaches for wireless sensor network applications and cloud analytics. In: IEEE Tenth International Conference on Intelligent Sensors, Sensor Networks and Information Processing (ISSNIP), April 2015, pp. 1–5.

Parameswaran, S., & Wolf, T. 2008. Embedded systems security—an overview. *Design Automation for Embedded Systems*, 12(3), pp. 173–183.

Park, J.S., & Chandramohan, P. 2004. Component recovery approaches for survivable distributed systems. In: 37th Hawaii International Conference on Systems Sciences (HICSS-37), Big Island, Hawaii, January 2004.

Park, J.S., Chandramohan, P., Devarajan, G., & Giordano, J. 2005. Trusted component sharing by runtime test and immunization for survivable distributed systems. In: IFIP International Information Security Conference (pp. 127–142). Springer US.

Park, J.S., Chandramohan, P., Suresh, A.T., Giordano, J., & Kwiat, K. 2009. Component survivability for mission-critical distributed systems. *Journal of Automatic and Trusted Computing (JoATC)*.

Park, J.S., Chandramohan, P., Suresh, A.T., Giordano, J., & Kwiat, K. 2013. Component survivability at runtime for mission-critical distributed systems. *Journal of Supercomputing*, (2013), 66 (3): pp. 1390–1417.

Porambage, P., Kumar, P., Schmitt, C., Gurtov, A., & Ylianttila, M. 2013. Certificate-based pairwise key establishment protocol for wireless sensor networks. In: IEEE 16th International Conference on Computational Science and Engineering (CSE), December 2013, pp. 667–674.

Porambage, P., Schmitt, C., Kumar, P., Gurtov, A., & Ylianttila, M. 2014. Two-phase authentication protocol for wireless sensor networks in distributed IoT applications. In: Wireless Communications and Networking Conference (WCNC), April 2014, pp. 2728–2733.

Qian, Y., Tipper, D., Krishnamurthy, P., & Joshi, J. 2010. *Information Assurance: Dependability and Security in Networked Systems*. Morgan Kaufmann, 2010.

Rabaey, J.M. 2015. The human intranet: where swarms and humans meet. In: Proceedings of the 2015 Design, Automation & Test in Europe Conference & Exhibition, EDA Consortium, March 09–13, 2015, pp. 637–640.

Razavi, B., & Wooley, B.A. 1992. Design techniques for high-speed, high-resolution comparators. *IEEE Journal of Solid-state Circuits*, 27(12), pp. 1916–1926.

Russell, D., & Gangemi, G.T. 1991. *Computer Security Basics*. O'Reilly Media.

Sabahi, F., & Movaghar, A. 2008. Intrusion detection: a survey. In: Third International Conference on Systems and Networks Communications, ICSNC'08, October 2008, pp. 23–26.

Santamarta, R. 2012. Project basecamp-attacking control logix. In: Report for 5th SCADA Security Scientific Symposium, Miami Beach, Florida, January 2012.

Schoenfield, B.S. 2015. *Securing Systems: Applied Security Architecture and Threat Models*. CRC Press.

Seba, V., Modlic, B., & Sisul, G. 2013. System model with adaptive modulation and frequency hopping in wireless networks. In: Global Information Infrastructure Symposium, October 2013, pp. 1–3.

Standards for Efficient Cryptography – SEC 4: Elliptic Curve Qu-Vanstone Implicit Certificate Scheme (ECQV), Version 0.97, March 9, 2011, Certicom Research, 32 pages.

Strobel, D., Oswald, D., Richter, B., Schellenberg, F., & Paar, C. 2014. Microcontrollers as (in) security devices for pervasive computing applications. *Proceedings of the IEEE*, 102(8), pp. 1157–1173.

Torrieri, D. 2015. *Principles of Spread-Spectrum Communication Systems*. Springer.

Tseng, Y.W., Liao, C.Y., & Hung, T.H. 2015. An embedded system with realtime surveillance application. 2015 International Symposium on Next-Generation Electronics (ISNE), Taipei, 2015, pp. 1–4.

Ukil, A., Sen, J., & Koilakonda, S. 2011. Embedded security for Internet of Things. In: IEEE 2nd National Conference on Emerging Trends and Applications in Computer Science (NCETACS), March 2011, pp. 1–6.

Unger, S., & Timmermann, D. 2015. DPWSec: devices profile for web services security. In: IEEE Tenth International Conference on Intelligent Sensors, Sensor Networks and Information Processing (ISSNIP), April 2015, pp. 1–6.

Veltri, L., Cirani, S., Ferrari, G., & Busanelli, S. 2013. Batch-based group key management with shared key derivation in the Internet of Things. In: IEEE 9th International Wireless Communications and Mobile Computing Conference (IWCMC), July 2013, pp. 1688–1693.

Wang, L., & Ranjan, R. 2015. Processing distributed internet of things data in clouds. *IEEE Cloud Computing*, 2(1), pp. 76–80.

Wu, C.H.J., & Irwin, J.D. 2013. *Introduction to Computer Networks and Cybersecurity*. CRC Press.

Xiang, W., Zexi, Z., Ying, L., & Yi, Z. 2013. A Design of Security Module to Protect Program Execution in Embedded System. Green Computing and Communications (GreenCom), 2013 IEEE and Internet of Things (iThings/CPSCom), IEEE International Conference on and IEEE Cyber, Physical and Social Computing, Beijing, 2013, pp. 1750–1755.

Xiaojun, Z., Kofi, A., Shoaib, E., Gareth, H., Huosheng, H., Dongbing, G. & Klaus, D. 2015. A Method for Detecting Abnormal Program Behavior on Embedded Devices, in IEEE Transactions on Information Forensics and Security, vol. 10, no. 8, pp. 1692–1704, Aug. 2015.

Yan, L., Zhang, Y., Yang, L.T., & Ning, H. (Eds.). 2008. *The Internet of Things: From RFID to the Next-Generation Pervasive Networked Systems*. CRC Press.

Yang, J.C., Hao, P.A.N.G., & Zhang, X. 2013. Enhanced mutual authentication model of IoT. *The Journal of China Universities of Posts and Telecommunications*, 20, pp. 69–74.

Yang, Y., Zhou, J., Wang, F., & Shi, C. 2014. An LPI design for secure burst communication systems. In: IEEE China Summit & International Conference on Signal and Information Processing (ChinaSIP), July 2014, pp. 631–635.

Yuan, Y., Wang, C., Wang, C., Zhang, B., Zhu, S., & Zhu, N. 2015. A novel algorithm for embedding dynamic virtual network request. In: IEEE 2nd International Conference on Information Science and Control Engineering (ICISCE), April 2015, pp. 28–32.

Yun, M., & Yuxin, B. 2010. Research on the architecture and key technology of Internet of Things (IoT) applied on smart grid. In: IEEE International Conference on Advances in Energy Engineering (ICAEE), June 2010, pp. 69–72.

Zhai, X., Appiah, K., Ehsan, S., Howells, G., Hu, H., Gu, D., & McDonald-Maier, K.D. 2015. A method for detecting abnormal program behavior on embedded devices. *IEEE Transactions on Information Forensics and Security*, 10(8), pp. 1692–1704.

Zhou, H. 2012. *The Internet of Things in the Cloud: A Middleware Perspective*. CRC Press.

Zhou, L., & Chao, H.C. 2011. Multimedia traffic security architecture for the internet of things. *IEEE Network*, 25(3), pp. 35–40.

CHAPTER 3

A SECURE UPDATE MECHANISM FOR INTERNET OF THINGS DEVICES

MARTIN GOLDBERG

U.S. Department of Defense, Fort Meade, MD, USA

3.1 INTRODUCTION

This chapter proposes a mechanism for securely updating IoT devices across networks and devices of any form factor or function. After all, even a children's toy can be used as an attack vector. Achieving complete IoT security can only be done through a holistic approach and by including security during the design phase. Developers interested in creating IoT devices have several security problems they must deal with. While not an exhaustive list, several of the problems are administering devices, proper authentication and authorization, securing communications, and firmware security. This chapter will only address updating IoT devices which is an essential part of IoT security (Aboba et al. 2004). This mechanism will focus on securely getting an update to the device through an untrusted network and verifying that the update is authentic.

3.1.1 Defining IoT Device

An IoT device is defined as having network capabilities and contains at least a part of the application logic (Kortuem et al. 2010). Having network capability does not necessarily mean connected to the Internet, but just the ability to perform t ransmission control protocol (TCP)/ i nternet protocol (IP) communications on its own. Devices that have no network capabilities and exchange data via a USB connection, for example, are not covered in this chapter. There is also the paradigm of using another device to provide temporary network capabilities. For example, meters that require an individual to connect a device so that meter can transmit its data are also not covered in this chapter. Having a part of the application logic, such as being able to process some of the sensor data, logic on what data to retain and transmit, etc.,

Cyber-Assurance for the Internet of Things, First Edition. Edited by Tyson T. Brooks.
© 2017 by The Institute of Electrical and Electronic Engineers, Inc. Published 2017 by John Wiley & Sons, Inc.

is what separates an IoT device from a radio frequency identification (RFID) tag, barcode, or a quick response (QR) code even though all of them are part of the IoT ecosystem.

This chapter defines an update as either updating both the operating system and application or just either the application or operating system running on an IoT device. This determination is made because in some cases it may be difficult to cleanly separate the operating system from the application (OWASP 2015). It should also be noted that addressing vulnerabilities in the underlying operating system is just as important as addressing vulnerabilities within the application code. This guidance is also not limited to any particular type of functionality so long as the definition of an IoT device is met. This chapter does not address all problems with updates. This chapter addresses performing updates to IoT devices in a manner that is secure, and is also based on security standards that the IoT device will need to implement to carry out its functions. The goal of this secure update mechanism is to make recommendations that would cause minimal increases in processing and memory requirements so that it could be used by IoT devices running on constrained platforms and on constrained networks.

3.2 IMPORTANCE OF IOT SECURITY

By the year 2010, the number of devices connected to the Internet exceeded the global population of 6.8 billion people with 12.5 billion connected devices (Evans 2011). It is being estimated that, by 2020, the number of connected devices will rise to roughly 50 billion (Evans 2011). IoT is being heralded as the driver of the fourth industrial revolution (Löffler & Tschiesner 2013). It is also enabling products that have life spans measured in decades, such as traffic lights, wind turbines, etc., to be connected. In short, IoT devices will be very prevalent and they will be long-lived, which means IoT devices deployed that cannot be updated after the discovery of a security vulnerability will be a major concern (Covington & Carskadeen 2013).

How we interact with IT systems, one another, our surroundings, and even money has already begun to change. With these changes come even greater threats. Traditionally, individuals and corporations worry about financial loss through identity theft or loss of personal/corporate intellectual property. Moving forward, physical well-being will become a concern as IoT starts connecting products from industries such as health care, public infrastructure, energy/utilities, and transportation that have had products that were, in the past, not connected. With so many new-to-the-Internet things coming online, a new term has been coined "The Internet of Insecure Things" (PWNIE 2015). Vendors who are new to being connected are going through the same growing pains as vendors who have been making connected products for some time now. The IoT ecosystem also lacks standards for vendors, both new and old, to follow. As a result of both of these situations, more attack surfaces for both home and enterprise networks are becoming available (Covington & Carskadeen 2013).

3.2.1 Importance of Updating

Citing home routers as an example, a survey was conducted where researchers found that home routers used software that was 4–5 years older than the release date of the router and the average age of the Linux operating system (OS) was 4 years (Schneier 2014; Tripwire 2014). Having old non-updated software is an exploit waiting to happen. In Brazil, 4.5 million digital subscriber line (DSL) routers were compromised and in December 2013, Symantec reported on a worm that specifically targets routers, cameras, and other IoT devices (Hayashi 2013).

Few would argue against the importance of keeping any system up-to-date, as a means to add functionality, fix bugs, and of course to enhance security. What is sometimes forgotten is that how a system is updated is just as important as the update itself. An update loses all value if its integrity cannot be verified, if that update can be altered in transit making it malicious, or if an unauthorized party is allowed to perform a malicious update. In the case of IoT, depending on the functionality of the device, the results of a malicious update could cause irreparable damage within the physical world. (Covington & Carskadeen 2013).

3.3 APPLYING THE DEFENSE IN-DEPTH STRATEGY FOR UPDATING

To achieve a secure update mechanism for IoT devices, a defense in-depth strategy must be used to incorporate two important security controls (Rubel et al. 2005). The first being a secure transport mechanism between the IoT device and the source of its update over what can be assumed to be an untrusted network. The second is validating the integrity of the update prior to it being installed. It could be argued that having one or the other of these security controls should suffice; however, having both aligns with the information assurance (IA) strategy of defense-in-depth (CSSP 2009).

By following this defense-in-depth strategy, an IoT system owner would force an attacker to defeat both security controls before achieving his/her goal. Without a secure transport, an attacker could make several attempts to cause an IoT device to accept a malicious update; there would be no mechanism in place to prevent the attempted update, or to prevent repeated attempts; this gap leaves the attacker the opportunity to adjust his/her trajectory if not initially successful. While it is true that the second security control, update validation, alone will prevent the attacker from installing compromised software, the availability of the IoT devices will be at risk if it is spending a large amount of time processing and failing invalid updates. Depending on the processing capabilities of the individual devices, the effort to validate the update could take a significant amount of time, increasing the impact of the attacker's denial of service. In this scenario, the device will also not receive its valid update as its resources are taxed and focused on validating the known bad software package. Conversely, by only using a secure transport, the transport security control does not provide a complete security posture. Should an attacker find a flaw in the secure transport security control, there is nothing stopping the attacker from sending a malicious update and having potentially adverse effect on the IoT device itself or the connectivity to the network from the IoT device itself.

3.4 A STANDARDS APPROACH

To support the greatest number of IoT devices possible, the mechanism proposed by this chapter will focus on IoT devices that are constrained devices (e.g., 8-bit microcontrollers with small amounts of random access memory (RAM) and read-only memory (ROM)) operating on constrained networks (e.g., 6LowPAN, small packet size, subject to packet loss (Montenegro et al. 2007; Hartke & Bergmann 2012; Shelby et al. 2014). This makes taking an approach that must leverage IoT security standards a critical requirement. The mechanism for updating has to use security already being used to keep any additional changes for the purposes of updating to a minimum. It is also a reasonable expectation that non-constrained IoT devices should have less trouble with implementing this mechanism.

3.4.1 Secure Transport

By the time of this writing, work toward standardizing IoT has begun. Thus far, the bulk of the work has been toward moving away from proprietary protocols for the purposes of interoperability and alleviating the need for gateways (Roman et al. 2011; Ishaq et al. 2013). However, with the creation of the constrained application protocol (CoAP), there is the ability to use datagram transport layer security (DTLS) for session security (Rescorla & Modadugu 2012). The use of DTLS is being even further refined by the DTLS In Constrained Environments (DICE) Working Group by taking in account of algorithms that can be used by constrained devices on constrained network (IETF 2013). The Constrained RESTful Environments (CoRE) Working Group, along with bringing the representational state transfer (REST) software architecture style to IoT systems, is looking to incorporate security by looking at DICE, the cryptographic message syntax (CMS), and the extensible authentication protocol (EAP) (Fielding 2000; Aboba et al. 2004; Housley 2009). The combination of the three will bring the potential for session security, object security, and device authentication.

The DICE Working Group's implementation of DTLS and its incorporation into CoAP and CoRE make DTLS arguably the best choice for providing the secure transport for the proposed secure update mechanism (Garcia-Morchon et al. 2013; Keoh et al. 2013). DTLS is a complete security protocol with its ability to perform authentication, key exchange, and confidentiality; it would protect the update while being transferred over a network. Although it would be ideal to use the existing DTLS standard as is, it was not designed to be used by either constrained devices or on constrained networks. The DICE Working Group is moving toward solving these problems by working toward (IEFTF 2013):

- defining DTLS profile(s) that are reasonably implementable on constrained devices,
- adapting DTLS for constrained networks, and
- supporting multicast messages, assuming the IoT devices in a multicast group are provisioned by a group key of some type.

Transport layer security (TLS), and therefore DTLS, supports three credential types for authentication: pre-shared secrets, raw public keys, and certificates (Tschofenig & Fossait 2015):

- Pre-shared secrets: For this credential type, the IoT device is configured with a shared secret and an identifier. This shared secret and identifier need to be shared with any host that this IoT device needs to communicate with.
- Raw public keys: A public/private key pair, typically associated with some identifier, is stored on the IoT device. To authenticate to any other host, the appropriate credential has to be known. If the other end uses raw public key as well, then their public key needs to be provisioned (out-of-band) to the IoT device.
- Certificates: The use of certificates requires the IoT device to store the public key (as part of the certificate) as well as the private key. The certificate will contain the identifier of the IoT device as well as various other attributes. Both sides communicating are assumed to be in possession of a trust anchor store that contains Certificate Authority (CA) certificates and, in case of certificate pinning, end-entity certificates. Similarly, to the other credentials the IoT device needs information about which entity to use which certificate with. Without a trust anchor store on the IoT device, it will not be possible to perform certificate validation.

Of the three credential types, certificates is recommended, although the most complex, it does offer the ability to revoke and update certificates. At minimum, raw public keys can also be used, while it is recommended to not use pre-shared secrets. In addition to not being able to provide mutual authentication or the ability to easily change should the secret be revealed, the use of pre-shared secrets would require additional crypto functionality which would increase the necessary code base. This concept is explained in Section 3.4.2.

3.4.2 Update Verification

Combining the guidance laid out by the Federal Information Processing Standard (FIPS) 186-4, Digital Signature Standard (DSS), and the Protection Profile for Mobile Device Fundamentals, the use of the RSA Digital Signature Algorithm (RDSA) or Elliptic Curve Digital Signature Algorithm (ECDSA) is recommended for verifying the integrity of data (and the identity of the signer) (PUB 1995; NIAP 2014). Although a mobile device is a higher functioning device than a constrained device, the protection profile for mobile device fundamentals provides an excellent example of a device with relatively low memory and processing being updated over an untrusted network. When used in conjunction with FIPS 180-4 Secure Hash Standard (SHS), RDSA and ECDSA seem like the ideal choice to provide the update verification security control. However, studies have shown that elliptic curve cryptography (ECC) performs much better than RSA on mobile platforms and constrained devices, making ECDSA the ideal choice (Gura et al. 2004; Gupta & Silakari 2011).

Back in November 2007, the National Institute of Standards and Technology (NIST) announced the SHA-3 competition to replace SHA-2. (GPO 2015). The intention of this announcement was to create a new family of Hash algorithms that can seamlessly substitute SHA-2 in existing applications in the event of a discovery of a practical attack against SHA-2. Part of the evaluation criteria was the computational efficiency and memory requirements of the candidate algorithms for the purposes of running on constrained devices. Although, there were no plans to test the algorithms on a constrained platform, submitters were asked to include a written statement on the advantages and disadvantages of running on an 8-bit processor and the community evaluating these submissions was asked to conduct their own tests on constrained platforms. In October 2012, NIST officially selected Keccak (pronounced "catch-ack") as the winner of the SHA-3 competition and in August 2015, Keccak officially became part of FIPS 180-4 as SHA-3 (Aumasson et al. 2008; Boutin 2012; GPO 2015).

In response to NIST's call to the community to test on constrained platforms, several studies were performed on the five finalists: Blake (Aumasson et al. 2010), Gr0stl (Gauravaram et al. 2009), JH (Wu 2011), Keccak (Bertoni et al. 2009), and Skein (Ferguson 2010). In the studies, Keccak performed overall very well in testing (Kavun et al. 2012; Alshaikhli et al. 2012). In August 2015, along with FIPS 180-4 being updated with a hash algorithm that performs well on constrained devices, the DICE Working Group published version 17 of their profile for using TLS/DTLS for IoT devices. In version 17, the organization made the cryptographic cipher suite TLS_ECDHE_ECDSA_WITH_AES_128_CCM_8 mandatory for use with certificates and raw public key (Tschofenig & Fossati 2015). This TLS/DTLS profile requires the use of ECDSA and is currently making use of SHA-2. Since the ability to seamlessly substitute SHA-3 for SHA-2 was one of the core requirements for SHA-3, it should not be long before this cipher suite will be using Keccak (GPO 2015). By having an IoT device follow this standard for the secure transport security control, no additional crypto functionality would be needed to implement the update verification security control. The pre-shared secrets credential type mandates TLS_PSK_WITH_AES_128_CCM_8, which has no need for performing a key agreement and therefore does not include ECDSA. Use of this cipher suite would require additional crypto functionality to implement the update verification security control.

3.5 CONCLUSION

It is all too often that during the design phase security comes second and when it is considered it is only considered in terms of securing the functionality of the product. Consideration for maintaining, which includes updating, is often left for last. This applies to IoT devices, and virtually any product. One of the chief concerns for developing on a constrained device is, obviously, keeping the memory footprint and processing to a minimum. However, by following standards and leveraging the crypto functions required to secure the devices functionality, meaning it will need this anyway, it is possible to have a secure update mechanism without significantly increasing the load on a constrained device.

REFERENCES

Aboba, B., Blunk, L., Vollbrecht, J., Carlson, J., & Levkowetz, H. 2004. Extensible authentication protocol (EAP). IETF Standards Track, RFC 3748, June 2004.

Alshaikhli, I.F., Alahmad, M.A., & Munthir, K. 2012. Comparison and analysis study of SHA-3 finalists. In: IEEE International Conference on Advanced Computer Science Applications and Technologies (ACSAT), November 2012, pp. 366–371.

Aumasson, J.P., Henzen, L., Meier, W., & Phan, R.C.W. 2008. SHA-3 proposal BLAKE. Submission to NIST (Round 3).

Bertoni, G., Daemen, J., Peeters, M., & Van Assche, G. 2009. KECCAK sponge function family main document. Submission to NIST (Round 2), 3, p. 30.

Covington, M.J., & Carskadden, R. 2013. Threat implications of the Internet of Things. In: IEEE 5th International Conference on Cyber Conflict (CyCon), June 2013, pp. 1–12.

CSSP. 2009. Recommended practice: improving industrial control systems cybersecurity with defense-in-depth strategies. US-CERT Defense In Depth, October 2009.

Evans, D. 2011. The Internet of Things: how the next evolution of the Internet is changing everything. CISCO White Paper, pp. 1–11.

Ferguson, N., Lucks, S., Schneier, B., Whiting, D., Bellare, M., Kohno, T., Callas, J., & Walker, J., 2010. The Skein hash function family. Submission to NIST (Round 3), 7(7.5), p. 3.

Fielding, R.T. 2000. Architectural styles and the design of network-based software architectures. Doctoral Dissertation, University of California, Irvine, CA.

Garcia-Morchon, O., Keoh, S.L., Kumar, S., Moreno-Sanchez, P., Vidal-Meca, F., & Ziegeldorf, J.H. 2013. Securing the IP-based Internet of Things with HIP and DTLS. In: Proceedings of the Sixth ACM Conference on Security and Privacy in Wireless and Mobile Networks, April 2013, pp. 119–124.

Gauravaram, P., Knudsen, L.R., Matusiewicz, K., Mendel, F., Rechberger, C., Schläffer, M., & Thomsen, S.S. 2009. Grøstl – a SHA-3 candidate. In: Dagstuhl Seminar Proceedings. Schloss Dagstuhl-Leibniz-Zentrum für Informatik.

Gupta, K., & Silakari, S. 2011. ECC over RSA for asymmetric encryption: a review. *International Journal of Computer Science Issues*, 8(3), p. 2.

Gura, N., Patel, A., Wander, A., Eberle, H., & Shantz, S.C. 2004. Comparing elliptic curve cryptography and RSA on 8-bit CPUs. In: *Cryptographic Hardware and Embedded Systems – CHES 2004*. Springer, Berlin/Heidelberg, pp. 119–132.

Hartke, K., & Bergmann, O. 2012. Datagram Transport Layer Security in Constrained Environments. draft-hartke-core-codtls-02 (WiP), IETF, 2012. Available at http://www.ietf.org/proceedings/83/slides/slides-83-lwig-2.pdf.

Hayashi, K. 2013. Linux Worm Targeting Hidden Devices. Symantec [online], 27(11). Available at http://www.symantec.com/connect/blogs/linux-worm-targeting-hidden-devices.

Housley, R. 2009. RFC 5652-Cryptographic Message Syntax (CMS). Available at https://tools.ietf.org/html/rfc5652.

Ishaq, I., Carels, D., Teklemariam, G.K., Hoebeke, J., Abeele, F.V.D., Poorter, E.D., Moerman, I., & Demeester, P. 2013. IETF standardization in the field of the Internet of Things (IoT): a survey. *Journal of Sensor and Actuator Networks*, 2(2), pp. 235–287.

Kavun, E.B., & Yalcin, T. 2012. On the suitability of SHA-3 finalists for lightweight applications. In: The Third SHA-3 Candidate Conference, Washington, DC, March 22–23, 2012.

Keoh, S., Kumar, S., & Garcia-Morchon, O. 2013. Securing the IP-based Internet of Things with DTLS.Working Draft, LWIG Working Group, February 2013.

Kortuem, G., Kawsar, F., Fitton, D., & Sundramoorthy, V. 2010. Smart objects as building blocks for the Internet of Things. *IEEE Internet Computing*, 14(1), pp. 44–51.

Löffler, M., & Tschiesner, A. 2013. The Internet of Things and the future of manufacturing. McKinsey & Company, 4. Available at http://www.futurenautics.com/wp-content/uploads/2013/10/Internet-of-Things-and-future-of-manufacturing.pdf.

Montenegro, G., Kushalnagar, N., Hui, J., & Culler, D. 2007. Transmission of IPv6 packets over IEEE 802.15.4 networks. Internet proposed standard, RFC 4944, September 2007.

National Information Assurance Partnership (NIAP). 2014. Protection Profile for Mobile Device Fundamentals, Version 2, December 2014.

OWASP Internet of Things Project, The Open Web Application Security Project. Available at https://www.owasp.org/index.php/OWASP_Internet_of_Things_Top_Ten_Project. Accessed on July 9, 2015.

PUB, F. 1995. Secure hash standard. *Public Law*, 100, p. 235.

PWNIE Express. 2015. The Internet of evil things: the rapidly emerging threat of high risk hardware. Available at http://www.internetofevilthings.com/. Accessed on April 15, 2015.

Rescorla, E., & Modadugu, N. 2012. Datagram Transport Layer Security Version 1.2, January 2012.

Roman, R., Najera, P., & Lopez, J. 2011. Securing the Internet of Things. *IEEE Computer*, 44(9), pp. 51–58.

Rubel, P., Ihde, M., Harp, S., & Payne, C. 2005. Generating policies for defense in depth. In: IEEE 21st Annual Computer Security Applications Conference, December 2005, p. 10.

Schneier, B. 2014. The Internet of things is wildly insecure—and often unpatchable. *Schneier on Security*, January 6, 2014.

Shelby, Z., Hartke, K., & Bormann, C. 2014. The constrained application protocol (CoAP) (No. RFC 7252). Available at https://www.rfc-editor.org/info/rfc7252.

Tripwire. 2014. SOHO Wireless Router (In) Security. Tripwire VERT Research Report. Available at http://www.tripwire.com/register/soho-wireless-router-insecurity/showMeta/2/. Accessed on February 25, 2014.

Tschofenig, H., & Fossati, T. 2015. TLS/DTLS Profiles for the Internet of Things. Internet-Draft draft-ietf-dice-profile-17.txt, IETF Secretariat, October 2015, pg. 1-59. Available at https://tools.ietf.org/html/draft-ietf-dice-profile-17.

U.S. Government Publishing Office (GPO). 2015. Federal Register, vol. 80, no. 150.

Wu, H. 2011. The hash function JH. Submission to NIST (Round 3), p. 6.

PART II

TRUST IMPACT

CHAPTER 4

SECURITY AND TRUST MANAGEMENT FOR THE INTERNET OF THINGS: AN RFID AND SENSOR NETWORK PERSPECTIVE

M. BALA KRISHNA

University School of Information and Communication Technology, Guru Gobind Singh Indraprastha University, Dwarka, New Delhi, India

4.1 INTRODUCTION

With emerging trends in information and communication technology (ICT), the wireless communication networks facilitate security in cyber-physical networking systems (CPNS) using ubiquitous and pervasive devices that are connected. The Internet of Things (IoT) is a new paradigm of cyber-physical systems that combines ubiquitous and pervasive components, Internet protocol (IP)-based network, radio-frequency identification (RFID) devices, cloud computing services, mobile *ad hoc*, and sensor networks into a single framework; this ensures trusted communication between the connected IoT objects. IoT defines unique object identity based on electronic product code (EPC). Security and trust in IoT protocols are primarily based on authentication, non-repudiation, validation, and confidentiality. Energy-aware security and trust management schemes minimize the delay overhead and save energy in RFID devices, sensors, actuators, and smart devices. Trust management schemes establish cooperative communication between the IoT objects for real-time applications.

The architecture of IoT aims at connecting heterogeneous devices and facilitate and support security and trust in the network (Gubbi et al. 2013). IoT integrates cloud computing technology with RFID, actuators and sensor network devices. Embedding RFID tags improve monitoring and coordinating tasks for IoT-based systems. Device-to-device (D2D) and machine-to-machine (M2M) also collectively contribute to the emerging field of IoT. Figure 4.1 represents the security and trust in IoT connected systems.

Cyber-Assurance for the Internet of Things, First Edition. Edited by Tyson T. Brooks.
© 2017 by The Institute of Electrical and Electronic Engineers, Inc. Published 2017 by John Wiley & Sons, Inc.

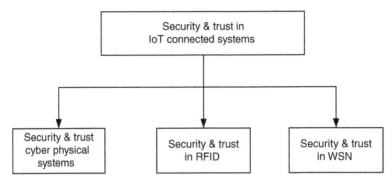

FIGURE 4.1   Security and trust in IoT connected systems. Reproduced with permission of IEEE.

Ad hoc and sensor networks operate in the unlicensed spectrum with limited processing, storage and energy level. The nodes being deployed in remote and hostile environments challenge the security issue of the network. Hence, cryptographic techniques based on symmetric and asymmetric key management are used in *ad hoc* and sensor networks (Boukerch et al. 2007). In resource constraint environment, adaptive and energy-efficient security protocols define the constraints of varying packet size and dynamic network traffic conditions (Prasithsangaree & Krishnamurthy 2004). Trust management protocols attributed with (i) cooperative and intelligent communication and (ii) confidence between the source node and base station inhibit the malicious attacks by intruders and secures the network (Burmester et al. 2007; Lopez et al. 2010).

4.1.1   Issues and Challenges in Security and Trust Management

With an increase in the number of Internet and multimedia-based services, the intruders use audio or video files for data hiding and compromise the network. Multimedia traffic security for IoT resolves the security issues of intruders for multimedia-based applications (Zhou & Cha 2011). Security challenges in IP-based IoT consider Internet protocol security (IPSec) features (Heer et al. 2011). Security and privacy in distributed IoT consider heterogeneous network authentic configurations (Roman 2013). Datagram transport layer security (DTLS) used in low power WPAN considers two-way authentication in IoT to establish the secure communications channel (Kothmayr et al. 2013). One of the major issues consists of security limitations within IoT systems themselves.

4.1.1.1   *Security Limitations in IoT Systems*   There are certain areas that present security limitations in the trust management aspect of IoT systems. These limitations are also there as the IoT device will experience problems during deployment. Therefore, the three main limitations include:

- **Architectural compatibility** – IoT is a collection of distributed heterogeneous network comprising RFID, sensors, actuators, smartphones, Bluetooth, Wi-Fi access points, and so on. Each technology supports a distinct type of security protocols. IoT defines a common integrated framework and establishes security in the heterogeneous network.

- **Functional differences** – The active and sleep schedules of distributed systems mostly differ with one another causing the key validation periods also to vary for the communicating devices. The limited power resources and constrained bandwidth lead to functional differences in the network. Irrespective of functional differences, frequent key verification process measures the degree of trust and invalidates the intruded paths of the network.

- **Deliberate delaying and modification** – Sparse intermediate relay nodes delay the performance of IoT. Intruders deliberately delay the network by causing traffic congestion along the active route paths. The malicious nodes compromise the secure keys, modify the data and forward (or drop) the message toward the destination node.

4.1.2 Design Metrics in Security and Trust Management Systems

With respect to security and trust management, the following properties of trust pertain specifically to the IoT:

4.1.2.1 *Degree of Reputation (d_R)*   Degree of reputation as a function of public and private keys exchanged between the nodes, $(Key_{Public}, Key_{Private})$ and number of previous transmissions $(PktTr_{Previous})$ is given as follows:

$$d_R = \Phi((Key_{Public}, Key_{Private}), PktTr_{Previous}) \tag{4.1}$$

4.1.2.2 *Degree of Trust (d_T)*   Degree of trust as a function of maximum available bandwidth B_{Max}, transmission or reception power P (μJ-bytes/sec), and number of key mismatches $key_{mismatches}$ is given as follows (Boukerch et al. 2007):

$$d_T = \Psi(B_{Max}, P, key_{mismatches}) \tag{4.2}$$

4.1.2.3 *Degree of Communication (d_C)*   Degree of communication as a function of degree of reputation d_R and degree of trust rate d_T is given as follows:

$$d_C = \Theta(d_R, d_T) \tag{4.3}$$

Φ, Ψ, and Θ estimate the degree of reputation, trust, and communication for active nodes in the network.

4.1.2.4 Trusted Node   Node $x(t)$ is considered to be a trusted node if and only if it satisfies the following condition:

$$x(t) = \frac{x_{n(ACK)} + x_{n(NACK)}}{x_{n(keyExchg)}} = \begin{cases} 1 & \text{trusted nodes} \\ 0 & \text{non-trusted nodes} \end{cases}, \text{ where } x(t) \in G(X_{tm}) \quad (4.4)$$

where $G(X_{tm})$ represents the group of trusted members, $x_{n(ACK)}$ and $x_{n(NACK)}$ are the number of successful and failed transactions recorded by the server and $x_{n(keyExchg)}$ represents the number of keys exchanged by the node $x(t)$.

4.2 SECURITY AND TRUST IN THE INTERNET OF THINGS

In the IoT, cloud-enabled features create virtual environments that manage and control the resources in the IoT networks. Security keys define the mechanisms for access control, authentication, confidentiality, and non-repudiation within IoT communication channel(s). Service-oriented architecture (SOA) for IoT middleware consists of modules such as service composition, service management, and object abstraction (Atzori et al. 2010). The service component layer features the concurrent services offered by systems which generate the workflow in executable SOA processes. Service components use web service definition languages to define SOA workflows. Service management deals with the dynamic discovery of objects and devices, while monitoring their respective functional status through the configuration of state of objects. Leveraging SOA, Table 4.1 describes the components of IoT and its respective connectivity services (Gubbi et al. 2013).

IoT functional modes, as shown in Figure 4.2, are classified as follows (Roman et al. 2013):

i. **Centralized mode** – The serving entity such as database server or cloud provides data and services to heterogeneous connected devices working in the passive mode. Centralized IoT servers provide interface standards and configuration parameters for the customer-centric systems. The decisiveness and network intelligence is within the control of centralized servers.

**TABLE 4.1   Components and Connectivity in IoT.
Reproduced with permission of IEEE**

Components	Connectivity Services
RFID	Near-field communication
Sensor and actuators	Routers, switches
6LoWPAN	Routers, switches, 4G/LTE
Mobile devices	4G/LTE, cloud virtualization
Internet-enabled components	4G/LTE, cloud virtualization

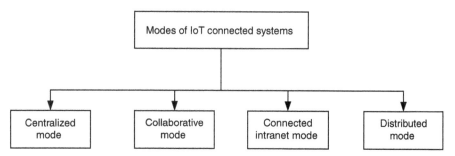

FIGURE 4.2 Modes of IoT connected systems. Reproduced with permission of IEEE.

ii. **Collaborative mode** – Collaboration between multiple servers and cloud entities enable the exchange of data and services IoT enabled applications. The user can select services from multiple service providers and configure his application.

iii. **Connected intranet mode** – Intranet defines customer-oriented services based on the available local data and shares the policies with central serving entities. Global database is updated with the local information obtained from distinctive intranet entities of IoT.

iv. **Distributed mode** – Distributed mode allows intranets to evolve into medium- and large-scale interconnected systems and collaborate with the local and global services. This mode enables the connected components to access global data repositories and support cloud-centric services.

4.2.1 Heterogeneity in IoT Security Management

The Web of Things (WoT) is the collection of heterogeneous devices, servers, and network configured to invoke standard web interface and communicate with each other. Sensor networks, RFIDs, M2M, D2D communications, and cloud computing contribute a major role in IoT. Existing security and trust models for sensor networks mainly focus on the establishment of energy efficient secure route paths with a minimum hop count (Atzori et al. 2010). This technique aims to reduce the energy consumption, packet delay, and communication overhead in the network. IoT devices differ in terms of frame formats, active or sleep periods, security algorithms, packet delivery ratio, and resource sharing capabilities (Atzori et al. 2010). Heterogeneous devices trying to communicate with one another compete for same networking and spectral resources. The heterogeneity issues in IoT security management are given as follows:

- Device naming and addressing
- Data integrity
- Device heterogeneity
- Interoperability

- High-speed communication
- Scalability
- Resilience to attacks
- Security and privacy

Object abstraction component coordinates with the heterogeneous devices by using single language and processing system that comprises two sub-layers, namely, the interface sub-layer and the communication sub-layers. IoT secure systems define authentication, access control, confidentiality, policy enforcement, privacy and secure middleware to mitigate threats in the network (Sicari et al. 2015; Ashraf & Habaebi 2015). IoT security systems are enhanced by using autonomic monitoring and analyzing the node behavior. Frequent updates and storage decisions are based on the level of intrusions in IoT systems.

4.2.2 Security Management in IoT Systems

Future networks enable the electronic and electrical devices (with embedded chips) to connect with each other using D2D and M2M technologies. RFID tags attached to patients and employee organizations interact with host server based on human computer interaction (HCI). Heterogeneous IoT devices rely on third-party server interventions for the re-buffering of data packets and secure message exchanges. Operational aspects of heterogeneous IoT devices based on three phases are given as follows (Nguyen et al. 2015):

i. **Bootstrap phase** – The pre-requisite conditions are defined TO INITIATE the communication between two unknown heterogeneous nodes. Valid device identity, enabling technology, type of service, number of secure keys, and the encryption algorithms are selected by IoT server to establish the secure channel.

ii. **Operational phase** – Messages exchanged between the nodes are based on the number of secure keys and an encryption algorithm. Cipher text is created based on the pre-shared keys and a secure transaction is COMPLETED in this phase.

iii. **Maintenance and reboot-strapping phase** – This phase is invoked after the successful transaction by receiving an ACKNOWLEDGEMENT from the destination nodes. The pre-shared keys are maintained by IoT servers to monitor the behavior of nodes during transactions. The degree of trust awarded to each node is shared with IoT server to ensure security and trust across the connecting devices in the network. The authentication schemes are broadly classified as: (i) shared-secret keys, (ii) static public keys, (iii) certificate-based keys, (iv) public-identifier keys, and (v) unique-identity-based keys (Saied et al. 2014).

A key distribution center (KDC) distributes the group keys and supports members to leave or join a communications session at any period of time (e.g., through dynamic behavior) in a multicast session (Veltri et al. 2013). Group key management decreases the overhead in security protocols. The tasks performed by the key distribution technique are as follows: (1) generate group key, (2) maintain secure group association, (3) update group membership, and (4) re-assigning of new group key for the compromised paths of the network. A member leaving the session is categorized into (i) pre-determined leave (Pre-Leave) (ii) unpredictable leave (Unpre-Leave). The group key as a function of Pre-Leave, Unpre-Leave and time stamp t_i handles the types of member leaving the secure session.

4.2.3 Trust Management in IoT Systems

The IoT ensures data reliability, user privacy and the trusted communication by defining objective and subjective trust properties between the sender, intermediate, and the receiver nodes (Yan et al. 2014). The trust levels of sender node based on earlier transactions are decided as follows:

i. Objective properties: authentic, reliable, and reputed
ii. Subjective Properties: benevolent and honest

The receiver node must be willing to trust the sender node and act in agreement with the security policies implemented by the sender. Figure 4.3 illustrates the features of IoT Trust Management Protocols (IoTTMP) (Yan et al. 2014; Borgia 2014).

4.2.3.1 Features of IoT Trust Management Protocols   The IoTTMP functions as an IoT-based protocol in which more than one node encountering each other or (involved in an interaction activity) can directly observe each other and exchange trust evaluation toward others (Veltri et al 2013). These activities, as displayed in Figure 4.3, are described as follows:

- **Event monitors and data collectors** – Basic services such as event monitoring, storing, and updating the behavior of authorized devices, servers, gateway, relay nodes, and access points are performed by IoTTMP.
- **Privacy preservers and secure mediators** – Device information, user profile information, and node access rights are preserved by IoT trust protocols. Privacy-based IoT and lightweight security protocols preserve, process, and analyze the security protocols to validate the nodes in the channel.
- **Fusion and mining manager** – Reliable fusion and mining algorithms are applied to process voluminous data from servers and online applications. Data are extracted, transformed, and loaded (ETL process) to the database servers. The authenticity and privacy of the data are preserved while applying the mining, fusion algorithms, and knowledge discovery in databases (KDD) systems on the data which address the queries of authentic users.
- **Secured robust transmission manager** – Only authentic devices are allowed to interact with the server. The behavior of each node per transaction in a complete

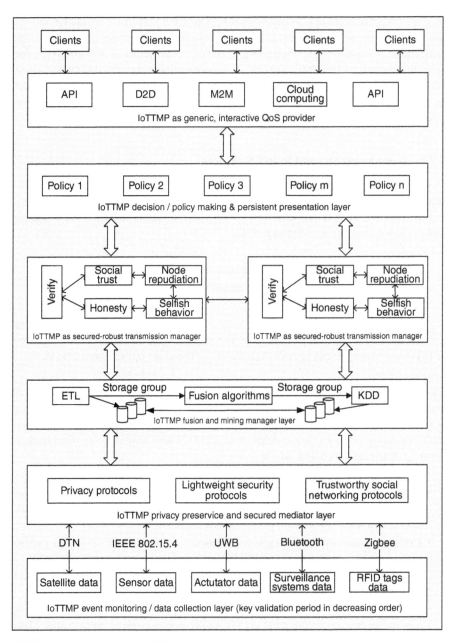

FIGURE 4.3   Features of IoT Trust Management Protocols. Reproduced with permission of IEEE.

session is analyzed in terms of the degree of trust with neighboring nodes, and estimates the direct and indirect trust levels of the network.

- **Efficient policy maker and persistent presenter** – Efficient decision makers define the trust relations between communicating objects and guide them to collaborate with each other. IoTTMP provides persistent data to the trusted members of the network.
- **Generic and interactive QoS provider** – IoTTMP are applied in generic and interactive applications that support multi-linguistic operating systems with varying network platforms. QoS is based on the cost of accuracy and time to transmit the data in the network.

4.2.3.2 *Functionality of IoT Trust Management Systems*   Trustworthy services are based on parameters such as authorization (access control), authentication (valid user), session life cycle, key management, and node behavioral information based on trust and reputation (Zhu et al. 2015). Security and trust management in IoT systems are based on the knowledge, supervision, and biometric parameters that validate the device and their respective services. An identity-based trust framework consists of front-end tools to authorize access control and restrict the unauthorized entities into the system (Gessner et al. 2012). Based on the valid ID and access certificate, the device informs the nature of the query, the resources required and the type of service. Then, the IoT server grants the access control with the existing operational policies. The IoT trust management systems monitor the authorization periods, identifies the life cycles and the nodes' behavior. This information further creates root identity and digital signature(s) and subsequent pseudonyms for unrevealing the transactions in a real-time application.

Distributed trust management in IoT-based SOA supports interoperability across heterogeneous devices in wired and social networks (Chen et al. 2014). The connected IoT devices send feedback that define direct or indirect trust based on node interaction level, trust level, social impact level, and cohesion level of server nodes in the network. The social relationship of IoT is a function of visited location, user-device interaction (direct or indirect), friendship group(s) and social group(s). This approach uses the adaptive filtering technique by combining the direct and indirect trust feedback to minimize the rate of trust bias across the nodes in IoT. This method provides high degree of trust with positive user interaction. This protocol is resilient if the rate of malicious nodes is less than 40% so that the convergence time and trust bias are maintained in the safe state.

4.3 RADIO FREQUENCY IDENTIFICATION: EVOLUTION AND APPROACHES

Radio frequency identification (RFID) tags consist of small wireless microchips which are limited to short range data transmission. RFID tags are embedded in credit or debit cards, driving licenses, employee identity cards, secret documents, passports, etc., which are used to retrieve or update private information of the user (Sun et al. 2008a). RFID systems extend their services from burglar alarms at an individual home to acute military surveillance systems. RFID is a potential technological countermeasure to address the issues of cloned tags of genuine goods such as electronic items, mechanical spare parts, textiles, toys, and household items, and safeguards the authenticity of the original manufacturer (Lehtonen et al. 2007). The information is read out by exchanging an unique secret key shared by the manufacturer and tag readers. Embedded advanced key technology in RFID increases the cost of production. Emerging technology such as near-field communication (NFC) in smart mobiles function as transponders and Electronic Product Code (EPC) readers verify the RFID and assures the genuine product (Langheinrich et al. 2009). Pair-wise public and private key encryption methods are applied in RFID enabled devices to ensure trust between the user and manufacturer. Cost-to-break systems in Universal Product Code (UPC) consisting of 14 digits and EPC are developed to reduce the cost of product vulnerability and safeguard the duplicity of products. RFID tag designers aim to create secured and sophisticated code to increase the trust level with the customers (Marquardt et al. 2010).

4.3.1 Categories of RFID Product Authentication

RFID tags are extensively used for product authentication and are broadly categorized as follows (Lehtonen et al. 2007): feature-based authentication, content-based authentication, and location-based authentication, as shown in Figure 4.4. The primary field of a RFID tag consists of three parameters: the type of product (month, year), the level of security, and the location of product (such as the manufacturer's name and address).

4.3.1.1 Feature-Based RFID The features of the product such as physical dimensions, electrical specifications (voltage, power), and surface pattern are specified in RFID tags. Manufacturers use digital signatures and product specification to generate unique RFID product tags, and the key validation process avoid duplicity of RFID tags.

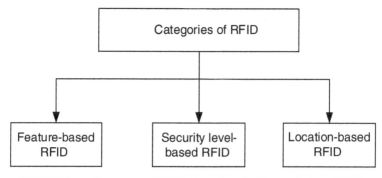

FIGURE 4.4 Categories of RFID. Reproduced with permission of IEEE.

4.3.1.2 Adversaries of Feature-Based RFID   Adversaries can compromise RFID signals by compromising the integrity of an RFID signal to append malicious logic to that signal to exploit a defect in the relationship between two components, in order to compromise a security property in one of those components. For products such as bags, shoes, and electronic gadgets manufactured by different companies, they all have similar physical specifications. Other identical objects use feature-based RFID tags that duplicate similar products. Distinguishing genuine products RFID signals increases the complexity and trust levels of the product.

4.3.1.3 Security Level-Based RFID   Expensive items such as jewelry, watches, and secret documents require high-level security as compared to the items such as bags, shoes, and electronic gadgets. Embedding secret keys in RFID tags and enable access rights to authentic tag readers reduces the effects of cloning in RFID technology. Tag readers use symmetric keys generated by the advanced encryption standard (AES) to secure RFID products. Another method to define the RFID tag is to generate non-clonable physical functions with combinations of a large number of logical gates and integrated circuits (ICs) to counter effect the intruders of RFID.

4.3.1.4 Adversaries of Security Level-Based RFID   Since the tag memory is limited, symmetric key encryption techniques are used in RFID. By using reverse engineering techniques, an adversary can break down the symmetric keys to lower the degree of trust between the customer and manufacturer (Arbit et al. 2014). As such, the components that perform security functions, and those that access or manipulate sensitive data or resources become more vulnerable.

4.3.1.5 Location-Based RFID   Location-based RFID tags (i.e., track-and-trace) define the location specification of an authentic product manufacturer (Lehtonen et al. 2007). This method identifies the duplicate or cloned product. Serializing the product number is based on the product class, such as global or local identity, that define the item number. EPC tags consist of Unique Item Identifier (UII) field of 96 bits and a global unique product specific number. This method is resistant to cloned products and can generate false alarms in multi-level secure systems that are read by the previous tag reader. Advance versions of the track-and-trace technique update the central server periodically when the tag reader reads the RFID product (Arbit et al. 2014). The cloned objects at familiar or unfamiliar locations are identified and counterfeited as duplicate products.

4.3.1.6 Adversaries of Location-Based RFID   Location-based RFIDs are primarily used when the supply chain for development is small. The complexity of location-based RFID increases when multiple products are used with identical location codes and further fabricate the genuine product.

4.3.2 RFID Solutions for Sensor Networks

RFID tags use ultra-high frequency for short-range communication within 1–10 m. The tags respond to a message broadcast of tag readers which further lead to collisions. The intruders can disable the supply chain for the RFID solution through any component in the supply chain (manufacturer-dealer-vendor-customer) (Marquardt et al. 2010). Hence, tag silencing and constant key updates per transaction improve the degree of privacy in RFID applications. Furthermore, the coordination between manufacturers, vendors, and customers is necessary for RFID applications.

A linear congruential generator (LCG) uses lightweight cipher blocks and pseudo-random numbers to generate security keys for RFID-based sensor networks (Sun et al. 2008a). Security attacks exist at various layers as follows: (i) sensor nodes can be physically attacked or and accessed by the intruders to retrieve the sensitive information. A denial-of-service (DoS) attack is performed by jamming a node blocking the signals from its base station and forcing the sensor node from transmitting signals to the base station (ii) link layer attacks manipulate the size of a frame format and manipulates the size of duty cycles, (iii) network layer attacks include spoofing, flooding, and altering of route paths and data packets between the source and destination nodes. The messages are embedded with pseudo-random numbers using fixed factors such as multiplier, increment, and modulus operators. Prime numbers define the basic parameters that are made public to estimate the permutations to encrypt the message. Multiplier and the modulus operators are avoided to reduce the complexity of key estimation from a large number of permutations. RFID tags with known values of the multiplier, increment, and modulus operators are sent to the valued customer.

4.3.3 RFID Protocols and Performance Aspects

The following represent some performance aspects associated with RFID protocols:

4.3.3.1 Sustainable Security with RFIDs
Malicious nodes apply key revival algorithms and brute force methods to obtain the security keys attached to RFID tags. Eavesdroppers tamper parts of the vital information stored in RFID tags or change passwords such that manufacturers will not be able to retrieve information (e.g., DoS attacks) from the tag. RFID tags sustain minimal information changes in the boundary areas of the tag. RFID operates within a short distance and is vulnerable to attacks. The survivability of RFID tags can be improved by enabling the tags to respond within a pre-defined distance range. RFID tags are restricted to evaluate bit-wise operations and hash functions, but the tag readers exchange separate keys with each tag to authorize the RFID. RFID surveillance system enhances the performance by using three-way communications among the forward channel, backward channel, and enterprise channels and maintains the degree of corrupt tags to a minimum level (Zuo et al. 2010).

4.3.3.2 RFID Tags in Customer Shopping
With an increase in the e-commerce business, tracing tagged objects and tracking the electronic articles through surveillance (electronic article surveillance) has become easy for manufacturers and customers (Melia-Segui et al. 2013). Features of RFID in shopping areas include the following:

- Operational improvement techniques include the installation of tag printers and commissioning equipment to modify or re-label the items with new costs, serial numbering, and stock keeping,
- Using handheld tag reader in uncovered zones of shopping area gives the quick updates for real-time stock inventory,
- RFID systems are used in point-of-sale systems for quick pricing of labels and avoid long queues in the market,
- RFID monitoring systems are installed at doors and entrance to generate alarms during the theft in shopping malls and,
- Virtual RFID systems allow 3D figures of garments and adjust the garment shape. This helps the customer to choose appropriate garment size in locating the selected item.

4.3.3.3 *Missing-Tag Detection*   RFID tags are used to count the number of goods, animals in large farms, birds in the sanctuary, and so on. Missing tag protocols identify the missed or lost items (due to theft or accident) based on the count and identify the number of missed items based on individual tag identity. Time slot-based protocols address the problem of multiple low-band tags competing for channels. The overhead and detection time are proportional to the number of missing tags. The protocol execution time should be less so that the complications of missing tags, updating the goods, and moving the goods from warehouse to containers are maintained at a minimum. Techniques such as base-line, two-phase, and three-phase protocols improve the missing-tag identification, reduce the overhead and decrease the time duration (Li et al. 2013a).

4.3.3.4 *Session-Based Security using RFID*   RFID technology is significantly applied in closed-loop and open-loop applications. In closed-loop RFID applications, the tags are utilized for a dedicated purpose and only authorized tag readers can retrieve the tag information. Closed-loop RFID systems share a unique master key with tag readers irrespective of organization and location. This system does not conceal the information stored on tags. The closed-loop tag manipulation becomes easy for attackers who snoop in the surrounding areas of the tag reader. Open-loop RFID systems use encrypted "handle" or random number-based keys that are communicated via specific channels to the required tag reader to retrieve the information. Hence, the tags are passive and embedded with session-based keys and secure access modules (Wang et al. 2014). In open-loop RFID systems, low-cost tags are used by tag readers in real-time applications. The privacy is protected for suspected-to-be-compromised tags by temporarily blocking the non-reversible operations.

4.4 SECURITY AND TRUST IN WIRELESS SENSOR NETWORKS

Sensor nodes deployed randomly in hostile environments that sense, aggregate, and transmit the information to the base station use multi-hop communications. Sensor

TABLE 4.2   Types of Security Threats and Attacks in Sensor Networks. Reproduced with permission of IEEE

Type of Security Attack	Nature of Attack	Proposed Security and Trust System
Bad mouthing attack	Malicious nodes defame the trusted nodes or increase the trust values of compromised nodes.	Direct trust rate is more than the threshold value and indirect trust considers mean and variance of probability (Sun et al. 2008b)
Colluding and mobile attack	After retrieving the secret keys, the malicious nodes attack the trusted nodes and broadcast the compromised nodes as valid nodes.	Verify and validate time-based sequence numbers of secret key broadcast message (SKBM) and authentication key disclosure message (AKDM) (Tas & Tosun 2011).
Node inconsistencies	Nodes act as untrusted nodes and create inconsistency in the network.	Validate the number of awards and penalties to assess the degree of trust for consistent and inconsistent nodes (Deng et al. 2009).
Node selfishness	Nodes act as non-cooperative nodes and disobey the neighboring nodes.	Measure the probability of node selfishness based on the rate of energy consumption (Bao et al. 2012)
Malicious impersonation attack (e.g., man-in-the middle)	Malicious nodes impersonate the trusted cloud and service providers to target the users.	Measure the cost, trust, and reputation degrees of service provider (Zhu et al. 2015)

nodes are vulnerable to attacks such as spoofing, DoS, colluding and others. Security protocols based on authentication and cryptographic methods ensure the trust across the sensor nodes in the network. In distributed and hierarchical sensor networks, the base station authenticates and assigns the secure keys to sensor nodes in the network. The node reputation depends on the number of successful and unsuccessful transactions for the active session. Table 4.2 represents the types of security threats and attacks in sensor networks.

In large-scale multi-hop communication networks, the cost of key exchange increases between the cluster head node (CH) and sensor nodes in the network. Therefore, mobile sink nodes are deployed in the network to monitor the behavior of sensor nodes and avoid intrusions in the network. Key revocation techniques are invoked when the rate of intrusion increases across the route paths of the network. Symmetric polynomial-based shared keys with reverse hash tags reduces the cryptographic overhead in the sensor network (Wang et al. 2011).

Security and trust management schemes ensure reliable packet transmission between the nodes, and trust management schemes secure the routing paths by providing session-based node identity for packet transmission in the network. Ensuring trust between the sender and receiver node is the primary concern in applications such as military applications, object tracking, and alarm monitoring system, health care systems, and so on. Trust management schemes are centered on reputation-based systems and localization techniques in sensor networks (Srinivasan et al. 2008; Yao et al. 2006).

4.4.1   Trust Management Protocols in Sensor Networks

Static and mobile heterogeneous nodes contribute directly to distributed sensor networks based on cooperative communication and shared spectral resources. The degree of trust defines the quality of services provided by sensor nodes and ensures reliable and robust routing paths in the network (Shaikh et al. 2009). Degree of trust between the networked nodes can be enhanced by using the FRiMA attributes, as illustrated in Figure 4.5, and can be defined as follows (Sun et al. 2008b):

a. **F**aster decision making – When the forwarding node(s) are found to be untrustworthy, then alternative node(s) must be selected to establish the new route paths

b. **Ri**sk adaption – The resource availability and node behavior are predicted within the risk threshold levels

c. **M**alicious behavior detection – Continuous monitoring of node behavior and secure attacks in the network

d. **A**ssessment of quantitative system level security – Assessing the degree of trust across the nodes in sub-network and gateway nodes in the network

4.4.1.1   *Trust-Based Security Solution*   A trust-based security solution (TBSS) provides the confidentiality, access control, and authentication in a network. Since the CH nodes perform data gathering and data aggregation tasks, the trust management schemes vary within each cluster (Ahamed et al. 2009). In reputed-based trust management, the sensor node with threshold bounded energy functions as a data gathering node, a disseminating node and supports the trust management process (Zia et al. 2008). Privacy preserving needs high internal coordination between the nodes and does not reveal the sensitive information to third-party nodes. Resource-aware and quality-aware location monitoring systems help in gathering and aggregating the information from sensor nodes with accuracy (Chow et al. 2011).

4.4.1.2   *Zone-Based Trust Management*   Zone-based trust management systems assume the base station as a fully trusted entity that analyzes the behavior of member nodes at multiple levels (Deng et al. 2009; Ho et al. 2012). Three-level trust awareness method functions as follows: (i) detect the nodes that frequently forge their data, (ii) measure the level of inconsistencies, and (iii) evaluate the node trust levels

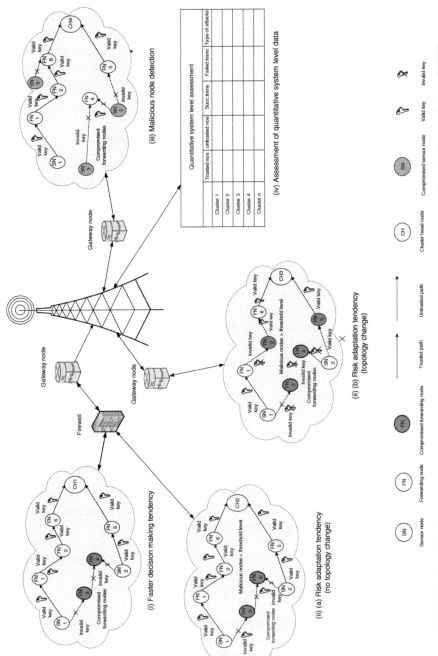

FIGURE 4.5 FRiMA attributes of trust management protocols in sensor networks. Reproduced with permission of IEEE.

during active transactions (Deng et al. 2009). Outlier analysis identifies the node that forges their data frequently, and the base station as gateway node measures the zone transmission inconsistencies using direct or indirect communication. The measured node conflicts are compared with local minimal and maximal values at single and multiple parent levels of the node. Based on these comparisons, a node is penalized or awarded by the parent node with bad or good reputation value. The average node trustworthiness is measured by analyzing the node behavior between the previous transaction period and current transaction period.

A static zone-based sensor network system allows each zone to analyze its reputation levels and update them periodically with the base station. Each zone consists of a group of secure localized nodes with low synchronization and minimum overhead (Ho et al. 2012). An aggregator node from each zone elects its member nodes and sends the aggregated trust levels to the base station. The node behavior after each transaction is evaluated to estimate the trust levels of each zone which is further compared with the threshold levels defined by the base station. The base station preserves the trust levels of each zone based on the number of compromised nodes in each zone. This approach is used for densely compromised nodes in a single zone that can further compromise multiple zones in the network. Periodically, the network operator and base station preloads the secret key, and verifies and validates the reliable active sensor node for each session.

4.4.1.3 Hierarchical Trust Management

In cluster-based sensor networks, the CHs monitor the behavior of one-hop and two-hop neighbors and evaluate the degree of trust across the inter and intra-cluster regions of the network. Hierarchical probabilistic models considers step-wise trust evaluation in which the base station estimates the behavior of CHs and awards the degree of trust to each CH node (Bao et al. 2011; Bao et al. 2012). Further, the CH node evaluates the peer-to-peer trust of every sensor node and identifies the malicious nodes within the cluster. The forwarding nodes observe the social behavior of neighboring nodes and send the information to CHs and the base station. Thus, the base station evaluates the degree of trust objective and validates the paths in the networks.

4.4.1.4 Lightweight Direct and Indirect Trust Management

A lightweight trust decision scheme defines the set of compromised nodes and uncompromised nodes and assigns the degree of trust (0 to 1) to the CH (Li et al. 2013b). This technique considerably reduces the rekeying process and the transmission overheads. The CH node measures the degree of trust by monitoring the node behavior and interaction level with the neighboring nodes (the number of overheard and retransmissions). Based on the status of node behavior, the CH node for reference assigns the degree of indirect trust to the respective sensor nodes, which is not shared with the neighboring nodes.

4.4.1.5 Reputation-Based Trust Management

The tasks performed by the trust and reputation model in sensor networks is categorized as follows: (1) gathering client information and service parameters, and forming a path between the gateway nodes, service providers, and network servers and (2) the service provider and server are assigned valid scores based on response time and the number of successful transaction histories (Mármol & Pérez 2009); this phase forms the rank evaluation to facilitate reputation in the network. (3) The path with maximum score and reputed servers are selected that define route paths and (4) the selected server is decided based on precise and error-free services required by the clients. The server reputation is defined in terms of rewards, punishments, and degree of trust per transaction.

The services of sensor networks can be enhanced by using the services of cloud computing technology that controls and monitors large number of data resources, networking servers, database servers, base stations, connecting components (routers, switches, and controllers), and service providers with distinct functional features and support high degree of trust and reputation across different entities in the network. Reputation-based trust management with cloud and sensor networks estimates the services based on resource cost and number of successful interactions in the network (Chunsheng et al. 2015).

4.5 APPLICATIONS OF INTERNET OF THINGS AND RFID IN REAL-TIME ENVIRONMENT

Low-power, low-cost sensor nodes are deployed randomly in hostile environments, and the IoT provides the flexibility to deploy authentic mobile elements in real-time environment to collect the data from source nodes and forward this information to base station for processing (Borgia et al. 2014). Near-field communication devices such as smartphones, tag readers, and parking meters transmit at 106–424 kilobits per second (kbps) within a range of 10 cm. RFID enabled devices transmit at 640 kbps within a range of 3–10 m. Sensor nodes transmit at 250 kbps covering a distance of 10–100 m. Horizontal application model consists of smart devices and tag readers that collect the physical data from source nodes or RFID tags (Borgia et al. 2014). Further, data is forwarded to the base station for IoT servers for the querying and processing of tasks. Table 4.3 represents the properties of RFIDs with respect to sensor networks and IoT (Marquardt et al. 2010).

4.5.1 Vehicular IoT

Embedding IoT sensors on cars, buses and autonomous vehicles facilitate enhanced navigation in the road and traffic management in crowded cities (Gerla et al. 2014). IoT vehicular sensors support system intelligence based on services (such as restaurants, parks, hospitals, and banks), travel schedule, and low-traffic routes of the city. This further reduces the complexity of the traditional vehicular grid and support autonomous serving needs Internet and cloud-connected vehicles. This technology leads to the design of autonomous vehicles with unmanned and self-driving capability. IoT sensors check the pollution level of vehicles and contribute to the clean environment. The service of IoT vehicular sensor for Internet and cloud-connected autonomous vehicles are highlighted as follows:

TABLE 4.3 Properties of RFIDs with respect to WSN and IoT. Reproduced with permission of IEEE

Properties	Relevance to Wireless Sensor Networks and Internet of Things	Advantages	Disadvantages
Identification and sensing	Reveal the identities, location and message to authentic sensor nodes, smart devices, and servers in the neighborhood	People, animals, goods, and documents	Intruders can track movement of security personnel equipment and vital documents.
Invisibility of tags	Authentic nodes must be seized to compromise the node behavior	Small in size and can be embedded in layers unknown to the user	Can be misused by the snoopers and defaulters
Invisibility of tag usage	Increases the reliability of network services	Tags can be read multiple times.	Malicious card readers can read valid information
Unique identity	Event monitoring and warning systems	Global unique identity distinguishes the genuine product.	Authentic goods can be forged if the tag reader supports multiple scans of same product.
Availability	Sensor nodes and networking devices can be tracked at any instant and issue an alarm that threaten the privacy of network.	Once activated, the tags respond to valid requests.	Information can be sent to malicious node.
Autonomy	Base stations install tag readers to trace the presence of nodes and devices in the network.	Tags are read by unique readers and do not respond to other wireless equipment such as mobile scanners and secure camera.	Special equipment is installed at entry and exit points to monitor the presence of RFID-enabled devices.
Passive	Long withstanding and unused tags are vulnerable and degrade the privacy of network.	Do not transmit signals	Intruders identify the long withstanding RFID devices to compromise the product and network.

i. Timely-alert messages: Provide information regarding traffic-free routes, work in progress at various location routes of the city, location and types of service centers, and issue alarm message for crossing the speed limits.

ii. Service-oriented messages: Provide route maps to restaurants, banks, business centers, hospitals, critical routes (that are accident prone) of the city.

iii. Collaborative service messages: Monitoring vehicular speed limits and recording the duration of vehicles parked with the license number and user identity. Sharing the collaborative service information with police personnel will identify the location of vehicular accidents and burglary in the city.

iv. Vehicular grid and cloud-based service messages: RFID tags are embedded in vehicles to monitor, trace, and track the vehicle movements and share this information in IoT cloud to generate a vehicular grid. Global positioning system (GPS) and controller area network (CAN) bus sensor tracking systems are used to retrieve the location positions of vehicles.

4.5.2 Advance Services in Internet of Things

Advanced IoT (AIoT) identifies and connects the nodes, devices, servers, etc., and uses add-on tools to manage the services of connected components in the IoT (Zhang & Mitton 2011). Distributed IoT architecture enables node interaction with respect to network services in varying traffic conditions. Object naming in AIoT maps the object ID with an IP address of a service provider and a unified object description language (UODL) addresses cloud computing issues in distributed systems. This provides flexibility to enable the devices (IoT-based) with policies and services (network access rights, tariff services of network operators) based on user specifications. The hexadecimal format of AIoT identity field comprises the model number, serial number, location identity, and manufacturer code with month and year. After verifying the unique code from each field of the tag, an action is triggered to delete the item code from the database and perform a database update. AIoT architecture consists of the following four modules (Zhang & Mitton 2011):

1. Advanced Object Naming Service (AONS)
2. Service Supplier Domain (SSD)
3. IoT user device with standard interface
4. Destination Object

The AONS module matches the object ID and IP address of the supplier server. The transactions are enabled for objects with valid standard identity (SID) that allows public naming service of the route paths for matching actions specified by SSD. Public key IDs are correlated and actual transactions are committed through the exchange of private keys, and the SSD services are updated. Service Supplier Domain reduces the complexity of supplier server through action engine (AE) and object server. AIoT standard interface embedded in AIoT user device guides the user to invoke the corresponding AIoT objects present in the network neighborhood area. Operations such as ADD, DELETE, and UPDATE are performed, and the information is stored in the Object Servers of SSD.

4.6 FUTURE RESEARCH DIRECTIONS AND CONCLUSION

IoT security systems aim to overcome the barriers in distributed systems. RFID tags with secure, intelligent algorithms, sensor network with dynamic key management and IoT-enabled devices for delay tolerant networks, and ubiquitous networks form the innovative research area in IoT technology. Security, trust, and reputation for IoT-based connecting components are evaluated at regular intervals using cloud computing services. Security and trust systems for complex distributed systems that define reusable and intelligent objects need to be applied in IoT-based applications.

IoT combines the aspects of ubiquitous, pervasive, RFID, cloud and sensor network technologies with the Internet-enabled services. Automation of knowledge, devices, vehicles, and IoT are the basic features of cyber-physical systems. This chapter features functional aspects of security and trust management in IoT-enabled devices, RFID and sensor network. RFID, WSNs, and smartphones form the key components in IoT technology. The degree of trust and reputation define the security attributes in IoT. Architecture and functional aspects of trust management protocols in IoT, RFID, and sensor network are elucidated in detail. This chapter highlights the features of distributed trust management in IoT. The significance of RFIDs in maintaining the security and trust in IoT-enabled devices is due to tag traceability. Key management and degree of trust, repudiation in sensor network establishes cooperative communication across the nodes in the network.

REFERENCES

Ahamed, S.I., Kim, D., Hasan, C.S., & Zulkernine, M. 2009. Towards developing a trust-based security solution. In: Proceedings of the 2009 ACM symposium on Applied Computing, March 2009, pp. 2204–2205.

Arbit, A., Oren, Y., & Wool, A. 2014. A secure supply-chain RFID system that respects your privacy. *Pervasive Computing, IEEE*, 13(2), pp. 52–60.

Ashraf, Q.M., & Habaebi, M.H. 2015. Autonomic schemes for threat mitigation in Internet of Things. *Journal of Network and Computer Applications*, 49, pp. 112–127.

Atzori, L., Iera, A., & Morabito, G. 2010. The Internet of things: a survey. *Computer Networks*, 54(15), pp. 2787–2805.

Bao, F., Chen, I.R., Chang, M., & Cho, J.H. 2011. Trust-based intrusion detection in wireless sensor networks. In: 2011 IEEE International Conference on Communications, pp. 1–6.

Bao, F., Chen, I.R., Chang, M., & Cho, J.H. 2012. Hierarchical trust management for wireless sensor networks and its applications to trust-based routing and intrusion detection. *IEEE Transactions on Network and Service Management*, 9(2), pp. 169–183.

Boukerch, A., Xu, L., & El-Khatib, K. 2007. Trust-based security for wireless ad hoc and sensor networks. *Computer Communications*, 30(11), pp. 2413–2427.

Borgia, E. 2014. The Internet of Things vision: key features, applications and open issues. *Computer Communications*, 54, pp. 1–31.

Burmester, M., Kotznanikolaou, P., & Douligeris, C. 2007. Security in Mobile Ad-hoc Networks. In: *Network Security Current Status and Future Directions*, D.N.S. Christos Douligeris (Ed.). Wiley-IEEE Press, John Wiley & Sons Inc., pp. 355–371.

Chen, R., Guo, J., & Bao, F. 2014, April. Trust management for service composition in SOA-based IoT systems. In: 2014 IEEE Wireless Communications and Networking Conference, pp. 3444–3449.

Chow, C.Y., Mokbel, M.F., & He, T. 2011. A privacy-preserving location monitoring system for wireless sensor networks. *IEEE Transactions on Mobile Computing*, 10(1), pp. 94–107.

Deng, H., Jin, G., Sun, K., Xu, R., Lyell, M., & Luke, J.A. 2009. Trust-aware in-network aggregation for wireless sensor networks. In: Global Telecommunications Conference, 2009. GLOBECOM November 2009, pp. 1–8.

Gerla, M., Lee, E.K., Pau, G., & Lee, U. 2014. Internet of vehicles: From intelligent grid to autonomous cars and vehicular clouds. In: 2014 IEEE World Forum on Internet of Things, March 2014, pp. 241–246.

Gessner, D., Olivereau, A., Segura, A.S., & Serbanati, A. 2012. Trustworthy infrastructure services for a secure and privacy-respecting Internet of Things. In: 2012 IEEE 11th International Conference on Trust, Security and Privacy in Computing and Communications, June 2012, pp. 998–1003.

Gubbi, J., Buyya, R., Marusic, S., & Palaniswami, M. 2013. Internet of Things (IoT): a vision, architectural elements, and future directions. *Future Generation Computer Systems*, 29(7), pp. 1645–1660.

Kothmayr, T., Schmitt, C., Hu, W., Brünig, M., & Carle, G. 2013. DTLS based security and two-way authentication for the Internet of Things. *Ad Hoc Networks*, 11(8), pp. 2710–2723.

Heer, T., Garcia-Morchon, O., Hummen, R., Keoh, S.L., Kumar, S.S., & Wehrle, K. 2011. Security Challenges in the IP-based Internet of Things. *Wireless Personal Communications*, 61(3), pp. 527–542.

Ho, J.W., Wright, M., & Das, S.K. 2012. ZoneTrust: Fast zone-based node compromise detection and revocation in wireless sensor networks using sequential hypothesis testing. *IEEE Transactions on Dependable and Secure Computing*, 9(4), pp. 494–511.

Langheinrich, M. 2009. A survey of RFID privacy approaches. *Personal and Ubiquitous Computing*, 13(6), pp. 413–421.

Lehtonen, M.O., Michahelles, F., & Fleisch, E. 2007. Trust and security in RFID-based product authentication systems. *IEEE Systems Journal*, 1(2), pp. 129–144.

Li, T., Chen, S., & Ling, Y. 2013a. Efficient protocols for identifying the missing tags in a large RFID system. *IEEE/ACM Transactions on Networking*, 21(6), pp. 1974–1987.

Li, X., Zhou, F., & Du, J. 2013b. LDTS: a lightweight and dependable trust system for clustered wireless sensor networks. *IEEE Transactions on Information Forensics and Security*, 8(6), pp. 924–935.

Lopez, J., Roman, R., Agudo, I., & Fernandez-Gago, C. 2010. Trust management systems for wireless sensor networks: Best practices. *Computer Communications*, 33(9), pp. 1086–1093.

Mármol, F.G., & Pérez, G.M. 2009. TRMSim-WSN, trust and reputation models simulator for wireless sensor networks. In: IEEE International Conference on Communications, ICC'09, June 2009, pp. 1–5.

Marquardt, N., Taylor, A.S., Villar, N., & Greenberg, S. 2010. Rethinking RFID: awareness and control for interaction with RFID systems. In: Proceedings of the SIGCHI Conference on Human Factors in Computing Systems, April 2010, pp. 2307–2316.

Melià-Seguí, J., Pous, R., Carreras, A., Morenza-Cinos, M., Parada, R., Liaghat, Z., & De Porrata-Doria, R. 2013. Enhancing the shopping experience through RFID in an actual retail store. In: Proceedings of the 2013 ACM conference on Pervasive and ubiquitous computing adjunct publication, September 2013, pp. 1029–1036.

Nguyen, K.T., Laurent, M., & Oualha, N. 2015. Survey on secure communication protocols for the Internet of Things. *Ad Hoc Networks*, 32, pp. 17–31.

Prasithsangaree, P., & Krishnamurthy, P. 2004. On a framework for energy-efficient security protocols in wireless networks. *Computer Communications*, 27(17), pp. 1716–1729.

Roman, R., Zhou, J., & Lopez, J. 2013. On the features and challenges of security and privacy in distributed Internet of things. *Computer Networks*, 57(10), pp. 2266–2279.

Saied, Y.B., Olivereau, A., Zeghlache, D., & Laurent, M. 2014. Lightweight collaborative key establishment scheme for the Internet of Things. *Computer Networks*, 64, pp. 273–295.

Sicari, S., Rizzardi, A., Grieco, L.A., & Coen-Porisini, A. 2015. Security, privacy and trust in Internet of Things: The road ahead. *Computer Networks*, 76, pp. 146–164.

Shaikh, R.A., Jameel, H., d'Auriol, B.J., Lee, H., Lee, S., & Song, Y.J. 2009. Group-based trust management scheme for clustered wireless sensor networks. *IEEE Transactions on Parallel and Distributed Systems*, 20(11), pp. 1698–1712.

Srinivasan, A., Li, F., & Wu, J. 2008. A novel CDS-based reputation monitoring system for wireless sensor networks. In: 28th International Conference on Distributed Computing Systems Workshops, June 2008, pp. 364–369.

Sun, B., Xiao, Y., Li, C.C., Chen, H.H., & Yang, T.A. 2008a. Security co-existence of wireless sensor networks and RFID for pervasive computing. *Computer Communications*, 31(18), pp. 4294–4303.

Sun, Y., Han, Z., & Liu, K.R. 2008b. Defense of trust management vulnerabilities in distributed networks. *Communications Magazine, IEEE*, 46(2), pp. 112–119.

Tas, B., & Tosun, A.Ş. 2011. Mobile assisted key distribution in wireless sensor networks. In: 2011 IEEE International Conference on Communications, June 2011, pp. 1–6.

Veltri, L., Cirani, S., Busanelli, S., & Ferrari, G. 2013. A novel batch-based group key management protocol applied to the Internet of Things. *Ad Hoc Networks*, 11(8), pp. 2724–2737.

Wang, L.M., Jiang, T., & Zhu, X.Y. 2011. Updatable key management scheme with intrusion tolerance for unattended wireless sensor network. In: 2011 IEEE Global Telecommunications Conference, GLOBECOM, December 2011, pp. 1–5.

Wang, J., Floerkemeier, C., & Sarma, S.E. 2014. Session-based security enhancement of RFID systems for emerging open-loop applications. *Personal and Ubiquitous Computing*, 18(8), pp. 1881–1891.

Yan, Z., Zhang, P., & Vasilakos, A.V. 2014. A survey on trust management for Internet of Things. *Journal of network and computer applications*, 42, pp. 120–134.

Yao, Z., Kim, D., & Doh, Y. 2006. PLUS: Parameterized and localized trust management scheme for sensor networks security. In: 2006 IEEE International Conference on Mobile Ad hoc and Sensor Systems, October 2006, pp. 437–446.

Zhang, L., & Mitton, N. 2011. Advanced Internet of things. In: Internet of things, 2011 International Conference on and 4th International Conference on Cyber, Physical and Social Computing, iThings/CPSCom, October 2011, pp. 1–8.

Zhou, L., & Chao, H.C. 2011. Multimedia traffic security architecture for the Internet of things. *IEEE Network*, 25(3), pp. 35–40.

Zhu, C., Nicanfar, H., Leung, V.C., & Yang, L.T. 2015. An authenticated trust and reputation calculation and management system for cloud and sensor networks integration. *IEEE Transactions on Information Forensics and Security*, 10(1), pp. 118–131.

Zia, T.A. 2008. Reputation-based trust management in wireless sensor networks. In: ISSNIP 2008. International Conference on Intelligent Sensors, Sensor Networks and Information Processing, December 2008, pp. 163–166.

Zuo, Y. 2010. RFID survivability quantification and attack modeling. In: Proceedings of the Third ACM Conference on Wireless Network Security, March 2010, pp. 13–18.

CHAPTER 5

THE IMPACT OF IoT DEVICES ON NETWORK TRUST BOUNDARIES

NICOLE NEWMEYER

U.S. Department of Defense, Fort Meade, MD, USA

5.1 INTRODUCTION

The growth of the Internet of Things (IoT) market today owes much of its success to the increasing conveniences the combinations of devices can provide to consumers. Those consumers range from home users to vehicle manufacturers, to retail, and industrial complexes; their use cases are as varied as their environments, and each has a separate segment of the IoT market dedicated to their needs.[1] Unfortunately, convenience is far from the only factor that should be taken into consideration when deciding whether to integrate IoT devices with existing infrastructure. One factor that is too often minimized is the impact of the individual IoT devices on the security posture of the network. This concept had been discussed from a mobile focus for years; by 2007, much had been published on the potential impact of this technology evolution; much of the concern is immediately applicable to the position of IoT devices today. The primary issue was often referenced as a boundary issue, some described it as "the line that currently divides these handheld devices from typical network computers will become very unclear" (Derr 2007). With the evolution of IoT devices, this issue is currently exacerbated by the absence of an agreed upon security architecture for IoT; there are a variety of working groups discussing the issue, but none are close to a consensus. The current spread of protocols that fall within the IoT realm make it difficult to define consistent protocol security or interoperability standards as well. As the IoT industry, as a whole, grows more mature, these security mechanisms will undoubtedly face more scrutiny; to account for their current absence, today it is the responsibility of the network owner to make risk determinations regarding the inclusion of IoT devices.

---

[1] http://www.beechamresearch.com/download.aspx?id=41

Cyber-Assurance for the Internet of Things, First Edition. Edited by Tyson T. Brooks.
© 2017 by The Institute of Electrical and Electronic Engineers, Inc. Published 2017 by John Wiley & Sons, Inc.

5.2   TRUST BOUNDARIES

Traditionally system trust boundaries have been defined statically; it was always possible for a system owner to quantify the exact devices that were connected to his or her network. Over time, as wireless computing devices became more widely adopted and integrated with enterprise networks, system owners were forced to adjust their concept of static trust to one that included laptops, tablets, and all other corporate devices that connected into the network wirelessly. Wireless intrusion detection (WID) and wireless intrusion prevention systems (WIPS) were widely deployed to help monitor the new trust boundary and mitigate the risk associated with the introduction of the (then) newly adopted technology. While networks with integrated wireless endpoint and midpoint devices have more complicated architecture than traditional wired networks, they are still static networks from the perspective of trust decisions. The system owners explicitly define which devices and types of communication are included within the trusted segment of their networks and are aware of each device's communication capabilities.

As IoT devices creep into enterprise networks, sometimes without the awareness of the system owner, neither the traditional trust boundary definition nor the modified definitions for networks with wireless components are sufficient. Current WIDS/WIPS are structured to focus on standardized radio frequency (RF) protocols that are primarily used in wireless and mobile computing. While some support short-range protocols such as Bluetooth or Bluetooth Low Energy, the nature of the short-range protocols themselves limits the effectiveness of most current WIDS architectures. As short-range protocols such as Bluetooth Low Energy, ZigBee, and Z-Wave are designed for communication over much shorter distances than the 802.11a/b/g/n suites that current WIDS/WIPS are designed to focus on, there is an extremely high likelihood that a device communicating over a short-range RF protocol would not be visible to a currently deployed WIDS/WIPS. As an example, a fitness band communicating using Bluetooth Low Energy could optimally be expected to pair with another device within 10 m, but, with a slightly different class of radio, the communication distance could be as short as 1 m; in an enterprise scenario, that would mean a user would always have to be within 10 m (generously) of a WIDS/WIPS in order for their fitness band communications to be visible to the system (Lee et al. 2007). Given that current best practices for WIDS/WIPS deployments often recommend one WIDS/WIPS node for every five wireless APs, it becomes even more unlikely that the fitness band would be visible to the WIDS/WIPS. Without focusing too heavily on the intrusion detection and prevention as it relates to IoT devices and protocols, the realization that the current WIDS/WIDS strategy is ineffective against the short-range RF protocols often used in IoT capabilities is a vital component in scoping the concern surrounding network trust boundaries and IoT devices.

A structure for defining trust boundaries for IoT devices must take into account the current lack of comprehensive intrusion detection or prevention system for IoT capabilities. It is that understanding that will help an enterprise system owner comprehend the differences that IoT devices will force in their networks. As the IoT market is incredibly broad, determining an approach to defining a trust boundary also necessitates an understanding of the potential IoT verticals that could interact with the enterprise networks. This approach focuses on the system owner's efforts, and should minimize the types of IoT protocols and devices that are taken into consideration. An example of this decision process would be including consumer and home devices, as an employee could bring these devices into the enterprise environment, including smart building and green building devices, as they are potentially already in the enterprise environment, but intentionally not including industrial distribution systems and protocols, as the enterprise does not interact with materials handling, materials pipelines, or conveyance systems.

The potential complications to this decision process arise when a system owner is unaware of potential interactions between an IoT vertical and the enterprise for which the trust boundaries are being defined. This could easily occur due to the breadth and complexity of IoT technologies; an example of this oversight would be a system owner making the determination that there is no need to take transportation and vehicle telematics systems into account, based on the specific enterprise not working with transportation in any way. Unfortunately, that decision would also cause the system owner to miss a number of IoT technologies that could have significant access to their core network; parking sensor systems, telematics from vehicles parking or traveling within a short distance of the enterprise facilities, and traffic signals within close proximity of the facility all have the potential to attempt communication with components within the enterprise network. These categorization decisions also have to be updated on a regular basis. As IoT technologies continue to evolve, and commercial adoption increases, IoT verticals that may legitimately not interact with an enterprise network today could have the potential to interact in the future. The IoT market is far from static, system owners will have to adapt their approach and security measures with the evolving IoT technologies.

The initial determination of which IoT verticals to focus on is only the beginning of the process. A system owner must then understand the breadth of communication mechanisms possible for the categories of IoT devices they intend to initially address. This understanding is crucial, as many IoT devices are capable of communicating over more than one mechanism. Looking at mobile devices, smartphones communicate over traditional cellular, Wi-Fi, and Bluetooth, among a number of other types of RF. The network owner must be aware of these possibilities; this awareness could prevent a device within the trusted network segment from being monitored on its Wi-Fi interface, but ignored on its backup cellular communication path that sends status information to the manufacturer and potentially others if compromised. Developing this understanding is complicated by the speed of evolution of the IoT market.

Smart watches provide a recent example of the concern; after consumers purchased the devices, they were provided a software update that activated an additional Wi-Fi capability to a device that was constructed with a Wi-Fi chip, but initially deployed with only a cellular communication capability. Another concern to the system owner are devices, such as snack machines that are delivered and installed with a primary and backup communications mechanism designed to send status information to the manufacturer or servicing organization. These devices fall well within the assumed physical trust boundary of the enterprise, but are not maintained or monitored by enterprise systems. The potential risk implications need to be taken into account by the system owner, who may not be aware of the multiple communications paths included within the device or the networks to which the device is designed to connect to.

Once this understanding has been developed, the system owner must then take into account the potential different approval levels of IoT devices within the enterprise network. This can be addressed by dividing the trust boundary discussion into two sides: how an approved IoT device affects the security posture when accepted into the trust boundary of a network, and how an unapproved IoT device affects the security posture when interacting with devices that fall within the trust boundary of a network. Each category of IoT device can be assessed to have a different impact when included within the trust boundary of the network, or intentionally excluded. From this perspective, two primary example IoT devices can effectively illustrate the complexities of each decision a network owner could make. Smart TVs and wearable fitness monitors will serve as basic examples of devices that most network owners will be forced to make risk decisions about in the near future. Given a relatively new building with some automation capability, such as motion sensing lights, dual factor authentication entry systems, and building control that adjusts temperature, it is possible to make high-level risk assessments based on separate use cases for each use of the smart TV and wearable fitness monitor.

5.2.1 Trusted Device

As IoT devices become more integrated with technologies that are traditionally a component of enterprise networks, it is now necessary to define trust boundaries that include specific IoT devices. These trust boundaries need to address every potential communication path of the included devices, as well as all of the potential networks the devices will attempt to connect to. This will become more complicated as devices are produced with broader communication capabilities and secondary communication paths designed to activate when primary paths are not available.

While many are focused on the consumer and home-focused IoT products, the range of capabilities that will be introduced into an enterprise or office building scenario is growing every day. Environmental optimization capabilities, often referenced as green building technologies, are frequently required in new construction or when a facility is being rehabilitated. These capabilities, including motion sensors, smart light bulbs, air quality sensors, door locks, and parking optimization sensors, have not traditionally been included in network security or information technology discussions; however, as the RF footprint and connectivity of these devices continues to increase, considering how to address them from an assurance standpoint will be necessary. Other technologies, more obviously associated with use in an enterprise setting, are currently included within the trust boundary of the network; however, most of those devices are being assessed from a traditional perspective and not from a connected, IoT perspective.

A first example is the smart TV scenario. Within this context, smart TV addresses any television that connects to the Internet for software updates, attempts to retrieve or display content from a cloud service, or requires RF connectivity to perform a predetermined function. While this capability obviously has relevance within a home scenario, it also has significant bearing on the enterprise scenario. With the smart TV market growing at an estimated 21% annually through 2018 with over 90% of sets actually connected by 2016, it will become increasingly difficult to purchase a television that is not a smart TV in the near future (O'Neill 2015). While most enterprises do not use televisions in the same way that home consumers do, there are still quite a few use cases for televisions in the enterprise environment. Welcome displays, security operations center monitors, video teleconferencing (VTC) systems, presentation displays, all rely on the same television models as are available to the consumer market; and as a result, they have the same level of connectivity as a person's smart TV in the home. With that level of connectivity comes even more work for the system owner. One specific use case can be used to explain the additional perspective necessary: addressing the smart TV as a connected television that the network owner intends to use as a conference room display mechanism. To support this use case, the smart TV would be connected directly into the business's computer network. While this would easily enable leveraging the smart TV to support briefings and VTC sessions, it also adds an unmanaged wireless device with a direct connection to the information stored within the core of the network. The system owner may not have configured the wireless interface of the smart TV, and may not have even been aware of its existence; but many smart TVs are configured by default to communicate over wireless (cellular or Wi-Fi) to the device manufacturer's cloud or to the reseller's monitoring system for maintenance purposes. The risk of such a connection increases with the level of trust placed in the smart TV, and the tiers of data it has access to.

The risk could be said to increase further if the system owner is not aware of the different communications paths the smart TV natively supports. For instance, if the system owner is aware of the smart TV's Wi-Fi communication with the manufacturers and monitors that communication path, but is unaware of the secondary cellular backhaul configuration, it would be possible to miss a compromise. The system owner also should take into account any possible interactions between the smart TV and the building's automation systems; if the smart TV is considered to fall within the trust boundary of the computer network and the smart TV communicates in any way with the building automation or control systems, the building control systems are technically then an extension of that trust relationship. If the system owner does not have complete insight into every device directly and indirectly connected to his or her network, it will be impossible to make accurate risk decisions. By now, it should be beginning to sound like an incredible amount of work for the system owner; and unfortunately that may be accurate, until monitoring technologies catch up with the needs of the system owner; but this advance in monitoring technology will not happen until the system owner understands the true breadth of implications of the evolution of IoT.

This evolution relates not only to basic communications functionality of IoT devices, but it has impacts throughout the entire device lifecycle. Exploring a few examples within the same use case of a smart TV being used for a presentation display system will help illustrate some of the dependencies. First, the upgrade process, both hardware and software, must be considered. In many commercial enterprises, technology refresh procedures are driven by requirements in a contract, whether that contract stipulates that desktops must be no older than three years, or that the devices must be currently supported by the manufacturer for software upgrades, or any other variant. From the perspective of a system owner, it would be expected that the upgraded devices would be at a minimum of the current version that supports the minimum requirements of the enterprise; and it would be a reasonable assumption that the device's security posture would be similar to the device it was replacing. Unfortunately, those assumptions no longer hold true. As the IoT market expands, an enterprise upgrading their presentation system could easily select the current version of the same television display they have currently installed in their facility without realizing that it now comes with additional communication capability or that a new version of a device could automatically be added to an approved products list because it met the basic functional or security requirements on paper, without the knowledge that the newer version now required a wireless connection out of the enterprise network; then, throughout the enterprise, administrators could easily assume that the new connectivity was approved and leverage that communications path for enterprise needs.

From the perspective of the system owner, the concern associated with hardware upgrades should be mirrored by the level of concern associated with software upgrade paths. Many smart TVs currently connect back to the manufacturer's cloud to check for software updates, and if available the updates are installed over the wireless connection (whether primary or secondary). As there are no unified standards across IoT verticals, or even within verticals, a system owner has to question what assurance there is in these upgrades. While some do perform these upgrades over secure hypertext transfer protocol (S-HTTP), there is no broad standard; these examples are not intended to indicate that no manufacturer is including security in their products, just that it is the responsibility of the system owner to ensure that the products that fall within their networks do meet their enterprise's security standards.

Once a system owner is confident that an IoT device meets the security standards of the enterprise, more assessments need to be completed before including the device within the network's trust boundary. If the device communicates using mechanisms that the enterprise's current monitoring and defense systems are not capable of covering, the system owner must find a way to mitigate that gap. This includes not only the intrusion detection and prevention systems, but the analytic components and the display interface with the network security professionals as well. The communications mechanism and protocols are not the only concern, unfortunately; throughput begins to become a serious concern if an enterprise's sensor network is not ready for the additional influx of raw data that multiple IoT devices will bring. From the analytic perspective, traffic from these approved devices must be quantified in a way that allows the analyst to determine which traffic is normal and which traffic is abnormal; in the current, uncoordinated IoT market, this could easily require the creation of specific analytics for each type of communication from each type of device.

With the understanding of communication capabilities of an IoT device, monitoring and analytic capabilities that support both positive and negative identification of activity from the IoT device, the system owner has all of the building blocks for developing a trust model for the device in question. Again, referencing the smart TV being used in a presentation system, the use case is critical to making the trust decisions. At this point, the system owner is capable of determining what devices and areas of the network the smart TV needs access to in order to function as intended. Once those areas are identified, the system owner must assess what external communications are required by the device and make a risk decision based on the monitoring and defensive capabilities that are available to cover the gaps. For instance, historically the television used for presentation may have been connected directly into the network and could have been addressable by any number of computers to drive the display. Once that television is upgraded to a smart TV, the network owner could determine that the new preferred connection model would be directly to a single computer, with no further credentials to the network. In this new architecture, the smart TV is still within the trust boundary, as it has access to trusted data within the network and does connect to trusted machines, but it does not have unfettered access to the entire trusted core of the network. This approach could be used to minimize potential intellectual property exposure if there was a compromise leveraging the smart TV's external communication capabilities.

Despite the breadth of understanding and work required, the smart TV example is one of the simplest and cleanest, as it does not change the nature of the trust boundary; it is still static, device-specific, and quantifiable. The network owner is aware of all of the approved network components, and can monitor all of the approved components for signs of compromise. Building on that required understanding, whether it is understanding that the system owner holds, or understanding that has been developed and integrated into monitoring and defensive capabilities, addressing untrusted devices becomes even more complex.

5.2.2 Untrusted Device

Developing upon the understanding built while assessing how to include an IoT device as a trusted component of the enterprise network, the system owner then has to address the more complex portion of the IoT evolution: untrusted devices. Untrusted devices can become exponentially more difficult to handle than trusted devices, especially if they are not enterprise-owned, or if they travel between enterprise networks. Using the simplest decomposition, there are two primary categories of untrusted devices: approved but untrusted, and unapproved and untrusted. Approved by untrusted devices are devices that the system owner has approved for interaction with enterprise systems, but does not have access to any trusted enterprise network components. Unapproved and untrusted devices are just as straightforward, they are devices that have not been approved for any interaction with enterprise systems, and do not have access to any trusted enterprise network components.

5.2.2.1 *Approved but Untrusted*   One category of devices currently at the forefront of the "approved by untrusted" category is wearable fitness devices. Even that category can be used to reference a broad array of individual capabilities, from fitness bands to sensors embedded in clothing, to sensors adhered to the body during exercise

sessions; to simplify the issue as much as possible, initially only fitness bands will be discussed. Wearable fitness devices pose a similar, but in some ways more complex, issue for the system owner. While the smart TV will have a fairly fixed location and power consumption posture, wearable fitness devices are inconstant. They can never be expected to have a fixed location, and often support multiple communications protocols; one benefit is that there is very little reason to consider a wearable fitness device as having an equivalent level of trust to a core network server. Given that lower expectation of trust, a system owner must then be concerned with what accesses, intentional or unintentional, are being provided to these devices. If users are connecting their fitness devices to resources controlled by the system owner for charging or syncing purposes, which connectivity must be taken into account when determining what level of trust is being extended to these devices? Are they being provided access to sensitive intellectual property by using a computer as a proxy? If that is a concern of the system owner, can the enterprise's monitoring capabilities detect that behavior? While a fitness band currently may not have a significant amount of storage or transmission capability, a system owner should never assume that as the technology evolves the capacity of the devices will not change. Such devices and tertiary connectivity to the trusted core network may not be of concern to a particular enterprise system owner based on the currently available technology, but that decision needs to be repeatedly evaluated as IoT devices become more capable.

A simple software upgrade, such as one enabling mesh communication may be enough to change a system owner's trust posture for wearable fitness devices. Where previously a system owner may not have cared if employees charged their devices using the USB interface of the enterprise computers, once that device has the capability to communicate with any other fitness band or small sensor using mesh, such as in the upcoming Bluetooth release, the system owner may determine that additional functionality changes the risk posture significantly enough to force a change in the trust model for the enterprise systems. In that case, the system owner would then need to ensure the monitoring systems could detect if that USB connection was being made after the change in trust boundaries, to help mitigate unintentional compromise.

While there is currently a glut of protocols used across IoT devices, there are a few that are leveraged across many IoT verticals. That commonality provides significant benefits regarding streamlining communication, and it also has the potential of causing concern; this is especially true in the case where the communications security mechanisms surrounding the use of the protocol are not defined or adhered to appropriately, specifically referencing authentication, identification, and integrity measures discussed in subsequent chapters. One extremely compelling example is the potential interconnection between smart building control systems and a wearable fitness device. Many smart building and green building technologies are being built to leverage protocols and chipsets that have already been tested and widely used; this benefits the manufacturers because it is a component they can drop in to an existing design without significant additional work. However, if the protocols are not being used to effectively leverage all of the included security benefits of the protocol suite, additional risk is incurred by the system owners. Within smart building and green building systems, that would mean ensuring every communication, both sensor-to-sensor and sensor-to-hub, verified the identity of the sender and receiver, as well as verified the integrity of the message (among other actions). As the smart building and green building IoT technologies are still evolving, it could be perceived as reasonable to assume that certain device manufacturers have not yet implemented that level of security into their components, whether they are smart light bulbs, carbon dioxide sensors, or motion sensors. If that is the case, and the building's control systems are communicating over low-energy Bluetooth in the same way that a user's wearable fitness device is, that opens the door for the components to identify each other using basic Bluetooth Low Energy functionalities; which does mean that information is being exchanged. Assuming that the enterprise system owner can gain access to the detailed information about the smart building and green building sensors deployed across the enterprise, the system owner must weigh the potential consequences of these connections, whether robust or intermittent, and take the implications into account when making every risk decision relating to IoT devices.

To further increase the complexity of the systems, the enterprise's monitoring and network defense capabilities must be capable of identifying both the approved and unapproved types of communication to effectively enforce the trust model decisions that were made by the system owner. Again, using the wearable fitness device as an example, the monitoring system must have an effective means of tracking low energy Bluetooth and other short-range transmission protocols, and the systems must be able to differentiate between normal use of the fitness band and unapproved use; in this case, that could be connection over USB to an enterprise computer, or communication with smart building components that support the same protocol suites. This only differs from the monitoring requirements in the trusted device use case in one primary way, even the approved communication should not be connecting to the trusted enterprise network; so the monitoring systems must be able to both identify the approved communication and all systems involved in the communication.

Wearable fitness devices can be used to illustrate one additional aspect of the potential assurance concern when introducing IoT devices into an enterprise network, the transiency of the devices themselves. When viewing a traditional, static, enterprise network, most devices will not be mobile enough to connect regularly at multiple points in the enterprise network. Wearable fitness devices do not fall within that same pattern. Moving to every room the enterprise employee accesses, the wearable fitness devices have the potential to touch numerous components within the enterprise network; from the system owner's perspective, that means that every piece of the network must have the same monitoring and defensive capabilities against any potential compromise from these devices. The next connectivity behavior of wearable fitness devices that needs to be considered by a system owner is their connection to remote untrusted networks. Many enterprises have already developed trust models that allow enterprise-owned laptops or tablets to connect to both the trusted network and untrusted networks, often securing the communications with a virtual private network (VPN) and segregating the components of the trusted core network that can be accessed remotely. The wearable fitness devices differ significantly from the laptops from a trust perspective; the laptops are trusted devices, expected to connect into the enterprise's core network. The wearable fitness devices, in this use case, are approved to be within the enterprise network's boundaries, but are not trusted and able to access any sensitive enterprise data. So, the VPN solution in the laptop trust model does not directly apply to the wearable fitness device concern, but the system owner must still develop a risk acceptance or mitigation plan that addresses the connection of IoT devices to remote untrusted networks as well as the enterprise network.

5.2.2.2 Unapproved and Untrusted The final, and potentially easiest to classify, category of IoT devices to be addressed from the system owner's perspective are unapproved and untrusted devices. Effectively, these are IoT devices that a system owner has either explicitly disapproved from connecting to enterprise networks, or has not made an acceptance decision on at the time in question. The simpler of the two use cases is a device that has been explicitly disapproved from connecting to enterprise networks. As an example, a system owner could have made the risk decision to not allow any smart building or smart home controllers, other than those integrated within the facility to connect to the enterprise's trusted network. This decision would prevent unintentional communications from a neighboring facility to connect to the enterprise, as well as any employees bringing in home or building control devices to experiment on. Solely making the risk decision is merely the first step. The system owner then has to ensure that monitoring and network defensive systems can identify the disapproved traffic, in a way that separates it from the approved smart building traffic, and make access decisions based on that identification. A second example would be a neighboring business's smart TV beaconing on its wireless interfaces, potentially attempting to connect to one of the enterprise wireless networks. The monitoring systems would need to differentiate between the traffic of approved enterprise owned smart TVs and the external untrusted smart TVs, when they potentially are the same make and model; if the identity and authentication components of the communication have not yet been implemented, the system owner's job becomes even more difficult. Referencing previous sections, this entails a detailed understanding of the communications capabilities of the disapproved devices as well as the approved devices, to allow the monitoring systems to differentiate between the traffic.

That process, while onerous, is feasible for an explicitly disapproved device; but, the system owner also has to be able to handle devices that trust decisions have not been made for yet. As an example, the wearable fitness device market has expanded quite a bit within the past year; multiple clothing manufacturers have been exploring the integration of fitness sensors into clothing lines, whether clothing designed for exercise or other purposes. Without an understanding of the capabilities of these sensors, or the processing power included in the product, it would be reasonable for a system owner to wait to make a trust decision while gathering information. Unfortunately, the rate of market evolution is moving so rapidly that it would be entirely feasible for an employee to unknowingly purchase clothing with embedded fitness sensors and wear it into the enterprise facility. While the current capabilities of embedded fitness sensors make the chance of compromise low, if a compromise were to occur, both the employee and system owner could be completely unaware of the entry vector. Monitoring and defense systems would only be capable of identifying and characterizing the traffic if it were protocols already supported by the systems. Until the IoT market converges on protocols and security standards, it will continue to be a game of catching up for the system owners. This scenario is essentially the unknown scenario, where it is not possible for a system owner to be prepared for an unknown device type, unknown security posture, and unknown potential communications capability, to interact with network security appliances that may or may not be able to detect unapproved behavior.

While the challenges for the system owner increase with untrusted devices, it is not a category that can be ignored when determining trust boundaries and making risk decisions. The negative detection capabilities in monitoring and network defense systems are equally as important as the positive identification capabilities. As the IoT market continues to evolve, much of the effort will fall on the system owner to ensure awareness of the potential concerns associated with including IoT devices within the enterprise network's trust boundaries.

5.3   RISK DECISIONS AND CONCLUSION

Recommending that a system owner be cognizant of every trust boundary connection in making all risk decisions is not a significant deviation from most traditional information assurance security recommendations; however, with some IoT devices, additional challenges are included in that recommendation. To make those trust and risk assessments, a system owner would need the capability to identify IoT devices within their network. While this capability exists for many devices that are now considered to fall within the IoT spectrum, there are just as many that are not yet included in commercial monitoring capabilities; in some cases this functionality would be difficult to develop in a reliable way, as the RF protocols are designed for short-range communications that do not necessarily transmit across an entire facility. A system owner with an existing network monitoring system including an intrusion detection and wireless intrusion detection may be under the false impression that their existing detection mechanisms are suitable for this new technology. But there is not yet a solution that addresses the issue across the entire IoT spectrum, and there may never be.

Identifying IoT devices that contact or cross network trust boundaries is merely the first stage of capability that a system owner will need to achieve. Following identification, the owner will need the ability to determine whether the IoT device is introducing any additional vulnerability into his or her system. In itself, that will be an incredibly difficult and time consuming effort; until there are more broad reaching security standards across the IoT spectrum, determining the security level of an individual IoT device will require analysis of that specific device as it relates to the system owner's network. If the device passes this level of scrutiny, the system owner must then determine whether there are any inherent security concerns within the IoT device itself.

Addressing all of these basic components will then allow the system owner to assess whether the inclusion of the IoT device affects the trust boundary of his/her network. Not only is that an inordinate amount of work today, it will likely continue to be until broader security mechanisms are in place across more sectors of the IoT market. From the system owner perspective, broad reaching security mechanisms in individual IoT devices will not be enough. They will still need to have a thorough understanding of the trust boundary of their network, and the implications of adding devices as well as intentionally excluding devices. Many will question the necessity of this step, but its importance becomes obvious with a brief glance into recent network history. The IoT concept is by no means the first disruptive technology that has expanded or adjusted the trust boundary of any network. The initial wave of wireless network access, specifically 802.11, forced system owners to question what security implications adding an AP to their network would bring; the collective push to address those issues when raised resulted in the addition of security protocols to the 802.11 framework. As network bandwidths increased, system owners and corporations had to quantify and identify a path forward to enable employees to connect from remote sites. As technology evolution continued to speed forward, system owners were faced with merging traditional computer and voice networks to deploy Voice-over-Internet Protocol (VoIP) systems and unified communications infrastructure. Many system owners are currently struggling with the implications of the bring-your-own-device (BYOD) concept; wherein approved, or not, these scenarios potentially create sensitive business operations on personal devices. All of these scenarios required the system owner to understand their existing network trust boundary and make an assessment of the risk involved with expanding it to support the new technology/capability set. The inclusion of IoT on a broader scale is merely the next in a series of expansions in the widely held concept of what comprises a network, and what network security truly means.

REFERENCES

Derr, K.W. 2007. Nightmares with mobile devices are just around the corner! In: IEEE International Conference on Portable Information Devices, PORTABLE07, May 2007, pp. 1–5.

Lee, J.S., Su, Y.W. & Shen, C.C., 2007. A comparative study of wireless protocols: Bluetooth, UWB, ZigBee, and Wi-Fi. In: 33rd Annual Conference of the IEEE Industrial Electronics Society, IECON 2007, November 2007. pp. 46–51.

O'Neill, J., 2015. Smart TV adoption – and connectivity – soars; will 4K stunt its growth? Available at http://www.ooyala.com/videomind/blog/smart-tv-adoption-%E2%80%93-and-connectivity-%E2%80%93-soars-will-4k-stunt-its-growth. Accessed on April 15, 2015.

PART III

WEARABLE AUTOMATION PROVENANCE

CHAPTER 6

WEARABLE IoT COMPUTING: INTERFACE, EMOTIONS, WEARER'S CULTURE, AND SECURITY/PRIVACY CONCERNS

ROBERT MCCLOUD,[1] MARTHA LERSKI,[2] JOON PARK,[3] and TYSON T. BROOKS[3]

[1]Department of Computer Science, Sacred Heart University, Fairfield, CT, USA
[2]Library, Lehman College, City University of New York, Bronx, NY, USA
[3]School of Information Studies, Syracuse University, Syracuse, NY, USA

6.1 INTRODUCTION

The debate about whether the wearable technology economy generates $10 billion or $100 billion underscores the deeply entrenched and complex nature of this industry. By 2020, consumer data collected from wearable devices are estimated to drive 5% of sales from the Global 1000 and the number of smartphone applications (apps) requesting to share consumer data will increase twofold by 2015, indicating a rise in the number of marketers or proprietors who seek access to customer profile data.[1] Today, wearable devices such as Google Glass, Apple Watch, and Fitbit Flex are affecting how we live our day-to-day lives, helping us keep connected and improving productivity. For instance, from the steps tracked, Fitbit computes the distance travelled, the calories burned, and the number of active minutes (Goode 2013). Activating an additional setting enables it to track sleep patterns. Users can set daily step goals, with a default goal of 10,000 steps. Once Fitbit detects that the goal is met, the user receives a congratulatory vibration on his/her wrist. The user can also access the Fitbit website, where a dashboard graphically illustrates accomplishments. In addition, an available sync links to smart phones, allowing continuous update checking. It is also possible to use social media to keep in touch with friends or make new friends through data sharing.

[1] http://www.gartner.com/newsroom/id/2603215

Cyber-Assurance for the Internet of Things, First Edition. Edited by Tyson T. Brooks.
© 2017 by The Institute of Electrical and Electronic Engineers, Inc. Published 2017 by John Wiley & Sons, Inc.

177

6.2 DATA ACCURACY IN WEARABLE COMPUTING

In 2013, writing in "Information disclosure on mobile devices: re-examining privacy calculus with actual user behavior," Keith et al. (2013) concluded that about 40% of registered participants provided at least some false information. Researchers also found that the potential for consumers to provide inaccurate information makes it difficult to determine whether a consumer intends to provide accurate information as opposed to simply information of some sort (Boehner et al. 2005). Accuracy of how you intend to provide information represents a further complication. Although it is not a wearable application, Facebook is frequently studied as an example of this conundrum. Hull (2015, p. 11–12) reported on a Columbia University student study the following:

"93.8% of participants revealed some information that they did not want disclosed. Given our sample, it is virtually certain that most other Facebook users have similar problems. On the other hand, we note that 84.6% of participants are hiding information that they wish to share. In other words, the user interface design is working against the very purpose of online social networking. Between these two figures, every single participant had at least one sharing violation. Either result alone would justify changes; taken together, the case is quite compelling."

As human computer interaction (HCI) emerged as a recognized field of study, the philosophical cognition structure was thought to be sufficient. It was assumed that we could apply computational terms to a model of how the mind works. This led to emotion being treated as an add-on to cognition. Palen and Bødker (2008) addressed such a treatment would enable us to obtain meaningful, analyzable data about the affective nature of any HCI experience. So far, research on wearable activity trackers has concentrated on validating their accuracy. Takacs et al. (2014) concluded, "No significant differences were noted between Fitbit One step count outputs and observer counts, and concordance was substantial (0.97–1.00)." Boehner et al. (2005) argued that emotion should be viewed as interaction and focus on an emotional HCI as one in which a person's social setting, culture, and interaction play a part in the HCI. The researchers conclude that an HCI system should play a supportive role and it should help users understand the full range of their emotional experience. For wearable computing, we might infer that the user will have an emotional experience with the device. Anger, annoyance, joy, and surprise can be part of the Fitbit experience; that a wearable computer can be closely bound to emotions is partially made possible by its constant presence.

6.3 INTERFACE AND CULTURE

The virtual reward has been a part of game design for many years. Going back to the beginning of the Super Mario Brothers series, Nintendo embedded virtual rewards in any number of on screen objects. The idea is taken a step farther in the Mario Kart series. At the conclusion of a race, your driver might cry or be happy, depending on how well you did against the opposition.

Fitbit initially sent users encouragement notes and reward icons as they approached or exceeded goals. This strategy was not viewed with approval by our subjects. One wrote, "I got an e-mail from Fitbit explaining a new icon reward that I can show off on social media…I for one thought it was slightly immature…" While the icon strategy was not popular, one other reward was mentioned at some point by every subject: the vibration that comes from Fitbit when one reaches his/her daily steps goal. A vibration can be a virtual reward in the traditional sense. However, it definitely is part of the wearable computer interface.

The first interface characteristic to note about the vibration, or "buzz" as most subjects call it, is how readily the young computer scientists accepted Fitbit's standards. For example, only two subjects mentioned changing the goals established by Fitbit. One wrote, "After setting my daily goals for the various tasks the device holds, I'm noticing as days go on I am checking my Fitbit more and more." The other noted that he had lowered the step goal because he wanted to feel the buzz sooner.

One person, who did not like the device, wrote, "Looks like Fitbit hasn't really suede [*sic*] me much to work out more. Looks like I've only reached my step goal a total of 5 times out of the month haha." Even though he did not reach his goal, this person did *accept* the goal established by Fitbit. In this sense, the interface established itself as the expert. One thinks of Huizinga's game theory. When someone plays a game, he/she agrees to enter the game's world and abide by its rules. Almost all subjects viewed the Fitbit HCI as establishing rules for the fitness-tracking game. They willingly enter the Fitbit world, "You'll be happy to know that I finally took to the Fitbit buzz but it took some extra work out of my ordinary… and I actually treated myself to extra dessert knowing that I accomplished my goals tonight…"

The Fitbit buzz is a virtual reward made physical. It makes HCI come alive on your skin. Some of the recipients stated "and I got the buzz today!… I stopped right in my tracks…I told my friend right away. I felt super accomplished!" This is the same sense of accomplishment we observed when talking with gamers who had bought a new game and played it for many hours straight through to completion. One enters the game's world and accepts the games praise when achieving its goals. To say that these goals are artificial is irrelevant. They are real in terms of the game. The Fitbit buzz is much like Huizinga's soccer game. You can be alone on the field and kick the ball into the goal over and over. The action has no meaning. But, when you kick the ball into the goal during the game, it acquires tremendous significance.

6.4 EMOTION AND PRIVACY

Palen and Bødker (2008) point out that emotion in HCI is both experiential and social. With that in mind, we check the emotional context of Fitbit during the subjects' opening day with the interface. Initial emotional reactions to Fitbit varied in both direction and intensity. In general, we agree that emotions are a part of the "always there" background (Palen & Bødker 2008). To foreground them in an analytical, as opposed to the descriptive, way would have resulted in isolation that impoverished the descriptive experience. It is interesting that no participant asked about privacy as the interface was set up. In fact, many participants were eager to share their data with friends. It is not clear whether they felt their data would naturally be protected or whether they simply did not address the issue. There seems to be an assumption that Fitbit would not implicitly violate the user privacy.

Emotions also play a role in users' level of sharing of data via social networking. It also may affect whether they accurately note information (Park et al. 2014). Preibusch (2013) argues that, without appropriate methodologies to analyze and associate privacy behaviors, research in the field may not accurately reflect consumer concerns or related action or inaction. He uses the economic model of privacy as control over information and defines privacy as "an individual's ability to personally control the collection, use and proliferation of information about herself" with the aim to gauge existing modes of understanding the individual's sensitivity to privacy. Arguing that studies with hypothetical privacy concerns are inadequate, he also notes that "observed actions can be used to infer their level of privacy concern" and notes that in the European Union (2016), almost 57% of consumers are "concerned that they have been asked for unnecessary information in the past and that data they provided to companies may be repurposed." Among types of privacy-enhancing behaviors are the refusal to share information and the falsification of details and also consumer concerns can bear upon selection of devices (Schwartz 2013). Emphasis on studying observed actions works only if one considers befuddlement an action (Preibusch 2013). Many subjects do not understand the privacy regulations they are asked to read, or do not take time to study the policies' legal implications; or, they make the economic decision to trade privacy for immediate gratification. That is, they cannot activate the application without first agreeing to the terms of use.

By making privacy dependent on user action, the opt-out policy is effectively implemented. That gives control to the application or site and for business purposes, it is nearly always in the site's best interest to control user privacy settings. The most effective way to do this is through densely worded, involved policy statements. To truly ensure privacy, the user should be granted total privacy at the outset, and then given the option to give up some or all of that privacy through opting-in. Arguments in favor of opt-out minimize and commoditize the subject. These arguments do not recognize subject privacy as a right. Compared to many sites, the Fitbit privacy appears clear and unambiguous. From a typographic view, the fact that this policy is printed in 12 point Helvetica adds to its legibility. To make the policy even more readable, Fitbit could put it in a two-column, ragged-right format with increased leading. However, compared to the web standard, they good job of creating legibility. Fitbit also includes the "Privacy Pledge" – "We pledge to respect your privacy, to be transparent about our data practices, to keep your data safe, to never sell your personal data, to let you decide how your information is shared, and to only collect data that help us improve our products and services."

The Privacy Pledge is not as comprehensive as it appears (Fitbit 2015). To fully understand Fitbit privacy, the user must click on the Cookie Policy link. There Fitbit tells us, "We use the following third-party advertising cookies to present you with opportunities to purchase Fitbit products on our Site; and retargeting cookies, to present you with Fitbit advertising on other websites based on your interaction on our

Sites and other websites." Fitbit compromises our privacy under the guise of doing us the favor of using cookies to provide our information to advertising companies. Included in these is DoubleClick, the data-collection ad company owned by Google. Also among the 13 data-collecting advertising providers are Google Adwords conversion, AOL's Advertising.Com, Twitter Advertising, Facebook Custom Audiences, and Yahoo's Genome. Your Fitbit activity is automatically stored and provided to all the big advertising data collectors in the Internet world.

Fitbit tells the user that, if you do not want these advertisers to have your data, you must go to each site individually, read that site's privacy policy, and then make your decision. Fitbit provides no one-click option to give the user protection. It would not be a difficult programming task to provide that option. Perhaps, Fitbit does not choose to offer it because such an option would deprive company of revenue. Fitbit commoditizes its users. That choice is linguistically disguised as an "opportunity" to purchase products from other sites.

6.5   PRIVACY PROTECTION POLICIES FOR WEARABLE DEVICES

Following New York Senator Charles Schumer's request for the Federal Trade Commission's mandatory opt-out requirement, Fitbit announced new policies addressing the protection of personal health data (Schumer 2014). To opt-out or to opt-in has long been a contentious topic among ethicists. The feeling is that the current opt-out requirement places the burden of privacy on the consumer, who must find policy options, read, and understand them, then make a decision. Recognizing that most users do not take the time to read fine print and policy statements, companies generally require them to opt-out, or change, the built-in data-sharing features. This places the burden of protection upon the often-ignorant consumer. Too often, that consumer becomes the unwitting aid in forfeiting privacy. If the standard were changed to opt-in, then the consumer would have to consciously decide to allow data sharing. Opt-out makes him/her consciously decide not to allow data sharing. The difference may sound subtle, but it is significant when one realizes that there is a third choice: to do nothing. That is effecting opting in. By setting the default at opt-in, sites take advantage of the fact that many users take the do-nothing option.

In Rahman et al. (2013), the researchers warn that "The careless integration of health data into social networks is fraught with privacy and security vulnerabilities." The researchers suggest there is a "critical challenge for the research community: to develop new security approaches." And, one example of these is to check the relationship between stride length and basal metabolic rate (BMR) (Rahman et al. 2013). If the relationship between these two does not meet expectations, the data are rejected on the assumption that an injection attack has compromised the data. The warning is further enhanced in "A longitudinal study of information privacy on mobile devices," (Keith et al. 2014). Here, the researchers note that users may not be aware of imbalances of power and state that "concurrently, consumers may believe that they are firmly in control of the risky situation regardless of the asymmetries of information between themselves and the app provider" (Keith et al. 2013).

It is pretty clear that the most-effective solution comes from ethics and not technology. Voluntarily, developers and applications publishers should change the opt-out standard to one that depends on a user opting in. From a commercial standpoint, it might seem naive to think profit-seeking companies would voluntarily abandon a practice that yields valuable marketing data. However, if they took the research from suggestions and made users aware that their data would be part of a global collection dedicated to further research, then users might well opt in (Rahman et al. 2013). Further, the users who did decide to opt in would be providing careful data. With the current opt-out strategy in place, it is not at all uncommon for users to intentionally provide misleading or false data (Keith et al. 2013; Preibusch 2013).

Fitbit users, specifically those who choose to use wearable devices, face unique challenges not only in satisfying security imperatives but also in privacy imperatives. The types of data that will be stored in the system should also be assessed for any potential privacy information. If privacy data is to be held within these devices, then, the wearable devices under consideration should be assessed for the impact it will have on the overall user. The architecture used for wearable services creates unique legal and regulatory situations that impact privacy objectives. Privacy in wearable technology has to consider the individual's contractual and statutory rights to control his/her own information, including decisions about submitting, using, disclosing, and protecting the data. Privacy considerations, including export concerns, data control and ownership, information standards, enforcement of memoranda of understanding (MoU), and memoranda of agreement (MoA) will need to be re-evaluated and re-engineered. Security and privacy can and should be simultaneously addressed by identifying distinct objectives, overlapping requirements, and integrated implementation in evaluating wearable provider service offerings. To ensure compliance with privacy requirements, strategies to promote transparency into the wearable provider's operations will be required.

6.6 PRIVACY/SECURITY CONCERNS ABOUT WEARABLE DEVICES

While wearable devices bring various benefits to the users, they also introduce new concerns, especially in terms of security and privacy (Thierer 2015). The current level of wearable mobile computing penetration is a much-debated topic among security experts. What researchers agree on is that organizations are almost certain to become more involved in wearable cybercrime over time. The line between online illicit activities toward wearable technology will increasingly blur, as will the distinction between licit and illicit activities. In other words, as crime increasingly penetrates the wearable mobile computing market, efforts to crack down comprehensively may produce widespread active collaboration with other sorts of pernicious hackers.

Rahman et al. (2013) studied the communication between Fitbit, its base-station, and its web server which identified vulnerabilities including cleartext login information and hypertext transfer protocol (HTTP) data processing exposing the devices to injecting data into trackers and associated social network accounts. Zhou and

Piramuthu's (2014) research identified that wearable fitness trackers involved in sensor-based information are not primarily designed with a goal to eliminate effects associated with issues related to privacy/security but identified that the measurement of embedded sensors in this technology is still vulnerable. Dehling et al. (2015) found that 95.63% of applications considered posting at least some potential damage through information security and privacy infringements. The researchers divided applications into two archetypes: archetypes AT4 and AT5, which included fitness *ad hoc* tools and fitness trackers (Dehling et al. 2015). Rouse (2012) argues that security for mobile devices is currently "bolted on" near the end of the software development life cycle. Similarly, Garitano (2015) writes that in order to create secure, privacy-aware and dependable embedded systems (ES), the design process must tackle security, privacy, and dependability (SPD) from the beginning, which will provide robust systems. The commonality of these researchers identifies the need for more robust, embedded security processes and technologies for privacy protection. Privacy protection is essential for all wearable technology, especially those that contain substantial amounts of personally identifiable information (PII) (OECD 2013). The use of wearable technologies should sustain and improve, not erode, the privacy protection provided in all statutes and policies relating to the collection, use and disclosure of personal information and the means of protecting this information is of the upmost importance.

The wearable threat to individual security and privacy will drive the proliferation of wearable embedded networked devices. Increasingly, virtually every wearable object will have an Internet Protocol (IP) address and will be on a network utilizing the IPv6 protocol. Every wearable object worth more than a few dollars will therefore be potentially "hackable" – meaning people will not only be able to collect PII data about that wearable object (directly or via a central server) but they will also potentially be able to control it remotely. Already, we have seen glimmerings of this hacking of everyday wearable objects with the laboratory success that security researchers have had hacking radio frequency identification (RFID)-enabled systems such as Xiao et al. (2006), Chen et al. (2009), Hancke et al. (2010), and Marquardt et al. (2010). Malicious innovators, who can scale mass attacks, have the potential for mass disruption and theft on a scale previously unimaginable for wearable technology. Thus, embedded security technologies must be used to separate processes and this PPI data since the ability to capture this data to determine one's identity poses a grave threat to traditional notions of privacy.

6.7 EXPECTATIONS ABOUT FUTURE WEARABLE DEVICES

Organizations will have to develop data privacy policies that will determine the issues related to data privacy and describe how these issues will be handled and determine the information and data security protection that will be required for the delivered system(s), application(s), database(s), server(s), and website(s) to achieve an acceptable level of risk to prevent unauthorized intrusions (Pagallo, 2011). All those participating in the research had some feelings toward the wearable technology.

Similarly, there was an agreement that the Fitbit HCI altered behavior. Everyone reported doing something different, from taking late-night walks, to parking farther away from the store, to using stairs instead of elevators, to establishing steps-per-day competitions on social media, to drinking more water to be in better shape for exercise.

Social media's impact on student fitness goal motivation was less significant than the physical feedback provided by the device itself. Security and privacy literature indicates that, perhaps in a broader group of users, social media feedback might become a significant factor, thereby exposing users to greater risks. The "Self-reflection and Self-understanding" component of Persuasion Strategies include "context-aware" activity monitoring that permits users to place their progress together with location information or identification of individuals. Ertürk (2008) introduced the framework for security continuous monitoring in large-scale application. This helps the users to make associations between their physical activeness and factors that affect their activity (Li et al. 2012). In this context, privacy setting options via a device's design and interface might best reflect the way that Keith et al. (2014) structured their research, such that participants' personal information could be made publicly available "unless they set their privacy settings to restrict their data to "friends only" or "nobody." Participants were aware that the mobile application was capable of sending personal information to remote servers" (Dimakopoulos & Magoulas 2009).

Will wearable devices be the next big thing for the security industry? The rapid evolution of wearable computing via wireless technology means literally billions of potential hackers will be carrying the tools to hack, or to be hacked, on them. This may be done initially to steal personal information or to take data stored locally on wearable devices. But as wearable devices become increasingly smart and are able to access corporate and other private information networks, every wearable device becomes a potential security threat. Undetected threats in wearable devices may be transferrable to corporate networks and from there deployed for further malicious purposes. Even more suggestively, each of these wearable devices will not only be a potential target for hackers, they will also be a potential vehicle for hackers to use to attack any other device.

REFERENCES

Boehner, K., DePaula, R., Dourish, P., & Sengers, P. 2005. Affect: from information to interaction. In: Proceedings of the 4th decennial conference on Critical computing: between sense and sensibility, August 2005, pp. 59–68.

Chen, C.Y., Kuo, C.P., & Chien, F.Y. 2009. An exploration of RFID information security and privacy. In: 2009 Joint Conferences on Pervasive Computing (JCPC), December 2009, pp. 65–70.

Dehling, T., Gao, F., Schneider, S., & Sunyaev, A. 2015. Exploring the far side of mobile health: information security and privacy of mobile health apps on iOS and Android. *JMIR mHealth and uHealth*, 3(1):e8. Available at http://mhealth.jmir.org/2015/1/e8/.

Dimakopoulos, D.N., & Magoulas, G.D. 2009. Interface design and evaluation of a personal information space for mobile learners. *International Journal of Mobile Learning and Organisation*, 3(4), pp. 440–463.

Ertürk, V. 2008. A framework based on continuous security monitoring. Doctoral Dissertation, Middle East Technical University, Ankara, Turkey.

European Union, 2016. European Commission – Press release: Agreement on Commission's EU data protection reform will boost Digital Single Market. Available at http://europa.eu/rapid/press-release_IP-15-6321_en.htm. Accessed on February 11, 2016.

Fitbit, 2015. Fitbit Privacy Policy (FPP). Available at http://www.fitbit.com/privacy. Accessed on May 5, 2015.

Garitano, I., Fayyad, S., & Noll, J. 2015. Multi-metrics approach for security, privacy and dependability in embedded systems. *Wireless Personal Communications*, 81(4), pp. 1359–1376.

Goode, L. 2013. Comparing wearables: Fitbit Flex vs. Jawbone Up and more. Available at https://www.allthingsd.com/20130715/fitbit-flex-vs-jawbone-up-and-more-a-wearables-comparison/. Accessed on May 4, 2015.

Hancke, G.P., Markantonakis, K., & Mayes, K.E. 2010. Security challenges for user-oriented RFID applications within the Internet of Things. *Journal of Internet Technology*, 11(3), pp. 307–313.

Hull, G. 2015. Successful failure: what Foucault can teach us about privacy self-management in a world of Facebook and Big Data. *Ethics and Information Technology*, 17(2), pp. 89–101.

Keith, M.J., Babb, J.S., & Lowry, P.B. 2014. A longitudinal study of information privacy on mobile devices. In: 2014 47th Hawaii International Conference on System Sciences, January 2014, pp. 3149–3158.

Keith, M.J., Thompson, S.C., Hale, J., Lowry, P.B., & Greer, C. 2013. Information disclosure on mobile devices: re-examining privacy calculus with actual user behavior. *International Journal of Human-Computer Studies*, 71(12), pp. 1163–1173.

Li, I., Dey, A.K., & Forlizzi, J. 2012. Using context to reveal factors that affect physical activity. *ACM Transactions on Computer-Human Interaction (TOCHI)*, 19(1), p. 7.

Marquardt, N., Taylor, A.S., Villar, N., & Greenberg, S. 2010. Rethinking RFID: awareness and control for interaction with RFID systems. In: Proceedings of the SIGCHI Conference on Human Factors in Computing Systems, April 2010, pp. 2307–2316.

OECD, 2013. 2013 OECD Privacy Guidelines. Available at http://www.oecd.org/internet/ieconomy/privacy-guidelines.htm. Accessed on February 9, 2016.

Pagallo, U. 2011. ISPs & rowdy web sites before the law: should we change today's safe harbour clauses? *Philosophy & Technology*, 24(4), pp. 419–436.

Palen, L., & Bødker, S. 2008. Don't get emotional. In: *Affect and Emotion in Human-Computer Interaction*. Springer, Berlin Heidelberg, pp. 12–22.

Park, J.S., Kwiat, K.A., Kamhoua, C.A., White, J., & Kim, S. 2014. Trusted online social network (OSN) services with optimal data management. *Computers & Security*, 42, pp. 116–136.

Preibusch, S. 2013. Guide to measuring privacy concern: review of survey and observational instruments. *International Journal of Human-Computer Studies*, 71(12), pp. 1133–1143.

Rahman, M., Carbunar, B., & Banik, M. 2013. Fit and vulnerable: attacks and defenses for a health monitoring device. arXiv:1304.5672.

Rouse, J. 2012. Mobile devices–the most hostile environment for security? *Network Security*, 2012(3), pp. 11–13.

Schumer, C. 2014, After Push by Schumer, Fitbit Announces New Privacy Policies Aimed at Protecting Personal Health Data. Available at https://www.highbeam.com/doc/1G1-379551602.html. Accessed on August 10, 2014.

Schwartz, P.M. 2013. The EU-US Privacy Collision: A Turn to Institutions and Procedures'. *Harvard Law Review*, 126, 1966–1975.

Takacs, J., Pollock, C.L., Guenther, J.R., Bahar, M., Napier, C., & Hunt, M.A. 2014. Validation of the Fitbit One activity monitor device during treadmill walking. *Journal of Science and Medicine in Sport*, 17(5), pp. 496–500.

Thierer, A.D. 2015. The Internet of Things and Wearable Technology: Addressing Privacy and Security Concerns without Derailing Innovation. *Richmond Journal of Law & Technology*, 21(6), pp. 1–31 (2015). Available at SSRN: http://papers.ssrn.com/sol3/Papers.cfm?abstract_id=2494382

Xiao, Y., Shen, X., Sun, B.O., & Cai, L. 2006. Security and privacy in RFID and applications in telemedicine. *Communications Magazine, IEEE*, 44(4), pp. 64–72.

Zhou, W., & Piramuthu, S. 2014. Security/privacy of wearable fitness tracking IoT devices. In: 9th Iberian Conference on Information Systems and Technologies (CISTI), June 2014, pp. 1–5.

CHAPTER 7

ON VULNERABILITIES OF IoT-BASED CONSUMER-ORIENTED CLOSED-LOOP CONTROL AUTOMATION SYSTEMS

MARTIN MURILLO

University of Notre Dame, Notre Dame, IN, USA

7.1 INTRODUCTION

Automation or automatic control is the utilization of various types of control systems and schemes to accomplish basic or complex electrical, mechanical or other tasks with minimum or no human intervention. The area of automation flourished catalyzed by automobile manufacturing, the assembly line, industrial processes, and space exploration. Nowadays different types of automation approaches are utilized in electronic or mechanical processes present in everyday life.

One characteristic of automation, particularly when applied to industry, is the utilization of specialized hardware and resilient communication protocols. With the relatively recent advent of small powerful devices, reliable Internet interconnectivity, and appropriate standards, industry automation systems are gradually inheriting various elements and even architectures of the information technology (IT) field. For example, processor-based devices are replacing microcontroller-based devices and IP-based wired and wireless communication networks are replacing serial wire communication.

Consumer-oriented systems such as home heating and air-conditioning systems, cars, "smart" infrastructure, and many others are also benefitting from both, the IT and the industrial automation fields. The IT area provides unprecedented hardware and software power, and the automation area provides a wealth of complex control laws, algorithms, and decades of automation experience. The incorporation of physical devices to the Internet and the adoption of IT technologies have positive implications in the efficiency of production processes. It is also opening the door for innovation like no other time in history. However, it can also introduce unprecedented risks where the incumbent technologies are at the mercy of knowledgeable attackers that act based on myriads of dictates. This is particularly relevant when some every-day life systems are critical enough that any compromise or malfunction could imply the loss of human life, in addition to economic losses. For instance, an ill-designed home heating system might not have enough safeguards and be vulnerable to attackers that could increase the temperature levels to prohibitive ranges; this, in some cases, might have serious implications on individuals while they are resting at night. More complex systems that are becoming critical might present wider implications to the public.

Already existing vulnerabilities are being compounded with the fact that IoT devices are growing dramatically and are expected to outnumber legacy devices in the coming years (Sanchez et al. 2014). Huge sets of these devices could present similar vulnerabilities due to the fact that these are supplied by the same manufacturer, utilize similar protocols, or run the same applications. Attacks can potentially spread to millions of users and infrastructure and produce unprecedented economic and human losses that could override any gains and efficiencies that were gained that far. The concerns above are not limited to currently isolated consumer-oriented applications such as home heating or air-conditioning systems. Consumer-oriented processes such as smart infrastructure and smart metering are gradually being incorporated into the operation of industrial processes such as the smart grid; this means that the repercussions of widespread compromise of consumer devices might in turn have detrimental effects on industrial processes which can have wider repercussions.

Because IoT devices and systems are currently being applied in critical applications whose operations rely heavily on sensor readings to provide closed loop automation, wrong sensor data or unavailable sensor data could have a critical effect on the user and third parties. Similarly, because some of these applications are relying heavily on centralized service providers, the compromise of central systems could pose serious consequences to users. The identification of system vulnerabilities in such architectures can help put preventive measures and inform all stakeholders of the implications of different decisions and actions.

While plenty of literature has emerged in very recent years that deal with the repercussions of attacks on industrial systems, there is not much literature addressing the compromising of consumer-oriented processes in the context of IoT devices and automation. This chapter will address two specific areas where vulnerabilities can pose high risks: (i) feedback loops and (ii) the utilization of centralized service providers. It seeks to fill the void present in this area in a more informative way while at the same time, raise awareness of important issues. Our goal is to highlight vulnerabilities in an area that is gradually being the target of a mix of contributions encompassing specialized subjects such as automatic control theory, control systems engineering, information technology, data science, technical standards, Internet governance, and many others. Because of its relationship and synergy with industrial control systems, this chapter will also briefly deal with appropriate concepts in this area.

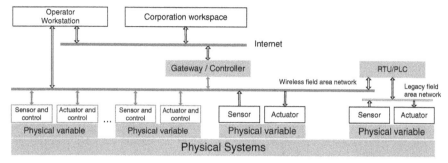

FIGURE 7.1   Generalized example of an industrial control system that has adopted various IoT elements and architecture. *Source*: Cárdenas et al. 2011. HOTSEC'08: Proceedings of the 3rd Conference on Hot Topics in Security. Reproduced with permission of IEEE.

7.2 INDUSTRIAL CONTROL SYSTEMS AND HOME AUTOMATION CONTROL

Control systems have been at the core of critical infrastructure, manufacturing, and industrial plants for decades. The area is very mature and specialized, relying heavily on control theory, resilient hardware, protocols, and communications. Several control applications can be labeled as safety-critical as they perform vital functions in weapons systems, national critical infrastructure, electric power generation and distribution, oil and natural gas distribution, water and waste-water treatment, transportation systems, health-care systems, and many others (Cárdenas et al. 2011). Over 80% of critical control system infrastructure is currently owned by private enterprises and have direct repercussions on public or national security (Cárdenas et al. 2011). This infrastructure ranges from a nuclear reactor owned by a private enterprise to a chemical manufacturing facility that is located in the proximity of a city.

Figure 7.1 illustrates a general architecture of an industrial process. The process utilizes a mix of IoT elements (gradually incorporated to these systems) and industrial control elements. At the lowest level sits the physical system that is under control. The physical system can range from a single process such as the control of the level of the water of a tank (with only one physical variable) to a complex process such as the production of a chemical component that involves the coordination of various processes, each having tens of variables.

Depending on the nature of the physical system, its subsystems can be in a single location or distributed in many locations thousands of miles away. Remote terminal units (RTU) or programmable logic controllers (PLC) assure that the overall system runs autonomously, under the supervision of a remote human operator whose main task is to set the operating parameters, attend any alarms, and coordinate maintenance. The figure contrasts two types of architectures: a hierarchical architecture (that is widely used today) based on "non-smart[1]" sensor/actuator elements controlled by

---

[1] Purdue model.

one or many RTUs or PLCs; and a more flattened IoT-based architecture where most functions of RTUs and PLCs have been adopted by a central controller and the sensors and actuators themselves. The figure represents a system located in a single physical location; similar systems located in various locations utilize reliable Internet connectivity in order to achieve automation.

While the diagram of Figure 7.1 is laid out mainly for illustrative purposes, it does represent a small portion of current industrial control systems, where IoT elements and corresponding architectures are being incorporated for controlling various processes. The hierarchical architecture of the "legacy" system represents the vast majority of critical industrial systems today; it is expected that industrial processes adopt the more flattened architecture at higher rates in the coming years (Chi et al. 2014). This adoption implies the following changes:

- While keeping their functions, RTUs and PLCs will incorporate new wireless standards (i.e., mesh networking-based) at lower layers and IP-based at higher layers; this will enable them to communicate through application layer standards.[2] Depending on the application and its requirements (i.e., cost, resources, computing power, harsh environments), RTUs and PLCs could be replaced, absorbed, or transformed into more mainstream microprocessor-based computers.
- Sensors and actuators have built-in computers that allow these devices to not only receive remote commands but to also collaborate with controllers, whether these are PLCs, RTUs, or other devices.
- Wired field area networks configured in serial or daisy chain modes are now replaced with wireless mesh networks characterized by utilizing specialized OSI lower layer protocols based on spread spectrum technologies.[3] Further resiliency is reached through the implementation of mesh networking technologies that are inherently self-healing.
- Because of these systems must work in real-time in a synchronous manner, these networks are centrally coordinated for the allocation of communication time periods for each device
- The IP-based communication protocols at the field area networks and local area networks offer ubiquitousness to operators, management, and other stakeholders.

Figure 7.2 illustrates a possible architecture of an IoT-based consumer-oriented system. It can represent a heating or air-conditioning system of a house; or heating, ventilating, and air conditioning (HVAC) systems that are present in larger infrastructure. Field devices (sensors and actuators) measure physical variables such as temperature and humidity; they also operate devices such as furnace relays or stepper

---

[2] Such as the Constrained Application Protocol (CoAP), which is an application layer protocol for resource constrained devices.

[3] Spread spectrum protocols (physical layer) are resilient to noise of harsh environments, such as industrial facilities. They sacrifice speed by resilience. Spread spectrum is generally associated with "frequency hopping" for achieving resiliency.

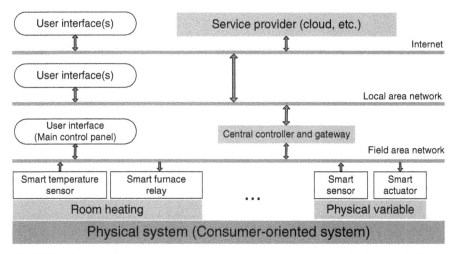

FIGURE 7.2   An IoT-enabled home automation system. Reproduced with permission of IEEE.

motors. Sensors and actuators are now "smarter" as they have built-in computers that enable them to communicate with other devices and process requests coming from controllers or from other parties. They might also have certain levels of autonomy through built-in algorithms. The central controller holds control algorithms, coordinates these field devices, and serves as a gateway for remote access to the devices, given that the appropriate policies are set.

The controller and the field devices (i.e., smart devices) share raw operational data, raw informational data, instructions, or status information. These instructions can be manipulator information or operational parameters or settings, such as desired temperature, efficiency modes, or control and feedback gain parameters. These devices can be characterized by communicating though IP protocols for constrained devices.[4] They generally utilize resilient physical layer protocols[5] at lower layers and mesh networking at higher layers. The controller is connected to the user's local area network which is in turn connected to the Internet. It is possible that the local area network and the field area network are physically unified if all devices communicate through similar physical layer protocols; however, the real-time nature of some automation systems will require specialized protocols that are resilient to noise and network congestion (Gomez & Paradells 2010).

As illustrated in Figure 7.3, depending on the application, the system provider is now an integral part of the architecture and can have the following roles:

i. Provides ubiquitousness to the user by enabling him to have complete control of the system from anywhere, given that the user has access to the Internet;

---

[4] 6LoWPAN (IPv6 over low power wireless personal area networks).
[5] Spread spectrum such as the IEEE 802.15.4.

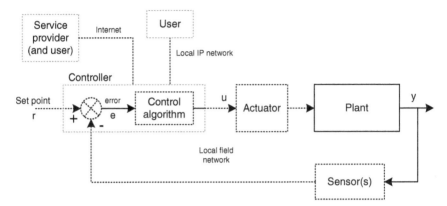

FIGURE 7.3 Diagram of a generic home control system. Note how the inclusion of a service provider and a local IP network allows the user to adjust set points from different locations. Reproduced with permission of IEEE.

ii. Updates different control system parameters depending on user request or on the request of automated supervisory functions programmed by the user or set by the service provider through analyzing historical data;

iii. Sends alarms to the user or "third-party" service providers;

iv. Logs operational data that is used for advanced functions, such as learning user's energy utilization for its integration with the smart grid;

v. Provides enhanced functions to the user;

vi. Assists in firmware and software updates, provides applications, and many others.

The emergence of IoT devices, architectures, and their potentials and the desire to automate processes for energy efficiency reasons is leading to replace old thermostat wired-based systems by the recently depicted architecture. The following changes are important to highlight:

- A microcontroller-based control panel and regulating box that communicates through wires is turned into a microprocessor-based computer with the ability to communicate wirelessly with sensors (heat measuring devices) and actuators (furnace relays) utilizing resilient communication protocols.

- The heating device now incorporates a wireless module that has two purposes: to receive remote commands wirelessly and to operate the heating or air-conditioning device relays and stepper motors accordingly.

- The sensing device(s) are now part of a feedback loop that sends periodic measurements to the central controller wirelessly.

- Wireless infrastructure that communicates with appropriate protocols has replaced cabling that was used for communications. Remaining communications wiring is expected to eventually disappear.

7.3 VULNERABILITY IDENTIFICATION

The inheriting of IoT elements and architectures from the IT field and the operational laws and algorithms from the control systems field brings unprecedented potentials such as energy efficiency,[6] autonomous operation, ubiquitousness, and opens the door for further innovation. However, it also inherits vulnerabilities from the IT field which now have physical implications. Because of the novelty of this intersection, such vulnerabilities might be unknown or not be a consideration issue(s) to the average information technology (IT) practitioner or control systems designer or practitioner.

Areas of control system theory such as adaptive control, robust control, optimal control, fault detection and estimation, supervisory control, and others have contributed immensely in alleviating system errors, uncertainties, disturbances, and even equipment failures (Hwang et al. 2010). Basic proportional negative feedback itself is a means to "fix" errors. These areas are very mature, readily implementable through algorithms, and they can be instrumental in the detection and mitigation of failures and some attacks in industrial control systems and other infrastructure automation systems (Amin et al. 2009).

However, attackers, in addition to being highly knowledgeable in IT systems and exploits, might also be experts in control system theory and practice. This introduces an entirely new challenge as the targeted compromising of a system also implies the potential compromising of the very algorithms and parameters that regulate the control system (Krotofil & Cárdenas 2013). Because these algorithms are software-based, run over operating systems, and reside in microprocessor-based hardware, attackers can not only change parameters, but also alter the very code that composes the algorithms. Furthermore, attackers could introduce subtle changes in measured values that even supervisory control agents would not be able to detect utilizing mainstream approaches (Krotofil & Cárdenas 2013; Tiwari 2015).

New approaches for detecting attacks based on Big Data and artificial intelligence are certainly changing the paradigm and will be instruments in the next generation of detection and mitigation systems (Qin 2014). The consumer-oriented environment and infrastructure, that will encompass millions of small automated control systems that are potentially vulnerable, will certainly also benefit from newer approaches of detection. In this case, however, various operations will be carried out by service providers or other "third-party" stakeholders. The main reason of incorporating other parties is because consumer-oriented devices are generally energy-constrained and require external resources for their operation, in similar ways some personal devices such as smartphones do for computing-demanding or resource-dependent operations.

Aside of the actions of disgruntled employees that have a deep knowledge of systems, perhaps no other example is more representative of a major targeted attack as the Stuxnet worm that affected various critical infrastructures around the world,

---

[6] These approaches also are being favored by climate change mitigation institutions, which have funding and decision-making stakes, particularly when applied to urban areas.

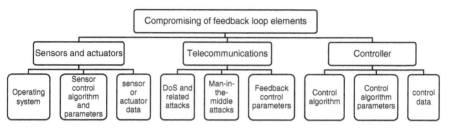

FIGURE 7.4 Elements of a feedback loop, that have the potential of being compromised. Reproduced with permission of IEEE.

where attackers utilized not-yet-known IT weaknesses[7] in order to alter the values being read by the nuclear centrifuge sensors (Abrams & Weiss 2008; Matrosov et al. 2010). The lessons learned from such incident were plenty, including the awareness on how far institutions and individuals can go to sabotage infrastructure; and how vulnerable infrastructure that is deemed secure can be to these types of attacks. As IoT devices become more common and more attractive due to their numbers and mass potential, already existing exploitation code will be readily available to carry out attacks. Remote attacks by individuals, groups, or nation states are quite attractive as they can be carried out remotely and anonymously, quite inexpensively, and with minimum risks for the attacking party.

Figure 7.3 illustrates the block diagram and communication paths of a generic feedback control system that can be found in home control or other consumer-oriented infrastructure. Dashed lines indicate wireless Internet protocol (IP) or other protocol-based communication. Similarly, dashed block diagrams indicate IP-enabled, central processing unit (CPU)-based devices. We argue that all dashed-lined elements have the potential of being compromised.

7.3.1 Open-Loop to Closed-Loop Systems Vulnerability Implications

In open-loop control systems, controllers do not use feedback to determine whether its output has achieved the desired goal of the input. One typical example of an open-loop architecture is a sprinkler system that is set to run at specific hours of the day; the system, regardless of whether it has rained or not will activate the sprinklers at the hours that were preprogrammed by the user. Had the sprinkler system had a humidity sensor and such measurement was taken into consideration before turning on the sprinklers, such system would be considered a closed-loop system.

Figure 7.4 illustrates a general closed-loop system; the system is characterized by the dynamic nature of the plant and the feedback created by the sensor measurements. The system depends on a desired input value (or setpoint) specified by the user and current or past outputs of the system as measured by sensors. Sensors are a key element of automation, as without them, feedback control would not be possible. The emergence of inexpensive sensors, applications that act on such measurements,

---

[7] Also known as Zero-day attacks

the desire for automation and efficiency, and the interconnectedness of devices in an IoT context (car systems, smart infrastructure, mobile phones) is incorporating closed-loop schemes to what used to be open-loop systems; simply put, monitoring and measuring is evolving into automatic control.

Closed loop controllers utilized in consumer-oriented devices such as home heating and air conditioning can be of the type bang–bang, also called hysteresis controller. A bang–bang controller is characterized by its switching abruptly between two states (on or off) in order to get the system reach target levels set by the user. Bang–bang operation is determined by the difference between the user's set point and the actual value measured by the sensor. This controller provides smooth operation in either state and it is considered a form of optimal control (Naidu 2002). These controllers are often used to control a device (or plant) that accepts a binary input, such as the actuator (relay) of a home heating furnace.

As sensor technologies get incorporated into home automation systems and more energy-efficient plants (i.e., furnaces) emerge,[8] bang–bang control will be just one of many approaches utilized. Another type of controller, proportional control, can be utilized when a bang–bang control is not appropriate. In the case of the cruise control of a car, for example, applying full gas or no gas to the car (bang–bang) will naturally not provide appropriate results. A more appropriate approach to maintain constant speed is to apply proportionate control; this would consist in subtracting the measured speed from the desired speed and gradually applying appropriate gas levels according to such difference (see Figure 7.4). Complex sets of interconnected control systems have tens of hundreds of sensors and actuators and are governed by different types of control schemes such as these. These systems are the core of industries such as oil, gas, water, nuclear, electric grid, and others. These are also gradually being incorporated into consumer-oriented infrastructure.

7.3.2 The Compromising of the Feedback Loop Elements

The adoption of feedback control schemes by consumer-oriented systems and the adoption of IoT elements by new and already existing closed-loop systems can introduce a wide gamma of vulnerabilities. The most obvious is the disruption of feedback loop elements, an essential part of automation (Murillo & Slipp 2009).

Figure 7.4 follows an operational approach to describe a general categorization of vulnerabilities of feedback systems. It categorizes vulnerabilities in three wide areas: sensors and actuators, telecommunication infrastructure, and the controller. We briefly elaborate on each of these.

7.3.2.1 Sensors and Actuators One of the main precepts of the IoT paradigm is that "intelligent" capabilities will be infused into current "dumb" elements, such as isolated sensors and actuators. This is facilitated, in most cases, by their evolution from microcontroller or hard-wired devices into operating system-based devices.

---

[8] Climate change mitigation is expected to affect government policies that will favor energy efficiency; this, in turn, is also expected to foster innovation in various fields.

These now offer an unprecedented amount of capabilities which are not limited to their ability to communicate through IP protocols, but also to their capacity of autonomous work and "decision-making." This naturally introduces unprecedented efficiencies and potentials as the capabilities of these devices are put in a collaboratory environment.

One of the implications of these changes is that control system algorithms operate as applications (i.e., services) over such operating systems, thus indeed inheriting all vulnerabilities of mainstream IT systems. As illustrated in Figure 7.6, these range from operating system (OS) compromises to the altering of operational data and the very parameters of the control algorithms. Furthermore, because these devices are generally resource constrained, emphasis must be put to the real-time nature of the algorithms, rather than file system encryption, for instance. This implies that schemes such as certificate operations and asymmetric key cryptography will need to have conservative footprints, compared to more powerful systems.

7.3.2.2 Telecommunications Feedback loops in consumer-oriented automation systems are generally carried out through resilient physical layer standards that guarantee time slots to each device, in addition to utilizing IP-based mesh protocols. Depending on the standard, this can imply the presence of a coordinating agent, which can also serve as a gateway, as illustrated in Figures 7.2 and 7.3. This ensures that feedback is provided on a real-time basis, an important requirement of feedback control systems, which can become unstable under delays.

These networks, however, are quite vulnerable to several types of communications attacks, such as denial of service (DoS) attacks, man-in-the-middle attacks, and many others (Raza et al. 2009) These are obviously the result of the use of IT exploits in order to gain access to nodes or coordinators; or the use of impersonation attacks to carry out what appear to be legitimate transactions. Attackers can also utilize similar exploits to access devices and reconfigure feedback control parameters, degrading the system gradually. There is a wealth of possibilities for attackers knowledgeable in the area (Alcaraz & Lopez 2010; Padmavathi & Shanmugapriya 2009). Overall, the disruption of feedback loops can be in the form of:

   i. disrupting sensor to controller or actuator to controller communications,
   ii. compromising feedback data integrity (altering sensor measurements),
  iii. affecting timeliness of the data (availability), or
  iv. simply connecting to the wrong sensor due to impersonation attacks or attacks that change sensor table parameters.

7.3.2.3 Controller Similar attacks as the ones carried out to sensors and actuators can be carried out against the controller, which is generally a more powerful device. As illustrated in Figures 7.2 and 7.3, the controller can also be a gateway that has direct connection to a local area network and the Internet. The controller can be considered a part of the feedback loop as it makes important decisions based on sensor measurements and desired levels dictated by the user. When feedback control parameters housed in the controller are changed by knowledgeable attackers, mainstream control system detection methods will not work, particularly when attackers have used unknown exploits to access the infrastructure.

Home automation, the smart grid, and cloud utilization are catalyzing the adoption of service providers or other third party stakeholders in order to leverage some of the capabilities needed for resource optimization, ubiquitousness, and collaborative schemes. As we will see, this practice in turn will further introduce other risks and vulnerabilities that can have wide implications.

7.3.3 The Compromising of the New Player: The Service Provider

The roots of the various types of attacks now include the compromising of a new stakeholder, which is also one of the most trusted entities, a service provider. New generations of consumer-oriented automation systems might (at different degrees) depend on these stakeholders in order to be part of a more global automation system, such as the smart grid or even driverless cars. In this case, the degree of coupling of the operational portion will depend on various factors such as the level of automation desired, efficiency, and even national and international regulations.

Home automation and smart infrastructure are increasing their utilization of service providers in order to provide ubiquitousness, availability, optimization, and enable and facilitate the user's remote administrative capabilities. The user can then remotely connect to his target system, this being house-heating system, intruder detection, energy efficiency system, or other systems or devices. The service provider can additionally be a gateway for alarms, software and firmware updates, and other actions. In the era of Big Data, data collected by service providers will be used to provide additional features, including providing intelligence to different stakeholders and the user himself. Figures 7.1 and 7.2 depicts the role of the service provider in a general context.

An immediate concern that arises because of these dependencies is the risks associated with these stakeholders being an essential component for the control and automatic operation of consumer products. And this is not an unfounded concern, as several personal devices[9] already depend heavily on service providers and can be deemed useless if no connection to the Internet or a dedicated network is available. The implications of this operational relationship and dependency in the event of an attack can bring frightening detrimental effects. Depending on the degree at which the service provider is involved in the operation of a system, a total compromise would imply the remote command of millions of homes or other infrastructure, including the injection of code that could set the home control system unusable or an instrument to cause physical harm or to carry out remote attacks. Less aggressive forms of attacks could consist of the gathering of target private information for selling in the market. There is a plethora of vulnerabilities for potential attacks; these attacks could arise because of a myriad of reasons and the most important condition, appropriate technical knowledge, is accessible to anyone.

---

[9] Chrome notebooks and various mobile applications

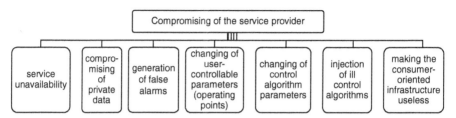

FIGURE 7.5   Possible consequences of the compromising of a service provider. Reproduced with permission of IEEE.

As Figure 7.5 illustrates, the implications and consequences that arise because of the compromising of the service provider can be many; these include the following: service unavailability, compromising of private data, generation of false alarms, changing of user-controllable parameters (operating points), changing of control algorithm parameters, injection of ill control algorithms, and ultimately making the consumer-oriented infrastructure useless.

It is important to note that attacks to service providers have so far been relegated to the compromise of personal or institutional data. The utilization of service providers to compromise IoT control infrastructure is not a known fact. Thus, the implications of such are not yet well-known. In contrast, the compromising of IoT elements to carry out mainstream IT attacks is a documented fact (Abadi & Kremer 2014).

7.4 MODELING AND SIMULATION OF BASIC ATTACKS TO CONTROL LOOPS AND SERVICE PROVIDERS

What would the consequences of the exploitation of such vulnerabilities look like in a real-life system? This section adopts already existing attack models to create a mathematical description of a generic consumer-oriented system that utilizes the two resources identified as vulnerable: feedback loops and the service provider (Huang et al. 2009; Cárdenas et al. 2011; Teixeria et al. 2012; Foroush & Martinez 2014). We then link this discussion, basic mathematical models, and real-life examples to see how real-life impacts of different types of attacks would look like.

First, consider a linear time invariant plant whose dynamics is expressed by the following equation:

$$\mathbf{x}(k+1) = \mathbf{A}\mathbf{x}(k) + \mathbf{B}\mathbf{u}(k)$$
$$\mathbf{y}(k) = \mathbf{C}\mathbf{x}(k) \tag{7.1}$$

Where $k \in \mathbb{N}$. $\mathbf{x}(k) \in \mathbb{R}^n$ denotes the state vector and $\mathbf{u}(k) \in \mathbb{R}^p$ denotes the input vector over which the user or the service provider has leverage. $\mathbf{y}(k) \in \mathbb{R}^q$ denotes the output vector composed of sensor measurements. $\mathbf{y}(k) = \{y_1(k), \ldots, y_q(k)\}$ represents the set of q sensors measurements. $y_i(k)$ denotes the measurement by sensor i at time k.

With this in mind, let $\tilde{\mathbf{y}}(k) \in \mathbb{R}^q$ denote the controller input data at time k; the control system utilizes those values to perform actions to maintain operational goals (Cárdenas et al. 2008) Similarly, let $\tau_a = \{\tau_s, \dots, \tau_e\}$, where $\tau_e \geq \tau_s$, represent the attack duration. A general sensor attack model in that interval can be expressed as

$$\tilde{y}_i(k) = \begin{cases} y_i(k), & \text{for } k \notin \tau_a \\ a_i(k), & \text{for } k \in \tau_a, \end{cases} \tag{7.2}$$

Where the $a_i(k)$ signal is a generalized result of the attack, whether it is an integrity or a DoS attack. In the latter case, $a_i(k) = y_i(\tau_s)$, where $y_i(\tau_s)$ is the last measurement received before the DoS attack (Cárdenas et al. 2011); in the case of an integrity attack, $a_i(k)$ can represent any arbitrary signal resulting from such attacks.

Under ideal conditions (i.e., the absence of noise and other disturbances in the state and output), the resiliency of the plant is increased through state feedback and the addition of a reference input:

$$\mathbf{u}(k) = \mathbf{r}(k) - \mathbf{K}\mathbf{y}(k) \tag{7.3}$$

Where $\mathbf{r}(k) \in \mathbb{R}^P$ is a vector of desired reference inputs and $\mathbf{K} \in \mathbb{R}^{p \times q}$ is a feedback control matrix that is chosen appropriately so that the overall system is stable and fulfills other requirements. The resulting system can then be expressed as

$$\begin{aligned} \mathbf{x}(k+1) &= (\mathbf{A} - \mathbf{BKC})\mathbf{x}(k) + \mathbf{B}\mathbf{r}(k) \\ \mathbf{y}(k) &= \mathbf{C}\mathbf{x}(k) \end{aligned} \tag{7.4}$$

Then the compromising of the service provider can be expressed as the following equation:

$$\mathbf{x}(k+1) = (\mathbf{A} - \mathbf{BKC})\mathbf{x}(k) + \mathbf{B}\tilde{\mathbf{r}}(k) \tag{7.5}$$

Where $\tilde{\mathbf{r}}(k)$ represents the result of targeted attacks to the reference signal, whether in the case of the compromising of the service provider or the compromising of any relevant element in the user's system.

Similarly, the set of p reference values can be represented by $r(k) = \{r_1(k), \dots, r_p(k)\}$, where $r_i(k)$ denotes the reference signal i at time k. For the sake of simplicity, we assume that the system is periodically being updated.[10]

Then let $\mathbf{r}(k) \in \mathbb{R}^P$ denote the reference input data at time k, based on which the control system performs actions to maintain the plant at $\mathbf{r}(k)$. Similarly, let $\tau_a = \{\tau_s, \dots, \tau_e\}$, where $\tau_e \geq \tau_s$, represent the attack duration. We assume that this attack is a form of mutually exclusive attack, represented by the following equation:

$$\tilde{r}_i(k) = \begin{cases} \tau_i(k), & \text{for } k \notin \tau_a \\ a_i(k), & \text{for } k \in \tau_a, \end{cases} \tag{7.6}$$

With such attack models in mind, we next simulate the behavior of a home heating system.

---

[10] Note that another appropriate approach can also be the utilization of discrete event modeling.

7.5 ILLUSTRATING VARIOUS ATTACKS THROUGH A BASIC HOME HEATING SYSTEM MODEL

Consider the following equations that represent a general description of a heating system and the house dynamics (Mathworks 2015):

$$\frac{dQ}{dt} = (T_h - T_r) \cdot Mdot \cdot c \tag{7.7}$$

$$\left(\frac{dQ}{dt}\right)_{losses} = \frac{T_r - T_{out}}{R_{eq}} \tag{7.8}$$

$$\frac{dT_r}{dt} = \frac{1}{M_{air} \cdot c} \cdot \left(\frac{dQ_h}{dt} - \frac{dQ_{losses}}{dt}\right) \tag{7.9}$$

Where:

$\frac{dQ}{dt}$ is the heat flow from the heater into the rooms,

c is the heat capacity of air at constant pressure,

Mdot is the air mass flow rate through the heater (Kg h^{-1}),

T_h is the temperature of hot air from heater,

T_r is the current room air temperature,

M_{air} is the mass of air inside the house,

and R_{eq} is the equivalent thermal resistance of the house.

7.5.1 Compromise of the Reference Signals

Assuming unity feedback is provided to the system formed by equations (7.7)–(7.9), the result of the compromising of the service provider or the user's infrastructure can be the altering of reference input signal $\mathbf{r}(k)$ into $\tilde{\mathbf{r}}(k)$ for $\tau_a \geq \tau_s$.

$$\tilde{r}_i(k) = \begin{cases} r_i(k) = 20, & \text{for } k < 5\,\text{s} \\ a_i(k) = 30, & \text{for } k \geq 5\,\text{s} \end{cases} \tag{7.10}$$

As equation (7.10) implies, the system runs in nominal conditions specified by the user, with a reference temperature of $r(k) = 20°C$. At time $k = 5$, the compromised system overrides the user's set point to $r(k) = 30$ for time $k \geq 5$.

This overriding can be done as part of a valid service provider reconfiguration; however, attackers have overridden the service provider's system databases or appropriate structures with undesired values. The overriding of the reference signals can also be due to the compromising of any of the user's devices that run remote configuration applications through CoAP, for example; the compromising of the controller (as defined in Figure 7.4) can also be a cause of this overriding.

Figure 7.6 illustrates the effects of such compromise. Note that under normal conditions, the unity feedback does a good job in keeping the temperature at nominal

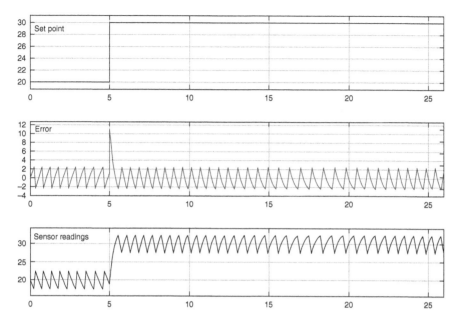

FIGURE 7.6 Results of the compromising of a service provider or the controller where the set point $r(k)$ is changed from 20°C to 30°C at $k = 5$ hours. Reproduced with permission of IEEE.

values set by the user. The overriding of the reference input (set point) as the result of system compromise has appropriate response of the feedback system, which in spite of the incorrect values, ensures that the system runs under new "nominal" conditions dictated by the trusted service provider.

7.5.2 Compromise of the Feedback System: Persistent DoS Attack

Among many others, compromise of the feedback system can be the result of DoS attacks, man-in-the-middle attacks, or simply rendering the feedback elements such as sensors and actuators useless through mainstream IT approaches. The simulation implements unity feedback to the system formed by equations (7.8) and (7.9). The system carries normal operation with $\tilde{y}_i(k) = y_i(k)$ for $0 \leq k < 5$. The feedback loop is compromised at $k \geq 5$, where $\tilde{y}_i(k) = 0$. For the sake of generalization and illustration, it is assumed that the feedback loop delivers a value of 0 (zero) to the controller for $\tau_a \geq \tau_s$. Equation (7.11) and (7.12) illustrate the uncompromised system and the system under DoS attack respectively.

$$\mathbf{x}(k + 1) = (\mathbf{A} - \mathbf{BKC})\,\mathbf{x}(k) + \mathbf{Br}(k) \tag{7.11}$$

$$\mathbf{x}(k + 1) = \mathbf{Ax}(k) + \mathbf{Br}(k) \tag{7.12}$$

Figure 7.7 illustrates the effects of such compromise. Note the degradation or the error signal at $k \geq 5$. The controller processes the error signal as valid and

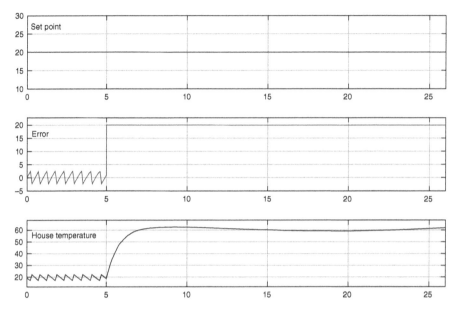

FIGURE 7.7   Effects of a DoS attack. The feedback loop is compromised at $k \geq 5$ hours, where $\tilde{y}_i(k) = 0$. Reproduced with permission of IEEE.

correspondingly increments the heating which reaches levels of 60°C. While this situation can seem farfetched, ill-designed systems and appliances that do not provide adequate safeguards could indeed provide such outputs. As stated earlier in the chapter, the control systems field provides a wide range of tools that can help mitigate such compromises; however, these will have limited impacts in the face of attacks carried out by knowledgeable stakeholders.

7.5.3 Compromise of the Feedback System: Changing a Gain Parameter or Compromising the Data Integrity of the Feedback Loop

Aside reference inputs (set points), gain parameters are elements that are often readily altered (by operators in industrial control systems) in order to obtain desired outputs. We apply unity feedback to the system formed by equations (7.7)–(7.9). In this case, however, we multiply such unity feedback by a factor of 0.5 for $k \geq 5$, to simulate the compromise of such parameter. The system runs at nominal conditions for $0 \leq k < 5$. Equation (7.13) illustrates the result of introducing this factor, represented by $\tilde{\mathbf{K}}$. Figure 7.8 illustrates the impacts of such compromise.

$$\mathbf{x}(k + 1) = (\mathbf{A} - \mathbf{B}\tilde{\mathbf{K}}\mathbf{C})\mathbf{x}(k) + \mathbf{B}\mathbf{r}(k) \tag{7.13}$$

In a separate simulation, we simulate results of a feedback loop data integrity attack that adds a factor of -10 to such feedback for $k \geq 5$. As in the first case, the system

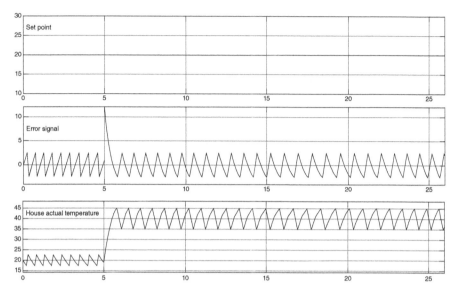

FIGURE 7.8   Attack to the feedback system: unity feedback is altered by a factor of 0.5 for $k \geq 5$. The system runs at nominal conditions for $0 \leq k < 5$. Reproduced with permission of IEEE.

runs at nominal conditions for $0 \leq k < 5$. Equation (7.14) illustrates the result of the addition of the faction, represented by $\mathbf{L}$.

$$\mathbf{x}(k + 1) = (\mathbf{A} - \mathbf{BKC} + \mathbf{L})\,\mathbf{x}(k) + \mathbf{B}r(k) \tag{7.14}$$

Figures 7.8 and 7.9 illustrate the effects of such compromises. The controller processes the feedback signal as valid and increments the heating which reaches levels of 40°C and 30°C. These types of attacks are very plausible and represent one of the first attacks to industrial infrastructure, the Stuxnet worm. One of the goals of this worm was indeed focused at altering sensor readings of real physical values. While the control systems field provides a wide range of tools that can help mitigate compromises, these would generally not be able to counteract attacks whose effects appear to be completely valid. Various service provider-based schemes are expected to fill in such void.

7.6   A GLIMPSE OF POSSIBLE ECONOMIC CONSEQUENCES OF ADDRESSED ATTACKS

The implications of the consequences of these potential attacks are many, including the safety of individuals, the integrity of systems that depend on the infrastructure, and economic costs. Figures 7.10 and 7.11 contrast the heating costs of the same infrastructure under two different conditions. Figure 7.10 refers to a non-compromised

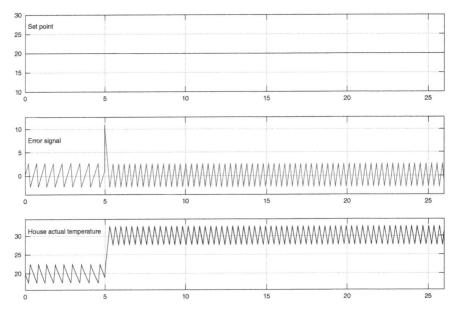

FIGURE 7.9   Attack to the feedback system: unity feedback is altered by adding a factor of -10 for $k \geq 5$ in order to simulate the results of a data integrity attack. The system runs at nominal conditions for $0 \leq k < 5$. Reproduced with permission of IEEE.

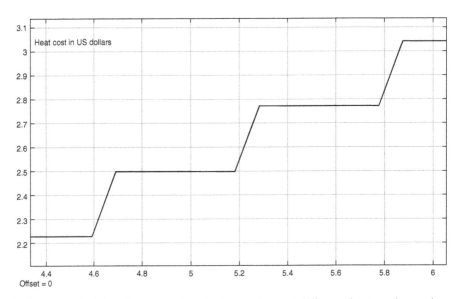

FIGURE 7.10   Home heating system: heating costs in US dollars under normal operation. Reproduced with permission of IEEE.

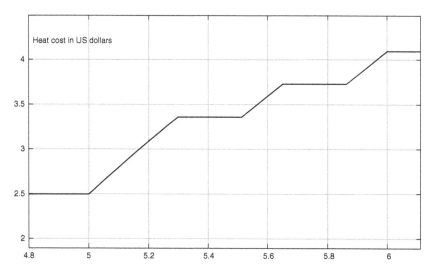

FIGURE 7.11   Home heating system: heating costs in US dollars under data integrity attack. Factor of −10 is added to the feedback loop at k ≥ 5. Reproduced with permission of IEEE.

system, while Figure 7.11 refers to a compromised system. Both depict an interval of 1 hour (5 ≤ k < 6). As can be seen, the difference in heating costs between these two scenarios for 1 hour is approximately one dollar, using very conservative assumptions. This implies that the consequences of a service provider-induced widespread attack to millions of homes could have overall costs of tens of millions of dollars in a single hour.

However, the impacts of these attacks are not relegated to economic costs, but these impacts can resonate harshly into the operation of the electric grid. The result of a sudden or unexpected surge of demand of electricity has been well-documented and can be potentially damaging, particularly given the random nature of these attacks (Albert et al. 2004).

7.7   DISCUSSION AND CONCLUSION

Based on current trends and discourses centered around IoT, we have developed and utilized a general infrastructure architecture and mathematical model of a consumer-oriented system. We have utilized such architecture in order to identify two new elements that can make these systems highly vulnerable. These two elements, feedback control systems and service providers, have core responsibilities in the autonomous operation of consumer-oriented systems; they are also relatively new players in the association of IoT and the automation of these systems.

We have simulated the results of different types of attacks through the utilization of already available general dynamic models of the system. No safeguards (such as saturation values to represent physical limits) were implemented for the sake of highlighting the raw effects of attacks. The simulations show overall expected system responses. The compromising of feedback elements through arbitrary changes critically affects the system, taking the home temperature to unacceptably high levels. DoS and data integrity attacks were shown to have very unpredictable effects due to the correcting effects that negative feedback loop provides. Service provider-induced attacks on user set points naturally have the desired negative effects in which the control system follows the dictates of the trusted provider.

The simulation of the effects of the attacks underlines the highly adverse consequences of the compromising of these new players in the new area where IoT and automation systems are integrated. Besides stopping system operation, operating in a "safe" area, or providing redundancy through various means, the field of control system theory offers various approaches to partially mitigate the effects of this type of failure; however, no control law approach will replace the real-time measurements of significant variables or detect set point changes that mimic valid operator requests (Gu & Niculescu 2003; Sztipanovits et al. 2012; Tiwari 2015).

These operational findings are not new, as they constitute basic knowledge of control theory and industrial control systems. However, new insights applied to every-day consumer products are important in order to have better insights on the repercussions of ill-designed systems, uninformed hastily-designed systems, the inclusion of inappropriate hardware, the inclusion of software and services that fail to take into consideration critical consequences, and even the development of protocols and standards that are based on limited view of this new interdisciplinary field. It also brings into attention the role of service providers and the high-stake nature of services that might bring negative repercussions to individuals and communities, if appropriate safeguards, design principles, adherence to standards and regulations, and processes are not taken into consideration.

The chapter and simulations also bridged some concepts of different disciplines highlighting the risks associated with different decisions. The innovation process is generally led by the availability of powerful devices, the fulfillment of immediate operational needs, and the dictates of technical individuals and institutions; these at times disregard the damaging potentials that ill decisions can bring to individuals.

A basic general model was utilized to symbolize the underlying control systems of more complex infrastructure such as driverless cars, the smart grid, and others. The implications of the compromise of the service provider and feedback loops can also be readily applicable to industrial control systems, which are gradually adopting similar IoT infrastructure.

REFERENCES

Abadi, M., & Kremer, S. (Eds.). 2014. *Principles of Security and Trust: Third International Conference, POST 2014, Held as Part of the European Joint Conferences on Theory and Practice of Software, ETAPS 2014, Grenoble, France, April 5–13, 2014, Proceedings*, vol. 8414. Springer.

Abrams, M., & Weiss, J. 2008. Malicious control system cyber security attack case study–Maroochy Water Services, Australia. The MITRE Corporation, McLean, VA.

Albert, R., Albert, I., & Nakarado, G.L. 2004. Structural vulnerability of the North American power grid. *Physical Review E*, 69(2), pp. 025103.

Alcaraz, C., & Lopez, J. 2010. A security analysis for wireless sensor mesh networks in highly critical systems. *IEEE Transactions on Systems, Man, and Cybernetics, Part C: Applications and Reviews*, 40(4), pp. 419–428.

Amin, S., Cárdenas, A.A., & Sastry, S.S. 2009. Safe and secure networked control systems under denial-of-service attacks. In: *Hybrid Systems: Computation and Control*. Springer, Berlin Heidelberg.

Cárdenas, A.A., Amin, S., Lin, Z.S., Huang, Y.L., Huang, C.Y., & Sastry, S. 2011. Attacks against process control systems: risk assessment, detection, and response. In: Proceedings of the 6th ACM Symposium on Information, Computer and Communications Security, March 2011, pp. 355–366.

Cárdenas, A.A., Amin, S., & Sastry, S. 2008. Research Challenges for the Security of Control Systems. In: HotSec, July 2008.

Chi, Q., Yan, H., Zhang, C., Pang, Z., & Da Xu, L. 2014. A reconfigurable smart sensor interface for industrial WSN in IoT environment. *IEEE Transactions on Industrial Informatics*, 10(2), pp. 1417–1425.

Foroush, H., & Martinez, S. 2014. On triggering control of single-input linear systems under pulse-width modulated dos signals. *SIAM Journal on Control and Optimization*, pp. 1–31. Available at http://fausto.dynamic.ucsd.edu/sonia/papers/data/2013_HSF-SM.pdf.

Gomez, C., & Paradells, J. 2010. Wireless home automation networks: a survey of architectures and technologies. *IEEE Communications Magazine*, 48(6), pp. 92–101.

Gu, K., & Niculescu, S.I. 2003. Survey on recent results in the stability and control of time-delay systems. *Journal of Dynamic Systems, Measurement, and Control*, 125(2), pp. 158–165.

Huang, Y.L., Cárdenas, A.A., Amin, S., Lin, Z.S., Tsai, H.Y., & Sastry, S. 2009. Understanding the physical and economic consequences of attacks on control systems. *International Journal of Critical Infrastructure Protection*, 2(3), pp. 73–83.

Hwang, I., Kim, S., Kim, Y., & Seah, C.E. 2010. A survey of fault detection, isolation, and reconfiguration methods. *IEEE Transactions on Control Systems Technology*, 18(3), pp. 636–653.

Krotofil, M. & Cárdenas, A.A. 2013. Resilience of process control systems to cyber-physical attacks. In: *Secure IT Systems*. Springer, Berlin Heidelberg, pp. 166–182.

Mathworks 2015. Thermal model of a house. Available at http://www.mathworks.com/help/simulink/examples/thermal-model-of-a-house.html. Accessed on April 3, 2016.

Matrosov, A., Rodionov, E., Harley, D., & Malcho, J. 2010. Stuxnet under the microscope. *ESET LLC (September 2010)*.

Murillo, M.J., & Slipp, J.A. 2009. Demo abstract: application of WINTeR industrial testbed to the analysis of closed-loop control systems in wireless sensor networks. In: International Conference on Information Processing in Sensor Networks, IPSN, April 2009, pp. 409–410.

Naidu, D.S. 2002. *Optimal Control Systems*. CRC press.

Padmavathi, D. G., & Shanmugapriya, M. 2009. A survey of attacks, security mechanisms and challenges in wireless sensor networks. arXiv:0909.0576.

Qin, S.J. 2014. Process data analytics in the era of big data. *AIChE Journal*, 60(9), pp. 3092–3100.

Raza, S., Slabbert, A., Voigt, T., & Landernas, K. 2009. Security considerations for the WirelessHART protocol. In: IEEE Conference on Emerging Technologies & Factory Automation, EFTA, September 2009, pp. 1–8.

Sanchez, L., Muñoz, L., Galache, J.A., Sotres, P., Santana, J.R., Gutierrez, V., Ramdhany, R., Gluhak, A., Krco, S., Theodoridis, E., & Pfisterer, D. 2014. SmartSantander: IoT experimentation over a smart city testbed. *Computer Networks*, 61, pp. 217–238.

Sztipanovits, J., Koutsoukos, X., Karsai, G., Kottenstette, N., Antsaklis, P., Gupta, V., Goodwine, B., Baras, J., & Wang, S. 2012. Toward a science of cyber–physical system integration. *Proceedings of the IEEE*, 100(1), pp. 29–44.

Teixeira, A., Pérez, D., Sandberg, H., & Johansson, K.H. 2012. Attack models and scenarios for networked control systems. In: Proceedings of the 1st International Conference on High Confidence Networked Systems, April 2012, pp. 55–64.

Tiwari, A. 2015. Attacking a Feedback Controller. *Electronic Notes in Theoretical Computer Science*, 317, pp. 141–153.

CHAPTER 8

BIG DATA COMPLEX EVENT PROCESSING FOR INTERNET OF THINGS PROVENANCE: BENEFITS FOR AUDIT, FORENSICS, AND SAFETY

MARK UNDERWOOD
Krypton Brothers, Albany, NY, USA
NIST Big Data Public Working Group – Security/Privacy Subgroup, Albany, NY, USA

8.1 OVERVIEW OF COMPLEX EVENT PROCESSING

Malcolm Gladwell's lesson of engineering pragmatism has parallels for securing information in IoT. Some IoT subsystems will be far less robust than others. They may be more easily compromised, subject to rapid design changes to meet market conditions, stripped of what an enterprise software developer would consider to be adequate assurance measures, or the subsystems may simply have been repurposed from their original purpose for an unanticipated use. For these and other reasons, ensuring the integrity of IoT information across sometimes loosely federated networks involves more than traditional network defense and edge protection.

The lifecycle of a sensor varies greatly. A widely used oxygen sensor used to monitor output and health of vehicle catalytic converters should be replaced after 60,000 miles, says the manufacturer. Oxygen sensor failure in cars is comparatively benign, but the explosion of a Proton-M booster rocket carrying three navigation satellites in 2013 was caused by a faulty sensor configuration. Some implantable defibrillation leads used for sensing electrical events have "limited lifetime" warranties but a 2008 report cited "inappropriate sensing due to conductor or insulation fracture, sensing lead adapter failure, loose set screws, or frank dislodgement can lead to over-sensing of electrical noise with resultant inappropriate shocks" (Tung et al. 2008). Systems that rely on these sensors require considerable knowledge about the sensors, their

Cyber-Assurance for the Internet of Things, First Edition. Edited by Tyson T. Brooks.
© 2017 by The Institute of Electrical and Electronic Engineers, Inc. Published 2017 by John Wiley & Sons, Inc.

calibration, test conditions, manufacturers' recommended maintenance procedures – not to mention guidance on how to interpret their data streams.

Is an out-of-bounds measurement from a sensor compromised through a man-in-the-middle attack, or simply producing spurious measures due to conditions of high heat? Despite the drive toward increased dataset variety, and while Big Data has had a correspondingly large impact on containerization and DevOps, the impact on information assurance (IA) has been incremental (Hendler 2014). This chapter surveys approaches to leverage Big Data techniques to enhance IoT provenance, which is itself only one of multiple measures needed to improve information assurance. A number of thus far loosely connected approaches are identified. Each is addressed in this chapter. A concluding section suggests possible future direction.

The concept of complex event processing (CEP) has matured since the late 90s, though the underlying concepts were not foreign to those working in sensor fusion and other real-time systems. For example, some investigators explored ways in which event structures could be modeled in (Scott 1982; Van Der Aalst 1998; Reinartz et al. 2015). Connections were also seen in even earlier modeling languages as well (Hoare 1978; Milner 1980).

More recently, two texts aimed at broader audiences presented useful book-length summaries of CEP. The first, based in part on earlier work by Luckham and Frasca (1998), introduced CEP to the business community (Luckham 2011). The other, by Etzion and Niblett (2010), was aimed at experienced software engineers, but still from a practical frame of reference. This chapter embraces the general framework presented by Etzion and Niblett (2010) as useful for the purpose of studying the role of CEP in strengthening provenance awareness and supporting provenance query for audit, forensics and safety.

CEP has been an integral part of security information and event management (SIEM) for some time, so much so that its scalability has been a concern (Vianello et al. 2013; Rosa et al. 2015). Rosa et al. (2015, p. 1) goes so far as to argue that:

> … a SIEM system is not only a sensible choice, but rather a mandatory component, as demonstrated by several examples such as: the Sarbanes-Oxley Act of 2002, Sec 103 (Auditing, Quality Control, and Independence Standards and Rules) which regulates the use of log collection, processing and retention for any traded company in the US (Sarbanes-Oxley Act 2002); the Payment Card Industry (PCI) council requisites for Data Security Standards (as stated by Requirement 10 "Track and monitor all access to network resources and cardholder data") (Payment Card Industry Data Security Standard version 2.0 2010); the North American Electric Reliability Corporation (NERC) CIP-009-2 Critical Infrastructure Protection (CIP-009-2 2009); or the Information Technology Infrastructure Library (ITIL) framework, which encompasses components for incident response in line with the role of the SIEM concept (Steinberg et al. 2011; Rosa et al. 2015).

CEP can play other roles beyond IA to enhance IoT information security. While not a focus of this chapter, those roles are mentioned. Both Lundberg (2006) and Progress Software (2009), providers of commercial CEP tools, cite quality of service

(QoS) and service-level assurance as enterprise benefits gained from CEP. The scope of this chapter is intentionally limited; its purpose is to suggest a potentially fruitful approach which can enhance IoT provenance – especially in audit, forensics, and safety – but also for IA more generally.

8.2 THE NEED: IoT SECURITY CHALLENGES IN AUDIT, FORENSICS, AND SAFETY

IoT is expected to stress existing technical, legal, and organizational frameworks in many ways, but especially for audit, forensics, and safety. As part of their introduction to what was termed "a forensics-aware ecosystem for IoT," Zawoad and Hasan (2015, p. 279) expressed the challenge this way:

> ... *[The] existing digital forensics tools and procedures do not fit with the IoT environment. The large number of IoT devices will generate massive amount of possible evidence* [Ed: Big Data Volume], *which will bring new challenges for all aspects of data management. Investigators will find it very challenging to collect evidence from the highly distributed IoT infrastructures. The wide variety of IoT devices will also raise problem in data analysis because of the heterogeneous formats of data* [Ed: Big Data Variety]. *Reliability of the evidence can also be questionable since the attacker can tamper with the evidence residing in the IoT devices* [Ed: Big Data Provenance, which some experts group with Veracity]. *On the other hand, the IoT can offer new opportunities to investigators. Since the IoT devices share local physical information, an investigator can use such information to establish facts about a criminal incident.*

A systems architect employing a CEP approach, even just as a conceptual overlay, encourages design-time explicit representation of IoT events. For many devices, "startup," "discovery," "test," "failover," "decommission," "reset," "self-identity," and "transmit latitude/longitude" each represents not only events, but entire groups of interrelated events. Analytics in support of audit, forensics, and network protection can be specified as design-time system requirements, rather than relying upon whatever logs happen to be provided by device manufacturers and operating systems. Because provenance operates at the intersection of IoT security and privacy, IoT system managers must consider proactive means to address it.

8.2.1 Provenance Defined for Risk Areas in IoT Audit and Safety

A concise definition of provenance was offered by Braun et al. (2008, p. 1): "a causality graph with annotations," specifically a directed acyclic graph (DAG). Each node is an entity of some sort, and edges are some sort of casual relationship, and the edges of the graph need to be preserved for provenance preservation. This observation is worth emphasizing. Provenance is different from other data (and metadata) because the design pattern for "cycles" does not apply. Braun et al. (2008, p. 1) writes: "Since time always moves forward, cycles are nonsensical. We may not know whether the chicken preceded the egg but clearly one came first. Provenance is not a tree because an entity may have multiple inputs… Provenance is valuable because it allows us to track a result back to its sources… Data ancestry can be more or less sensitive than the data itself. Thus provenance security cannot be trivially subsumed by existing security systems."

More broadly, Braun et al. (2008, p. 1) suggests that provenance is "metadata that represents the ancestry of an object," a lay notion inherited from art history. Provenance is immutable, they assert. Because this is not a characteristic of most commercial file system implementations, investigators such as Sultana and Bertino (2013) proposed extending file system capabilities to support queries on provenance, eliminating redundant provenance data, and securing provenance by using a security policy database that allows administration of the level of provenance granularity (e.g., with processes, applications, users, file attributes). Perhaps in opposition to these more ubiquitous file system approaches, others have suggested specialized file systems to ensure immutability, tailored to the characteristics of sensor systems (Ledlie & Holland 2005).

Big Data is changing the nature of work for Chief Security Officers (CSO), auditors, and forensic investigators. IoT will gradually add volume, velocity, and variety to their work. Taken at face value, this will be seen by most as a good thing, perhaps after an awkward period of IT infrastructure realignment. But, beneath this surfeit of data are fundamental problems in recognizing what is relevant for a particular analytic task. What is relevant can be domain-dependent, time-dependent, or role-dependent. Establishing relevance for IoT provenance was the focus for Bauer's conceptual model the researcher named "A Common Architecture of Data Provenance and the Internet of Things." In most discussions of IoT provenance, privacy, integrity, completeness, and confidentiality are central if not essential (Bauer and Schreckling 2013). This tends to be true for Big Data only at the purported point of origin, such as where medical records data are collected; less care with providence may be taken as information grows distant from the point of origin. Less often, systems are architected with provenance as a central consideration. For example, linkability and unlinkability refer to mechanisms by which provenance (especially personal information) can be linked to data, or, in the case of unlinkability, the extent to which anonymity is preserved. In Bauer and Schreckling (2013) conceptual model, unlinkability is a guarantee that certain provenance data are confidential. Linkability, working in concert with transparency, ensures traceability of actions taken on data across "different interconnected smart [IoT] objects" (Braun et al. 2008, Section 4.3ff).

To address this problem, Braun et al. (2008) proposes a provenance event handler to control computation on provenance data. IoT networks are likely to feature greater device heterogeneity (Big Data variety), hence more diverse provenance. Whether Bauer and Schreckling (2013) approach or another is best for a particular scenario, many IoT networks which will touch consumers (utilities, smart cars, and insurers) directly or indirectly must contend with provenance, or (in the case of breaches in the United States) face possible actions from the Federal Trade Commission.

When setting forth requirements for auditors, forensic investigators, and safety engineering, Bauer and Schreckling (2013) conceptual model offers much for IoT system architects to consider. Yet some will argue that it overlooks a key feature of cloud-based, elastic, reconfigurable systems. CEP is an approach that can assist in working with Big Data by establishing what data are relevant. The notion of "point in time" is an intrinsic factor, whereas most applications built in the last two decades only keep a few timestamps associated with a transaction. CEP incorporates temporal components in the very definition of events. CEP facilitates automated reasoning about events and also provides a basis for human investigations not anticipated by an IoT system's original architects.

Provenance is often overlooked as an integral component of the IoT. The following is a partial list of the provenance, audit, and safety stressors that many anticipate will be placed on IoT systems. While each item is not fully explored here, the purpose of the list is to highlight the importance of provenance.

- IoT network heterogeneity is the IoT parallel to Big Data variety: many audit types, many safety concerns.
- Need for life cycle management of "smart" sensors.
- Increased IoT man-in-the-middle attack exposure.
- Need for significantly more complex federated configuration management across sensor and traditional IoT systems.
- More complex maintenance environments.
- Need for integrated systems management tools that require steady data streams, such as integrated vehicle health management (Jennions 2013).
- A push toward decentralized CEP for IoT real-time analytics will indirectly create demand for forensics to support the validity of data sources and associated reasoning system results (Govindarajan et al. 2014).
- Some organizations may pursue IoT ontologies, such as those based on ISO 15926 or MIMOSA for managing cross-domain risk.
- Big Data requirements could include privacy traceability for PII and de-identified derivatives that can also support IA.
- IA support may be needed to support new brute force Big Data applications, such as extended use of multimedia, especially video.
- Use of named data networks for distributed sensor repositories may require auxiliary provenance systems (Ledlie & Holland 2005).
- Experts, including Jon Hudson at Brocade, have suggested the use of Big Data systems to save entire configuration, binaries, reference datasets, setup, calibration, test, simulation, people, and institutions involved – captured through real-time network traffic and saved in Big Data lakes such as the Hadoop File System.

8.3 CHALLENGES TO CEP ADOPTION IN IoT SETTINGS

The use of CEP in IoT security settings faces many challenges. Some of these challenges are domain-specific, such as the volume of data associated with others that are characteristics of the types of systems that may be integrated. Problems in common representation of time may be ignored by system architects until unanticipated use cases bring them to the surface (Chen et al. 2014). The so-called "point in time" problem occurs in many domains. With sensor data, the characteristics of a sensor's stream might change before and after an upgrade or an environmental event, such as a fire or intrusion.

Example 8.1 The local railroad operator issues an automated message indicating that a signal outage occurred, but the message does not identify the start time or duration of the outage. Was the railroad signal tampered with, or is this purely a maintenance issue? Should ordinary signal filtering proceed, or is this an exceptional circumstance? □

While the use of IoT ontologies is seen as a major future breakthrough, the current lack of ontology interoperability is limiting the adoption of current device and physics ontologies that could otherwise be employed to establish baseline performance data against which security threats could be assessed (Bock & Gruninger 2005; Underwood et al. 2015). Developers lack proficiency in the use of CEP programming practices. Etzion and Niblett (2010) surveyed three CEP implementation styles developers should be familiar with. Some observers might interpret these as design patterns:

- Stream-oriented
- Rule-oriented
- Imperative style (e.g., Apama MonitorScript)

It may be necessary for IoT architects to integrate domain-specific event elements into common provenance assurance "dashboards." This effort may be nontrivial; consider the challenges of a city-sized temperature monitoring application (Park & Heidemann 2008). Provenance in IoT can address issues of data confidence, ownership, and reliability. This was observed in the context of traditional databases by (Buneman et al. 2001). In IoT systems, attackers can exploit data aberrations already present in data streams to insert malicious code, divert attention, or interrupt critical surveillance or monitoring systems. CEP models can model these attack vectors as event types. Scalability issues may arise when accessing distributed provenance data given workflow constraints.

While the problem of software construction from reusable parts is not new, constructing systems for smart energy systems, integrating multiple devices, and mixing real-time and transaction-oriented systems are likely to exacerbate the problem (Garlan et al. 1995). Unclear connections will often surface among IoT software representations of states, functional roles, types of security, information reliability, and communication models (Bauer and Schreckling 2013). This problem was noted by Kim et al. (2014) in a project designed to integrate IoT devices using the business process execution language (BPEL): "A technical difficulty in IoT computing is to manage the heterogeneity of IoT devices in terms of their network protocol supported, interface language, data exchange scheme, and type of mobility provided" (Kim et al. 2014).

Researchers have identified special problems associated with real-time sensor network provenance which designers must address (Le-Phuoc & Hauswirth 2009). Some systems, especially those developed for municipal applications, may rely upon legacy supervisory control and data acquisition (SCADA), enterprise resource planning (ERP), utility and other applications which are not properly instrumented to identify exceptions, perform logging or detect unusual man-in-the-middle attacks that were not possible before the legacy application became part of a broader IoT solution. Application rule embedding is common in much legacy software. This weak transparency is common for embedded sensor management, especially when assumptions were made about sensor or channel security or reliability. In order to expose internal events to a CEP system, it may be necessary to use static program analysis or mining of dependence graphs (Chang et al. 2008).

Fault tolerance in IoT systems may be bolted on after-the-fact, resulting in unnecessary cost and management complexity. Addressing all aspects of fault – from prevention to detection to corruption – due in part to sensor or network failure or network attack, should be an integral part of an IoT design, following design patterns analogous to those used for detecting sensor abnormalities (Negiz & Cinar 1992). IoT software test environments may not accurately reflect the security or information assurance risks that will be faced when they are deployed. This could be due to scalability limitations, or to a failure to account for complex interactions between events. The IoT Security Fabric Design Pattern One of the findings of the NIST Big Data Public Working Group is that Big Data requires a fabric approach (NIST 2015a). The fabric approach is integrated into the group's early reference architecture (Chang et al. 2008), but the design pattern is not well-established and will require adaptation for IoT. Is an IoT fabric different? The group believes it is not significantly different from other Big Data systems, such as the Spotify recommender, Netflix or other high-volume, high-velocity applications.

8.4 CEP AND IoT SECURITY VISUALIZATION

Future research is needed to address IoT security visualization. The role CEP can play in this varies, but a potentially key capability is to reduce false positives. False positives are a well-known limitation of SIEMs which employ Big Data technologies to collect or sift logs. CEP can organize meaningful subsets of that data into interconnected contexts that would otherwise require traditional analysts to engage in trial and error methods. How should provenance be visualized for network defense and alert consoles? Even though there is no standard for event instances or types, there are numerous instances represented (Etzion and Niblett 2010, p. 79). A CEP design pattern typically includes event producers, event consumers, temporal markings, and the like. Representing these visually is already achieved in some CEP tools such as Websphere's Business Events Design tool. Moving from these process representations to supporting security analysts is a more direct path than attempting to visualize raw packet flow.

That said, there are prerequisites for CEP to play such a role. While representing temporal data is intrinsic to CEP, standards for representing it are not widely adopted. There have been attempts to improve available techniques to represent events digitally in ways that facilitate both machine processing and human interaction, but these are not fully developed. One attempt was researched by Pustejovsky et al. (2007), which was a specification language for event annotation in documents in which it tries to standardize representation of event ordering, duration, and subordination.

Audit and forensics disciplines have general principles that will influence IoT systems designs. In addition, there are specific regulatory scenarios which IoT architects would do well to study. A 2015 example was the release of information from two laboratories demonstrating that the German auto maker Volkswagen had contributed to what one academician-columnist called "the Internet of Cheating Things" (Tufekci 2015). A simplistic description of this scenario might consider the onboard vehicle software simply an IoT end point. That would be missing an important facet of the regulatory milieu in which auto manufacturing operates. As mentioned earlier, "test" is a common IoT device event, consisting of a network of related conditions, components, and security measures. "Validation" is the term used in psychometrics to define the method by which a psychological test actually measures what it claims to measure. To validate the performance of a software-enabled device like a smart car, emissions test requires both validation and, as Bauer and Schreckling (2013) asserts, transparency.

Some experts believe the problem will not only get worse, but is regularly occurring without detection. Security writer Bruce Schneier (2015), addressing the VW scenario, worried that "computers allow people to cheat in ways that are new. Because the cheating is encapsulated in software, the malicious actions can happen at a far remove from the testing itself. Because the software is "smart" in ways that normal objects are not, the cheating can be subtler and harder to detect ... and they will cheat smarter. For all of VW's brazenness, its cheating was obvious once people knew to look for it. Far cleverer would be to make the cheating look like an accident. Overall, software quality is so bad that products ship with thousands of programming mistakes" (Schneier 2015).

What CEP brings to the table is a model for establishing what the NIST Cyber Physical Systems Public Working Group referred to as "an accurate 'trail of provenance'" in its first draft for public comment (NIST 2015b). Complex event processing, coupled with other well-understood design patterns, can expose test conditions, operating assumptions regarding pre-existing conditions (e.g., vehicle is currently being tested for emissions), alert mechanisms, and other configuration parameters. A similar regulatory scenario faces organizations that must process health-care data in the United States. Such firms are subject to comparatively strict regulation under Health Information Portability and Accountability Act (HIPAA). The advent of digital patient health records and wearable medical devices brings IoT into a US health care regulatory framework.

In a paper provocatively titled "Let SDN Be Your Eyes," Bates et al. (2014) proposed that software-defined networks (SDN) present "interesting new opportunities for network forensics," observing that "the network itself can be used as a part of observation." Adapting data provenance to the domain of network provenance, they note that "within the context of the data center, network provenance can be used to trace back traffic and discover the cause of a [network] event." The approach taken is to construct a "provenance graph" which can be queried to "replay" network events (Zhou et al. 2011). The authors envision a pure SDN data center which can be instrumented with "Provenance Verification Points" that can perform forensic analysis or act as passive monitors.

An SDN thus provisioned could embed CEP capabilities itself, or relay messages to a separate CEP processing resource which can host more complex, rich models of device-, domain-, or ontology-dependent event representations. Systems capable of inference-making, accessing prior history or attack templates and past annotations could provide another avenue for both defense and forensics. Livingston et al. note that "as annotation efforts expand to capture more complex information, annotations will need to be able to refer to knowledge structures formally defined in terms of more atomic knowledge structures" (Livingston et al. 2013).

Many smart IoT devices will likely require periodic upgrades, and it seems unlikely that the current model for a house system administration role would be sufficient for performing this duty on hundreds of thousands of potentially diverse nodes. Rather it seems likely that smart devices will be self-updating, with self-administered software becoming increasingly ubiquitous. These updates will be delivered as data over IoT networks, and present a reliability as well as a security risk as the provenance for those updates could be difficult to establish. Rollback might be difficult or impossible with some devices, yet testing sensor network integrity across multiple devices might not be feasible. Orchestrating configuration changes might well entail approaches that integrate CEP with more conventional techniques. Such methods would ideally allow both forensic rewind-and-replay as well as features to enhance resilience while systems are live.

8.5 SUMMARY

There is considerable overlap between the techniques employed to enhance IoT systems for audit, privacy policy transparency, and forensics. Taken together, these approaches represent possible elements in an overall risk management framework. The IoT life cycle perspective is likely to call for Big Data and CEP resources at all project phases: planning, simulation, operations, maintenance, and failure analysis.

Methods considered when addressing IoT IA will likely revisit previous design patterns, including middleware, intelligent agents, and provenance for distributed systems. Any one of these could be combined in an integrated risk framework such as the NBD-PWG security fabric to improve IoT information assurance (Chang et al. 2008). Future versions of the NBD-PWG effort is expected to integrate current defensive countermeasures with a workflow model. Work in scientific workflows such as Zhao et al. 2008), DataOne D-OPM may prove to be helpful design patterns, though they are not hosted atop Big Data frameworks at this point.

Meanwhile, other studies demonstrate the use of "provenance wrappers" and elsewhere suggest a means of representing information assurance attributes in ways that facilitate reasoning over such properties in a workflow (Moitra et al. 2009). These approaches could be adapted for DevOps in Big Data frameworks, which may become *de facto* sensor data standard repositories.

Improvements in IoT information systems provenance can be made in several areas:

- **Provenance benefits for IoT audit.** Whether audit data can be trusted may seem like a straightforward problem of signature analysis, but the problem extends beyond simple logging.
- **Provenance benefits for IoT digital forensics.** Systematic treatment of IoT devices in information systems consists of a judicious selection of domain-specific, device-specific practices, and the use of more general design patterns applicable across CEP.
- **The return of ETL.** The role of ETL has recently been subordinated by widespread adoption of Big Data schemes that argue for collection of large-scale raw data sets without pre-filtering. For some IoT settings, however, this approach may not scale. Etzion and Niblett (2010, p. 176) devote considerable attention to the role of filtering and transformation in event networks. Products such as Syncsort's DMX-h, designed to work with Hadoop data lakes, could serve a useful purpose in filtering, for example, SIEM logs or producing unified data collections from disparate data sources that specialized processor-agents might ingest.
- **Provenance benefits for IoT system safety and resilience**. Systems that are designed with an eye to possible data quality deterioration or interruption will likely need to build or adopt manufacturer-supplied device models. While this introduces complexity and additional software configuration management effort, it can also improve the potential for improved safety and resilience.
- **False positive reduction.** In a survey of risks associated with critical infrastructure networks including smart grid, SCADA, and industrial control, Knapp & Langill (2014) cited numerous instances where false positives could interfere not only with proper interpretation of events, but could lead to erroneous network deactivation or other adverse effects. The problem of false positives in IoT networks built from numerous, low-cost, weather-exposed, non-secured sensors could be serious. Abimbola et al. (2006) demonstrated the problems that false positives introduced into intrusion detection systems. The effects go beyond automated systems. As shown in a work by Thompson et al. (2006), the burden of false positives can adversely affect the performance of human monitors. In some instances, such as in a medical setting, the result could be fatal, as in a recent Long Island nursing home case (Lam 2015).

Cognitive aspects of event perception remain poorly understood in communities where systems requirements are developed (Zacks & Swallow 2007). This lack is likely to result in security or oversight lapses, with an attendant need for increased demand for IoT forensics capabilities. As the number and variety of devices grows, including both sensors and digital collectors, the burden on systems and human operators is likely to encroach on reliability, even privacy expectations, in unpredictable ways.

8.6 CONCLUSION

It is another "engineer's lament" that perfection is the enemy of the good. Producing fully assured IoT systems may be beyond the capabilities of all but academic scenarios. That is not to say there is no role for the safety engineer, or that there is not plenty of brushed-metal sheen to the technology, safety engineers employ. Addressing the challenge of IoT system imperfections and compromises – especially those brought about by determined attackers or sheer configuration complexity – will require steady computational and human incremental improvements.

Systematic use of CEP can improve on current information assurance practices, especially if its paradigms and design practices are more widely incorporated into IoT architectures. At the same time, education and training for developer and IoT user communities will be needed. In the aviation community where safety practices have a long history, technological improvements are accompanied by research into how crews and ground personnel are to receive alerts and displays from sensor systems. In a recent study of human factors in the design of flight deck displays, a Federal Aviation Administration (FAA) report included recommendations such as the following (Yeh et al. 2013, section 8.1):

- The latency period induced by the display system, particularly for alerts, should not be excessive and should take into account the criticality of the alert and the required crew response time to minimize propagation of the failure condition.
- Timely alerts for each phase of flight should be provided when any operating limit is reached or exceeded for the required power plant parameter.
- Alerting conditions such as establishing how airplane system conditions or operational events that require an alert (e.g., engine overheating, wind shear), will be determined.
- Provide individual alerts for each function essential for safe operation.
- Alerting messages should differentiate between normal and abnormal indications.
- The number and type of alerts required should be determined by the unique situations that are being detected and by the crew procedures required to address those situations.

These representative requirements from FAA researchers set forth to guide cockpit designers illustrate commonalities between IoT security engineering and the more mature aviation safety engineering. It may be reasonable to expect that for some critical IoT systems, simulation, test, avionics-like instrumentation, and black box-like forensics capabilities will be similar in nature, but even more complex to develop and manage. The complexity presents both opportunity and risk. IoT system attacks can take place across multiple fronts where protections are not cost-effective or feasible. On the other hand, CEP affords additional opportunities for detection, remediation, or resilience. System architects are well-advised to consider mechanisms to tolerate failure, whether system and service resilience are seen as a control problem or a call for a better decision support for operator-managers (Kocsis et al. 2008; Snediker et al. 2008).

REFERENCES

Abimbola, A.A., Munoz, J.M., & Buchanan, W.J. 2006. Investigating false positive reduction in http via procedure analysis. In: International Conference on Networking and Services, 2006, ICNS, July 2006, pp. 87–87.

Bates, A., Butler, K., Haeberlen, A., Sherr, M., & Zhou, W. 2014. Let SDN be your eyes: Secure forensics in data center networks. In: Proceedings of the NDSS Workshop on Security of Emerging Network Technologies (SENT'14), February 2014.

Bauer, S., & Schreckling, D. 2013. Data Provenance in the Internet of Things. In: EU Project COMPOSE, Conference Seminar.

Bock, C., & Gruninger, M., 2005. PSL: a semantic domain for flow models. *Software & Systems Modeling*, 4(2), pp. 209–231.

Braun, U., Shinnar, A., & Seltzer, M.I. 2008. Securing Provenance. In: HotSec, July 2008.

Buneman, P., Khanna, S., & Wang-Chiew, T. 2001. Why and where: A characterization of data provenance. In: *Database Theory – ICDT 2001*. Springer, Berlin Heidelberg, pp. 316–330.

Chang, R.Y., Podgurski, A., & Yang, J. 2008. Discovering neglected conditions in software by mining dependence graphs. *IEEE Transactions on Software Engineering*, 34(5), pp. 579–596.

Chen, P., Plale, B., & Aktas, M.S. 2014. Temporal representation for mining scientific data provenance. *Future Generation Computer Systems*, 36, pp. 363–378.

Etzion, O., & Niblett, P. 2010. *Event Processing in Action*. Manning Publications Co.

Garlan, D., Allen, R., & Ockerbloom, J. 1995. Architectural mismatch or why it's hard to build systems out of existing parts. In: Proceedings of the 17th International Conference on Software Engineering, April 1995, pp. 179–185.

Govindarajan, N., Simmhan, Y., Jamadagni, N., & Misra, P. 2014. Event processing across edge and the cloud for Internet of Things applications. In: Proceedings of the 20th International Conference on Management of Data, Computer Society of India, December 2014, pp. 101–104.

Hendler, J. 2014. Data Integration for Heterogenous Datasets. *Big Data*, 2(4), pp. 205–215.

Hoare, C.A.R. 1978. *Communicating Sequential Processes*. Springer, New York, pp. 413–443.

Jennions, I.K. 2013. *Integrated Vehicle Health Management: The Technology (Integrated Vehicle Health Management (IVHM))*. Society of Automotive Engineers.

Kim, S.D., Lee, J.Y., Kim, D.Y., Park, C.W., & La, H.J. 2014. Modeling BPEL-Based Collaborations with Heterogeneous IoT Devices. In: IEEE 12th International Conference on Dependable, Autonomic and Secure Computing (DASC), August 2014, pp. 289–294.

Knapp, E.D., & Langill, J.T., 2014. *Industrial Network Security: Securing Critical Infrastructure Networks for Smart Grid, SCADA, and Other Industrial Control Systems*. Syngress.

Kocsis, I., Csertán, G., Pásztor, P.L., & Pataricza, A. 2008. Dependability and security metrics in controlling infrastructure. In: Second International Conference on Emerging Security Information, Systems and Technologies, SECURWARE'08, August 2008, pp. 368–374.

Lam, C. 2015. Ex-aide in Medford nursing home death testifies staff ignored warning alarms for 2 hours, *Newsday*. Available at http://www.newsday.com/long-island/suffolk/medford-nursing-home-staff-ignored-warning-alarms-for-2-hours-witness-in-death-case-says-1.10496777. Accessed on June 15, 2015.

Lange, R.J. 2010. Provenance aware sensor networks for real-time data analysis.

Ledlie, J., & Holland, D.A. 2005. Provenance-aware sensor data storage. In: 21st IEEE International Conference on Data Engineering Workshops, 2005, April 2005, pp. 1189–1189.

Le-Phuoc, D., & Hauswirth, M. (2009). Linked open data in sensor data mashups. In Proceedings of the 2nd International Conference on Semantic Sensor Networks-Volume 522 (pp. 1–16). CEUR-WS. org.

Livingston, K.M., Bada, M., Hunter, L.E., & Verspoor, K. 2013. Representing annotation compositionality and provenance for the Semantic Web. *Journal of Biomedical Semantics*, 4, p. 38.

Luckham, D.C. 2011. *Event Processing for Business: Organizing the Real-time Enterprise*. John Wiley & Sons.

Luckham, D.C., & Frasca, B. 1998. Complex event processing in distributed systems. Computer Systems Laboratory Technical Report CSL-TR-98-754. Stanford University, Stanford, CA.

Lundberg, A. 2006. Leverage complex event processing to improve operational performance. *Business Intelligence Journal*, 11(1), p. 55.

Milner, R. 1980. *A Calculus of Communicating Systems*. Springer-Verlag, Berlin; New York.

Moitra, A., Barnett, B., Crapo, A., & Dill, S.J. 2009. Data provenance architecture to support information assurance in a multi-level secure environment. In: MILCOM 2009 - 2009 IEEE Military Communications Conference, October 2009, pp. 1–7.

National Institute of Standards and Technology (NIST), 2015a. NIST Big Data Interoperability Framework, vol. 4, Available at https://s3.amazonaws.com/nist-sgcps/cpspwg/pwgglobal/CPS_PWG_Draft_Framework_for_Cyber-Physical_Systems_Release_0_8_September_2015.pdf. Accessed on September 30, 2015.

National Institute of Standards and Technology (NIST), 2015b. Draft Framework for Cyber-Physical Systems, *NIST*. Available at http://www.cpspwg.org/Portals/3/docs/CPS%20PWG%20Draft%20Framework%20for%20Cyber-Physical%20Systems%20Release%200.8%20September%202015.pdf. Accessed on September 30, 2015.

Negiz, A., & Cinar, A., 1992. On the detection of multiple sensor abnormalities in multivariate processes. In: American Control Conference, 1992, June 1992, pp. 2364–2368.

Park, U., & Heidemann, J. 2008. Provenance in sensornet republishing. In: *Provenance and Annotation of Data and Processes*. Springer, Berlin Heidelberg, pp. 280–292.

Progress Software 2009. Managing Assurance from Customer to Network to Service with Complex Event Processing. Available at http://media.techtarget.com/Syndication/ENTERPRISE_APPS/ManagingAssurance_CEP.pdf. Accessed on May 1, 2015.

Pustejovsky, J., Littman, J., & Saurí, R. 2007. Arguments in TimeML: events and entities. Lecture Notes in Computer Science, 4795, p. 107.

Reinartz, C., Metzger, A., & Pohl, K. 2015. Model-based verification of event-driven business processes. In: Proceedings of the 9th ACM International Conference on Distributed Event-Based Systems, June 2015, pp. 1–9.

Rosa, L., Alves, P., Cruz, T., Simões, P., & Monteiro, E. 2015. A comparative study of correlation engines for security event management. In: The Proceedings of the 10th International Conference on Cyber Warfare and Security (ICCWS 2015), Academic Conferences Limited, February 2015, p. 277.

Schneier, B. 2015. VW scandal could just be the beginning. Available at https://www.schneier.com/essays/archives/2015/09/vw_scandal_could_jus.html. Accessed on September 7, 2015.

Scott, D.S., 1982. Domains for denotational semantics. In: *Automata, Languages and Programming*. Springer, Berlin Heidelberg, pp. 577–610.

Snediker, D.E., Murray, A.T., & Matisziw, T.C. 2008. Decision support for network disruption mitigation. *Decision Support Systems*, 44(4), pp. 954–969.

Steinberg, R.A., Rudd, C., Lacy, S., & Hanna, A. 2011. *ITIL Service Operation*. TSO.

Sultana, S. & Bertino, E., 2013. A file provenance system. In: Proceedings of the 3rd ACM Conference on Data and Application Security and Privacy, February 2013, pp. 153–156.

Thompson, R.S., Rantanen, E.M., & Yurcik, W. 2006. Network intrusion detection cognitive task analysis: textual and visual tool usage and recommendations. In: *Proceedings of the Human Factors and Ergonomics Society Annual Meeting*, October 2006, vol. 50(5). SAGE Publications, pp. 669–673.

Tufekci, Z. 2015. Volkswagen and the era of cheating software, *New York Times*, p. A35.

Tung, R., Zimetbaum, P., & Josephson, M.E. 2008. A critical appraisal of implantable cardioverter-defibrillator therapy for the prevention of sudden cardiac death. *Journal of the American College of Cardiology*, 52(14), pp. 1111–1121.

Underwood, M., Gruninger, M., & Obrst, L. 2015. Internet of things: Toward smart networked systems and societies. The Ontology Summit 2015 communiqué. *Applied Ontology*, 10(3), p. 4.

Van der Aalst, W.M. 1998. The application of Petri nets to workflow management. *Journal of Circuits, Systems, and Computers*, 8(01), pp. 21–66.

Vianello, V., Gulisano, V., Jimenez-Peris, R., Patiño-Martínez, M., Torres, R., Diaz, R., & Prieto, E., 2013. A scalable SIEM correlation engine and its application to the olympic games IT infrastructure. In: 18th International Conference on Availability, Reliability and Security (ARES), 2013 September, pp. 625–629.

Yeh, M., Jin Jo, Y., Donovan, C., & Gabree, S. 2013. Human factors considerations in the design and evaluation of flight deck displays and controls. United States Department of Transportation in the interest of information exchange, Washington.

Zacks, J.M., & Swallow, K.M. 2007. Event segmentation. *Current Directions in Psychological Science*, 16(2), pp. 80–84.

Zawoad, S., & Hasan, R., 2015. FAIoT: Towards building a forensics aware eco system for the Internet of Things. In: IEEE International Conference on Services Computing (SCC), June 2015, pp. 279–284.

Zhao, J., Goble, C., Stevens, R., & Turi, D. 2008. Mining Taverna's semantic web of provenance. *Concurrency and Computation: Practice and Experience*, 20(5), pp. 463–472.

Zhou, W., Fei, Q., Narayan, A., Haeberlen, A., Loo, B.T., & Sherr, M. 2011. Secure network provenance. In: Proceedings of the Twenty-Third ACM Symposium on Operating Systems Principles, October 2011, pp. 295–310.

PART IV

CLOUD ARTIFICIAL INTELLIGENCE CYBER-PHYSICAL SYSTEMS

CHAPTER 9

A STEADY-STATE FRAMEWORK FOR ASSESSING SECURITY MECHANISMS IN A CLOUD-OF-THINGS ARCHITECTURE

TYSON T. BROOKS and LEE McKNIGHT

School of Information Studies, Syracuse University, Syracuse, NY, USA

VARIABLE NOMENCLATURE

The following are notations of variables and parameters used in this chapter:

C_N	represents the set of communication nodes in the CoT
d	represents the distance in the total communication path
L_{tot}	represents total performance path loss for each communication node in the CoT
T	physical and virtual things used to process data in a CoT environment
SM	represents a network thing characterized by one or more security mechanisms
T_S	represents the total security of the IoT system is approximately the sum of all the things with associated security mechanisms and/or controls
RM	represents a reader, authenticator, tag, etc., mechanism
H	represents the subset of P whose security elements that have human security configuration flaw
TE	represents the subset of P whose security elements that have a technical error
$H\&TE$	represents the subset of P whose elements are sectors that have human security configuration flaws and technical errors

Cyber-Assurance for the Internet of Things, First Edition. Edited by Tyson T. Brooks.
© 2017 by The Institute of Electrical and Electronic Engineers, Inc. Published 2017 by John Wiley & Sons, Inc.

P	represents probability of occurrence that sectors are vulnerable due to human security configuration flaws, technical errors or both
$P(SM_{SteadyState})_v$	the probability of occurrence of the steady state for sector v
$SM_{SteadyState}$	the steady-state event that a sector is vulnerable
v	represents the security mechanisms that are vulnerable
n	represents the security mechanisms that are not vulnerable
$P(x)$	the subset of v and $-P(x)$
$P(N)$	represents the likelihood of occurrence of a non-vulnerable CoT Sector
$P(V)$	represents the likelihood of occurrence of a vulnerable CoT sector
A_v	the event that sector v is vulnerable

9.1 INTRODUCTION

The ability to process large amounts of data with the integration of the Internet of Things (IoT) and cloud computing environments means organizations can trade sophisticated security estimation techniques for more accurate and simple models. As data are received and processed by digital sensors/tags/actuators, information will be fed directly into the IoT/cloud computing network for computation (or storage) and non-digital information has to be encoded to become digital information before it can be processed. The architecture supporting this new environment and the wide application of modern information technology (IT) will turn the network into an unobstructed, grid-style entity with revolutionary changes in data transmission methods, modes, and processing alike. The more data processed in these new and potentially unsecured architectures, the more undetectable vulnerabilities become.

Organizations have recognized the need for timely access to comprehensive, accurate, timely, and relevant information on which to base important business decisions (Brooks 2009b). Traditional system analysis and control methods can not explicitly consider the impacts toward the IoT architecture. It is usually assumed that all IoT system "things/objects" (e.g., smart devices) data will be received and processed timely, accurately, and reliably. At its essence, cloud computing enables organizations to utilize instantly provisioned scalable IT resources on a pay-per-use basis (Brooks et al. 2012b). These resources can be rapidly provisioned and released with minimal management effort or service provider interaction (Brooks & McKnight 2013). The capacity to recycle these services across the organization requires the integration of technologies including internets/intranets/extranets, e-mail, data warehousing, data mining, and workflow/document management systems (Brooks 2009a). Any cloud, regardless of its service deployment or architecture, can be internal or external: internal clouds reside inside an organization's network security perimeter while external clouds reside outside the same perimeter (Stallings & Stallings 1997). Cloud architectures designed for Big Data analysis are optimized to maximize input/output (I/O) throughput and minimize hardware costs. Virtual servers and virtual private networks provide the ability to quickly reconfigure available cloud resources on demand and provide the necessary security assurance (Rimal et al. 2011). Virtual computing environments are most often compromised due to the intentional exploitation of defects that arise from inherent deficiencies in the virtual computing environment's production environment (Brooks et al. 2012a). These features allow a single application to scale to thousands of machines, and each machine added increases the processing and storage capacity linearly.

The IoT network is a huge and complex system comprised of numerous devices and high-tech equipment and technology, which has wide coverage and involves a very broad scope of content (Qian & Wang 2012). The IoT operates as an interconnected grid network consisting of various types of networks (e.g., client/server, cloud, wireless) so that information can be transmitted in various forms including sound, word, image, and multimedia (Qian & Wang 2012). Working under the high demands of time-effectiveness, accuracy, stability, and information security, IoT data processing and operations of the system itself are very complicated. The IoT will create a huge network of billions or trillions of "Things" communicating each other (Chen et al. 2014b). In the IoT, smart things/objects are expected to become active participants in business and information and social processes, where they are enabled to interact and communicate amongst themselves and with the environment by exchanging data and information sensed about the environment, while reacting autonomously to the real/physical-world events and influencing it by running processes that trigger actions and create services with or without direct human intervention (Weber 2010). The IoT has the purpose of providing an IT infrastructure, facilitating the exchanges of things in a secure and reliable manner (Chunming et al. 2012).

9.2 BACKGROUND

In the IoT paradigm, many of the objects that surround us will be on the network in one form or another; radio frequency identification (RFID) and wireless sensor network (WSN) technologies will rise to meet this new challenge, in which information and communication systems are invisibly embedded in the environment around us (Gubbi et al. 2013). At face value, the IoT is an integrated part of the "Future Internet" including existing and evolving Internet and network developments, and could be conceptually defined as a dynamic global network infrastructure with self-configuring capabilities based on standard and interoperable communication protocols where physical and virtual "things" have identities, physical attributes, and virtual personalities, use intelligent interfaces, and are seamlessly integrated into the information network (Weber 2010).

Cloud computing platforms are defined primarily by scalability, both in terms of ability to grow and efficiency at large-scale, and revenue generation and cost savings (Mazzucco et al. 2010). Developed in response to the challenges of storing large amounts of data, cloud computing platforms are designed to enable breakthroughs for organizations seeking to extract important information from multiple, large data sets. Historically, cloud architectures were designed for Big Data analysis for optimization to maximize I/O throughput and minimize hardware costs (Abadi 2009). An analytic cloud capability should be part of a larger data processing and storage pipeline. Well-defined services for Cloud-of-Things (CoT) can be built and deployed over cloud resources to allow various organizations to all benefit from the economies of scale possible through an enterprise-wide infrastructure.

For the IoT, it is necessary to develop a CoT covering the physical and wireless space. In IoT operations, there will be no boundary to the cyberspace realm which will extend to anywhere on the Internet. Therefore, the CoT is not only confined to the actual IoT network with devices, hardware, and software, but should also involve the whole dimensions of a CoT strategy. In this CoT-dimensional environment for the IoT, the main mode of transmission of information is wireless (e.g., ultra-short wave, satellite). In terms of the IoT, the CoT platform must combine defense and security into a single, unified entity. Each of the CoT components not only can act separately and independently in a particular time segment and area during operations, but must also be integrated to form a single operation system. Hence, the CoT platform not only has to cover and connect the various systems in the IoT network, but should also be able to separate or realign the various components based on configuration changes.

With respect to the IoT network for information flow, the CoT platform should cover the sensor and information networks for the IoT so that the networks can work together as a whole. This also includes malicious detection, information transmission, and processing networks into the CoT platform and ensuring full network coverage and linkage in all the areas where information has to reach. With regard to the level of operations, the CoT platform should achieve the integration of various security controls (e.g., access, authentication), essential IoT elements and processes (e.g., integration of systemic power from the smart grid, sensors, tags) even from the integration of new processes and information implementations (Yahav et al. 2013). For example, the smart grid relies heavily on the underlying communication network to collect system information and transfer control signals (Subashini & Kavitha 2011). Therefore, the failures of switches, communication links, and servers will downgrade the communication network performance and threaten the security of the smart grid (Subashini & Kavitha 2011). In practice, attackers can disable a switch, a communication server, or a communication link by launching a denial-of-services/distributed denial-of-service (DoS/DDoS) attack; or they can simply destroy these devices physically if not well protected. Even without an attacker, these devices may also experience random hardware/software faults. It is therefore important to quantitatively measure the impacts of device failures on the overall performance of the IoT network.

IoT networks use high-capacity and high-speed transmission of data processing and full compatibility in various formats. To meet this requirement, the IoT network provides many different methods of data transmissions; these various transmission modes and methods are used in combination, and in particular, through the development of optical cables and satellite systems for long-distance transmissions. The bandwidth of IoT data transmissions is extensive; various frequencies such as high frequency (HF), extremely low frequency (ELF), and ultra-high frequency (UHF) are utilized and with the bandwidths being allocated automatically according to the properties of the information transmitted. Furthermore, the IoT system has a high compatibility which can handle various formats of information such as voice, data, images, and multi-media documents at the same time. The capability of uninterrupted wireless data processing at any time and under any circumstances, through standardization of transmission of information in various systems in the IoT, is required even under hostile conditions to satisfy the requests of devices accessing the IoT network. As such, physical layer monitoring through a CoT will be essential in the IoT network.

9.2.1 Related Work

Presently, there is no existing "steady-state" framework specifically designed for a CoT architecture. However, in the area of network resiliency under attack, Chen et al. (2014a) researched a fusion-based defense mechanism to mitigate the damage caused by an intentional attack and analyzed the critical value for the percolation-based connectivity under intentional attacks of an IoT infrastructure. Chen et al. (2014a) research implemented a fusion-based defense mechanism on the Internet router-level topology and a European power grid, producing both analytical results and empirical network data showing that the proposed mechanism greatly enhances the network robustness to prevent IoT infrastructure from disruption. Chen and Hero's (2014) research introduced new methods for evaluating and improving resilience of network connectivity to attacks or failures on nodes of the network using a new centrality measure called edge rewiring that quantifies sensitivity of the size of the largest connected component to node removals. Using the topology of the power grid of western US states, this research showed that the power grid topology is especially vulnerable to nodal attacks and in particular, by using our new centrality measure, an attacker could reduce the largest component size by nearly a factor of two by only targeting 0.2% of the nodes (Chen & Hero 2014). Chen and Cheng (2015) developed a sequential defense mechanism based on sequential hypothesis test in complex networks with an aim of enhancing the network robustness of networked engineering systems. Chen and Cheng's (2015) research developed a mechanism which provides timely and efficient defense against random and intentional attacks by sequentially acquiring binary attack status of each node in descending degree order. By implementing this mechanism on the canonical complex network models as well as the empirical network data extracted from the World Wide Web (WWW), the Internet, the European super grid, and the US power grid topology, the results validate the effectiveness and reliability of this mechanism against fatal attacks and based on the performance analysis and network configurations, several approaches including link addition, topology adjustment, and detection capability enhancement are elucidated to guarantee robust operations of the entire system (Chen & Hero 2014).

With both cloud computing and IoT approaches, issues of complexity of the steady-state approach and how quickly a decision can really be made must be considered before and during the actual steady state implementation can occur (Harmonosky et al. 1997). Further, there is often the underlying assumption that steady-state analysis may not always be the best approach and the long-term effects upon system performance of short-term probability decisions are not specifically considered (Harmonosky et al. 1997). Since the number of devices to be controlled in the CoT will be rather large, most processing control actions will be completed based on extended information throughout the network. Therefore, the traffic of the CoT communication network will be very congested. In addition, existing communication networks are not open-access networks, which are relatively independent and do not have many interfaces with external networks. Because of these characteristics of the CoT, the impact of not having a steady-state framework to analysis the new architecture creates a significant risk.

9.3 ESTABLISHING A FRAMEWORK FOR CoT ANALYSIS

The basic task of the steady-state model for the CoT will be to support the defense for the CoT network through detecting technical loopholes and topographic structures from the various CoT networks and the data/information stored inside the system. By determining tactical and technical parameters of CoT wireless equipment and systems, discovering irregularities of electronic tags and their threat levels and analyzing tags/readers strong and weak APs provide the interoperability for organizing and carrying out CoT defense. The steady-state model will support the CoT network, devices, and system performance through its normal functions. The concrete tasks are mainly, through multiple means and methods, to guarantee the normal operations of a user's own computing device or network system and processing of secure data transmissions and support defending against malicious intrusions.

The above assumption, however, may no longer hold true for satellite networks, mobile networks, embedded systems, wireless networks, RFID, and even the Internet. For example, since the number of smart devices in the future smart grid environment can be massive (e.g., a single distribution network may cover thousands of distributed generators, electric vehicles, and controllable loads), and each smart device needs to exchange status information, market-related information, and control signals with the control center in the future; thus the data traffic can be extremely heavy (Yan et al. 2013). On the other hand, since a communication channel does not currently exist between distributed smart devices and an existing cloud center, the most economical way to implement the CoT will be by utilizing existing general-purpose communication networks (e.g., the Internet or mobile phone network).

Since a general communication network is a public characteristic and usually covers a large geographical space, the communication delay and data loss will be non-neglectable and can significantly degrade the control system performance. The performance of the CoT has great impacts on these types of operations and must be taken into consideration. The CoT architecture includes the traditional cloud computing models (i.e., software-as-a-service (SaaS), platform-as-a-service (PaaS), infrastructure-as-a-service (IaaS)) with the inclusion of IoT components such as ubiquitous connectivity technologies (e.g., machine-to-machine (M2M), RFID, WSN, supervisory control and data acquisition (SCADA)) and devices (e.g., sensors, actuators, controllers) over wireless networks (Xia 1996; Ghosh et al. 2010; Rimal et al. 2011). Leveraging the China Communications Standards Association (CCSA)

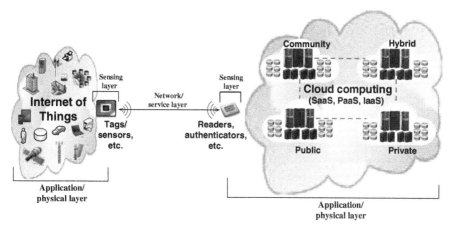

FIGURE 9.1   A future CoT architecture comprising IoT components with embedded tags, sensors, etc., providing secure wireless frames to CoT readers, authenticators, etc., for integration and interoperability with cloud computing environments. Reproduced with permission of IEEE.

reference model for the IoT (Chen et al. 2014a), the CoT includes three functional sectors as follows: (1) sensing sector which connects sensors, controllers, RFID readers, and location sensing device (e.g., GPS) to the network/service sector, (2) network/service sector which includes networks (e.g., 4G, IPv6 over low-power wireless personal area networks (6LoWPANs), urban low-power and lossy networks (U-LLNs), optical fiber networks, satellite networks) utilizing web protocols (e.g., constrained application protocols (CoAP) for CoT devices used by different CoT applications, and (3) the application/physical sector which includes cloud and IoT hardware components and common function and open application programming interfaces (API) for interoperability. A generic CoT architecture is displayed in Figure 9.1.

The steady state of the CoT framework provides the ability to be able to rate the effectiveness of various composed security solutions at countering both random and intentionally introduced vulnerabilities during defined operational states (e.g., development, maintenance, production). Many researchers consider the steady state security related quality attributes to be a part of the system dependability[1] (Kopetz et al. 1995; Laprie 1995; Madan et al. 2004). Through vulnerability analysis, a resultant rating is not intended as an absolute rating but used as a relative comparison to other security solutions. For example, it could be used to compare the efficiency of a composed security solution to an equivalent smart grid architecture or of a solution with $\underline{n}$ levels to one with $n + 1$ or $n - 1$ levels. Having a well-defined framework for doing so will be important for providing repeatable and consistent assessments of proposed security solutions made up of multiple levels of system components. The initial use of this analysis will be to assess security control (e.g.,

---

[1] Dependability is defined as the property of computer system such that reliance can justifiably be placed on the service it delivers (Chen et al. 2014; Chen & Cheng 2015).

access controls, authentication, authorization, encryption, identity management, cryptography) mechanisms, but this analytic approach should be extensible to assessing other non-technical security solutions (e.g., fences, guards, locks) as well.

The security-critical components of a network can be represented by an idealized network of things, each of which can be characterized in such a way as to incorporate it into the CoT architecture. These CoT "Things" (which can also be known as objects) that represent hardware and software may be considered physical, whereas more abstract security services may be considered virtual (Liang et al. 2011). Physical things are tangible, or directly observable, and encompass security components such as smart devices, routers, switches, firewalls, servers, etc. Virtual things are intangible and encompass more ephemeral security controls such as encryption, access control policies, security software, physical security, etc. Each thing may have one or more access points where they are connected to the other things in the CoT network.

9.3.1 Defining Path Loss for System Performance

As displayed in Figure 9.2, the CoT architecture can be divided into three layers, that is, the application/physical, sensing, and network/services. The "things/objects" within the CoT are responsible for the processing, transferring, and collecting of information respectively, and jointly determine the overall performance of the CoT system. Mathematical models for computing, communication, and "things\objects" sensing components must first be developed and integrated with existing system models to form the model of the CoT architecture. Similar to traditional systems, the CoT system can be formulated using differential/algebraic equations, respectively. The main difference between a CoT system and a standard IT system lies in that the CoT system usually has several discrete working environments (i.e., states) made up of various standard IT systems. Therefore, identifying the transition between

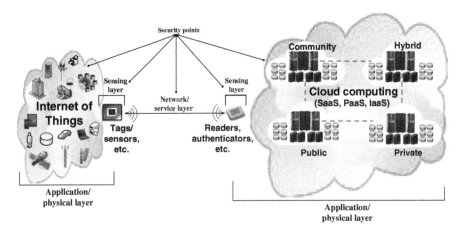

FIGURE 9.2 A depiction of security points in a future CoT architecture. Reproduced with permission of IEEE.

different working states is of the upmost importance, the architecture models can be conveniently integrated to form the comprehensive system models of the CoT architecture.

Since the CoT architecture is a network of systems, its basic state can therefore be formulated as a network flow model. Any CoT architecture, sensing devices, and some computing devices are the sources of information flow, their functions are to generate information and then eject into the communication network. Other computing devices are at the end of information flow, since they are used to receive the information and conduct necessarily analysis. The communication network is responsible for transferring information and information exchange devices (e.g., routers and switches), determining the transmission path of each data packet, or in other words, determining the directions of information flows (Vermesan et al. 2011). Determining the path loss of this communication due to attenuation is crucial in planning the CoT to assist in interference estimations and frequency assignments (Yan et al. 2013).

Therefore, system performance for the CoT can be formulated as follows: C_N is the set of communication nodes in the CoT where each node can represent a computing AP, communication or sensing device, or their combination. d represents the distance in the total communication path and L_{tot} is the total path loss during communications. As it relates to the total path loss for each communication node in the CoT (Yan et al. 2013), it is described by:

$$L_{tot}(d) = \left(\frac{\lambda}{4\Pi d_0}\right)^2 x \left(\frac{d}{d_0}\right)^{C_n} \tag{9.1}$$

Using the equation(9.1), the performance analysis of the CoT can be carried out. When the information volume injected into the node and link does not exceed their exchange and transmission limits, the CoT will begin its "steady state." Since the data packets are passed directly to and from the actual physical transmission medium and bypass layers three through seven of the communications protocol,[2] the synchronous signals are sent as rapidly as possible between the actual devices. Based on the traffic of the CoT network, a data packet will have seven different passes through the communications protocol to select and therefore, the CoT may have several differing working states. The purpose of the analysis is to establish a feasible working environment based on solving equation (9.1). By performing this first analysis, the performance information flows of all the links in the CoT network can be obtained, and whether a CoT network is able to support the operation of a specific control can then be determined.

---

[2] In the Open System Interconnection (OSI) model, a communication network can be divided into seven layers (i.e., physical, data link, network, transport, session, presentation, application layers) based on their functions.

9.3.2 Foundations of the Steady-State Framework

The discussion to this point has used a broad, somewhat vague definition of network thing, T, both physical and virtual. Specific things must be further defined, even imperfectly, in order to better advance discussion of the framework. Each thing will be generically characterized by the following constants: T, physical and virtual things[3] used to process data in a CoT environment. For example, encryption is a good example of a virtual security thing as it will have a security value which is essentially infinite since the encrypting thing must be configured and functioning properly.

Since a network cyber-attack can bypass existing security controls, a security thing has a high probability of being able to bypass any identical security thing with an identical configuration. Therefore, only the first identical thing an adversary encounters contributes to the overall security of the network. Any additional identical things are considered to have security points to provide security, as seen in Figure 9.2. Realistically, there will be other infrastructures, but this simple case will serve as an initial example.

Each network thing can be characterized by one or more security mechanisms, SM, that define an objective, quantitative measure of the security provided by that thing in the context of the larger CoT network. SM must provide some insight into the effectiveness of security controls provided by the thing and alternatively, SM can represent the difficulty seen by a hacker attempting to bypass the security controls provided by that thing. In either case, SM is a function of configuration, cost, and time of the security mechanism. Finally, there must be series and parallel addition operations for SM. Cyber-attacks by hackers can be characterized as attempts to penetrate or bypass network thing along one or more paths through the network. Breaching confidentiality and integrity might require a hacker to completely penetrate the security-critical things and denying availability could be as easy as overtaking an outward-facing wireless device.

The output of SM must be both useful to a user of the security framework and be comprised of realistically obtainable data. Instead of attempting to define the success rate for a network attack as a function of resources expended, one can consider the resources required to successfully attack a network thing with a reasonable success rate. Here, a "success rate" is not precisely defined, but can be thought of a level of accomplishment relatively constant and sets the output of T to be simply a measure of the resources required to launch a reasonably successful attack on a network thing.

Appropriately simplifying assumptions about the input to SM can be determined by considering the most likely characteristics of the function. For most network components, there is a minimum level of security configuration(s) required if the component is to function properly, though the security offered by a base configuration is not likely to be ideal. If significant effort or expertise is expended to secure the component, the security almost certainly increases, though even a perfectly configured device cannot be considered perfectly secure due to the prevalence of previously

---

[3] Physical and virtual things may be further characterized by whether or not any security is used to protect the confidentiality, integrity, and availability of data at different locations in the CoT network.

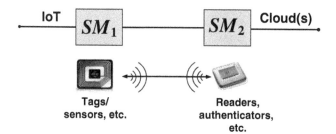

FIGURE 9.3 Network connection between two network things/objects transmitting data wirelessly. Reproduced with permission of IEEE.

unknown "zero-day" attacks. This option, shown in Figure 9.3, is less detailed but perhaps no less accurate, given the objective nature of security data-gathering process and the generic classification of network things. Defining the security function in this manner will allow users of the framework to readily estimate their security for a given resource expenditure for a given thing as well as the entire network. Security things in series could force a hacker to penetrate a thing in order to achieve some goal (e.g., to gain access to data), increasing the overall security of the system. Therefore, the security of the overall system is approximately the sum of things with associated security mechanisms and/or controls T_S. The series case is depicted by two things arranged linearly as shown in Figure 9.3.

In this case, the total security T_S of two independent network things T, and its corresponding security mechanisms SM_1 and SM_2 can be approximated for a series of independent things as follows:

$$T_S = T(SM_1) + T(SM_2) \tag{9.2}$$

In the example that follows, when two network things are connected analogously, as shown in Figure 9.4, the relationship becomes more complex, as a hacker is presented with multiple paths to achieve the same goal, and the overall security of the system is potentially diminished. A hacker with knowledge of the network topology will always choose to attack the weaker of the two things, or attack the thing that is most susceptible to the hacker's technical strengths.

This implies that SM_1 cannot be greater than the least SM_2 in the parallel network, if they both need to transmit data to a reader, tag, authenticator, etc., mechanism (RM_1). An additional complication is that each thing increases the attack surface of the parallel network, potentially allowing an adversary to choose an attack vector tailored to their strengths. It is possible, and perhaps probable that the overall security of the network might even be less than the minimum security of the thing taken individually.

For only two parallel things, this simplifies to:

$$SM = (SM_1 SM_2)/RM_1 \tag{9.3}$$

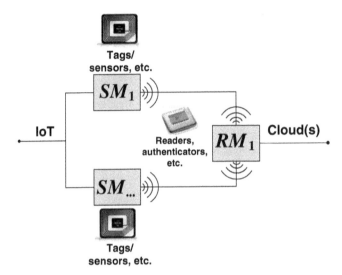

FIGURE 9.4   Parallel connection between two network things and one reader/authenticator for a cloud computing environment. Reproduced with permission of IEEE.

Therefore, an initial proposal for parallel addition is that security adds in a reciprocal:

$$SM = \frac{\left(SM_1^{-1} + SM_2^{-2} + \ldots + SM_N^{-N}\right)^{-N}}{RM_N} \tag{9.4}$$

If SM_1 and SM_N are not independent, a more complex relationship may be used if the precision gained warrants the effort expended. For example, if several readers with the same security configuration are used in one or more cloud computing environment, the overall security may not be any higher than the security of the first, as any attack that penetrates the first reader can readily be repeated to get through subsequent readers at little additional effort.

9.4   THE CoT STEADY-STATE FRAMEWORK

The CoT sensing, network/service and application/physical sectors consist of a collection of complex process and functions that will include providing security services. A sector that provides authorization services, for example, may consist of the actual encryption/decryption functions, configuration management functions, identity management, and key and certificate management functions. Treating all of that complexities as a CoT sector allows inclusion of a broad range of threats to the performance of a critical security control/function without having to deal with the details of each component. For the purposes of this analysis, each CoT sector is generally considered to be completely independent of others. Subsequent enhancements to this analysis approach should consider more realistic cases where the security levels are not completely independent, where they are administered by the same process, for example.

The steady state of a CoT sector characterizes the sector as being vulnerable or not. There is a single state defined to represent all non-vulnerable conditions, but multiple states are defined to represent the vulnerable conditions. Limiting the set of vulnerable states is important to keep the analysis achievable, so there must be some important assumptions that drive and bound the definition of the vulnerable steady state. Vulnerable CoT steady states are characterized as follows. (1) vulnerability causation: consideration is given to whether the vulnerability occurred through intentional or unintentional causes from either a human security configuration flaw, a technical error, or both, as it pertains to a network thing; (2) the CoT steady state for each CoT condition sector which could consist of an identified human security configuration flaws (e.g., device designs, patching, weak passwords), technical errors (e.g., unexpected verification conditions, invalid processing transactions, data inconsistence's) or both, which could lead to exploitation into the CoT network by a hacker; and (3) its impact (e.g., "high" causing severe damage, "medium" causing moderate damage, and "low" causing minimum damage) of the vulnerabilities considered from the perspective of the harm caused if exploited. The taxonomy shown in Figure 9.5 is provided to capture the above characteristics and identifies specific CoT steady states for each vulnerability area for a CoT sector that needs to be analyzed.

While each CoT sector is individually assigned a steady-state condition, the overall approach and value are to analyze the combination of the levels and determine how well they work together to thwart hacker attacks. Each combination of steady state of all levels being analyzed is referred to herein as a CoT steady-state case and each CoT steady-state case must be individually analyzed. As an example, assume a security control that uses two forms of successive access control and authentication to protect data being sent over the Internet via the CoT network. The threat is assumed to be coming remotely from hackers who are presently on the Internet. The hackers goal is to counter the confidentiality, integrity, and availability levels to recover underlying

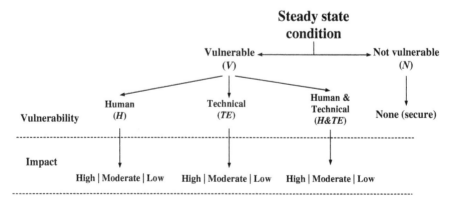

FIGURE 9.5 Steady-state taxonomy for the CoT sectors. Reproduced with permission of IEEE.

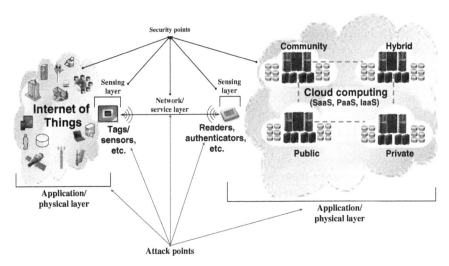

FIGURE 9.6   Attack points for the CoT sectors. Reproduced with permission of IEEE.

data and/or to penetrate the enclave network through specific attack points at the CoT application/physical, sensing, and network/service sectors security points as shown in Figure 9.6.

The CoT framework is only used for calculating the occurrence of the initial CoT steady state. To reiterate, a CoT sector is a collection of complex and secure functions, controls and activities that together provide sensing, network/services, and application/physical services. This proposed CoT steady-state framework is still theoretical and need sufficient vulnerability data for validity since security is absolutely critical to the framework's ability to accurately assess the security of a realistic CoT architecture. Following the logic in the taxonomy in Figure 9.7, a CoT sector can either be vulnerable or not vulnerable (not both). Therefore, in probability for events H, TE, and $H\&TE$, using the inclusion–exclusion principle (Papoulis & Pillai 2002), the Venn diagram becomes, for $n = 3$:

The vulnerabilities conditions are things of the set P consisting of identified human security configuration flaws, technical errors, or both. Thus, P has three subsets of interest as shown below:

$$P = \{H, TE, H\&TE\} \tag{9.5}$$

where:

H is the subset of P whose security elements have human security configuration flaw.

TE is the subset of P whose security elements have a technical error.

$H\&TE$ is the subset of P whose elements are sectors that have human security configuration flaws and technical errors.

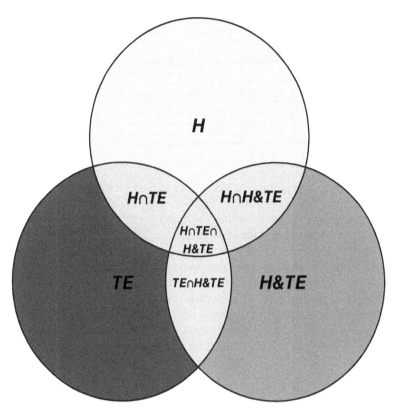

FIGURE 9.7   CoT Venn diagram. Reproduced with permission of IEEE.

Therefore, we can determine the following:

$$
\begin{aligned}
P = H_1 \cup TE_2 \cup H\&TE_3 &= P(H_1) + P(TE_2) + P(H\&TE_3) \\
&\quad -P(H_1 \cap TE_2) - P(H_1 - H\&TE_3) - P(TE_2 \cap H\&TE_3) \\
&\quad +P(H_1 \cap TE_2 \cap H\&TE_3)
\end{aligned}
\tag{9.6}
$$

Since each CoT sector is assumed to be independent, combining probabilities of occurrence for multiple CoT sectors is done by multiplying the probabilities for the CoT steady states of each sector for each combination of states. As defined earlier, each combination of CoT steady states for one or more CoT sectors is referred to as a CoT steady-state case. The probability of occurrence for each CoT steady-state case can be calculated referencing the PIE Theorem for probability (Durrett 2010):

$$
P\left(\bigcup_{v=1}^{n} A_v\right) = \sum_{SM=1}^{n} (-1)^{SM+1} \sum P\left(A_{v_1} \cap \ldots \cap A_{v_{SM}}\right),
\tag{9.7}
$$

Therefore,

$$P(SteadyState) = \prod_{v=1}^{n \geq 1} P(SM_{SteadyState})_v \tag{9.8}$$

where: $P(SM_{SteadyState})_v$ = the probability of occurrence of the steady state for sector v:

  v represents the security mechanisms sectors that are vulnerable

  n represents the security mechanisms sectors that are not vulnerable

With a method for weighting the occurrence of CoT steady-state cases, it is now possible to calculate a solution value. The first step is to establish some minimum criteria for judging whether the security solution is effective or not under various steady-state combinations. For the security mechanisms discussed herein, the criterion is that at least one sector of security (e.g., encryption, authorization) must be intact in order for the solution to be considered secure and effective. Next, the analysis of all the CoT steady-state cases for the solution is performed, noting for each combination how many sectors of protection are intact. Finally, calculate the probability of occurrence for each CoT steady-state case and then calculate the security solution. Using the binomial theorem (Brualdi 1992), this can be done by tallying the probabilities of those CoT steady-state cases that meet the minimum criteria:

$$P(SteadyState) = \sum_{v=0}^{n} (-1)^v \binom{n}{v} = (1-1)^n \tag{9.9}$$

9.4.1 Hypothetical Performance Evaluation

The analysis approach described in Section 9.4 will be applied to current thinking regarding the encryption of an ICD (e.g., smartphone) to a cloud computing environment. The problem to be solved with the encryption solution is to ensure the ICD is able to connect to the cloud environment. The architecture that will be analyzed is one that consists of a single layer of host-based encryption. While this single layer of encryption solution is assumed to not be secure enough, the analysis will be done to establish a quantitative baseline for the single layer of encryption.

In Figure 9.8, let us assume that an interception attack is taking place amongst an ICD (e.g., smartphone) sending data to a cloud computing environment via an IPv6 over a 6LoWPAN. Data communications across the IoT network/service circuits can be intercepted and disclosed. The ICD data packets are unencrypted and subject to interception by sniffer type software applications that may be employed by an attacker. The disclosure of any information if the ICD data packets are intercepted while in transit on the network could possibly reveal password/logon information and theoretically allow unauthorized access to attackers who may be inclined to harm the IoT system in some way.

However, in equation (9.4), we do not account for any empty set (not vulnerable) sectors against this interception attack. As such, suppose n sectors (e.g., application/

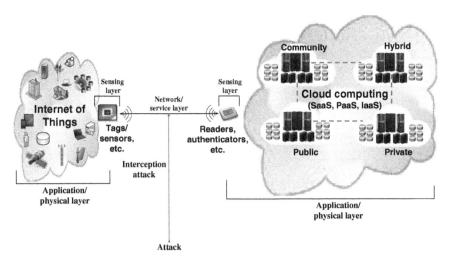

FIGURE 9.8   Interception attack. Reproduced with permission of IEEE.

physical, sensing, network/service) are identified as "not vulnerable" in illogical order, so what is the chance that at least one sector is vulnerable to the interception attack? Let $SM_{SteadyState}$ be the steady-state event that sector (i.e., network/service layer) v is vulnerable, then:

$$P(SM_{SteadyState}) = \frac{(n-1)!}{n!} = \frac{1}{n} \tag{9.10}$$

Similarly,

$$P(A_{v_1} \cap \ldots \cap A_{v_{SM_{SteadyState}}}) = \frac{(n - SM_{SteadyState})!}{n!} \tag{9.11}$$

Therefore, the event that at least one sector is vulnerable to an interception attack is

$$P = \sum_{v=1}^{SM_{SteadyState}} (-1)^{SM_{SteadyState}+1} \sum P(A_i \cap \ldots \cap A_{i_{SM_{SteadyState}}}$$

$$P = \sum_{v=1}^{SM_{SteadyState}} (-1)^{SM_{SteadyState}+1} \binom{n}{v} \frac{(n - SM_{SteadyState})!}{n!} \tag{9.12}$$

$$P = \sum_{i=1}^{SM_{SteadyState}} (-1)^{SM_{SteadyState}+1} \frac{1}{SM_{SteadyState}!}$$

$$P = 1 - \frac{1}{2} + \frac{1}{3!} - \ldots \pm \frac{1}{n!}$$

Furthermore, the secure solution can be calculated tallying the probabilities of the steady-state cases that meet the minimum criteria. For the inception attack, only one steady-state case met the minimum requirement of providing a secure solution; therefore, the derivation of the steady-state exponent can be calculated as follows:

$$SM^x_{SteadyState} = 1 + v + v^2/2 + v^3/3! + \dots . \tag{9.13}$$

Therefore, the probability that a steady-state event in the network/service sector is vulnerable is

$$P(SM_{SteadyState}) = 1 - SM^{-1}_{SteadyState} = 0.6 \tag{9.14}$$

Since each CoT sector is assumed to be independent, combining probabilities of occurrence for multiple CoT sectors with vulnerabilities would contribute to a 0.6 (or 60%) chance of an inception attack in the above-referenced example in at least one sector (in this case the network/sensor layer). The minimum essential requirement for this environment is that the network/sensor sector provides some level of encryption protection to provide at least a 40% chance of secure data-in-transit communications.

9.5 CONCLUSION

Information security is of the upmost importance in the CoT and the recognition of valid "things/objects" is essential. The CoT architecture will be one of the most powerful platforms for computer networking. A wide range of communication networks, from a single local area network (LAN) to global satellite networks will support in this new CoT environment. With the incorporation of a broad suite of protocols and technologies, new development environments to enable modeling of all CoT network types and technologies to perform both fluid simulation and discrete event simulation will be used to analyze network performance and obtain key performance indices.

Because of the availability of "random access" functions in the CoT and the heavy utilization and mutual penetration of various kinds of operational measures, the CoT system will possess a function of automatic identity recognition and needs a steady-state framework for measuring security components and mechanisms of computing devices, communication networks, and sensing devices. First of all, the CoT system should automatically recognize and verify the identities of "things/objects" that have gained random access to the CoT system; it should be able to distinguish whether the information that has entered the CoT system is valid from legitimate sources or a potential adversary. The environment surrounding the CoT is extremely harsh and there are many factors posing tremendous threats to the validity of its architecture which can seriously affect the functions of the CoT system and even its existence.

Therefore, future research on this CoT steady-state framework and how they should be able to monitor the CoT environmental parameters automatically and issue warnings in time to respective individuals or organizations is warranted. When an attack, which is threatening the security of the CoT system has escalated to a certain level to reach safety coefficient values, the CoT system should be able to carry out an evaluation of the level of safety automatically. While issuing warnings and providing detection and protection automatically, the CoT system should also be able to connect to corresponding counter-attack systems or defense systems in accordance to CoT standards to give protection to the CoT system and to launch effective counter-attacks.

The framework developed here should be further researched and influenced by vulnerability data from a CoT architecture. This or other probability frameworks will be used for weighting the cyber-attack occurrence on CoT architectures. An ideal security solution would yield perfect security information about the CoT architecture, given detailed configuration and maintenance information as inputs. Ideally, this output information would be a list (or plot) of attack success probabilities for a widely varying range of attacker capabilities and resources against the CoT. Unfortunately, there is no quick or easy solution which can quickly and reliably measure the security of a thing, much less a CoT network, so vulnerability data for the CoT must be further researched and simplified.

REFERENCES

Abadi, D.J. 2009. Data management in the cloud: limitations and opportunities. *IEEE Data Engineering Bulletin*, 32(1), pp. 3–12.

Brooks, T. 2009a. Principles for implementing a service-oriented enterprise architecture. *SOA Magazine*, Issue XXIX, May/June 2009.

Brooks, T. 2009b. Service-oriented enterprise architecture (SOEA) conceptual design through data architecture. *Journal of Enterprise Architecture*, 5(4), pp. 16–26.

Brooks, T., & McKnight, L. 2013. Securing wireless grids: architecture designs for secure wiglet-to-wiglet interfaces. *International Journal of Information and Network Security*, 2(1), p. 1.

Brooks, T., Caicedo, C., & Park, J. 2012a. Security challenges and countermeasures for trusted virtualized computing environments. In: IEEE World Congress on Internet Security, Guelph, ON, June 10–12, 2012, pp. 117–122.

Brooks, T., Robinson, J., & McKnight, L. 2012b. Conceptualizing a secure wireless cloud. *International Journal of Cloud Computing and Services Science*, 1(3), p. 89.

Brualdi, R.A. 1992. Introductory combinatorics. *Learning*, 4(5), p. 6.

Chen, P.Y., & Cheng, S.M. 2015. Sequential defense against random and intentional attacks in complex networks. *Physical Review E*, 91(2), p. 022805.

Chen, P.Y., & Hero, A.O. 2014. Assessing and safeguarding network resilience to nodal attacks. *IEEE Communications Magazine,* 52(11), pp. 138–143.

Chen, P.Y., Cheng, S.M., & Chen, K.C. 2014a. Information fusion to defend intentional attack in Internet of Things. *IEEE Internet of Things Journal*, 1(4), pp. 337–348.

Chen, S., Xu, H., Liu, D., Hu, B., & Wang, H. 2014b. A vision of IoT: applications, challenges, and opportunities with China perspective. *IEEE Internet of Things Journal*, 1(4), pp. 349–359.

Chunming, Z., Yun, Z., Yingjiang, W., and Shuwen, D. 2012. A Stochastic Dynamic Model of Computer Viruses, Discrete Dynamics in Nature and Society, vol. 2012, Article ID 264874, pp. 1–16.

Durrett, R. 2010. *Probability: Theory and Examples*. Cambridge University Press.

Ghosh, R., Trivedi, K.S., Naik, V.K., & Kim, D.S. 2010. End-to-end performability analysis for infrastructure-as-a-service cloud: an interacting stochastic models approach. In: IEEE 16th Pacific Rim International Symposium on Dependable Computing, Tokyo, December 13–15, 2010, pp. 125–132.

Gubbi, J., Buyya, R., Marusic, S., & Palaniswami, M. 2013. Internet of Things (IoT): A vision, architectural elements, and future directions. *Future Generation Computer Systems*, 29(7), pp. 1645–1660.

Kopetz, H., Braun, M., Ebner, C., Kruger, A., Millinger, D., Nossal, R., & Schedl, A. 1995. The design of large real-time systems: the time-triggered approach. In Real-Time Systems Symposium, 1995. Proceedings., 16th IEEE (pp. 182–187). IEEE.

Harmonosky, C.M., Farr, R.H., & Ni, M.C. 1997. Selective rerouting using simulated steady state system data. In: Proceedings of the 29th Winter simulation conference, Atlanta, Georgia, USA, December 7–10, 1997, pp. 1293–1298.

Laprie, J.C. 1995. Dependability of computer systems: concepts, limits, improvements. In: Proceedings of the IEEE Sixth International Symposium on Software Reliability Engineering, Toulouse, October 24–27, 1995, pp. 2–11.

Liang, H., Huang, D., Cai, L.X., Shen, X., & Peng, D. 2011. Resource allocation for security services in mobile cloud computing. In: IEEE Conference on Computer Communications Workshops (INFOCOM WKSHPS), Shanghai, April 10–15, 2011, pp. 191–195.

Madan, B.B., Goševa-Popstojanova, K., Vaidyanathan, K., & Trivedi, K.S. 2004. A method for modeling and quantifying the security attributes of intrusion tolerant systems. *Performance Evaluation*, 56(1), pp. 167–186.

Mazzucco, M., Dyachuk, D., & Deters, R. 2010. Maximizing cloud providers' revenues via energy aware allocation policies. In: IEEE 3rd International Conference on Cloud Computing (CLOUD), Miami, FL, July 5–10, 2010, pp. 131–138.

Papoulis, A., & Pillai, S.U. 2002. *Probability, Random Variables, and Stochastic Processes*. Tata McGraw-Hill Education.

Qian, Z., & Wang, Y. 2012. IoT technology and application. *Acta Electronica Sinica*, 40(5), pp. 1023–1028.

Rimal, B.P., Jukan, A., Katsaros, D., & Goeleven, Y. 2011. Architectural requirements for cloud computing systems: an enterprise cloud approach. *Journal of Grid Computing*, 9(1), pp. 3–26.

Subashini, S., & Kavitha, V. 2011. A survey on security issues in service delivery models of cloud computing. *Journal of Network and Computer Applications*, 34(1), pp. 1–11.

Vermesan, O., Friess, P., Guillemin, P., Gusmeroli, S., Sundmaeker, H., Bassi, A., Jubert, I.S., Mazura, M., Harrison, M., Eisenhauer, M., & Doody, P. 2011. Internet of Things strategic research roadmap. In: Internet of Things-Global Technological and Societal Trends, pp. 9–52.

Weber, R.H. 2010. Internet of Things–new security and privacy challenges. *Computer Law & Security Review*, 26(1), pp. 23–30.

Xia, H.H. 1996. An analytical model for predicting path loss in urban and suburban environments. In: PIMRC'96, Seventh IEEE International Symposium on Personal, Indoor and Mobile Radio Communications, vol. 1, Taipei, October 15–18, 1996, pp. 19–23.

Yahav, I., Karaesmen, I., & Raschid, L. 2013. Managing on-demand computing services with heterogeneous customers. In: Proceedings of the 2013 Winter Simulation Conference: Simulation: Making Decisions in a Complex World, Washington, DC, December 8–11, 2013, pp. 5–16.

Yan, Y., Qian, Y., Sharif, H., & Tipper, D. 2013. A survey on smart grid communication infrastructures: Motivations, requirements and challenges. *IEEE Communications Surveys & Tutorials*, 15(1), pp. 5–20.

CHAPTER 10

AN ARTIFICIAL INTELLIGENCE PERSPECTIVE ON ENSURING CYBER-ASSURANCE FOR THE INTERNET OF THINGS

UTKU KÖSE

Computer Sciences Application and Research Center, Usak University, Usak, Turkey

10.1 INTRODUCTION

As technological improvements arise, humanity continues to grow into a new type of world providing more practical ways of using smart devices in daily life activities. New products with new communication devices ensure effectiveness in our daily activities providing an important role in shaping our future. If we focus more on the latest technological developments, we can see that using smart devices has become a principle that promises efficiency, speed, and practicality for all tasks. Typical tasks like using personal clouds to store vast amount of data, sharing data amongst other users throughout the world or transforming data into new forms of knowledge have made it a necessity to use complex computer systems and networks – also known as the Internet. Because of endless security challenges, computer and communication systems have to continue to incorporate new approaches, methods, and techniques to process data securely for all its users.

The technology challenge facing the Internet of Things (IoT) requires a multidisciplined approach to artificial intelligence (AI) systems engineering and it is critical that the IoT effort address cyber-assurance (e.g., embedded, automatic security processing) for rapid responses to significant IoT activities. AI can provide the principles and technologies to unify these systems to deliver the IoT end-state goal of a secure system of systems for greatly enhanced interoperability, scalability, performance, and agility. Ultimate success requires steadfast technology development to

Cyber-Assurance for the Internet of Things, First Edition. Edited by Tyson T. Brooks.
© 2017 by The Institute of Electrical and Electronic Engineers, Inc. Published 2017 by John Wiley & Sons, Inc.

traverse the many obstacles that inhibit any transformational initiative. The AI aspect of this effort also demands a strong approach to extensive coordination within the IoT development lifecycle with numerous external organizations developing these new smart products.

In general, the IoT can be defined as a world-wide, Internet-based structure that allows the exchange of goods and services (Weber & Weber 2010). But this definition is a view on the general function of the IoT. From a different perspective, we can explain the concept of IoT as the wide connection of physical devices in order to form an interactive. Briefly, the IoT is also defined as a networked interconnection of everyday objects, which are often equipped with ubiquitous intelligence (Xia et al. 2012). The novelty of the IoT is connected with providing world "smart objects" (Kopetz 2011). The IoT structure is formed by the creation of different components like computers, smart devices, network infrastructure, software components, etc. The IoT offers an interactive connection between the physical world and computer systems in order to obtain improved efficiency, accuracy, and economic advantages (Evans 2011; Reddy 2014).

10.2   AI-RELATED CYBER-ASSURANCE RESEARCH FOR THE IoT

Focusing on recent information security literature, it can be seen that there is no direct research on AI for cyber-assurance solutions specifically for the IoT. Therefore, this research area is still immature and has great potential. However, some research provide key areas enabling researchers to think more about alternative, intelligent ways of providing such solutions. Since cyber-assurance will be a vital area in the future, the research aspect of AI enables cyber-assurance for the IoT to effectively define many security activities in parallel to achieve results faster and build research momentum.

Recent research has been closely related to AI-based cyber-assurance for the IoT. In their research, (Aman & Snekkenes (2015) introduce a model for an autonomic, event-driven, adaptive security (EDAS) approach for the IoT. In this EDAS approach, the researchers determined that any intentional or unintentional risks are investigated in case of any security situation changes reported by the things in the monitored IoT systems (Aman & Snekkenes 2015). The researchers correlated different events in time and space to reduce any false alarms and provided a mechanism to predict attacks before they are realized (Aman & Snekkenes 2015). Additionally, the researchers also determined that risks are responded to autonomically by utilizing a runtime adaptation ontology and the mitigation action is chosen after assessing essential information, such as the risk faced, user preferences, device capabilities, and service requirements through selecting an optimal mitigation action in a particular adverse situation (Aman & Snekkenes 2015). Madhura et al. (2015) discusses security and privacy issues in the IoT through an intelligent community security system (ICSS). This research determined that the ICSS provides several subsystems, such as vehicle management subsystem (VMS), surrounding security subsystem (SSS), central information processing system (CIPS), property management subsystem (PMS), fire and theft prevention subsystem (FTPS) etc., for IoT security (Madhura et al. 2015). Their research also identified a wireless communication approach belonging to the CIPS connecting all subsystems which are capable of automatic changes and giving timely warnings for ensuring security in the IoT (Madhura et al. 2015).

Greensmith's (2015) research focuses on usage of an artificial immune systems approach to achieve security in IoT. This work discusses the challenges in intelligent mechanisms and proposes a responsive version of the deterministic Dendritic Cell Algorithm technique (Greensmith 2015). Greensmith's (2015) research identifies that the responsive artificial immune system will need to be developed to meet these future challenges through proposing the incorporation of a model of T-cell responses. Katasonov et al. (2008) provides research on UBIWARE, which is a set of tools providing means for effective development of agents and adapters and a run-time environment for operations. This research describes the author's vision of a middleware for the IoT, which will allow creation of self-managed complex systems, in particular industrial ones, consisting of distributed and heterogeneous components of different nature (Katasonov et al. 2008).

Liu et al.'s (2011) research detects security threats in the IoT through the mechanisms of an artificial immune system applied to the IoT environment. Liu et al. (2011) developed an application method of immune theory to the IoT environment constructed through a method of intrusion detection, and an immature detector, mature detector, and memory detector which are defined to detect attacks in the IoT. The researchers were able to adapt the complicated and changeful environment of the IoT, using detectors which evolved dynamically to detect mutated IoT attacks and the attacks detected by detectors in the IoT are combined with the attack information library to alarm the manager in the IoT (Liu et al. 2011). Chen et al. (2012) also identified research on the usage of an artificial immune system approach in cyber-assurance. The author's research on an artificial immune-based theory model for distributed intrusion detection in IoT has been introduced and realizes detecting intrusion of IoT in distribution and parallelity Chen et al. (2012). From a general perspective, the approach designed in Chen et al. (2012) has similar features and functions with the approach proposed by Liu et al. (2011).

Chen et al.'s (2012) research on artificial immune-based distributed intrusion detection identifies another artificial immune system which also introduces a security situation sense model for ensuring a secure IoT system. This research focuses briefly on the structure of a security threat sense sub-model, formulation mechanism provided for security threat intensity and also structure of the security situation assessment sub-model Chen et al. (2012). Additionally, Liu et al. (2013) also produces similar work to the development of an artificial immune system security efforts in IoT systems. This research on artificial immune systems looks to achieve the desired end-state security that satisfies the IoT's operational needs at fixed, mobile, and embedded variants. In pursuing the end-state security objective, the IoT will primarily apply a cyber-assurance-driven approach to ensure that the future AI needs of the IoT are given rigorous design attention. A summary of recent works relating AI-based cyber-assurance for the IoT is identified in Table 10.1.

TABLE 10.1 Research AI-based Cyber-Assurance for the IoT. Reproduced with permission of IEEE.

Year	Authors	Work
2015	W. Aman, and E. Snekkenes	EDAS: an evaluation prototype for autonomic event-driven adaptive security in the Internet of Things
2015	P.M. Madhura, N. Bilurkar, P. Jain, and J. Ranjith	A survey on Internet of Things: security and privacy issues
2015	J. Greensmith	Securing the Internet of Things with responsive artificial immune systems
2013	C. Liu, Y. Zhang, Z. Cai, J. Yang, and L. Peng	Artificial immunity-based security response model for the Internet of Things
2012	R. Chen, C.M. Liu, and C. Chen	An artificial immune-based distributed intrusion detection model for the Internet of Things
2012	R. Chen, C.M. Liu, and L.X. Xiao	A security situation sense model based on artificial immune system in the Internet of Things
2011	C. Liu, J. Yang, Y. Zhang, R. Chen, and J. Zeng	Research on immunity-based intrusion detection technology for the Internet of Things
2008	A. Katasonov, O. Kaykova, O. Khriyenko, S. Nikitin, and V.Y. Terziyan	Smart semantic middleware for the Internet of Things

10.3 MULTIDISCIPLINARY INTELLIGENCE ENABLING OPPORTUNITIES WITH AI

AI is an active research field, which focuses on simulating human thinking style/behaviors or intelligent dynamics occurring in the nature, in order to provide effective and accurate solutions for real-world-based problems (Jaffe 2015; Amyx 2015; Ashton 2015; Meek 2015). An AI approach does not demand the discarding of current IoT systems to start anew. On the contrary, it enables the utilization of existing technology assets by integrating select functionality into the IoT.

However, this "intelligence enabling" of AI for new IoT systems could be a best practice for quickly building out an IoT system by maximizing the leverage of existing systems. For example, an AI process for applications enabling services could differ from the design process for a traditional system by allowing for parallel execution through a bottom-up approach where only existing systems' functionality that provides value to the greater community of IoT systems (i.e., delivering security services) is selected for service enabling and application services. This enabling creates a set of service "building blocks" that are utilized to deliver the security capabilities. These building blocks become security assets incorporated into the IoT architecture reflected in key security artifacts.

10.3.1 A Generic Approach for AI for Different Disciplines

Defining and designing infrastructure services in parallel with IoT system and security service enabling design efforts provide several benefits. Some of the most compelling A.I. delivers a security infrastructure that is driven by the needs of the device level services; reducing the risk of cyber-attacks through gradual systems migration and evolutionary growth as the IoT matures, reduces overall IoT system cost through a just-in-time approach to infrastructure services that requires an investment only after a clear needs emerge. This allows for early successes to build program momentum and for gradual organizational change.

In order to better understand the usage of AI, the following explains a general process of integrating AI into the IoT (Figure 10.1):

- **Using AI directly on the target problem:** To achieve overall IoT system agility and adaptability, IoT system functions that were once performed by monolithic components are now implemented as a set of embedded services interacting with one another. Each individual embedded service being thoroughly tested "to the spec" does not necessarily mean the aggregated IoT system will have the expected behavior. Therefore, the AI process should shift its focus from application-centric performance of internal system logic to the "composite" system behavior pertaining to the IoT.

- **Using as step(s) in the solution process:** The integration life cycle can no longer be a sequential waterfall process for AI activities for the IoT. Because each individual security service or security service family may have its own development timeline, waiting to start overall IoT system integration until all security services to be developed and unit-tested is neither cost-effective nor necessary. Rather, the solution should incrementally incorporate integration of security services as they become available, constantly testing the overall IoT system behavior along the way. This heightens the need for IoT test harnesses, prototypes, and simulators that can act as a surrogate while the true security service capabilities are being developed.

FIGURE 10.1 A schema explaining how AI could be used in different disciplines. Reproduced with permission of IEEE.

- **Using as a hybrid model for the target problem:** In the "System of Systems" environment of IoT, the distributed nature of a security services network also places a greater burden on the overall process to quantify and ensure the Quality of Service (QoS) characteristics (e.g., user response time, latencies, data throughput) of the aggregated IoT system as well as the individual services. Using a hybrid model for AI for the architecture of the IoT and its dependencies on external IoT networks and systems imply that its integration and environments cannot be self-contained. Instead, these environments must be themselves connection-based and fully interoperable.
- **Using before or after the solution process:** Failure to account for AI solutions may not only result in prolonged development cycles but more importantly, it can lead to an AI system that does not meet the IoT needs in an operational environment. Therefore, AI integration should be used before or after new IoT product development activities as an integral part of the development process and carefully planned right from the start.

10.4 FUTURE RESEARCH ON AI-BASED CYBER-ASSURANCE FOR IoT

By taking the related research developments into account, it is also possible to have some ideas about what can be possible in the future regarding AI-based cyber-assurance for IoT. Of course, new developments in AI technologies and the formulation of cyber-assurance integration strategies involving a combination of advanced embedded processes, prototyping tools, and enhanced security designed will lead the next generation of research. The research will also seek to illuminate broader organizational impacts on business processes and the global impact of AI-based cyber-assurance solutions for the IoT.

Some future research areas for AI-based cyber-assurance for IoT can be identified as follows:

- The use of artificial immune systems for ensuring secure IoT systems. Current research does not indicate that the artificial immune system is the only AI method which is capable of developing security functions for the IoT. In contrast, other AI approaches, methods, and techniques, which are similar to the artificial immune systems could be used for cyber-assurance-related activities.
- Coordination with the AI architecture and IoT development efforts to ensure full traceability to security threads, operational situations, and IoT system models to validate IoT system architecture and design will be needed.
- The development of test harnesses for security services interoperability at functional, interface, and transport levels of all AI products.
- Integration of embedded capabilities such as integrated models, associative algorithms, and predictive tools for all AI-related products.
- Continued support in producing AI/cyber-assurance metrics, best practices, lessons learned, and documentation.

10.5 CONCLUSION

In closing, the IoT is one of the most innovative approaches that will make it possible to achieve global device connectivity in the future. Although it is highly debated that the technology influence in our daily lives may make us ever more dependent on technology, the growth of AI within the IoT will also continue. As seen from some of the latest research developments, our present environment is highly connected with collaborative, self-thinking smart devices. This interconnected process is not only applicable to the IoT but also in AI as the main research fields in creating intelligent machines of the future. This chapter briefly provides the possibility of the usage of AI for cyber-assurance for the IoT. Although AI in the context of cyber-assurance still needs further research and refinement, it is a good point to begin the discussing regarding "intelligent cyber-assurance" for the IoT.

REFERENCES

Aman, W., & Snekkenes, E. 2015. EDAS: an evaluation prototype for autonomic event-driven adaptive security in the Internet of Things. *Future Internet*, 7(3), pp. 225–256.

Amyx, S. 2015. Wearing your intelligence: how to apply artificial intelligence in aearables and IoT. *Wired.* Available at http://www.wired.com/insights/2014/12/wearing-your-intelligence/. Accessed on May 13, 2015.

Ashton, K. 2015. When IoT meets artificial intelligence. *waylay.io*. Available at http://www.waylay.io/blog-iot-meets-artificial-intelligence.html. Accessed on May 13, 2015.

Chen, R., Liu, C.M., & Chen, C. 2012. An artificial immune-based distributed intrusion detection model for the Internet of Things. *Advanced Materials Research*, 366, pp. 165–168).

Chen, R., Liu, C.M., & Xiao, L.X. 2011. A security situation sense model based on artificial immune system in the Internet of Things. *Advanced Materials Research*, 403, pp. 2457–2460.

Evans, D. 2011. The Internet of Things: how the next evolution of the internet is changing everything. *CISCO white paper*, 1, pp. 1–11.

Gérald, S. 2010. The Internet of Things: between the revolution of the Internet and the metamorphosis of objects, H. Sundmaeker, P. Guillemin, P. Friess, & S. Woelffle, (Eds.). In: Forum American Bar Association, pp. 11–24, Feb. 2010.

Greensmith, J. 2015. Securing the Internet of Things with responsive artificial immune systems. In: Proceedings of the 2015 Genetic and Evolutionary Computation Conference, New York, NY, July 2015, pp. 113–120.

Jaffe, M. 2015. IoT won't work without artificial intelligence. *Wired.* Available at http://www.wired.com/insights/2014/11/iot-wont-work-without-artificial-intelligence/. Accessed on May 13, 2015.

Katasonov, A., Kaykova, O., Khriyenko, O., Nikitin, S., & Terziyan, V.Y. 2008. Smart semantic middleware for the Internet of Things. In: Proceedings of the 5th International Conference on Informatics in Control, Automation and Robotics, 8, pp. 169–178.

Kopetz, H. 2011. Internet of things. In: *Real-time Systems*. Springer, US, pp. 307–323.

Liu, C., Yang, J., Zhang, Y., Chen, R., & Zeng, J. 2011. Research on immunity-based intrusion detection technology for the internet of things. In: IEEE 2011 Seventh International Conference on Natural Computation, vol. 1, Shanghai, July 26–28, pp. 212–216.

Liu, C., Zhang, Y., Cai, Z., Yang, J., & Peng, L. 2013. Artificial immunity-based security response model for the internet of things. *Journal of Computers*, 8(12), pp. 3111–3118.

Madhura, P.M., Bilurkar, N., Jain, P., & Ranjith, J. 2015. A survey on Internet of Things: security and privacy issues. *International Journal of Innovative Technology and Research*, 3(3), pp. 2069–2074.

Meek, A. 2015. Connecting artificial intelligence with the Internet of Things. *The Guardian*. Available at http://www.theguardian.com/technology/2015/jul/24/artificial-intelligence-internet-of-things. Accessed on July 24, 2015.

Reddy, A.S. 2014. Reaping the benefits of the Internet of Things. *Cognizant Reports*. Available at https://www.cognizant.com/InsightsWhitepapers/Reaping-the-Benefits-of-the-Internet-of-Things.pdf May 2014.

Weber, R.H., & Weber, R. 2010. *Internet of Things: Legal Perspectives*, vol. 49. Springer Science+Business Media.

Xia, F., Yang, L.T., Wang, L., & Vinel, A. 2012. Internet of Things. *International Journal of Communication Systems*, 25(9), p. 1101.

CHAPTER 11

PERCEIVED THREAT MODELING FOR CYBER-PHYSICAL SYSTEMS

CHRISTOPHER LEBERKNIGHT

Department of Computer Science, Montclair State University, Montclair, NJ, USA

11.1 INTRODUCTION

Many strategies and models used for information security (INFOSEC) often fail to simultaneously consider the threats to information due to a lack of adequate physical security controls (McCumber 1991; Schou et al. 2004). One common approach for securing information is to incorporate any number of available intrusion detection tools into an organization's security infrastructure. However, while there are several software applications aimed at detecting intrusions at the network, operating system (OS) or application layer, there are far less intrusion detection applications available for physical security. Physical security is a critical component used to safeguard employees and prevent unauthorized access to critical infrastructures. However, the need and importance of new software-based physical security intrusion detection systems is amplified by the dependency of INFOSEC on physical security.

The terms INFOSEC and information assurance (IA) are often used interchangeably; however, they are intrinsically different. The main difference between these two definitions is that IA is defined to include INFOSEC, but also incorporates restoration of information systems. To present a more comprehensive approach to security this paper places a greater emphasis on IA. The Committee on National Security Systems defines IA as "Measures that protect and defend information and information systems by ensuring their availability, integrity, authentication, confidentiality, and non-repudiation. These measures include providing for restoration of information systems by incorporating protection, detection, and reaction capabilities.[1]"

IA is typically addressed from a logical security perspective due to the large volume of digitally stored information. Consequently, many organizations fail to evaluate

---

[1] https://www.ncsc.gov/nittf/docs/CNSSI-4009_National_Information_Assurance.pdf

Cyber-Assurance for the Internet of Things, First Edition. Edited by Tyson T. Brooks.
© 2017 by The Institute of Electrical and Electronic Engineers, Inc. Published 2017 by John Wiley & Sons, Inc.

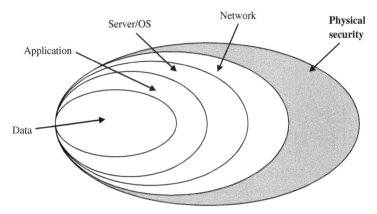

FIGURE 11.1 Security independencies. Reproduced with permission of IEEE.

the risk of information being compromised due to poor physical security (Forte & Power 2007). Physical security, as the first line of defense, is a critical component of the overall security plan and the interdependence of the distinct functions within physical and logical security can expose several unforeseen vulnerabilities. Based on the diagram illustrated in Figure 11.1, regardless of the number of controls and policies within inner security layers, without adequate physical security controls an organization might as well not have any security at all. If there is a breach in the physical security layer, then one should assume all other layers can also be compromised. Threats to physical security and hence information becomes even more compounded with the proliferation of information stored on wireless devices such as smartphones and laptops.

In addition to reasons to improve physical security within the private sector, there are also increasing concerns to enhance logical security within the public sector due to threats against technologies, known as supervisory control and data acquisition (SCADA) systems, used to control critical infrastructures. SCADA systems are widely used in the management of critical infrastructure such as electricity and water distribution systems, and currently there is little understanding of how to best protect SCADA systems from malicious attacks (Dawson et al. 2006). For example, the August 2003 blackout in North America underscored the delicate and critical role information technologies can play in supporting other infrastructure.

In that massive outage, three failures of information technology systems – alarm systems, software, and other computerized controls – were associated at least in part with the outage.[2] In 1999, the Olympic Pipeline in Washington experienced a major failure due to the failure of its computer control system, which ultimately led to an inability to control pressure resulting in three deaths. In 2004, a Sasser worm was able to disrupt an oil and gas platform in the Gulf of Mexico for a couple of days. Hacking and other cyber-attacks have disrupted energy and other infrastructure

---

[2] https://emp.lbl.gov/publications/final-report-august-14-2003-blackout.

facilities. Information technology has numerous interconnections in the water supply and wastewater treatment sector, and vulnerabilities have surfaced in areas such as the inability to track contaminants or properly characterize flow rates (Zimmerman and Horan 2004). Interdependency between information technologies and transportation infrastructure is also noteworthy.

Quite a number of examples exist where airline travel was halted due to computer failures in air controller operations or within other airport operations, such as ticketing or automated baggage handling systems (Zimmerman and Restrepo 2006). While these examples demonstrate the need to improve software and information technologies to better protect against cyber-attacks on critical infrastructures, new approaches for improving physical security should also be considered. Intruders will take the path of least resistance which may either be through a physical intrusion or cyber-attack. Therefore, it is imperative that an organization's overall security framework consider the components, controls, limitations, and interdependencies of physical security as well as logical security. Specifically, when designing INFOSEC policies physical security should not be overlooked. Therefore, the threat to critical infrastructures and the interdependencies of physical and logical security underscores the requirement to investigate new technologies to improve physical security.

The threats from attacks on information such as theft of corporate intellectual property and damage to physical assets and national security with respect to critical infrastructures indicate that a more holistic and comprehensive approach to security is required. While there have been several advancements to improve security controls within many of the inner layers in Figure 11.1, less notable advancements have been made with respect to physical security. The one exception is the field of biometrics which is aimed at improving physical security by using various identity verification strategies. However, aside from biometric technologies which are primarily stand-alone hardware devices there is very limited research which has provided a *software-based* approach to improve physical security. To fully understand the need for better physical security software systems a brief review of physical security and the associated software limitations are presented in the following section.

11.2 OVERVIEW OF PHYSICAL SECURITY

A physical security system (PSS) is designed to employ a complementary combination of six components: (1) intrusion detection and assessment, (2) entry and search control, (3) barriers, (4) communications, (5) testing and maintenance, and (6) support systems, which are used to deter, detect, and delay an attack.[3] The communications component consists of telephones, radios, and alarms which serve as the security backbone, enabling coordination and synchronization of events between all other components in the system. Another mechanism used to communicate and

---

[3] http://www.globalsecurity.org/military/library/policy/army/fm/3-19-30/ch2.htm, p. 5.

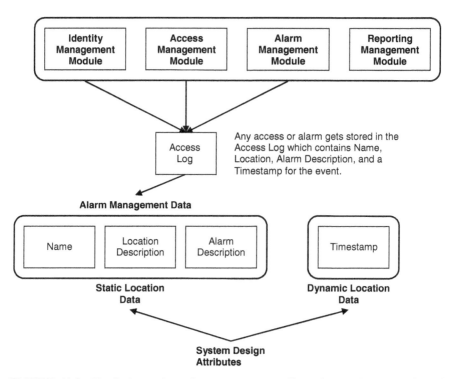

FIGURE 11.2 Physical security software components. Reproduced with permission of IEEE.

monitor security incidents is by using a physical security software application. The main components are illustrated in Figure 11.2. The three main components consist of: (1) an identity management module, (2) an access management module, and (3) an alarm management module. The identity management module is used to add or modify an individual's contact information to the system such as the individual's name, phone, or badge id. The access management module is used to configure access, for an individual within the system, to a particular location during specified times. The alarm management module is used to configure and clear alarm notifications. All events triggered by the access control or intrusion detection system are transmitted to the application. Information from the three modules as well as a timestamp are collectively sent to a log and displayed within the application interface. There are several limitations with the information that is transmitted to the physical security software application.

For example, information originating from the intrusion detection components and transmitted to the software system is extremely limited due to the capabilities of the underlying technology. In most cases the technology used for intrusion detection consists of interior or exterior sensors which often generate false alarms due to environments such as wind or interference from animals and do not provide any meaningful details other than the notification that an event has occurred. With respect to access control systems, the available information is often of a static nature, and there may be other dynamic information which, if made available, could help to improve an individual's perception of threat. Due to the poor quality of information generated from the intrusion detection and access control sub-systems, security professionals often lose trust in the physical security application and rely on knowledge and experience to assess a threat. This may at first make sense, however, considering different individuals process the same information differently and each individual has a different background, knowledge, and experience, the perceived versus actual threat can vary from person to person. Therefore, the software system should be designed to incorporate a higher degree of information quality and provide an automated decision process which facilitates decision-making. However, to design such a system first requires a thorough understanding of the challenges surrounding behavioral decision-making and previous decision support system research.

11.3 RELEVANCE TO GROUNDED THEORY

The main objective of this research is to understand the factors which influence an individual's perception of threat in an effort to build a theory for designing a physical security intrusion based-decision support systems. To understand why and how the perceptions change could not be captured through survey or by analyzing official data, since these methods would strip away the context and not reveal the richness and complexity involved in the decision-making process. A grounded theory approach through an iterative process of analytical induction was initially considered to help precipitate the construction of our perceived threat theory for decision support systems design (Fielding et al. 1998; Glaser & Straus 1968). However, the grounded theory approach rejects the use of literature to generate themes, concepts, or relationships between them and relies solely on the data for theory building (Rubin & Rubin 2005). After careful examination of various qualitative research methods and due to the vast amount of extant literature on decision support systems design, it was concluded that the most appropriate method for our research might be realized by employing a different design method known as front-end-loaded grounded theory (DeLuca et al. 2008).

11.3.1 Different Design Modes of the Approach

The front-end-loaded grounded theory method (FGTM) begins with a set of constructs or codes based on the analysis of previous literature, but also allows the introduction of new constructs which may emerge during the course of content analysis (DeLuca et al. 2008). Therefore, the FGTM approach provides for greater flexibility by leveraging results from previous research which can serve as a catalyst for the theory construction and also help guide in the design of specific interview questions which may lead to more fruitful analysis.

11.3.2   Grounded Theory and Qualitative and Quantitative Methods

In addition, this research employs a hybrid approach to grounded theory by incorporating quantitative results which were collected during several simulated paper-based scenarios involving physical security intrusions. The quantitative results corresponded to the participant's selection of threat levels and feelings toward specified probability of intrusions at particular locations. The analysis was used in conjunction with the analysis of semi-structured interviews to understand the relation of cognitive factors and probabilistic values inherent in making decisions under uncertainty. The main intention was to investigate any correlations and overall impact on perceived threat.

11.4   THEORETICAL MODEL CONSTRUCTION

In previous research we developed a research model which claimed that in addition to several situational characteristics an individual's perception of threat is strongly influenced by specific cognitive properties (Leberknight et al. 2008). The identification of the five situational characteristics illustrated in Figure 11.3 is based on features which were absent in current systems and provided dynamic information. This lack of dynamic information and use of static information are illustrated in Figure 11.2. Ultimately, a system which has the capability to provide dynamic

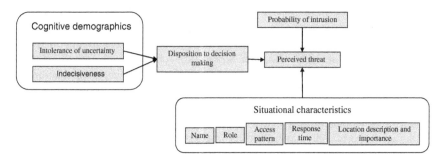

Contributing Literature

Illusion of control (Langer 1975; Langer & Roth 1975; Wortman 1975).

Decision support system (Ashford & Kasper 2003; Kasper 1996; Davis et al. 1991; Kottemann et al. 1994; Melone et al. 1995; Morton 1983; Wortman 1975)

Information presentation (Tractinsky & Meyer 1999; Lim & Benbasat 2000)

Threat rigidity (Staw et al. 1981; Barnett & Pratt 2000)

Risk assessment (Alberts et al. 2003; den Braber et al. 2007; Jones 2007; Karabacak & Sogukpinar 2005; Page et al. 2007; Suh & Han 2003; Yavagal et al. 2005)

Cognitive factors (Berenbaum et al. 2007; Dugas et al. 2001; Frost & Shows et al. 1993; Rassin et al. 2007)

FIGURE 11.3   Perceived threat model. Reproduced with permission of IEEE.

TABLE 11.1   Research Questions. Reproduced with permission of IEEE.

RQ 1: *What factors need to be considered when designing a system to improve an individual's perception of threat?*

Sub-question	Question
What situational characteristics influence an	RQ 1-1 individual's perception of threat?
What cognitive characteristics influence an	RQ 1-2 individual's perception of threat?

information will result in a higher perceived information quality. In addition, the probability of intrusion construct in Figure 11.3 was used to exercise our model under varying degrees of uncertainty. The fundamental premise for our research model is that, regardless of the situation, individuals have a specific baseline or disposition to decision-making which is influenced by two psychological factors: (1) indecisiveness and (2) intolerance of uncertainty. These two factors are collectively known as cognitive demographics which function as the determinants for a new construct known as disposition toward decision-making. The review and synthesis of previous psychology and decision support systems research which contributed to the development of the perceived threat model is illustrated in Figure 11.3.

The theoretical foundation of the research model, in Figure 11.3, and subsequent analysis is based on the FGTM first proposed by DeLuca et al. (2008). FGTM begins with a set of constructs or codes based on the analysis of previous literature, but also allows for the introduction of new constructs which may emerge during the course of content analysis. This is contrasted with the more pervasive grounded theory method developed by Glaser and Straus (1968) which generally begins with the researcher coding text into phrases with the goal of uncovering a theory (DeLuca et al. (2008). The overarching goal of this research is to evaluate the research model in an effort to derive a set of input requirements for a decision support systems-based PSS, and aid in the development of a decision support systems design theory with specific emphasis on perceived threat. Several questions which are summarized in Table 11.1 were created to help guide the research process and help answer our main hypothesis, **H1:**

H1:   Perceived threat is a construct that depends on the social context and disposition toward decision-making of the user.

11.5 EXPERIMENT

The model was tested using a series of semi-structured interview questions and an experimental task. The task was used to vary the quality of information, and the semi-structured interviews helped to elucidate the subject's responses in the task and investigate their perceptions of model constructs. The use of an experimental task was necessary to instill a sense of realism regarding the simulation of an actual security intrusion and attempt to induce threat-rigidity effects (Staw et al. 1981).

This research method has been widely employed in previous research as a means to evaluate model constructs (Keil et al. 2000; Nicolaou & McKnight 2006; Tsiros & Mittal 2000; Webster & Trevino 1995; Yoo & Alavi 2001).

11.5.1 Semi-Structured Interviews

A total of 10 questions were designed to elicit responses regarding indecisiveness and intolerance of uncertainty. Five questions were aimed at evaluating the subjects' disposition to decision-making via indecisiveness and five questions for the intolerance of uncertainty construct. The questions were adapted from scales used in previous research (Dugas et al. 2004; Germeijs & De Boeck 2002; Rassin & Muris 2005). In addition, 15 other questions were created to capture individual responses regarding the task. The task provided the means to present the situational characteristics along with the probability of intrusion variable.

11.5.2 Triangulation

Triangulation was taken into consideration to address general concerns for validity and reliability. Essentially, triangulation refers to using different methods to verify the convergence of results across all methods for some phenomena under investigation. Triangulation is achieved, consistent with Malhotra and Grover (1998), by utilizing multiple items for both the indecisiveness and intolerance of uncertainty constructs. In addition, the task and interviews were administered to two different populations with varying degrees of physical security experience and responsibilities. The roles of each subject ranged from junior employees to senior administration. This helped to ensure different points of view would be captured and factored into the analysis. In an effort to reduce measurement errors, a pre-test of the experiment was also conducted.

11.5.3 Pre-testing

Prior to administering the task and semi-structured interviews a pre-test was conducted to ensure the task and questions in the interview were clear and unambiguous. Four Ph.D. students who had taken courses on quantitative and qualitative research methods were selected to participate in the pre-test. Each subject was given the experimental task and interview questions and several grammatical and notational changes were implemented based on their feedback.

11.5.4 Qualitative Interview Guidelines

To improve the reliability and validity of the data for subsequent analysis, the interviews were conducted based on the dramaturgical model proposed by Myers & Newman (2007). The model suggests seven guidelines, summarized in Table 11.2, which can be used to enhance the performance of the interview process and quality of the data.

TABLE 11.2   Guidelines for Successful Interviews. Reproduced with permission of IEEE.

Guideline	Description
Situating the researcher as actor	Assuming that the researcher is the interviewer, it is important for the researcher to "situate" themselves before the interview takes place.
Minimize social dissonance	Minimize anything that may lead to the interviewee to feel uncomfortable.
Represent various "voices"	In qualitative research it is usually necessary to interview a variety of people within an organization.
Everyone is an interpreter	This guideline recognizes that subjects are creative interpreters of their worlds as we are of theirs.
Use mirroring in questions and answers	Mirroring is taking the words and phrases the subjects use in constructing a subsequent question or comment: mirroring their comments. This allows the researcher to focus on the subjects' world and uses their language rather than imposing yours.
Flexibility	Semi-structured and unstructured interviewing uses an incomplete script and so requires flexibility, improvisation, and openness.
Confidentiality of disclosures	It is important for researchers to keep transcripts/records and the technology confidential and secure.

11.5.5 Description of Subjects

Ten physical security experts were recruited, from two different locations, using e-mail advertisements. The decision to test the model in two different locations was to eliminate any bias which might result from certain security variables within an organizational setting. For example, security variables, such as the required degree of security or frequent attempts to breach security will vary depending on the location. These variables can influence an individual's perception of threat. Therefore, a university and military installation were identified as the two locations which would have a good degree of differences regarding the security variables and therefore perception of threat. Six subjects from the university location and four subjects from a military installation participated in the study.

The grounded theory approach recommends that theoretical sampling be used instead of random sampling. In theoretical sampling, the focus is in getting theoretically useful cases that confirms, extends, and sharpens the theoretical framework from as many aspects as possible (Glaser & Straus 1968). In this study, the focus was on getting subjects with a wide range of physical security experience. The subject's physical security responsibilities ranged from junior to senior executive and their experience ranged from 2 years to 30 years. On average, each subject in the study had 14.4 years of physical security experience with a standard deviation of 9.6 years. A summary of the subject demographics by age, race, and gender, for the qualitative study is provided in Figure 11.4.

Subject Demographics
Age, Race and Gender

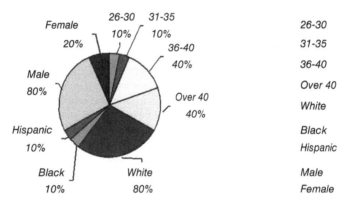

FIGURE 11.4 Demographics. Reproduced with permission of IEEE.

11.5.6 Procedure

Following the recruitment of the 10 subjects, each subject was contacted to schedule an appointment to participate in the task and interview. The appointments were scheduled such that only one subject participated in the experiment at a time. During the appointment and prior to beginning the experiment, each subject was informed of the purpose of the experiment and the amount of time required for their participation. This information was also provided upon initial contact or recruitment of the subjects using an e-mail advertisement. In addition, each subject was informed of their consent to participate and right to withdraw from the study at any time. Subsequently, a training script was used to ensure that each subject received a consistent overview of access control systems and instructions on completing the task. Next the task was administered to each subject, and afterward the subject was given a brief semi-structured interview. Each subject completed the task and interview in a quiet, private office or lab setting to ensure no distractions or discomfort while participating in the experiment.

The interviews were audio recorded with the consent of the subjects which was received prior to beginning the experiment. The audio recordings were necessary in order to create accurate transcriptions for content analysis. On average each subject completed the task and experiment within 1 hour. The task consisted of 10 different scenarios with various predefined probabilities of intrusion. Each scenario was based on the location in which the physical security subject worked. Each subject had their own a priori subjective estimate of the likelihood of an intrusion. That is, prior to receiving any information, individuals had an estimate of an intrusion occurring at a particular location based on previous experience or other assumptions about the importance of the location. Therefore, each subject was asked to rate the likelihood of an intrusion at five different locations and the associated threat levels should an intrusion actually occur at one of the locations.

The threat levels ranged from one to five corresponding to least to most threatening. The next set of scenarios controlled the probability of intrusion variable and some of the constructs relating to situational characteristics. Specifically, the location, name of the individual accessing the location, and their role were controlled. With different values for the probability of intrusion and the situational characteristics, the subjects were then asked to rate the threat level. The probability of intrusion variable was used to examine the perception of threat by controlling the quality of information. The quality of information is in part due to the source from which the information originated. For this research, the source is a biometric keypad and the probability of an intrusion is the probability that the keypad identifies an intruder. As with any biometric, or in any situation with a high degree of uncertainty, all outcomes are viewed in probabilistic terms. Therefore, the biometric probability output is only used for clarity and any other data source could also be used.

By controlling the probability of intrusion variable the quality of information and hence the underlying technology is evaluated. The introduction of the probability of intrusion variable after the first set of scenarios was to gauge the difference between the a priori likelihood of an intrusion and the associated threat level, and the threat level based on the assigned probability of intrusion values. This was designed to explore the range of probability of intrusion values which change the perception of threat from the a priori value. An example of the scenarios designed to capture the perception of threat based on a prior likelihood of an intrusion and after the probability of intrusion variable is introduced is depicted in Figures 11.5 and 11.6. Subjects were asked to indicate the likelihood of an intrusion at five different locations and the associated threat level using Figure 11.5. Subsequently, subjects were given two different scenarios using the same locations, but different information regarding the probability of an intrusion and the name of the person. For the purposes of this experiment, subjects were informed that the source used to provide information regarding the person's name and probability of intrusion was made possible by the biometric keypad.

The probability of intrusion, denoted as PI in Figures 11.6 and 11.7, refers to the probability that the person accessing the location is who he or she claims to be.

Subjects were then required to assign a threat based on the information that was provided. After completing the two scenarios and assigning threat levels to each of the five locations the subjects were interviewed regarding their responses. The main objective of the semi-structured interviews was to identify what factors influenced their choice of the threat level based on the information presented in the task.

11.6 RESULTS

To investigate and evaluate the perceived threat research model, an experimental paper based task simulating 10 different physical security scenarios was provided to

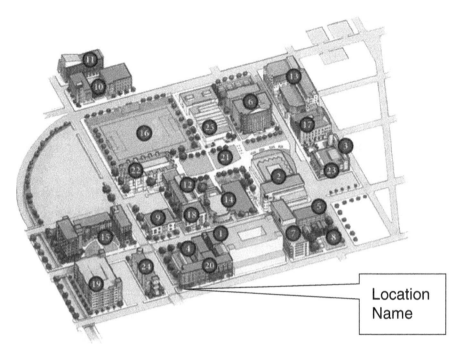

Location Name

Location Number	PI	Threat Level $(1-5)$
13		
7		
2		
11		
15		

FIGURE 11.5 Posterior perception of threat. Reproduced with permission of IEEE.

10 physical security experts. The objective of the task was to inject a sense of realism into the experiment and examine the effect of different variables on the individual's perception of threat.

Subsequently, the 10 subjects were interviewed to provide a deeper insight into the effect of the constructs within the proposed model based on their responses in the task.

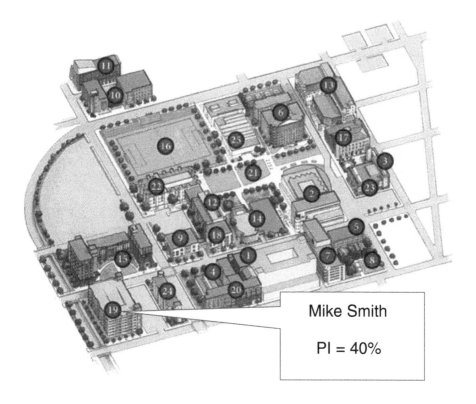

Location	Number	Threat Level $(1 - 5)$
	19	
	7	
	2	
	11	
	15	

FIGURE 11.6 Posterior perception of threat. Reproduced with permission of IEEE.

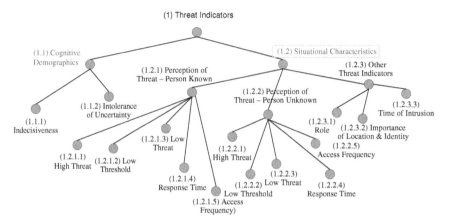

FIGURE 11.7   Initial conceptual model. Reproduced with permission of IEEE.

11.6.1   Initial Conceptual Model

The interviews for the 10 physical security experts were audio recorded and transcribed using NVivo software developed by QSR International (http://www. qsrinternational.com/). NVivo was used to perform a content analysis on the transcriptions by automating the assignment of text to codes in a decision tree structure. The mapping of nodes within the tree hierarchy produced a conceptual map of codes which facilitated the evaluation of the proposed model and the emergence of new constructs. This process of investigating a priori and emerging concepts or codes in qualitative systems research is based on the FGTM, first proposed by (DeLuca et al. (2008). The conceptual map of codes was created by assigning the responses from each of the 10 transcriptions into the 2 a priori codes: cognitive demographics and situational characteristics. This model, illustrated in Figure 11.7, was further refined in two separate stages by iteratively evaluating the responses within each of the two nodes.

The model contains a root node or code labeled as "Threat Indicators" which has two child nodes corresponding to responses relating to either cognitive demographics (left) or situational characteristics (right). The two stages of the analysis begin with further refinement of the situational characteristic node followed by further refinement of the cognitive demographic node.

11.6.2   Analysis of Situational Characteristics

The situational characteristics sub-tree contains all of the subjects' responses regarding their perception of threat based on the two scenarios in the task. The main distinction between the two scenarios was that in scenario one the name of the individual allegedly accessing the locations was known, while in scenario two the name of the individual allegedly accessing the locations was not known. In both scenarios,

TABLE 11.3   Codes and Descriptions for Situational Characteristics. Reproduced with permission of IEEE.

Scenario Codes	Description
High threat	Location, which if compromised, would create the highest threat
Low threshold	Probability of intrusion value to be considered a low threat
Low threat	Location, which if compromised, would create the lowest threat
Response time	Average time for security personnel to arrive on the scene
Access frequency	No. of times an individual accessed a location

it is assumed that the individual accessing the location is using the proper security credentials but it is unknown whether the individual is actually authorized. The access control system provides a mechanism to extract and transmit the name of the individual to security personnel. One objective of the scenarios was to determine if knowledge of the individuals name influenced the subjects' perception of threat. The codes for the descendant nodes of the two scenarios (person known vs. person unknown in Figure 11.7) are summarized in Table 11.3.

In regards to the first three codes, all of the locations within the paper-based scenarios were annotated with a probability of intrusion value. Initially, the subjects were asked to rate the chance of an intrusion for several locations. Subsequently, the same locations were used in the scenarios with a fixed probability of intrusion values. The objective was to investigate whether the introduction of an automated probability of intrusion estimate would alter their perception of the threat from their initial estimate. Again, the subjects were informed that the access control system provided a mechanism to extract and transmit the probability of intrusion value to security personnel. The probability of intrusion values were the same for both scenarios. After the subjects answered questions directly related to their responses in the two scenarios, they were asked what other factors they considered when evaluating a potential threat. Their responses were all related to situational characteristics and were coded as "Other Threat Indicators" node. The description of codes which emerged (Figure 11.7) is summarized in Table 11.4.

Once the text or responses were coded, the next step was to compare and contrast the responses between the two scenarios corresponding to the two sub-trees. This would elucidate whether knowledge of the individual's name accessing a location

TABLE 11.4   Situational Characteristics Emergent Codes. Reproduced with permission of IEEE.

Emergent Codes	Description
Role	Role of individual accessing a location
Time of intrusion	Perception of threat in relation to time of intrusion
Importance of location vs. identity	Perception of threat with respect to location vs. identity of individual allegedly accessing a location

would influence their perception of threat. That is, if security personnel knew the individual accessing a location, would their perception of the threat be different than if they did not know the person accessing the location? The result of the analysis indicated that the knowledge of the individual's name accessing the locations did not influence the subjects' perception of threat. However, the existence or absence of knowledge regarding the individual precipitated the emergence of another construct, the role of the individual. However, the responses were mixed regarding the subjects perception of threat based on the individual's role. Subsequent analysis of the transcriptions revealed that the single most important factor influencing the perception of threat, regarding the characteristics of the individual accessing the location, was the individual's access frequency. That is, knowing whether the individual normally accessed the location had a greater impact on the subjects' perception of threat compared to the individual's name or role within the organization.

In addition to the characteristics surrounding the individual accessing the location, participant responses indicated that there were several characteristics relating to the location being accessed which also influenced the subjects' perception of threat. The conceptual map of codes relating to location-specific characteristics influencing threat perception is illustrated in Figure 11.8. The main causes of concern with respect to the location or building characteristics included the impact or consequence of a threat in different locations as well as the reputation of the organization to the outside community. The potential impact of a threat was dependent on whether the location was in a secluded or populated area, and whether the building contained a large number of individual or physical assets. Different subjects rated the same location as both a high threat and low threat. After further analysis into the conflicting perceptions of threat, the main reason behind the two different viewpoints was based on whether the subjects analyzed the threat from a physical security or anti-terrorism perspective.

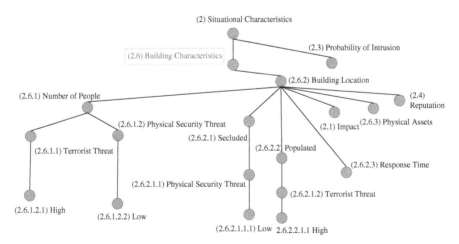

FIGURE 11.8   Conceptual map of situational characteristics – building.

A location which has limited security and is open to the public is less of a physical security threat, but more of a terrorist threat. In certain instances, both parameters exist and therefore the significance of this finding for designers would be to evaluate the benefit of incorporating a count of the number of individuals in the location during the time of the incident. Since current access control systems record the timestamp and ID of the individual accessing the location, a possible improvement in the perceived threat might be facilitated by displaying the total number of individuals in the location. In addition to the building characteristics and factors surrounding the individual accessing different locations in the scenarios, the effect of the probability of an intrusion in different locations on the subjects' perception of threat was also examined.

However, first, based on the proposed model in Figure 11.8, the cognitive demographics, which relate to an individual's disposition to decision-making is analyzed. It is hypothesized that the perception of threat is also affected by an individual's cognitive demographics. Considering the multitude of aforementioned variables which may influence threat perception, an investigation into the effects of cognitive demographics may provide additional insight into the design features of a decision support systems-based IDS.

11.6.3 Analysis of Cognitive Demographics

The two main constructs in this research relating to an individual's cognitive demographics are indecisiveness and intolerance of uncertainty. These two constructs were used to measure an individual's disposition to decision-making. The conjecture is that the perception of threat depends on the situational characteristics and the degree of the disposition to decision-making. A conceptual map of the coded nodes for the cognitive demographics and their relation are presented in a tree hierarchy in Figure 11.9.

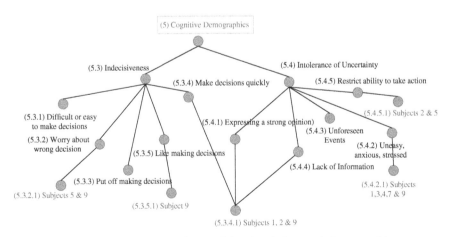

FIGURE 11.9 Conceptual map of situational characteristics – cognitive.

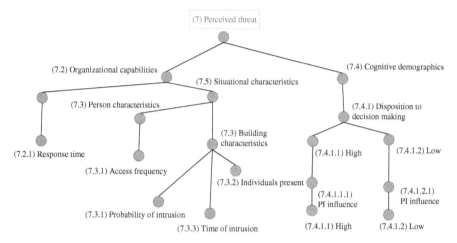

FIGURE 11.10   Proposed model of perceived threat. Reproduced with permission of IEEE.

The sub-tree on the left of Figure 11.10 coded the different dimensions of inde-cisiveness, while the sub-tree on the right coded different dimensions of intolerance of uncertainty. The leaf nodes correspond to the subject(s) who shared a character-istic or dimension associated with indecisiveness or intolerance of uncertainty. The analysis of coded responses for the leaf nodes yielded several interesting results. First, 3 subjects were not present in the map at all (subject 6, 8, and 10); second, 3 subjects (subjects 3, 4, and 7) only appeared one time in the map; and third, 1 subject appeared twice (subject 5). The term "appeared" refers to the number of parents for each child node. These subjects were considered to have a high disposi-tion toward decision-making since they demonstrated a lower frequency of responses to questions relating to indecisiveness and intolerance to uncertainty. Furthermore, 2 subjects appeared 4 times (subjects 1 and 2) in the map and 1 subject appeared 6 times (subject 9) in the map. These subjects were considered to have a low disposi-tion toward decision-making since they demonstrated a higher frequency of responses to questions relating to indecisiveness and intolerance to uncertainty.

Thus far, the responses extracted from the interviews regarding the cognitive demographics and situational characteristics have been analyzed. Several subjects have demonstrated varying degrees regarding a disposition toward decision-making and several factors regarding the situational characteristics which influenced per-ceived threat have been identified. An interesting question to explore is how does a subject's cognitive demographics impact her/his perception of threat, given the probability of an intrusion? The results can help explain whether an individual's perception of threat is more influenced by the probability of an intrusion, situational characteristics, or both. This may ultimately provide details on which characteris-tics or features should be incorporated into the design and which mechanisms or policies might enable increased decision quality. To explore these issues, each of the subject's responses to the task were analyzed. The results concluded that the perception of threat is more influenced by the probability of intrusion value for individuals who exhibit a low disposition toward decision-making compared to individuals who exhibit a high disposition toward decision-making.

11.7 DISCUSSION

The investigation into the proposed model of perceived threat consisted of a content analysis of 10 interview transcriptions and the analysis of responses in the experimental task. The results of the collective analyses precipitated several key factors which could aid designers in the development of future intrusion detection systems. The primary concepts, which emerged, relating to an individual's perception of threat are divided into three categories. The first category corresponds to the organizational capabilities such as response time. Respondents indicated that the response time is strongly influenced by the number of available resources and that a longer response time would increase their perception of threat. Therefore, a mechanism which could provide the estimated time to respond to a physical security incident would help to improve threat perception. The second category is related to situational characteristics. The content analysis of the transcriptions served to further expand the specific threat indicators into person characteristics and building characteristics.

In regards to the person characteristics, the most significant factor which would help to assess the severity of a physical intrusion was access frequency. The name and role of the individual was less significant compared to whether or not it was normal for the individual to access the location. Therefore, mechanism which could provide the access frequency for an individual would help to improve threat perception. In terms of the building characteristics, the time of the intrusion and the number of individuals present in the location influenced the subjects' perception of threat. The concept relating to the number of individuals in a particular location influenced the subjects' perception of threat depending on whether they were assessing the threat from a physical security or anti-terrorist perspective. The two different perspectives led to extreme opposite perceptions of the threat. Therefore, to reduce the ambiguity between the two perspectives, future development of software-based intrusion detection systems should consider incorporating a feature which can provide details on the number of people present in a particular location. Another design consideration is the time of intrusion. However, while significant, this feature is already available in many commercial systems and is only mentioned to accurately describe the main concepts which emerged during the analysis.

In addition, to the time of intrusion, and the number of people in the location, another factor which influenced the subjects' perception of threat, with respect to building characteristics, was the probability of intrusion. However, by analyzing the subjects' responses in the scenarios regarding prior and posterior probabilities and the associated threat levels it was determined that interpretation of the probability of intrusion value was related to an individual's cognitive demographics. The analysis of the coded text for the cognitive demographic concept revealed that some subjects responded to questions in the interview which would indicate a higher degree of indecisiveness and intolerance of uncertainty compared to other subjects.

Specifically, some subjects were observed to have characteristics consistent with a low disposition toward decision-making and while analyzing the response in the task relating to the probability of intrusion value it was determined that subjects with a low disposition toward decision-making were more likely to be influenced by the probability of intrusion value and less likely to rely on other situational characteristics to assess a threat compared to subjects with a high disposition toward decision-making. The significance of this result, from a design perspective, is that a system which provides a probability of intrusion statistic may require more accuracy or precision for subjects with a high disposition toward decision-making compared to subjects with a low disposition. Therefore, the importance or influence of situational characteristics on perceived threat should be viewed in light of the individual's cognitive demographics or disposition toward decision-making. As a result, the system should provide a mechanism which adjusts and adapts to an individual's perceived threat based on cognitive demographics and situational characteristics. This will be discussed in greater detail in following section, future research. A summary of all of the concepts which emerged is illustrated in Figure 11.10.

11.8 FUTURE RESEARCH

Due to the myriad of situational characteristics, cognitive demographics, and other factors not addressed in this research, incorporating all of the factors into a single system can be an extremely overwhelming and futile task. As a result, the discussion of the features presented in the previous section may best be realized in the implementation of a decision support systems, which learns the decision of a human operator in several different scenarios. With respect to a system which generates a probability of intrusion, such as biometric-based access control technologies, the system can dynamically adjust the appropriate security setting at any particular checkpoint based on the information learned from the human operator during a training stage. Subsequently, the operators learned perception of threat can be used to provide automated decisions regarding the detection of an intrusion and the appropriate course of action. While it is not the intention of this research to fully explore and evaluate development and usability issues surrounding such a system and the interface or mock-up, illustrated in Figure 11.11, the illustration helps to highlight the key features which emerged during the analyses of the situational characteristics (access frequency and person count) and cognitive demographics.

Subsequently, a brief description of the automated decision process is described. The mock-up presents the user with information, such as the access frequency for the individual accessing the location, the number of individuals present in the location, the estimated response time, and a probability of intrusion for the particular location. In addition, to compensate for the low number of alternative solutions during a threatening situation, strong visualization techniques are incorporated into the design to promote the formulation of new ideas and solutions (Ashford & Kasper 2003).

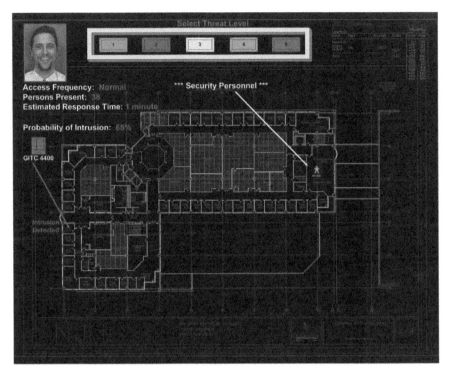

FIGURE 11.11   Behavioral biometric IDS. Reproduced with permission of IEEE.

The specific action that results from receiving the information is dependent on four parameters: (1) The access frequency for the person accessing the location (based on historical access logs), (2) the number of persons present at the location, (3) the estimated time to respond to the location, (4) and the probability of intrusion. For example, based on the biometric keypad the probability of intrusion would relate to the deviation of an individual's current keystroke pattern from the keystroke pattern in his/her profile. However, the probability of intrusion statistic generated by any other mechanism would suffice as well. A classification algorithm such as the iterative Dichotomiser 3 (ID3) algorithm, developed by Quinlan (1987), could be employed, to generate the smallest decision tree using all of the four parameters as input nodes. The ID3 algorithm could be used to learn an individual perception of threat during several scenarios and suggest the most appropriate threat level given the 4 parameters. The sensitivity of the pattern matching or score relating to the probability of intrusion performed by any biometric access technology or the collection other significant parameters used in the computation of the probability could be adjusted to each individual based on the individual's perception of threat during a training stage. For example, when a higher degree of security is required due to the time of day or an individual who has a high disposition toward decision-making, the probability metric could be adjusted or increased. As discussed in the previous section, subjects with a high disposition toward decision-making may require a higher or more accurate

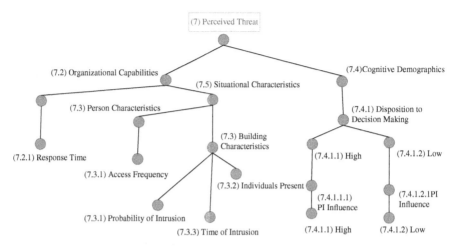

FIGURE 11.12   Final model of perceived threat. Reproduced with permission of IEEE.

probability of intrusion value in order to have any effect on the individual's perception of threat. However, this has to be considered with caution as the unfortunate consequence of increased security is quite often a decrease in usability.

11.9 CONCLUSION

This chapter presented the analysis of each of the three constructs, cognitive demographics, situational characteristics, and probability of intrusion, based on the perceived threat model (Leberknight et al 2008). The final model (Figure 11.12) encapsulating all of the results as well as the design implications is illustrated below.

Several findings were presented based on a content analysis of the interview transcriptions and the examination of responses in the experimental task. While previous research has reported the significance of situational characteristics on perceived threat, this research identified several new concepts which emerged during the analysis of the situational characteristics. Specifically, results from this research discussed the identification of building or location characteristics and the different perceptions of threat based on either a physical security or anti-terrorist perspective.

In addition, the content analysis of the cognitive demographic construct demonstrated that subjects had different dispositions toward decision-making. This result was subsequently linked to the participant's responses in the experimental task and the findings revealed that, subjects with a low disposition toward decision-making rated locations with higher probability of intrusions as a high threat, compared to subjects with a high disposition supporting our main hypothesis which claimed:

H1:   Perceived threat is a construct that depends on the social context and disposition toward decision-making of the user.

This implies that the probability of intrusion had a stronger impact on perceived threat for individuals with a low disposition toward decision-making compared to individuals with a high disposition toward decision-making.

REFERENCES

Alberts, C., Dorofee, A., Stevens, J., & Woody, C. 2003. *Introduction to the OCTAVE Approach.* Carnegie Mellon University, Pittsburgh, PA.

Ashford, B.M., & Kasper, G.M. 2003. A test of the theory of DSS design for user calibration: the effects of expressiveness and visibility on user calibration. In: SIGHCI 2003 Proceedings, p. 18.

Barnett, C.K., & Pratt, M.G. 2000. From threat-rigidity to flexibility – toward a learning model of autogenic crisis in organizations. *Journal of Organizational Change Management*, 13(1), pp. 74–88.

Berenbaum, H., Thompson, R.J., & Bredemeier, K. 2007. Perceived threat: exploring its association with worry and its hypothesized antecedents. *Behaviour Research and Therapy*, 45(10), pp. 2473–2482.

Davis, F.D., Kottemann, J.E., & Remus, W.E. 1991. What-if analysis and the illusion of control. In: IEEE Proceedings of the Twenty-Fourth Annual Hawaii International Conference on System Sciences, vol. iii, January 8–11, 1991, Kauai, HI, pp. 452–460.

Dawson, R., Boyd, C., Dawson, E., & Nieto, J.M.G. 2006. SKMA: a key management architecture for SCADA systems. In: Proceedings of the 2006 Australasian workshops on Grid computing and e-research, vol. 54, January 2006, Australian Computer Society, Inc., Darlinghurst, Australia, pp. 183–192.

DeLuca, D., Gallivan, M.J., & Kock, N. 2008. Furthering information systems action research: a post-positivist synthesis of four dialectics. *Journal of the Association for Information Systems*, 9(2), p. 48.

den Braber, F., Hogganvik, I., Lund, M.S., Stølen, K., & Vraalsen, F. 2007. Model-based security analysis in seven steps – a guided tour to the CORAS method. *BT Technology Journal*, 25(1), pp. 101–117

Dugas, M.J., Buhr, K., & Ladouceur, R. 2004. The Role of Intolerance of Uncertainty in Etiology and Maintenance.

Dugas, M.J., Gosselin, P., & Ladouceur, R. 2001. Intolerance of uncertainty and worry: Investigating specificity in a nonclinical sample. *Cognitive Therapy and Research*, 25(5), pp. 551–558.

Fielding, N.G., Lee, N.F.R.M., & Lee, R.M. 1998. *Computer Analysis and Qualitative Research.* Sage.

Forte, D., & Power, R. 2007. Physical security–overlook it at your own peril. *Computer Fraud & Security*, 2007(8), pp. 16–20.

Frost, R.O., & Shows, D.L. 1993. The nature and measurement of compulsive indecisiveness. *Behaviour Research and Therapy*, 31(7), pp. 683–692.

Germeijs, V., & De Boeck, P. 2002. A measurement scale for indecisiveness and its relationship to career indecision and other types of indecision. *European Journal of Psychological Assessment*, 18(2), p. 113.

Glaser, B.G., Strauss, A.L., & Elizabeth S. 1968. The discovery of grounded theory; strategies for qualitative research. *Nursing Research*, 17(4), 364.

Jones, A. 2007. A framework for the management of information security risks. *BT Technology Journal*, 25(1), pp. 30–36.

Karabacak, B., & Sogukpinar, I. 2005. ISRAM: information security risk analysis method. *Computers & Security*, 24(2), pp. 147–159.

Kasper, G.M. 1996. A theory of decision support system design for user calibration. *Information Systems Research*, 7(2), pp. 215–232.

Keil, M., Tan, B.C., Wei, K.K., Saarinen, T., Tuunainen, V., & Wassenaar, A. 2000. A cross-cultural study on escalation of commitment behavior in software projects. *MIS quarterly*, 24(2), pp. 299–325.

Kottemann, J.E., Davis, F.D., & Remus, W.E. 1994. Computer-assisted decision making: performance, beliefs, and the illusion of control. *Organizational Behavior and Human Decision Processes*, 57(1), pp. 26–37.

Langer, E.J. 1975. The illusion of control. *Journal of Personality and Social Psychology*, 32(2), p. 311.

Langer, E.J., & Roth, J. 1975. Heads I win, tails it's chance: the illusion of control as a function of the sequence of outcomes in a purely chance task. *Journal of Personality and Social Psychology*, 32(6), pp. 951–955.

Leberknight, C.S., Widmeyer, G.R., & Recce, M.L. 2008. Decision support for perceived threat in the context of intrusion detection systems. In: AMCIS 2008 Proceedings, p. 317.

Lim, K.H., & Benbasat, I. 2000. The effect of multimedia on perceived equivocality and perceived usefulness of information systems. *MIS quarterly*, 24(3), pp. 449–471.

Malhotra, M.K., & Grover, V. 1998. An assessment of survey research in POM: from constructs to theory. *Journal of Operations Management*, 16(4), pp. 407–425.

McCumber, J. 1991. Information systems security: a comprehensive model. In: Proceedings of the 14th National Computer Security Conference, October 1991.

Melone, N.P., McGuire, T.W., Chan, L.W., & Gerwing, T.A. 1995. Effects of DSS, modeling, and exogenous factors on decision quality and confidence. In: IEEE Proceedings of the Twenty-Eighth Hawaii International Conference on System Sciences, vol. iii, January 3–6, 1995, Wailea, HI, pp. 152–159.

Morton, M.S.S. 1983. State of the art of research in management support systems. Report no. 107, CISR Working paper, Center for Information Systems Research, Sloan School of Management, Massachusetts Institute of Technology, pp. 1473–1483.

Myers, M.D., & Newman, M. 2007. The qualitative interview in IS research: examining the craft. *Information and Organization*, 17(1), pp. 2–26.

Nicolaou, A.I., & McKnight, D.H. 2006. Perceived information quality in data exchanges: effects on risk, trust, and intention to use. *Information Systems Research*, 17(4), pp. 332–351.

Page, V., Dixon, M., & Choudhury, I. 2007. Security risk mitigation for information systems. *BT Technology Journal*, 25(1), pp. 118–127.

Quinlan, J.R. 1987. Simplifying decision trees. *International Journal of Man-Machine Studies*, 27(3), pp. 221–234.

Rassin, E., & Muris, P. 2005. To be or not to be… indecisive: gender differences, correlations with obsessive–compulsive complaints, and behavioural manifestation. *Personality and Individual Differences*, 38(5), pp. 1175–1181.

Rassin, E., Muris, P., Franken, I., Smit, M., & Wong, M. 2007. Measuring general indecisiveness. *Journal of Psychopathology and Behavioral Assessment*, 29(1), pp. 60–67.

Rubin, H.J., & Rubin, I.S. (2005). *Qualitative Interviewing: The Art of Hearing Data*. Sage, Thousand Oaks, CA.

Schou, C.D., Frost, J., & Maconachy, W. 2004. Information assurance in biomedical informatics systems. *Engineering in Medicine and Biology Magazine*, 23(1), pp. 110–118.

Staw, B.M., Sandelands, L.E., & Dutton, J.E. 1981. Threat rigidity effects in organizational behavior: a multilevel analysis. *Administrative Science Quarterly*, 26(4), pp. 501–524.

Suh, B., & Han, I. 2003. The IS risk analysis based on a business model. *Information & Management*, 41(2), pp. 149–158.

Tractinsky, N., & Meyer, J. 1999. Chartjunk or goldgraph? Effects of presentation objectives and content desirability on information presentation. *MIS Quarterly*, 23(3), pp. 397–420.

Tsiros, M., & Mittal, V. 2000. Regret: a model of its antecedents and consequences in consumer decision making. *Journal of Consumer Research*, 26(4), 401–417.

Webster, J., & Trevino, L.K. 1995. Rational and social theories as complementary explanations of communication media choices: two policy-capturing studies. *Academy of Management Journal*, 38(6), pp. 1544–1572.

Wortman, C.B. 1975. Some determinants of perceived control. *Journal of Personality and Social Psychology*, 31(2), p. 282.

Yavagal, D.S., Lee, S.W., Ahn, G.J., & Gandhi, R.A. 2005. Common criteria requirements modeling and its uses for quality of information assurance (QoIA). In: Proceedings of the 43rd annual Southeast regional conference, vol. 2, March 2005, New York, NY, pp. 130–135.

Yoo, Y., & Alavi, M. 2001. Media and group cohesion: relative influences on social presence, task participation, and group consensus. *MIS Quarterly*, 25(3), pp. 371–390.

Zimmerman, R., & Horan, T.A. 2004. *Digital Infrastructures: Enabling Civil and Environmental Systems through Information Technology*. Psychology Press.

Zimmerman, R., & Restrepo, C.E. 2006. Information Technology (IT) and Critical Infrastructure Interdependencies for Emergency Response. In Proceedings of the 3rd ISCRAM Conference (B. Van de Walle and M. Turoff, eds.), Newark, NJ (USA), May 2006, pp. 382–386.

APPENDIX A

LIST OF IEEE INTERNET OF THINGS STANDARDS[1]

Below is a listing of IEEE published standards related to the Internet of Things as of March 2016.

IEEE 754^{TM}-2008 – IEEE Standard for Floating-Point Arithmetic

   Description: This standard specifies interchange and arithmetic formats and methods for binary and decimal floating-point arithmetic in computer programming environments. This standard specifies exception conditions and their default handling. An implementation of a floating-point system conforming to this standard may be realized entirely in software, entirely in hardware, or in any combination of software and hardware. For operations specified in the normative part of this standard, numerical results and exceptions are uniquely determined by the values of the input data, sequence of operations, and destination formats, all under user control.

IEEE 802.1AS^{TM}-2011 – IEEE Standard for Local and Metropolitan Area Networks – Timing and Synchronization for Time-Sensitive Applications in Bridged Local Area Networks

   Description: This standard defines a protocol and procedures for the transport of timing over bridged and virtual bridged local area networks. It includes the transport of synchronized time, the selection of the timing source (i.e., best

---

[1] http://standards.ieee.org/innovate/iot/stds.html

Cyber-Assurance for the Internet of Things, First Edition. Edited by Tyson T. Brooks.

master), and the indication of the occurrence and magnitude of timing impairments (i.e., phase and frequency discontinuities). The PDF of this standard is available at the IEEE Get Program. The "IEEE Get Program" grants public access to view and download individual PDFs of select standards at no charge. Visit http://standards.ieee.org/about/get/index.html for details.

IEEE 802.1Q™-2011 – IEEE Standard for Local and Metropolitan Area Networks – Media Access Control (MAC) Bridges and Virtual Bridged Local Area Networks

Description: This standard specifies how the MAC service is supported by virtual bridged local area networks, the principles of operation of those networks, and the operation of VLAN-aware ridges, including management, protocols, and algorithms. Incorporates IEEE Std 802.1Q-2005, IEEE Std 802.1ad-2005, IEEE Std 802.1ak-2007, IEEE Std 802.1ag-2007, IEEE Std 802.1ah-2008, IEEE Std 802-1Q-2005/Cor-1-2008, IEEE Std 802.1ap-2008, IEEE Std 802.1Qaw-2009, IEEE Std 802.1Qay-2009, IEEE Std 802.1aj-2009, IEEE Std 802.1Qav-2009, IEEE Std Qau-2010, and IEEE Std Qat-2010. The PDF of this standard is available at no cost, compliments of the IEEE 802 group. http://grouper.ieee.org/groups/802/1/

IEEE 802.3™-2012 – IEEE Standard for Ethernet

Description: Ethernet local area network operation is specified for selected speeds of operation from 1 Mb/s to 100 Gb/s using a common media access control (MAC) specification and management information base (MIB). The Carrier Sense Multiple Access with Collision Detection (CSMA/CD) MAC protocol specifies shared medium (half duplex) operation, as well as full duplex operation. Speed specific Media Independent Interfaces (MIIs) allow use of selected physical layer devices (PHY) for operation over coaxial, twisted-pair or fiber optic cables. System considerations for multi-segment shared access networks describe the use of Repeaters that are defined for operational speeds up to 1000 Mb/s. Local area network (LAN) operation is supported at all speeds. Other specified capabilities include various PHY types for access networks, PHYs suitable for metropolitan area network applications, and the provision of power over selected twisted-pair PHY types.

IEEE 802.3.1™-2011 – IEEE Standard for Management Information Base (MIB) Definitions for Ethernet

Description: The Management Information Base (MIB) module specifications for IEEE Std 802.3, also known as Ethernet, are contained in this standard. It includes the Structure of Management Information Version 2 (SMIv2) MIB module specifications formerly produced and published by the Internet Engineering Task Force (IETF), and the Guidelines for the Definition of Managed Objects (GDMO) MIB modules formerly specified within IEEE Std 802.3, as well as extensions resulting from amendments to IEEE Std 802.3. The SMIv2 MIB modules are intended for use with the Simple Network Management Protocol (SNMP), commonly used to manage Ethernet.

IEEE 802.11™-2012 – IEEE Standard for Information Technology – Telecommunications and Information Exchange Between Systems – Local and Metropolitan Area Networks – Specific Requirements Part 11: Wireless LAN Medium Access Control (MAC) and Physical Layer (PHY)
Description: This revision specifies technical corrections and clarifications to IEEE Std 802.11 for wireless local area networks (WLANS) as well as enhancements to the existing medium access control (MAC) and physical layer (PHY) functions. It also incorporates Amendments 1 to 10 published in 2008 to 2011. The PDF of this standard is available at http://standards.ieee.org/about/get/802/802.11.html at no cost, compliments of the IEEE 802 GET program.

IEEE 802.11ad™-2012 – IEEE Standard for Local and Metropolitan Area Networks – Specific Requirements – Part 11: Wireless LAN Medium Access Control (MAC) and Physical Layer (PHY) Specifications – Amendment 3: Enhancements for Very High Throughput in the 60 GHz Band
Description: This amendment defines modifications to both the IEEE 802.11 physical layers (PHYs) and the IEEE 802.11 medium access control layer (MAC) to enable operation in frequencies around 60 GHz and capable of very high throughput.

IEEE 802.15.1™-2005 – IEEE Standard for Information Technology – Telecommunications and Information Exchange Between Systems – Local and Metropolitan Area Networks – Specific Requirements. – Part 15.1: Wireless Medium Access Control (MAC) and Physical Layer (PHY) Specifications for Wireless Personal Area Networks (WPANs)
Description: Methods for communicating devices in a personal area network (PAN) are covered in this standard.

IEEE 802.15.2™-2003 – IEEE Recommended Practice for Information Technology – Telecommunications and Information Exchange Between Systems – Local and Metropolitan Area Networks – Specific Requirements Part 15.2: Coexistence of Wireless Personal Area Networks with Other Wireless Devices Operating in Unlicensed Frequency Bands
Description: This recommended practice addresses the issue of coexistence of wireless local area networks and wireless personal area networks. These wireless networks often operate in the same unlicensed band. This recommended practice describes coexistence mechanisms that can be used to facilitate coexistence of wireless local area networks (i.e., IEEE Std 802.11b1999) and wireless personal area networks (i.e., IEEE Std 802.15.1-2002).

IEEE 802.15.3™-2003 – IEEE Standard for Information Technology – Telecommunications and Information Exchange Between Systems – Local and Metropolitan Area Networks – Specific Requirements Part 15.3: Wireless Medium Access Control (MAC) and Physical Layer (PHY) Specifications for High Rate Wireless Personal Area Networks (WPANs) Amendment 1: Mac Sublayer

Description: The protocol and compatible interconnection of data and multimedia communication equipment via 2.4 GHz radio transmissions in a wireless personal area network (WPAN) using low power and multiple modulation formats to support scalable data rates is defined in this standard. The medium access control (MAC) sublayer protocol supports both isochronous and asynchronous data types.

IEEE 802.15.3c^{TM}-2009 – IEEE Standard for Information Technology – Local and Metropolitan Area Networks – Specific Requirements – Part 15.3: Amendment 2: Millimeter-Wave-Based Alternative Physical Layer Extension

Description: This amendment defines an alternative physical layer (PHY) for IEEE Std 802.15.3-2003. Three PHY modes have been defined that enable data rates in excess of 5 Gb/s using the 60 GHz band. A beam forming protocol has been defined to improve the range of communicating devices. Aggregation and block acknowledgment have been defined to improve the medium access control (MAC) efficiency at the high data rates provided for by the PHY. The "IEEE Get Program" grants public access to view and download individual PDFs of select standards at no charge. Visit http://standards.ieee.org/about/get/index.html for details.

IEEE 802.15.4^{TM}-2011 – IEEE Standard for Local and Metropolitan Area Networks – Part 15.4: Low-Rate Wireless Personal Area Networks (LR-WPANs)

Description: The protocol and compatible interconnection for data communication devices using low-data-rate, low-power, and low-complexity short-range radio frequency (RF) transmissions in a wireless personal area network (WPAN) were defined in IEEE Std 802.15.4-2006. In this revision, the market applicability of IEEE Std 802.15.4 is extended, the ambiguities in the standard are removed, and the improvements learned from implementations of IEEE Std 802.15.4-2006 are included. The PDF of this standard is available at no cost, compliments of the GETIEEE802 program located at http://standards.ieee.org/about/get/index.html

IEEE 802.15.4e^{TM}-2012 – IEEE Standard for Local and Metropolitan Area Networks – Part 15.4: Low-Rate Wireless Personal Area Networks (LR-WPANs) Amendment 1: MAC Sublayer

Description: IEEE Std 802.15.4-2011 is amended by this standard. The intention of this amendment is to enhance and add functionality to the IEEE 802.15.4 MAC to (a) better support the industrial markets and (b) permit compatibility with modifications being proposed within the Chinese WPAN. The PDF of this standard is available at no cost, compliments of the IEEEGET802 program at http://standards.ieee.org/getieee802/download/802.15.4e-2012.pdf

IEEE 802.15.4f^{TM}-2012 – IEEE Standard for Local and Metropolitan Area Networks – Part 15.4: Low-Rate Wireless Personal Area Networks

(LR-WPANs) Amendment 2: Active Radio Frequency Identification (RFID) System Physical Layer (PHY)

Description: This amendment provides two PHYs (MSK and LRP UWB) that can be used in a wide range of applications requiring various combinations of low cost, low energy consumption, multiyear battery life, reliable communications, precision location, and reader options. This PHY standard supports the performance and flexibility needed for future mass deployments of highly populated autonomous active RFID systems anywhere in the world.

IEEE 802.15.4g™-2012 – IEEE Standard for Local and Metropolitan Area Networks – Part 15.4: Low-Rate Wireless Personal Area Networks (LR-WPANs) Amendment 3: Physical Layer (PHY) Specifications for Low-Data-Rate, Wireless, Smart Metering Utility Networks

Description: In this amendment to IEEE Std 802.15.4-2011, outdoor low-data-rate, wireless, smart metering utility network requirements are addressed. Alternate PHYs are defined as well as only those MAC modifications needed to support their implementation.

IEEE 802.15.4j™-2013 – IEEE Standard for Information Technology – Telecommunications and Information Exchange Between Systems – Local and Metropolitan Area Networks – Specific Requirements – Part 15.4: Wireless Medium Access Control (MAC) and Physical Layer (PHY) Specifications for Low Rate Wireless Personal Area Networks (WPANs) Amendment: Alternative Physical Layer Extension to Support Medical Body Area Network (MBAN) Services Operating in the 2360–2400 MHz Band

Description: In this amendment to IEEE Std 802.15.4TM-2011, a physical layer for IEEE 802.15.4 in the 2360 MHz to 2400 MHz band which complies with Federal Communications Commission (FCC) MBAN rules is defined. Modifications to the MAC needed to support this new physical layer are also defined in this amendment.

IEEE 802.15.5™-2009 – IEEE Recommended Practice for Information Technology – Telecommunications and Information Exchange Between Systems – Local and Metropolitan Area Networks – Specific Requirements Part 15.5: Mesh Topology Capability in Wireless Personal Area Networks (WPANs)

Description: This IEEE-recommended practice defines the architectural framework that enables WPAN devices to promote interoperable, stable, and scalable wireless mesh topologies and, if needed, to provide the amendment text to the current WPAN standards that is required to implement this recommended practice.

IEEE 802.15.6™-2012 – IEEE Standard for Information Technology – Telecommunications and Information Exchange Between Systems – Local and Metropolitan Area Networks – Specific Requirements – Part 15.6:

Wireless Medium Access Control (MAC) and Physical Layer (PHY) Specifications for Wireless Personal Area Networks (WPANs)

Description: Short-range, wireless communications in the vicinity of, or inside, a human body (but not limited to humans) are specified in this standard. It uses existing industrial scientific medical (ISM) bands as well as frequency bands approved by national medical and/or regulatory authorities. Support for quality of service (QoS), extremely low power, and data rates up to 10 Mbps is required while simultaneously complying with strict non-interference guidelines where needed. This standard considers effects on portable antennas due to the presence of a person (varying with male, female, skinny, heavy, etc.), radiation pattern shaping to minimize the specific absorption rate (SAR) into the body, and changes in characteristics as a result of the user motions. The PDF of this standard is available at no cost at http://standards.ieee.org/about/get/802/802.15.html, compliments of the IEEE 802 working group.

IEEE 802.15.7™-2011 – IEEE Standard for Local and Metropolitan Area Networks – Part 15.7: Short-Range Wireless Optical Communication Using Visible Light

Description: A PHY and a MAC layer for short-range optical wireless communications using visible light in optically transparent media are defined. The visible light spectrum extends from 380 nm to 780 nm in wavelength. The standard is capable of delivering data rates sufficient to support audio and video multimedia services and also considers mobility of the visible link, compatibility with visible-light infrastructures, impairments due to noise and interference from sources like ambient light and a MAC layer that accommodates visible links. The standard adheres to applicable eye safety regulations. The PDF of this standard is available for free download, compliments of the IEEE GET Program. For more details go to http://standards.ieee.org/getieee802/

IEEE 802.16™-2012 – IEEE Standard for Air Interface for Broadband Wireless Access Systems

Description: This standard specifies the air interface, including the medium access control layer (MAC) and physical layer (PHY), of combined fixed and mobile point-to-multipoint broadband wireless access (BWA) systems providing multiple services. The MAC is structured to support the WirelessMAN-SC, WirelessMAN-OFDM, and WirelessMAN-OFDMA PHY specifications, each suited to a particular operational environment. The standard enables rapid worldwide deployment of innovative, cost-effective, and interoperable multivendor broadband wireless access products, facilitates competition in broadband access by providing alternatives to wireline broadband access, encourages consistent worldwide spectrum allocation, and accelerates the commercialization of broadband wireless access systems.

IEEE 802.16p™-2012 – IEEE Standard for Air Interface for Broadband Wireless Access Systems Amendment: Enhancements to Support Machine-to-Machine Applications

Description: Enhancements to the Wireless MAN-OFDMA Air Interface, an air interface designated as "IMT-2000" by the International Telecommunication Union-Radio communication Sector (ITU-R), are specified by this amendment. The enhancements provide improved support for machine-to-machine applications. The PDF of this standard is available at no charge, compliments of the GETIEEE802 standards program located at http://standards.ieee.org/about/get/index.html

IEEE 802.16.1b™-2012 – IEEE Standard for WirelessMAN-Advanced Air Interface for Broadband Wireless Access Systems – Amendment: Enhancements to Support Machine-to-Machine Applications
Description: Enhancements to the Wireless MAN-Advanced Air Interface, an air interface designated as "IMT-Advanced" by the International Telecommunication Union–Radio communication Sector (ITU-R), are specified in this standard. Improved support for machine-to-machine applications are provided by these enhancements. The PDF of this standard is available at no cost, compliments of the GETIEEE802 program located at http://standards.ieee.org/about/get/index.html

IEEE 802.22™-2011 – IEEE Standard for Information Technology – Telecommunications and Information Exchange Between Systems Wireless Regional Area Networks (WRAN) – Specific Requirements Part 22: Cognitive Wireless RAN Medium Access Control (MAC) and Physical Layer (PHY) Specifications: Policies and Procedures for Operation in the TV Bands
Description: This standard specifies the air interface, including the cognitive medium access control layer (MAC) and physical layer (PHY), of point-to-multipoint wireless regional area networks comprised of a professional fixed base station with fixed and portable user terminals operating in the VHF/UHF TV broadcast bands between 54 MHz and 862 MHz.

IEEE 802.22.1™-2010 – IEEE Standard for Information Technology – Telecommunications and Information Exchange Between Systems – Local and Metropolitan Area Networks – Specific Requirements Part 22.1: Standard to Enhance Harmful Interference Protection for Low-Power Licensed Devices Operating in TV Broadcast Bands
Description: This standard defines the protocol and data formats for communication devices forming a beaconing network that are used to protect low-power, licensed devices operating in television broadcast bands from harmful interference generated by license-exempt devices, such as wireless regional area networks (WRAN), intended to operate in the same bands. The devices being protected are devices licensed as secondary under Title 47, Part 74, Subpart H in the USA and equivalent devices in other regulatory domains.

IEEE 802.22.2™-2012 – IEEE Standard for Information Technology – Telecommunications and Information Exchange Between Systems – Local and Metropolitan Area Networks – Specific Requirements Part 22.2: Installation and Deployment of IEEE 802.22 Systems

Description: Engineering practices for the installation and deployment of IEEE 802.22 systems are discussed in this recommended practice.

IEEE 1284™-2000 – IEEE Standard Signaling Method for a Bidirectional Parallel Peripheral Interface for Personal Computers
Description: A signaling method for asynchronous, fully interlocked, bidirectional parallel communications between hosts and printers or other peripherals is defined. A functional subset of the signaling method may be implemented on personal computers (PCs) or equivalent parallel port hardware with new software. New electrical interfaces, cabling, and interface hardware that provides improved performance while retaining backward compatibility with this subset is detailed.

IEEE 1285™-2005 – IEEE Standard for Scalable Storage Interface (S/SUP 2/I)
Description: A scalable interface between mass-storage devices and controlling hardware/software is specified in this standard. The interface is optimized for low-latency interconnects, and assumes that the processor/controller and the storage device can often be co-located on the same printed-circuit board. The interface can also be used with longer-distance bus-like interconnects, including (but not limited to) IEEE Std 1394-1995 Serial Bus and IEEE Std 1596-1992 Scalable Coherent Interface.

IEEE 1301.3™-1992 – IEEE Standard for a Metric Equipment Practice for Microcomputers – Convection-Cooled with 2.5 mm Connectors
Description: Dimension requirements are presented for subracks, plug-in units, printed boards, and backplanes to be used in conjunction with IEEE Std 1301-1991 and with a 2.5 mm connector as defined in IEC 48B (Central Office) 245. The general arrangement, dimensions, and environmental requirements are covered. This standard may be used with other IEEE Std 1301.x connector implementations in the subrack.

IEEE 1377™-2012 – IEEE Standard for Utility Industry Metering Communication Protocol Application Layer (End Device Data Tables)
Description: Common structures are provided in this standard for encoding data in communication between end devices (meters, home appliances, IEEE 1703 nodes) and utility enterprise collection and control systems using binary codes and Extensible Markup Language (XML) content. The advanced metering infrastructure (AMI) and smart grid requirements are addressed as identified by the Office of Electricity Delivery and Energy Reliability of the U.S. Department of Energy and by the Smart Metering Initiative of the Ontario Ministry of Energy (Canada) and of Measurement Canada. Sets of tables are exposed that are grouped together into sections that pertain to a particular feature-set and related function such as time-of-use, load profile, security, power quality, and more. Each standard table set (data model) can be expanded or restricted by the manufacturer of the IEEE 1377 device or home appliance using XML/TDL descriptive registered syntax (XML-based Table Definition Language) and enterprise data-value management using EDL (Exchange Data

Language) in a manner that is machine readable. Published jointly with NEMA and Measurement Canada, Tables are provided in support of gas, water, and electric sensors and related appliances. Tables are also provided for network configuration and management by referencing its companion standard IEEE Std 1703TM-2012. IEEE Std 1377-2012 is co-published as ANSI C12.19 and MC12.19.

IEEE 1394^{TM}-2008 – IEEE Standard for a High-Performance Serial Bus
Description: This standard provides specifications for a high-speed serial bus that supports both asynchronous and isochronous communication and integrates well with most IEEE standard 32-bit and 64-bit parallel buses. It is intended to provide a low-cost interconnect between cards on the same backplane, cards on other backplanes, and external peripherals. Interfaces to longer distance transmission media (such as unshielded twisted pair (UTP), optical fiber, and plastic optical fiber (POF)) allow the interconnection to be extended throughout a local network. This standard follows the command and status register (CSR) architecture of IEEE Std 1212 trade-2001.

IEEE 1451.0^{TM}-2007 – IEEE Standard for a Smart Transducer Interface for Sensors and Actuators – Common Functions, Communication Protocols, and Transducer Electronic Data Sheet (TEDS) Formats
Description: This standard provides a common basis for members of the IEEE 1451 family of standards to be interoperable. It defines the functions that are to be performed by a transducer interface module (TIM) and the common characteristics for all devices that implement the TIM. It specifies the formats for transducer electronic data sheets (TEDS). It defines a set of commands to facilitate the setup and control of the TIM as well as reading and writing the data used by the system. Application programming interfaces (APIs) are defined to facilitate communications with the TIM and with applications

IEEE 1547^{TM}-2003 – IEEE Standard for Interconnecting Distributed Resources with Electric Power Systems
Description: This standard is the first in the 1547 series of interconnection standards and is a benchmark milestone demonstrating the open consensus process for standards development. Traditionally, utility electric power systems (EPS grid or utility grid) were not designed to accommodate active generation and storage at the distribution level. As a result, there are major issues and obstacles to an orderly transition to using and integrating distributed power resources with the grid. The lack of uniform national interconnection standards and tests for interconnection operation and certification, as well as the lack of uniform national building, electrical, and safety codes, are understood. IEEE Std 1547 and its development demonstrate a model for ongoing success in establishing additional interconnection agreements, rules, and standards, on a national, regional, and state level. IEEE Std 1547 has the potential to be used in federal legislation and rule making and state public utilities commission (PUC) deliberations, and by over 3000 utilities in formulating technical requirements for interconnection agreements for distributed generators powering the electric

grid. This standard focuses on the technical specifications for, and testing of, the interconnection itself. It provides requirements relevant to the performance, operation, testing, safety considerations, and maintenance of the interconnection. It includes general requirements, response to abnormal conditions, power quality, islanding, and test specifications and requirements for design, production, installation evaluation, commissioning, and periodic tests. The stated requirements are universally needed for interconnection of distributed resources (DR), including synchronous machines, induction machines, or power inverters/converters and will be sufficient for most installations. The criteria and requirements are applicable to all DR technologies, with aggregate capacity of 10 MVA or less at the point of common coupling, interconnected to electric power systems at typical primary and/or secondary distribution voltages. Installation of DR on radial primary and secondary distribution systems is the main emphasis of this document, although installation of DR on primary and secondary network distribution systems is considered. This standard is written considering that the DR is a 60 Hz source.

IEEE 1547.1^{TM}-2005 – IEEE Standard Conformance Test Procedures for Equipment Interconnecting Distributed Resources with Electric Power Systems

Description: This standard specifies the type, production, and commissioning tests that shall be performed to demonstrate that the interconnection functions and equipment of the distributed resources (DR) conform to IEEE Std 1547.

IEEE 1547.2^{TM}-2008 – IEEE Application Guide for IEEE Std 1547^{TM}, IEEE Standard for Interconnecting Distributed Resources with Electric Power Systems

Description: In this paper, technical background and application details to support understanding of IEEE Std 1547-2003 are provided. The guide facilitates the use of IEEE Std 1547-2003 by characterizing various forms of distributed resource (DR) technologies and their associated interconnection issues. It provides background and rationale of the technical requirements of IEEE Std 1547-2003. It also provides tips, techniques, and rules of thumb, and it addresses topics related to DR project implementation to enhance the user's understanding of how IEEE Std 1547-2003 may relate to those topics. This guide is intended for use by engineers, engineering consultants, and knowledgeable individuals in the field of DR. The IEEE 1547 series of standards is cited in the Federal Energy Policy Act of 2005, and this guide is one document in the IEEE 1547 series.

IEEE 1547.3^{TM}-2007 – IEEE Guide for Monitoring, Information Exchange, and Control of Distributed Resources Interconnected with Electric Power Systems

Description: This guide is intended to facilitate the interoperability of distributed resources (DR) and help DR project stakeholders implement monitoring, information exchange, and control (MIC) to support the technical and business operations of DR and transactions among the stakeholders. The focus is on MIC between DR controllers and stakeholder entities with direct communication interactions. This guide incorporates information modeling, use case approaches, and a pro forma information exchange template and introduces the concept of an information exchange interface. The concepts and approaches are compatible with historical approaches to establishing and satisfying MIC needs. The IEEE 1547 trade series of standards is cited in the U.S. Federal Energy Policy Act of 2005, and this guide is one document in the IEEE 1547 series. This guide is primarily concerned with MIC between the DR unit controller and the outside world. However, the concepts and methods should also prove helpful to manufacturers and implementers of communications systems for loads, energy management systems, SCADA, electric power system and equipment protection, and revenue metering. The guide does not address the economic or technical viability of specific types of DR. It provides use case methodology and examples (e.g., examples of DR unit dispatch, scheduling, maintenance, ancillary services, and reactive supply). Market drivers will determine which DR applications become viable. This document provides guidelines rather than mandatory requirements or prioritized preferences.

IEEE 1547.4™-2011 – IEEE Guide for Design, Operation, and Integration of Distributed Resource Island Systems with Electric Power Systems
Description: Alternative approaches and good practices for the design, operation, and integration of distributed resource (DR) island systems with electric power systems (EPS) are provided. This includes the ability to separate from and reconnect to part of the area EPS while providing power to the islanded EPSs. This guide includes the DRs, interconnection systems, and participating EPSs.

IEEE 1547.6™-2011 – IEEE Recommended Practice for Interconnecting Distributed Resources with Electric Power Systems Distribution Secondary Networks
Description: Recommendations and guidance for distributed resources (DR) interconnected on the distribution secondary networks, including both spot networks and grid networks, are provided. This document gives an overview of distribution secondary network systems design, components, and operation; describes considerations for interconnecting DR with networks; and provides potential solutions for the interconnection of DR on network distribution systems. IEEE Std 1547.6-2011 is part of the IEEE 1547(TM) series of standards. IEEE Std 1547-2003 provides mandatory requirements for the interconnection of DR with EPSs and focuses primarily on radial distribution circuit interconnections. For DR interconnected on networks, all of IEEE Std 1547-2003 needs to be satisfied. IEEE Std 1547.6-2011 was specifically developed to provide additional information in regard to interconnecting DR with distribution secondary networks.

IEEE 1609.2™-2013 – IEEE Standard for Wireless Access in Vehicular Environments – Security Services for Applications and Management Messages

Description: Secure message formats and processing for use by wireless access in vehicular environments (WAVE) devices, including methods to secure WAVE management messages and methods to secure application messages are defined in this standard. It also describes administrative functions necessary to support the core security functions.

IEEE 1609.3™-2010 – IEEE Standard for Wireless Access in Vehicular Environments (WAVE) – Networking Services
Description: Wireless access in vehicular environments (WAVE) networking services provides services to WAVE devices and systems. Layers 3 and 4 of the open system interconnect (OSI) model and the Internet Protocol (IP), User Datagram Protocol (UDP), and Transmission Control Protocol (TCP) elements of the Internet model are represented. Management and data services within WAVE devices are provided.

IEEE 1609.4™-2010 – IEEE Standard for Wireless Access in Vehicular Environments (WAVE) – Multi-Channel Operation
Description: Multi-channel wireless radio operations, wireless access in vehicular environments (WAVE) mode, medium access control (MAC), and physical layers (PHYs), including the operation of control channel (CCH) and service channel (SCH) interval timers, parameters for priority access, channel switching and routing, management services, and primitives designed for multi-channel operations are described in this standard.

IEEE 1609.11™-2010 – IEEE Standard for Wireless Access in Vehicular Environments (WAVE) – Over-the-Air Electronic Payment Data Exchange Protocol for Intelligent Transportation Systems (ITS)
Description: This standard specifies the electronic payment service layer and profile for payment and identity authentication, and payment data transfer for dedicated short range communication (DSRC)-based applications in wireless access in vehicular environments. This standard defines a basic level of technical interoperability (vehicle-to-roadside) for electronic payment equipment, that is, onboard unit (OBU) and roadside unit (RSU) using WAVE. It does not provide a full solution for interoperability, and it does not define other parts of the electronic payment system, other services, other technologies and non-technical elements of payment interoperability. This standard is not intended to define technology and processes to activate and store data into the OBU (personalization), nor the applications using the payment service.

IEEE 1609.12™-2012 – IEEE Standard for Wireless Access in Vehicular Environments (WAVE) – Identifier Allocations
Description: Wireless access in vehicular environments (WAVE) is specified in the IEEE 1609 family of standards, within which a number of identifiers are used. This document describes the use of these identifiers, indicates identifier values that have been allocated for use by WAVE systems, and specifies the allocation of values of identifiers specified in the WAVE standards.

IEEE 1675™-2008 – IEEE Standard for Broadband Over Powerline Hardware 1900.1-2008 IEEE Standard Definitions and Concepts for Dynamic

Spectrum Access: Terminology Relating to Emerging Wireless Networks, System Functionality, and Spectrum Management
Description: Testing and verification standards for the commonly used hardware, primarily couplers, and enclosures, for broadband over power line (BPL) installations, and installation methods to enable compliance with applicable codes and standards are provided in this standard.

IEEE 1701™-2011 – IEEE Standard for Optical Port Communication Protocol to Complement the Utility Industry End Device Data Tables
Description: This standard provides multi-source and "plug and play" environment for the millions of metering devices in the field now and the future using the ANSI Type 2 optical port interface. It solves the problems associated with single source systems and with multi-source systems based upon proprietary communications protocols. Electric, water, and gas utilities and corresponding vendors can realize cost savings which ultimately shall benefit the client consumers of the utilities.

IEEE 1702™-2011 – IEEE Standard for Telephone Modem Communication Protocol to Complement the Utility Industry End Device Data Tables
Description: This standard provides multisource and "plug and play" environment for the millions of metering devices in the field now and in the future using the telephone modem communication interface. It solves the problems associated with single-source systems and with multisource systems based upon proprietary communications protocols. Electric, water, and gas utilities and corresponding vendors can realize cost savings that ultimately shall benefit the client consumers of the utilities.

IEEE 1703™-2012 – IEEE Standard for Local Area Network/Wide Area Network (LAN/WAN) Node Communication Protocol to complement the Utility Industry End Device Data Tables
Description: A set of application layer messaging services are provided in this standard that are applicable for the enterprise and end device ends of an advanced metering infrastructure (AMI). The application services include those useful for managing the AMI network assets defined by this standard. These messages may be transported over a wide range of underlying network transports such as TCP/IP, UDP, IEEE 802.11, IEEE 802.15.4 IEEE 802.16, PLC, and SMS over GSM, over a wide range of physical media. Additionally, interfaces are defined for a communication module and a local port (e.g., an IEEE 1701 optical port).The described protocol is tailored for, but not limited to, the transport of IEEE 1377 Table data. Also, a means by which information can be sent in a secure manner using AES-128 and the EAX' mode is provided in this standard. This standard was developed jointly with ANSI (published as ANSI C12.22) and Measurement Canada (published as MC12.22).

IEEE 1775™-2010 – IEEE Standard for Power Line Communication Equipment – Electromagnetic Compatibility (EMC) Requirements – Testing and Measurement Methods

Description: Electromagnetic compatibility (EMC) criteria and consensus test and measurements procedures for broadband over power line (BPL) communication equipment and installations are presented. Existing national and international standards for BPL equipment and installations are referenced. This standard does not include the specific emission limits, which are subject to national regulations.

IEEE 1815™-2012 – IEEE Standard for Electric Power Systems Communications – Distributed Network Protocol (DNP3) 2200-2012 IEEE Standard Protocol for Stream Management in Media Client Devices
Description: The DNP3 protocol structure, functions, and interoperable application options (subset levels) are specified. The simplest application level is intended for low-cost distribution feeder devices, and the most complex for full-featured systems. The appropriate level is selected to suit the functionality required in each device. The protocol is suitable for operation on a variety of communication media consistent with the makeup of most electric power communication systems.

IEEE 1888™-2011 – IEEE Standard for Ubiquitous Green Community Control Network Protocol
Description: The standard describes remote control architecture of digital community, intelligent building groups, and digital metropolitan networks; specifies interactive data format between devices and systems; and gives a standardized generalization of equipment, data communication interface, and interactive message in this digital community network. The digital community remote control network opens interfaces for public administration, public service, property management service, and individual service, which enables intelligent interconnection, collaboration service, remote surveillance, and central management to be feasible.

IEEE 1900.1™-2008 – IEEE Standard Definitions and Concepts for Dynamic Spectrum Access: Terminology Relating to Emerging Wireless Networks, System Functionality, and Spectrum Management
Description: This standard provides definitions and explanations of key concepts in the fields of spectrum management, cognitive radio, policy-defined radio, adaptive radio, software-defined radio, and related technologies. The document goes beyond simple, short definitions by providing amplifying text that explains these terms in the context of the technologies that use them. The document also describes how these technologies interrelate and create new capabilities while at the same time providing mechanisms supportive of new spectrum management paradigms such as dynamic spectrum access.

IEEE 1900.2™-2008 – IEEE Recommended Practice for the Analysis of In-band and Adjacent Band Interference and Coexistence Between Radio Systems
Description: Technical guidelines are provided in this recommended practice for analyzing the coexistence or, alternatively, the interference between

radio systems, operating in the same spectrum assignment or between different spectrum assignments.

IEEE 1900.4™-2009 – IEEE Standard for Architectural Building Blocks Enabling Network-Device Distributed Decision Making for Optimized Radio Resource Usage in Heterogeneous Wireless Access Networks
Description: The building blocks comprising (i) network resource managers, (ii) device resource managers, and (iii) the information to be exchanged between the building blocks, for enabling coordinated network-device distributed decision making that will aid in the optimization of radio resource usage, including spectrum access control, in heterogeneous wireless access networks are defined. The standard is limited to the architectural and functional definitions at a first stage. The corresponding protocols definition related to the information exchange will be addressed at a later stage.

IEEE 1900.4a™-2011 – IEEE Standard for Architectural Building Blocks Enabling Network-Device Distributed Decision Making for Optimized Radio Resource Usage in Heterogeneous Wireless Access Networks Amendment 1: Architecture and Interfaces for Dynamic Spectrum Access Networks in White Space Frequency Bands
Description: Additional components of the IEEE 1900.4 system are defined in this amendment to enable mobile wireless access service in white space frequency bands without any limitation on used radio interface (physical and media access control layers, carrier frequency, etc.).

IEEE 1901™-2010 – IEEE Standard for Broadband over Power Line Networks: Medium Access Control and Physical Layer Specifications
Description: A standard for high-speed communication devices via electric power lines, so called broadband over power line (BPL) devices, is defined. Transmission frequencies below 100 MHz are used. All classes of BPL devices can use this standard, including BPL devices used for the first-mile/last-mile connection to broadband services as well as BPL devices used in buildings for local area networks (LANs), smart energy applications, transportation platforms (vehicle) applications, and other data distribution. The balanced and efficient use of the power line communications channel by all classes of BPL devices is the main focus of this standard, defining detailed mechanisms for coexistence and interoperability between different BPL devices, and ensuring that desired bandwidth and quality of service may be delivered. The necessary security questions are addressed to ensure the privacy of communications between users and to allow the use of BPL for security sensitive services.

IEEE 1902.1™-2009 – IEEE Standard for Long Wavelength Wireless Network Protocol
Description: This standard defines the air interface for radiating transceiver radio tags using long wavelength signals (kilometric and hectometric frequencies, <450 kHz). Conforming devices can have very low power consumption (a few microwatts on average), while operating over medium ranges (0.5 to 30 meters) and at low data transfer speeds (300–9600 bps). They are well

suited for visibility networks, sensors, effectors and battery operated displays. This standard fills a gap between non-network-based RFID standards (e.g., ISO/IEC CD 15961-3, ISO 18000-6C or ISO 18000-7) and existing high bandwidth network standards such as IEEE Std 802.11 trade and IEEE 802.15.4 trade.

IEEE 1905.1™-2013 – IEEE Draft Standard for a Convergent Digital Home Network for Heterogeneous Technologies
Description: An abstraction layer for multiple home networking technologies that provides a common interface to widely deployed home networking technologies is defined in this standard: IEEE 1901 over power lines, IEEE 802.11 for wireless, Ethernet over twisted pair cable, and MoCA 1.1 over coax. Connectivity selection for transmission of packets arriving from any interface or application is supported by the 1905.1 abstraction layer. Modification to the underlying home networking technologies is not required by the 1905.1 layer, and hence it does not change the behavior or implementation of existing home networking technologies. Introduced by the 1905.1 specification is a layer between layers 2 and 3 that abstracts the individual details of each interface, aggregates available bandwidth, and facilitates seamless integration. The 1905.1 also facilitates end-to-end quality of service (QoS) while simplifying the introduction of new devices to the network, establishing secure connections, extending network coverage, and facilitating advanced network management features including discovery, path selection, auto-configuration, and quality of service (QoS) negotiation.

IEEE 2200™-2012 – IEEE Standard Protocol for Stream Management in Media Client Devices
Description: Interfaces for intelligently distributing and replicating content over heterogeneous networks to portable and intermediate devices with local storage are defined.

IEEE 2030™-2011 – IEEE Guide for Smart Grid Interoperability of Energy Technology and Information Technology Operation with the Electric Power System (EPS), End-Use Applications, and Loads
Description: IEEE Std 2030 provides alternative approaches and best practices for achieving smart grid interoperability. It is the first all-encompassing IEEE standard on smart grid interoperability providing a roadmap directed at establishing the framework in developing an IEEE national and international body of standards based on cross-cutting technical disciplines in power applications and information exchange and control through communications. IEEE Std 2030 establishes the smart grid interoperability reference model (SGIRM) and provides a knowledge base addressing terminology, characteristics, functional performance and evaluation criteria, and the application of engineering principles for smart grid interoperability of the electric power system with end-use applications and loads. A system of systems approach to smart grid interoperability lays the foundation on which IEEE Std 2030 establishes the SGIRM as a design tool that inherently allows for extensibility, scalability, and upgradeability. The IEEE 2030 SGIRM defines three integrated architectural perspectives: power

systems, communications technology, and information technology. Additionally, it defines design tables and the classification of data flow characteristics necessary for interoperability. Guidelines for smart grid interoperability, design criteria, and reference model applications are addressed with emphasis on functional interface identification, logical connections and data flows, communications and linkages, digital information management, and power generation usage.

IEEE 11073-00101™-2008 – IEEE Standard for Health Informatics – PoC Medical Device Communication – Part 00101: Guide – Guidelines for the Use of RF Wireless Technology
Description: N/A

IEEE 11073-10102™-2012 – IEEE Standard for Health informatics – Point-of-Care Medical Device Communication – Nomenclature – Annotated ECG
Description: The base IEEE 11073-10101 Nomenclature is extended by this standard to provide support for ECG annotation terminology. It may be used either in conjunction with other IEEE 11073 standards (e.g., ISO/IEEE 11073-10201:2001) or independently with other standards. The major subject areas addressed by the nomenclature include ECG beat annotations, wave component annotations, rhythm annotations, and noise annotations. Additional "global" and "per-lead" numeric observation identifiers, ECG lead systems, and additional ECG lead identifiers also are defined.

IEEE 11073-10103™-2012 – IEEE Standard for Health Informatics – Point-of-Care Medical Device Communication – Nomenclature – Implantable Device, Cardiac
Description: The base nomenclature provided in IEEE 11073 to support terminology for implantable cardiac devices is extended in this standard. Devices within the scope of this nomenclature are implantable devices such as pacemakers, defibrillators, devices for cardiac resynchronization therapy, and implantable cardiac monitors. The discrete terms necessary to convey a clinically relevant summary of the information obtained during a device interrogation are defined in this nomenclature. To improve workflow efficiencies, cardiology and electrophysiology practices require the management of summary interrogation information from all vendor devices and systems in a central system such as an electronic health records (EHR) system or a device clinic management system. To address this requirement, the Implantable Device, Cardiac (IDC) Nomenclature defines a standard-based terminology for device data. The nomenclature facilitates the transfer of data from the vendor proprietary systems to the clinic EHR or device clinic management system. Additional files can be found at http://standards.ieee.org/downloads/11073/11073-10103-2012/ if not attached to the PDF.

IEEE 11073-10201™-2004 – IEEE Standard for Health Informatics – Point-of-Care Medical Device Communication – Part 10201: Domain Information Model

Description: Within the context of the ISO/IEEE 11073 family of standards for point-of-care (POC) medical device communication (MDC), this standard provides an abstract object-oriented domain information model that specifies the structure of exchanged information, as well as the events and services that are supported by each object. All elements are specified using abstract syntax (ASN.1) and may be applied to many different implementation technologies, transfer syntaxes, and application service models. Core subjects include medical, alert, system, patient, control, archival, communication, and extended services. Model extensibility is supported, and a conformance model and statement template is provided.

IEEE 11073-10404™-2010 – IEEE Standard for Health Informatics – Personal Health Device Communication Part 10404: Device Specialization – Pulse Oximeter
Description: Adoption of IEEE Std 11073-10404-2008. Within the context of the ISO/IEEE 11073 family of standards for device communication, this standard establishes a normative definition of communication between personal telehealth pulse oximetry devices and compute engines (e.g., cell phones, personal computers, personal health appliances, set top boxes) in a manner that enables plug-and-play (PnP) interoperability. It leverages appropriate portions of existing standards including ISO/IEEE 11073 terminology, information models, application profile standards, and transport standards. It specifies the use of specific term codes, formats, and behaviors in telehealth environments restricting optionality in base frameworks in favor of interoperability. This standard defines a common core of communication functionality for personal telehealth pulse oximeters

IEEE 11073-10406™-2011 – IEEE Standard for Health Informatics – Personal Health Device Communication Part 10406: Device Specialization – Basic Electrocardiograph (ECG) (1- to 3-lead ECG)
Description: Within the context of the ISO/IEEE 11073 family of standards for device communication, a normative definition of the communication between personal basic electrocardiograph (ECG) devices and managers (e.g., cell phones, personal computers, personal health appliances, and set top boxes) in a manner that enables plug-and-play interoperability is established in this standard. Appropriate portions of existing standards including ISO/IEEE 11073 terminology and IEEE 11073-20601 information models are leveraged. The use of specific term codes, formats, and behaviors in telehealth environments restricting optionality in base frameworks in favor of interoperability is specified. A common core of communication functionality for personal telehealth basic ECG (1- to 3-lead ECG) devices is defined. Monitoring ECG devices are distinguished from diagnostic ECG equipment with respect to including support for wearable ECG devices, limiting the number of leads supported by the equipment to three, and not requiring the capability of annotating or analyzing the detected electrical activity to determine known cardiac phenomena. This standard is consistent with the base framework and allows multifunction

implementations by following multiple device specializations (e.g., ECG and respiration rate).

IEEE 11073-10407™-2010 – IEEE Standard for Health Informatics Personal Health Device Communication Part 10407: Device Specialization Blood Pressure Monitor

Description: Adoption of IEEE Std 11073-10407-2008. Within the context of the ISO/IEEE 11073 family of standards for device communication, this standard establishes a normative definition of communication between personal telehealth blood pressure monitor devices and compute engines (e.g., cell phones, personal computers, personal health appliances, and set top boxes) in a manner that enables plug-and-play interoperability. It leverages appropriate portions of existing standards including ISO/IEEE 11073 terminology, information models, application profile standards, and transport standards. It specifies the use of specific term codes, formats, and behaviors in telehealth environments restricting optionality in base frameworks in favor of interoperability. This standard defines a common core of communication functionality for personal telehealth blood pressure monitors

IEEE 11073-10408™-2010 – IEEE Standard for Health Informatics Personal Health Device Communication Part 10408: Device Specialization Thermometer

Description: Adoption of IEEE Std 11073-10408-2008 Within the context of the ISO/IEEE 11073 family of standards for device communication, this standard establishes a normative definition of communication between personal telehealth thermometer devices and compute engines (e.g., cell phones, personal computers, personal health appliances, and set top boxes) in a manner that enables plug-and-play interoperability. It leverages appropriate portions of existing standards including ISO/IEEE 11073 terminology, information models, application profile standards, and transport standards. It specifies the use of specific term codes, formats, and behaviors in telehealth environments restricting optionality in base frameworks in favor of interoperability. This standard defines a common core of communication functionality for personal telehealth thermometer devices.

IEEE 11073-10415™-2010 – IEEE Standard for Health Informatics Personal Health Device Communication Part 10415: Device Specialization Weighing Scale 11073-10420-2010 IEEE Standard for Health Informatics – Personal Health Device Communication Part 10420: Device Specialization – Body Composition Analyzer

Description: Adoption of IEEE Std 11073-10415-2008. Within the context of the ISO/IEEE 11073 family of standards for device communication, this standard establishes a normative definition of communication between personal telehealth weighing scale devices and compute engines (e.g., cell phones, personal computers, personal health appliances, and set top boxes) in a manner that enables plug-and-play interoperability. It leverages appropriate portions of existing standards including ISO/IEEE 11073 terminology, information models, application profile standards, and transport standards. It specifies the use of specific term codes, formats, and behaviors in telehealth environments restricting optionality in base frameworks in favor of interoperability. This standard defines a common core of communication functionality for personal telehealth weighing scales.

IEEE 11073-10417™-2011 – IEEE Standard for Health Informatics Personal Health Device Communication Part 10417: Device Specialization Glucose Meter

Description: Within the context of the ISO/IEEE 11073 family of standards for device communication, a normative definition of communication between personal telehealth glucose meter devices and compute engines (e.g., cell phones, personal computers, personal health appliances, and set top boxes) is established by this standard in a manner that enables plug-and play interoperability. Appropriate portions of existing standards are leveraged, including ISO/IEEE 11073 terminology, information models, application profile standards, and transport standards. The use of specific term codes, formats, and behaviors in telehealth environments restricting optionality in base frameworks in favor of interoperability are specified. A common core of communication functionality for personal telehealth glucose meters is defined in this standard.

IEEE 11073-10418™-2011 – IEEE Standard for Health Informatics – Personal Health Device Communication – Device Specialization – International Normalized Ratio (INR) Monitor

Description: A normative definition of communication between personal telehealth international normalized ratio (INR) devices (agents) and managers (e.g., cell phones, personal computers, personal health appliances, and set top boxes) is established in this standard in a manner that enables plug-and-play interoperability. Work done in other ISO/IEEE 11073 standards is leveraged, including existing terminology, information profiles, application profile standards, and transport standards. The use of specific term codes, formats, and behaviors in telehealth environments restricting optionality in base frameworks in favor of interoperability is specified. A common core of functionality of INR devices is defined in this standard. In the context of personal health devices, the measurement of the prothrombin time (PT) that is used to assess the level of anticoagulant therapy and its presentation as the international normalized ratio compared to the prothrombin time of normal blood plasma is referred to in INR monitoring. Applications of the INR monitor include the management of the therapeutic level of anticoagulant used in the treatment of a variety of conditions. The data modeling and its transport shim layer according to ISO/IEEE 11073-20601:2010 are provided by this standard, and the measurement method is not specified.

IEEE 11073-10420™-2010 – IEEE Standard for Health Informatics – Personal Health Device Communication Part 10420: Device Specialization – Body Composition Analyzer

Description: Within the context of the ISO/IEEE 11073 family of standards for device communication, this standard establishes a normative definition of the communication between personal body composition analyzing devices and managers (e.g., cell phones, personal computers, personal health appliances, set top boxes) in a manner that enables plug-and-play interoperability. It leverages appropriate portions of existing standards including ISO/IEEE 11073 terminology and IEEE 11073-20601(TM) information models. It specifies the use of specific term codes, formats, and behaviors in telehealth environments restricting optionality in base frameworks in favor of interoperability. This standard defines a common core of communication functionality for personal telehealth body composition analyzer devices. In this context, body composition analyzer devices are being used broadly to cover body composition analyzer devices that measure body impedances, and compute the various body components including body fat from the impedance

IEEE 11073-10441™-2008 – IEEE Standard for Health Informatics – Personal Health Device Communication – Part 10441: Device Specialization – Cardiovascular Fitness and Activity Monitor
Description: Within the context of the ISO/IEEE 11073 family of standards for device communication, this standard establishes a normative definition of communication between personal telehealth cardiovascular fitness and activity monitor devices and compute engines (e.g., cell phones, personal computers, personal health appliances, and set top boxes) in a manner that enables plug-and-play interoperability. It leverages appropriate portions of existing standards including ISO/IEEE 11073 terminology, information models, application profile standards, and transport standards. It specifies the use of specific term codes, formats, and behaviors in telehealth environments restricting optionality in base frameworks in favor of interoperability. This standard defines a common core of communication functionality for personal telehealth cardiovascular fitness and activity monitor devices.

IEEE 11073-30300™-2004 – IEEE Standard for Health informatics – Point-of-Care Medical Device Communication – Transport Profile – Infrared
Description: This standard establishes a connection-oriented transport profile and physical layer suitable for medical device communications that use short-range infrared wireless. This standard defines communications services and protocols that are consistent with specifications of the Infrared Data Association (IrDA) and are optimized for point-of-care (POC) applications at or near the patient.

IEEE 11073-30400™-2010 – IEEE Standard for Health Informatics – Point-of-Care Medical Device Communication Part 30400: Interface Profile – Cabled Ethernet
Description: The application of the Ethernet family (IEEE Std 802.3-2008) of protocols for use in medical device communication is addressed in this document. The scope is limited to referencing the appropriate Ethernet family specifications and calling out any specific special needs or requirements of the

ISO/IEEE 11073 environment, with a particular focus on easing interoperability and controlling costs.

IEEE 14575^{TM}-2000 – IEEE Standard for Heterogeneous Interconnect (HIC) (Low-Cost, Low-Latency Scalable Serial Interconnect for Parallel System Construction)
Description: Enabling the construction of high-performance, scalable, modular, parallel systems with low system integration cost is discussed. Complementary use of physical connectors and cables, electrical properties, and logical protocols for point-to-point serial scalable interconnect, operating at speeds of 10–200 Mb/s and at 1 Gb/s in copper and optic technologies, is described.

IEEE 21450^{TM}-2010 – IEEE Standard for Information Technology – Smart Transducer Interface for Sensors and Actuators – Common Functions, Communication Protocols, and Transducer Electronic Data Sheet (TEDS) Formats
Description: Adoption of IEEE Std 1451.0-2007. This standard provides a common basis for members of the IEEE 1451 family of standards to be interoperable. It defines the functions that are to be performed by a transducer interface module (TIM) and the common characteristics for all devices that implement the TIM. It specifies the formats for transducer electronic data sheets (TEDS). It defines a set of commands to facilitate the setup and control of the TIM as well as reading and writing the data used by the system. Application programming interfaces (APIs) are defined to facilitate communications with the TIM and with applications.

IEEE 21451-1^{TM}-2010 – IEEE Standard for Information Technology – Smart Transducer Interface for Sensors and Actuators – Part 1: Network Capable Application Processor (NCAP) Information Model
Description: Adoption of IEEE Std 1451.1-1999. This standard defines an object model with a network-neutral interface for connecting processors to communication networks, sensors, and actuators. The object model containing blocks, services, and components specifies interactions with sensors and actuators and forms the basis for implementing application code executing in the processor.

IEEE 21451-2^{TM}-2010 – IEEE Standard for Information Technology – Smart Transducer Interface for Sensors and Actuators – Part 2: Transducer to Microprocessor Communication Protocols and Transducer Electronic Data Sheet (TEDS) Formats
Description: Adoption of IEEE Std 1451.2-1997. A digital interface for connecting transducers to microprocessors is defined. A transducer electronic data sheet (TEDS) and its data formats are described. An electrical interface, read and write logic functions to access the TEDS and a wide variety of transducers are defined. This standard does not specify signal conditioning, signal conversion, or how the TEDS data is used in applications.

IEEE 21451-4^{TM}-2010 – IEEE Standard for Information Technology – Smart Transducer Interface for Sensors and actuators – Part 4: Mixed-Mode

Communication Protocols and Transducer Electronic Data Sheet (TEDS) Formats
Description: Adoption of IEEE Std 1451.2-1997. A digital interface for connecting transducers to microprocessors is defined. A transducer electronic data sheet (TEDS) and its data formats are described. An electrical interface, read and write logic functions to access the TEDS and a wide variety of transducers are defined. This standard does not specify signal conditioning, signal conversion, or how the TEDS data is used in applications.

IEEE 21451-7™-2011 – IEEE Standard for Smart Transducer Interface for Sensors and Actuators – Transducers to Radio Frequency Identification (RFID) Systems Communication Protocols and Transducer Electronic Data Sheet Formats
Description: ISO/IEC/IEEE 21451-7:2011 defines data formats to facilitate communications between radio frequency identification (RFID) systems and smart RFID tags with integral transducers (sensors and actuators). It defines new transducer electronic data sheet (TEDS) formats based on the ISO/IEC/IEEE 21451 series of standards. It also defines a command structure and specifies the communication methods with which the command structure is designed to be compatible.

Below is a partial listing of IEEE standards in development related to the Internet of Things as of March 2016.

802.11af-2013 – IEEE Standard for Information Technology – Telecommunications and Information Exchange Between Systems – Local and Metropolitan Area Networks – Specific Requirements – Part 11: Wireless LAN Medium Access Control (MAC) and Physical Layer (PHY) Specifications Amendment 5: Television White Spaces (TVWS) Operation
Description: Enhancements to the IEEE 802.11 physical layers (PHYs) and medium access control (MAC) sublayer to support operation in the white spaces in television bands are defined. (The PDF of this standard is available at no cost, compliments of the GETIEEE802 program, located at http://standards.ieee.org/getieee802/

IEEE P802.11ah™ – IEEE Draft Standard for Information Technology – Telecommunications and Information Exchange Between Systems – Local and Metropolitan Area Networks – Specific Requirements – Part 11: Wireless LAN Medium Access Control (MAC) and Physical Layer (PHY) Specifications: Amendment – Sub 1 GHz License-Exempt Operation
Description: The purpose of this amendment defines operation of license-exempt IEEE 802.11 wireless networks in frequency bands below 1 GHz excluding the TV white space bands. This amendment defines an orthogonal frequency division multiplexing (OFDM) physical layer (PHY) operating in the license-exempt bands below 1 GHz, e.g., 868–868.6 MHz (Europe), 950–958 MHz (Japan), 314–316 MHz, 430–434 MHz, 470–510 MHz, and

779–787 MHz (China), 917–923.5 MHz (Korea) and 902–928 MHz (USA), and enhancements to the IEEE 802.11 medium access control (MAC) to support this PHY, and provides mechanisms that enable coexistence with other systems in the bands including IEEE 802.15.4 and IEEE P802.15.4g. The data rates defined in this amendment optimize the rate vs range performance of the specific channelization in a given band. This amendment also adds support for transmission range up to 1 km and data rates >100 kbit/s while maintaining the IEEE 802.11 WLAN user experience for fixed, outdoor, point to multi point applications.

IEEE P802.11ai^{TM} – IEEE Draft Standard for Information Technology – Telecommunications and Information Exchange Between Systems – Local and Metropolitan Area Networks – Specific Requirements – Part 11: Wireless LAN Medium Access Control (MAC) and Physical Layer (PHY) Specifications: Amendment – Fast Initial Link Setup
Description: This amendment defines mechanisms that provide IEEE 802.11 networks with fast initial link set-up methods which do not degrade the security offered by Robust Security Network Association (RSNA) already defined in IEEE 802.11. This amendment defines modifications to the IEEE 802.11 medium access control layer (MAC) to enable a fast initial link set-up of IEEE 802.11 stations (STAs).

IEEE P802.15.4j^{TM} – IEEE Draft Standard for Information Technology – Telecommunications and Information Exchange Between Systems – Local and Metropolitan Area Networks – Specific Requirements – Part 15.4: Wireless Medium Access Control (MAC) and Physical Layer (PHY) Specifications for Low Rate Wireless Personal Area Networks (WPANs) Amendment: Alternative Physical Layer Extension to Support Medical Body Area Network (MBAN) Services Operating in the 2360–2400 MHz Band
Description: In this amendment to IEEE Std 802.15.4TM-2011, a physical layer for IEEE 802.15.4 in the 2360 MHz to 2400 MHz band which complies with Federal Communications Commission (FCC) MBAN rules is defined. Modifications to the MAC needed to support this new physical layer are also defined in this amendment.

IEEE P802.15.4k^{TM} – IEEE Draft Standard for Local and Metropolitan Area Networks – Part 15.4: Wireless Medium Access Control (MAC) and Physical Layer (PHY) Specifications for Low Rate Wireless Personal Area Networks (WPANs) Amendment – Physical Layer (PHY) Specifications for Low Energy, Critical Infrastructure Monitoring Networks (LECIM)
Description: Two PHYs (DSSS and FSK) that support critical infrastructure monitoring applications are provided in this amendment to IEEE Std 802.15.4TM-2011. In addition, only those MAC modifications needed to support the implementation of the two PHYs are described in this amendment. The PDF of this standard is available at no cost, compliments of the GETIEEE802 program. For more information visit their web page at http://standards.ieee.org/about/get/802/802.15.html

IEEE P802.15.4m™ – IEEE Draft Standard for Local and Metropolitan Area Networks Part 15.4: Low Rate Wireless Personal Area Networks (LR-WPANs) Amendment: TV White Space Between 54 MHz and 862 MHz Physical Layer.
Description: In this amendment to IEEE Std 802.15.4(TM)-2011, outdoor low-data-rate, wireless, television white space (TVWS) network requirements are addressed. Alternate physical layers (PHYs) are defined as well as only the medium access control (MAC) modifications needed to support their implementation. (The PDF of this standard is available at no cost, compliments of the GETIEEE program, located at http://standards.ieee.org/about/get/index.html)

IEEE P802.15.4n™ – IEEE Draft Standard for Local and Metropolitan Area Networks – Part 15.4: Low-Rate Wireless Personal Area Networks (LR-WPANs) Amendment: Physical Layer Utilizing Dedicated Medical Bands in China
Description: This amendment defines a physical layer for IEEE Std. 802.15.4 utilizing the approved 174–216 MHz, 407–425 MHz and 608–630 MHz medical bands in China. This amendment defines modifications to the medium access control (MAC) layer needed to support this new physical layer.

IEEE P802.15.4p™ – IEEE Draft Standard for Local and Metropolitan Area Networks – Part 15.4: Low-Rate Wireless Personal Area Networks (LR-WPANs) Amendment: Positive Train Control (PTC) System Physical Layer
Description: This amendment to IEEE Std 802.15.4(TM)-2011 specifies a PHY for use in equipment intended to address rail transportation industry needs and to meet US positive train control (PTC) regulatory requirements and similar regulatory requirements in other parts of the world. In addition, the amendment describes only those MAC changes needed to support this PHY. (The PDF of this standard is available at no charge, compliments of the GETIEEE802 program http://standards.ieee.org/getieee802/

IEEE P802.15.4q™ – IEEE Draft Standard for Local and Metropolitan Area Networks – Part 15.4: Wireless Medium Access Control (MAC) and Physical Layer (PHY) Specifications for Low Rate Wireless Personal Area Networks (WPANs) Amendment – Physical Layer (PHY) Specifications for Low Energy, Critical Infrastructure Monitoring Networks (LECIM)
Description: This amendment defines an ultra-low power (ULP) physical layer operating in sub 1 GHz and 2.4 GHz license exempt bands supporting typical data rates up to 1 Mbps. This amendment also defines the necessary MAC changes required for supporting the new ULP physical layer. The desired peak power consumption for the PHY should be typically less than 15 mW.

IEEE P802.15.8™ – IEEE Draft Standard for Wireless Medium Access Control (MAC) and Physical Layer (PHY) Specifications for Peer Aware Communications (PAC)
Description: The purpose is to provide a global standard for scalable, low power, and highly reliable wireless communications for emerging services

such as social networking, advertising, gaming, streaming, and emergency services. Existing standards may be able to provide parts of the envisioned PAC services, but no single standard provides infrastructureless peer-aware communications with fully distributed coordination. This standard defines PHY and MAC mechanism for wireless personal area networks (WPAN) peer aware communications (PAC) optimized for peer to peer and infrastructureless communications with fully distributed coordination. PAC features include: discovery for peer information without association, discovery signaling rate typically greater than 100 kbps, discovery of the number of devices in the network, scalable data transmission rates, typically up to 10 Mbps, group communications with simultaneous membership in multiple groups, typically up to 10, relative positioning, multihop relay, security, and operational in selected globally available unlicensed/licensed bands below 11 GHz capable of supporting these requirements

IEEE P802.15.9™ – IEEE Draft Recommended Practice for Transport of Key Management Protocol (KMP) Datagrams
Description: This recommended practice describes support for transporting KMPs datagrams to support the security functionality present in IEEE Std 802.15.4. This recommended practice defines a message exchange framework based on information elements as a transport method for key management protocol (KMP) datagrams and guidelines for the use of some existing KMPs with IEEE Std 802.15.4. This recommended practice does not create a new KMP.

IEEE P802.16n™ – IEEE Draft Standard for Local and Metropolitan Area Networks Part 16: Air Interface for Broadband Wireless Access Systems
Description: Enhancements to the wireless MAN-OFDMA air interface to support higher reliability networks are specified in this amendment to IEEE Std 802.16-2012.

IEEE P802.21d™ – IEEE Draft Standard for Local and Metropolitan Area Networks – Part 21: Media Independent Handover Services Amendment: Multicast Group Management
Description: Mechanisms to enable multicast group management for MIH services is specified in this standard. The specification defines management primitives and messages that enable a user to join, leave or update group membership and security mechanisms to protect multicast communication.

IEEE P802.22b™ – IEEE Draft Standard for Information Technology – Telecommunications and Information Exchange Between Systems Wireless Regional Area Networks (WRAN) – Specific Requirements Part 22: Cognitive Wireless RAN Medium Access Control (MAC) and Physical Layer (PHY) Specifications: Policies and Procedures for Operation in the TV Bands Amendment: Enhancement for Broadband Services and Monitoring Applications
Description: This standard specifies alternate physical layer (PHY) and necessary medium access control layer (MAC) enhancements to IEEE std. 802.22-2011 for operation in very high frequency (VHF)/ultra high frequency (UHF)

TV broadcast bands between 54 MHz and 862 MHz to support enhanced broadband services and monitoring applications. The standard supports aggregate data rates greater than the maximum data rate supported by the IEEE Std. 802.22-2011. This standard defines new classes of 802.22 devices to address these applications and supports more than 512 devices in a network. This standard also specifies techniques to enhance communications among the devices and makes necessary amendments to the cognitive, security & parameters and connection management clauses. This amendment supports mechanisms to enable coexistence with other 802 systems in the same band.

IEEE P1451.2™ – IEEE Draft Standard for a Smart Transducer Interface for Sensors and Actuators – Serial Point-to-Point Interface
Description: A digital interface for connecting transducers to microprocessors is defined. A TEDS and its data formats are described. An elctrical interface, read and write logic functions to access the TEDS and a wide variety of transducers are defined. This standard does not specify signal conditioning, signal conversion, or how the TEDS data is used in applications.

IEEE P1451.4a™ – IEEE Draft Standard for a Smart Transducer Interface for Sensors and Actuators – Mixed-Mode Communication Protocols and Transducer Electronic Data Sheet (TEDS) Formats – Amendment
Description: The amendments reflect the need of industry and correct errors in the existing standard. The scope of the proposed changes include: 1) the correction of errors, both editorial and technical of the existing standard, 2) the creation of new parameters in the transducer electronic data sheets (TEDS), TEDS templates, and hooks that can make it easier for other industrial users to apply and use this standard, 3) the provision for interface with the IEEE 1451 standard to enable users to access IEEE 1451.4 transducers via a network, and 4) consideration of provision for global transducer identification.

IEEE P1547.7™ – IEEE Draft Guide to Conducting Distribution Impact Studies for Distributed Resource Interconnection
Description: IEEE Std 1547.7(TM) is part of the IEEE 1547(TM) series of standards. Whereas IEEE Std 1547(TM)-2003 provides mandatory requirements for the interconnection of distributed resources (DR) with electric power systems (EPS), this guide does not presume the interconnection is IEEE 1547(TM) compliant. Further, this guide does not interpret IEEE Std 1547(TM) or other standards in the IEEE 1547(TM) series, and this guide does not provide additional requirements or recommended practices related to the other IEEE 1547(TM) documents. However, DR interconnection may contribute to resultant conditions that could exceed what was normally planned for and built into the distribution system. This guide provides alternative approaches and good practices for engineering studies of the potential impacts of a DR or aggregate DR interconnected to the electric power distribution system. This guide describes criteria, scope, and extent for those engineering studies. Study scope and extent are described as functions of identifiable characteristics of the DR, the EPS, and the interconnection. The intent includes promoting impact study

consistency while helping identify only those studies that should be performed based on technically transparent criteria for the DR interconnection.

IEEE P1547.8™ – IEEE Draft Recommended Practice for Establishing Methods and Procedures that Provide Supplemental Support for Implementation Strategies for Expanded Use of IEEE Standard 1547.

Description: The purpose of the methods and procedures provided in this recommended practice is to provide more flexibility in determining the design and processes used in expanding the implementation strategies used for interconnecting distributed resources with electric power systems. Further, based on IEEE Std 1547 requirements, the purpose of this recommended practice is to provide the knowledge base, experience, and opportunities for greater utilization of the interconnection and its applications. This recommended practice applies to the requirements set forth in IEEE Std 1547 and provides recommended methods that may expand the usefulness and utilization of IEEE Std 1547 through the identification of innovative designs, processes, and operational procedures.

IEEE P1609.0™ – IEEE Draft Guide for Wireless Access in Vehicular Environments (WAVE) – Architecture

Description: The wireless access in vehicular environments (WAVE) architecture and services necessary for WAVE devices to communicate in a mobile vehicular environment are described in this guide. It is meant to be used in conjunction with the family of IEEE 1609 standards as of its publication date. These include IEEE Std 1609.2™, IEEE Standard Security Services for Applications and Management Messages, IEEE Std 1609.3 Networking Services, IEEE Std 1609.4 Multi-Channel Operation, IEEE Std 1609.11 Over-the-Air Electronic Payment Data Exchange Protocol for Intelligent Transportation Systems (ITS), IEEE Std 1609.12 Identifier Allocations, and IEEE Std 802.11 in operation outside the context of a basic service set.

IEEE P1609.5™ – IEEE Draft Standard for Wireless Access in Vehicular Environments (WAVE) – Communication Manager
Description: N/A

IEEE P1704™ – IEEE Draft Standard for Utility Industry End Device Communications Module
Description: N/A

IEEE P1705™ – IEEE Draft Standard for Compliance Testing to Utility Industry Metering Communications Protocol Standards
Description: N/A

IEEE P1828™ – IEEE Draft Standard for Systems with Virtual Components
Description: N/A

IEEE P1856™ – IEEE Draft Standard Framework for Prognostics and Health Management of Electronic Systems
Description: The purpose of this standard is to classify and define the concepts involved in prognostics and health management of electronic systems, and to

provide a standard framework that assists practitioners in the development of business cases, and the selection of approaches, methodologies, algorithms, condition monitoring equipment, and strategies for implementing prognostics for electronic systems. This standard covers all aspects of prognostics and health management of electronic systems, including definitions, approaches, algorithms, sensors and sensor selection, data collection, storage and analysis, anomaly detection, diagnosis, metrics, life cycle cost of implementation, return on investment and documentation. This standard describes a normative framework for classifying PHM capability and for planning the development of PHM for a system or product. The use of this standard is not required throughout the industry. This standard provides information to aid practitioners in the selection of PHM strategies and approaches to meet their needs.

IEEE P1888.1[TM] **– IEEE Draft Standard for a Ubiquitous Community Network: Control and Management**
Description: This standard describes network gateway access, control, and management; specifies control and management requirements; defines the system architecture, communication sequences, and enhanced functions for the protocols defined in IEEE 1888[TM], "Ubiquitous Green Community Control Network Protocol"; and extends the protocols and interfaces based on the requirements. This standard shall provide enhanced protocols, workflows, and message formats for the network gateway under control and management, such as registration, access, control, event handling, configuration, status querying, etc.

IEEE P1888.2[TM] **– IEEE Draft Standard for Ubiquitous Green Community Control Network: Heterogeneous Networks Convergence and Scalability**
Description: This standard describes heterogeneous networks convergence and scalability, specifies the requirements of network convergence, extends the system architecture defined in IEEE Std 1888(TM), IEEE Standard for Ubiquitous Green Community Control Network Protocol, with two new IEEE 1888(TM) Components, that is, the reconfigurable resolution server (RRS) and the intelligent application resolver (IAR), and generalizes primitive data type expressions and explicit field-bus data type management in IEEE 1888 systems. This standard enables IEEE 1888 systems to interoperate with heterogeneous access networks efficiently and improves the efficiency, flexibility, scalability and manageability of IEEE 1888 systems.

IEEE P1888.3[TM] **– IEEE Draft Standard for Ubiquitous Green Community Control Network: Security**
Description: The enhanced security management function for the protocol defined in IEEE 1888(TM), "Ubiquitous Green Community Control Network Protocol," is described in this standard. Security requirements, system security architecture definitions, and a standardized description of authentication and authorization, along with security procedures and protocols, are specified. This standard can help avoid unintended data disclosure to the public and unauthorized access to resources, while providing enhanced integrity and

confidentiality of transmitted data in the ubiquitous green community control network.

IEEE P1900.7™ – IEEE Draft Standard for Radio Interface for White Space Dynamic Spectrum Access Radio Systems Supporting Fixed and Mobile Operation

Description: This standard enables the development of cost-effective, multi-vendor white space dynamic spectrum access radio systems capable of inter-operable operation in white space frequency bands on a non-interfering basis to incumbent users in these frequency bands. This standard facilitates a variety of applications, including the ones capable to support high mobility, both low-power and high-power, short-, medium, and long-range, and a variety of network topologies. This standard is a baseline standard for a family of other standards that are expected to be developed focusing on particular applications, regulatory domains, etc. This standard specifies a radio interface including medium access control (MAC) sublayer(s) and physical (PHY) layer(s) of white space dynamic spectrum access radio systems supporting fixed and mobile operation in white space frequency bands, while avoiding causing harmful interference to incumbent users in these frequency bands. The standard provides means to support P1900.4a for white space management and P1900.6 to obtain and exchange sensing related information (spectrum sensing and geolocation information).

IEEE P1901.2™ – IEEE Draft Standard for Low Frequency (Less Than 500 kHz) Narrow Band Power Line Communications for Smart Grid Applications

Description: A worldwide standard for narrowband power line communications (PLC) via alternating current, direct current, and non-energized electric power lines using frequencies below 500 kHz. Data rates of up to 500 kb/s are supported. The field of use includes smart grid applications. Coexistence mechanisms that can be used by other PLC technologies operating below 500 kHz are also included. These coexistence mechanisms may be used separately from the rest of the standard.

IEEE P1904.1™-Conformance 01 – IEEE Draft Standard for Conformance Test Procedures for Service Interoperability in Ethernet Passive Optical Networks, IEEE Std 1904.1 Package A-Conformance 01 – IEEE Draft Standard for Conformance Test Procedures for Service Interoperability in Ethernet Passive Optical Networks, IEEE Std 1904.1 Package A

Description: This standard specifies a suite of conformance tests for system-level requirements of Ethernet passive optical network (EPON) equipment, defined in IEEE 1904.1 Package A.

IEEE P1904.1™-Conformance 02 – IEEE Draft Standard for Conformance Test Procedures for Service Interoperability in Ethernet Passive Optical Networks, IEEE Std 1904.1 Package B

Description: This standard specifies a suite of conformance tests for system-level requirements of Ethernet passive optical network (EPON) equipment, defined in IEEE 1904.1 Package B.

IEEE P1904.1™-Conformance 03 – IEEE Draft Standard for Conformance Test Procedures for Service Interoperability in Ethernet Passive Optical Networks, IEEE Std 1904.1 Package C
Description: This standard specifies a suite of conformance tests for system-level requirements of Ethernet passive optical network (EPON) equipment, defined in IEEE 1904.1 Package C.

IEEE P1907.1™ – IEEE Draft Standard for Network-Adaptive Quality of Experience (QoE) Management Scheme for Real-Time Mobile Video Communications
Description: The purpose of this standard is to enable network operators, application developers, service/content providers, and end-users to develop, deploy and utilize collaborative services that employ real-time 2-way and multi-party video connectivity within any mobile browser, application, game, device, or service platform. This Standard defines an End-to-End Quality of Experience (E2E QoE) Management Scheme for real-time video communication systems, including those operating in resource varying environments. The scheme utilizes correlation of both subjective and objective E2E QoE with received real-time video data (stream header and/or video signal), application-level Quality of Service (QoS) measurements, and network-level QoS measurements. The standard defines a human visual perception-based E2E QoE Metric and the methodology of correlating this metric to real-time video data, application/network-level QoS measurements, the capabilities of user devices, and subjective user factors. It also defines the subjective viewing test procedures to facilitate the benchmarking and sharing of real-time video test sequence databases and QoE/QoS reporting databases for real-time mobile visual communications. The standard defines network adaptive video encoding and decoding algorithms utilizing device-based E2E QoE-driven feedback and, where available, network-based E2E QoE-driven feedback to achieve real-time adaptation according to available device and/or network resources. The standard defines real-time device-based and network-based feedback control mechanisms that can be used to regulate E2E QoE by one or more of: application-level objective measurement and reporting of the actual received real-time video signal quality; network-level objective measurement and reporting of the in-transit real-time video signal quality; application-level measurement and reporting of device and/or network resources and QoS performance; and network-level measurement and reporting of device and/or network resources and QoS performance.

IEEE P2030.1™ – IEEE Draft Guide for Electric-Sourced Transportation Infrastructure
Description: This guideline provides methods that can be utilized by utilities, manufacturers, transportation providers, infrastructure developers and end

users of electric-sourced vehicles and related infrastructure to develop and support systems that allow increased utilization of electric sourced transportation. The transition to alternative-fuel vehicles, including those that use electricity, is inevitable. Servicing of the limited number of electric vehicles operating today can be absorbed by current generation and distribution capacity. The existence of a few hundred thousand of these vehicles, however, is just the first step in a long-term trend. Preparing for rapid growth in electric vehicle use is necessary since new and upgraded supporting infrastructure, whether charging stations, generating capacity or enhanced transmission systems, requires time for deployment. To reduce the amount of new generation required and better utilize the existing generation, energy efficiency methods for electric sourced transportation based on an end-to-end systems approach are outlined in this document. Standards that exist and research that is being performed are pointed out in this document. Where new standards are needed, they are pointed out in this document. This document supports utilities in planning for the most economic method of production to support increasing transportation loads. This document allows manufacturers to understand the standardization requirements and bring products to fruition as the supporting systems and methods are developed and standardized. This document allows end users to understand technologies that can be implemented for their transportation energy needs. A phased implementation is suggested in this document and is based on economic considerations for technologies available today and technologies being developed. While regional political and regulatory issues may alter these methods, this document does not consider the wide range of regional differences available. It is incumbent on the user of the guide to understand the financial differences that these factors may have on their specific planning requirements. This document does not consider non-road forms of transportation. This document provides guidelines that can be used by utilities, manufacturers, transportation providers, infrastructure developers and end users of electric-sourced vehicles and related support infrastructure in addressing applications for road-based personal and mass transportation. This guide provides a knowledge base addressing terminology, methods, equipment, and planning requirements for such transportation and its impacts on commercial and industrial systems including, for example, generation, transmission, and distribution systems of electrical power. This guide provides a roadmap for users to plan for short, medium, and long-term systems.

IEEE P2301^{TM} – IEEE Draft Guide for Cloud Portability and Interoperability Profiles (CPIP)
Description: The purpose of this guide is to assist cloud computing vendors and users in developing, building, and using standards-based cloud computing products and services, which should lead to increased portability, commonality, and interoperability. Cloud Computing systems contain many disparate elements. For each element there are often multiple options, each with different externally visible interfaces, file formats, and operational conventions. In

many cases these visible interfaces, formats, and conventions have different semantics. This guide enumerates options, grouped in a logical fashion called "profiles," for such definitions of interfaces, formats, and conventions, from a variety of sources. In this way, cloud ecosystem participants will tend towards more portability, commonality, and interoperability, growing the cloud computing adoption rate overall. This guide advises cloud computing ecosystem participants (cloud vendors, service providers, and users) of standards-based choices in areas such as application interfaces, portability interfaces, management interfaces, interoperability interfaces, file formats, and operation conventions. This guide groups these choices into multiple logical profiles, which are organized to address different cloud personalities.

IEEE P2302[TM] **– IEEE Draft Standard for Intercloud Interoperability and Federation (SIIF)**
Description: This standard creates an economy amongst cloud providers that is transparent to users and applications, which provides for a dynamic infrastructure that can support evolving business models. In addition to the technical issues, appropriate infrastructure for economic audit and settlement must exist. This standard defines topology, functions, and governance for cloud-to-cloud interoperability and federation. Topological elements include clouds, roots, exchanges (which mediate governance between clouds), and gateways (which mediate data exchange between clouds). Functional elements include name spaces, presence, messaging, resource ontologies (including standardized units of measurement), and trust infrastructure. Governance elements include registration, geo-independence, trust anchor, and potentially compliance and audit. The standard does not address intra-cloud (within cloud) operation, as this is cloud implementation-specific, nor does it address proprietary hybrid-cloud implementations.

IEEE P3333.1[TM] **– IEEE Draft Standard for the Quality Assessment of Three Dimensional (3D) Displays, 3D Contents and 3D Devices based on Human Factors**
Description: N/A

IEEE P3333.2[TM] **– IEEE Draft Standard for Three-Dimensional Model Creation Using Unprocessed 3D Medical Data**
Description: N/A

IEEE P11073-10423[TM] **– IEEE Draft Standard for Health Informatics – Personal Health Device Communication – Device Specialization – Sleep Monitor**
Description: This standard addresses a need for an openly defined, independent standard for controlling information exchange to and from personal health devices (agents) and managers (e.g., cell phones, personal computers, personal health appliances, set top boxes). Interoperability is key to growing the potential market for these devices and enabling people to be better informed participants in the management of their health. Within the context of the ISO/IEEE 11073

family of standards for device communication, this standard establishes a normative definition of the communication between personal health sleep quality monitor devices and managers (e.g., cell phones, personal computers, personal health appliances, set top boxes) in a manner that enables plug-and-play interoperability. It leverages appropriate portions of existing standards including ISO/IEEE 11073 terminology, information models, application profile standards, and transport standards. It specifies the use of specific term codes, formats, and behaviors in telehealth environments restricting optionality in base frameworks in favor of interoperability. This standard defines a common core of communication functionality for personal health sleep monitor devices. In this context, sleep monitor devices are defined as devices that have successfully recorded the night's sleep-wake cycle (or possibly sleep stages and REM) and other qualitative and quantitative measures of sleep.

IEEE P11073-10424™ – IEEE Draft Standard for Health informatics – Personal Health Device Communication – Device Specialization – Sleep Apnea Breathing Therapy Equipment

Description: This standard addresses a need for an openly defined, independent standard for controlling information exchange to and from personal health devices (agents) and managers (e.g., cell phones, personal computers, personal health appliances, and set top boxes). Interoperability is key to growing the potential market for these devices and to enabling people to be better informed participants in the management of their health. Within the context of the ISO/IEEE 11073 family of standards for device communication, this standard establishes a normative definition of the communication between sleep apnea breathing therapy equipment and managers (e.g., cell phones, personal computers, personal health appliances, set top boxes) in a manner that enables plug-and-play interoperability. It leverages appropriate portions of existing standards including ISO/IEEE 11073 terminology, information models, application profile standards, and transport standards. It specifies the use of specific term codes, formats, and behaviors in telehealth environments restricting optionality in base frameworks in favor of interoperability. This standard defines a common core of communication functionality for sleep apnea breathing therapy equipment. In this context, sleep apnea breathing therapy equipment are defined as devices that are intended to alleviate the symptoms of a patient who suffers from sleep apnea by delivering a therapeutic breathing pressure to the patient. Sleep apnea breathing therapy equipment are primarily used in the home health-care environment by a lay operator without direct professional supervision.

IEEE P11073-10419™ – IEEE Draft Standard for Health Informatics – Personal Health Device Communication – Device Specialization – Insulin Pump

Description: Within the context of the ISO/IEEE 11073 family of standards for device communication, a normative definition of communication between personal telehealth insulin pump devices and compute engines (e.g., cell phones, personal computers, personal health appliances, set top boxes) in a manner that enables plug-and-play interoperability, is established in this standard. Appropriate portions of existing standards including ISO/IEEE 11073 terminology, information models, application profile standards, and transport standards are leveraged. The use of specific term codes, formats, and behaviors in telehealth environments restricting optionality in base frameworks in favor of interoperability are specified. A common core of communication functionality for personal telehealth insulin pump devices is defined.

IEEE P21451-001™ – IEEE Draft Recommended Practice for Signal Treatment Applied to Smart Transducers

Description: The purpose is to define a standardized and universal framework that allows smart transducers to extract features of the signal being generated and measured. With the definition of these practices, the raw data can be converted into information and then into knowledge. In this context, knowledge means understanding of the nature of the transducer signal. This understanding can be shared with the system and other transducers in order to form a platform for sensory knowledge fusion. This recommended practice defines signal processing algorithms and data structure in order to share and to infer signal and state information of an instrumentation or control system. These algorithms are based on their own signal and also on the transducers attached to the system. The recommended practice also defines the commands and replies for requesting information and algorithms for shape analysis such as exponential, sinusoidal, impulsive noise, noise, and tendency.

IEEE P21451-1™ – IEEE Draft Standard for Smart Transducer Interface for Sensors and Actuators – Common Network Services

Description: In the family of IEEE 1451 standards, there are no common network services defined for IEEE 1451 smart transducers to communicate transducer data and information to and from a network accommodating various network services, such as Hypertext Transfer Protocol (HTTP) services, Internet Protocol (IP) services, Web services, and Extensible Messaging and Presence Protocol (XMPP) services. The purpose of this standard is to define a set of common network services for smart transducers. This standard provides means for smart transducer interoperability. This standard defines a set of common network services for communication with IEEE 1451 smart transducers invoking IEEE 1451.0 transducer services.

IEEE P21451-1-4™ – IEEE Draft Standard for a Smart Transducer Interface for Sensors, Actuators, and Devices – eXtensible Messaging and Presence Protocol (XMPP) for Networked Device Communication

Description: The purpose of this standard is to provide session initiation and protocol transport for sensors, actuators, and devices. The standard addresses issues of security, scalability, and interoperability. This standard can provide significant cost savings and reduce complexity, leveraging current instrumentation and devices used in industry. This standard defines a method for transporting IEEE 1451 messages over a network using eXtensible Messaging and

Presence Protocol (XMPP) to establish session initiation, secure communication, and characteristic identification between networked client and server devices using device meta identification information based on the IEEE 1451 transducer electronic data sheets (TEDS).

IEEE P62704-4™ – IEEE Draft Standard for Determining the Peak Spatial-Average Specific Absorption Rate (SAR) in the Human Body from Wireless Communications Devices, 30 MHz – 6 GHz: General Requirements for Using the Finite Element Method (FEM) for SAR Calculations and Specific Requirements for Modeling Vehicle-Mounted Antennas and Personal Wireless Devices

Description: Document will not contain a purpose clause This standard describes the concepts, techniques, models, validation procedures, uncertainties and limitations of the finite-element method when used for determining the spatial-peak specific absorption rate (SAR) in standardized anatomical models exposed to wireless communication devices, including vehicle-mounted antennas and personal wireless devices, such as hand-held mobile phones. Guidance on modeling such devices and benchmark data for simulation is provided; model contents, meshing and test positions of the anatomical models are defined. This document does not recommend specific SAR values since these are found in other documents, e.g., IEEE C95.1-2005 (IEEE Standard for Safety Levels with Respect to Human Exposure to Radio Frequency Electromagnetic Fields, 3 kHz to 300 GHz.).

APPENDIX B

GLOSSARY

802.11 Standard the generic name of a family of protocols and standards used for wireless networking; these standards define the rules for communication.

802.11i Standard an amendment to the 802.11 Standard; 802.11i uses Wi-Fi Protected Access (WPA) and Advanced Encryption Standard (AES) as a replacement for RC4 encryption.

Access control a security technique that can be used to regulate who or what can view or use resources in a computing environment.

Actuators a type of motor that is responsible for moving or controlling a mechanism or system.

Advanced persistent threats a set of stealthy and continuous computer hacking processes, often orchestrated by human(s) targeting a specific entity; usually targets organizations and/or nations for business or political motives.

Advanced RISC machines a family of reduced instruction set computing (RISC) architectures for computer processors, configured for various environments, developed by British company ARM Holdings.

Adversary generally considered to be a person, group, or force that opposes and/or attacks; a malicious entity whose aim is to prevent the users of a computer system from achieving their goal (confidential, privacy, integrity, and availability of data).

Adware malicious software that is intended to hijack a system into displaying advertisements, sometimes for dubious services that themselves are malicious.

Cyber-Assurance for the Internet of Things, First Edition. Edited by Tyson T. Brooks.
© 2017 by The Institute of Electrical and Electronic Engineers, Inc. Published 2017 by John Wiley & Sons, Inc.

Algorithm a procedure or formula for solving a problem.

Archetype a formal reusable model of a domain concept.

Artificial intelligence intelligence exhibited by computers.

Assurance a measure of confidence that the security features and architecture of information systems and networks are secured correctly and enforce the security policy in place for those systems and networks. See Information Assurance.

Asymmetric encryption an encryption algorithm that requires two different keys for encryption and decryption; these keys are commonly referred to as the public and private keys; asymmetric algorithms are slower than symmetric algorithms and the speed of encryption may be different from the speed of decryption; asymmetric algorithms are either used to exchange symmetric session keys or to digitally sign a message. RSA and ECC are examples of asymmetric algorithms.

Attacker (also see Hackers) a person or other entity such as a computer program that attempts to cause harm to an information system.

Authentication the process of identifying an individual, usually based on a username and password

Authenticity assurance that an entity claiming an identity does possess the right to use it.

Authorization the function of specifying access rights to resources related to information security and computer security in general and to access control in particular.

Automatic control (also see Automation) the utilization of various types of control systems and schemes to accomplish basic or complex electrical, mechanical, or other tasks with minimum or no human intervention.

Automation (also see Automatic Control) the utilization of various types of control systems and schemes to accomplish basic or complex electrical, mechanical, or other tasks with minimum or no human intervention.

Availability assurance that information or services are available or accessible under all conditions that it is supposed to be.

Big Data a broad term for data sets so large or complex that traditional data processing applications are inadequate. Challenges include analysis, capture, data curation, search, sharing, storage, transfer, visualization, and information privacy.

Bluetooth a wireless technology standard for exchanging data over short distances (using short-wavelength UHF radio waves in the ISM band from 2.4 to 2.485 GHz) from fixed and mobile devices, and building personal area networks (PANs). Invented by telecom vendor Ericsson in 1994, it was originally conceived as a wireless alternative to RS-232 data cables. It can connect several devices, overcoming problems of synchronization.

Bring your own device refers to the policy of permitting employees to bring personally owned mobile devices (laptops, tablets, and smart phones) to their workplace, and to use those devices to access privileged company information and applications.

C2 see Command-and-Control Server.

Central processing unit the electronic circuitry within a computer that carries out the instructions of a computer program by performing the basic arithmetic, logical, control, and input/output (I/O) operations specified by the instructions.

Certificate authority an entity that issues digital certificates.

Certificate revocation lists one of two common methods when using a public key infrastructure for maintaining access to servers in a network.

Cloud computing a model for enabling convenient, on-demand network access to a shared pool of configurable computing resources (e.g., networks, servers, storage, applications, and services) that can be rapidly provisioned and released with minimal management effort or service provider interaction; can be utilized into the following three categories: infrastructure-as-a-service (IaaS), platform-as-a-service (PaaS), and software-as-a-service (SaaS).

Cloud-of-Things the integration of cloud computing and Internet of Things architecture environments.

Cluster head used in wireless sensor networks to collect data from a respective cluster's nodes and then forward the aggregated data to a wireless base station.

Command-and-control server a server configured to centrally manage and control activities of many other servers (i.e., a "C2" server); hackers often use a C2 server to remotely control activities of zombie computers as they manage their botnets.

Common industrial protocol a major component within the NetLinx Open Network Architecture, and it provides you with four common features: common control services – provides you with a standard set of messaging services for all three networks within the NetLinx architecture.

Confidentiality assurance that information is accessible or readable only by entities with requisite rights.

CONOPS expresses the characteristics for a proposed system from a user's perspective; also describes the user organization, mission, and objectives from an integrated systems point of view.

Constrained Application Protocol a software protocol intended to be used in very simple electronics devices that allows them to communicate interactively over the Internet; particularly targeted for small low power sensors, switches, valves and similar components that need to be controlled or supervised remotely, through standard Internet networks.

Constrained IP network has limited packet sizes, may exhibit a high degree of packet loss and may have a substantial number of devices that may be powered off at any point in time but periodically begin operations for brief periods of time.

Constrained RESTful Environments realizes the Representational State Transfer architecture in a suitable form for the most constrained nodes (e.g., 8-bit microcontrollers with limited memory) and networks (e.g., IPv6 over low-power wireless personal area networks (6LoWPANs); is aimed at machine-to-machine (M2M) applications such as smart energy and building automation.

Control system a device, or set of devices, that manages, commands, directs, or regulates the behavior of other devices or systems. Industrial control systems are used in industrial production for controlling equipment or machines.

Cookie a digital "breadcrumb" in the form of a small file left behind after visiting a website; these files are sometimes beneficial to the user, storing usernames or passwords for faster access later, but sometimes can "phone home," tracking the user's Internet activity for advertising, data mining, or other purposes.

Crypto domain-specific language a language designed from the development of cryptographic algorithms.

Crypto engine for key management supports the key management functions in support of the custom cryptographic processors.

Cryptographic Message Syntax the IETF's standard for cryptographically protected messages; can be used to digitally sign, digest, authenticate, or encrypt any form of digital data.

Cryptographic processor a processor designed to support high performance cryptographic algorithms.

Cryptography the practice and study of techniques for secure communication in the presence of third parties (e.g., adversaries).

Cyber-assurance the justified confidence that networked systems are adequately secure to meet operational needs, even in the presence of attacks, failures, accidents, and unexpected events.

Cyber-attack any type of offensive maneuver employed by individuals or whole organizations that targets computer information systems, infrastructures, computer networks, and/or personal computer devices by various means of malicious acts usually originating from an anonymous source that steals, alters, or destroys a specified target by hacking into a susceptible system.

Cyber-physical system the integration of computation, networking, and physical processes using embedded computers, network monitors and controls the physical processes, with feedback loops where physical processes affect computations and vice versa.

Cyberspace the notional environment in which communication over computer networks occurs.

Cyber-security focuses on protecting computers, networks, programs, and data from unintended or unauthorized access, change, or destruction.

Cyclomatic a software metric (measurement) used to indicate the complexity of a program. It is a quantitative measure of the number of linearly independent paths through a program's source code.

Data-at-rest a term referring to inactive data which are stored physically in any digital form (e.g., databases, data warehouses, spreadsheets, archives, tapes, off-site backups, mobile devices).

Datagram transport layer security provides communications security for datagram protocols; allows datagram-based applications to communicate in a way that is designed to prevent eavesdropping, tampering, or message forgery.

Data-in-transit information that flows over the public or untrusted network such as the internet and data which flows in the confines of a private network such as a corporate or enterprise local area network (LAN).

Defense-in-depth an information assurance concept in which multiple layers of security controls (defense) are placed throughout an information technology system to prevent an intrusion or malicious action.

Denial of service an attempt to make a machine or network resource unavailable to its intended users, such as to temporarily, indefinitely interrupt or suspend services of a host connected to the Internet.

Dependability defined as the property of computer system such that reliance can justifiably be placed on the service it delivers.

Digital certificate certifies the ownership of a public key by the named subject of the certificate.

Direct digital control the automated control of a condition or process by a digital device (computer).

Eavesdropping secretly listening to the private conversation of others without their consent.

Elliptic Curve Diffie-Hellman an anonymous key agreement protocol that allows two parties, each having an elliptic curve public–private key pair, to establish a shared secret over an insecure channel.

Elliptic Curve Menezes-Qu-Vanstone a key agreement performed using elliptical curves rather than traditional integers; is authenticated so it does not suffer man-in-the-middle (MitM) attacks.

Embedded computing system a computer system with a dedicated function within a larger mechanical or electrical system, often with real-time computing constraints. It is embedded as part of a complete device often including hardware and mechanical parts.

Embedded system security the reduction of vulnerabilities and protection against threats in software running on embedded devices.

Extensible Authentication Protocol an authentication framework frequently used in wireless networks and point-to-point connections; is defined in RFC 3748, which made RFC 2284 obsolete, and was updated by RFC 5247.

eXtensible Markup Language a markup language that defines a set of rules for encoding documents in a format which is both human-readable and machine-readable.

Extranet a website that allows controlled access to partners, vendors, and suppliers or an authorized set of customers – normally to a subset of the information accessible from an organization's intranet.

Extremely low frequency the ITU designation for electromagnetic radiation (radio waves) with frequencies from 3 to 30 Hz, and corresponding wavelengths from 100,000 to 10,000 kilometers.

Federal Information Processing Standard 180-4, Secure Hash Standard a set of cryptographically secure hash algorithms specified by the National Institute of Standards and Technology (NIST); the current version of the SHS standard is the document NIST FIPS 180-4, which specifies seven Secure Hash Algorithms: SHA-1, SHA-224, SHA-256, SHA-384, SHA-512, SHA-512/224, and SHA-512/256.

Federal Information Processing Standard 186-4, Digital Signature Standard a Federal Information Processing Standard for digital signatures. It was proposed by the National Institute of Standards and Technology (NIST) in August 1991 for use in their Digital Signature Standard (DSS) and adopted as FIPS 186 in 1993; four revisions to the initial specification have been released: FIPS 186-1 in 1996, FIPS 186-2 in 2000, FIPS 186-3 in 2009, and FIPS 186-4 in 2013.

Field-programmable gate array an integrated circuit designed to be configured by a customer or a designer after manufacturing.

Firewall a program that filters incoming and outgoing traffic in a computer network using a set of permissions; traffic that is permitted is free to travel through the firewall, while those that are restricted are unable to enter or exit the system.

Fortification to apply automatic embedded network protection techniques in ICD devices for protecting IoT devices and networks during a cyber-attack.

Graphical user interface software representation of information used to view information on and/or used to operate computers.

Hacker someone who seeks and exploits weaknesses in a computer system or computer network, may be motivated by a multitude of reasons, such as profit, protest, challenge, enjoyment, or evaluates those weaknesses to assist in removing them.

Hardware-Assisted Flow Integrity eXtension defense against code-reuse attacks exploiting backward edges (returns); provides fine-grained and practical protection, and serves as an enabling technology for future control-flow integrity instantiations.

Hashed refers to a method where a discrete algorithm is applied against a string of information. The resulting unique "hashed" value is appended to the string of information and sent with the information to the distant end; the receiver applies the algorithm to the string of information and compares the hashed values; if they are the same, the receiver has reasonable assurance that the message has not been tampered within transit; this technique often is used to maintain the integrity of information.

Heating, ventilating, and air conditioning the technology of indoor and vehicular environmental comfort. Its goal is to provide thermal comfort and acceptable indoor air quality. HVAC system design is a sub-discipline of mechanical engineering, based on the principles of thermodynamics, fluid mechanics, and heat transfer. Refrigeration is sometimes added to the field's abbreviation as HVAC&R or HVACR, or ventilating is dropped as in HACR (such as the designation of HACR-rated circuit breakers).

High frequency the ITU designation for the range of radio frequency electromagnetic waves (radio waves) between 3 and 30 MHz.

Hub a device that provides a physical communication device that permits several computers and devices to communicate with each other; hubs do not have the intelligence of routers, which read addressing and forwarding data to desired recipients; when a signal is received by a hub, it is broadcast to all the systems connected to the hub.

Human–computer interaction an area of research and practice that emerged in the early 1980s, initially as a specialty area in computer science embracing cognitive science and human factors engineering.

Hypertext Transfer Protocol an application protocol for distributed, collaborative, hypermedia information systems; is the foundation of data communication for the World Wide Web.

Information assurance the practice of assuring information and managing risks related to the use, processing, storage, and transmission of information or data and the systems and processes used for those purposes.

Information technology the application of computers and telecommunications equipment to store, retrieve, transmit, and manipulate data, often in the context of a business or other enterprise.

Infrastructure-as-a-service the capability provided to the consumer is to rent processing, storage, networks, and other fundamental computing resources where the consumer is able to deploy and run arbitrary software, which can include operating systems and applications; includes the foundational elements, such as storage, operating system instances, network, and identity management upon which development platforms and application can be layered.

Integrity assurance that information is created, modified, and deleted only by entities with the rights to do so.

International Telecommunications Union the international organization that coordinates worldwide telecommunications. It is part of the United Nations. Originally it was based in France and known as the CCITT, an acronym by which it is still widely known. It seeks to obtain agreement on the setting of and adherence to international standards for data telecommunications.

Internet the global communication network that allows almost all computers worldwide to connect and exchange information.

Internet-connected devices devices which can sense, communicate, compute, and potentially actuate and can have intelligence, multimodal interfaces, physical/virtual identities and attributes; can be sensors, radio frequency identification, social media, clickstreams, business transactions, actuators (such as machines/equipment fitted with sensors and deployed for mining, oil exploration or manufacturing operations), lab instruments (such as high-energy physics synchrotron), and smart consumer appliance (TV, phone, and so on).

Internet Engineering Task Force develops and promotes voluntary Internet standards, in particular the standards that comprise the Internet Protocol suite (TCP/IP); an open standards organization, with no formal membership or membership requirements with all participants and managers as volunteers, though their work is usually funded by their employers or sponsors.

Internet Protocol the principal communications protocol in the Internet Protocol suite for relaying datagrams across network boundaries and is a routing function enabling internetworking.

Internet Protocol version 4 the fourth version in the development of the Internet Protocol (IP). It is one of the core protocols of standards-based internetworking methods in the Internet, and was the first version deployed for production in the ARPANET in 1983.

Internet Protocol version 6 the most recent version of the Internet Protocol (IP), the communications protocol that provides an identification and location system for computers on networks and routes traffic across the Internet.

Internet of Things comprises billions of Internet-connected devices (ICD) or "things" each of which can sense, communicate, compute, and potentially actuate and can have intelligence, multimodal interfaces, physical/virtual identities, and attributes.

Intranet a computer network that uses Internet Protocol technology to share information, operational systems, or computing services within an organization; refers to a network within an organization.

Key management people, process, and technology coordinated to keep track of encryption keys to ensure availability of encrypted data.

Legacy system an old method, technology, computer system, or application program, of, relating to, or being a previous or outdated computer system; often a pejorative term, referencing a system as "legacy" often implies that the system is out of date or in need of replacement.

Local area networks a group of computers that are connected together in a localized area to communicate with one another and share resources such as a printer.

Low-power and lossy networks are made up of many embedded devices with limited power, memory, and processing resources; are interconnected by a variety of links, such as IEEE 802.15.4, Bluetooth, low power Wi-Fi, wired, or other low power powerline communication (PLC) links; are transitioning to an end-to-end IP-based solution to avoid the problem of non-interoperable networks interconnected by protocol translation gateways and proxies.

MAC address the identifying code given to a specific device to identify that device on a local network.

Machine-to-machine refers to technologies that allow both wireless and wired systems to communicate with other devices of the same type. M2M is a broad term as it does not pinpoint specific wireless or wired networking, information, and communications technology.

Malware an umbrella term used to refer to a variety of forms of hostile or intrusive software, including computer viruses, worms, trojan horses, ransomware, spyware, adware, scareware, and other malicious programs which can take the form of executable code, scripts, active content, and other software.

Media access control the lower sublayer of the data link layer (layer 2) of the seven-layer OSI model; the MAC sublayer provides addressing and channel access control mechanisms that make it possible for several terminals or network nodes to communicate within a multiple access network that incorporates a shared medium, for example, an Ethernet network.

Microcontroller (sometimes abbreviated μC, uC or MCU) a small computer on a single integrated circuit containing a processor core, memory, and programmable input/output peripherals.

Morris worm the first computer distributed via the Internet released on November 2, 1988.

National Institute of Standards and Technology a unit of the U.S. Commerce Department; formerly known as the National Bureau of Standards, which promotes and maintains measurement standards; also has active programs for encouraging and assisting industry and science to develop and use these standards.

Next-generation network a body of key architectural changes in telecommunication core and access networks. The general idea behind the next-generation network is that one network transports all information and services (voice, data, and all sorts of media such as video) by encapsulating these into packets, similar to those used on the Internet. Next-generation networks are commonly built around the Internet Protocol (IP), and therefore the term "all IP" is also sometimes used to describe the transformation of formerly telephone-centric networks towards next-generation networks.

Non-repudiation assurance that an action can be irrefutably bound to an accountable entity.

Open authorization an open standard for authorization which provides client applications a secure delegated access to server resources on behalf of a resource owner; specifies a process for resource owners to authorize third-party access to their server resources without sharing their credentials.

Packet the unit of data that is routed between an origin and a destination on the Internet or any other packet-switched network.

Personal area networks a computer network used for data transmission among devices such as computers, telephones, and personal digital assistants.

Personally identifiable information any data that could potentially identify a specific individual; any information that can be used to distinguish one person from another.

Physical objects a tangible and visible entity.

Platform-as-a-service (PaaS) provides the ability to lease an application development environment through an additional abstraction level, instead of supplying a virtualized infrastructure, in which systems run on a software platform.

Pre-shared key a shared secret which was previously shared between the two parties using some secure channel before it needs to be used.

Programmable logic controller a digital computer used for automation of typically industrial electromechanical processes, such as control of machinery on factory assembly lines, amusement rides, or light fixtures; used in many machines and industries.

Protocol a defined set of rules and regulations that determine how data are transmitted in telecommunications and computer networking.

Public key a key that belongs to a principal and is revealed to everyone; in order for everyone to trust that the public key really belongs to the principal, the public key is embedded in a digital certificate; is used to encrypt messages that are sent to the principal as well as to verify the signature of the principal.

Public key certificates are an electronic document used to prove ownership of a public key; the certificate includes information about the key, information about its owner's identity, and the digital signature of an entity that has verified the certificate's contents are correct; if the signature is valid, and the person examining the certificate trusts the signer, then they know they can use that key to communicate with its owner.

Public key cryptography a cryptographic algorithm that uses split keys to allow a user to keep the private component while allowing others to identify the user using a public component.

Quality of service the idea that transmission rates, error rates, and other characteristics can be measured, improved, and, to some extent, guaranteed in advance.

Radio frequency identification small electronic devices that consist of a small chip and an antenna which is typically capable of carrying 2000 bytes of data or less and must be scanned to retrieve the identifying information.

Random-access memory the temporary memory of a computer system.

Recognition includes the identification of a cyber-attack being performed leading to the fortification of smart ICDs before gaining access to IoT networks and systems.

Re-establishment a means to return the ICDs to its operational condition after a cyber-attack through remapping to a different network route.

Remote terminal units a microprocessor-controlled electronic device that interfaces objects in the physical world to a distributed control system or SCADA (supervisory control and data acquisition) system by transmitting telemetry data to a master system, and by using messages from the master supervisory system to control connected object.

Representational state transfer the software architectural style of the World Wide Web which gives a coordinated set of constraints to the design of components in a distributed hypermedia system that can lead to a higher performing and more maintainable architecture.

Return-oriented programming a computer security exploit technique that allows an attacker to execute code in the presence of security defenses such as non-executable memory and code signing.

Risk a measure of the extent to which an entity is threatened by a potential circumstance or event, and is typically a function of (i) the adverse impacts that would arise if the circumstance or event occurs and (ii) the likelihood of occurrence.

Sandbox environment the enforcement of access control by a native programming language such that an applet can only access limited resources; provides excellent protection against accidental or malicious destruction or abuse of local resources, it does not address the security issues related to authentication, authorization, privacy, integrity, and nonrepudiation.

Secret key a key used by a symmetric algorithm to encrypt and decrypt data.

Secure Hash Algorithm a message-digest algorithm that digests a message of arbitrary size to 160 bits.

Secure packet mechanism initiates counter-measures to confine data and stop processing if malicious activity is found amongst the plain text and cipher text in an ICD sensor agent.

Secure sockets layer the standard security technology for establishing an encrypted link between a web server and a browser; ensures that all data passed between the web server and browsers remain private and integral.

Security control processor ensures that a cryptographic processor and the input/output (I/O) processors perform in a manner that provides channel separation between the active channels flowing through the ICD sensor agent.

Sensor a tool that is designed to detect something and then to respond by taking a specific action; any of various devices designed to detect, measure, or record physical phenomena, as radiation, heat, or blood pressure, and to respond, as by transmitting information, initiating changes, or operating controls.

Smart device an electronic device, generally connected to other devices or networks via different protocols such as Bluetooth, Wi-Fi, and 3G, that can operate to some extent interactively and autonomously.

Smart grid a system which includes a variety of operational and energy measures including smart meters, smart appliances, renewable energy resources, and energy efficiency resources; electronic power conditioning and control of the production and distribution of electricity are important aspects of the smart grid.

Smart TV a television set or set-top box with integrated Internet and Web 2.0 features and is an example of technological convergence between computers and television sets and set-top boxes.

Software-as-a-service offers network accessible applications customizable by a user to a limited degree utilizing a security model developed by the provider.

Spoofing attack a situation in which one person or program successfully masquerades as another by falsifying data and thereby gaining an illegitimate advantage.

Steady state the normal operating condition for an information system.

Stop and wait automatic repeat request also can be referred to as Alternating bit protocol; is a method used in telecommunications to send information between two connected devices; ensures that information is not lost due to dropped packets and that packets are received in the correct order.

Stuxnet worm a computer worm that targets industrial control systems that are used to monitor and control large-scale industrial facilities like power plants, dams, waste processing systems and similar operations; it allows the attackers to take control of these systems without the operators knowing.

Supervisory control and data acquisition a system operating with coded signals over communication channels so as to provide control of remote equipment (using typically one communication channel per remote station).

Survivability the capability of an entity to continue its mission even in the presence of cyber-attacks, internal failures, or accidents.

Symmetric algorithm an algorithm where the same key can be used for encryption and decryption.

Telematic an interdisciplinary field encompassing telecommunications, vehicular technologies, road transportation, road safety, electrical engineering (sensors, instrumentation, wireless communications, etc.), and computer science (multimedia, Internet, etc.).

Thing (also see Internet-Connected Device) network of physical objects embedded with electronics, software, sensors, and network connectivity, which enables these objects to collect and exchange data.

Threat an event with the potential to impact an information system adversely via unauthorized access.

Token an object that represents something else, such as another object (either physical or virtual). A security token is a physical device, such as a special Smart Card, that together with something that a user knows, such as a PIN, will enable authorized access to a computer system or network.

Transmission Control Protocol a core protocol of the Internet Protocol suite; it originated in the initial network implementation in which it complemented the Internet Protocol (IP).

Transport layer security a protocol that ensures privacy between communicating applications and their users on the Internet; ensures that no third party may eavesdrop or tamper with any message; is the successor to the Secure Sockets Layer.

Trust boundaries a term in computer science and security used to describe a boundary where program data or execution changes its level of "trust" the term refers to any distinct boundary within which a system trusts all sub-systems (including data).

Ubiquitous computing a concept in software engineering and computer science where computing is made to appear anytime and everywhere. In contrast to desktop computing, ubiquitous computing can occur using any device, in any location, and in any format.

Ultra-high frequency the ITU designation for radio frequencies in the range between 300 MHz and 3 GHz, also known as the decimeter band as the wavelengths range from one meter to one decimeter.

V_{cc} a positive-voltage supply and the collector terminal of bipolar transistors is connected to the V_{cc} supply or to a load which connects to V_{cc}.

Virtual machine an operating system (OS) or application environment that is installed on software which imitates dedicated hardware.

Virtual private network extends a private network across a public network, such as the Internet. It enables users to send and receive data across shared or public networks as if their computing devices were directly connected to the private network, and thus are benefiting from the functionality, security, and management policies of the private network; is created by establishing a virtual point-to-point connection through the use of dedicated connections, virtual tunneling protocols, or traffic encryption.

Virtual world a computer-based online community environment that is designed and shared by individuals so that they can interact in a custom-built, simulated world.

Virtualization the use of virtual machines in a network environment, often as a way to create a secure testing environment for software updates, or in off-site, cloud storage. See also Virtual machine.

Virus often colloquially used as a term for any malicious code, including rootkits, Trojans, and worms, viruses are a subset of malware that are specifically designed to be self-replicating by invading other files or programs, similar to viruses in nature.

Voice over Internet Protocol a form of digital telephony where live audio is encoded and passed over the Internet much like traditional phone signals.

Vulnerability an exploitable flaw or weakness in an information infrastructure.

Wearable Technology clothing and accessories incorporating computer and advanced electronic technologies; is part of the network of physical objects or "things" embedded with electronics, software, sensors, and connectivity to enable objects to exchange data with a manufacturer, operator and/or other connected devices, without requiring human intervention.

Websocket a protocol providing full-duplex communication channels over a single TCP connection; standardized by the IETF as RFC 6455 in 2011, and the WebSocket API in Web IDL is being standardized by the W3C.

Wireless using radio, microwaves, etc. (as opposed to wires or cables) to transmit signals.

Wireless frequency the set of legally allowed wireless local area network channels using IEEE 802.11 protocols, mostly sold under the trademark Wi-Fi; the 802.11 workgroup currently documents use in five distinct frequency ranges: 2.4 GHz, 3.6 GHz, 4.9 GHz, 5 GHz, and 5.9 GHz bands.

Wireless intrusion detection monitors the radio spectrum for the presence of unauthorized, rogue access points and the use of wireless attack tools; the system monitors the radio spectrum used by wireless LANs, and immediately alerts a systems administrator whenever a rogue access point is detected. Conventionally it is achieved by comparing the MAC address of the participating wireless devices.

Wireless intrusion prevention systems a network device that monitors the radio spectrum for the presence of unauthorized access points (intrusion detection), and can automatically take countermeasures (intrusion prevention).

Wireless local area network a wireless computer network that links two or more devices using a wireless distribution method (often spread-spectrum or OFDM radio) within a limited area such as a home, school, computer laboratory, or office building.

Wireless sensor network spatially distributed autonomous sensors to monitor physical or environmental conditions, such as temperature, sound, and pressure, and to cooperatively pass their data through the network to a main location.

World Wide Web an information space where documents and other web resources are identified by uniform resource locators, interlinked by hypertext links, and can be accessed via the Internet.

Zero-day (also known as zero-hour or 0-day) vulnerability is an undisclosed and uncorrected computer application vulnerability that could be exploited to adversely affect the computer programs, data, additional computers or a network; also known as a "zero-day" because once a flaw becomes known, the programmer or developer has zero days (before disclosure) to fix it.

ZigBee a IEEE 802.15.4-based specification for a suite of high-level communication protocols used to create personal area networks with small, low-power digital radios.

Z-Wave a wireless communications specification designed to allow devices at home (lighting, access controls, entertainment systems, and household appliances, for example) to communicate with one another for the purposes of home automation.

APPENDIX C

CSBD THERMOSTAT REPORT

Cyber-Assurance for the Internet of Things, First Edition. Edited by Tyson T. Brooks.
© 2017 by The Institute of Electrical and Electronic Engineers, Inc. Published 2017 by John Wiley & Sons, Inc.

1   command Theory

Built: 19 August 2015
Parent Theories: list

1.1   Datatypes

command = PR privcmd | NP npriv

npriv = Status

privcmd = Set num | EU | DU

1.2   Definitions

[npriv_CASE]

$\vdash \forall x\ v_0.\ (\textbf{case}\ x\ \textbf{of}\ \text{Status} \Rightarrow v_0) = (\lambda m.\ v_0)\ (\text{npriv2num}\ x)$

1.3   Theorems

[command_distinct_thm]

$\vdash \forall a'\ a.\ \text{PR}\ a \neq \text{NP}\ a'$

[command_nchotomy_thm]

$\vdash \forall cc.\ (\exists p.\ cc = \text{PR}\ p) \lor \exists n.\ cc = \text{NP}\ n$

[npriv_nchotomy_thm]

$\vdash \forall a.\ a = \text{Status}$

[privcmd_distinct_thm]

$\vdash (\forall a.\ \text{Set}\ a \neq \text{EU}) \land (\forall a.\ \text{Set}\ a \neq \text{DU}) \land \text{EU} \neq \text{DU}$

[privcmd_nchotomy_thm]

$\vdash \forall pp.\ (\exists n.\ pp = \text{Set}\ n) \lor (pp = \text{EU}) \lor (pp = \text{DU})$

[set_command_11]

$\vdash (\forall a\ a'.\ (\text{PR}\ a = \text{PR}\ a') \iff (a = a')) \land$
$\quad \forall a\ a'.\ (\text{NP}\ a = \text{NP}\ a') \iff (a = a')$

[set_privcmd_11]

$\vdash \forall a\ a'.\ (\text{Set}\ a = \text{Set}\ a') \iff (a = a')$

2   principal Theory

Built: 19 August 2015
Parent Theories: cipher

2.1   Datatypes

keyPrinc = CA | Server | Utility num

principal =
    Role keyPrinc
 | Key (keyPrinc pKey)
 | Keyboard
 | Owner num
 | Account num num

3   option Theory

Built: 21 May 2015
Parent Theories: one, sum, normalForms

3.1   Datatypes

option = NONE | SOME 'a

3.2   Definitions

[IS_NONE_DEF]

  ⊢ ($\forall x$. IS_NONE (SOME x) $\iff$ F) $\wedge$ (IS_NONE NONE $\iff$ T)

[IS_SOME_DEF]

  ⊢ ($\forall x$. IS_SOME (SOME x) $\iff$ T) $\wedge$ (IS_SOME NONE $\iff$ F)

[NONE_DEF]

  ⊢ NONE = option_ABS (INR ())

[OPTION_APPLY_def]

  ⊢ ($\forall x$. NONE <*> x = NONE) $\wedge$ $\forall f$ x. SOME f <*> x = OPTION_MAP f x

[OPTION_BIND_def]

  ⊢ ($\forall f$. OPTION_BIND NONE f = NONE) $\wedge$
    $\forall x$ f. OPTION_BIND (SOME x) f = f x

[OPTION_CHOICE_def]

  ⊢ ($\forall m_2$. OPTION_CHOICE NONE m_2 = m_2) $\wedge$
    $\forall x$ m_2. OPTION_CHOICE (SOME x) m_2 = SOME x

[OPTION_GUARD_def]

  ⊢ (OPTION_GUARD T = SOME ()) $\wedge$ (OPTION_GUARD F = NONE)

[OPTION_IGNORE_BIND_def]

$\vdash \forall m_1\ m_2.\ \text{OPTION\_IGNORE\_BIND}\ m_1\ m_2 = \text{OPTION\_BIND}\ m_1\ (\text{K}\ m_2)$

[OPTION_JOIN_DEF]

$\vdash (\text{OPTION\_JOIN NONE} = \text{NONE}) \wedge \forall x.\ \text{OPTION\_JOIN}\ (\text{SOME}\ x) = x$

[OPTION_MAP2_DEF]

$\vdash \forall f\ x\ y.$
    $\text{OPTION\_MAP2}\ f\ x\ y =$
    if $\text{IS\_SOME}\ x \wedge \text{IS\_SOME}\ y$ **then** $\text{SOME}\ (f\ (\text{THE}\ x)\ (\text{THE}\ y))$
    else NONE

[OPTION_MAP_DEF]

$\vdash (\forall f\ x.\ \text{OPTION\_MAP}\ f\ (\text{SOME}\ x) = \text{SOME}\ (f\ x)) \wedge$
  $\forall f.\ \text{OPTION\_MAP}\ f\ \text{NONE} = \text{NONE}$

[option_REP_ABS_DEF]

$\vdash (\forall a.\ \text{option\_ABS}\ (\text{option\_REP}\ a) = a) \wedge$
  $\forall r.\ (\lambda x.\ \text{T})\ r \iff (\text{option\_REP}\ (\text{option\_ABS}\ r) = r)$

[OPTREL_def]

$\vdash \forall R\ x\ y.$
    $\text{OPTREL}\ R\ x\ y \iff$
    $(x = \text{NONE}) \wedge (y = \text{NONE}) \vee$
    $\exists x_0\ y_0.\ (x = \text{SOME}\ x_0) \wedge (y = \text{SOME}\ y_0) \wedge R\ x_0\ y_0$

[some_def]

$\vdash \forall P.\ (\text{some})\ P = $ **if** $\exists x.\ P\ x$ **then** $\text{SOME}\ (\varepsilon x.\ P\ x)$ **else** NONE

[SOME_DEF]

$\vdash \forall x.\ \text{SOME}\ x = \text{option\_ABS}\ (\text{INL}\ x)$

[THE_DEF]

$\vdash \forall x.\ \text{THE}\ (\text{SOME}\ x) = x$

3.3 Theorems

[EXISTS_OPTION]

$\vdash (\exists opt.\ P\ opt) \iff P\ \text{NONE} \vee \exists x.\ P\ (\text{SOME}\ x)$

[FORALL_OPTION]

$\vdash (\forall opt.\ P\ opt) \iff P\ \text{NONE} \wedge \forall x.\ P\ (\text{SOME}\ x)$

[IF_EQUALS_OPTION]

$\vdash$ $(((\text{if } P \text{ then SOME } x \text{ else NONE}) = \text{NONE}) \iff \neg P) \wedge$
$(((\text{if } P \text{ then NONE else SOME } x) = \text{NONE}) \iff P) \wedge$
$(((\text{if } P \text{ then SOME } x \text{ else NONE}) = \text{SOME } y) \iff P \wedge (x = y)) \wedge$
$(((\text{if } P \text{ then NONE else SOME } x) = \text{SOME } y) \iff \neg P \wedge (x = y))$

[IF_NONE_EQUALS_OPTION]

$\vdash$ $(((\text{if } P \text{ then } X \text{ else NONE}) = \text{NONE}) \iff P \Rightarrow \text{IS\_NONE } X) \wedge$
$(((\text{if } P \text{ then NONE else } X) = \text{NONE}) \iff \text{IS\_SOME } X \Rightarrow P) \wedge$
$(((\text{if } P \text{ then } X \text{ else NONE}) = \text{SOME } x) \iff P \wedge (X = \text{SOME } x)) \wedge$
$(((\text{if } P \text{ then NONE else } X) = \text{SOME } x) \iff \neg P \wedge (X = \text{SOME } x))$

[IS_NONE_EQ_NONE]

$\vdash$ $\forall x. \text{ IS\_NONE } x \iff (x = \text{NONE})$

[NOT_IS_SOME_EQ_NONE]

$\vdash$ $\forall x. \neg\text{IS\_SOME } x \iff (x = \text{NONE})$

[NOT_NONE_SOME]

$\vdash$ $\forall x. \text{ NONE} \neq \text{SOME } x$

[NOT_SOME_NONE]

$\vdash$ $\forall x. \text{ SOME } x \neq \text{NONE}$

[OPTION_APPLY_MAP2]

$\vdash$ $\text{OPTION\_MAP } f \ x \ \texttt{<*>} \ y = \text{OPTION\_MAP2 } f \ x \ y$

[OPTION_APPLY_o]

$\vdash$ $\text{SOME } (\text{o}) \ \texttt{<*>} \ f \ \texttt{<*>} \ g \ \texttt{<*>} \ x = f \ \texttt{<*>} \ (g \ \texttt{<*>} \ x)$

[OPTION_BIND_cong]

$\vdash$ $\forall o_1 \ o_2 \ f_1 \ f_2.$
    $(o_1 = o_2) \wedge (\forall x. \ (o_2 = \text{SOME } x) \Rightarrow (f_1 \ x = f_2 \ x)) \Rightarrow$
    $(\text{OPTION\_BIND } o_1 \ f_1 = \text{OPTION\_BIND } o_2 \ f_2)$

[OPTION_BIND_EQUALS_OPTION]

$\vdash$ $((\text{OPTION\_BIND } p \ f = \text{NONE}) \iff$
    $(p = \text{NONE}) \vee \exists x. \ (p = \text{SOME } x) \wedge (f \ x = \text{NONE})) \wedge$
    $((\text{OPTION\_BIND } p \ f = \text{SOME } y) \iff$
    $\exists x. \ (p = \text{SOME } x) \wedge (f \ x = \text{SOME } y))$

[option_case_compute]

$\vdash$ $\text{option\_CASE } x \ e \ f = \text{if IS\_SOME } x \text{ then } f \ (\text{THE } x) \text{ else } e$

[option_case_ID]

$\vdash$ $\forall x. \text{ option\_CASE } x \text{ NONE SOME} = x$

$[\text{option\_case\_SOME\_ID}]$

$\vdash \forall x.\ \text{option\_CASE}\ x\ x\ \text{SOME} = x$

$[\text{OPTION\_CHOICE\_EQ\_NONE}]$

$\vdash (\text{OPTION\_CHOICE}\ m_1\ m_2 = \text{NONE}) \iff (m_1 = \text{NONE}) \wedge (m_2 = \text{NONE})$

$[\text{option\_CLAUSES}]$

$\vdash (\forall x\ y.\ (\text{SOME}\ x = \text{SOME}\ y) \iff (x = y)) \wedge$
$\quad (\forall x.\ \text{THE}\ (\text{SOME}\ x) = x) \wedge (\forall x.\ \text{NONE} \neq \text{SOME}\ x) \wedge$
$\quad (\forall x.\ \text{SOME}\ x \neq \text{NONE}) \wedge (\forall x.\ \text{IS\_SOME}\ (\text{SOME}\ x) \iff \text{T}) \wedge$
$\quad (\text{IS\_SOME NONE} \iff \text{F}) \wedge (\forall x.\ \text{IS\_NONE}\ x \iff (x = \text{NONE})) \wedge$
$\quad (\forall x.\ \neg\text{IS\_SOME}\ x \iff (x = \text{NONE})) \wedge$
$\quad (\forall x.\ \text{IS\_SOME}\ x \Rightarrow (\text{SOME}\ (\text{THE}\ x) = x)) \wedge$
$\quad (\forall x.\ \text{option\_CASE}\ x\ \text{NONE SOME} = x) \wedge$
$\quad (\forall x.\ \text{option\_CASE}\ x\ x\ \text{SOME} = x) \wedge$
$\quad (\forall x.\ \text{IS\_NONE}\ x \Rightarrow (\text{option\_CASE}\ x\ e\ f = e)) \wedge$
$\quad (\forall x.\ \text{IS\_SOME}\ x \Rightarrow (\text{option\_CASE}\ x\ e\ f = f\ (\text{THE}\ x))) \wedge$
$\quad (\forall x.\ \text{IS\_SOME}\ x \Rightarrow (\text{option\_CASE}\ x\ e\ \text{SOME} = x)) \wedge$
$\quad (\forall v\ f.\ \text{option\_CASE NONE}\ v\ f = v) \wedge$
$\quad (\forall x\ v\ f.\ \text{option\_CASE}\ (\text{SOME}\ x)\ v\ f = f\ x) \wedge$
$\quad (\forall f\ x.\ \text{OPTION\_MAP}\ f\ (\text{SOME}\ x) = \text{SOME}\ (f\ x)) \wedge$
$\quad (\forall f.\ \text{OPTION\_MAP}\ f\ \text{NONE} = \text{NONE}) \wedge (\text{OPTION\_JOIN NONE} = \text{NONE}) \wedge$
$\quad \forall x.\ \text{OPTION\_JOIN}\ (\text{SOME}\ x) = x$

$[\text{OPTION\_GUARD\_COND}]$

$\vdash \text{OPTION\_GUARD}\ b = \textbf{if}\ b\ \textbf{then}\ \text{SOME}\ ()\ \textbf{else}\ \text{NONE}$

$[\text{OPTION\_GUARD\_EQ\_THM}]$

$\vdash ((\text{OPTION\_GUARD}\ b = \text{SOME}\ ()) \iff b) \wedge$
$\quad ((\text{OPTION\_GUARD}\ b = \text{NONE}) \iff \neg b)$

$[\text{OPTION\_IGNORE\_BIND\_thm}]$

$\vdash (\text{OPTION\_IGNORE\_BIND NONE}\ m = \text{NONE}) \wedge$
$\quad (\text{OPTION\_IGNORE\_BIND}\ (\text{SOME}\ v)\ m = m)$

$[\text{OPTION\_JOIN\_EQ\_SOME}]$

$\vdash \forall x\ y.\ (\text{OPTION\_JOIN}\ x = \text{SOME}\ y) \iff (x = \text{SOME}\ (\text{SOME}\ y))$

$[\text{OPTION\_MAP2\_cong}]$

$\vdash \forall x_1\ x_2\ y_1\ y_2\ f_1\ f_2.$
$\quad (x_1 = x_2) \wedge (y_1 = y_2) \wedge$
$\quad (\forall x\ y.\ (x_2 = \text{SOME}\ x) \wedge (y_2 = \text{SOME}\ y) \Rightarrow (f_1\ x\ y = f_2\ x\ y)) \Rightarrow$
$\quad (\text{OPTION\_MAP2}\ f_1\ x_1\ y_1 = \text{OPTION\_MAP2}\ f_2\ x_2\ y_2)$

$[\text{OPTION\_MAP2\_NONE}]$

$\vdash (\text{OPTION\_MAP2}\ f\ o_1\ o_2 = \text{NONE}) \iff (o_1 = \text{NONE}) \vee (o_2 = \text{NONE})$

$\lceil$OPTION_MAP2_SOME$\rceil$

$\vdash$ (OPTION_MAP2 f o_1 o_2 = SOME v) $\iff$

$\exists x_1\ x_2.\ (o_1 = \text{SOME } x_1) \land (o_2 = \text{SOME } x_2) \land (v = f\ x_1\ x_2)$

$\lceil$OPTION_MAP2_THM$\rceil$

$\vdash$ (OPTION_MAP2 f (SOME x) (SOME y) = SOME (f x y)) $\land$

(OPTION_MAP2 f (SOME x) NONE = NONE) $\land$

(OPTION_MAP2 f NONE (SOME y) = NONE) $\land$

(OPTION_MAP2 f NONE NONE = NONE)

$\lceil$OPTION_MAP_COMPOSE$\rceil$

$\vdash$ OPTION_MAP f (OPTION_MAP g x) = OPTION_MAP ($f \circ g$) x

$\lceil$OPTION_MAP_CONG$\rceil$

$\vdash \forall opt_1\ opt_2\ f_1\ f_2.$

$(opt_1 = opt_2) \land (\forall x.\ (opt_2 = \text{SOME } x) \Rightarrow (f_1\ x = f_2\ x)) \Rightarrow$

(OPTION_MAP f_1 opt_1 = OPTION_MAP f_2 opt_2)

$\lceil$OPTION_MAP_EQ_NONE$\rceil$

$\vdash \forall f\ x.\ (\text{OPTION\_MAP } f\ x = \text{NONE}) \iff (x = \text{NONE})$

$\lceil$OPTION_MAP_EQ_NONE_both_ways$\rceil$

$\vdash$ ((OPTION_MAP f x = NONE) $\iff$ (x = NONE)) $\land$

((NONE = OPTION_MAP f x) $\iff$ (x = NONE))

$\lceil$OPTION_MAP_EQ_SOME$\rceil$

$\vdash \forall f\ x\ y.$

(OPTION_MAP f x = SOME y) $\iff \exists z.\ (x = \text{SOME } z) \land (y = f\ z)$

$\lceil$OPTREL_MONO$\rceil$

$\vdash (\forall x\ y.\ P\ x\ y \Rightarrow Q\ x\ y) \Rightarrow \text{OPTREL } P\ x\ y \Rightarrow \text{OPTREL } Q\ x\ y$

$\lceil$OPTREL_refl$\rceil$

$\vdash (\forall x.\ R\ x\ x) \Rightarrow \forall x.\ \text{OPTREL } R\ x\ x$

$\lceil$SOME_11$\rceil$

$\vdash \forall x\ y.\ (\text{SOME } x = \text{SOME } y) \iff (x = y)$

$\lceil$SOME_APPLY_PERMUTE$\rceil$

$\vdash f \text{ <*> SOME } x = \text{SOME } (\lambda f.\ f\ x) \text{ <*> } f$

$\lceil$some_elim$\rceil$

$\vdash Q\ ((\text{some})\ P) \Rightarrow (\exists x.\ P\ x \land Q\ (\text{SOME } x)) \lor (\forall x.\ \neg P\ x) \land Q\ \text{NONE}$

$\lceil$some_EQ$\rceil$

$\vdash$ ((some $x.\ x = y$) = SOME y) $\land$ ((some $x.\ y = x$) = SOME y)

$\lceil$some_F$\rceil$

$\vdash$ (some $x.$ F) = NONE

$\lceil$some_intro$\rceil$

$\vdash (\forall x.\ P\ x \Rightarrow Q\ (\text{SOME } x)) \land ((\forall x.\ \neg P\ x) \Rightarrow Q\ \text{NONE}) \Rightarrow Q\ ((\text{some})\ P)$

$\lceil$SOME_SOME_APPLY$\rceil$

$\vdash$ SOME f <*> SOME x = SOME (f x)

4 cipher Theory

Built: 19 August 2015
Parent Theories: list

4.1 Datatypes

$asymMsg$ = Ea ('princ pKey) ('message option)

$digest$ = hash ('message option)

$pKey$ = pubK 'princ | privK 'princ

$symKey$ = sym num

$symMsg$ = Es symKey ('message option)

4.2 Definitions

[deciphP_def]

$\vdash$ (deciphP key (Ea (privK P) (SOME x)) =
   if key = pubK P **then** SOME x **else** NONE) $\wedge$
   (deciphP key (Ea (pubK P) (SOME x)) =
   if key = privK P **then** SOME x **else** NONE) $\wedge$
   (deciphP k_1 (Ea k_2 NONE) = NONE)

[deciphS_def]

$\vdash$ (deciphS k_1 (Es k_2 (SOME x)) =
   if k_1 = k_2 **then** SOME x **else** NONE) $\wedge$
   (deciphS k_1 (Es k_2 NONE) = NONE)

[sign_def]

$\vdash$ $\forall pubKey\ dgst$. sign $pubKey\ dgst$ = Ea $pubKey$ (SOME $dgst$)

[signVerify_def]

$\vdash$ $\forall pubKey\ signature\ msgContents$.
   signVerify $pubKey\ signature\ msgContents$ $\iff$
   (SOME (hash $msgContents$) = deciphP $pubKey\ signature$)

4.3 Theorems

[asymMsg_one_one]

$\vdash$ $\forall a_0\ a_1\ a_0'\ a_1'$.
   (Ea $a_0\ a_1$ = Ea $a_0'\ a_1'$) $\iff$ (a_0 = a_0') $\wedge$ (a_1 = a_1')

$\lfloor$deciphP_clauses$\rfloor$

$\vdash (\forall P \; text.$
 $(\text{deciphP} \; (\text{pubK} \; P) \; (\text{Ea} \; (\text{privK} \; P) \; (\text{SOME} \; text)) =$
 $\text{SOME} \; text) \wedge$
 $(\text{deciphP} \; (\text{privK} \; P) \; (\text{Ea} \; (\text{pubK} \; P) \; (\text{SOME} \; text)) =$
 $\text{SOME} \; text)) \wedge$
$(\forall k \; P \; text.$
 $(\text{deciphP} \; k \; (\text{Ea} \; (\text{privK} \; P) \; (\text{SOME} \; text)) = \text{SOME} \; text) \iff$
 $(k = \text{pubK} \; P)) \wedge$
$(\forall k \; P \; text.$
 $(\text{deciphP} \; k \; (\text{Ea} \; (\text{pubK} \; P) \; (\text{SOME} \; text)) = \text{SOME} \; text) \iff$
 $(k = \text{privK} \; P)) \wedge$
$(\forall x \; k_2 \; k_1 \; P_2 \; P_1.$
 $(\text{deciphP} \; (\text{pubK} \; P_1) \; (\text{Ea} \; (\text{pubK} \; P_2) \; (\text{SOME} \; x)) = \text{NONE}) \wedge$
 $(\text{deciphP} \; k_1 \; (\text{Ea} \; k_2 \; \text{NONE}) = \text{NONE})) \wedge$
$\forall x \; P_2 \; P_1. \; \text{deciphP} \; (\text{privK} \; P_1) \; (\text{Ea} \; (\text{privK} \; P_2) \; (\text{SOME} \; x)) = \text{NONE}$

$\lfloor$deciphP_one_one$\rfloor$

$\vdash (\forall P_1 \; P_2 \; text_1 \; text_2.$
 $(\text{deciphP} \; (\text{pubK} \; P_1) \; (\text{Ea} \; (\text{privK} \; P_2) \; (\text{SOME} \; text_2)) =$
 $\text{SOME} \; text_1) \iff (P_1 = P_2) \wedge (text_1 = text_2)) \wedge$
$(\forall P_1 \; P_2 \; text_1 \; text_2.$
 $(\text{deciphP} \; (\text{privK} \; P_1) \; (\text{Ea} \; (\text{pubK} \; P_2) \; (\text{SOME} \; text_2)) =$
 $\text{SOME} \; text_1) \iff (P_1 = P_2) \wedge (text_1 = text_2)) \wedge$
$(\forall p \; c \; P \; msg.$
 $(\text{deciphP} \; (\text{pubK} \; P) \; (\text{Ea} \; p \; c) = \text{SOME} \; msg) \iff$
 $(p = \text{privK} \; P) \wedge (c = \text{SOME} \; msg)) \wedge$
$(\forall enMsg \; P \; msg.$
 $(\text{deciphP} \; (\text{pubK} \; P) \; enMsg = \text{SOME} \; msg) \iff$
 $(enMsg = \text{Ea} \; (\text{privK} \; P) \; (\text{SOME} \; msg))) \wedge$
$(\forall p \; c \; P \; msg.$
 $(\text{deciphP} \; (\text{privK} \; P) \; (\text{Ea} \; p \; c) = \text{SOME} \; msg) \iff$
 $(p = \text{pubK} \; P) \wedge (c = \text{SOME} \; msg)) \wedge$
$\forall enMsg \; P \; msg.$
 $(\text{deciphP} \; (\text{privK} \; P) \; enMsg = \text{SOME} \; msg) \iff$
 $(enMsg = \text{Ea} \; (\text{pubK} \; P) \; (\text{SOME} \; msg))$

$\lfloor$deciphS_clauses$\rfloor$

$\vdash (\forall k \; text. \; \text{deciphS} \; k \; (\text{Es} \; k \; (\text{SOME} \; text)) = \text{SOME} \; text) \wedge$
$(\forall k_1 \; k_2 \; text.$
 $(\text{deciphS} \; k_1 \; (\text{Es} \; k_2 \; (\text{SOME} \; text)) = \text{SOME} \; text) \iff$
 $(k_1 = k_2)) \wedge$
$(\forall k_1 \; k_2 \; text.$
 $(\text{deciphS} \; k_1 \; (\text{Es} \; k_2 \; (\text{SOME} \; text)) = \text{NONE}) \iff k_1 \neq k_2) \wedge$
$\forall k_1 \; k_2. \; \text{deciphS} \; k_1 \; (\text{Es} \; k_2 \; \text{NONE}) = \text{NONE}$

$\lfloor$deciphS_one_one$\rfloor$

$\vdash (\forall k_1 \; k_2 \; text_1 \; text_2 .$
    $(\text{deciphS} \; k_1 \; (\text{Es} \; k_2 \; (\text{SOME} \; text_2)) = \text{SOME} \; text_1) \iff$
    $(k_1 = k_2) \land (text_1 = text_2)) \land$
  $\forall enMsg \; text \; key .$
    $(\text{deciphS} \; key \; enMsg = \text{SOME} \; text) \iff$
    $(enMsg = \text{Es} \; key \; (\text{SOME} \; text))$

[digest_one_one]

$\vdash \forall a \; a' . (\text{hash} \; a = \text{hash} \; a') \iff (a = a')$

[option_distinct]

$\vdash \forall x . \; \text{NONE} \neq \text{SOME} \; x$

[option_one_one]

$\vdash \forall x \; y . (\text{SOME} \; x = \text{SOME} \; y) \iff (x = y)$

[pKey_distinct_clauses]

$\vdash (\forall a' \; a . \; \text{pubK} \; a \neq \text{privK} \; a') \land \forall a' \; a . \; \text{privK} \; a' \neq \text{pubK} \; a$

[pKey_one_one]

$\vdash (\forall a \; a' . (\text{pubK} \; a = \text{pubK} \; a') \iff (a = a')) \land$
  $\forall a \; a' . (\text{privK} \; a = \text{privK} \; a') \iff (a = a')$

[sign_one_one]

$\vdash \forall pubKey_1 \; pubKey_2 \; m_1 \; m_2 .$
    $(\text{sign} \; pubKey_1 \; (\text{hash} \; m_1) = \text{sign} \; pubKey_2 \; (\text{hash} \; m_2)) \iff$
    $(pubKey_1 = pubKey_2) \land (m_1 = m_2)$

[signVerify_one_one]

$\vdash (\forall P \; m_1 \; m_2 .$
    $\text{signVerify} \; (\text{pubK} \; P) \; (\text{Ea} \; (\text{privK} \; P) \; (\text{SOME} \; (\text{hash} \; (\text{SOME} \; m_1))))$
      $(\text{SOME} \; m_2) \iff (m_1 = m_2)) \land$
  $(\forall signature \; P \; text .$
    $\text{signVerify} \; (\text{pubK} \; P) \; signature \; (\text{SOME} \; text) \iff$
    $(signature = \text{sign} \; (\text{privK} \; P) \; (\text{hash} \; (\text{SOME} \; text)))) \land$
  $\forall text_2 \; text_1 \; P_2 \; P_1 .$
    $\text{signVerify} \; (\text{pubK} \; P_1) \; (\text{sign} \; (\text{privK} \; P_2) \; (\text{hash} \; (\text{SOME} \; text_2)))$
      $(\text{SOME} \; text_1) \iff (P_1 = P_2) \land (text_1 = text_2)$

[signVerifyOK]

$\vdash \forall P \; msg .$
    $\text{signVerify} \; (\text{pubK} \; P) \; (\text{sign} \; (\text{privK} \; P) \; (\text{hash} \; (\text{SOME} \; msg)))$
    $(\text{SOME} \; msg)$

[symKey_one_one]

$\vdash \forall a \; a' . (\text{sym} \; a = \text{sym} \; a') \iff (a = a')$

[symMsg_one_one]

$\vdash \forall a_0 \; a_1 \; a_0' \; a_1' .$
    $(\text{Es} \; a_0 \; a_1 = \text{Es} \; a_0' \; a_1') \iff (a_0 = a_0') \land (a_1 = a_1')$

5 satList Theory

Built: 28 January 2016

Parent Theories: aclDrules

5.1 Definitions

⌊satList_def⌋

⊢ ∀ M Oi Os $formList$.
(M,Oi,Os) satList $formList$ ⟺
FOLDR $(\lambda x\ y.\ x \wedge y)$ T (MAP $(\lambda f.\ (M,Oi,Os)$ sat $f)$ $formList)$

5.2 Theorems

⌊satList_conj⌋

⊢ ∀ l_1 l_2 M Oi Os.
(M,Oi,Os) satList $l_1 \wedge (M,Oi,Os)$ satList l_2 ⟺
(M,Oi,Os) satList $(l_1$ ++ $l_2)$

⌊satList_CONS⌋

⊢ ∀ h t M Oi Os.
(M,Oi,Os) satList $(h::t)$ ⟺
(M,Oi,Os) sat $h \wedge (M,Oi,Os)$ satList t

⌊satList_nil⌋

⊢ (M,Oi,Os) satList []

6 vm1a Theory

Built: 28 January 2016

Parent Theories: satList

6.1 Datatypes

configuration =
    CFG (('command inst, 'principal, 'd, 'e) Form -> bool)
        ('state -> ('command inst, 'principal, 'd, 'e) Form)
        (('command inst, 'principal, 'd, 'e) Form list)
        (('command inst, 'principal, 'd, 'e) Form list) 'state
        ('output list)

inst = CMD 'command | TRAP

trType = discard | trap 'inst | exec 'inst

6.2 Definitions

$\lceil$CFGInterpret_def$\rceil$

$\vdash$ CFGInterpret (M, Oi, Os)
  (CFG *inputTest stateInterp context* $(x::ins)$ *state*
     outStream) $\Longleftrightarrow$
 (M, Oi, Os) satList *context* $\wedge$ (M, Oi, Os) sat x $\wedge$
 (M, Oi, Os) sat *stateInterp state*

$\lceil$TR_def$\rceil$

$\vdash$ TR =
  $(\lambda a_0\ a_1\ a_2\ a_3.$
    $\forall TR'.$
      $(\forall a_0\ a_1\ a_2\ a_3.$
        $(\exists inputTest\ P\ NS\ M\ Oi\ Os\ Out\ s\ certs\ stateInterp\ cmd$
          ins outs.
          $(a_0 = (M, Oi, Os))$ $\wedge$ $(a_1 = $ exec $($CMD $cmd))$ $\wedge$
          $(a_2 =$
          CFG *inputTest stateInterp certs*
            $(P$ says prop $($CMD $cmd)::ins)\ s\ outs)$ $\wedge$
          $(a_3 =$
          CFG *inputTest stateInterp certs ins*
            $(NS\ s\ ($exec $($CMD $cmd)))$
            $(Out\ s\ ($exec $($CMD $cmd))::outs))$ $\wedge$
          inputTest $(P$ says prop $($CMD $cmd))$ $\wedge$
          CFGInterpret (M, Oi, Os)
            (CFG *inputTest stateInterp certs*
              $(P$ says prop $($CMD $cmd)::ins)\ s\ outs))$ $\vee$
        $(\exists inputTest\ P\ NS\ M\ Oi\ Os\ Out\ s\ certs\ stateInterp\ cmd$
          ins outs.
          $(a_0 = (M, Oi, Os))$ $\wedge$ $(a_1 = $ trap $($CMD $cmd))$ $\wedge$
          $(a_2 =$
          CFG *inputTest stateInterp certs*
            $(P$ says prop $($CMD $cmd)::ins)\ s\ outs)$ $\wedge$
          $(a_3 =$
          CFG *inputTest stateInterp certs ins*
            $(NS\ s\ ($trap $($CMD $cmd)))$
            $(Out\ s\ ($trap $($CMD $cmd))::outs))$ $\wedge$
          inputTest $(P$ says prop $($CMD $cmd))$ $\wedge$
          CFGInterpret (M, Oi, Os)
            (CFG *inputTest stateInterp certs*
              $(P$ says prop $($CMD $cmd)::ins)\ s\ outs))$ $\vee$
        $(\exists inputTest\ NS\ M\ Oi\ Os\ Out\ s\ certs\ stateInterp\ cmd\ x$
          ins outs.
          $(a_0 = (M, Oi, Os))$ $\wedge$ $(a_1 = $ discard$)$ $\wedge$
          $(a_2 =$
          CFG *inputTest stateInterp certs* $(x::ins)\ s$
            outs$)$ $\wedge$
          $(a_3 =$

$$\text{CFG } inputTest \ stateInterp \ certs \ ins$$
$$(NS \ s \ \texttt{discard}) \ (Out \ s \ \texttt{discard::}outs)) \ \wedge$$
$$\neg inputTest \ x) \ \Rightarrow$$
$$TR' \ a_0 \ a_1 \ a_2 \ a_3) \ \Rightarrow$$
$$TR' \ a_0 \ a_1 \ a_2 \ a_3)$$

6.3 Theorems

⌊configuration_one_one⌋

$\vdash \forall a_0 \ a_1 \ a_2 \ a_3 \ a_4 \ a_5 \ a_0' \ a_1' \ a_2' \ a_3' \ a_4' \ a_5'.$
  (CFG $a_0 \ a_1 \ a_2 \ a_3 \ a_4 \ a_5$ = CFG $a_0' \ a_1' \ a_2' \ a_3' \ a_4' \ a_5'$) $\iff$
  $(a_0 = a_0') \ \wedge \ (a_1 = a_1') \ \wedge \ (a_2 = a_2') \ \wedge \ (a_3 = a_3') \ \wedge$
  $(a_4 = a_4') \ \wedge \ (a_5 = a_5')$

⌊inst_distinct_clauses⌋

$\vdash (\forall a. \ \text{CMD } a \neq \text{TRAP}) \ \wedge \ \forall a. \ \text{TRAP} \neq \text{CMD } a$

⌊TR_cases⌋

$\vdash \forall a_0 \ a_1 \ a_2 \ a_3.$
  TR $a_0 \ a_1 \ a_2 \ a_3 \ \iff$
  ($\exists inputTest \ P \ NS \ M \ Oi \ Os \ Out \ s \ certs \ stateInterp \ cmd \ ins$
    $outs.$
    $(a_0 = (M, Oi, Os)) \ \wedge \ (a_1 = \texttt{exec} \ (\text{CMD } cmd)) \ \wedge$
    $(a_2 =$
    CFG $inputTest \ stateInterp \ certs$
      $(P \ \texttt{says prop} \ (\text{CMD } cmd)::ins) \ s \ outs) \ \wedge$
    $(a_3 =$
    CFG $inputTest \ stateInterp \ certs \ ins$
      $(NS \ s \ (\texttt{exec} \ (\text{CMD } cmd)))$
      $(Out \ s \ (\texttt{exec} \ (\text{CMD } cmd))::outs)) \ \wedge$
    $inputTest \ (P \ \texttt{says prop} \ (\text{CMD } cmd)) \ \wedge$
    CFGInterpret (M, Oi, Os)
      (CFG $inputTest \ stateInterp \ certs$
        $(P \ \texttt{says prop} \ (\text{CMD } cmd)::ins) \ s \ outs)) \ \vee$
  ($\exists inputTest \ P \ NS \ M \ Oi \ Os \ Out \ s \ certs \ stateInterp \ cmd \ ins$
    $outs.$
    $(a_0 = (M, Oi, Os)) \ \wedge \ (a_1 = \texttt{trap} \ (\text{CMD } cmd)) \ \wedge$
    $(a_2 =$
    CFG $inputTest \ stateInterp \ certs$
      $(P \ \texttt{says prop} \ (\text{CMD } cmd)::ins) \ s \ outs) \ \wedge$
    $(a_3 =$
    CFG $inputTest \ stateInterp \ certs \ ins$
      $(NS \ s \ (\texttt{trap} \ (\text{CMD } cmd)))$
      $(Out \ s \ (\texttt{trap} \ (\text{CMD } cmd))::outs)) \ \wedge$
    $inputTest \ (P \ \texttt{says prop} \ (\text{CMD } cmd)) \ \wedge$
    CFGInterpret (M, Oi, Os)
      (CFG $inputTest \ stateInterp \ certs$
        $(P \ \texttt{says prop} \ (\text{CMD } cmd)::ins) \ s \ outs)) \ \vee$

$\exists$ *inputTest NS M Oi Os Out s certs stateInterp cmd x ins*
outs .
  $(a_0 = (M,Oi,Os)) \land (a_1 = \text{discard}) \land$
  $(a_2 = \text{CFG } inputTest\ stateInterp\ certs\ (x::ins)\ s\ outs) \land$
  $(a_3 =$
   CFG *inputTest stateInterp certs ins* (*NS s* discard)
    (*Out s* discard::*outs*)) $\land$ $\neg inputTest\ x$

[TR_discard_cmd_rule]

$\vdash$ TR (M,Oi,Os) discard
  (CFG *inputTest stateInterp certs* $(x::ins)$ *s outs*)
  (CFG *inputTest stateInterp certs ins* (*NS s* discard)
   (*Out s* discard::*outs*)) $\iff$ $\neg inputTest\ x$

[TR_EQ_rules_thm]

$\vdash$ (TR (M,Oi,Os) (exec (CMD *cmd*))
   (CFG *inputTest stateInterp certs*
    (P says prop (CMD *cmd*)::*ins*) *s outs*)
   (CFG *inputTest stateInterp certs ins*
    (*NS s* (exec (CMD *cmd*)))
    (*Out s* (exec (CMD *cmd*))::*outs*)) $\iff$
  inputTest (P says prop (CMD *cmd*)) $\land$
  CFGInterpret (M,Oi,Os)
   (CFG *inputTest stateInterp certs*
    (P says prop (CMD *cmd*)::*ins*) *s outs*)) $\land$
  (TR (M,Oi,Os) (trap (CMD *cmd*))
   (CFG *inputTest stateInterp certs*
    (P says prop (CMD *cmd*)::*ins*) *s outs*)
   (CFG *inputTest stateInterp certs ins*
    (*NS s* (trap (CMD *cmd*)))
    (*Out s* (trap (CMD *cmd*))::*outs*)) $\iff$
  inputTest (P says prop (CMD *cmd*)) $\land$
  CFGInterpret (M,Oi,Os)
   (CFG *inputTest stateInterp certs*
    (P says prop (CMD *cmd*)::*ins*) *s outs*)) $\land$
  (TR (M,Oi,Os) discard
   (CFG *inputTest stateInterp certs* $(x::ins)$ *s outs*)
   (CFG *inputTest stateInterp certs ins* (*NS s* discard)
    (*Out s* discard::*outs*)) $\iff$ $\neg inputTest\ x$)

[TR_exec_cmd_rule]

$\vdash$ $\forall inputTest\ certs\ stateInterp\ P\ cmd\ ins\ s\ outs$.
  ($\forall M\ Oi\ Os$.
   CFGInterpret (M,Oi,Os)
    (CFG *inputTest stateInterp certs*
     (P says prop (CMD *cmd*)::*ins*) *s outs*) $\Rightarrow$
   (M,Oi,Os) sat prop (CMD *cmd*)) $\Rightarrow$
  $\forall NS\ Out\ M\ Oi\ Os$.

TR (M,Oi,Os) (exec (CMD cmd))
  (CFG $inputTest$ $stateInterp$ $certs$
    (P says prop (CMD cmd)::ins) s $outs$)
  (CFG $inputTest$ $stateInterp$ $certs$ ins
    (NS s (exec (CMD cmd)))
    (Out s (exec (CMD cmd))::$outs$)) $\iff$
$inputTest$ (P says prop (CMD cmd)) $\wedge$
CFGInterpret (M,Oi,Os)
  (CFG $inputTest$ $stateInterp$ $certs$
    (P says prop (CMD cmd)::ins) s $outs$) $\wedge$
(M,Oi,Os) sat prop (CMD cmd)

[TR_ind]
$\vdash \forall TR'.$
  ($\forall inputTest$ P NS M Oi Os Out s $certs$ $stateInterp$ cmd ins
    $outs$.
    $inputTest$ (P says prop (CMD cmd)) $\wedge$
    CFGInterpret (M,Oi,Os)
      (CFG $inputTest$ $stateInterp$ $certs$
        (P says prop (CMD cmd)::ins) s $outs$) $\Rightarrow$
    TR' (M,Oi,Os) (exec (CMD cmd))
      (CFG $inputTest$ $stateInterp$ $certs$
        (P says prop (CMD cmd)::ins) s $outs$)
      (CFG $inputTest$ $stateInterp$ $certs$ ins
        (NS s (exec (CMD cmd)))
        (Out s (exec (CMD cmd))::$outs$))) $\wedge$
  ($\forall inputTest$ P NS M Oi Os Out s $certs$ $stateInterp$ cmd ins
    $outs$.
    $inputTest$ (P says prop (CMD cmd)) $\wedge$
    CFGInterpret (M,Oi,Os)
      (CFG $inputTest$ $stateInterp$ $certs$
        (P says prop (CMD cmd)::ins) s $outs$) $\Rightarrow$
    TR' (M,Oi,Os) (trap (CMD cmd))
      (CFG $inputTest$ $stateInterp$ $certs$
        (P says prop (CMD cmd)::ins) s $outs$)
      (CFG $inputTest$ $stateInterp$ $certs$ ins
        (NS s (trap (CMD cmd)))
        (Out s (trap (CMD cmd))::$outs$))) $\wedge$
  ($\forall inputTest$ NS M Oi Os Out s $certs$ $stateInterp$ cmd x ins
    $outs$.
    $\neg inputTest$ x $\Rightarrow$
    TR' (M,Oi,Os) discard
      (CFG $inputTest$ $stateInterp$ $certs$ (x::ins) s $outs$)
      (CFG $inputTest$ $stateInterp$ $certs$ ins (NS s discard)
      (Out s discard::$outs$))) $\Rightarrow$
  $\forall a_0$ a_1 a_2 a_3. TR a_0 a_1 a_2 a_3 $\Rightarrow$ TR' a_0 a_1 a_2 a_3

[TR_rules]
  $\vdash$ ($\forall inputTest$ P NS M Oi Os Out s $certs$ $stateInterp$ cmd ins
    $outs$.

$inputTest\ (P$ says prop (CMD $cmd))\ \wedge$
CFGInterpret (M,Oi,Os)
  (CFG $inputTest\ stateInterp\ certs$
    $(P$ says prop (CMD $cmd)::ins)\ s\ outs)\ \Rightarrow$
TR (M,Oi,Os) (exec (CMD $cmd))$
  (CFG $inputTest\ stateInterp\ certs$
    $(P$ says prop (CMD $cmd)::ins)\ s\ outs)$
  (CFG $inputTest\ stateInterp\ certs\ ins$
    $(NS\ s$ (exec (CMD $cmd)))$
    $(Out\ s$ (exec (CMD $cmd))::outs)))\ \wedge$
$(\forall inputTest\ P\ NS\ M\ Oi\ Os\ Out\ s\ certs\ stateInterp\ cmd\ ins$
  $outs\,.$
  $inputTest\ (P$ says prop (CMD $cmd))\ \wedge$
  CFGInterpret (M,Oi,Os)
    (CFG $inputTest\ stateInterp\ certs$
      $(P$ says prop (CMD $cmd)::ins)\ s\ outs)\ \Rightarrow$
  TR (M,Oi,Os) (trap (CMD $cmd))$
    (CFG $inputTest\ stateInterp\ certs$
      $(P$ says prop (CMD $cmd)::ins)\ s\ outs)$
    (CFG $inputTest\ stateInterp\ certs\ ins$
      $(NS\ s$ (trap (CMD $cmd)))$
      $(Out\ s$ (trap (CMD $cmd))::outs)))\ \wedge$
$\forall inputTest\ NS\ M\ Oi\ Os\ Out\ s\ certs\ stateInterp\ cmd\ x\ ins\ outs\,.$
$\neg inputTest\ x\ \Rightarrow$
TR (M,Oi,Os) discard
  (CFG $inputTest\ stateInterp\ certs\ (x::ins)\ s\ outs)$
  (CFG $inputTest\ stateInterp\ certs\ ins\ (NS\ s$ discard)
    $(Out\ s$ discard::outs))

[TR_strongind]

$\vdash\ \forall TR'\,.$
  $(\forall inputTest\ P\ NS\ M\ Oi\ Os\ Out\ s\ certs\ stateInterp\ cmd\ ins$
    $outs\,.$
    $inputTest\ (P$ says prop (CMD $cmd))\ \wedge$
    CFGInterpret (M,Oi,Os)
      (CFG $inputTest\ stateInterp\ certs$
        $(P$ says prop (CMD $cmd)::ins)\ s\ outs)\ \Rightarrow$
    $TR'\ (M,Oi,Os)$ (exec (CMD $cmd))$
      (CFG $inputTest\ stateInterp\ certs$
        $(P$ says prop (CMD $cmd)::ins)\ s\ outs)$
      (CFG $inputTest\ stateInterp\ certs\ ins$
        $(NS\ s$ (exec (CMD $cmd)))$
        $(Out\ s$ (exec (CMD $cmd))::outs)))\ \wedge$
  $(\forall inputTest\ P\ NS\ M\ Oi\ Os\ Out\ s\ certs\ stateInterp\ cmd\ ins$
    $outs\,.$
    $inputTest\ (P$ says prop (CMD $cmd))\ \wedge$
    CFGInterpret (M,Oi,Os)
      (CFG $inputTest\ stateInterp\ certs$
        $(P$ says prop (CMD $cmd)::ins)\ s\ outs)\ \Rightarrow$

TR' (M,Oi,Os) (trap (CMD cmd))
  (CFG $inputTest$ $stateInterp$ $certs$
    (P says prop (CMD cmd)::ins) s $outs$)
  (CFG $inputTest$ $stateInterp$ $certs$ ins
    (NS s (trap (CMD cmd)))
    (Out s (trap (CMD cmd))::$outs$))) $\wedge$
($\forall inputTest$ NS M Oi Os Out s $certs$ $stateInterp$ x ins $outs$.
  $\neg inputTest$ x $\Rightarrow$
  TR' (M,Oi,Os) discard
    (CFG $inputTest$ $stateInterp$ $certs$ (x::ins) s $outs$)
    (CFG $inputTest$ $stateInterp$ $certs$ ins (NS s discard)
      (Out s discard::$outs$))) $\Rightarrow$
$\forall a_0$ a_1 a_2 a_3. TR a_0 a_1 a_2 a_3 $\Rightarrow$ TR' a_0 a_1 a_2 a_3

[TR_trap_cmd_rule]

$\vdash$ $\forall inputTest$ $stateInterp$ $certs$ P cmd ins s $outs$.
  ($\forall M$ Oi Os.
    CFGInterpret (M,Oi,Os)
      (CFG $inputTest$ $stateInterp$ $certs$
        (P says prop (CMD cmd)::ins) s $outs$) $\Rightarrow$
      (M,Oi,Os) sat prop TRAP) $\Rightarrow$
  $\forall NS$ Out M Oi Os.
    TR (M,Oi,Os) (trap (CMD cmd))
      (CFG $inputTest$ $stateInterp$ $certs$
        (P says prop (CMD cmd)::ins) s $outs$)
      (CFG $inputTest$ $stateInterp$ $certs$ ins
        (NS s (trap (CMD cmd)))
        (Out s (trap (CMD cmd))::$outs$)) $\Longleftrightarrow$
    $inputTest$ (P says prop (CMD cmd)) $\wedge$
    CFGInterpret (M,Oi,Os)
      (CFG $inputTest$ $stateInterp$ $certs$
        (P says prop (CMD cmd)::ins) s $outs$) $\wedge$
    (M,Oi,Os) sat prop TRAP

[TRrule0]

$\vdash$ TR (M,Oi,Os) (exec (CMD cmd))
    (CFG $inputTest$ $stateInterp$ $certs$
      (P says prop (CMD cmd)::ins) s $outs$)
    (CFG $inputTest$ $stateInterp$ $certs$ ins
      (NS s (exec (CMD cmd)))
      (Out s (exec (CMD cmd))::$outs$)) $\Longleftrightarrow$
  $inputTest$ (P says prop (CMD cmd)) $\wedge$
  CFGInterpret (M,Oi,Os)
    (CFG $inputTest$ $stateInterp$ $certs$
      (P says prop (CMD cmd)::ins) s $outs$)

[TRrule1]

$\vdash$ TR (M,Oi,Os) (trap (CMD cmd))
    (CFG $inputTest$ $stateInterp$ $certs$

$(P$ says prop (CMD cmd)::ins) s $outs$)
$(CFG$ $inputTest$ $stateInterp$ $certs$ ins
$(NS$ s (trap (CMD cmd)))
$(Out$ s (trap (CMD cmd)))::$outs$)) $\iff$
$inputTest$ (P says prop (CMD cmd)) $\land$
CFGInterpret (M, Oi, Os)
$(CFG$ $inputTest$ $stateInterp$ $certs$
$(P$ says prop (CMD cmd)::ins) s $outs$)

[trType_distinct_clauses]

$\vdash$ ($\forall a$. discard $\neq$ trap a) $\land$ ($\forall a$. discard $\neq$ exec a) $\land$
($\forall a'$ a. trap a $\neq$ exec a') $\land$ ($\forall a$. trap a $\neq$ discard) $\land$
($\forall a$. exec a $\neq$ discard) $\land$ $\forall a'$ a. exec a' $\neq$ trap a

7 vm2a Theory

Built: 28 January 2016

Parent Theories: vm1a

7.1 Datatypes

$configuration_2$ =
CFG2 ('input -> ('command inst, 'principal, 'd, 'e) Form)
('cert -> ('command inst, 'principal, 'd, 'e) Form)
(('command inst, 'principal, 'd, 'e) Form -> bool)
('cert list)
('state -> ('command inst, 'principal, 'd, 'e) Form)
('input list) 'state ('output list)

7.2 Definitions

[CFG2Interpret_def]

$\vdash$ CFG2Interpret (M, Oi, Os)
$(CFG2$ $inputInterpret$ $certInterpret$ $inputTest$ $certs$
$stateInterpret$ (x::ins) $state$ $outStream$) $\iff$
(M, Oi, Os) satList MAP $certInterpret$ $certs$ $\land$
(M, Oi, Os) sat $inputInterpret$ x $\land$
(M, Oi, Os) sat $stateInterpret$ $state$

[TR2_def]

$\vdash$ TR2 =
(λa_0 a_1 a_2 a_3.
$\forall TR_2'$.
($\forall a_0$ a_1 a_2 a_3.
($\exists inputInterpret$ $certInterpret$ $inputTest$ x NS M Oi Os
Out $state$ $certs$ $stateInterpret$ cmd ins $outStream$.
(a_0 = (M, Oi, Os)) $\land$ (a_1 = exec (CMD cmd)) $\land$

$(a_2 =$

  CFG2 *inputInterpret certInterpret inputTest certs*
    stateInterpret $(x::ins)$ *state outStream*) $\wedge$

$(a_3 =$

  CFG2 *inputInterpret certInterpret inputTest certs*
    stateInterpret ins (*NS state* (exec (CMD *cmd*)))
    (*Out state* (exec (CMD *cmd*))::*outStream*)) $\wedge$

inputTest (*inputInterpret x*) $\wedge$

CFG2Interpret (M, Oi, Os)

  (CFG2 *inputInterpret certInterpret inputTest*
    certs stateInterpret $(x::ins)$ *state*
    outStream)) $\vee$

($\exists$ *inputInterpret certInterpret inputTest x NS M Oi Os*
  Out state certs stateInterpret cmd ins outStream.

  $(a_0 = (M, Oi, Os)) \wedge (a_1 = $ trap (CMD *cmd*)) $\wedge$

  $(a_2 =$

    CFG2 *inputInterpret certInterpret inputTest certs*
      stateInterpret $(x::ins)$ *state outStream*) $\wedge$

  $(a_3 =$

    CFG2 *inputInterpret certInterpret inputTest certs*
      stateInterpret ins (*NS state* (trap (CMD *cmd*)))
      (*Out state* (trap (CMD *cmd*))::*outStream*)) $\wedge$

  inputTest (*inputInterpret x*) $\wedge$

  CFG2Interpret (M, Oi, Os)

    (CFG2 *inputInterpret certInterpret inputTest*
      certs stateInterpret $(x::ins)$ *state*
      outStream)) $\vee$

($\exists$ *inputInterpret certInterpret inputTest x NS M Oi Os*
  Out state certs stateInterpret cmd ins outStream.

  $(a_0 = (M, Oi, Os)) \wedge (a_1 = $ discard) $\wedge$

  $(a_2 =$

    CFG2 *inputInterpret certInterpret inputTest certs*
      stateInterpret $(x::ins)$ *state outStream*) $\wedge$

  $(a_3 =$

    CFG2 *inputInterpret certInterpret inputTest certs*
      stateInterpret ins (*NS state* discard)
      (*Out state* discard::*outStream*)) $\wedge$

  $\neg$*inputTest* (*inputInterpret x*)) $\Rightarrow$

TR_2' a_0 a_1 a_2 a_3) $\Rightarrow$

TR_2' a_0 a_1 a_2 a_3)

7.3 Theorems

[TR2_cases]

$\vdash \forall a_0$ a_1 a_2 a_3.

  TR2 a_0 a_1 a_2 a_3 $\Longleftrightarrow$

    ($\exists$ *inputInterpret certInterpret inputTest x NS M Oi Os Out*
      state certs stateInterpret cmd ins outStream.

      $(a_0 = (M, Oi, Os)) \wedge (a_1 = $ exec (CMD *cmd*)) $\wedge$

$(a_2 =$
  CFG2 *inputInterpret certInterpret inputTest certs*
    stateInterpret $(x::ins)$ *state outStream*$) \wedge$
$(a_3 =$
  CFG2 *inputInterpret certInterpret ins* $(NS$ *state* $(\texttt{exec } (\texttt{CMD } cmd)))$
    $(Out$ *state* $(\texttt{exec } (\texttt{CMD } cmd)))::outStream)) \wedge$
inputTest $(inputInterpret\ x) \wedge$
CFG2Interpret (M, Oi, Os)
  $(CFG2$ *inputInterpret certInterpret inputTest certs*
    stateInterpret $(x::ins)$ *state outStream*$)) \vee$
$(\exists inputInterpret\ certInterpret\ inputTest\ x\ NS\ M\ Oi\ Os\ Out$
  state certs stateInterpret cmd ins outStream.
  $(a_0 = (M, Oi, Os)) \wedge (a_1 = \texttt{trap } (\texttt{CMD } cmd)) \wedge$
  $(a_2 =$
    CFG2 *inputInterpret certInterpret inputTest certs*
      stateInterpret $(x::ins)$ *state outStream*$) \wedge$
  $(a_3 =$
    CFG2 *inputInterpret certInterpret inputTest certs*
      stateInterpret ins $(NS$ *state* $(\texttt{trap } (\texttt{CMD } cmd)))$
      $(Out$ *state* $(\texttt{trap } (\texttt{CMD } cmd)))::outStream)) \wedge$
  inputTest $(inputInterpret\ x) \wedge$
  CFG2Interpret (M, Oi, Os)
    $(CFG2$ *inputInterpret certInterpret inputTest certs*
      stateInterpret $(x::ins)$ *state outStream*$)) \vee$
$\exists inputInterpret\ certInterpret\ inputTest\ x\ NS\ M\ Oi\ Os\ Out$
  state certs stateInterpret cmd ins outStream.
  $(a_0 = (M, Oi, Os)) \wedge (a_1 = \texttt{discard}) \wedge$
  $(a_2 =$
    CFG2 *inputInterpret certInterpret inputTest certs*
      stateInterpret $(x::ins)$ *state outStream*$) \wedge$
  $(a_3 =$
    CFG2 *inputInterpret certInterpret inputTest certs*
      stateInterpret ins $(NS$ *state* $\texttt{discard})$
      $(Out$ *state* $\texttt{discard}::outStream)) \wedge$
  $\neg inputTest$ $(inputInterpret\ x)$

$\lfloor$TR2_discard_cmd_rule$\rfloor$

$\vdash$ TR2 (M, Oi, Os) discard
  $(CFG2$ *inputInterpret certInterpret inputTest certs*
    stateInterpret $(x::ins)$ *state outStream*$)$
  $(CFG2$ *inputInterpret certInterpret inputTest certs*
    stateInterpret ins $(NS$ *state* $\texttt{discard})$
    $(Out$ *state* $\texttt{discard}::outStream)) \Longleftrightarrow$
  $\neg inputTest$ $(inputInterpret\ x)$

$\lfloor$TR2_EQ_rules_thm$\rfloor$

$\vdash$ (TR2 (M, Oi, Os) $(\texttt{exec } (\texttt{CMD } cmd))$)
  $(CFG2$ *inputInterpret certInterpret inputTest certs*

$stateInterpret\ (x::ins)\ state\ outStream)$
$(\text{CFG2}\ inputInterpret\ certInterpret\ inputTest\ certs$
$stateInterpret\ ins\ (NS\ state\ (\text{exec}\ (\text{CMD}\ cmd)))$
$(Out\ state\ (\text{exec}\ (\text{CMD}\ cmd))::outStream))\ \Longleftrightarrow$
$inputTest\ (inputInterpret\ x)\ \wedge$
$\text{CFG2Interpret}\ (M,Oi,Os)$
$(\text{CFG2}\ inputInterpret\ certInterpret\ inputTest\ certs$
$stateInterpret\ (x::ins)\ state\ outStream))\ \wedge$
$(\text{TR2}\ (M,Oi,Os)\ (\text{trap}\ (\text{CMD}\ cmd))$
$(\text{CFG2}\ inputInterpret\ certInterpret\ inputTest\ certs$
$stateInterpret\ (x::ins)\ state\ outStream)$
$(\text{CFG2}\ inputInterpret\ certInterpret\ inputTest\ certs$
$stateInterpret\ ins\ (NS\ state\ (\text{trap}\ (\text{CMD}\ cmd)))$
$(Out\ state\ (\text{trap}\ (\text{CMD}\ cmd))::outStream))\ \Longleftrightarrow$
$inputTest\ (inputInterpret\ x)\ \wedge$
$\text{CFG2Interpret}\ (M,Oi,Os)$
$(\text{CFG2}\ inputInterpret\ certInterpret\ inputTest\ certs$
$stateInterpret\ (x::ins)\ state\ outStream))\ \wedge$
$(\text{TR2}\ (M,Oi,Os)\ \text{discard}$
$(\text{CFG2}\ inputInterpret\ certInterpret\ inputTest\ certs$
$stateInterpret\ (x::ins)\ state\ outStream)$
$(\text{CFG2}\ inputInterpret\ certInterpret\ inputTest\ certs$
$stateInterpret\ ins\ (NS\ state\ \text{discard})$
$(Out\ state\ \text{discard}::outStream))\ \Longleftrightarrow$
$\neg inputTest\ (inputInterpret\ x))$

⌈TR2_exec_cmd_rule⌋
$\vdash\ \forall inputInterpret\ certInterpret\ inputTest\ certs\ stateInterpret$
$x\ cmd\ ins\ state\ outStream.$
$(\forall M\ Oi\ Os.$
$\text{CFG2Interpret}\ (M,Oi,Os)$
$(\text{CFG2}\ inputInterpret\ certInterpret\ inputTest\ certs$
$stateInterpret\ (x::ins)\ state\ outStream)\ \Rightarrow$
$(M,Oi,Os)\ \text{sat prop}\ (\text{CMD}\ cmd))\ \Rightarrow$
$\forall NS\ Out\ M\ Oi\ Os.$
$\text{TR2}\ (M,Oi,Os)\ (\text{exec}\ (\text{CMD}\ cmd))$
$(\text{CFG2}\ inputInterpret\ certInterpret\ inputTest\ certs$
$stateInterpret\ (x::ins)\ state\ outStream)$
$(\text{CFG2}\ inputInterpret\ certInterpret\ inputTest\ certs$
$stateInterpret\ ins\ (NS\ state\ (\text{exec}\ (\text{CMD}\ cmd)))$
$(Out\ state\ (\text{exec}\ (\text{CMD}\ cmd))::outStream))\ \Longleftrightarrow$
$inputTest\ (inputInterpret\ x)\ \wedge$
$\text{CFG2Interpret}\ (M,Oi,Os)$
$(\text{CFG2}\ inputInterpret\ certInterpret\ inputTest\ certs$
$stateInterpret\ (x::ins)\ state\ outStream)\ \wedge$
$(M,Oi,Os)\ \text{sat prop}\ (\text{CMD}\ cmd)$

⌈TR2_iff_TR_discard_thm⌋
$\vdash\ \forall NS\ Out\ outStream\ state\ certs\ certs_2\ ins\ ins_2\ stateInterpret$
$inputInterpret\ certInterpret\ inputTest.$

TR2 (M, Oi, Os) discard
  (CFG2 *inputInterpret certInterpret inputTest certs*$_2$
    stateInterpret $(x::ins_2)$ *state outStream*)
  (CFG2 *inputInterpret certInterpret inputTest certs*$_2$
    stateInterpret ins$_2$ (*NS state* discard)
    (*Out state* discard::*outStream*)) $\Longleftrightarrow$
TR (M, Oi, Os) discard
  (CFG *inputTest stateInterpret certs*
    (*inputInterpret* $x::ins$) *state outStream*)
  (CFG *inputTest stateInterpret certs ins*
    (*NS state* discard) (*Out state* discard::*outStream*))

[TR2_ind]

$\vdash \forall TR_2'.$
  ($\forall$ *inputInterpret certInterpret inputTest x NS M Oi Os Out*
    state certs stateInterpret cmd ins outStream.
    inputTest (*inputInterpret x*) $\wedge$
    CFG2Interpret (M, Oi, Os)
      (CFG2 *inputInterpret certInterpret inputTest certs*
        stateInterpret $(x::ins)$ *state outStream*) $\Rightarrow$
    TR_2' (M, Oi, Os) (exec (CMD *cmd*))
      (CFG2 *inputInterpret certInterpret inputTest certs*
        stateInterpret $(x::ins)$ *state outStream*)
      (CFG2 *inputInterpret certInterpret inputTest certs*
        stateInterpret ins (*NS state* (exec (CMD *cmd*)))
        (*Out state* (exec (CMD *cmd*))::*outStream*))) $\wedge$
  ($\forall$ *inputInterpret certInterpret inputTest x NS M Oi Os Out*
    state certs stateInterpret cmd ins outStream.
    inputTest (*inputInterpret x*) $\wedge$
    CFG2Interpret (M, Oi, Os)
      (CFG2 *inputInterpret certInterpret inputTest certs*
        stateInterpret $(x::ins)$ *state outStream*) $\Rightarrow$
    TR_2' (M, Oi, Os) (trap (CMD *cmd*))
      (CFG2 *inputInterpret certInterpret inputTest certs*
        stateInterpret $(x::ins)$ *state outStream*)
      (CFG2 *inputInterpret certInterpret inputTest certs*
        stateInterpret ins (*NS state* (trap (CMD *cmd*)))
        (*Out state* (trap (CMD *cmd*))::*outStream*))) $\wedge$
  ($\forall$ *inputInterpret certInterpret inputTest x NS M Oi Os Out*
    state certs stateInterpret cmd ins outStream.
    $\neg$*inputTest* (*inputInterpret x*) $\Rightarrow$
    TR_2' (M, Oi, Os) discard
      (CFG2 *inputInterpret certInterpret inputTest certs*
        stateInterpret $(x::ins)$ *state outStream*)
      (CFG2 *inputInterpret certInterpret inputTest certs*
        stateInterpret ins (*NS state* discard)
        (*Out state* discard::*outStream*))) $\Rightarrow$
  $\forall a_0 \ a_1 \ a_2 \ a_3$. TR2 $a_0 \ a_1 \ a_2 \ a_3 \Rightarrow TR_2' \ a_0 \ a_1 \ a_2 \ a_3$

[TR2_rules]

⊢ (∀ *inputInterpret certInterpret inputTest x NS M Oi Os Out*
    state certs stateInterpret cmd ins outStream.
    inputTest (*inputInterpret x*) ∧
    CFG2Interpret (*M,Oi,Os*)
      (CFG2 *inputInterpret certInterpret inputTest certs*
        stateInterpret (*x::ins*) *state outStream*) ⇒
    TR2 (*M,Oi,Os*) (exec (CMD *cmd*))
      (CFG2 *inputInterpret certInterpret inputTest certs*
        stateInterpret (*x::ins*) *state outStream*)
      (CFG2 *inputInterpret certInterpret inputTest certs*
        stateInterpret ins (*NS state* (exec (CMD *cmd*)))
        (*Out state* (exec (CMD *cmd*))::*outStream*))) ∧
  (∀ *inputInterpret certInterpret inputTest x NS M Oi Os Out*
    state certs stateInterpret cmd ins outStream.
    inputTest (*inputInterpret x*) ∧
    CFG2Interpret (*M,Oi,Os*)
      (CFG2 *inputInterpret certInterpret inputTest certs*
        stateInterpret (*x::ins*) *state outStream*) ⇒
    TR2 (*M,Oi,Os*) (trap (CMD *cmd*))
      (CFG2 *inputInterpret certInterpret inputTest certs*
        stateInterpret (*x::ins*) *state outStream*)
      (CFG2 *inputInterpret certInterpret inputTest certs*
        stateInterpret ins (*NS state* (trap (CMD *cmd*)))
        (*Out state* (trap (CMD *cmd*))::*outStream*))) ∧
  ∀ *inputInterpret certInterpret inputTest x NS M Oi Os Out*
    state certs stateInterpret cmd ins outStream.
    ¬*inputTest* (*inputInterpret x*) ⇒
    TR2 (*M,Oi,Os*) discard
      (CFG2 *inputInterpret certInterpret inputTest certs*
        stateInterpret (*x::ins*) *state outStream*)
      (CFG2 *inputInterpret certInterpret inputTest certs*
        stateInterpret ins (*NS state* discard)
        (*Out state* discard::*outStream*))

[TR2_strongind]

⊢ ∀ TR_2'.
    (∀ *inputInterpret certInterpret inputTest x NS M Oi Os Out*
      state certs stateInterpret cmd ins outStream.
      inputTest (*inputInterpret x*) ∧
      CFG2Interpret (*M,Oi,Os*)
        (CFG2 *inputInterpret certInterpret inputTest certs*
          stateInterpret (*x::ins*) *state outStream*) ⇒
      TR_2' (*M,Oi,Os*) (exec (CMD *cmd*))
        (CFG2 *inputInterpret certInterpret inputTest certs*
          stateInterpret (*x::ins*) *state outStream*)
        (CFG2 *inputInterpret certInterpret inputTest certs*
          stateInterpret ins (*NS state* (exec (CMD *cmd*)))
          (*Out state* (exec (CMD *cmd*))::*outStream*))) ∧

$(\forall\, inputInterpret\ certInterpret\ inputTest\ x\ NS\ M\ Oi\ Os\ Out$
$state\ certs\ stateInterpret\ cmd\ ins\ outStream\,.$
$inputTest\ (inputInterpret\ x)\ \wedge$
$\text{CFG2Interpret}\ (M,Oi,Os)$
$\quad(\text{CFG2}\ inputInterpret\ certInterpret\ inputTest\ certs$
$\quad\quad stateInterpret\ (x::ins)\ state\ outStream)\ \Rightarrow$
$TR_2'\ (M,Oi,Os)\ (\text{trap}\ (\text{CMD}\ cmd))$
$\quad(\text{CFG2}\ inputInterpret\ certInterpret\ inputTest\ certs$
$\quad\quad stateInterpret\ (x::ins)\ state\ outStream)$
$\quad(\text{CFG2}\ inputInterpret\ certInterpret\ inputTest\ certs$
$\quad\quad stateInterpret\ ins\ (NS\ state\ (\text{trap}\ (\text{CMD}\ cmd)))$
$\quad\quad(Out\ state\ (\text{trap}\ (\text{CMD}\ cmd))::outStream)))\ \wedge$
$(\forall\, inputInterpret\ certInterpret\ inputTest\ x\ NS\ M\ Oi\ Os\ Out$
$state\ certs\ stateInterpret\ ins\ outStream\,.$
$\neg inputTest\ (inputInterpret\ x)\ \Rightarrow$
$TR_2'\ (M,Oi,Os)\ \text{discard}$
$\quad(\text{CFG2}\ inputInterpret\ certInterpret\ inputTest\ certs$
$\quad\quad stateInterpret\ (x::ins)\ state\ outStream)$
$\quad(\text{CFG2}\ inputInterpret\ certInterpret\ inputTest\ certs$
$\quad\quad stateInterpret\ ins\ (NS\ state\ \text{discard})$
$\quad\quad(Out\ state\ \text{discard}::outStream)))\ \Rightarrow$
$\forall\, a_0\ a_1\ a_2\ a_3.\ \text{TR2}\ a_0\ a_1\ a_2\ a_3\ \Rightarrow\ TR_2'\ a_0\ a_1\ a_2\ a_3$

$\lfloor\text{TR2\_trap\_cmd\_rule}\rfloor$

$\vdash\ \forall\, inputInterpret\ certInterpret\ inputTest\ certs\ stateInterpret$
$x\ cmd\ ins\ state\ outStream\,.$
$(\forall\, M\ Oi\ Os\,.$
$\quad\text{CFG2Interpret}\ (M,Oi,Os)$
$\quad\quad(\text{CFG2}\ inputInterpret\ certInterpret\ inputTest\ certs$
$\quad\quad\quad stateInterpret\ (x::ins)\ state\ outStream)\ \Rightarrow$
$\quad(M,Oi,Os)\ \text{sat prop TRAP})\ \Rightarrow$
$\forall\, NS\ Out\ M\ Oi\ Os\,.$
$\quad\text{TR2}\ (M,Oi,Os)\ (\text{trap}\ (\text{CMD}\ cmd))$
$\quad\quad(\text{CFG2}\ inputInterpret\ certInterpret\ inputTest\ certs$
$\quad\quad\quad stateInterpret\ (x::ins)\ state\ outStream)$
$\quad\quad(\text{CFG2}\ inputInterpret\ certInterpret\ inputTest\ certs$
$\quad\quad\quad stateInterpret\ ins\ (NS\ state\ (\text{trap}\ (\text{CMD}\ cmd)))$
$\quad\quad\quad(Out\ state\ (\text{trap}\ (\text{CMD}\ cmd))::outStream))\ \Longleftrightarrow$
$\quad inputTest\ (inputInterpret\ x)\ \wedge$
$\quad\text{CFG2Interpret}\ (M,Oi,Os)$
$\quad\quad(\text{CFG2}\ inputInterpret\ certInterpret\ inputTest\ certs$
$\quad\quad\quad stateInterpret\ (x::ins)\ state\ outStream)\ \wedge$
$\quad(M,Oi,Os)\ \text{sat prop TRAP}$

$\lfloor\text{TR2rule0}\rfloor$

$\vdash\ \text{TR2}\ (M,Oi,Os)\ (\text{exec}\ (\text{CMD}\ cmd))$
$\quad(\text{CFG2}\ inputInterpret\ certInterpret\ inputTest\ certs$
$\quad\quad stateInterpret\ (x::ins)\ state\ outStream)$
$\quad(\text{CFG2}\ inputInterpret\ certInterpret\ inputTest\ certs$

$$stateInterpret\ ins\ (NS\ state\ (exec\ (CMD\ cmd)))$$
$$(Out\ state\ (exec\ (CMD\ cmd))::outStream)) \iff$$
$$inputTest\ (inputInterpret\ x) \land$$
$$CFG2Interpret\ (M,Oi,Os)$$
$$(CFG2\ inputInterpret\ certInterpret\ inputTest\ certs$$
$$stateInterpret\ (x::ins)\ state\ outStream)$$

|TR2rule1|

$\vdash$ TR2 (M,Oi,Os) (trap (CMD cmd))
$$(CFG2\ inputInterpret\ certInterpret\ inputTest\ certs$$
$$stateInterpret\ (x::ins)\ state\ outStream)$$
$$(CFG2\ inputInterpret\ certInterpret\ inputTest\ certs$$
$$stateInterpret\ ins\ (NS\ state\ (trap\ (CMD\ cmd)))$$
$$(Out\ state\ (trap\ (CMD\ cmd))::outStream)) \iff$$
$$inputTest\ (inputInterpret\ x) \land$$
$$CFG2Interpret\ (M,Oi,Os)$$
$$(CFG2\ inputInterpret\ certInterpret\ inputTest\ certs$$
$$stateInterpret\ (x::ins)\ state\ outStream)$$

8 thermo1 Theory

Built: 28 January 2016

Parent Theories: vm1a, principal, command

8.1 Datatypes

$mode$ = enabled | disabled

$output$ = report state | flag command | null

$state$ = State mode num

8.2 Definitions

|isAuthenticated_def|

$\vdash$ (isAuthenticated
   (Name Keyboard quoting Name (Owner $ownerID$) says
   prop (CMD cmd)) $\iff$ T) $\land$
  (isAuthenticated
   (Name (Key (pubK Server)) quoting
   Name (Owner $ownerID$) says prop (CMD cmd)) $\iff$ T) $\land$
  (isAuthenticated
   (Name (Key (pubK Server)) quoting
   Name (Role (Utility $utilityID$)) says prop (CMD cmd)) $\iff$
  T) $\land$ (isAuthenticated TT $\iff$ F) $\land$ (isAuthenticated FF $\iff$ F) $\land$
  (isAuthenticated (prop v) $\iff$ F) $\land$
  (isAuthenticated (notf v_1) $\iff$ F) $\land$

$(\text{isAuthenticated } (v_2 \text{ andf } v_3) \iff \text{F}) \wedge$

$(\text{isAuthenticated } (v_4 \text{ orf } v_5) \iff \text{F}) \wedge$

$(\text{isAuthenticated } (v_6 \text{ impf } v_7) \iff \text{F}) \wedge$

$(\text{isAuthenticated } (v_8 \text{ eqf } v_9) \iff \text{F}) \wedge$

$(\text{isAuthenticated } (v_{10} \text{ says TT}) \iff \text{F}) \wedge$

$(\text{isAuthenticated } (v_{10} \text{ says FF}) \iff \text{F}) \wedge$

$(\text{isAuthenticated } (\text{Name } v132 \text{ says prop } v_{66}) \iff \text{F}) \wedge$

$(\text{isAuthenticated } (v133 \text{ meet } v134 \text{ says prop } v_{66}) \iff \text{F}) \wedge$

(isAuthenticated
   (Name (Role $v174$) quoting Name (Role $v164$) says
      prop (CMD $v142$)) $\iff$ F) $\wedge$

(isAuthenticated
   (Name (Key $v175$) quoting Name (Role CA) says
      prop (CMD $v142$)) $\iff$ F) $\wedge$

(isAuthenticated
   (Name (Key $v175$) quoting Name (Role Server) says
      prop (CMD $v142$)) $\iff$ F) $\wedge$

(isAuthenticated
   (Name (Key (pubK CA)) quoting
   Name (Role (Utility $v184$)) says prop (CMD $v142$)) $\iff$ F) $\wedge$

(isAuthenticated
   (Name (Key (pubK (Utility $v190$))) quoting
   Name (Role (Utility $v184$)) says prop (CMD $v142$)) $\iff$ F) $\wedge$

(isAuthenticated
   (Name (Key (privK $v187$)) quoting
   Name (Role (Utility $v184$)) says prop (CMD $v142$)) $\iff$ F) $\wedge$

(isAuthenticated
   (Name Keyboard quoting Name (Role $v164$) says
      prop (CMD $v142$)) $\iff$ F) $\wedge$

(isAuthenticated
   (Name (Owner $v176$) quoting Name (Role $v164$) says
      prop (CMD $v142$)) $\iff$ F) $\wedge$

(isAuthenticated
   (Name (Account $v177$ $v178$) quoting Name (Role $v164$) says
      prop (CMD $v142$)) $\iff$ F) $\wedge$

(isAuthenticated
   (Name $v154$ quoting Name (Key $v165$) says
      prop (CMD $v142$)) $\iff$ F) $\wedge$

(isAuthenticated
   (Name $v154$ quoting Name Keyboard says prop (CMD $v142$)) $\iff$
   F) $\wedge$

(isAuthenticated
   (Name (Role $v192$) quoting Name (Owner $v166$) says
      prop (CMD $v142$)) $\iff$ F) $\wedge$

(isAuthenticated
   (Name (Key (pubK CA)) quoting Name (Owner $v166$) says
      prop (CMD $v142$)) $\iff$ F) $\wedge$

(isAuthenticated
   (Name (Key (pubK (Utility $v206$))) quoting

```
      Name (Owner v166) says prop (CMD v142)) ⟺ F) ∧
(isAuthenticated
   (Name (Key (privK v203)) quoting Name (Owner v166) says
    prop (CMD v142)) ⟺ F) ∧
(isAuthenticated
   (Name (Owner v194) quoting Name (Owner v166) says
    prop (CMD v142)) ⟺ F) ∧
(isAuthenticated
   (Name (Account v195 v196) quoting Name (Owner v166) says
    prop (CMD v142)) ⟺ F) ∧
(isAuthenticated
   (Name v154 quoting Name (Account v167 v168) says
    prop (CMD v142)) ⟺ F) ∧
(isAuthenticated
   (v155 meet v156 quoting Name v144 says prop (CMD v142)) ⟺
 F) ∧
(isAuthenticated
   ((v157 quoting v158) quoting Name v144 says
    prop (CMD v142)) ⟺ F) ∧
(isAuthenticated
   (v135 quoting v145 meet v146 says prop (CMD v142)) ⟺ F) ∧
(isAuthenticated
   (v135 quoting v147 quoting v148 says prop (CMD v142)) ⟺
 F) ∧
(isAuthenticated (v135 quoting v136 says prop TRAP) ⟺ F) ∧
(isAuthenticated (v10 says notf v67) ⟺ F) ∧
(isAuthenticated (v10 says (v68 andf v69)) ⟺ F) ∧
(isAuthenticated (v10 says (v70 orf v71)) ⟺ F) ∧
(isAuthenticated (v10 says (v72 impf v73)) ⟺ F) ∧
(isAuthenticated (v10 says (v74 eqf v75)) ⟺ F) ∧
(isAuthenticated (v10 says v76 says v77) ⟺ F) ∧
(isAuthenticated (v10 says v78 speaks_for v79) ⟺ F) ∧
(isAuthenticated (v10 says v80 controls v81) ⟺ F) ∧
(isAuthenticated (v10 says reps v82 v83 v84) ⟺ F) ∧
(isAuthenticated (v10 says v85 domi v86) ⟺ F) ∧
(isAuthenticated (v10 says v87 eqi v88) ⟺ F) ∧
(isAuthenticated (v10 says v89 doms v90) ⟺ F) ∧
(isAuthenticated (v10 says v91 eqs v92) ⟺ F) ∧
(isAuthenticated (v10 says v93 eqn v94) ⟺ F) ∧
(isAuthenticated (v10 says v95 lte v96) ⟺ F) ∧
(isAuthenticated (v10 says v97 lt v98) ⟺ F) ∧
(isAuthenticated (v12 speaks_for v13) ⟺ F) ∧
(isAuthenticated (v14 controls v15) ⟺ F) ∧
(isAuthenticated (reps v16 v17 v18) ⟺ F) ∧
(isAuthenticated (v19 domi v20) ⟺ F) ∧
(isAuthenticated (v21 eqi v22) ⟺ F) ∧
(isAuthenticated (v23 doms v24) ⟺ F) ∧
(isAuthenticated (v25 eqs v26) ⟺ F) ∧
(isAuthenticated (v27 eqn v28) ⟺ F) ∧
```

$$(\text{isAuthenticated } (v_{29} \text{ lte } v_{30}) \iff \text{F}) \wedge$$
$$(\text{isAuthenticated } (v_{31} \text{ lt } v_{32}) \iff \text{F})$$

[mode_CASE]

$\vdash \forall x \; v_0 \; v_1.$

$(\textbf{case } x \textbf{ of } \text{enabled} \Rightarrow v_0 \mid \text{disabled} \Rightarrow v_1) =$
$(\lambda m. \textbf{ if } m = 0 \textbf{ then } v_0 \textbf{ else } v_1) \; (\text{mode2num } x)$

[thermo1NS_def]

$\vdash (\text{thermo1NS } (\text{State } opMode \; temp) \; \text{discard} = \text{State } opMode \; temp) \wedge$
$\quad (\text{thermo1NS } (\text{State } opMode \; temp)$
$\qquad (\text{exec } (\text{CMD } (\text{PR } (\text{Set } newTemp)))) =$
$\quad \text{State } opMode \; newTemp) \wedge$
$\quad (\text{thermo1NS } (\text{State } opMode \; temp) \; (\text{exec } (\text{CMD } (\text{PR } \text{EU}))) =$
$\quad \text{State enabled } temp) \wedge$
$\quad (\text{thermo1NS } (\text{State } opMode \; temp) \; (\text{exec } (\text{CMD } (\text{PR } \text{DU}))) =$
$\quad \text{State disabled } temp) \wedge$
$\quad (\text{thermo1NS } (\text{State } opMode \; temp) \; (\text{exec } (\text{CMD } (\text{NP } \text{Status}))) =$
$\quad \text{State } opMode \; temp) \wedge$
$\quad (\text{thermo1NS } (\text{State } opMode \; temp)$
$\qquad (\text{trap } (\text{CMD } (\text{PR } (\text{Set } newTemp)))) =$
$\quad \text{State } opMode \; temp) \wedge$
$\quad (\text{thermo1NS } (\text{State } opMode \; temp) \; (\text{trap } (\text{CMD } (\text{PR } \text{EU}))) =$
$\quad \text{State } opMode \; temp) \wedge$
$\quad (\text{thermo1NS } (\text{State } opMode \; temp) \; (\text{trap } (\text{CMD } (\text{PR } \text{DU}))) =$
$\quad \text{State } opMode \; temp)$

[thermo1Out_def]

$\vdash (\text{thermo1Out } (\text{State enabled } temp)$
$\qquad (\text{exec } (\text{CMD } (\text{PR } (\text{Set } newTemp)))) =$
$\quad \text{report } (\text{State enabled } newTemp)) \wedge$
$\quad (\text{thermo1Out } (\text{State disabled } temp)$
$\qquad (\text{exec } (\text{CMD } (\text{PR } (\text{Set } newTemp)))) =$
$\quad \text{report } (\text{State disabled } newTemp)) \wedge$
$\quad (\text{thermo1Out } (\text{State enabled } temp) \; (\text{exec } (\text{CMD } (\text{PR } \text{EU}))) =$
$\quad \text{report } (\text{State enabled } temp)) \wedge$
$\quad (\text{thermo1Out } (\text{State disabled } temp) \; (\text{exec } (\text{CMD } (\text{PR } \text{EU}))) =$
$\quad \text{report } (\text{State enabled } temp)) \wedge$
$\quad (\text{thermo1Out } (\text{State enabled } temp) \; (\text{exec } (\text{CMD } (\text{PR } \text{DU}))) =$
$\quad \text{report } (\text{State disabled } temp)) \wedge$
$\quad (\text{thermo1Out } (\text{State disabled } temp) \; (\text{exec } (\text{CMD } (\text{PR } \text{DU}))) =$
$\quad \text{report } (\text{State disabled } temp)) \wedge$
$\quad (\text{thermo1Out } (\text{State enabled } temp) \; (\text{exec } (\text{CMD } (\text{NP } \text{Status}))) =$
$\quad \text{report } (\text{State enabled } temp)) \wedge$
$\quad (\text{thermo1Out } (\text{State disabled } temp) \; (\text{exec } (\text{CMD } (\text{NP } \text{Status}))) =$
$\quad \text{report } (\text{State disabled } temp)) \wedge$
$\quad (\text{thermo1Out } (\text{State enabled } temp)$
$\qquad (\text{trap } (\text{CMD } (\text{PR } (\text{Set } newTemp)))) =$

flag (PR (Set *newTemp*))) ∧
(thermo1Out (State disabled *temp*)
  (trap (CMD (PR (Set *newTemp*)))) =
flag (PR (Set *newTemp*))) ∧
(thermo1Out (State enabled *temp*) (trap (CMD (PR EU))) =
flag (PR EU)) ∧
(thermo1Out (State disabled *temp*) (trap (CMD (PR EU))) =
flag (PR EU)) ∧
(thermo1Out (State enabled *temp*) (trap (CMD (PR DU))) =
flag (PR DU)) ∧
(thermo1Out (State disabled *temp*) (trap (CMD (PR DU))) =
flag (PR DU)) ∧
(thermo1Out (State enabled *temp*) discard = null) ∧
(thermo1Out (State disabled *temp*) discard = null)

⌊thermoStateInterp_def⌋

⊢ (thermoStateInterp *utilityID* *privcmd* (State enabled *temp*) =
  Name (Role (Utility *utilityID*)) controls
  prop (CMD (PR *privcmd*))) ∧
  (thermoStateInterp *utilityID* *privcmd* (State disabled *temp*) =
  Name (Role (Utility *utilityID*)) says
  prop (CMD (PR *privcmd*)) impf prop TRAP)

8.3 Theorems

⌊npriv_Safe⌋

⊢ ∀*npriv* *state*. thermo1NS *state* (exec (CMD (NP *npriv*))) = *state*

⌊output_one_one⌋

⊢ (∀*a* *a'*. (report *a* = report *a'*) ⟺ (*a* = *a'*)) ∧
  ∀*a* *a'*. (flag *a* = flag *a'*) ⟺ (*a* = *a'*)

⌊privcmd_Security_Sensitive⌋

⊢ ∀*privcmd*.
    ∃*state*. thermo1NS *state* (exec (CMD (PR *privcmd*))) ≠ *state*

⌊state_one_one⌋

⊢ ∀a_0 a_1 a_0' a_1'.
    (State a_0 a_1 = State a_0' a_1') ⟺ (a_0 = a_0') ∧ (a_1 = a_1')

⌊trap_safe_flag⌋

⊢ ∀*privcmd* *state*.
    (thermo1NS *state* (trap (CMD (PR *privcmd*))) = *state*) ∧
    (thermo1Out *state* (trap (CMD (PR *privcmd*))) =
     flag (PR *privcmd*))

9   thermo1Certs Theory

Built: 28 January 2016
Parent Theories: thermo1

9.1   Definitions

[certs_def]

⊢ ∀ *ownerID utilityID cmd npriv privcmd*.
    certs *ownerID utilityID cmd npriv privcmd* =
    [Name (Owner *ownerID*) controls prop (CMD *cmd*);
    reps (Name Keyboard) (Name (Owner *ownerID*))
      (prop (CMD *cmd*));
    reps (Name (Role Server)) (Name (Owner *ownerID*))
      (prop (CMD *cmd*));
    Name (Role CA) controls
    Name (Key (pubK Server)) speaks_for Name (Role Server);
    Name (Key (pubK CA)) speaks_for Name (Role CA);
    Name (Key (pubK CA)) says
    Name (Key (pubK Server)) speaks_for Name (Role Server);
    reps (Name (Role Server))
      (Name (Role (Utility *utilityID*)))
      (prop (CMD (NP *npriv*)));
    reps (Name (Role Server))
      (Name (Role (Utility *utilityID*)))
      (prop (CMD (PR *privcmd*)));
    Name (Role (Utility *utilityID*)) controls
    prop (CMD (NP *npriv*))]

9.2   Theorems

[CA_Server_key_lemma]

⊢ (M, Oi, Os) sat
  Name (Role CA) controls
  Name (Key (pubK Server)) speaks_for Name (Role Server) ⇒
  (M, Oi, Os) sat
  Name (Key (pubK CA)) speaks_for Name (Role CA) ⇒
  (M, Oi, Os) sat
  Name (Key (pubK CA)) says
  Name (Key (pubK Server)) speaks_for Name (Role Server) ⇒
  (M, Oi, Os) sat
  Name (Key (pubK Server)) speaks_for Name (Role Server)

[CFGInterpret_exec_Keyboard_Owner_cmd]

⊢ ∀ *NS Out outs s ins npriv privcmd cmd ownerID utilityID M Oi*
    Os.
    CFGInterpret (M, Oi, Os)

```
    (CFG isAuthenticated
      (thermoStateInterp utilityID privcmd)
      (certs ownerID utilityID cmd npriv privcmd)
      (Name Keyboard quoting Name (Owner ownerID) says
       prop (CMD cmd)::ins) s outs) ⇒
  TR (M,Oi,Os) (exec (CMD cmd))
    (CFG isAuthenticated
      (thermoStateInterp utilityID privcmd)
      (certs ownerID utilityID cmd npriv privcmd)
      (Name Keyboard quoting Name (Owner ownerID) says
       prop (CMD cmd)::ins) s outs)
    (CFG isAuthenticated
      (thermoStateInterp utilityID privcmd)
      (certs ownerID utilityID cmd npriv privcmd) ins
      (NS s (exec (CMD cmd)))
      (Out s (exec (CMD cmd))::outs)) ∧
  (M,Oi,Os) sat prop (CMD cmd)
```

⌈CFGInterpret_exec_KServer_Owner_cmd⌋

```
⊢ ∀NS Out outs s ins npriv privcmd cmd ownerID utilityID M Oi
    Os .
  CFGInterpret (M,Oi,Os)
    (CFG isAuthenticated
      (thermoStateInterp utilityID privcmd)
      (certs ownerID utilityID cmd npriv privcmd)
      (Name (Key (pubK Server)) quoting
       Name (Owner ownerID) says prop (CMD cmd)::ins) s
      outs) ⇒
  TR (M,Oi,Os) (exec (CMD cmd))
    (CFG isAuthenticated
      (thermoStateInterp utilityID privcmd)
      (certs ownerID utilityID cmd npriv privcmd)
      (Name (Key (pubK Server)) quoting
       Name (Owner ownerID) says prop (CMD cmd)::ins) s
      outs)
    (CFG isAuthenticated
      (thermoStateInterp utilityID privcmd)
      (certs ownerID utilityID cmd npriv privcmd) ins
      (NS s (exec (CMD cmd)))
      (Out s (exec (CMD cmd))::outs)) ∧
  (M,Oi,Os) sat prop (CMD cmd)
```

⌈CFGInterpret_exec_KServer_Utility_npriv⌋

```
⊢ ∀NS Out outs s ins npriv privcmd cmd ownerID utilityID M Oi
    Os .
  CFGInterpret (M,Oi,Os)
    (CFG isAuthenticated
      (thermoStateInterp utilityID privcmd)
      (certs ownerID utilityID cmd npriv privcmd)
```

```
                (Name (Key (pubK Server)) quoting
                 Name (Role (Utility utilityID)) says
                 prop (CMD (NP npriv))::ins) s outs) ⇒
        TR (M,Oi,Os) (exec (CMD (NP npriv)))
          (CFG isAuthenticated
              (thermoStateInterp utilityID privcmd)
              (certs ownerID utilityID cmd npriv privcmd)
              (Name (Key (pubK Server)) quoting
               Name (Role (Utility utilityID)) says
               prop (CMD (NP npriv))::ins) s outs)
            (CFG isAuthenticated
              (thermoStateInterp utilityID privcmd)
              (certs ownerID utilityID cmd npriv privcmd) ins
              (NS s (exec (CMD (NP npriv))))
              (Out s (exec (CMD (NP npriv)))::outs)) ∧
          (M,Oi,Os) sat prop (CMD (NP npriv))
```

⌐CFGInterpret_exec_KServer_Utility_privcmd⌐

```
 ⊢ ∀ NS Out outs temperature ins npriv privcmd cmd ownerID
       utilityID M Oi Os.
     CFGInterpret (M,Oi,Os)
       (CFG isAuthenticated
           (thermoStateInterp utilityID privcmd)
           (certs ownerID utilityID cmd npriv privcmd)
           (Name (Key (pubK Server)) quoting
            Name (Role (Utility utilityID)) says
            prop (CMD (PR privcmd))::ins)
           (State enabled temperature) outs) ⇒
       TR (M,Oi,Os) (exec (CMD (PR privcmd)))
         (CFG isAuthenticated
           (thermoStateInterp utilityID privcmd)
           (certs ownerID utilityID cmd npriv privcmd)
           (Name (Key (pubK Server)) quoting
            Name (Role (Utility utilityID)) says
            prop (CMD (PR privcmd))::ins)
           (State enabled temperature) outs)
         (CFG isAuthenticated
           (thermoStateInterp utilityID privcmd)
           (certs ownerID utilityID cmd npriv privcmd) ins
           (NS (State enabled temperature)
              (exec (CMD (PR privcmd))))
           (Out (State enabled temperature)
              (exec (CMD (PR privcmd)))::outs)) ∧
       (M,Oi,Os) sat prop (CMD (PR privcmd))
```

⌐CFGInterpret_Owner_Keyboard_thm⌐

```
 ⊢ ∀ M Oi Os.
     CFGInterpret (M,Oi,Os)
       (CFG isAuthenticated
```

$\quad$ (thermoStateInterp *utilityID* *privcmd*)
$\quad$ (certs *ownerID* *utilityID* *cmd* *npriv* *privcmd*)
$\quad$ (Name Keyboard quoting Name (Owner *ownerID*) says
$\quad\quad$ prop (CMD *cmd*):: *ins*) *s* *outs*) $\Rightarrow$
$\quad$ (*M*, *Oi*, *Os*) sat prop (CMD *cmd*)

[CFGInterpret_Owner_KServer_thm]

$\vdash \forall M\ Oi\ Os.$
$\quad$ CFGInterpret (*M*, *Oi*, *Os*)
$\quad\quad$ (CFG isAuthenticated
$\quad\quad\quad$ (thermoStateInterp *utilityID* *privcmd*)
$\quad\quad\quad$ (certs *ownerID* *utilityID* *cmd* *npriv* *privcmd*)
$\quad\quad\quad$ (Name (Key (pubK Server)) quoting
$\quad\quad\quad$ Name (Owner *ownerID*) says prop (CMD *cmd*):: *ins*) *s*
$\quad\quad\quad$ *outs*) $\Rightarrow$
$\quad\quad$ (*M*, *Oi*, *Os*) sat prop (CMD *cmd*)

[CFGInterpret_trap_KServer_Utility_privcmd]

$\vdash \forall NS\ Out\ outs\ temperature\ ins\ npriv\ privcmd\ cmd\ ownerID$
$\quad\quad utilityID\ M\ Oi\ Os.$
$\quad$ CFGInterpret (*M*, *Oi*, *Os*)
$\quad\quad$ (CFG isAuthenticated
$\quad\quad\quad$ (thermoStateInterp *utilityID* *privcmd*)
$\quad\quad\quad$ (certs *ownerID* *utilityID* *cmd* *npriv* *privcmd*)
$\quad\quad\quad$ (Name (Key (pubK Server)) quoting
$\quad\quad\quad$ Name (Role (Utility *utilityID*)) says
$\quad\quad\quad$ prop (CMD (PR *privcmd*)):: *ins*)
$\quad\quad\quad$ (State disabled *temperature*) *outs*) $\Rightarrow$
$\quad\quad$ TR (*M*, *Oi*, *Os*) (trap (CMD (PR *privcmd*)))
$\quad\quad\quad$ (CFG isAuthenticated
$\quad\quad\quad\quad$ (thermoStateInterp *utilityID* *privcmd*)
$\quad\quad\quad\quad$ (certs *ownerID* *utilityID* *cmd* *npriv* *privcmd*)
$\quad\quad\quad\quad$ (Name (Key (pubK Server)) quoting
$\quad\quad\quad\quad$ Name (Role (Utility *utilityID*)) says
$\quad\quad\quad\quad$ prop (CMD (PR *privcmd*)):: *ins*)
$\quad\quad\quad\quad$ (State disabled *temperature*) *outs*)
$\quad\quad\quad$ (CFG isAuthenticated
$\quad\quad\quad\quad$ (thermoStateInterp *utilityID* *privcmd*)
$\quad\quad\quad\quad$ (certs *ownerID* *utilityID* *cmd* *npriv* *privcmd*) *ins*
$\quad\quad\quad\quad$ (*NS* (State disabled *temperature*)
$\quad\quad\quad\quad\quad$ (trap (CMD (PR *privcmd*))))
$\quad\quad\quad\quad$ (*Out* (State disabled *temperature*)
$\quad\quad\quad\quad\quad$ (trap (CMD (PR *privcmd*))):: *outs*)) $\wedge$
$\quad\quad$ (*M*, *Oi*, *Os*) sat prop TRAP

[CFGInterpret_Utility_KServer_npriv_thm]

$\vdash \forall M\ Oi\ Os.$
$\quad$ CFGInterpret (*M*, *Oi*, *Os*)

```
        (CFG isAuthenticated
          (thermoStateInterp utilityID privcmd)
          (certs ownerID utilityID cmd npriv privcmd)
          (Name (Key (pubK Server)) quoting
          Name (Role (Utility utilityID)) says
          prop (CMD (NP npriv))::ins) s outs) ⇒
    (M,Oi,Os) sat prop (CMD (NP npriv))
```

[CFGInterpret_Utility_KServer_privcmd_thm]

```
⊢ ∀M Oi Os.
    CFGInterpret (M,Oi,Os)
      (CFG isAuthenticated
        (thermoStateInterp utilityID privcmd)
        (certs ownerID utilityID cmd npriv privcmd)
        (Name (Key (pubK Server)) quoting
        Name (Role (Utility utilityID)) says
        prop (CMD (PR privcmd))::ins)
        (State enabled temperature) outs) ⇒
    (M,Oi,Os) sat prop (CMD (PR privcmd))
```

[CFGInterpret_Utility_KServer_trap_thm]

```
⊢ ∀M Oi Os.
    CFGInterpret (M,Oi,Os)
      (CFG isAuthenticated
        (thermoStateInterp utilityID privcmd)
        (certs ownerID utilityID cmd npriv privcmd)
        (Name (Key (pubK Server)) quoting
        Name (Role (Utility utilityID)) says
        prop (CMD (PR privcmd))::ins)
        (State disabled temperature) outs) ⇒
    (M,Oi,Os) sat prop TRAP
```

[delegates_thm]

```
⊢ (M,Oi,Os) sat delegate quoting owner says cmd ⇒
  (M,Oi,Os) sat owner controls cmd ⇒
  (M,Oi,Os) sat reps delegate owner cmd ⇒
  (M,Oi,Os) sat cmd
```

[exec_Keyboard_Owner_cmd_Justified]

```
⊢ ∀NS Out outs s ins npriv privcmd cmd ownerID utilityID M Oi
    Os.
    TR (M,Oi,Os) (exec (CMD cmd))
      (CFG isAuthenticated
        (thermoStateInterp utilityID privcmd)
        (certs ownerID utilityID cmd npriv privcmd)
        (Name Keyboard quoting Name (Owner ownerID) says
        prop (CMD cmd)::ins) s outs)
      (CFG isAuthenticated
```

```
            (thermoStateInterp utilityID privcmd)
            (certs ownerID utilityID cmd npriv privcmd) ins
            (NS s (exec (CMD cmd)))
            (Out s (exec (CMD cmd))::outs)) ⇒
        (M,Oi,Os) sat prop (CMD cmd)
```

⌊exec_Keyboard_Owner_cmd_thm⌋

```
⊢ ∀NS Out M Oi Os.
    TR (M,Oi,Os) (exec (CMD cmd))
      (CFG isAuthenticated
        (thermoStateInterp utilityID privcmd)
        (certs ownerID utilityID cmd npriv privcmd)
        (Name Keyboard quoting Name (Owner ownerID) says
         prop (CMD cmd)::ins) s outs)
      (CFG isAuthenticated
        (thermoStateInterp utilityID privcmd)
        (certs ownerID utilityID cmd npriv privcmd) ins
        (NS s (exec (CMD cmd)))
        (Out s (exec (CMD cmd))::outs)) ⟺
    CFGInterpret (M,Oi,Os)
      (CFG isAuthenticated
        (thermoStateInterp utilityID privcmd)
        (certs ownerID utilityID cmd npriv privcmd)
        (Name Keyboard quoting Name (Owner ownerID) says
         prop (CMD cmd)::ins) s outs) ∧
    (M,Oi,Os) sat prop (CMD cmd)
```

⌊exec_KServer_Owner_cmd_Justified⌋

```
⊢ ∀NS Out outs s ins npriv privcmd cmd ownerID utilityID M Oi
    Os.
    TR (M,Oi,Os) (exec (CMD cmd))
      (CFG isAuthenticated
        (thermoStateInterp utilityID privcmd)
        (certs ownerID utilityID cmd npriv privcmd)
        (Name (Key (pubK Server)) quoting
         Name (Owner ownerID) says prop (CMD cmd)::ins) s
        outs)
      (CFG isAuthenticated
        (thermoStateInterp utilityID privcmd)
        (certs ownerID utilityID cmd npriv privcmd) ins
        (NS s (exec (CMD cmd)))
        (Out s (exec (CMD cmd))::outs)) ⇒
    (M,Oi,Os) sat prop (CMD cmd)
```

⌊exec_KServer_Owner_cmd_thm⌋

```
⊢ ∀NS Out M Oi Os.
    TR (M,Oi,Os) (exec (CMD cmd))
      (CFG isAuthenticated
```

      (thermoStateInterp *utilityID privcmd*)
      (certs *ownerID utilityID cmd npriv privcmd*)
      (Name (Key (pubK Server)) quoting
       Name (Owner *ownerID*) says prop (CMD *cmd*)::*ins*) *s*
      outs)
    (CFG isAuthenticated
      (thermoStateInterp *utilityID privcmd*)
      (certs *ownerID utilityID cmd npriv privcmd*) *ins*
      (*NS s* (exec (CMD *cmd*)))
      (*Out s* (exec (CMD *cmd*))::*outs*)) $\Longleftrightarrow$
  CFGInterpret (*M*,*Oi*,*Os*)
    (CFG isAuthenticated
      (thermoStateInterp *utilityID privcmd*)
      (certs *ownerID utilityID cmd npriv privcmd*)
      (Name (Key (pubK Server)) quoting
       Name (Owner *ownerID*) says prop (CMD *cmd*)::*ins*) *s*
      outs) $\wedge$ (*M*,*Oi*,*Os*) sat prop (CMD *cmd*)

[exec_KServer_Utility_npriv_Justified]

$\vdash \forall NS$ *Out outs s ins npriv privcmd cmd ownerID utilityID M Oi*
    Os.
    TR (*M*,*Oi*,*Os*) (exec (CMD (NP *npriv*)))
      (CFG isAuthenticated
        (thermoStateInterp *utilityID privcmd*)
        (certs *ownerID utilityID cmd npriv privcmd*)
        (Name (Key (pubK Server)) quoting
         Name (Role (Utility *utilityID*)) says
         prop (CMD (NP *npriv*))::*ins*) *s outs*)
      (CFG isAuthenticated
        (thermoStateInterp *utilityID privcmd*)
        (certs *ownerID utilityID cmd npriv privcmd*) *ins*
        (*NS s* (exec (CMD (NP *npriv*))))
        (*Out s* (exec (CMD (NP *npriv*)))::*outs*)) $\Rightarrow$
    (*M*,*Oi*,*Os*) sat prop (CMD (NP *npriv*))

[exec_KServer_Utility_npriv_thm]

$\vdash \forall NS$ *Out M Oi Os*.
    TR (*M*,*Oi*,*Os*) (exec (CMD (NP *npriv*)))
      (CFG isAuthenticated
        (thermoStateInterp *utilityID privcmd*)
        (certs *ownerID utilityID cmd npriv privcmd*)
        (Name (Key (pubK Server)) quoting
         Name (Role (Utility *utilityID*)) says
         prop (CMD (NP *npriv*))::*ins*) *s outs*)
      (CFG isAuthenticated
        (thermoStateInterp *utilityID privcmd*)
        (certs *ownerID utilityID cmd npriv privcmd*) *ins*
        (*NS s* (exec (CMD (NP *npriv*))))
        (*Out s* (exec (CMD (NP *npriv*)))::*outs*)) $\Longleftrightarrow$

```
CFGInterpret (M,Oi,Os)
  (CFG isAuthenticated
    (thermoStateInterp utilityID privcmd)
    (certs ownerID utilityID cmd npriv privcmd)
    (Name (Key (pubK Server)) quoting
     Name (Role (Utility utilityID)) says
     prop (CMD (NP npriv))::ins) s outs) ∧
  (M,Oi,Os) sat prop (CMD (NP npriv))
```

⌊exec_KServer_Utility_privcmd_Justified⌋

```
⊢ ∀NS Out outs temperature ins npriv privcmd cmd ownerID
    utilityID M Oi Os.
    TR (M,Oi,Os) (exec (CMD (PR privcmd)))
      (CFG isAuthenticated
        (thermoStateInterp utilityID privcmd)
        (certs ownerID utilityID cmd npriv privcmd)
        (Name (Key (pubK Server)) quoting
         Name (Role (Utility utilityID)) says
         prop (CMD (PR privcmd))::ins)
        (State enabled temperature) outs)
      (CFG isAuthenticated
        (thermoStateInterp utilityID privcmd)
        (certs ownerID utilityID cmd npriv privcmd) ins
        (NS (State enabled temperature)
          (exec (CMD (PR privcmd))))
        (Out (State enabled temperature)
          (exec (CMD (PR privcmd)))::outs)) ⇒
    (M,Oi,Os) sat prop (CMD (PR privcmd))
```

⌊exec_KServer_Utility_privcmd_thm⌋

```
⊢ ∀NS Out M Oi Os.
    TR (M,Oi,Os) (exec (CMD (PR privcmd)))
      (CFG isAuthenticated
        (thermoStateInterp utilityID privcmd)
        (certs ownerID utilityID cmd npriv privcmd)
        (Name (Key (pubK Server)) quoting
         Name (Role (Utility utilityID)) says
         prop (CMD (PR privcmd))::ins)
        (State enabled temperature) outs)
      (CFG isAuthenticated
        (thermoStateInterp utilityID privcmd)
        (certs ownerID utilityID cmd npriv privcmd) ins
        (NS (State enabled temperature)
          (exec (CMD (PR privcmd))))
        (Out (State enabled temperature)
          (exec (CMD (PR privcmd)))::outs)) ⟺
    CFGInterpret (M,Oi,Os)
      (CFG isAuthenticated
        (thermoStateInterp utilityID privcmd)
```

```
      (certs ownerID utilityID cmd npriv privcmd)
      (Name (Key (pubK Server)) quoting
       Name (Role (Utility utilityID)) says
       prop (CMD (PR privcmd))::ins)
      (State enabled temperature) outs) ∧
  (M,Oi,Os) sat prop (CMD (PR privcmd))
```

[isAuthenticated_clauses]

⊢ isAuthenticated
   (Name Keyboard quoting Name (Owner ownerID) says
    prop (CMD cmd)) ∧
  isAuthenticated
   (Name (Key (pubK Server)) quoting Name (Owner ownerID) says
    prop (CMD cmd)) ∧
  isAuthenticated
   (Name (Key (pubK Server)) quoting
    Name (Role (Utility utilityID)) says prop (CMD cmd)) ∧
  ¬isAuthenticated TT ∧ ¬isAuthenticated FF ∧
  ¬isAuthenticated (prop v) ∧ ¬isAuthenticated (notf v_1) ∧
  ¬isAuthenticated (v_2 andf v_3) ∧
  ¬isAuthenticated (v_4 orf v_5) ∧
  ¬isAuthenticated (v_6 impf v_7) ∧
  ¬isAuthenticated (v_8 eqf v_9) ∧
  ¬isAuthenticated (v_{10} says TT) ∧
  ¬isAuthenticated (v_{10} says FF) ∧
  ¬isAuthenticated (Name v132 says prop v_{66}) ∧
  ¬isAuthenticated (v133 meet v134 says prop v_{66}) ∧
  ¬isAuthenticated
    (Name (Role v174) quoting Name (Role v164) says
     prop (CMD v142)) ∧
  ¬isAuthenticated
    (Name (Key v175) quoting Name (Role CA) says
     prop (CMD v142)) ∧
  ¬isAuthenticated
    (Name (Key v175) quoting Name (Role Server) says
     prop (CMD v142)) ∧
  ¬isAuthenticated
    (Name (Key (pubK CA)) quoting
     Name (Role (Utility v184)) says prop (CMD v142)) ∧
  ¬isAuthenticated
    (Name (Key (pubK (Utility v190))) quoting
     Name (Role (Utility v184)) says prop (CMD v142)) ∧
  ¬isAuthenticated
    (Name (Key (privK v187)) quoting
     Name (Role (Utility v184)) says prop (CMD v142)) ∧
  ¬isAuthenticated
    (Name Keyboard quoting Name (Role v164) says
     prop (CMD v142)) ∧
  ¬isAuthenticated
```
```

(Name (Owner $v176$) quoting Name (Role $v164$) says
  prop (CMD $v142$)) $\wedge$
$\neg$isAuthenticated
  (Name (Account $v177$ $v178$) quoting Name (Role $v164$) says
  prop (CMD $v142$)) $\wedge$
$\neg$isAuthenticated
  (Name $v154$ quoting Name (Key $v165$) says prop (CMD $v142$)) $\wedge$
$\neg$isAuthenticated
  (Name $v154$ quoting Name Keyboard says prop (CMD $v142$)) $\wedge$
$\neg$isAuthenticated
  (Name (Role $v192$) quoting Name (Owner $v166$) says
  prop (CMD $v142$)) $\wedge$
$\neg$isAuthenticated
  (Name (Key (pubK CA)) quoting Name (Owner $v166$) says
  prop (CMD $v142$)) $\wedge$
$\neg$isAuthenticated
  (Name (Key (pubK (Utility $v206$))) quoting
  Name (Owner $v166$) says prop (CMD $v142$)) $\wedge$
$\neg$isAuthenticated
  (Name (Key (privK $v203$)) quoting Name (Owner $v166$) says
  prop (CMD $v142$)) $\wedge$
$\neg$isAuthenticated
  (Name (Owner $v194$) quoting Name (Owner $v166$) says
  prop (CMD $v142$)) $\wedge$
$\neg$isAuthenticated
  (Name (Account $v195$ $v196$) quoting Name (Owner $v166$) says
  prop (CMD $v142$)) $\wedge$
$\neg$isAuthenticated
  (Name $v154$ quoting Name (Account $v167$ $v168$) says
  prop (CMD $v142$)) $\wedge$
$\neg$isAuthenticated
  ($v155$ meet $v156$ quoting Name $v144$ says prop (CMD $v142$)) $\wedge$
$\neg$isAuthenticated
  (($v157$ quoting $v158$) quoting Name $v144$ says
  prop (CMD $v142$)) $\wedge$
$\neg$isAuthenticated
  ($v135$ quoting $v145$ meet $v146$ says prop (CMD $v142$)) $\wedge$
$\neg$isAuthenticated
  ($v135$ quoting $v147$ quoting $v148$ says prop (CMD $v142$)) $\wedge$
$\neg$isAuthenticated ($v135$ quoting $v136$ says prop TRAP) $\wedge$
$\neg$isAuthenticated (v_{10} says notf v_{67}) $\wedge$
$\neg$isAuthenticated (v_{10} says (v_{68} andf v_{69})) $\wedge$
$\neg$isAuthenticated (v_{10} says (v_{70} orf v_{71})) $\wedge$
$\neg$isAuthenticated (v_{10} says (v_{72} impf v_{73})) $\wedge$
$\neg$isAuthenticated (v_{10} says (v_{74} eqf v_{75})) $\wedge$
$\neg$isAuthenticated (v_{10} says v_{76} says v_{77}) $\wedge$
$\neg$isAuthenticated (v_{10} says v_{78} speaks_for v_{79}) $\wedge$
$\neg$isAuthenticated (v_{10} says v_{80} controls v_{81}) $\wedge$
$\neg$isAuthenticated (v_{10} says reps v_{82} v_{83} v_{84}) $\wedge$

$\neg$isAuthenticated (v_{10} says v_{85} domi v_{86}) $\wedge$
$\neg$isAuthenticated (v_{10} says v_{87} eqi v_{88}) $\wedge$
$\neg$isAuthenticated (v_{10} says v_{89} doms v_{90}) $\wedge$
$\neg$isAuthenticated (v_{10} says v_{91} eqs v_{92}) $\wedge$
$\neg$isAuthenticated (v_{10} says v_{93} eqn v_{94}) $\wedge$
$\neg$isAuthenticated (v_{10} says v_{95} lte v_{96}) $\wedge$
$\neg$isAuthenticated (v_{10} says v_{97} lt v_{98}) $\wedge$
$\neg$isAuthenticated (v_{12} speaks_for v_{13}) $\wedge$
$\neg$isAuthenticated (v_{14} controls v_{15}) $\wedge$
$\neg$isAuthenticated (reps v_{16} v_{17} v_{18}) $\wedge$
$\neg$isAuthenticated (v_{19} domi v_{20}) $\wedge$
$\neg$isAuthenticated (v_{21} eqi v_{22}) $\wedge$
$\neg$isAuthenticated (v_{23} doms v_{24}) $\wedge$
$\neg$isAuthenticated (v_{25} eqs v_{26}) $\wedge$
$\neg$isAuthenticated (v_{27} eqn v_{28}) $\wedge$
$\neg$isAuthenticated (v_{29} lte v_{30}) $\wedge$
$\neg$isAuthenticated (v_{31} lt v_{32})

[isAuthenticated_Owner_Keyboard_thm]

$\vdash$ isAuthenticated
    (Name Keyboard quoting Name (Owner *ownerID*) says
     prop (CMD *cmd*))

[isAuthenticated_Owner_KServer_thm]

$\vdash$ isAuthenticated
    (Name (Key (pubK Server)) quoting Name (Owner *ownerID*) says
     prop (CMD *cmd*))

[isAuthenticated_Utility_KServer_npriv_thm]

$\vdash$ isAuthenticated
    (Name (Key (pubK Server)) quoting
     Name (Role (Utility *utilityID*)) says
     prop (CMD (NP *npriv*)))

[isAuthenticated_Utility_KServer_privcmd_thm]

$\vdash$ isAuthenticated
    (Name (Key (pubK Server)) quoting
     Name (Role (Utility *utilityID*)) says
     prop (CMD (PR *privcmd*)))

[Ks_Owner_lemma]

$\vdash$ (M, Oi, Os) sat
  Name (Key (pubK Server)) quoting Name (Owner *ownerID*) says
  prop (CMD *cmd*) $\Rightarrow$
  (M, Oi, Os) sat Name (Owner *ownerID*) controls prop (CMD *cmd*) $\Rightarrow$
  (M, Oi, Os) sat
  reps (Name (Role Server)) (Name (Owner *ownerID*))
    (prop (CMD *cmd*)) $\Rightarrow$

(M, Oi, Os) sat
Name (Role CA) controls
Name (Key (pubK Server)) speaks_for Name (Role Server) $\Rightarrow$
(M, Oi, Os) sat
Name (Key (pubK CA)) speaks_for Name (Role CA) $\Rightarrow$
(M, Oi, Os) sat
Name (Key (pubK CA)) says
Name (Key (pubK Server)) speaks_for Name (Role Server) $\Rightarrow$
(M, Oi, Os) sat prop (CMD cmd)

$\lfloor$ks_owner_lemma$\rfloor$

$\vdash (M, Oi, Os)$ sat ks quoting $owner$ says prop (CMD cmd) $\Rightarrow$
(M, Oi, Os) sat $owner$ controls prop (CMD cmd) $\Rightarrow$
(M, Oi, Os) sat reps $server$ $owner$ (prop (CMD cmd)) $\Rightarrow$
(M, Oi, Os) sat ca controls ks speaks_for $server$ $\Rightarrow$
(M, Oi, Os) sat kca speaks_for ca $\Rightarrow$
(M, Oi, Os) sat kca says ks speaks_for $server$ $\Rightarrow$
(M, Oi, Os) sat prop (CMD cmd)

$\lfloor$ManualOperationA_lemma$\rfloor$

$\vdash (M, Oi, Os)$ sat
Name Keyboard quoting Name (Owner $ownerID$) says
prop (CMD cmd) $\Rightarrow$
(M, Oi, Os) sat Name (Owner $ownerID$) controls prop (CMD cmd) $\Rightarrow$
(M, Oi, Os) sat
reps (Name Keyboard) (Name (Owner $ownerID$))
  (prop (CMD cmd)) $\Rightarrow$
(M, Oi, Os) sat
reps (Name (Role Server)) (Name (Owner $ownerID$))
  (prop (CMD cmd)) $\Rightarrow$
(M, Oi, Os) sat
Name (Role CA) controls
Name (Key (pubK Server)) speaks_for Name (Role Server) $\Rightarrow$
(M, Oi, Os) sat
Name (Key (pubK CA)) speaks_for Name (Role CA) $\Rightarrow$
(M, Oi, Os) sat
Name (Key (pubK CA)) says
Name (Key (pubK Server)) speaks_for Name (Role Server) $\Rightarrow$
(M, Oi, Os) sat
reps (Name (Role Server)) (Name (Role (Utility $utilityID$)))
  (prop (CMD (NP $npriv$))) $\Rightarrow$
(M, Oi, Os) sat
reps (Name (Role Server)) (Name (Role (Utility $utilityID$)))
  (prop (CMD (PR $privcmd$))) $\Rightarrow$
(M, Oi, Os) sat
Name (Role (Utility $utilityID$)) controls
prop (CMD (NP $npriv$)) $\Rightarrow$
(M, Oi, Os) sat
Name (Role (Utility $utilityID$)) controls

prop (CMD (PR *privcmd*)) $\Rightarrow$
(M, Oi, Os) sat prop (CMD *cmd*)

|ManualOperationB_lemma|

$\vdash (M, Oi, Os)$ sat
  Name Keyboard quoting Name (Owner *ownerID*) says
  prop (CMD *cmd*) $\Rightarrow$
  (M, Oi, Os) sat Name (Owner *ownerID*) controls prop (CMD *cmd*) $\Rightarrow$
  (M, Oi, Os) sat
  reps (Name Keyboard) (Name (Owner *ownerID*))
    (prop (CMD *cmd*)) $\Rightarrow$
  (M, Oi, Os) sat
  reps (Name (Role Server)) (Name (Owner *ownerID*))
    (prop (CMD *cmd*)) $\Rightarrow$
  (M, Oi, Os) sat
  Name (Role CA) controls
  Name (Key (pubK Server)) speaks_for Name (Role Server) $\Rightarrow$
  (M, Oi, Os) sat
  Name (Key (pubK CA)) speaks_for Name (Role CA) $\Rightarrow$
  (M, Oi, Os) sat
  Name (Key (pubK CA)) says
  Name (Key (pubK Server)) speaks_for Name (Role Server) $\Rightarrow$
  (M, Oi, Os) sat
  reps (Name (Role Server)) (Name (Role (Utility *utilityID*)))
    (prop (CMD (NP *npriv*))) $\Rightarrow$
  (M, Oi, Os) sat
  reps (Name (Role Server)) (Name (Role (Utility *utilityID*)))
    (prop (CMD (PR *privcmd*))) $\Rightarrow$
  (M, Oi, Os) sat
  Name (Role (Utility *utilityID*)) controls
  prop (CMD (NP *npriv*)) $\Rightarrow$
  (M, Oi, Os) sat
  Name (Role (Utility *utilityID*)) says
  prop (CMD (PR *privcmd*)) impf prop TRAP $\Rightarrow$
  (M, Oi, Os) sat prop (CMD *cmd*)

|owner_Keyboard_lemma|

$\vdash (M, Oi, Os)$ sat
  Name Keyboard quoting Name (Owner *ownerID*) says
  prop (CMD *cmd*) $\Rightarrow$
  (M, Oi, Os) sat Name (Owner *ownerID*) controls prop (CMD *cmd*) $\Rightarrow$
  (M, Oi, Os) sat
  reps (Name Keyboard) (Name (Owner *ownerID*))
    (prop (CMD *cmd*)) $\Rightarrow$
  (M, Oi, Os) sat prop (CMD *cmd*)

|OwnerServerOperationA_lemma|

$\vdash (M, Oi, Os)$ sat
  Name (Key (pubK Server)) quoting Name (Owner *ownerID*) says

prop (CMD *cmd*) ⇒
(M, Oi, Os) sat Name (Owner *ownerID*) controls prop (CMD *cmd*) ⇒
(M, Oi, Os) sat
reps (Name Keyboard) (Name (Owner *ownerID*))
  (prop (CMD *cmd*)) ⇒
(M, Oi, Os) sat
reps (Name (Role Server)) (Name (Owner *ownerID*))
  (prop (CMD *cmd*)) ⇒
(M, Oi, Os) sat
Name (Role CA) controls
Name (Key (pubK Server)) speaks_for Name (Role Server) ⇒
(M, Oi, Os) sat
Name (Key (pubK CA)) speaks_for Name (Role CA) ⇒
(M, Oi, Os) sat
Name (Key (pubK CA)) says
Name (Key (pubK Server)) speaks_for Name (Role Server) ⇒
(M, Oi, Os) sat
reps (Name (Role Server)) (Name (Role (Utility *utilityID*)))
  (prop (CMD (NP *npriv*))) ⇒
(M, Oi, Os) sat
reps (Name (Role Server)) (Name (Role (Utility *utilityID*)))
  (prop (CMD (PR *privcmd*))) ⇒
(M, Oi, Os) sat
Name (Role (Utility *utilityID*)) controls
prop (CMD (NP *npriv*)) ⇒
(M, Oi, Os) sat
Name (Role (Utility *utilityID*)) controls
prop (CMD (PR *privcmd*)) ⇒
(M, Oi, Os) sat prop (CMD *cmd*)

[OwnerServerOperationB_lemma]

⊢ (M, Oi, Os) sat
  Name (Key (pubK Server)) quoting Name (Owner *ownerID*) says
  prop (CMD *cmd*) ⇒
  (M, Oi, Os) sat Name (Owner *ownerID*) controls prop (CMD *cmd*) ⇒
  (M, Oi, Os) sat
  reps (Name Keyboard) (Name (Owner *ownerID*))
    (prop (CMD *cmd*)) ⇒
  (M, Oi, Os) sat
  reps (Name (Role Server)) (Name (Owner *ownerID*))
    (prop (CMD *cmd*)) ⇒
  (M, Oi, Os) sat
  Name (Role CA) controls
  Name (Key (pubK Server)) speaks_for Name (Role Server) ⇒
  (M, Oi, Os) sat
  Name (Key (pubK CA)) speaks_for Name (Role CA) ⇒
  (M, Oi, Os) sat
  Name (Key (pubK CA)) says
  Name (Key (pubK Server)) speaks_for Name (Role Server) ⇒

(M, Oi, Os) sat
reps (Name (Role Server)) (Name (Role (Utility *utilityID*)))
  (prop (CMD (NP *npriv*))) $\Rightarrow$
(M, Oi, Os) sat
reps (Name (Role Server)) (Name (Role (Utility *utilityID*)))
  (prop (CMD (PR *privcmd*))) $\Rightarrow$
(M, Oi, Os) sat
Name (Role (Utility *utilityID*)) controls
prop (CMD (NP *npriv*)) $\Rightarrow$
(M, Oi, Os) sat
Name (Role (Utility *utilityID*)) says
prop (CMD (PR *privcmd*)) impf prop TRAP $\Rightarrow$
(M, Oi, Os) sat prop (CMD *cmd*)

[quoting_speaks_for_lemma]

$\vdash (M, Oi, Os)$ sat *kp* quoting Q says *cmd* $\Rightarrow$
(M, Oi, Os) sat *kp* speaks_for P $\Rightarrow$
(M, Oi, Os) sat P quoting Q says *cmd*

[root_ca_key_cert_thm]

$\vdash (M, Oi, Os)$ sat *ca* controls *ks* speaks_for *server* $\Rightarrow$
(M, Oi, Os) sat *kca* speaks_for *ca* $\Rightarrow$
(M, Oi, Os) sat *kca* says *ks* speaks_for *server* $\Rightarrow$
(M, Oi, Os) sat *ks* speaks_for *server*

[TR_exec_Keyboard_Owner_cmd_lemma]

$\vdash (\forall M\ Oi\ Os.$
    CFGInterpret (M, Oi, Os)
      (CFG isAuthenticated
        (thermoStateInterp *utilityID* *privcmd*)
        (certs *ownerID* *utilityID* *cmd* *npriv* *privcmd*)
        (Name Keyboard quoting Name (Owner *ownerID*) says
          prop (CMD *cmd*)::*ins*) *s* *outs*) $\Rightarrow$
     (M, Oi, Os) sat prop (CMD *cmd*)) $\Rightarrow$
  $\forall NS\ Out\ M\ Oi\ Os.$
    TR (M, Oi, Os) (exec (CMD *cmd*))
      (CFG isAuthenticated
        (thermoStateInterp *utilityID* *privcmd*)
        (certs *ownerID* *utilityID* *cmd* *npriv* *privcmd*)
        (Name Keyboard quoting Name (Owner *ownerID*) says
         prop (CMD *cmd*)::*ins*) *s* *outs*)
      (CFG isAuthenticated
        (thermoStateInterp *utilityID* *privcmd*)
        (certs *ownerID* *utilityID* *cmd* *npriv* *privcmd*) *ins*
        $(NS\ s$ (exec (CMD *cmd*)))
        $(Out\ s$ (exec (CMD *cmd*))::*outs*)) $\Longleftrightarrow$
    isAuthenticated
      (Name Keyboard quoting Name (Owner *ownerID*) says

        prop (CMD *cmd*)) ∧
    CFGInterpret (*M*, *Oi*, *Os*)
      (CFG isAuthenticated
        (thermoStateInterp *utilityID privcmd*)
        (certs *ownerID utilityID cmd npriv privcmd*)
        (Name Keyboard quoting Name (Owner *ownerID*) says
          prop (CMD *cmd*)::*ins*) *s outs*) ∧
    (*M*, *Oi*, *Os*) sat prop (CMD *cmd*)

[TR_exec_KServer_Owner_cmd_lemma]

⊢ (∀ *M Oi Os*.
    CFGInterpret (*M*, *Oi*, *Os*)
      (CFG isAuthenticated
        (thermoStateInterp *utilityID privcmd*)
        (certs *ownerID utilityID cmd npriv privcmd*)
        (Name (Key (pubK Server)) quoting
          Name (Owner *ownerID*) says prop (CMD *cmd*)::*ins*) *s*
        outs) ⇒
    (*M*, *Oi*, *Os*) sat prop (CMD *cmd*)) ⇒
  ∀ *NS Out M Oi Os*.
    TR (*M*, *Oi*, *Os*) (exec (CMD *cmd*))
      (CFG isAuthenticated
        (thermoStateInterp *utilityID privcmd*)
        (certs *ownerID utilityID cmd npriv privcmd*)
        (Name (Key (pubK Server)) quoting
          Name (Owner *ownerID*) says prop (CMD *cmd*)::*ins*) *s*
        outs)
      (CFG isAuthenticated
        (thermoStateInterp *utilityID privcmd*)
        (certs *ownerID utilityID cmd npriv privcmd*) *ins*
        (*NS s* (exec (CMD *cmd*)))
        (*Out s* (exec (CMD *cmd*)))::*outs*)) ⟺
    isAuthenticated
      (Name (Key (pubK Server)) quoting
        Name (Owner *ownerID*) says prop (CMD *cmd*)) ∧
    CFGInterpret (*M*, *Oi*, *Os*)
      (CFG isAuthenticated
        (thermoStateInterp *utilityID privcmd*)
        (certs *ownerID utilityID cmd npriv privcmd*)
        (Name (Key (pubK Server)) quoting
          Name (Owner *ownerID*) says prop (CMD *cmd*)::*ins*) *s*
        outs) ∧ (*M*, *Oi*, *Os*) sat prop (CMD *cmd*)

[TR_exec_KServer_Utility_cmd_lemma]

⊢ (∀ *M Oi Os*.
    CFGInterpret (*M*, *Oi*, *Os*)
      (CFG isAuthenticated
        (thermoStateInterp *utilityID privcmd*)
        (certs *ownerID utilityID cmd npriv privcmd*)

```
            (Name (Key (pubK Server)) quoting
             Name (Role (Utility utilityID)) says
             prop (CMD (NP npriv))::ins) s outs) ⇒
      (M,Oi,Os) sat prop (CMD (NP npriv))) ⇒
 ∀NS Out M Oi Os.
    TR (M,Oi,Os) (exec (CMD (NP npriv)))
      (CFG isAuthenticated
        (thermoStateInterp utilityID privcmd)
        (certs ownerID utilityID cmd npriv privcmd)
        (Name (Key (pubK Server)) quoting
         Name (Role (Utility utilityID)) says
         prop (CMD (NP npriv))::ins) s outs)
      (CFG isAuthenticated
        (thermoStateInterp utilityID privcmd)
        (certs ownerID utilityID cmd npriv privcmd) ins
        (NS s (exec (CMD (NP npriv))))
        (Out s (exec (CMD (NP npriv)))::outs))  ⟺
    isAuthenticated
      (Name (Key (pubK Server)) quoting
       Name (Role (Utility utilityID)) says
       prop (CMD (NP npriv))) ∧
    CFGInterpret (M,Oi,Os)
      (CFG isAuthenticated
        (thermoStateInterp utilityID privcmd)
        (certs ownerID utilityID cmd npriv privcmd)
        (Name (Key (pubK Server)) quoting
         Name (Role (Utility utilityID)) says
         prop (CMD (NP npriv))::ins) s outs) ∧
      (M,Oi,Os) sat prop (CMD (NP npriv))
```

[TR_exec_KServer_Utility_privcmd_lemma]

```
⊢ (∀M Oi Os.
      CFGInterpret (M,Oi,Os)
        (CFG isAuthenticated
          (thermoStateInterp utilityID privcmd)
          (certs ownerID utilityID cmd npriv privcmd)
          (Name (Key (pubK Server)) quoting
           Name (Role (Utility utilityID)) says
           prop (CMD (PR privcmd))::ins)
          (State enabled temperature) outs) ⇒
      (M,Oi,Os) sat prop (CMD (PR privcmd))) ⇒
  ∀NS Out M Oi Os.
    TR (M,Oi,Os) (exec (CMD (PR privcmd)))
      (CFG isAuthenticated
        (thermoStateInterp utilityID privcmd)
        (certs ownerID utilityID cmd npriv privcmd)
        (Name (Key (pubK Server)) quoting
         Name (Role (Utility utilityID)) says
         prop (CMD (PR privcmd))::ins)
```

```
              (State enabled temperature) outs)
          (CFG isAuthenticated
             (thermoStateInterp utilityID privcmd)
             (certs ownerID utilityID cmd npriv privcmd) ins
             (NS (State enabled temperature)
                (exec (CMD (PR privcmd))))
             (Out (State enabled temperature)
                (exec (CMD (PR privcmd)))::outs))  ⟺
      isAuthenticated
        (Name (Key (pubK Server)) quoting
         Name (Role (Utility utilityID)) says
         prop (CMD (PR privcmd))) ∧
      CFGInterpret (M,Oi,Os)
        (CFG isAuthenticated
           (thermoStateInterp utilityID privcmd)
           (certs ownerID utilityID cmd npriv privcmd)
           (Name (Key (pubK Server)) quoting
            Name (Role (Utility utilityID)) says
            prop (CMD (PR privcmd))::ins)
           (State enabled temperature) outs) ∧
      (M,Oi,Os) sat prop (CMD (PR privcmd))
```

[TR_trap_KServer_Utility_privcmd_lemma]

```
⊢ (∀ M Oi Os.
      CFGInterpret (M,Oi,Os)
        (CFG isAuthenticated
           (thermoStateInterp utilityID privcmd)
           (certs ownerID utilityID cmd npriv privcmd)
           (Name (Key (pubK Server)) quoting
            Name (Role (Utility utilityID)) says
            prop (CMD (PR privcmd))::ins)
           (State disabled temperature) outs) ⇒
      (M,Oi,Os) sat prop TRAP) ⇒
    ∀ NS Out M Oi Os.
      TR (M,Oi,Os) (trap (CMD (PR privcmd)))
        (CFG isAuthenticated
           (thermoStateInterp utilityID privcmd)
           (certs ownerID utilityID cmd npriv privcmd)
           (Name (Key (pubK Server)) quoting
            Name (Role (Utility utilityID)) says
            prop (CMD (PR privcmd))::ins)
           (State disabled temperature) outs)
        (CFG isAuthenticated
           (thermoStateInterp utilityID privcmd)
           (certs ownerID utilityID cmd npriv privcmd) ins
           (NS (State disabled temperature)
              (trap (CMD (PR privcmd))))
           (Out (State disabled temperature)
              (trap (CMD (PR privcmd)))::outs))  ⟺
```

```
isAuthenticated
  (Name (Key (pubK Server)) quoting
   Name (Role (Utility utilityID)) says
   prop (CMD (PR privcmd))) ∧
CFGInterpret (M, Oi, Os)
  (CFG isAuthenticated
    (thermoStateInterp utilityID privcmd)
    (certs ownerID utilityID cmd npriv privcmd)
    (Name (Key (pubK Server)) quoting
     Name (Role (Utility utilityID)) says
     prop (CMD (PR privcmd))::ins)
    (State disabled temperature) outs) ∧
(M, Oi, Os) sat prop TRAP
```

|trap_KServer_Utility_privcmd_Justified|

```
⊢ ∀ NS Out outs temperature ins npriv privcmd cmd ownerID
    utilityID M Oi Os.
  TR (M, Oi, Os) (trap (CMD (PR privcmd)))
    (CFG isAuthenticated
      (thermoStateInterp utilityID privcmd)
      (certs ownerID utilityID cmd npriv privcmd)
      (Name (Key (pubK Server)) quoting
       Name (Role (Utility utilityID)) says
       prop (CMD (PR privcmd))::ins)
      (State disabled temperature) outs)
    (CFG isAuthenticated
      (thermoStateInterp utilityID privcmd)
      (certs ownerID utilityID cmd npriv privcmd) ins
      (NS (State disabled temperature)
         (trap (CMD (PR privcmd))))
      (Out (State disabled temperature)
         (trap (CMD (PR privcmd)))::outs)) ⇒
    (M, Oi, Os) sat prop TRAP
```

|trap_KServer_Utility_privcmd_thm|

```
⊢ ∀ NS Out M Oi Os.
  TR (M, Oi, Os) (trap (CMD (PR privcmd)))
    (CFG isAuthenticated
      (thermoStateInterp utilityID privcmd)
      (certs ownerID utilityID cmd npriv privcmd)
      (Name (Key (pubK Server)) quoting
       Name (Role (Utility utilityID)) says
       prop (CMD (PR privcmd))::ins)
      (State disabled temperature) outs)
    (CFG isAuthenticated
      (thermoStateInterp utilityID privcmd)
      (certs ownerID utilityID cmd npriv privcmd) ins
      (NS (State disabled temperature)
         (trap (CMD (PR privcmd))))
```

$\quad$ (Out (State disabled $temperature$)
$\qquad$ (trap (CMD (PR $privcmd$)))::$outs$)) $\Longleftrightarrow$
CFGInterpret (M,Oi,Os)
$\quad$ (CFG isAuthenticated
$\qquad$ (thermoStateInterp $utilityID$ $privcmd$)
$\qquad$ (certs $ownerID$ $utilityID$ cmd $npriv$ $privcmd$)
$\qquad$ (Name (Key (pubK Server)) quoting
$\qquad$ Name (Role (Utility $utilityID$)) says
$\qquad$ prop (CMD (PR $privcmd$))::ins)
$\qquad$ (State disabled $temperature$) $outs$) $\wedge$
(M,Oi,Os) sat prop TRAP

[Unauthenticated_cmd_discarded]

$\vdash \forall NS$ Out $outs$ s ins $npriv$ $privcmd$ cmd $ownerID$ $utilityID$ M Oi
$\quad Os$.
$\quad$ TR (M,Oi,Os) discard
$\qquad$ (CFG isAuthenticated
$\qquad\quad$ (thermoStateInterp $utilityID$ $privcmd$)
$\qquad\quad$ (certs $ownerID$ $utilityID$ cmd $npriv$ $privcmd$)
$\qquad\quad$ (prop (CMD cmd)::ins) s $outs$)
$\qquad$ (CFG isAuthenticated
$\qquad\quad$ (thermoStateInterp $utilityID$ $privcmd$)
$\qquad\quad$ (certs $ownerID$ $utilityID$ cmd $npriv$ $privcmd$) ins
$\qquad\quad$ (NS s discard) (Out s discard::$outs$))

[Utility_npriv_Authorized_lemma]

$\vdash (M,Oi,Os)$ sat
$\quad$ Name (Key (pubK Server)) quoting
$\quad$ Name (Role (Utility $utilityID$)) says prop (CMD (NP $npriv$)) $\Rightarrow$
$\quad (M,Oi,Os)$ sat
$\quad$ Name (Role CA) controls
$\quad$ Name (Key (pubK Server)) speaks_for Name (Role Server) $\Rightarrow$
$\quad (M,Oi,Os)$ sat
$\quad$ Name (Key (pubK CA)) speaks_for Name (Role CA) $\Rightarrow$
$\quad (M,Oi,Os)$ sat
$\quad$ Name (Key (pubK CA)) says
$\quad$ Name (Key (pubK Server)) speaks_for Name (Role Server) $\Rightarrow$
$\quad (M,Oi,Os)$ sat
$\quad$ reps (Name (Role Server)) (Name (Role (Utility $utilityID$)))
$\qquad$ (prop (CMD (NP $npriv$))) $\Rightarrow$
$\quad (M,Oi,Os)$ sat
$\quad$ Name (Role (Utility $utilityID$)) controls
$\quad$ prop (CMD (NP $npriv$)) $\Rightarrow$
$\quad (M,Oi,Os)$ sat prop (CMD (NP $npriv$))

[utility_npriv_authorized_lemma]

$\vdash (M,Oi,Os)$ sat ks quoting $utility$ says prop (CMD (NP $npriv$)) $\Rightarrow$
$\quad (M,Oi,Os)$ sat ca controls ks speaks_for $server$ $\Rightarrow$

(M, Oi, Os) sat kca speaks_for ca $\Rightarrow$
(M, Oi, Os) sat kca says ks speaks_for $server$ $\Rightarrow$
(M, Oi, Os) sat reps $server$ $utility$ (prop (CMD (NP $npriv$))) $\Rightarrow$
(M, Oi, Os) sat $utility$ controls prop (CMD (NP $npriv$)) $\Rightarrow$
(M, Oi, Os) sat prop (CMD (NP $npriv$))

⌊Utility_privcmd_Authorized_lemma⌋

$\vdash (M, Oi, Os)$ sat
Name (Key (pubK Server)) quoting
Name (Role (Utility $utilityID$)) says
prop (CMD (PR $privcmd$)) $\Rightarrow$
(M, Oi, Os) sat
Name (Role CA) controls
Name (Key (pubK Server)) speaks_for Name (Role Server) $\Rightarrow$
(M, Oi, Os) sat
Name (Key (pubK CA)) speaks_for Name (Role CA) $\Rightarrow$
(M, Oi, Os) sat
Name (Key (pubK CA)) says
Name (Key (pubK Server)) speaks_for Name (Role Server) $\Rightarrow$
(M, Oi, Os) sat
reps (Name (Role Server)) (Name (Role (Utility $utilityID$)))
  (prop (CMD (PR $privcmd$))) $\Rightarrow$
(M, Oi, Os) sat
Name (Role (Utility $utilityID$)) controls
prop (CMD (PR $privcmd$)) $\Rightarrow$
(M, Oi, Os) sat prop (CMD (PR $privcmd$))

⌊utility_privcmd_authorized_lemma⌋

$\vdash (M, Oi, Os)$ sat
ks quoting $utility$ says prop (CMD (PR $privcmd$)) $\Rightarrow$
(M, Oi, Os) sat ca controls ks speaks_for $server$ $\Rightarrow$
(M, Oi, Os) sat kca speaks_for ca $\Rightarrow$
(M, Oi, Os) sat kca says ks speaks_for $server$ $\Rightarrow$
(M, Oi, Os) sat reps $server$ $utility$ (prop (CMD (PR $privcmd$))) $\Rightarrow$
(M, Oi, Os) sat $utility$ controls prop (CMD (PR $privcmd$)) $\Rightarrow$
(M, Oi, Os) sat prop (CMD (PR $privcmd$))

⌊Utility_privcmd_Trapped_lemma⌋

$\vdash (M, Oi, Os)$ sat
Name (Key (pubK Server)) quoting
Name (Role (Utility $utilityID$)) says
prop (CMD (PR $privcmd$)) $\Rightarrow$
(M, Oi, Os) sat
Name (Role CA) controls
Name (Key (pubK Server)) speaks_for Name (Role Server) $\Rightarrow$
(M, Oi, Os) sat
Name (Key (pubK CA)) speaks_for Name (Role CA) $\Rightarrow$
(M, Oi, Os) sat

Name (Key (pubK CA)) says
Name (Key (pubK Server)) speaks_for Name (Role Server) $\Rightarrow$
(M, Oi, Os) sat
reps (Name (Role Server)) (Name (Role (Utility *utilityID*)))
  (prop (CMD (PR *privcmd*))) $\Rightarrow$
(M, Oi, Os) sat
Name (Role (Utility *utilityID*)) says
prop (CMD (PR *privcmd*)) impf prop TRAP $\Rightarrow$
(M, Oi, Os) sat prop TRAP

[utility_privcmd_trapped_lemma]

$\vdash (M, Oi, Os)$ sat
  ks quoting *utility* says prop (CMD (PR *privcmd*)) $\Rightarrow$
  (M, Oi, Os) sat *ca* controls *ks* speaks_for *server* $\Rightarrow$
  (M, Oi, Os) sat *kca* speaks_for *ca* $\Rightarrow$
  (M, Oi, Os) sat *kca* says *ks* speaks_for *server* $\Rightarrow$
  (M, Oi, Os) sat reps *server utility* (prop (CMD (PR *privcmd*))) $\Rightarrow$
  (M, Oi, Os) sat
  utility says prop (CMD (PR *privcmd*)) impf prop TRAP $\Rightarrow$
  (M, Oi, Os) sat prop TRAP

[UtilityServerNonPrivA_lemma]

$\vdash (M, Oi, Os)$ sat
Name (Key (pubK Server)) quoting
Name (Role (Utility *utilityID*)) says prop (CMD (NP *npriv*)) $\Rightarrow$
(M, Oi, Os) sat Name (Owner *ownerID*) controls prop (CMD *cmd*) $\Rightarrow$
(M, Oi, Os) sat
reps (Name Keyboard) (Name (Owner *ownerID*))
  (prop (CMD *cmd*)) $\Rightarrow$
(M, Oi, Os) sat
reps (Name (Role Server)) (Name (Owner *ownerID*))
  (prop (CMD *cmd*)) $\Rightarrow$
(M, Oi, Os) sat
Name (Role CA) controls
Name (Key (pubK Server)) speaks_for Name (Role Server) $\Rightarrow$
(M, Oi, Os) sat
Name (Key (pubK CA)) speaks_for Name (Role CA) $\Rightarrow$
(M, Oi, Os) sat
Name (Key (pubK CA)) says
Name (Key (pubK Server)) speaks_for Name (Role Server) $\Rightarrow$
(M, Oi, Os) sat
reps (Name (Role Server)) (Name (Role (Utility *utilityID*)))
  (prop (CMD (NP *npriv*))) $\Rightarrow$
(M, Oi, Os) sat
reps (Name (Role Server)) (Name (Role (Utility *utilityID*)))
  (prop (CMD (PR *privcmd*))) $\Rightarrow$
(M, Oi, Os) sat
Name (Role (Utility *utilityID*)) controls
prop (CMD (NP *npriv*)) $\Rightarrow$

(M, Oi, Os) sat
Name (Role (Utility *utilityID*)) controls
prop (CMD (PR *privcmd*)) $\Rightarrow$
(M, Oi, Os) sat prop (CMD (NP *npriv*))

|UtilityServerNonPrivB_lemma|

$\vdash (M, Oi, Os)$ sat
Name (Key (pubK Server)) quoting
Name (Role (Utility *utilityID*)) says prop (CMD (NP *npriv*)) $\Rightarrow$
(M, Oi, Os) sat Name (Owner *ownerID*) controls prop (CMD *cmd*) $\Rightarrow$
(M, Oi, Os) sat
reps (Name Keyboard) (Name (Owner *ownerID*))
  (prop (CMD *cmd*)) $\Rightarrow$
(M, Oi, Os) sat
reps (Name (Role Server)) (Name (Owner *ownerID*))
  (prop (CMD *cmd*)) $\Rightarrow$
(M, Oi, Os) sat
Name (Role CA) controls
Name (Key (pubK Server)) speaks_for Name (Role Server) $\Rightarrow$
(M, Oi, Os) sat
Name (Key (pubK CA)) speaks_for Name (Role CA) $\Rightarrow$
(M, Oi, Os) sat
Name (Key (pubK CA)) says
Name (Key (pubK Server)) speaks_for Name (Role Server) $\Rightarrow$
(M, Oi, Os) sat
reps (Name (Role Server)) (Name (Role (Utility *utilityID*)))
  (prop (CMD (NP *npriv*))) $\Rightarrow$
(M, Oi, Os) sat
reps (Name (Role Server)) (Name (Role (Utility *utilityID*)))
  (prop (CMD (PR *privcmd*))) $\Rightarrow$
(M, Oi, Os) sat
Name (Role (Utility *utilityID*)) controls
prop (CMD (NP *npriv*)) $\Rightarrow$
(M, Oi, Os) sat
Name (Role (Utility *utilityID*)) says
prop (CMD (PR *privcmd*)) impf prop TRAP $\Rightarrow$
(M, Oi, Os) sat prop (CMD (NP *npriv*))

|UtilityServerPrivA_lemma|

$\vdash (M, Oi, Os)$ sat
Name (Key (pubK Server)) quoting
Name (Role (Utility *utilityID*)) says
prop (CMD (PR *privcmd*)) $\Rightarrow$
(M, Oi, Os) sat Name (Owner *ownerID*) controls prop (CMD *cmd*) $\Rightarrow$
(M, Oi, Os) sat
reps (Name Keyboard) (Name (Owner *ownerID*))
  (prop (CMD *cmd*)) $\Rightarrow$
(M, Oi, Os) sat
reps (Name (Role Server)) (Name (Owner *ownerID*))

(prop (CMD *cmd*)) ⇒
(M,Oi,Os) sat
Name (Role CA) controls
Name (Key (pubK Server)) speaks_for Name (Role Server) ⇒
(M,Oi,Os) sat
Name (Key (pubK CA)) speaks_for Name (Role CA) ⇒
(M,Oi,Os) sat
Name (Key (pubK CA)) says
Name (Key (pubK Server)) speaks_for Name (Role Server) ⇒
(M,Oi,Os) sat
reps (Name (Role Server)) (Name (Role (Utility *utilityID*)))
  (prop (CMD (NP *npriv*))) ⇒
(M,Oi,Os) sat
reps (Name (Role Server)) (Name (Role (Utility *utilityID*)))
  (prop (CMD (PR *privcmd*))) ⇒
(M,Oi,Os) sat
Name (Role (Utility *utilityID*)) controls
prop (CMD (NP *npriv*)) ⇒
(M,Oi,Os) sat
Name (Role (Utility *utilityID*)) controls
prop (CMD (PR *privcmd*)) ⇒
(M,Oi,Os) sat prop (CMD (PR *privcmd*))

|UtilityServerPrivB_lemma|

⊢ (M,Oi,Os) sat
  Name (Key (pubK Server)) quoting
  Name (Role (Utility *utilityID*)) says
  prop (CMD (PR *privcmd*)) ⇒
  (M,Oi,Os) sat Name (Owner *ownerID*) controls prop (CMD *cmd*) ⇒
  (M,Oi,Os) sat
  reps (Name Keyboard) (Name (Owner *ownerID*))
    (prop (CMD *cmd*)) ⇒
  (M,Oi,Os) sat
  reps (Name (Role Server)) (Name (Owner *ownerID*))
    (prop (CMD *cmd*)) ⇒
  (M,Oi,Os) sat
  Name (Role CA) controls
  Name (Key (pubK Server)) speaks_for Name (Role Server) ⇒
  (M,Oi,Os) sat
  Name (Key (pubK CA)) speaks_for Name (Role CA) ⇒
  (M,Oi,Os) sat
  Name (Key (pubK CA)) says
  Name (Key (pubK Server)) speaks_for Name (Role Server) ⇒
  (M,Oi,Os) sat
  reps (Name (Role Server)) (Name (Role (Utility *utilityID*)))
    (prop (CMD (NP *npriv*))) ⇒
  (M,Oi,Os) sat
  reps (Name (Role Server)) (Name (Role (Utility *utilityID*)))
    (prop (CMD (PR *privcmd*))) ⇒

(M, Oi, Os) sat
Name (Role (Utility *utilityID*)) controls
prop (CMD (NP *npriv*)) $\Rightarrow$
(M, Oi, Os) sat
Name (Role (Utility *utilityID*)) says
prop (CMD (PR *privcmd*)) impf prop TRAP $\Rightarrow$
(M, Oi, Os) sat prop TRAP

10   inMsgA Theory

Built: 28 January 2016
Parent Theories: vm1a, principal, command

10.1   Datatypes

msg =
    KB num command
  | MSG keyPrinc principal order
        ((order digest, keyPrinc) asymMsg)

order = ORD keyPrinc principal command

10.2   Definitions

⌊checkmsg_def⌋
 ⊢ (checkmsg
        (MSG *sender recipient* (ORD *originator role cmd*)
            signature) $\iff$
    signVerify (pubK *sender*) *signature*
      (SOME (ORD *originator role cmd*)) $\wedge$
    (*sender* = *originator*)) $\wedge$ (checkmsg (KB *ownerID cmd*) $\iff$ T)

⌊msgInterpret_def⌋
 ⊢ (msgInterpret
        (MSG *sender recipient* (ORD *originator role cmd*)
            signature) =
    if
      checkmsg
        (MSG *sender recipient* (ORD *originator role cmd*)
            signature)
    then
      Name (Key (pubK *sender*)) quoting Name *role* says
      prop (CMD *cmd*)
    else TT) $\wedge$
    (msgInterpret (KB *ownerID cmd*) =
    if checkmsg (KB *ownerID cmd*) **then**
      Name Keyboard quoting Name (Owner *ownerID*) says
      prop (CMD *cmd*)
    else TT)

10.3 Theorems

[checkKB_OK]

$\vdash \forall ownerID\ cmd$. **checkmsg** (KB $ownerID\ cmd$)

[checkMSG_OK]

$\vdash (\forall ownerID\ sender\ recipient\ originator\ role\ cmd$.
    $(sender = originator) \Rightarrow$
    checkmsg
      (MSG $sender\ recipient$ (ORD $originator\ role\ cmd$)
        (**sign** (privK $sender$)
          (**hash** (SOME (ORD $originator\ role\ cmd$)))))) $\wedge$
  $\forall ownerID\ sender\ recipient\ originator\ role\ cmd$.
    $sender \neq originator \Rightarrow$
    $\neg$**checkmsg**
      (MSG $sender\ recipient$ (ORD $originator\ role\ cmd$)
        (**sign** (privK $sender$)
          (**hash** (SOME (ORD $originator\ role\ cmd$))))))

[checkmsg_OK]

$\vdash ((\forall ownerID\ sender\ recipient\ originator\ role\ cmd$.
    $(sender = originator) \Rightarrow$
    checkmsg
      (MSG $sender\ recipient$ (ORD $originator\ role\ cmd$)
        (**sign** (privK $sender$)
          (**hash** (SOME (ORD $originator\ role\ cmd$))))))) $\wedge$
  $\forall ownerID\ sender\ recipient\ originator\ role\ cmd$.
    $sender \neq originator \Rightarrow$
    $\neg$**checkmsg**
      (MSG $sender\ recipient$ (ORD $originator\ role\ cmd$)
        (**sign** (privK $sender$)
          (**hash** (SOME (ORD $originator\ role\ cmd$)))))) $\wedge$
  $\forall ownerID\ cmd$. **checkmsg** (KB $ownerID\ cmd$)

[msg_distinct_thm]

$\vdash \forall a_3\ a_2\ a_1'\ a_1\ a_0'\ a_0$. KB $a_0\ a_1 \neq$ MSG $a_0'\ a_1'\ a_2\ a_3$

[msg_one_one]

$\vdash (\forall a_0\ a_1\ a_0'\ a_1'$.
    (KB $a_0\ a_1 =$ KB $a_0'\ a_1'$) $\iff$ $(a_0 = a_0') \wedge (a_1 = a_1')) \wedge$
  $\forall a_0\ a_1\ a_2\ a_3\ a_0'\ a_1'\ a_2'\ a_3'$.
    (MSG $a_0\ a_1\ a_2\ a_3 =$ MSG $a_0'\ a_1'\ a_2'\ a_3'$) $\iff$
    $(a_0 = a_0') \wedge (a_1 = a_1') \wedge (a_2 = a_2') \wedge (a_3 = a_3')$

[msgInterpretKB]

$\vdash (M, Oi, Os)$ **sat** **msgInterpret** (KB $ownerID\ cmd$) $\iff$
  (M, Oi, Os) **sat**
  Name Keyboard quoting Name (Owner $ownerID$) says
  prop (CMD cmd)

[msgInterpretMSG_denied]

⊢ *sender* ≠ *originator* ⇒
  (msgInterpret
    (MSG *sender* *recipient* (ORD *originator* *role* *cmd*)
      (sign (privK *sender*)
        (hash (SOME (ORD *originator* *role* *cmd*)))))) =
  TT)

[msgInterpretMSG_sender_originator_match]

⊢ msgInterpret
    (MSG *sender* *recipient* (ORD *sender* *role* *cmd*)
      (sign (privK *sender*)
        (hash (SOME (ORD *sender* *role* *cmd*))))) =
  Name (Key (pubK *sender*)) quoting Name *role* says
  prop (CMD *cmd*)

[order_one_one]

⊢ ∀ a_0 a_1 a_2 a_0' a_1' a_2'.
    (ORD a_0 a_1 a_2 = ORD a_0' a_1' a_2') ⟺
    (a_0 = a_0') ∧ (a_1 = a_1') ∧ (a_2 = a_2')

11 certA Theory

Built: 28 January 2016
Parent Theories: inMsgA, thermo1Certs

11.1 Datatypes

$cert_2$ =
    RCtrCert principal command
  | RRepsCert principal principal command
  | RCtrKCert keyPrinc keyPrinc keyPrinc
  | RKeyCert keyPrinc keyPrinc
  | KeyCert keyPrinc keyPrinc (keyPrinc pKey)
            (((keyPrinc × keyPrinc pKey) digest, keyPrinc)
            asymMsg)

11.2 Definitions

[cert2Interpret_def]

⊢ (cert2Interpret (RCtrCert P *cmd*) =
    if checkcert2 (RCtrCert P *cmd*) then
      Name P controls prop (CMD *cmd*)
    else TT) ∧
  (cert2Interpret (RRepsCert P Q *cmd*) =
    if checkcert2 (RRepsCert P Q *cmd*) then

```
      reps (Name P) (Name Q) (prop (CMD cmd))
   else TT) ∧
   (cert2Interpret (RCtrKCert ca keyKpr keyPpr) =
   if checkcert2 (RCtrKCert ca keyKpr keyPpr) then
     Name (Role ca) controls
     Name (Key (pubK keyKpr)) speaks_for Name (Role keyPpr)
   else TT) ∧
   (cert2Interpret (RKeyCert kppr ca) =
   if checkcert2 (RKeyCert kppr ca) then
     Name (Key (pubK kppr)) speaks_for Name (Role ca)
   else TT) ∧
   (cert2Interpret (KeyCert ca keyPpr (pubK keyRpr) signature) =
   if
     checkcert2 (KeyCert ca keyPpr (pubK keyRpr) signature)
   then
     Name (Key (pubK ca)) says
     Name (Key (pubK keyRpr)) speaks_for Name (Role keyPpr)
   else TT)
```

[certs2_def]

```
⊢ ∀ownerID utilityID cmd npriv privcmd.
     certs2 ownerID utilityID cmd npriv privcmd =
     [RCtrCert (Owner ownerID) cmd;
     RRepsCert Keyboard (Owner ownerID) cmd;
     RRepsCert (Role Server) (Owner ownerID) cmd;
     RCtrKCert CA Server Server; RKeyCert CA CA;
     KeyCert CA Server (pubK Server)
       (sign (privK CA) (hash (SOME (Server,pubK Server))));
     RRepsCert (Role Server) (Role (Utility utilityID))
       (NP npriv);
     RRepsCert (Role Server) (Role (Utility utilityID))
       (PR privcmd);
     RCtrCert (Role (Utility utilityID)) (NP npriv)]
```

[checkcert2_def]

```
⊢ (checkcert2 (RCtrCert P cmd)  ⟺  T) ∧
  (checkcert2 (RRepsCert P Q cmd)  ⟺  T) ∧
  (checkcert2 (RCtrKCert keyPpr Kq keyQpr)  ⟺  T) ∧
  (checkcert2 (RKeyCert kp keyPpr)  ⟺  T) ∧
  (checkcert2 (KeyCert CApr Ppr (pubK Rpr) signature)  ⟺
  signVerify (pubK CApr) signature (SOME (Ppr,pubK Rpr)))
```

11.3 Theorems

[cert2_distinct_thm]

```
⊢ (∀ a₂ a′₁ a₁ a′₀ a₀. RCtrCert a₀ a₁ ≠ RRepsCert a′₀ a′₁ a₂) ∧
  (∀ a₂ a′₁ a₁ a′₀ a₀. RCtrCert a₀ a₁ ≠ RCtrKCert a′₀ a′₁ a₂) ∧
  (∀ a′₁ a₁ a′₀ a₀. RCtrCert a₀ a₁ ≠ RKeyCert a′₀ a′₁) ∧
```

$(\forall a_3 \ a_2 \ a_1' \ a_1 \ a_0' \ a_0.$
$\quad$ RCtrCert $a_0 \ a_1 \neq$ KeyCert $a_0' \ a_1' \ a_2 \ a_3) \ \wedge$
$(\forall a_2' \ a_2 \ a_1' \ a_1 \ a_0' \ a_0.$
$\quad$ RRepsCert $a_0 \ a_1 \ a_2 \neq$ RCtrKCert $a_0' \ a_1' \ a_2') \ \wedge$
$(\forall a_2 \ a_1' \ a_1 \ a_0' \ a_0.$ RRepsCert $a_0 \ a_1 \ a_2 \neq$ RKeyCert $a_0' \ a_1') \ \wedge$
$(\forall a_3 \ a_2' \ a_2 \ a_1' \ a_1 \ a_0' \ a_0.$
$\quad$ RRepsCert $a_0 \ a_1 \ a_2 \neq$ KeyCert $a_0' \ a_1' \ a_2' \ a_3) \ \wedge$
$(\forall a_2 \ a_1' \ a_1 \ a_0' \ a_0.$ RCtrKCert $a_0 \ a_1 \ a_2 \neq$ RKeyCert $a_0' \ a_1') \ \wedge$
$(\forall a_3 \ a_2' \ a_2 \ a_1' \ a_1 \ a_0' \ a_0.$
$\quad$ RCtrKCert $a_0 \ a_1 \ a_2 \neq$ KeyCert $a_0' \ a_1' \ a_2' \ a_3) \ \wedge$
$\forall a_3 \ a_2 \ a_1' \ a_1 \ a_0' \ a_0.$ RKeyCert $a_0 \ a_1 \neq$ KeyCert $a_0' \ a_1' \ a_2 \ a_3$

[cert2_one_one]

$\vdash (\forall a_0 \ a_1 \ a_0' \ a_1'.$
$\quad$ (RCtrCert $a_0 \ a_1 =$ RCtrCert $a_0' \ a_1') \iff$
$\quad (a_0 = a_0') \wedge (a_1 = a_1')) \ \wedge$
$(\forall a_0 \ a_1 \ a_2 \ a_0' \ a_1' \ a_2'.$
$\quad$ (RRepsCert $a_0 \ a_1 \ a_2 =$ RRepsCert $a_0' \ a_1' \ a_2') \iff$
$\quad (a_0 = a_0') \wedge (a_1 = a_1') \wedge (a_2 = a_2')) \ \wedge$
$(\forall a_0 \ a_1 \ a_2 \ a_0' \ a_1' \ a_2'.$
$\quad$ (RCtrKCert $a_0 \ a_1 \ a_2 =$ RCtrKCert $a_0' \ a_1' \ a_2') \iff$
$\quad (a_0 = a_0') \wedge (a_1 = a_1') \wedge (a_2 = a_2')) \ \wedge$
$(\forall a_0 \ a_1 \ a_0' \ a_1'.$
$\quad$ (RKeyCert $a_0 \ a_1 =$ RKeyCert $a_0' \ a_1') \iff$
$\quad (a_0 = a_0') \wedge (a_1 = a_1')) \ \wedge$
$\forall a_0 \ a_1 \ a_2 \ a_3 \ a_0' \ a_1' \ a_2' \ a_3'.$
$\quad$ (KeyCert $a_0 \ a_1 \ a_2 \ a_3 =$ KeyCert $a_0' \ a_1' \ a_2' \ a_3') \iff$
$\quad (a_0 = a_0') \wedge (a_1 = a_1') \wedge (a_2 = a_2') \wedge (a_3 = a_3')$

[cert2A_lemma]

$\vdash (M, Oi, Os)$ sat
$\quad$ cert2Interpret (RCtrCert (Owner *ownerID*) *cmd*) $\iff$
$\quad (M, Oi, Os)$ sat Name (Owner *ownerID*) controls prop (CMD *cmd*)

[cert2B_lemma]

$\vdash (M, Oi, Os)$ sat
$\quad$ cert2Interpret (RRepsCert Keyboard (Owner *ownerID*) *cmd*) $\iff$
$\quad (M, Oi, Os)$ sat
$\quad$ reps (Name Keyboard) (Name (Owner *ownerID*)) (prop (CMD *cmd*))

[cert2C_lemma]

$\vdash (M, Oi, Os)$ sat
$\quad$ cert2Interpret
$\quad\quad$ (RRepsCert (Role Server) (Owner *ownerID*) *cmd*) $\iff$
$\quad (M, Oi, Os)$ sat
$\quad$ reps (Name (Role Server)) (Name (Owner *ownerID*))
$\quad\quad$ (prop (CMD *cmd*))

⌈cert2D_lemma⌋

⊢ (M, Oi, Os) sat cert2Interpret (RCtrKCert CA Server Server) ⟺
   (M, Oi, Os) sat
   Name (Role CA) controls
   Name (Key (pubK Server)) speaks_for Name (Role Server)

⌈cert2E_lemma⌋

⊢ (M, Oi, Os) sat cert2Interpret (RKeyCert CA CA) ⟺
   (M, Oi, Os) sat Name (Key (pubK CA)) speaks_for Name (Role CA)

⌈cert2F_lemma⌋

⊢ (M, Oi, Os) sat
   cert2Interpret
     (KeyCert CA Server (pubK Server)
       (sign (privK CA) (hash (SOME (Server,pubK Server))))) ⟺
   (M, Oi, Os) sat
   Name (Key (pubK CA)) says
   Name (Key (pubK Server)) speaks_for Name (Role Server)

⌈cert2G_lemma⌋

⊢ (M, Oi, Os) sat
   cert2Interpret
     (RRepsCert (Role Server) (Role (Utility *utilityID*))
       (NP *npriv*)) ⟺
   (M, Oi, Os) sat
   reps (Name (Role Server)) (Name (Role (Utility *utilityID*)))
     (prop (CMD (NP *npriv*)))

⌈cert2H_lemma⌋

⊢ (M, Oi, Os) sat
   cert2Interpret
     (RRepsCert (Role Server) (Role (Utility *utilityID*))
       (PR *privcmd*)) ⟺
   (M, Oi, Os) sat
   reps (Name (Role Server)) (Name (Role (Utility *utilityID*)))
     (prop (CMD (PR *privcmd*)))

⌈cert2I_lemma⌋

⊢ (M, Oi, Os) sat
   cert2Interpret
     (RCtrCert (Role (Utility *utilityID*)) (NP *npriv*)) ⟺
   (M, Oi, Os) sat
   Name (Role (Utility *utilityID*)) controls
   prop (CMD (NP *npriv*))

[cert2InterpretKeyCert]

$\vdash (M, Oi, Os)$ sat
  cert2Interpret
    (KeyCert ca P (pubK P)
      (sign (privK ca) (hash (SOME (P,pubK P))))) $\Longleftrightarrow$
  (M, Oi, Os) sat
  Name (Key (pubK ca)) says
  Name (Key (pubK P)) speaks_for Name (Role P)

[cert2InterpretRCtrCert]

$\vdash (M, Oi, Os)$ sat cert2Interpret (RCtrCert (Role P) cmd) $\Longleftrightarrow$
  (M, Oi, Os) sat Name (Role P) controls prop (CMD cmd)

[cert2InterpretRCtrKCert]

$\vdash (M, Oi, Os)$ sat cert2Interpret (RCtrKCert P Q Q) $\Longleftrightarrow$
  (M, Oi, Os) sat
  Name (Role P) controls
  Name (Key (pubK Q)) speaks_for Name (Role Q)

[cert2InterpretRKeyCert]

$\vdash (M, Oi, Os)$ sat cert2Interpret (RKeyCert P P) $\Longleftrightarrow$
  (M, Oi, Os) sat Name (Key (pubK P)) speaks_for Name (Role P)

[cert2InterpretRRepsCert]

$\vdash (M, Oi, Os)$ sat
  cert2Interpret (RRepsCert (Role P) (Role Q) cmd) $\Longleftrightarrow$
  (M, Oi, Os) sat
  reps (Name (Role P)) (Name (Role Q)) (prop (CMD cmd))

12 thermo2 Theory

Built: 28 January 2016
Parent Theories: certA, vm2a

12.1 Theorems

[CFG2Interpret_exec_Keyboard_Owner_cmd]

$\vdash \forall NS$ Out $outStream$ $state$ ins $npriv$ $privcmd$ cmd $ownerID$
    $utilityID$ M Oi Os.
  CFG2Interpret (M, Oi, Os)
    (CFG2 msgInterpret cert2Interpret isAuthenticated
      (certs2 $ownerID$ $utilityID$ cmd $npriv$ $privcmd$)
      (thermoStateInterp $utilityID$ $privcmd$)
      (KB $ownerID$ cmd::ins) $state$ $outStream$) $\Rightarrow$
    TR2 (M, Oi, Os) (exec (CMD cmd))
      (CFG2 msgInterpret cert2Interpret isAuthenticated

```
        (certs2 ownerID utilityID cmd npriv privcmd)
        (thermoStateInterp utilityID privcmd)
        (KB ownerID cmd::ins) state outStream)
    (CFG2 msgInterpret cert2Interpret isAuthenticated
        (certs2 ownerID utilityID cmd npriv privcmd)
        (thermoStateInterp utilityID privcmd) ins
        (NS state (exec (CMD cmd)))
        (Out state (exec (CMD cmd))::outStream)) ∧
    (M,Oi,Os) sat prop (CMD cmd)
```

[CFG2Interpret_exec_KServer_Owner_cmd]

```
⊢ ∀ NS Out M Oi Os outStream state ins privcmd npriv cmd
        utilityID ownerID.
    CFG2Interpret (M,Oi,Os)
        (CFG2 msgInterpret cert2Interpret isAuthenticated
            (certs2 ownerID utilityID cmd npriv privcmd)
            (thermoStateInterp utilityID privcmd)
            (MSG Server (Owner ownerID)
                (ORD Server (Owner ownerID) cmd)
                (sign (privK Server)
                    (hash
                        (SOME (ORD Server (Owner ownerID) cmd))))::
                    ins) state outStream) ⇒
        TR2 (M,Oi,Os) (exec (CMD cmd))
            (CFG2 msgInterpret cert2Interpret isAuthenticated
                (certs2 ownerID utilityID cmd npriv privcmd)
                (thermoStateInterp utilityID privcmd)
                (MSG Server (Owner ownerID)
                    (ORD Server (Owner ownerID) cmd)
                    (sign (privK Server)
                        (hash
                            (SOME (ORD Server (Owner ownerID) cmd))))::
                        ins) state outStream)
            (CFG2 msgInterpret cert2Interpret isAuthenticated
                (certs2 ownerID utilityID cmd npriv privcmd)
                (thermoStateInterp utilityID privcmd) ins
                (NS state (exec (CMD cmd)))
                (Out state (exec (CMD cmd))::outStream)) ∧
    (M,Oi,Os) sat prop (CMD cmd)
```

[CFG2Interpret_exec_KServer_Utility_npriv]

```
⊢ ∀ NS Out M Oi Os outStream state ins privcmd npriv cmd
        utilityID ownerID.
    CFG2Interpret (M,Oi,Os)
        (CFG2 msgInterpret cert2Interpret isAuthenticated
            (certs2 ownerID utilityID cmd npriv privcmd)
            (thermoStateInterp utilityID privcmd)
            (MSG Server (Role (Utility utilityID))
                (ORD Server (Role (Utility utilityID)) (NP npriv))
```

```
                    (sign (privK Server)
                      (hash
                        (SOME
                          (ORD Server (Role (Utility utilityID))
                            (NP npriv)))))::ins) state outStream) ⇒
      TR2 (M,Oi,Os) (exec (CMD (NP npriv)))
        (CFG2 msgInterpret cert2Interpret isAuthenticated
          (certs2 ownerID utilityID cmd npriv privcmd)
          (thermoStateInterp utilityID privcmd)
          (MSG Server (Role (Utility utilityID))
            (ORD Server (Role (Utility utilityID)) (NP npriv))
            (sign (privK Server)
              (hash
                (SOME
                  (ORD Server (Role (Utility utilityID))
                    (NP npriv)))))::ins) state outStream)
        (CFG2 msgInterpret cert2Interpret isAuthenticated
          (certs2 ownerID utilityID cmd npriv privcmd)
          (thermoStateInterp utilityID privcmd) ins
          (NS state (exec (CMD (NP npriv))))
          (Out state (exec (CMD (NP npriv)))::outStream)) ∧
      (M,Oi,Os) sat prop (CMD (NP npriv))
```

⌐CFG2Interpret_exec_KServer_Utility_privcmd⌐

```
⊢ ∀NS Out outStream temperature ins npriv privcmd cmd ownerID
    utilityID M Oi Os.
    CFG2Interpret (M,Oi,Os)
      (CFG2 msgInterpret cert2Interpret isAuthenticated
        (certs2 ownerID utilityID cmd npriv privcmd)
        (thermoStateInterp utilityID privcmd)
        (MSG Server (Role (Utility utilityID))
          (ORD Server (Role (Utility utilityID))
            (PR privcmd))
          (sign (privK Server)
            (hash
              (SOME
                (ORD Server (Role (Utility utilityID))
                  (PR privcmd)))))::ins)
        (State enabled temperature) outStream) ⇒
      TR2 (M,Oi,Os) (exec (CMD (PR privcmd)))
        (CFG2 msgInterpret cert2Interpret isAuthenticated
          (certs2 ownerID utilityID cmd npriv privcmd)
          (thermoStateInterp utilityID privcmd)
          (MSG Server (Role (Utility utilityID))
            (ORD Server (Role (Utility utilityID))
              (PR privcmd))
            (sign (privK Server)
              (hash
                (SOME
```

$$(ORD\ Server\ (Role\ (Utility\ \mathit{utilityID}))$$
$$(PR\ \mathit{privcmd}))))::\mathit{ins}$$
$$(State\ enabled\ \mathit{temperature})\ \mathit{outStream})$$
$$(CFG2\ msgInterpret\ cert2Interpret\ isAuthenticated$$
$$(certs2\ \mathit{ownerID}\ \mathit{utilityID}\ \mathit{cmd}\ \mathit{npriv}\ \mathit{privcmd})$$
$$(thermoStateInterp\ \mathit{utilityID}\ \mathit{privcmd})\ \mathit{ins}$$
$$(\mathit{NS}\ (State\ enabled\ \mathit{temperature})$$
$$(exec\ (CMD\ (PR\ \mathit{privcmd}))))$$
$$(\mathit{Out}\ (State\ enabled\ \mathit{temperature})$$
$$(exec\ (CMD\ (PR\ \mathit{privcmd})))::\mathit{outStream}))\ \wedge$$
$$(M,Oi,Os)\ \text{sat prop}\ (CMD\ (PR\ \mathit{privcmd}))$$

⌈CFG2Interpret_iff_CFGInterpret_Keyboard_Owner_cmd_lemma⌉

⊢ CFG2Interpret (M,Oi,Os)
   (CFG2 msgInterpret cert2Interpret isAuthenticated
     (certs2 $\mathit{ownerID}$ $\mathit{utilityID}$ cmd npriv $\mathit{privcmd}$)
     (thermoStateInterp $\mathit{utilityID}$ $\mathit{privcmd}$)
     (KB $\mathit{ownerID}$ $\mathit{cmd}::\mathit{ins_2}$) state $\mathit{outStream}$) $\iff$
 CFGInterpret (M,Oi,Os)
   (CFG isAuthenticated (thermoStateInterp $\mathit{utilityID}$ $\mathit{privcmd}$)
     (certs $\mathit{ownerID}$ $\mathit{utilityID}$ cmd npriv $\mathit{privcmd}$)
     (Name Keyboard quoting Name (Owner $\mathit{ownerID}$) says
      prop (CMD cmd)::ins) state $\mathit{outStream}$)

⌈CFG2Interpret_iff_CFGInterpret_KServer_Owner_cmd_lemma⌉

⊢ CFG2Interpret (M,Oi,Os)
   (CFG2 msgInterpret cert2Interpret isAuthenticated
     (certs2 $\mathit{ownerID}$ $\mathit{utilityID}$ cmd npriv $\mathit{privcmd}$)
     (thermoStateInterp $\mathit{utilityID}$ $\mathit{privcmd}$)
     (MSG Server (Owner $\mathit{ownerID}$)
        (ORD Server (Owner $\mathit{ownerID}$) cmd)
        (sign (privK Server)
           (hash (SOME (ORD Server (Owner $\mathit{ownerID}$) cmd))))::
         $\mathit{ins_2}$) state $\mathit{outStream}$) $\iff$
 CFGInterpret (M,Oi,Os)
   (CFG isAuthenticated (thermoStateInterp $\mathit{utilityID}$ $\mathit{privcmd}$)
     (certs $\mathit{ownerID}$ $\mathit{utilityID}$ cmd npriv $\mathit{privcmd}$)
     (Name (Key (pubK Server)) quoting
      Name (Owner $\mathit{ownerID}$) says prop (CMD cmd)::ins) state
    $\mathit{outStream}$)

⌈CFG2Interpret_iff_CFGInterpret_KServer_Utility_npriv_lemma⌉

⊢ CFG2Interpret (M,Oi,Os)
   (CFG2 msgInterpret cert2Interpret isAuthenticated
     (certs2 $\mathit{ownerID}$ $\mathit{utilityID}$ cmd npriv $\mathit{privcmd}$)
     (thermoStateInterp $\mathit{utilityID}$ $\mathit{privcmd}$)
     (MSG Server (Role (Utility $\mathit{utilityID}$))
        (ORD Server (Role (Utility $\mathit{utilityID}$))) (NP npriv))

```
        (sign (privK Server)
          (hash
            (SOME
              (ORD Server (Role (Utility utilityID))
                (NP npriv)))))::ins₂) state outStream)  ⟺
CFGInterpret (M,Oi,Os)
  (CFG isAuthenticated (thermoStateInterp utilityID privcmd)
    (certs ownerID utilityID cmd npriv privcmd)
    (Name (Key (pubK Server)) quoting
    Name (Role (Utility utilityID)) says
    prop (CMD (NP npriv))::ins) state outStream)
```

[CFG2Interpret_iff_CFGInterpret_KServer_Utility_trap_lemma]

```
⊢ CFG2Interpret (M,Oi,Os)
    (CFG2 msgInterpret cert2Interpret isAuthenticated
      (certs2 ownerID utilityID cmd npriv privcmd)
      (thermoStateInterp utilityID privcmd)
      (MSG Server (Role (Utility utilityID))
        (ORD Server (Role (Utility utilityID)) (PR privcmd))
        (sign (privK Server)
          (hash
            (SOME
              (ORD Server (Role (Utility utilityID))
                (PR privcmd)))))::ins₂)
      (State disabled temperature) outStream)  ⟺
  CFGInterpret (M,Oi,Os)
    (CFG isAuthenticated (thermoStateInterp utilityID privcmd)
      (certs ownerID utilityID cmd npriv privcmd)
      (Name (Key (pubK Server)) quoting
      Name (Role (Utility utilityID)) says
      prop (CMD (PR privcmd))::ins)
      (State disabled temperature) outStream)
```

[CFG2Interpret_Owner_Keyboard_thm]

```
⊢ ∀M Oi Os.
    CFG2Interpret (M,Oi,Os)
      (CFG2 msgInterpret cert2Interpret isAuthenticated
        (certs2 ownerID utilityID cmd npriv privcmd)
        (thermoStateInterp utilityID privcmd)
        (KB ownerID cmd::ins) state outStream) ⇒
    (M,Oi,Os) sat prop (CMD cmd)
```

[CFG2Interpret_Owner_KServer_thm]

```
⊢ ∀M Oi Os.
    CFG2Interpret (M,Oi,Os)
      (CFG2 msgInterpret cert2Interpret isAuthenticated
        (certs2 ownerID utilityID cmd npriv privcmd)
        (thermoStateInterp utilityID privcmd)
```

```
        (MSG Server (Owner ownerID)
          (ORD Server (Owner ownerID) cmd)
          (sign (privK Server)
            (hash
              (SOME (ORD Server (Owner ownerID) cmd))))::
            ins) state outStream) ⇒
    (M, Oi, Os) sat prop (CMD cmd)
```

[CFG2Interpret_trap_KServer_Utility_privcmd]

```
⊢ ∀ NS  Out outStream temperature ins npriv privcmd cmd ownerID
    utilityID M Oi Os.
  CFG2Interpret (M, Oi, Os)
    (CFG2 msgInterpret cert2Interpret isAuthenticated
      (certs2 ownerID utilityID cmd npriv privcmd)
      (thermoStateInterp utilityID privcmd)
      (MSG Server (Role (Utility utilityID))
        (ORD Server (Role (Utility utilityID))
          (PR privcmd))
        (sign (privK Server)
          (hash
            (SOME
              (ORD Server (Role (Utility utilityID))
                (PR privcmd)))))::ins)
      (State disabled temperature) outStream) ⇒
    TR2 (M, Oi, Os) (trap (CMD (PR privcmd)))
      (CFG2 msgInterpret cert2Interpret isAuthenticated
        (certs2 ownerID utilityID cmd npriv privcmd)
        (thermoStateInterp utilityID privcmd)
        (MSG Server (Role (Utility utilityID))
          (ORD Server (Role (Utility utilityID))
            (PR privcmd))
          (sign (privK Server)
            (hash
              (SOME
                (ORD Server (Role (Utility utilityID))
                  (PR privcmd)))))::ins)
        (State disabled temperature) outStream)
      (CFG2 msgInterpret cert2Interpret isAuthenticated
        (certs2 ownerID utilityID cmd npriv privcmd)
        (thermoStateInterp utilityID privcmd) ins
        (NS (State disabled temperature)
          (trap (CMD (PR privcmd))))
        (Out (State disabled temperature)
          (trap (CMD (PR privcmd)))::outStream)) ∧
    (M, Oi, Os) sat prop TRAP
```

[CFG2Interpret_Utility_KServer_npriv_thm]

```
⊢ ∀ M  Oi Os.
  CFG2Interpret (M, Oi, Os)
```

```
(CFG2 msgInterpret cert2Interpret isAuthenticated
    (certs2 ownerID utilityID cmd npriv privcmd)
    (thermoStateInterp utilityID privcmd)
    (MSG Server (Role (Utility utilityID))
        (ORD Server (Role (Utility utilityID)) (NP npriv))
        (sign (privK Server)
            (hash
                (SOME
                    (ORD Server (Role (Utility utilityID))
                        (NP npriv)))))::ins) state outStream) ⇒
(M,Oi,Os) sat prop (CMD (NP npriv))
```

[CFG2Interpret_Utility_KServer_privcmd_thm]

⊢ ∀M Oi Os.
    CFG2Interpret (M,Oi,Os)
```
(CFG2 msgInterpret cert2Interpret isAuthenticated
    (certs2 ownerID utilityID cmd npriv privcmd)
    (thermoStateInterp utilityID privcmd)
    (MSG Server (Role (Utility utilityID))
        (ORD Server (Role (Utility utilityID))
            (PR privcmd))
        (sign (privK Server)
            (hash
                (SOME
                    (ORD Server (Role (Utility utilityID))
                        (PR privcmd)))))::ins)
    (State enabled temperature) outStream) ⇒
(M,Oi,Os) sat prop (CMD (PR privcmd))
```

[CFG2Interpret_Utility_KServer_trap_thm]

⊢ ∀M Oi Os.
    CFG2Interpret (M,Oi,Os)
```
(CFG2 msgInterpret cert2Interpret isAuthenticated
    (certs2 ownerID utilityID cmd npriv privcmd)
    (thermoStateInterp utilityID privcmd)
    (MSG Server (Role (Utility utilityID))
        (ORD Server (Role (Utility utilityID))
            (PR privcmd))
        (sign (privK Server)
            (hash
                (SOME
                    (ORD Server (Role (Utility utilityID))
                        (PR privcmd)))))::ins)
    (State disabled temperature) outStream) ⇒
(M,Oi,Os) sat prop TRAP
```

[exec2_Keyboard_Owner_cmd_Justified]

⊢ ∀NS Out M Oi Os.
    TR2 (M,Oi,Os) (exec (CMD cmd))

```
    (CFG2 msgInterpret cert2Interpret isAuthenticated
      (certs2 ownerID utilityID cmd npriv privcmd)
      (thermoStateInterp utilityID privcmd)
      (KB ownerID cmd::ins) state outStream)
    (CFG2 msgInterpret cert2Interpret isAuthenticated
      (certs2 ownerID utilityID cmd npriv privcmd)
      (thermoStateInterp utilityID privcmd) ins
      (NS state (exec (CMD cmd)))
      (Out state (exec (CMD cmd))::outStream)) ⇒
  (M,Oi,Os) sat prop (CMD cmd)
```

⌈exec2_Keyboard_Owner_cmd_thm⌋

```
⊢ ∀NS Out M Oi Os.
    TR2 (M,Oi,Os) (exec (CMD cmd))
      (CFG2 msgInterpret cert2Interpret isAuthenticated
        (certs2 ownerID utilityID cmd npriv privcmd)
        (thermoStateInterp utilityID privcmd)
        (KB ownerID cmd::ins) state outStream)
      (CFG2 msgInterpret cert2Interpret isAuthenticated
        (certs2 ownerID utilityID cmd npriv privcmd)
        (thermoStateInterp utilityID privcmd) ins
        (NS state (exec (CMD cmd)))
        (Out state (exec (CMD cmd))::outStream)) ⟺
    CFG2Interpret (M,Oi,Os)
      (CFG2 msgInterpret cert2Interpret isAuthenticated
        (certs2 ownerID utilityID cmd npriv privcmd)
        (thermoStateInterp utilityID privcmd)
        (KB ownerID cmd::ins) state outStream) ∧
    (M,Oi,Os) sat prop (CMD cmd)
```

⌈exec2_KServer_Owner_cmd_Justified⌋

```
⊢ ∀NS Out M Oi Os.
    TR2 (M,Oi,Os) (exec (CMD cmd))
      (CFG2 msgInterpret cert2Interpret isAuthenticated
        (certs2 ownerID utilityID cmd npriv privcmd)
        (thermoStateInterp utilityID privcmd)
        (MSG Server (Owner ownerID)
          (ORD Server (Owner ownerID) cmd)
          (sign (privK Server)
            (hash
              (SOME (ORD Server (Owner ownerID) cmd))))::
              ins) state outStream)
      (CFG2 msgInterpret cert2Interpret isAuthenticated
        (certs2 ownerID utilityID cmd npriv privcmd)
        (thermoStateInterp utilityID privcmd) ins
        (NS state (exec (CMD cmd)))
        (Out state (exec (CMD cmd))::outStream)) ⇒
    (M,Oi,Os) sat prop (CMD cmd)
```

$[exec2\_KServer\_Owner\_cmd\_thm]$

$\vdash \forall NS\ Out\ M\ Oi\ Os.$
$\quad$ TR2 (M, Oi, Os) (exec (CMD cmd))
$\quad\quad$ (CFG2 msgInterpret cert2Interpret isAuthenticated
$\quad\quad\quad$ (certs2 $ownerID\ utilityID\ cmd\ npriv\ privcmd$)
$\quad\quad\quad$ (thermoStateInterp $utilityID\ privcmd$)
$\quad\quad\quad$ (MSG Server (Owner $ownerID$)
$\quad\quad\quad\quad$ (ORD Server (Owner $ownerID$) cmd)
$\quad\quad\quad\quad$ (sign (privK Server)
$\quad\quad\quad\quad\quad$ (hash
$\quad\quad\quad\quad\quad\quad$ (SOME (ORD Server (Owner $ownerID$) cmd))))::
$\quad\quad\quad\quad\quad$ ins) $state\ outStream$)
$\quad\quad$ (CFG2 msgInterpret cert2Interpret isAuthenticated
$\quad\quad\quad$ (certs2 $ownerID\ utilityID\ cmd\ npriv\ privcmd$)
$\quad\quad\quad$ (thermoStateInterp $utilityID\ privcmd$) ins
$\quad\quad\quad$ ($NS\ state$ (exec (CMD cmd)))
$\quad\quad\quad$ ($Out\ state$ (exec (CMD cmd))::$outStream$)) $\Longleftrightarrow$
$\quad$ CFG2Interpret (M, Oi, Os)
$\quad\quad$ (CFG2 msgInterpret cert2Interpret isAuthenticated
$\quad\quad\quad$ (certs2 $ownerID\ utilityID\ cmd\ npriv\ privcmd$)
$\quad\quad\quad$ (thermoStateInterp $utilityID\ privcmd$)
$\quad\quad\quad$ (MSG Server (Owner $ownerID$)
$\quad\quad\quad\quad$ (ORD Server (Owner $ownerID$) cmd)
$\quad\quad\quad\quad$ (sign (privK Server)
$\quad\quad\quad\quad\quad$ (hash
$\quad\quad\quad\quad\quad\quad$ (SOME (ORD Server (Owner $ownerID$) cmd))))::
$\quad\quad\quad\quad\quad$ ins) $state\ outStream$) $\wedge$
$\quad$ (M, Oi, Os) sat prop (CMD cmd)

$[exec2\_KServer\_Utility\_npriv\_Justified]$

$\vdash \forall NS\ Out\ outStream\ state\ ins\ npriv\ privcmd\ cmd\ ownerID$
$\quad\quad utilityID\ M\ Oi\ Os.$
$\quad$ TR2 (M, Oi, Os) (exec (CMD (NP $npriv$)))
$\quad\quad$ (CFG2 msgInterpret cert2Interpret isAuthenticated
$\quad\quad\quad$ (certs2 $ownerID\ utilityID\ cmd\ npriv\ privcmd$)
$\quad\quad\quad$ (thermoStateInterp $utilityID\ privcmd$)
$\quad\quad\quad$ (MSG Server (Role (Utility $utilityID$))
$\quad\quad\quad\quad$ (ORD Server (Role (Utility $utilityID$)) (NP $npriv$))
$\quad\quad\quad\quad$ (sign (privK Server)
$\quad\quad\quad\quad\quad$ (hash
$\quad\quad\quad\quad\quad\quad$ (SOME
$\quad\quad\quad\quad\quad\quad\quad$ (ORD Server (Role (Utility $utilityID$))
$\quad\quad\quad\quad\quad\quad\quad\quad$ (NP $npriv$)))))::ins) $state\ outStream$)
$\quad\quad$ (CFG2 msgInterpret cert2Interpret isAuthenticated
$\quad\quad\quad$ (certs2 $ownerID\ utilityID\ cmd\ npriv\ privcmd$)
$\quad\quad\quad$ (thermoStateInterp $utilityID\ privcmd$) ins
$\quad\quad\quad$ ($NS\ state$ (exec (CMD (NP $npriv$))))
$\quad\quad\quad$ ($Out\ state$ (exec (CMD (NP $npriv$)))::$outStream$)) $\Rightarrow$
$\quad$ (M, Oi, Os) sat prop (CMD (NP $npriv$))

|exec2_KServer_Utility_npriv_thm|

⊢ ∀NS Out M Oi Os.
   TR2 (M,Oi,Os) (exec (CMD (NP npriv)))
     (CFG2 msgInterpret cert2Interpret isAuthenticated
       (certs2 ownerID utilityID cmd npriv privcmd)
       (thermoStateInterp utilityID privcmd)
       (MSG Server (Role (Utility utilityID))
         (ORD Server (Role (Utility utilityID)) (NP npriv))
         (sign (privK Server)
          (hash
           (SOME
             (ORD Server (Role (Utility utilityID))
               (NP npriv)))))::ins) state outStream)
     (CFG2 msgInterpret cert2Interpret isAuthenticated
       (certs2 ownerID utilityID cmd npriv privcmd)
       (thermoStateInterp utilityID privcmd) ins
       $(NS$ state (exec (CMD (NP npriv))))
       $(Out$ state (exec (CMD (NP npriv)))::outStream)) ⟺
   CFG2Interpret (M,Oi,Os)
     (CFG2 msgInterpret cert2Interpret isAuthenticated
       (certs2 ownerID utilityID cmd npriv privcmd)
       (thermoStateInterp utilityID privcmd)
       (MSG Server (Role (Utility utilityID))
         (ORD Server (Role (Utility utilityID)) (NP npriv))
         (sign (privK Server)
          (hash
           (SOME
             (ORD Server (Role (Utility utilityID))
               (NP npriv)))))::ins) state outStream) ∧
   (M,Oi,Os) sat prop (CMD (NP npriv))

|exec2_KServer_Utility_privcmd_Justified|

⊢ ∀NS Out outStream temperature ins npriv privcmd cmd ownerID
   utilityID M Oi Os.
   TR2 (M,Oi,Os) (exec (CMD (PR privcmd)))
     (CFG2 msgInterpret cert2Interpret isAuthenticated
       (certs2 ownerID utilityID cmd npriv privcmd)
       (thermoStateInterp utilityID privcmd)
       (MSG Server (Role (Utility utilityID))
         (ORD Server (Role (Utility utilityID))
          (PR privcmd))
         (sign (privK Server)
          (hash
           (SOME
             (ORD Server (Role (Utility utilityID))
               (PR privcmd)))))::ins)
       (State enabled temperature) outStream)
     (CFG2 msgInterpret cert2Interpret isAuthenticated
       (certs2 ownerID utilityID cmd npriv privcmd)

```
          (thermoStateInterp utilityID privcmd) ins
          (NS (State enabled temperature)
            (exec (CMD (PR privcmd))))
          (Out (State enabled temperature)
            (exec (CMD (PR privcmd)))::outStream)) ⇒
      (M,Oi,Os) sat prop (CMD (PR privcmd))
```

⌊exec2_KServer_Utility_privcmd_thm⌋

```
⊢ ∀NS Out M Oi Os.
    TR2 (M,Oi,Os) (exec (CMD (PR privcmd)))
      (CFG2 msgInterpret cert2Interpret isAuthenticated
        (certs2 ownerID utilityID cmd npriv privcmd)
        (thermoStateInterp utilityID privcmd)
        (MSG Server (Role (Utility utilityID))
          (ORD Server (Role (Utility utilityID))
            (PR privcmd))
          (sign (privK Server)
            (hash
              (SOME
                (ORD Server (Role (Utility utilityID))
                  (PR privcmd)))))::ins)
        (State enabled temperature) outStream)
      (CFG2 msgInterpret cert2Interpret isAuthenticated
        (certs2 ownerID utilityID cmd npriv privcmd)
        (thermoStateInterp utilityID privcmd) ins
        (NS (State enabled temperature)
          (exec (CMD (PR privcmd))))
        (Out (State enabled temperature)
          (exec (CMD (PR privcmd)))::outStream)) ⟺
    CFG2Interpret (M,Oi,Os)
      (CFG2 msgInterpret cert2Interpret isAuthenticated
        (certs2 ownerID utilityID cmd npriv privcmd)
        (thermoStateInterp utilityID privcmd)
        (MSG Server (Role (Utility utilityID))
          (ORD Server (Role (Utility utilityID))
            (PR privcmd))
          (sign (privK Server)
            (hash
              (SOME
                (ORD Server (Role (Utility utilityID))
                  (PR privcmd)))))::ins)
        (State enabled temperature) outStream) ∧
    (M,Oi,Os) sat prop (CMD (PR privcmd))
```

⌊isAuthenticated2_Owner_Keyboard_thm⌋

```
⊢ isAuthenticated (msgInterpret (KB ownerID cmd))
```

⌊isAuthenticated2_Owner_KServer_thm⌋

⊢ isAuthenticated
    (msgInterpret
      (MSG Server (Owner *ownerID*)
        (ORD Server (Owner *ownerID*) cmd)
        (sign (privK Server)
          (hash (SOME (ORD Server (Owner *ownerID*) cmd))))))

⌐isAuthenticated2_Utility_KServer_npriv_thm⌐

⊢ isAuthenticated
    (msgInterpret
      (MSG Server (Role (Utility *utilityID*))
        (ORD Server (Role (Utility *utilityID*)) (NP *npriv*))
        (sign (privK Server)
          (hash
            (SOME
              (ORD Server (Role (Utility *utilityID*))
                (NP *npriv*)))))))

⌐isAuthenticated2_Utility_KServer_privcmd_thm⌐

⊢ isAuthenticated
    (msgInterpret
      (MSG Server (Role (Utility *utilityID*))
        (ORD Server (Role (Utility *utilityID*)) (PR *privcmd*))
        (sign (privK Server)
          (hash
            (SOME
              (ORD Server (Role (Utility *utilityID*))
                (PR *privcmd*)))))))

⌐TR2_exec_Keyboard_Owner_cmd_lemma⌐

⊢ (∀ M Oi Os.
    CFG2Interpret (M,Oi,Os)
      (CFG2 msgInterpret cert2Interpret isAuthenticated
        (certs2 *ownerID* *utilityID* cmd *npriv* *privcmd*)
        (thermoStateInterp *utilityID* *privcmd*)
        (KB *ownerID* cmd::ins) state outStream) ⇒
    (M,Oi,Os) sat prop (CMD cmd)) ⇒
  ∀ NS Out M Oi Os.
    TR2 (M,Oi,Os) (exec (CMD cmd))
      (CFG2 msgInterpret cert2Interpret isAuthenticated
        (certs2 *ownerID* *utilityID* cmd *npriv* *privcmd*)
        (thermoStateInterp *utilityID* *privcmd*)
        (KB *ownerID* cmd::ins) state outStream)
      (CFG2 msgInterpret cert2Interpret isAuthenticated
        (certs2 *ownerID* *utilityID* cmd *npriv* *privcmd*)
        (thermoStateInterp *utilityID* *privcmd*) ins
        (NS state (exec (CMD cmd)))
      (Out state (exec (CMD cmd))::outStream)) ⟺

isAuthenticated (msgInterpret (KB *ownerID* cmd)) ∧
CFG2Interpret (M, Oi, Os)
  (CFG2 msgInterpret cert2Interpret isAuthenticated
    (certs2 *ownerID* *utilityID* cmd *npriv* *privcmd*)
    (thermoStateInterp *utilityID* *privcmd*)
    (KB *ownerID* cmd::*ins*) *state* *outStream*) ∧
  (M, Oi, Os) sat prop (CMD *cmd*)

[TR2_exec_KServer_Owner_cmd_lemma]

⊢ (∀*M Oi Os*.
   CFG2Interpret (M, Oi, Os)
    (CFG2 msgInterpret cert2Interpret isAuthenticated
      (certs2 *ownerID* *utilityID* cmd *npriv* *privcmd*)
      (thermoStateInterp *utilityID* *privcmd*)
      (MSG Server (Owner *ownerID*)
        (ORD Server (Owner *ownerID*) *cmd*)
        (sign (privK Server)
         (hash
          (SOME (ORD Server (Owner *ownerID*) *cmd*))))::
        ins) *state* *outStream*) ⇒
  (M, Oi, Os) sat prop (CMD *cmd*)) ⇒
∀*NS Out M Oi Os*.
  TR2 (M, Oi, Os) (exec (CMD *cmd*))
    (CFG2 msgInterpret cert2Interpret isAuthenticated
      (certs2 *ownerID* *utilityID* cmd *npriv* *privcmd*)
      (thermoStateInterp *utilityID* *privcmd*)
      (MSG Server (Owner *ownerID*)
        (ORD Server (Owner *ownerID*) *cmd*)
        (sign (privK Server)
         (hash
          (SOME (ORD Server (Owner *ownerID*) *cmd*))))::
        ins) *state* *outStream*)
    (CFG2 msgInterpret cert2Interpret isAuthenticated
      (certs2 *ownerID* *utilityID* cmd *npriv* *privcmd*)
      (thermoStateInterp *utilityID* *privcmd*) *ins*
      (*NS state* (exec (CMD *cmd*)))
      (*Out state* (exec (CMD *cmd*))::*outStream*)) ⟺
  isAuthenticated
    (msgInterpret
      (MSG Server (Owner *ownerID*)
        (ORD Server (Owner *ownerID*) *cmd*)
        (sign (privK Server)
         (hash
          (SOME (ORD Server (Owner *ownerID*) *cmd*)))))) ∧
  CFG2Interpret (M, Oi, Os)
    (CFG2 msgInterpret cert2Interpret isAuthenticated
      (certs2 *ownerID* *utilityID* cmd *npriv* *privcmd*)
      (thermoStateInterp *utilityID* *privcmd*)
      (MSG Server (Owner *ownerID*)

```
              (ORD Server (Owner ownerID) cmd)
              (sign (privK Server)
                (hash
                  (SOME (ORD Server (Owner ownerID) cmd))))::
              ins) state outStream) ∧
      (M,Oi,Os) sat prop (CMD cmd)
```

TR2_exec_KServer_Utility_cmd_lemma

```
⊢ (∀ M Oi Os.
      CFG2Interpret (M,Oi,Os)
        (CFG2 msgInterpret cert2Interpret isAuthenticated
          (certs2 ownerID utilityID cmd npriv privcmd)
          (thermoStateInterp utilityID privcmd)
          (MSG Server (Role (Utility utilityID))
            (ORD Server (Role (Utility utilityID)) (NP npriv))
            (sign (privK Server)
              (hash
                (SOME
                  (ORD Server (Role (Utility utilityID))
                    (NP npriv)))))::ins) state
          outStream) ⇒
      (M,Oi,Os) sat prop (CMD (NP npriv))) ⇒
  ∀ NS Out M Oi Os.
    TR2 (M,Oi,Os) (exec (CMD (NP npriv)))
      (CFG2 msgInterpret cert2Interpret isAuthenticated
        (certs2 ownerID utilityID cmd npriv privcmd)
        (thermoStateInterp utilityID privcmd)
        (MSG Server (Role (Utility utilityID))
          (ORD Server (Role (Utility utilityID)) (NP npriv))
          (sign (privK Server)
            (hash
              (SOME
                (ORD Server (Role (Utility utilityID))
                  (NP npriv)))))::ins) state outStream)
      (CFG2 msgInterpret cert2Interpret isAuthenticated
        (certs2 ownerID utilityID cmd npriv privcmd)
        (thermoStateInterp utilityID privcmd) ins
        (NS state (exec (CMD (NP npriv))))
        (Out state (exec (CMD (NP npriv)))::outStream)) ⟺
    isAuthenticated
      (msgInterpret
        (MSG Server (Role (Utility utilityID))
          (ORD Server (Role (Utility utilityID)) (NP npriv))
          (sign (privK Server)
            (hash
              (SOME
                (ORD Server (Role (Utility utilityID))
                  (NP npriv))))))) ∧
    CFG2Interpret (M,Oi,Os)
```

```
        (CFG2 msgInterpret cert2Interpret isAuthenticated
          (certs2 ownerID utilityID cmd npriv privcmd)
          (thermoStateInterp utilityID privcmd)
          (MSG Server (Role (Utility utilityID))
            (ORD Server (Role (Utility utilityID))) (NP npriv))
            (sign (privK Server)
              (hash
                (SOME
                  (ORD Server (Role (Utility utilityID))
                    (NP npriv))))::ins) state outStream) ∧
  (M,Oi,Os) sat prop (CMD (NP npriv))
```

⌐TR2_exec_KServer_Utility_privcmd_lemma⌐

```
⊢ (∀ M  Oi  Os.
    CFG2Interpret (M,Oi,Os)
      (CFG2 msgInterpret cert2Interpret isAuthenticated
        (certs2 ownerID utilityID cmd npriv privcmd)
        (thermoStateInterp utilityID privcmd)
        (MSG Server (Role (Utility utilityID))
          (ORD Server (Role (Utility utilityID))
            (PR privcmd))
          (sign (privK Server)
            (hash
              (SOME
                (ORD Server (Role (Utility utilityID))
                  (PR privcmd)))))::ins)
        (State enabled temperature) outStream) ⇒
    (M,Oi,Os) sat prop (CMD (PR privcmd))) ⇒
∀ NS  Out  M  Oi  Os.
  TR2 (M,Oi,Os) (exec (CMD (PR privcmd)))
    (CFG2 msgInterpret cert2Interpret isAuthenticated
      (certs2 ownerID utilityID cmd npriv privcmd)
      (thermoStateInterp utilityID privcmd)
      (MSG Server (Role (Utility utilityID))
        (ORD Server (Role (Utility utilityID))
          (PR privcmd))
        (sign (privK Server)
          (hash
            (SOME
              (ORD Server (Role (Utility utilityID))
                (PR privcmd)))))::ins)
      (State enabled temperature) outStream)
    (CFG2 msgInterpret cert2Interpret isAuthenticated
      (certs2 ownerID utilityID cmd npriv privcmd)
      (thermoStateInterp utilityID privcmd) ins
      (NS (State enabled temperature)
        (exec (CMD (PR privcmd))))
      (Out (State enabled temperature)
        (exec (CMD (PR privcmd)))::outStream)) ⟺
```

```
isAuthenticated
  (msgInterpret
    (MSG Server (Role (Utility utilityID))
      (ORD Server (Role (Utility utilityID))
        (PR privcmd))
      (sign (privK Server)
        (hash
          (SOME
            (ORD Server (Role (Utility utilityID))
              (PR privcmd))))))) ∧
CFG2Interpret (M,Oi,Os)
  (CFG2 msgInterpret cert2Interpret isAuthenticated
    (certs2 ownerID utilityID cmd npriv privcmd)
    (thermoStateInterp utilityID privcmd)
    (MSG Server (Role (Utility utilityID))
      (ORD Server (Role (Utility utilityID))
        (PR privcmd))
      (sign (privK Server)
        (hash
          (SOME
            (ORD Server (Role (Utility utilityID))
              (PR privcmd))))) :: ins)
    (State enabled temperature) outStream) ∧
  (M,Oi,Os) sat prop (CMD (PR privcmd))
```

$\lfloor$ TR2_iff_TR_Keyboard_Owner_cmd $\rfloor$

```
⊢ ∀ M Oi Os ownerID utilityID ins ins₂ outStream NS Out state
  npriv privcmd cmd.
  TR2 (M,Oi,Os) (exec (CMD cmd))
    (CFG2 msgInterpret cert2Interpret isAuthenticated
      (certs2 ownerID utilityID cmd npriv privcmd)
      (thermoStateInterp utilityID privcmd)
      (KB ownerID cmd :: ins₂) state outStream)
    (CFG2 msgInterpret cert2Interpret isAuthenticated
      (certs2 ownerID utilityID cmd npriv privcmd)
      (thermoStateInterp utilityID privcmd) ins₂
      (NS state (exec (CMD cmd)))
      (Out state (exec (CMD cmd)) :: outStream)) ⟺
  TR (M,Oi,Os) (exec (CMD cmd))
    (CFG isAuthenticated
      (thermoStateInterp utilityID privcmd)
      (certs ownerID utilityID cmd npriv privcmd)
      (Name Keyboard quoting Name (Owner ownerID) says
        prop (CMD cmd) :: ins) state outStream)
    (CFG isAuthenticated
      (thermoStateInterp utilityID privcmd)
      (certs ownerID utilityID cmd npriv privcmd) ins
      (NS state (exec (CMD cmd)))
      (Out state (exec (CMD cmd)) :: outStream))
```

⌈TR2_iff_TR_KServer_Owner_cmd⌉

⊢ ∀ M Oi Os ownerID utilityID ins ins₂ outStream NS Out state
 npriv privcmd cmd.
  TR2 (M, Oi, Os) (exec (CMD cmd))
   (CFG2 msgInterpret cert2Interpret isAuthenticated
    (certs2 ownerID utilityID cmd npriv privcmd)
    (thermoStateInterp utilityID privcmd)
    (MSG Server (Owner ownerID)
      (ORD Server (Owner ownerID) cmd)
      (sign (privK Server)
        (hash
          (SOME (ORD Server (Owner ownerID) cmd))))::
          ins₂) state outStream)
   (CFG2 msgInterpret cert2Interpret isAuthenticated
    (certs2 ownerID utilityID cmd npriv privcmd)
    (thermoStateInterp utilityID privcmd) ins₂
    (NS state (exec (CMD cmd)))
    (Out state (exec (CMD cmd))::outStream)) ⟺
  TR (M, Oi, Os) (exec (CMD cmd))
   (CFG isAuthenticated
    (thermoStateInterp utilityID privcmd)
    (certs ownerID utilityID cmd npriv privcmd)
    (Name (Key (pubK Server)) quoting
    Name (Owner ownerID) says prop (CMD cmd)::ins) state
    outStream)
   (CFG isAuthenticated
    (thermoStateInterp utilityID privcmd)
    (certs ownerID utilityID cmd npriv privcmd) ins
    (NS state (exec (CMD cmd)))
    (Out state (exec (CMD cmd))::outStream))

⌈TR2_iff_TR_KServer_Utility_npriv⌉

⊢ ∀ M Oi Os ownerID utilityID ins ins₂ outStream NS Out state
 npriv privcmd cmd.
  TR2 (M, Oi, Os) (exec (CMD (NP npriv)))
   (CFG2 msgInterpret cert2Interpret isAuthenticated
    (certs2 ownerID utilityID cmd npriv privcmd)
    (thermoStateInterp utilityID privcmd)
    (MSG Server (Role (Utility utilityID))
      (ORD Server (Role (Utility utilityID)) (NP npriv))
      (sign (privK Server)
        (hash
          (SOME
            (ORD Server (Role (Utility utilityID))
              (NP npriv)))))::ins₂) state outStream)
   (CFG2 msgInterpret cert2Interpret isAuthenticated
    (certs2 ownerID utilityID cmd npriv privcmd)
    (thermoStateInterp utilityID privcmd) ins₂
    (NS state (exec (CMD (NP npriv))))

$(Out\ state\ (exec\ (CMD\ (NP\ npriv)))::outStream)) \Longleftarrow$

TR (M, Oi, Os) (exec (CMD (NP $npriv$)))

  (CFG isAuthenticated

    (thermoStateInterp $utilityID$ $privcmd$)

    (certs $ownerID$ $utilityID$ cmd $npriv$ $privcmd$)

    (Name (Key (pubK Server)) quoting

    Name (Role (Utility $utilityID$)) says

    prop (CMD (NP $npriv$))::ins) $state$ $outStream$)

  (CFG isAuthenticated

    (thermoStateInterp $utilityID$ $privcmd$)

    (certs $ownerID$ $utilityID$ cmd $npriv$ $privcmd$) ins

    (NS $state$ (exec (CMD (NP $npriv$))))

    (Out $state$ (exec (CMD (NP $npriv$)))::$outStream$))

|TR2_iff_TR_KServer_Utility_privcmd|

$\vdash \forall M\ Oi\ Os\ ownerID\ utilityID\ ins\ ins_2\ temperature\ outStream\ NS$

  $Out\ npriv\ privcmd\ cmd.$

  TR2 (M, Oi, Os) (exec (CMD (PR $privcmd$)))

    (CFG2 msgInterpret cert2Interpret isAuthenticated

      (certs2 $ownerID$ $utilityID$ cmd $npriv$ $privcmd$)

      (thermoStateInterp $utilityID$ $privcmd$)

      (MSG Server (Role (Utility $utilityID$))

        (ORD Server (Role (Utility $utilityID$))

          (PR $privcmd$))

        (sign (privK Server)

         (hash

          (SOME

            (ORD Server (Role (Utility $utilityID$))

             (PR $privcmd$)))))::ins_2)

      (State enabled $temperature$) $outStream$)

    (CFG2 msgInterpret cert2Interpret isAuthenticated

      (certs2 $ownerID$ $utilityID$ cmd $npriv$ $privcmd$)

      (thermoStateInterp $utilityID$ $privcmd$) ins_2

      (NS (State enabled $temperature$)

        (exec (CMD (PR $privcmd$))))

      (Out (State enabled $temperature$)

        (exec (CMD (PR $privcmd$))))::$outStream$)) $\Longleftarrow$

  TR (M, Oi, Os) (exec (CMD (PR $privcmd$)))

    (CFG isAuthenticated

      (thermoStateInterp $utilityID$ $privcmd$)

      (certs $ownerID$ $utilityID$ cmd $npriv$ $privcmd$)

      (Name (Key (pubK Server)) quoting

      Name (Role (Utility $utilityID$)) says

      prop (CMD (PR $privcmd$))::ins)

      (State enabled $temperature$) $outStream$)

    (CFG isAuthenticated

      (thermoStateInterp $utilityID$ $privcmd$)

      (certs $ownerID$ $utilityID$ cmd $npriv$ $privcmd$) ins

      (NS (State enabled $temperature$)

```
                (exec (CMD (PR privcmd))))
            (Out (State enabled temperature)
                (exec (CMD (PR privcmd)))::outStream))
```

|TR2_iff_TR_KServer_Utility_trap|

$\vdash \forall M\ Oi\ Os\ ownerID\ utilityID\ ins\ ins_2\ temperature\ outStream\ NS$
$\quad Out\ npriv\ privcmd\ cmd.$

```
    TR2 (M,Oi,Os) (trap (CMD (PR privcmd)))
        (CFG2 msgInterpret cert2Interpret isAuthenticated
            (certs2 ownerID utilityID cmd npriv privcmd)
            (thermoStateInterp utilityID privcmd)
            (MSG Server (Role (Utility utilityID))
                (ORD Server (Role (Utility utilityID))
                    (PR privcmd))
                (sign (privK Server)
                    (hash
                        (SOME
                            (ORD Server (Role (Utility utilityID))
                                (PR privcmd)))))::ins_2)
            (State disabled temperature) outStream)
        (CFG2 msgInterpret cert2Interpret isAuthenticated
            (certs2 ownerID utilityID cmd npriv privcmd)
            (thermoStateInterp utilityID privcmd) ins_2
            (NS (State disabled temperature)
                (trap (CMD (PR privcmd))))
            (Out (State disabled temperature)
                (trap (CMD (PR privcmd)))::outStream))  ⟺
    TR (M,Oi,Os) (trap (CMD (PR privcmd)))
        (CFG isAuthenticated
            (thermoStateInterp utilityID privcmd)
            (certs ownerID utilityID cmd npriv privcmd)
            (Name (Key (pubK Server)) quoting
            Name (Role (Utility utilityID)) says
            prop (CMD (PR privcmd))::ins)
            (State disabled temperature) outStream)
        (CFG isAuthenticated
            (thermoStateInterp utilityID privcmd)
            (certs ownerID utilityID cmd npriv privcmd) ins
            (NS (State disabled temperature)
                (trap (CMD (PR privcmd))))
            (Out (State disabled temperature)
                (trap (CMD (PR privcmd)))::outStream))
```

|TR2_trap_KServer_Utility_privcmd_lemma|

$\vdash (\forall M\ Oi\ Os.$

```
    CFG2Interpret (M,Oi,Os)
        (CFG2 msgInterpret cert2Interpret isAuthenticated
            (certs2 ownerID utilityID cmd npriv privcmd)
            (thermoStateInterp utilityID privcmd)
```

```
            (MSG Server (Role (Utility utilityID))
                (ORD Server (Role (Utility utilityID))
                    (PR privcmd))
                (sign (privK Server)
                    (hash
                        (SOME
                            (ORD Server (Role (Utility utilityID))
                                (PR privcmd)))))::ins)
            (State disabled temperature) outStream) ⇒
    (M,Oi,Os) sat prop TRAP) ⇒
∀ NS Out M Oi Os.
    TR2 (M,Oi,Os) (trap (CMD (PR privcmd)))
      (CFG2 msgInterpret cert2Interpret isAuthenticated
          (certs2 ownerID utilityID cmd npriv privcmd)
          (thermoStateInterp utilityID privcmd)
          (MSG Server (Role (Utility utilityID))
              (ORD Server (Role (Utility utilityID))
                  (PR privcmd))
              (sign (privK Server)
                  (hash
                      (SOME
                          (ORD Server (Role (Utility utilityID))
                              (PR privcmd)))))::ins)
          (State disabled temperature) outStream)
      (CFG2 msgInterpret cert2Interpret isAuthenticated
          (certs2 ownerID utilityID cmd npriv privcmd)
          (thermoStateInterp utilityID privcmd) ins
          (NS (State disabled temperature)
              (trap (CMD (PR privcmd))))
          (Out (State disabled temperature)
              (trap (CMD (PR privcmd)))::outStream)) ⟺
    isAuthenticated
        (msgInterpret
            (MSG Server (Role (Utility utilityID))
                (ORD Server (Role (Utility utilityID))
                    (PR privcmd))
                (sign (privK Server)
                    (hash
                        (SOME
                            (ORD Server (Role (Utility utilityID))
                                (PR privcmd))))))) ∧
    CFG2Interpret (M,Oi,Os)
        (CFG2 msgInterpret cert2Interpret isAuthenticated
            (certs2 ownerID utilityID cmd npriv privcmd)
            (thermoStateInterp utilityID privcmd)
            (MSG Server (Role (Utility utilityID))
                (ORD Server (Role (Utility utilityID))
                    (PR privcmd))
                (sign (privK Server)
```

```
              (hash
                (SOME
                  (ORD Server (Role (Utility utilityID))
                    (PR privcmd)))))::ins)
          (State disabled temperature) outStream) ∧
      (M,Oi,Os) sat prop TRAP
```

$\lfloor$ trap2_KServer_Utility_privcmd_Justified $\rfloor$

```
⊢ ∀NS Out outStream temperature ins npriv privcmd cmd ownerID
    utilityID M Oi Os.
  TR2 (M,Oi,Os) (trap (CMD (PR privcmd)))
    (CFG2 msgInterpret cert2Interpret isAuthenticated
      (certs2 ownerID utilityID cmd npriv privcmd)
      (thermoStateInterp utilityID privcmd)
      (MSG Server (Role (Utility utilityID))
        (ORD Server (Role (Utility utilityID))
          (PR privcmd))
        (sign (privK Server)
          (hash
            (SOME
              (ORD Server (Role (Utility utilityID))
                (PR privcmd)))))::ins)
      (State disabled temperature) outStream)
    (CFG2 msgInterpret cert2Interpret isAuthenticated
      (certs2 ownerID utilityID cmd npriv privcmd)
      (thermoStateInterp utilityID privcmd) ins
      (NS (State disabled temperature)
        (trap (CMD (PR privcmd))))
      (Out (State disabled temperature)
        (trap (CMD (PR privcmd)))::outStream)) ⇒
  (M,Oi,Os) sat prop TRAP
```

$\lfloor$ trap2_KServer_Utility_privcmd_thm $\rfloor$

```
⊢ ∀NS Out M Oi Os.
  TR2 (M,Oi,Os) (trap (CMD (PR privcmd)))
    (CFG2 msgInterpret cert2Interpret isAuthenticated
      (certs2 ownerID utilityID cmd npriv privcmd)
      (thermoStateInterp utilityID privcmd)
      (MSG Server (Role (Utility utilityID))
        (ORD Server (Role (Utility utilityID))
          (PR privcmd))
        (sign (privK Server)
          (hash
            (SOME
              (ORD Server (Role (Utility utilityID))
                (PR privcmd)))))::ins)
      (State disabled temperature) outStream)
    (CFG2 msgInterpret cert2Interpret isAuthenticated
      (certs2 ownerID utilityID cmd npriv privcmd)
```

(thermoStateInterp *utilityID priucmd*) *ins*

(*NS* (State disabled *temperature*)

   (trap (CMD (PR *privcmd*))))

(*Out* (State disabled *temperature*)

   (trap (CMD (PR *privcmd*)))::*outStream*)) ⟺

CFG2Interpret (*M*, *Oi*, *Os*)

  (CFG2 msgInterpret cert2Interpret isAuthenticated

    (certs2 *ownerID utilityID cmd npriv privcmd*)

    (thermoStateInterp *utilityID privcmd*)

    (MSG Server (Role (Utility *utilityID*))

      (ORD Server (Role (Utility *utilityID*))

        (PR *privcmd*))

     (sign (privK Server)

      (hash

        (SOME

          (ORD Server (Role (Utility *utilityID*))

           (PR *privcmd*)))))::*ins*)

    (State disabled *temperature*) *outStream*) ∧

(*M*, *Oi*, *Os*) sat prop TRAP

APPENDIX D

CSBD ACCESS-CONTROL LOGIC REPORT

Cyber-Assurance for the Internet of Things, First Edition. Edited by Tyson T. Brooks.
© 2017 by The Institute of Electrical and Electronic Engineers, Inc. Published 2017 by John Wiley & Sons, Inc.

1 aclfoundation Theory

Built: 14 August 2015

Parent Theories: list

1.1 Datatypes

Form =
```
    TT
  | FF
  | prop 'aavar
  | notf (('aavar, 'apn, 'il, 'sl) Form)
  | (andf) (('aavar, 'apn, 'il, 'sl) Form)
          (('aavar, 'apn, 'il, 'sl) Form)
  | (orf) (('aavar, 'apn, 'il, 'sl) Form)
          (('aavar, 'apn, 'il, 'sl) Form)
  | (impf) (('aavar, 'apn, 'il, 'sl) Form)
           (('aavar, 'apn, 'il, 'sl) Form)
  | (eqf) (('aavar, 'apn, 'il, 'sl) Form)
          (('aavar, 'apn, 'il, 'sl) Form)
  | (says) ('apn Princ) (('aavar, 'apn, 'il, 'sl) Form)
  | (speaks_for) ('apn Princ) ('apn Princ)
  | (controls) ('apn Princ) (('aavar, 'apn, 'il, 'sl) Form)
  | reps ('apn Princ) ('apn Princ)
          (('aavar, 'apn, 'il, 'sl) Form)
  | (domi) (('apn, 'il) IntLevel) (('apn, 'il) IntLevel)
  | (eqi) (('apn, 'il) IntLevel) (('apn, 'il) IntLevel)
  | (doms) (('apn, 'sl) SecLevel) (('apn, 'sl) SecLevel)
  | (eqs) (('apn, 'sl) SecLevel) (('apn, 'sl) SecLevel)
  | (eqn) num num
  | (lte) num num
  | (lt) num num
```

Kripke =
```
    KS ('aavar -> 'aaworld -> bool)
       ('apn -> 'aaworld -> 'aaworld -> bool) ('apn -> 'il)
       ('apn -> 'sl)
```

Princ =
```
    Name 'apn
  | (meet) ('apn Princ) ('apn Princ)
  | (quoting) ('apn Princ) ('apn Princ) ;
```

IntLevel = iLab 'il | il 'apn ;

SecLevel = sLab 'sl | sl 'apn

1.2 Definitions

$\lfloor \text{imapKS\_def} \rfloor$

   $\vdash \forall \textit{Intp Jfn ilmap slmap} .$
     $\text{imapKS } (\text{KS } \textit{Intp Jfn ilmap slmap}) = \textit{ilmap}$

$\lfloor \text{intpKS\_def} \rfloor$

   $\vdash \forall \textit{Intp Jfn ilmap slmap} .$
     $\text{intpKS } (\text{KS } \textit{Intp Jfn ilmap slmap}) = \textit{Intp}$

$\lfloor \text{jKS\_def} \rfloor$

   $\vdash \forall \textit{Intp Jfn ilmap slmap} . \text{ jKS } (\text{KS } \textit{Intp Jfn ilmap slmap}) = \textit{Jfn}$

$\lfloor \text{O1\_def} \rfloor$

   $\vdash \text{O1} = \text{PO one\_weakorder}$

$\lfloor \text{one\_weakorder\_def} \rfloor$

   $\vdash \forall x \; y. \text{ one\_weakorder } x \; y \iff \text{T}$

$\lfloor \text{po\_TY\_DEF} \rfloor$

   $\vdash \exists \textit{rep}. \text{ TYPE\_DEFINITION WeakOrder } \textit{rep}$

$\lfloor \text{po\_tybij} \rfloor$

   $\vdash (\forall a. \text{ PO } (\text{repPO } a) = a) \wedge$
    $\forall r. \text{ WeakOrder } r \iff (\text{repPO } (\text{PO } r) = r)$

$\lfloor \text{prod\_PO\_def} \rfloor$

   $\vdash \forall PO_1 \; PO_2 .$
     $\text{prod\_PO } PO_1 \; PO_2 = \text{PO } (\text{RPROD } (\text{repPO } PO_1) \; (\text{repPO } PO_2))$

$\lfloor \text{smapKS\_def} \rfloor$

   $\vdash \forall \textit{Intp Jfn ilmap slmap} .$
     $\text{smapKS } (\text{KS } \textit{Intp Jfn ilmap slmap}) = \textit{slmap}$

$\lfloor \text{Subset\_PO\_def} \rfloor$

   $\vdash \text{Subset\_PO} = \text{PO } (\subseteq)$

1.3 Theorems

$\lfloor \text{abs\_po11} \rfloor$

   $\vdash \forall r \; r' .$
     $\text{WeakOrder } r \Rightarrow \text{WeakOrder } r' \Rightarrow ((\text{PO } r = \text{PO } r') \iff (r = r'))$

$\lfloor \text{absPO\_fn\_onto} \rfloor$

   $\vdash \forall a. \; \exists r. \; (a = \text{PO } r) \wedge \text{WeakOrder } r$

⌊antisym_prod_antisym⌋

$\vdash \forall r \ s.$
  antisymmetric $r \wedge$ antisymmetric $s \Rightarrow$
  antisymmetric (RPROD $r \ s$)

⌊EQ_WeakOrder⌋

$\vdash$ WeakOrder (=)

⌊KS_bij⌋

$\vdash \forall M. \ M =$ KS (intpKS M) (jKS M) (imapKS M) (smapKS M)

⌊one_weakorder_WO⌋

$\vdash$ WeakOrder one_weakorder

⌊onto_po⌋

$\vdash \forall r.$ WeakOrder $r \iff \exists a. \ r =$ repPO a

⌊po_bij⌋

$\vdash (\forall a.$ PO (repPO a) $= a) \wedge$
  $\forall r.$ WeakOrder $r \iff$ (repPO (PO r) $= r$)

⌊PO_repPO⌋

$\vdash \forall a.$ PO (repPO a) $= a$

⌊refl_prod_refl⌋

$\vdash \forall r \ s.$ reflexive $r \wedge$ reflexive $s \Rightarrow$ reflexive (RPROD $r \ s$)

⌊repPO_iPO_partial_order⌋

$\vdash (\forall x.$ repPO $iPO \ x \ x) \wedge$
  $(\forall x \ y.$ repPO $iPO \ x \ y \wedge$ repPO $iPO \ y \ x \Rightarrow (x = y)) \wedge$
  $\forall x \ y \ z.$ repPO $iPO \ x \ y \wedge$ repPO $iPO \ y \ z \Rightarrow$ repPO $iPO \ x \ z$

⌊repPO_O1⌋

$\vdash$ repPO O1 = one_weakorder

⌊repPO_prod_PO⌋

$\vdash \forall po_1 \ po_2.$
  repPO (prod_PO $po_1 \ po_2$) = RPROD (repPO po_1) (repPO po_2)

⌊repPO_Subset_PO⌋

$\vdash$ repPO Subset_PO = ($\subseteq$)

⌊RPROD_THM⌋

$\vdash \forall r \ s \ a \ b.$
  RPROD $r \ s \ a \ b \iff r$ (FST a) (FST b) $\wedge s$ (SND a) (SND b)

[SUBSET_WO]

⊢ WeakOrder (⊆)

[trans_prod_trans]

⊢ ∀r s. transitive r ∧ transitive s ⇒ transitive (RPROD r s)

[WeakOrder_Exists]

⊢ ∃R. WeakOrder R

[WO_prod_WO]

⊢ ∀r s. WeakOrder r ∧ WeakOrder s ⇒ WeakOrder (RPROD r s)

[WO_repPO]

⊢ ∀r. WeakOrder r ⟺ (repPO (PO r) = r)

2   aclsemantics Theory

Built: 14 August 2015
Parent Theories: aclfoundation

2.1   Definitions

[Efn_def]

⊢ (∀Oi Os M. Efn Oi Os M TT = $\mathcal{U}$(:'v)) ∧
(∀Oi Os M. Efn Oi Os M FF = { }) ∧
(∀Oi Os M p. Efn Oi Os M (prop p) = intpKS M p) ∧
(∀Oi Os M f.
  Efn Oi Os M (notf f) = $\mathcal{U}$(:'v) DIFF Efn Oi Os M f) ∧
(∀Oi Os M f_1 f_2.
  Efn Oi Os M (f_1 andf f_2) =
  Efn Oi Os M f_1 ∩ Efn Oi Os M f_2) ∧
(∀Oi Os M f_1 f_2.
  Efn Oi Os M (f_1 orf f_2) =
  Efn Oi Os M f_1 ∪ Efn Oi Os M f_2) ∧
(∀Oi Os M f_1 f_2.
  Efn Oi Os M (f_1 impf f_2) =
  $\mathcal{U}$(:'v) DIFF Efn Oi Os M f_1 ∪ Efn Oi Os M f_2) ∧
(∀Oi Os M f_1 f_2.
  Efn Oi Os M (f_1 eqf f_2) =
  ($\mathcal{U}$(:'v) DIFF Efn Oi Os M f_1 ∪ Efn Oi Os M f_2) ∩
  ($\mathcal{U}$(:'v) DIFF Efn Oi Os M f_2 ∪ Efn Oi Os M f_1)) ∧
(∀Oi Os M P f.
  Efn Oi Os M (P says f) =
  {w | Jext (jKS M) P w ⊆ Efn Oi Os M f}) ∧
(∀Oi Os M P Q.
  Efn Oi Os M (P speaks_for Q) =

If Jext (jKS M) Q RSUBSET Jext (jKS M) P then $\mathcal{U}(:'v)$
else { }) ∧
($\forall$ Oi Os M P f.
Efn Oi Os M (P controls f) =
$\mathcal{U}(:'v)$ DIFF {w | Jext (jKS M) P w ⊆ Efn Oi Os M f} ∪
Efn Oi Os M f) ∧
($\forall$ Oi Os M P Q f.
Efn Oi Os M (reps P Q f) =
$\mathcal{U}(:'v)$ DIFF
{w | Jext (jKS M) (P quoting Q) w ⊆ Efn Oi Os M f} ∪
{w | Jext (jKS M) Q w ⊆ Efn Oi Os M f}) ∧
($\forall$ Oi Os M $intl_1$ $intl_2$.
Efn Oi Os M ($intl_1$ domi $intl_2$) =
if repPO Oi (Lifn M $intl_2$) (Lifn M $intl_1$) then $\mathcal{U}(:'v)$
else { }) ∧
($\forall$ Oi Os M $intl_2$ $intl_1$.
Efn Oi Os M ($intl_2$ eqi $intl_1$) =
(if repPO Oi (Lifn M $intl_2$) (Lifn M $intl_1$) then $\mathcal{U}(:'v)$
else { }) ∩
if repPO Oi (Lifn M $intl_1$) (Lifn M $intl_2$) then $\mathcal{U}(:'v)$
else { }) ∧
($\forall$ Oi Os M $secl_1$ $secl_2$.
Efn Oi Os M ($secl_1$ doms $secl_2$) =
if repPO Os (Lsfn M $secl_2$) (Lsfn M $secl_1$) then $\mathcal{U}(:'v)$
else { }) ∧
($\forall$ Oi Os M $secl_2$ $secl_1$.
Efn Oi Os M ($secl_2$ eqs $secl_1$) =
(if repPO Os (Lsfn M $secl_2$) (Lsfn M $secl_1$) then $\mathcal{U}(:'v)$
else { }) ∩
if repPO Os (Lsfn M $secl_1$) (Lsfn M $secl_2$) then $\mathcal{U}(:'v)$
else { }) ∧
($\forall$ Oi Os M $numExp_1$ $numExp_2$.
Efn Oi Os M ($numExp_1$ eqn $numExp_2$) =
if $numExp_1$ = $numExp_2$ then $\mathcal{U}(:'v)$ else { }) ∧
($\forall$ Oi Os M $numExp_1$ $numExp_2$.
Efn Oi Os M ($numExp_1$ lte $numExp_2$) =
if $numExp_1$ ≤ $numExp_2$ then $\mathcal{U}(:'v)$ else { }) ∧
$\forall$ Oi Os M $numExp_1$ $numExp_2$.
Efn Oi Os M ($numExp_1$ lt $numExp_2$) =
if $numExp_1$ < $numExp_2$ then $\mathcal{U}(:'v)$ else { }

[Jext_def]
⊢ ($\forall J$ s. Jext J (Name s) = J s) ∧
($\forall J$ P_1 P_2.
Jext J (P_1 meet P_2) = Jext J P_1 RUNION Jext J P_2) ∧
$\forall J$ P_1 P_2. Jext J (P_1 quoting P_2) = Jext J P_2 O Jext J P_1

[Lifn_def]
⊢ ($\forall M$ l. Lifn M (iLab l) = l) ∧
$\forall M$ $name$. Lifn M (il $name$) = imapKS M $name$

⌊Lsfn_def⌋

$\vdash (\forall M\ l.\ \text{Lsfn}\ M\ (\text{sLab}\ l) = l) \wedge$
$\quad \forall M\ name.\ \text{Lsfn}\ M\ (\text{sl}\ name) = \text{smapKS}\ M\ name$

2.2 Theorems

⌊andf_def⌋

$\vdash \forall Oi\ Os\ M\ f_1\ f_2.$
$\quad \text{Efn}\ Oi\ Os\ M\ (f_1\ \text{andf}\ f_2) = \text{Efn}\ Oi\ Os\ M\ f_1 \cap \text{Efn}\ Oi\ Os\ M\ f_2$

⌊controls_def⌋

$\vdash \forall Oi\ Os\ M\ P\ f.$
$\quad \text{Efn}\ Oi\ Os\ M\ (P\ \text{controls}\ f) =$
$\quad \mathcal{U}(:\text{'v})\ \text{DIFF}\ \{w\ |\ \text{Jext}\ (\text{jKS}\ M)\ P\ w \subseteq \text{Efn}\ Oi\ Os\ M\ f\} \cup$
$\quad \text{Efn}\ Oi\ Os\ M\ f$

⌊controls_says⌋

$\vdash \forall M\ P\ f.$
$\quad \text{Efn}\ Oi\ Os\ M\ (P\ \text{controls}\ f) = \text{Efn}\ Oi\ Os\ M\ (P\ \text{says}\ f\ \text{impf}\ f)$

⌊domi_def⌋

$\vdash \forall Oi\ Os\ M\ intl_1\ intl_2.$
$\quad \text{Efn}\ Oi\ Os\ M\ (intl_1\ \text{domi}\ intl_2) =$
$\quad \textbf{if}\ \text{repPO}\ Oi\ (\text{Lifn}\ M\ intl_2)\ (\text{Lifn}\ M\ intl_1)\ \textbf{then}\ \mathcal{U}(:\text{'v})$
$\quad \textbf{else}\ \{\,\}$

⌊doms_def⌋

$\vdash \forall Oi\ Os\ M\ secl_1\ secl_2.$
$\quad \text{Efn}\ Oi\ Os\ M\ (secl_1\ \text{doms}\ secl_2) =$
$\quad \textbf{if}\ \text{repPO}\ Os\ (\text{Lsfn}\ M\ secl_2)\ (\text{Lsfn}\ M\ secl_1)\ \textbf{then}\ \mathcal{U}(:\text{'v})$
$\quad \textbf{else}\ \{\,\}$

⌊eqf_def⌋

$\vdash \forall Oi\ Os\ M\ f_1\ f_2.$
$\quad \text{Efn}\ Oi\ Os\ M\ (f_1\ \text{eqf}\ f_2) =$
$\quad (\mathcal{U}(:\text{'v})\ \text{DIFF}\ \text{Efn}\ Oi\ Os\ M\ f_1 \cup \text{Efn}\ Oi\ Os\ M\ f_2) \cap$
$\quad (\mathcal{U}(:\text{'v})\ \text{DIFF}\ \text{Efn}\ Oi\ Os\ M\ f_2 \cup \text{Efn}\ Oi\ Os\ M\ f_1)$

⌊eqf_impf⌋

$\vdash \forall M\ f_1\ f_2.$
$\quad \text{Efn}\ Oi\ Os\ M\ (f_1\ \text{eqf}\ f_2) =$
$\quad \text{Efn}\ Oi\ Os\ M\ ((f_1\ \text{impf}\ f_2)\ \text{andf}\ (f_2\ \text{impf}\ f_1))$

$\lfloor$eqi_def$\rfloor$

$\vdash \forall Oi\ Os\ M\ intl_2\ intl_1$.

    Efn $Oi\ Os\ M\ (intl_2$ eqi $intl_1) =$

    (**if** repPO Oi (Lifn $M\ intl_2$) (Lifn $M\ intl_1$) **then** $\mathcal{U}(:$'v)

    else $\{\}$) $\cap$

    if repPO Oi (Lifn $M\ intl_1$) (Lifn $M\ intl_2$) **then** $\mathcal{U}(:$'v)

    else $\{\}$

$\lfloor$eqi_domi$\rfloor$

$\vdash \forall M\ intL_1\ intL_2$.

    Efn $Oi\ Os\ M\ (intL_1$ eqi $intL_2) =$

    Efn $Oi\ Os\ M\ (intL_2$ domi $intL_1$ andf $intL_1$ domi $intL_2$)

$\lfloor$eqn_def$\rfloor$

$\vdash \forall Oi\ Os\ M\ numExp_1\ numExp_2$.

    Efn $Oi\ Os\ M\ (numExp_1$ eqn $numExp_2) =$

    if $numExp_1 = numExp_2$ **then** $\mathcal{U}(:$'v) **else** $\{\}$

$\lfloor$eqs_def$\rfloor$

$\vdash \forall Oi\ Os\ M\ secl_2\ secl_1$.

    Efn $Oi\ Os\ M\ (secl_2$ eqs $secl_1) =$

    (**if** repPO Os (Lsfn $M\ secl_2$) (Lsfn $M\ secl_1$) **then** $\mathcal{U}(:$'v)

    else $\{\}$) $\cap$

    if repPO Os (Lsfn $M\ secl_1$) (Lsfn $M\ secl_2$) **then** $\mathcal{U}(:$'v)

    else $\{\}$

$\lfloor$eqs_doms$\rfloor$

$\vdash \forall M\ secL_1\ secL_2$.

    Efn $Oi\ Os\ M\ (secL_1$ eqs $secL_2) =$

    Efn $Oi\ Os\ M\ (secL_2$ doms $secL_1$ andf $secL_1$ doms $secL_2$)

$\lceil$FF_def$\rfloor$

$\vdash \forall Oi\ Os\ M$. Efn $Oi\ Os\ M$ FF $= \{\}$

$\lfloor$impf_def$\rfloor$

$\vdash \forall Oi\ Os\ M\ f_1\ f_2$.

    Efn $Oi\ Os\ M\ (f_1$ impf $f_2) =$

    $\mathcal{U}(:$'v) DIFF Efn $Oi\ Os\ M\ f_1 \cup$ Efn $Oi\ Os\ M\ f_2$

$\lceil$lt_def$\rfloor$

$\vdash \forall Oi\ Os\ M\ numExp_1\ numExp_2$.

    Efn $Oi\ Os\ M\ (numExp_1$ lt $numExp_2) =$

    if $numExp_1 < numExp_2$ **then** $\mathcal{U}(:$'v) **else** $\{\}$

$\lceil$lte_def$\rfloor$

$\vdash \forall Oi\ Os\ M\ numExp_1\ numExp_2$.

    Efn $Oi\ Os\ M\ (numExp_1$ lte $numExp_2) =$

    if $numExp_1 \leq numExp_2$ **then** $\mathcal{U}(:$'v) **else** $\{\}$

⌊meet_def⌋

$\vdash \forall J\ P_1\ P_2.$ Jext J $(P_1$ meet $P_2)$ = Jext J P_1 RUNION Jext J P_2

⌊name_def⌋

$\vdash \forall J\ s.$ Jext J (Name s) = $J\ s$

⌊notf_def⌋

$\vdash \forall Oi\ Os\ M\ f.$ Efn $Oi\ Os\ M$ (notf f) = $\mathcal{U}(:\text{'v})$ DIFF Efn $Oi\ Os\ M\ f$

⌊orf_def⌋

$\vdash \forall Oi\ Os\ M\ f_1\ f_2.$
   Efn $Oi\ Os\ M$ $(f_1$ orf $f_2)$ = Efn $Oi\ Os\ M\ f_1\ \cup$ Efn $Oi\ Os\ M\ f_2$

⌊prop_def⌋

$\vdash \forall Oi\ Os\ M\ p.$ Efn $Oi\ Os\ M$ (prop p) = intpKS $M\ p$

⌊quoting_def⌋

$\vdash \forall J\ P_1\ P_2.$ Jext J $(P_1$ quoting $P_2)$ = Jext J P_2 O Jext J P_1

⌊reps_def⌋

$\vdash \forall Oi\ Os\ M\ P\ Q\ f.$
   Efn $Oi\ Os\ M$ (reps $P\ Q\ f$) =
   $\mathcal{U}(:\text{'v})$ DIFF
   $\{w\mid$ Jext (jKS M) $(P$ quoting $Q)$ $w \subseteq$ Efn $Oi\ Os\ M\ f\} \cup$
   $\{w\mid$ Jext (jKS M) $Q\ w \subseteq$ Efn $Oi\ Os\ M\ f\}$

⌊says_def⌋

$\vdash \forall Oi\ Os\ M\ P\ f.$
   Efn $Oi\ Os\ M$ $(P$ says $f)$ =
   $\{w\mid$ Jext (jKS M) $P\ w \subseteq$ Efn $Oi\ Os\ M\ f\}$

⌊speaks_for_def⌋

$\vdash \forall Oi\ Os\ M\ P\ Q.$
   Efn $Oi\ Os\ M$ $(P$ speaks_for $Q)$ =
   if Jext (jKS M) Q RSUBSET Jext (jKS M) P **then** $\mathcal{U}(:\text{'v})$
   else $\{\}$

⌊TT_def⌋

$\vdash \forall Oi\ Os\ M.$ Efn $Oi\ Os\ M$ TT = $\mathcal{U}(:\text{'v})$

3 aclrules Theory

Built: 30 November 2015
Parent Theories: aclsemantics

3.1 Definitions

[sat_def]

$\vdash \forall M \ Oi \ Os \ f. \ (M,Oi,Os) \ \text{sat} \ f \ \Longleftrightarrow \ (\text{Efn} \ Oi \ Os \ M \ f = \mathcal{U}(:\text{'world}))$

3.2 Theorems

[And_Says]

$\vdash \forall M \ Oi \ Os \ P \ Q \ f.$
$\quad (M,Oi,Os) \ \text{sat} \ P \ \text{meet} \ Q \ \text{says} \ f \ \text{eqf} \ P \ \text{says} \ f \ \text{andf} \ Q \ \text{says} \ f$

[And_Says_Eq]

$\vdash (M,Oi,Os) \ \text{sat} \ P \ \text{meet} \ Q \ \text{says} \ f \ \Longleftrightarrow$
$\quad (M,Oi,Os) \ \text{sat} \ P \ \text{says} \ f \ \text{andf} \ Q \ \text{says} \ f$

[and_says_lemma]

$\vdash \forall M \ Oi \ Os \ P \ Q \ f.$
$\quad (M,Oi,Os) \ \text{sat} \ P \ \text{meet} \ Q \ \text{says} \ f \ \text{impf} \ P \ \text{says} \ f \ \text{andf} \ Q \ \text{says} \ f$

[Controls_Eq]

$\vdash \forall M \ Oi \ Os \ P \ f.$
$\quad (M,Oi,Os) \ \text{sat} \ P \ \text{controls} \ f \ \Longleftrightarrow \ (M,Oi,Os) \ \text{sat} \ P \ \text{says} \ f \ \text{impf} \ f$

[DIFF_UNIV_SUBSET]

$\vdash (\mathcal{U}(:\text{'a}) \ \text{DIFF} \ s \cup t = \mathcal{U}(:\text{'a})) \ \Longleftrightarrow \ s \subseteq t$

[domi_antisymmetric]

$\vdash \forall M \ Oi \ Os \ l_1 \ l_2.$
$\quad (M,Oi,Os) \ \text{sat} \ l_1 \ \text{domi} \ l_2 \ \Rightarrow$
$\quad (M,Oi,Os) \ \text{sat} \ l_2 \ \text{domi} \ l_1 \ \Rightarrow$
$\quad (M,Oi,Os) \ \text{sat} \ l_1 \ \text{eqi} \ l_2$

[domi_reflexive]

$\vdash \forall M \ Oi \ Os \ l. \ (M,Oi,Os) \ \text{sat} \ l \ \text{domi} \ l$

[domi_transitive]

$\vdash \forall M \ Oi \ Os \ l_1 \ l_2 \ l_3.$
$\quad (M,Oi,Os) \ \text{sat} \ l_1 \ \text{domi} \ l_2 \ \Rightarrow$
$\quad (M,Oi,Os) \ \text{sat} \ l_2 \ \text{domi} \ l_3 \ \Rightarrow$
$\quad (M,Oi,Os) \ \text{sat} \ l_1 \ \text{domi} \ l_3$

[doms_antisymmetric]

$\vdash \forall M \ Oi \ Os \ l_1 \ l_2.$
$\quad (M,Oi,Os) \ \text{sat} \ l_1 \ \text{doms} \ l_2 \ \Rightarrow$
$\quad (M,Oi,Os) \ \text{sat} \ l_2 \ \text{doms} \ l_1 \ \Rightarrow$
$\quad (M,Oi,Os) \ \text{sat} \ l_1 \ \text{eqs} \ l_2$

[doms_reflexive]

$\vdash \forall M\ Oi\ Os\ l.\ (M, Oi, Os)$ sat l doms l

[doms_transitive]

$\vdash \forall M\ Oi\ Os\ l_1\ l_2\ l_3.$
    (M, Oi, Os) sat l_1 doms $l_2 \Rightarrow$
    (M, Oi, Os) sat l_2 doms $l_3 \Rightarrow$
    (M, Oi, Os) sat l_1 doms l_3

[eqf_and_impf]

$\vdash \forall M\ Oi\ Os\ f_1\ f_2.$
    (M, Oi, Os) sat f_1 eqf $f_2 \iff$
    (M, Oi, Os) sat $(f_1$ impf $f_2)$ andf $(f_2$ impf $f_1)$

[eqf_andf1]

$\vdash \forall M\ Oi\ Os\ f\ f'\ g.$
    (M, Oi, Os) sat f eqf $f' \Rightarrow$
    (M, Oi, Os) sat f andf $g \Rightarrow$
    (M, Oi, Os) sat f' andf g

[eqf_andf2]

$\vdash \forall M\ Oi\ Os\ f\ f'\ g.$
    (M, Oi, Os) sat f eqf $f' \Rightarrow$
    (M, Oi, Os) sat g andf $f \Rightarrow$
    (M, Oi, Os) sat g andf f'

[eqf_controls]

$\vdash \forall M\ Oi\ Os\ P\ f\ f'.$
    (M, Oi, Os) sat f eqf $f' \Rightarrow$
    (M, Oi, Os) sat P controls $f \Rightarrow$
    (M, Oi, Os) sat P controls f'

[eqf_eq]

$\vdash$ (Efn $Oi\ Os\ M\ (f_1$ eqf $f_2) = \mathcal{U}(:\text{'b})) \iff$
    (Efn $Oi\ Os\ M\ f_1 =$ Efn $Oi\ Os\ M\ f_2)$

[eqf_eqf1]

$\vdash \forall M\ Oi\ Os\ f\ f'\ g.$
    (M, Oi, Os) sat f eqf $f' \Rightarrow$
    (M, Oi, Os) sat f eqf $g \Rightarrow$
    (M, Oi, Os) sat f' eqf g

[eqf_eqf2]

$\vdash \forall M\ Oi\ Os\ f\ f'\ g.$
    (M, Oi, Os) sat f eqf $f' \Rightarrow$
    (M, Oi, Os) sat g eqf $f \Rightarrow$
    (M, Oi, Os) sat g eqf f'

$\lfloor$eqf_impf1$\rfloor$

$\vdash \forall M \; Oi \; Os \; f \; f' \; g.$
(M,Oi,Os) sat f eqf $f' \Rightarrow$
(M,Oi,Os) sat f impf $g \Rightarrow$
(M,Oi,Os) sat f' impf g

$\lfloor$eqf_impf2$\rfloor$

$\vdash \forall M \; Oi \; Os \; f \; f' \; g.$
(M,Oi,Os) sat f eqf $f' \Rightarrow$
(M,Oi,Os) sat g impf $f \Rightarrow$
(M,Oi,Os) sat g impf f'

$\lfloor$eqf_notf$\rfloor$

$\vdash \forall M \; Oi \; Os \; f \; f'.$
(M,Oi,Os) sat f eqf $f' \Rightarrow$
(M,Oi,Os) sat notf $f \Rightarrow$
(M,Oi,Os) sat notf f'

$\lfloor$eqf_orf1$\rfloor$

$\vdash \forall M \; Oi \; Os \; f \; f' \; g.$
(M,Oi,Os) sat f eqf $f' \Rightarrow$
(M,Oi,Os) sat f orf $g \Rightarrow$
(M,Oi,Os) sat f' orf g

$\lfloor$eqf_orf2$\rfloor$

$\vdash \forall M \; Oi \; Os \; f \; f' \; g.$
(M,Oi,Os) sat f eqf $f' \Rightarrow$
(M,Oi,Os) sat g orf $f \Rightarrow$
(M,Oi,Os) sat g orf f'

$\lfloor$eqf_reps$\rfloor$

$\vdash \forall M \; Oi \; Os \; P \; Q \; f \; f'.$
(M,Oi,Os) sat f eqf $f' \Rightarrow$
(M,Oi,Os) sat reps $P \; Q \; f \Rightarrow$
(M,Oi,Os) sat reps $P \; Q \; f'$

$\lfloor$eqf_sat$\rfloor$

$\vdash \forall M \; Oi \; Os \; f_1 \; f_2.$
(M,Oi,Os) sat f_1 eqf $f_2 \Rightarrow$
$((M,Oi,Os)$ sat $f_1 \iff (M,Oi,Os)$ sat $f_2)$

$\lfloor$eqf_says$\rfloor$

$\vdash \forall M \; Oi \; Os \; P \; f \; f'.$
(M,Oi,Os) sat f eqf $f' \Rightarrow$
(M,Oi,Os) sat P says $f \Rightarrow$
$(M.Oi.Os)$ sat P savs f'

[eqi_Eq]

$\vdash \forall M \ Oi \ Os \ l_1 \ l_2.$
    (M, Oi, Os) sat l_1 eqi l_2 $\Longleftrightarrow$
    (M, Oi, Os) sat l_2 domi l_1 andf l_1 domi l_2

[eqs_Eq]

$\vdash \forall M \ Oi \ Os \ l_1 \ l_2.$
    (M, Oi, Os) sat l_1 eqs l_2 $\Longleftrightarrow$
    (M, Oi, Os) sat l_2 doms l_1 andf l_1 doms l_2

[Idemp_Speaks_For]

$\vdash \forall M \ Oi \ Os \ P.$ (M, Oi, Os) sat P speaks_for P

[Image_cmp]

$\vdash \forall R_1 \ R_2 \ R_3 \ u.$ $(R_1 \ O \ R_2) \ u \subseteq R_3$ $\Longleftrightarrow$ $R_2 \ u \subseteq \{y \mid R_1 \ y \subseteq R_3\}$

[Image_SUBSET]

$\vdash \forall R_1 \ R_2.$ R_2 RSUBSET R_1 $\Rightarrow$ $\forall w.$ $R_2 \ w \subseteq R_1 \ w$

[Image_UNION]

$\vdash \forall R_1 \ R_2 \ w.$ $(R_1$ RUNION $R_2) \ w = R_1 \ w \cup R_2 \ w$

[INTER_EQ_UNIV]

$\vdash (s \cap t = \mathcal{U}(:\text{'a})) \ \Longleftrightarrow \ (s = \mathcal{U}(:\text{'a})) \land (t = \mathcal{U}(:\text{'a}))$

[Modus_Ponens]

$\vdash \forall M \ Oi \ Os \ f_1 \ f_2.$
    (M, Oi, Os) sat f_1 $\Rightarrow$
    (M, Oi, Os) sat f_1 impf f_2 $\Rightarrow$
    (M, Oi, Os) sat f_2

[Mono_speaks_for]

$\vdash \forall M \ Oi \ Os \ P \ P' \ Q \ Q'.$
    (M, Oi, Os) sat P speaks_for P' $\Rightarrow$
    (M, Oi, Os) sat Q speaks_for Q' $\Rightarrow$
    (M, Oi, Os) sat P quoting Q speaks_for P' quoting Q'

[MP_Says]

$\vdash \forall M \ Oi \ Os \ P \ f_1 \ f_2.$
    (M, Oi, Os) sat
    P says $(f_1$ impf $f_2)$ impf P says f_1 impf P says f_2

[Quoting]

$\vdash \forall M \ Oi \ Os \ P \ Q \ f.$
    (M, Oi, Os) sat P quoting Q says f eqf P says Q says f

[Quoting_Eq]

$\vdash \forall M\ Oi\ Os\ P\ Q\ f.$
$\quad (M,Oi,Os)$ sat P quoting Q says $f \iff$
$\quad (M,Oi,Os)$ sat P says Q says f

[reps_def_lemma]

$\vdash \forall M\ Oi\ Os\ P\ Q\ f.$
$\quad$ Efn $Oi\ Os\ M$ (reps $P\ Q\ f$) =
$\quad$ Efn $Oi\ Os\ M$ (P quoting Q says f impf Q says f)

[Reps_Eq]

$\vdash \forall M\ Oi\ Os\ P\ Q\ f.$
$\quad (M,Oi,Os)$ sat reps $P\ Q\ f \iff$
$\quad (M,Oi,Os)$ sat P quoting Q says f impf Q says f

[sat_allworld]

$\vdash \forall M\ f.\ (M,Oi,Os)$ sat $f \iff \forall w.\ w \in$ Efn $Oi\ Os\ M\ f$

[sat_andf_eq_and_sat]

$\vdash (M,Oi,Os)$ sat f_1 andf $f_2 \iff$
$\quad (M,Oi,Os)$ sat $f_1 \wedge (M,Oi,Os)$ sat f_2

[sat_TT]

$\vdash (M,Oi,Os)$ sat TT

[Says]

$\vdash \forall M\ Oi\ Os\ P\ f.\ (M,Oi,Os)$ sat $f \Rightarrow (M,Oi,Os)$ sat P says f

[says_and_lemma]

$\vdash \forall M\ Oi\ Os\ P\ Q\ f.$
$\quad (M,Oi,Os)$ sat P says f andf Q says f impf P meet Q says f

[Speaks_For]

$\vdash \forall M\ Oi\ Os\ P\ Q\ f.$
$\quad (M,Oi,Os)$ sat P speaks_for Q impf P says f impf Q says f

[speaks_for_SUBSET]

$\vdash \forall R_3\ R_2\ R_1.$
$\quad R_2$ RSUBSET $R_1 \Rightarrow \forall w.\ \{w \mid R_1\ w \subseteq R_3\} \subseteq \{w \mid R_2\ w \subseteq R_3\}$

[SUBSET_Image_SUBSET]

$\vdash \forall R_1\ R_2\ R_3.$
$\quad (\forall w_1.\ R_2\ w_1 \subseteq R_1\ w_1) \Rightarrow$
$\quad \forall w.\ \{w \mid R_1\ w \subseteq R_3\} \subseteq \{w \mid R_2\ w \subseteq R_3\}$

$\lfloor$Trans_Speaks_For$\rfloor$

$\vdash \forall M\ Oi\ Os\ P\ Q\ R.$
    (M, Oi, Os) sat P speaks_for $Q \Rightarrow$
    (M, Oi, Os) sat Q speaks_for $R \Rightarrow$
    (M, Oi, Os) sat P speaks_for R

$\lfloor$UNIV_DIFF_SUBSET$\rfloor$

$\vdash \forall R_1\ R_2.\ R_1 \subseteq R_2 \Rightarrow (\mathcal{U}(:\text{'a})\ \text{DIFF}\ R_1 \cup R_2 = \mathcal{U}(:\text{'a}))$

$\lfloor$world_and$\rfloor$

$\vdash \forall M\ Oi\ Os\ f_1\ f_2\ w.$
    $w \in \text{Efn}\ Oi\ Os\ M\ (f_1\ \text{andf}\ f_2) \iff$
    $w \in \text{Efn}\ Oi\ Os\ M\ f_1 \wedge w \in \text{Efn}\ Oi\ Os\ M\ f_2$

$\lfloor$world_eq$\rfloor$

$\vdash \forall M\ Oi\ Os\ f_1\ f_2\ w.$
    $w \in \text{Efn}\ Oi\ Os\ M\ (f_1\ \text{eqf}\ f_2) \iff$
    $(w \in \text{Efn}\ Oi\ Os\ M\ f_1 \iff w \in \text{Efn}\ Oi\ Os\ M\ f_2)$

$\lfloor$world_eqn$\rfloor$

$\vdash \forall M\ Oi\ Os\ n_1\ n_2\ w.\ w \in \text{Efn}\ Oi\ Os\ m\ (n_1\ \text{eqn}\ n_2) \iff (n_1 = n_2)$

$\lfloor$world_F$\rfloor$

$\vdash \forall M\ Oi\ Os\ w.\ w \notin \text{Efn}\ Oi\ Os\ M\ \text{FF}$

$\lfloor$world_imp$\rfloor$

$\vdash \forall M\ Oi\ Os\ f_1\ f_2\ w.$
    $w \in \text{Efn}\ Oi\ Os\ M\ (f_1\ \text{impf}\ f_2) \iff$
    $w \in \text{Efn}\ Oi\ Os\ M\ f_1 \Rightarrow w \in \text{Efn}\ Oi\ Os\ M\ f_2$

$\lfloor$world_lt$\rfloor$

$\vdash \forall M\ Oi\ Os\ n_1\ n_2\ w.\ w \in \text{Efn}\ Oi\ Os\ m\ (n_1\ \text{lt}\ n_2) \iff n_1 < n_2$

$\lfloor$world_lte$\rfloor$

$\vdash \forall M\ Oi\ Os\ n_1\ n_2\ w.\ w \in \text{Efn}\ Oi\ Os\ m\ (n_1\ \text{lte}\ n_2) \iff n_1 \leq n_2$

$\lfloor$world_not$\rfloor$

$\vdash \forall M\ Oi\ Os\ f\ w.\ w \in \text{Efn}\ Oi\ Os\ M\ (\text{notf}\ f) \iff w \notin \text{Efn}\ Oi\ Os\ M\ f$

$\lfloor$world_or$\rfloor$

$\vdash \forall M\ f_1\ f_2\ w.$
    $w \in \text{Efn}\ Oi\ Os\ M\ (f_1\ \text{orf}\ f_2) \iff$
    $w \in \text{Efn}\ Oi\ Os\ M\ f_1 \vee w \in \text{Efn}\ Oi\ Os\ M\ f_2$

$\lfloor$world_says$\rfloor$

$\vdash \forall M\ Oi\ Os\ P\ f\ w.$
    $w \in \text{Efn}\ Oi\ Os\ M\ (P\ \text{says}\ f) \iff$
    $\forall v.\ v \in \text{Jext}\ (\text{jKS}\ M)\ P\ w \Rightarrow v \in \text{Efn}\ Oi\ Os\ M\ f$

$\lfloor$world_T$\rfloor$

$\vdash \forall M\ Oi\ Os\ w.\ w \in \text{Efn}\ Oi\ Os\ M\ \text{TT}$

4   aclDrules Theory

Built: 30 November 2015
Parent Theories: aclrules

4.1   Theorems

[Conjunction]

$\vdash \forall M \ Oi \ Os \ f_1 \ f_2.$
   (M, Oi, Os) sat $f_1 \Rightarrow$
   (M, Oi, Os) sat $f_2 \Rightarrow$
   (M, Oi, Os) sat f_1 andf f_2

[Controls]

$\vdash \forall M \ Oi \ Os \ P \ f.$
   (M, Oi, Os) sat P says $f \Rightarrow$
   (M, Oi, Os) sat P controls $f \Rightarrow$
   (M, Oi, Os) sat f

[Derived_Controls]

$\vdash \forall M \ Oi \ Os \ P \ Q \ f.$
   (M, Oi, Os) sat P speaks_for $Q \Rightarrow$
   (M, Oi, Os) sat Q controls $f \Rightarrow$
   (M, Oi, Os) sat P controls f

[Derived_Speaks_For]

$\vdash \forall M \ Oi \ Os \ P \ Q \ f.$
   (M, Oi, Os) sat P speaks_for $Q \Rightarrow$
   (M, Oi, Os) sat P says $f \Rightarrow$
   (M, Oi, Os) sat Q says f

[Disjunction1]

$\vdash \forall M \ Oi \ Os \ f_1 \ f_2. \ (M, Oi, Os)$ sat $f_1 \Rightarrow (M, Oi, Os)$ sat f_1 orf f_2

[Disjunction2]

$\vdash \forall M \ Oi \ Os \ f_1 \ f_2. \ (M, Oi, Os)$ sat $f_2 \Rightarrow (M, Oi, Os)$ sat f_1 orf f_2

[Disjunctive_Syllogism]

$\vdash \forall M \ Oi \ Os \ f_1 \ f_2.$
   (M, Oi, Os) sat f_1 orf $f_2 \Rightarrow$
   (M, Oi, Os) sat notf $f_1 \Rightarrow$
   (M, Oi, Os) sat f_2

[Double_Negation]

$\vdash \forall M \ Oi \ Os \ f. \ (M, Oi, Os)$ sat notf (notf f) $\Rightarrow (M, Oi, Os)$ sat f

⌊eqn_eqn⌋

$\vdash (M, Oi, Os)$ sat c_1 eqn $n_1 \Rightarrow$
(M, Oi, Os) sat c_2 eqn $n_2 \Rightarrow$
(M, Oi, Os) sat n_1 eqn $n_2 \Rightarrow$
(M, Oi, Os) sat c_1 eqn c_2

⌊eqn_lt⌋

$\vdash (M, Oi, Os)$ sat c_1 eqn $n_1 \Rightarrow$
(M, Oi, Os) sat c_2 eqn $n_2 \Rightarrow$
(M, Oi, Os) sat n_1 lt $n_2 \Rightarrow$
(M, Oi, Os) sat c_1 lt c_2

⌊eqn_lte⌋

$\vdash (M, Oi, Os)$ sat c_1 eqn $n_1 \Rightarrow$
(M, Oi, Os) sat c_2 eqn $n_2 \Rightarrow$
(M, Oi, Os) sat n_1 lte $n_2 \Rightarrow$
(M, Oi, Os) sat c_1 lte c_2

⌊Hypothetical_Syllogism⌋

$\vdash \forall M \ Oi \ Os \ f_1 \ f_2 \ f_3.$
(M, Oi, Os) sat f_1 impf $f_2 \Rightarrow$
(M, Oi, Os) sat f_2 impf $f_3 \Rightarrow$
(M, Oi, Os) sat f_1 impf f_3

⌊il_domi⌋

$\vdash \forall M \ Oi \ Os \ P \ Q \ l_1 \ l_2.$
(M, Oi, Os) sat il P eqi $l_1 \Rightarrow$
(M, Oi, Os) sat il Q eqi $l_2 \Rightarrow$
(M, Oi, Os) sat l_2 domi $l_1 \Rightarrow$
(M, Oi, Os) sat il Q domi il P

⌊INTER_EQ_UNIV⌋

$\vdash \forall s_1 \ s_2. \ (s_1 \cap s_2 = U(:\verb|'|a)) \iff (s_1 = U(:\verb|'|a)) \wedge (s_2 = U(:\verb|'|a))$

⌊Modus_Tollens⌋

$\vdash \forall M \ Oi \ Os \ f_1 \ f_2.$
(M, Oi, Os) sat f_1 impf $f_2 \Rightarrow$
(M, Oi, Os) sat notf $f_2 \Rightarrow$
(M, Oi, Os) sat notf f_1

⌊Rep_Controls_Eq⌋

$\vdash \forall M \ Oi \ Os \ A \ B \ f.$
(M, Oi, Os) sat reps $A \ B \ f \iff$
(M, Oi, Os) sat A controls B says f

[Rep_Says]

$\vdash \forall M \; Oi \; Os \; P \; Q \; f.$
(M, Oi, Os) sat reps $P \; Q \; f \Rightarrow$
(M, Oi, Os) sat P quoting Q says $f \Rightarrow$
(M, Oi, Os) sat Q says f

[Reps]

$\vdash \forall M \; Oi \; Os \; P \; Q \; f.$
(M, Oi, Os) sat reps $P \; Q \; f \Rightarrow$
(M, Oi, Os) sat P quoting Q says $f \Rightarrow$
(M, Oi, Os) sat Q controls $f \Rightarrow$
(M, Oi, Os) sat f

[Says_Simplification1]

$\vdash \forall M \; Oi \; Os \; P \; f_1 \; f_2.$
(M, Oi, Os) sat P says $(f_1 \text{ andf } f_2) \Rightarrow (M, Oi, Os)$ sat P says f_1

[Says_Simplification2]

$\vdash \forall M \; Oi \; Os \; P \; f_1 \; f_2.$
(M, Oi, Os) sat P says $(f_1 \text{ andf } f_2) \Rightarrow (M, Oi, Os)$ sat P says f_2

[Simplification1]

$\vdash \forall M \; Oi \; Os \; f_1 \; f_2. \; (M, Oi, Os)$ sat f_1 andf $f_2 \Rightarrow (M, Oi, Os)$ sat f_1

[Simplification2]

$\vdash \forall M \; Oi \; Os \; f_1 \; f_2. \; (M, Oi, Os)$ sat f_1 andf $f_2 \Rightarrow (M, Oi, Os)$ sat f_2

[sl_doms]

$\vdash \forall M \; Oi \; Os \; P \; Q \; l_1 \; l_2.$
(M, Oi, Os) sat sl P eqs $l_1 \Rightarrow$
(M, Oi, Os) sat sl Q eqs $l_2 \Rightarrow$
(M, Oi, Os) sat l_2 doms $l_1 \Rightarrow$
(M, Oi, Os) sat sl Q doms sl P

BIBLIOGRAPHY

Abad, C., Taylor, J., Sengul, C., Yurcik, W., Zhou, Y., & Rowe, K. 2003. Log correlation for intrusion detection: a proof of concept. In: IEEE Proceedings of the 19th Annual Computer Security Applications Conference, December 2003, pp. 255–264.

Abadi, D.J. 2009. Data management in the cloud: limitations and opportunities. *IEEE Data Engineering Bulletin*, 32(1), pp. 3–12.

Abadi, M., & Kremer, S. (Eds.). 2014. Principles of security and trust. In: Third International Conference, POST 2014, Held as Part of the European Joint Conferences on Theory and Practice of Software, ETAPS 2014, Vol. 8414, Grenoble, France, April 5–13, 2014, Springer.

Abadi, M., Burrows, M., Lampson, B., & Plotkin, G. 1993. A calculus for access control in distributed systems. *ACM Transactions on Programming Languages and Systems (TOPLAS)*, 15(4), pp. 706–734.

Abimbola, A.A., Munoz, J.M., & Buchanan, W.J. 2006. Investigating false positive reduction in http via procedure analysis. In: IEEE International Conference on Networking and Services, Slicon Valley, CA, July 16–18, 2006, pp. 87–87.

Aboba, B., Blunk, L., Vollbrecht, J., Carlson, J., & Levkowetz, H. 2004. Extensible authentication protocol (EAP). IETF standards track, RFC 3748, June 2004.

Abrams, M., & Weiss, J. 2008. *Malicious Control System Cyber Security Attack Case Study – Maroochy Water Services, Australia*. The MITRE Corporation, McLean, VA.

Agosta, G., & Pelosi, G. 2007. A domain specific language for cryptography. In: Proceedings of the Forum on Specification and Design Languages, Gières, France: ECSI, pp. 159–164.

Ahamed, S.I., Kim, D., Hasan, C.S., & Zulkernine, M. 2009. Towards developing a trust-based security solution. In: Proceedings of the 2009 ACM symposium on Applied Computing, March 2009, pp. 2204–2205.

Cyber-Assurance for the Internet of Things, First Edition. Edited by Tyson T. Brooks.
© 2017 by The Institute of Electrical and Electronic Engineers, Inc. Published 2017 by John Wiley & Sons, Inc.

Albert, R., Albert, I., & Nakarado, G.L. 2004. Structural vulnerability of the North American power grid. *Physical Review E*, 69(2), p. 025103.

Alberts, C., Dorofee, A., Stevens, J., & Woody, C. 2003. *Introduction to the OCTAVE Approach*. Carnegie Mellon University, Pittsburgh, PA.

Alberts, C., Ellison, R.J., & Woody, C. 2009. Cyber Assurance. 2009 CERT Research Report. Software Engineering Institute, Carnegie Mellon University. Available at http://resources.sei.cmu.edu/library/asset-view.cfm?assetid=77638.

Alcaraz, C., & Lopez, J. 2010. A security analysis for wireless sensor mesh networks in highly critical systems. *IEEE Transactions on Systems, Man, and Cybernetics, Part C: Applications and Reviews*, 40(4), pp. 419–428.

Alshaikhli, I.F., Alahmad, M.A., & Munthir, K. 2012. Comparison and analysis study of SHA-3 finalists. In: International Conference on Advanced Computer Science Applications and Technologies (ACSAT), November 2012, pp. 366–371.

Aman, W., & Snekkenes, E. 2015. EDAS: an evaluation prototype for autonomic event-driven adaptive security in the Internet of Things. *Future Internet*, 7(3), pp. 225–256.

Amin, S., Cárdenas, A.A., & Sastry, S.S. 2009. Safe and secure networked control systems under denial-of-service attacks. In: *Hybrid Systems: Computation and Control*. Springer, Berlin/Heidelberg, pp. 31–45.

Amyx, S. 2015. Wearing your intelligence: how to apply artificial intelligence in wearables and IoT. *Wired*. Available at http://www.wired.com/insights/2014/12/wearing-your-intelligence/. Accessed on May 13, 2015.

Anderson, E.A., Irvine, C.E., & Schell, R.R. 2004. Subversion as a Threat in Information Warfare, *Journal of Information Warfare*, 3(2), June 2004, pp. 52–65.

Ansilla, J.D., Vasudevan, N., JayachandraBensam, J., & Anunciya, J.D. 2015. Data security in Smart Grid with hardware implementation against DoS attacks. In: IEEE International Conference on Circuit, Power and Computing Technologies, March 2015, pp. 1–7.

Arbit, A., Oren, Y., & Wool, A. 2014. A secure supply-chain RFID system that respects your privacy. *Pervasive Computing*, 13(2), pp. 52–60.

Arias, O., Davi, L., Hanreich, M., Jin, Y., Koeberl, P., Paul, D., Sadeghi, A.R., & Sullivan, D. 2015. Hafix: hardware-assisted flow integrity extension. In: 52nd Design Automation Conference, San Francisco, CA, June 8–12, 2015, pp. 1–6.

Asensio, Á., Blanco, T., Blasco, R., Marco, Á., & Casas, R. 2015. Managing emergency situations in the smart city: the smart signal. *Sensors*, 15(6), pp. 14370–14396.

Ashford, B.M., & Kasper, G.M. 2003. A test of the theory of DSS design for user calibration: the effects of expressiveness and visibility on user calibration. In: SIGHCI 2003 Proceedings, January 1, 2003, p. 18.

Ashraf, Q.M., & Habaebi, M.H. 2015. Autonomic schemes for threat mitigation in Internet of Things. *Journal of Network and Computer Applications*, 49, pp. 112–127.

Ashton, K. 2015. When IoT meets artificial intelligence. *Waylay.io*. Available at http://www.waylay.io/blog-iot-meets-artificial-intelligence.html. Accessed on May 13, 2015.

Atzori, L., Iera, A., & Morabito, G. 2010. The internet of things: a survey. *Computer Networks*, 54(15), pp. 2787–2805.

Aumasson, J.P., Henzen, L., Meier, W., & Phan, R.C.W. 2008. SHA-3 proposal BLAKE. Submission to NIST (Round 3).

Babar, S., Stango, A., Prasad, N., Sen, J., & Prasad, R. 2011. Proposed embedded security framework for Internet of Things (IoT). In: IEEE 2nd International Conference on Wireless Communication, Vehicular Technology, Information Theory and Aerospace & Electronic Systems Technology, February 2011, pp. 1–5.

Bai, Q., Giugni, S., Williamson, D., & Taylor, J. (Eds.). 2013. *Data Provenance and Data Management in eScience.* Springer.

Ballardie, A. 1996. Scalable multicast key distribution. RFC 1949, May 1996.

Bao, F., Chen, I.R., Chang, M., & Cho, J.H. 2011. Trust-based intrusion detection in wireless sensor networks. In: IEEE International Conference on Communications (ICC), June 2011, pp. 1–6.

Bao, F., Chen, I.R., Chang, M., & Cho, J.H. 2012. Hierarchical trust management for wireless sensor networks and its applications to trust-based routing and intrusion detection. *IEEE Transactions on Network and Service Management*, 9(2), pp. 169–183.

Barnett, C.K., & Pratt, M.G. 2000. From threat-rigidity to flexibility-Toward a learning model of autogenic crisis in organizations. *Journal of Organizational Change Management*, 13(1), pp. 74–88.

Bates, A., Butler, K., Haeberlen, A., Sherr, M., & Zhou, W. 2014. Let SDN be your eyes: secure forensics in data center networks. In: Proceedings of the NDSS Workshop on Security of Emerging Network Technologies, San Diego, CA, February 23, 2014.

Bauer, S., & Schreckling, D. 2013. Data provenance in the Internet of Things. In: EU Project COMPOSE, Conference Seminar.

Berenbaum, H., Thompson, R.J., & Bredemeier, K. 2007. Perceived threat: Exploring its association with worry and its hypothesized antecedents. *Behaviour Research and Therapy*, 45(10), pp. 2473–2482.

Bertoni, G., Daemen, J., Peeters, M., & Van Assche, G. 2009. Keccak sponge function family main document. Submission to NIST (Round 2), 3, p. 30.

Biba, K.J. 1977. Integrity considerations for secure computer systems. No. MTR-3153-REV-1. MITRE Corp., Bedford, MA.

Bizeul, D. 2007. Russian business network study. Unpublished paper.

Bobade, S.D., & Mankar, V.R. 2015. VLSI architecture for an area efficient Elliptic Curve Cryptographic processor for embedded systems. In: IEEE International Conference on Industrial Instrumentation and Control (ICIC), Pune, May 28–30, 2015, pp. 1038–1043.

Bock, C., & Gruninger, M. 2005. PSL: a semantic domain for flow models. *Software & Systems Modeling*, 4(2), pp. 209–231.

Boehner, K., DePaula, R., Dourish, P., & Sengers, P. 2005. Affect: from information to interaction. In: Proceedings of the 4th Decennial Conference on Critical Computing: Between Sense and Sensibility, New York, August 2005, pp. 59–68.

Borgia, E. 2014. The Internet of Things vision: key features, applications and open issues. *Computer Communications*, 54, pp. 1–31.

Boukerch, A., Xu, L., & El-Khatib, K. 2007. Trust-based security for wireless ad hoc and sensor networks. *Computer Communications*, 30(11), pp. 2413–2427.

Brauer, W. 1987. *Petri Nets: Applications and Relationships to Other Models of Concurrency*, vol. 2. Springer-Verlag.

Braun, U., Shinnar, A., & Seltzer, M.I. 2008. Securing provenance. In: Proceedings of the 3rd USENIX Workshop on Hot Topics in Security (HotSec), San Jose, CA, July 2008.

Brooks, T. 2009. Principles for implementing a service-oriented enterprise architecture. *SOA Magazine*, Issue XXIX, May/June 2009.

Brooks, T. 2009. Service-oriented enterprise architecture (SOEA) conceptual design through data architecture. *Journal of Enterprise Architecture*, 5(4), pp. 16–26.

Brooks, T., & McKnight, L. 2013. Securing wireless grids: architecture designs for secure wiglet-to-wiglet interfaces. *International Journal of Information and Network Security*, 2(1), p. 1.

Brooks, T., Caicedo, C., & Park, J. 2012. Security challenges and countermeasures for trusted virtualized computing environments. In: IEEE World Congress on Internet Security (World-CIS), Guelph, ON, June 10–12, 2012, pp. 117–122.

Brooks, T., Kaarst-Brown, M., Caicedo, C., Park, J., & McKnight, L. 2013. A failure to communicate: security vulnerabilities in the gridstreamx edgeware application. In: IEEE 8th International Conference on Internet Technology and Secured Transactions (ICITST), December 2013, pp. 516–523.

Brooks, T., Kaarst-Brown, M., Caicedo, C., Park, J., & McKnight, L.W. 2014. Secure the edge? Understanding the risk towards wireless grids Edgeware technology. *International Journal of Internet Technology and Secured Transactions*, 5(3), pp. 191–222.

Brooks, T., Robinson, J., & McKnight, L. 2012. Conceptualizing a secure wireless cloud. *International Journal of Cloud Computing and Services Science*, 1(3), p. 89.

Brualdi, R.A. 1992. Introductory combinatorics. *Learning*, 4(5), p. 6.

Buneman, P., Khanna, S., & Wang-Chiew, T. 2001. Why and where: a characterization of data provenance. In: *Database Theory – ICDT 2001*. Springer, Berlin/Heidelberg, pp. 316–330.

Burbridge, T., & Harrison, M. 2009. Security considerations in the design and peering of RFID discovery services. In: IEEE International Conference on RFID, Orlando, FL, April 27–28, 2009, pp. 249–256.

Burmester, M., Kotznanikolaou, P., & Douligeris, C. 2007. Security in mobile ad-hoc networks. In: *Network Security Current Status and Future Directions*, Wiley-IEEE Press, pp. 355–371.

Cárdenas, A.A., Amin, S., & Sastry, S. 2008. Research challenges for the security of control systems. In: Proceedings of the 3rd USENIX Workshop on Hot Topics in Security (HotSec), San Jose, CA, July 2008.

Cárdenas, A.A., Amin, S., Lin, Z.S., Huang, Y.L., Huang, C.Y., & Sastry, S. 2011. Attacks against process control systems: risk assessment, detection, and response. In: Proceedings of the 6th ACM Symposium on Information, Computer and Communications Security, March 2011, pp. 355–366.

Carvajal, R.G., Ramírez-Angulo, J., López-Martín, A.J., Torralba, A., Galán, J.A.G., Carlosena, A., & Chavero, F.M. 2005. The flipped voltage follower: a useful cell for low-voltage low-power circuit design. *IEEE Transactions on Circuits and Systems I: Regular Papers*, 52(7), pp. 1276–1291.

Castellani, A.P., Gheda, M., Bui, N., Rossi, M., & Zorzi, M. 2011. Web services for the Internet of Things through CoAP and EXI. In: IEEE International Conference on Communications Workshops (ICC), June 2011, pp. 1–6.

Chang, R.Y., Podgurski, A., & Yang, J. 2008. Discovering neglected conditions in software by mining dependence graphs. *IEEE Transactions on Software Engineering*, 34(5), pp. 579–596.

Chasaki, D., & Wolf, T. 2010. Design of a secure packet processor. In: ACM/IEEE Symposium on Architectures for Networking and Communications Systems, October 2010, pp. 1–10.

Chen, C.Y., Kuo, C.P., & Chien, F.Y. 2009. An exploration of RFID information security and privacy. In: IEEE Joint Conferences on Pervasive Computing, December 2009, pp. 65–70.

Chen, P., Plale, B., & Aktas, M.S. 2014. Temporal representation for mining scientific data provenance. *Future Generation Computer Systems*, 36, pp. 363–378.

Chen, P.Y., & Cheng, S.M. 2015. Sequential defense against random and intentional attacks in complex networks. *Physical Review E*, 91(2), p. 022805.

Chen, P.Y., & Hero, A.O. 2014. Assessing and safeguarding network resilience to nodal attacks. *IEEE Communications Magazine*, 52(11), pp. 138–143.

Chen, P.Y., Cheng, S.M., & Chen, K.C. 2014. Information fusion to defend intentional attack in internet of things. *IEEE Internet of Things Journal*, 1(4), pp. 337–348.

Chen, R., Guo, J., & Bao, F. 2014. Trust management for service composition in SOA-based IoT systems. In: IEEE Wireless Communications and Networking Conference, April 2014, pp. 3444–3449.

Chen, R., Liu, C.M., & Chen, C. 2012. An artificial immune-based distributed intrusion detection model for the Internet of Things. *Advanced Materials Research*, 366, pp. 165–168.

Chen, R., Liu, C.M., & Xiao, L.X. 2011. A security situation sense model based on artificial immune system in the internet of things. *Advanced Materials Research*, 403, pp. 2457–2460.

Chen, S., Xu, H., Liu, D., Hu, B., & Wang, H. 2014. A vision of IoT: applications, challenges, and opportunities with china perspective. *IEEE Internet of Things Journal*, 1(4), pp. 349–359.

Chi, Q., Yan, H., Zhang, C., Pang, Z., & Da Xu, L. 2014. A reconfigurable smart sensor interface for industrial WSN in IoT environment. *IEEE Transactions on Industrial Informatics*, 10(2), pp. 1417–1425.

Chin, S.K., & Older, S.B. 2010. *Access Control, Security, and Trust: A Logical Approach.* CRC press.

Chow, C.Y., Mokbel, M.F., & He, T. 2011. A privacy-preserving location monitoring system for wireless sensor networks. *IEEE Transactions on Mobile Computing*, 10(1), pp. 94–107.

Cirani, S., Picone, M., Gonizzi, P., Veltri, L., & Ferrari, G. 2015. IoT-OAS: an OAuth-based authorization service architecture for secure services in IoT scenarios. *IEEE Sensors Journal,* 15(2), pp. 1224–1234.

Clark, D.D., Wroclawski, J., Sollins, K.R., & Braden, R. 2002. Tussle in cyberspace: defining tomorrow's internet. *ACM SIGCOMM Computer Communication Review*, 32(4), pp. 347–356.

Committee on National Security Systems (CNSS) Instruction. 2010. 4009 National Information Assurance (IA) Glossary.

Conovalu, S., & Park, J. 2015. Cybersecurity strategies for smart grids. In: The International Conference on Information and Network Security, Shanghai, China, July 29–30, 2015.

Conway, L. 2012. Reminiscences of the VLSI revolution: how a series of failures triggered a paradigm shift in digital design. *IEEE Solid-State Circuits Magazine*, 4(4), pp. 8–31.

Cordesman, A.H., & Cordesman, J.G. 2002. *Cyber-Threats, Information Warfare, and Critical Infrastructure Protection: Defending the US Homeland.* Greenwood Publishing Group.

Covington, M.J., & Carskadden, R. 2013. Threat implications of the Internet of Things. In: IEEE 5th International Conference on Cyber Conflict, Tallinn, June 4–7, 2013, pp. 1–12.

CSSP, D. 2009. Recommended practice: improving industrial control systems cybersecurity with defense-in-depth strategies. US-CERT Defense In Depth, October 2009.

Curts, R.J., & Campbell, D.E. 2015. Cybersecurity requires a clear systems engineering approach as a basis for its cyberstrategy. *Cybersecurity Policies and Strategies for Cyberwarfare Prevention*, p. 102.

Czybik, B., Hausmann, S., Heiss, S., & Jasperneite, J. 2013. Performance evaluation of MAC algorithms for real-time Ethernet communication systems. In: 11th IEEE International Conference on Industrial Informatics (INDIN), July 2013, pp. 676–681.

Da Xu, L., He, W., & Li, S. 2014. Internet of things in industries: a survey. *IEEE Transactions on Industrial Informatics*, 10(4), pp. 2233–2243.

Davidson, S.B., Boulakia, S.C., Eyal, A., Ludäscher, B., McPhillips, T.M., Bowers, S., Anand, M.K., & Freire, J. 2007. Provenance in scientific workflow systems. *IEEE Data Engineering Bulletin*, 30(4), pp. 44–50.

Davis, F.D., Kottemann, J.E., & Remus, W.E. 1991. What-if analysis and the illusion of control. In: Proceedings of the Twenty-Fourth Annual Hawaii International Conference on System Sciences, Vol. iii, Kauai, HI, January 8–11, 1991, pp. 452–460.

Dawson, R., Boyd, C., Dawson, E., & Nieto, J.M.G. 2006. SKMA: a key management architecture for SCADA systems. In: Proceedings of the 2006 Australasian Workshops on Grid computing and e-research, Vol. 54, January 2006, Australian Computer Society, Inc., Darlinghurst, Australia, pp. 183–192.

Dehling, T., Gao, F., Schneider, S., & Sunyaev, A. 2015. Exploring the far side of mobile health: information security and privacy of mobile health apps on iOS and Android. *JMIR mHealth and uHealth*, 3(1), e8. Available at http://mhealth.jmir.org/2015/1/e8/.

DeLuca, D., Gallivan, M.J., & Kock, N. 2008. Furthering information systems action research: a post-positivist synthesis of four dialectics. *Journal of the Association for Information Systems*, 9(2), p. 48.

den Braber, F., Hogganvik, I., Lund, M.S., Stølen, K., & Vraalsen, F. 2007. Model-based security analysis in seven steps – a guided tour to the CORAS method. *BT Technology Journal*, 25(1), pp. 101–117.

Deng, H., Jin, G., Sun, K., Xu, R., Lyell, M., & Luke, J.A. 2009. Trust-aware in-network aggregation for wireless sensor networks. In: IEEE Global Telecommunications Conference (GLOBECOM 2009), November 2009, pp. 1–8.

Derr, K.W. 2007. Nightmares with mobile devices are just around the corner! In: IEEE International Conference on Portable Information Devices (PORTABLE07), May 2007, pp. 1–5.

Dierks, T. & Rescorla, E. 2008. The Transport Layer Security (TLS) Protocol Version 1.2. IETF RFC 5246, 2008. Available at http://www.ietf.org/rfc/rfc5246.txt.

Dimakopoulos, D.N., & Magoulas, G.D. 2009. Interface design and evaluation of a personal information space for mobile learners. *International Journal of Mobile Learning and Organisation*, 3(4), pp. 440–463.

Dlamini, M., Venter, H., Eloff, J., & Mitha, Y. 2012. *Authentication in the Cloud: A Risk-Based Approach*. University of Pretoria.

Du, W., Deng, J., Han, Y.S., Varshney, P.K., Katz, J., & Khalili, A. 2005. A pairwise key predistribution scheme for wireless sensor networks. *ACM Transactions on Information and System Security (TISSEC)*, 8(2), pp. 228–258.

Dugas, M.J., Buhr, K., & Ladouceur, R. 2004. The Role of Intolerance of Uncertainty in Etiology and Maintenance. Dugas, Michel J.; Buhr, Kristin; Ladouceur, Robert Heimberg, Richard G. (Ed); Turk, Cynthia L. (Ed); Mennin, Douglas S. (Ed). (2004). Generalized anxiety disorder: Advances in research and practice (pp. 143–163). New York, NY, US: Guilford Press, xvi, 446 pp.

Dugas, M.J., Gosselin, P., & Ladouceur, R. 2001. Intolerance of uncertainty and worry: investigating specificity in a nonclinical sample. *Cognitive Therapy and Research*, 25(5), pp. 551–558.

Durrett, R. 2010. *Probability: Theory and Examples.* Cambridge University Press.

Elbe, A., Janssen, N., & Sedlak, H. 2003. Cryptographic processor. U.S. Patent Application 10/461,913.

Eliasson, J., Pereira, P.P., Makitaavola, H., Delsing, J., Nilsson, J., & Gebart, J. 2014. A feasibility study of SOA-enabled networked rock bolts. In: IEEE Emerging Technology and Factory Automation (ETFA), Barcelona, September 16–19, 2014, pp. 1–8.

Engebretson, P. 2013. *The Basics of Hacking and Penetration Testing: Ethical Hacking and Penetration Testing Made Easy.* Elsevier.

Ertürk, V. 2008. A framework based on continuous security monitoring. Doctoral dissertation, Middle East Technical University.

Etzion, O., & Niblett, P. 2010. *Event Processing in Action.* Manning Publications.

European Union. 2016. European Commission – Press release: Agreement on Commission's EU data protection reform will boost Digital Single Market. Available at http://europa.eu/rapid/press-release_IP-15-6321_en.htm. Accessed on February 11, 2016.

Evans, D. 2011. The Internet of Things: how the next evolution of the internet is changing everything. CISCO white paper, 1, pp.1–11.

Ferguson, N., Lucks, S., Schneier, B., Whiting, D., Bellare, M., Kohno, T., Callas, J., & Walker, J. 2010. The Skein hash function family. Submission to NIST (Round 3), 7(7.5), p. 3.

Ferraiolo, D., & Kuhn, R. 1992. Role-based access controls. In: 15th NISTNCSC National Computer Security Conference, Baltimore, MD, October 13–16, 1992, pp. 554–563.

Fielding, N.G., Lee, N.F.R.M., & Lee, R.M. 1998. *Computer Analysis and Qualitative Research.* Sage.

Fielding, R.T. 2000. Architectural styles and the design of network-based software architectures. Doctoral dissertation, University of California, Irvine.

Fitbit. 2015. Fitbit Privacy Policy (FPP). Available at http://www.fitbit.com/privacy. Accessed on May 5, 2015.

Flood, P., & Schukat, M. 2014. Peer to peer authentication for small embedded systems: a zero-knowledge-based approach to security for the Internet of Things. In: IEEE 10th International Conference on Digital Technologies (DT), Zilina, July 9–11, 2014, pp. 68–72.

Foroush, H., & Martinez, S. 2014. On triggering control of single-input linear systems under pulse-width modulated DOS signals. *SIAM Journal on Control and Optimization.* pp. 1–31. Available at http://fausto.dynamic.ucsd.edu/sonia/papers/data/2013_HSF-SM.pdf.

Forte, D., & Power, R. 2007. Physical security – overlook it at your own peril. *Computer Fraud & Security*, 2007(8), pp. 16–20.

Frost, R.O., & Shows, D.L. 1993. The nature and measurement of compulsive indecisiveness. *Behaviour Research and Therapy*, 31(7), pp. 683-IN2.

Gao, Z., & Ansari, N. 2005. Tracing cyber attacks from the practical perspective. *IEEE Communications Magazine*, 43(5), pp. 123–131.

Garcia-Morchon, O., Keoh, S.L., Kumar, S., Moreno-Sanchez, P., Vidal-Meca, F., & Ziegel-dorf, J.H. 2013. Securing the IP-based internet of things with HIP and DTLS. In: Proceedings of the Sixth ACM Conference on Security and Privacy in Wireless and Mobile Networks, New York, April 2013, pp. 119–124.

Garitano, I., Fayyad, S., & Noll, J. 2015. Multi-metrics approach for security, privacy and dependability in embedded systems. *Wireless Personal Communications*, 81(4), pp. 1359–1376.

Garlan, D., Allen, R., & Ockerbloom, J. 1995. Architectural mismatch or why it's hard to build systems out of existing parts. In: Proceedings of the 17th International Conference on Software Engineering, New York, April 1995, pp. 179–185.

Gauravaram, P., Knudsen, L.R., Matusiewicz, K., Mendel, F., Rechberger, C., Schläffer, M., & Thomsen, S.S. 2009. Grøstl – a SHA-3 candidate. In: Dagstuhl Seminar Proceedings, Schloss Dagstuhl-Leibniz-Zentrum für Informatik.

Gérald, S. 2010. The Internet of Things: between the revolution of the Internet and the metamorphosis of Objects, H. Sundmaeker, P. Guillemin, P. Friess, & S. Woelffle, (Eds.). In: Forum American Bar Association, pp. 11–24, Feb. 2010.

Gerla, M., Lee, E.K., Pau, G., & Lee, U. 2014. Internet of vehicles: from intelligent grid to autonomous cars and vehicular clouds. In: IEEE World Forum on Internet of Things (WF-IoT), Seoul, March 6–8, 2014, pp. 241–246.

Germeijs, V., & De Boeck, P. 2002. A measurement scale for indecisiveness and its relationship to career indecision and other types of indecision. *European Journal of Psychological Assessment*, 18(2), p. 113.

Gessner, D., Olivereau, A., Segura, A.S., & Serbanati, A. 2012. Trustworthy infrastructure services for a secure and privacy-respecting Internet of Things. In: IEEE 11th International Conference on Trust, Security and Privacy in Computing and Communications (TrustCom), Liverpool, June 25–27, 2012, pp. 998–1003.

Ghosh, R., Trivedi, K.S., Naik, V.K., & Kim, D.S. 2010. End-to-end performability analysis for infrastructure-as-a-service cloud: an interacting stochastic models approach. In: IEEE 16th Pacific Rim International Symposium on Dependable Computing (PRDC), Tokyo, December 13–15, 2010, pp. 125–132.

Gladwell, M. 2015. The engineer's lament. *New Yorker*, pp. 46–55.

Glaser, B.G., Anselm, L., & Elizabeth, S. 1968. The discovery of grounded theory; strategies for qualitative research. *Nursing Research* 17(4), p. 364.

Goel, S., Hong, Y., Papakonstantinou, V., & Kloza, D. 2015. *Smart Grid Security*. Springer, London.

Gomez, C., & Paradells, J. 2010. Wireless home automation networks: a survey of architectures and technologies. *IEEE Communications Magazine*, 48(6), pp. 92–101.

Goode, L. 2013. Comparing Wearables: Fitbit Flex vs. Jawbone Up and More. *Health and Fitness*. Available at https://www.allthingsd.com/20130715/fitbit-flex-vs-jawbone-up-and-more-a-wearables-comparison/. Accessed on May 4, 2015.

Gope, P., & Hwang, T. 2015. Untraceable sensor movement in distributed IoT infrastructure. *IEEE Sensors Journal*, 15(9), pp. 5340–5348.

Gordon, M.J., & Melham, T.F. 1993. *Introduction to HOL: A Theorem Proving Environment for Higher Order Logic*. Cambridge University Press, New York.

Govindarajan, N., Simmhan, Y., Jamadagni, N., & Misra, P. 2014. Event processing across edge and the cloud for internet of things applications. In: Proceedings of the 20th International

Conference on Management of Data. Computer Society of India, Mumbai, India, December 2014, pp. 101–104.

Graham, J., Olson, R., & Howard, R. (Eds.). 2010. *Cyber Security Essentials*. CRC Press.

Greensmith, J. 2015. Securing the Internet of Things with responsive artificial immune systems. In: Proceedings of the 2015 on Genetic and Evolutionary Computation Conference, New York, July 2015, pp. 113–120.

Gu, K., & Niculescu, S.I. 2003. Survey on recent results in the stability and control of time-delay systems. *Journal of Dynamic Systems, Measurement, and Control*, 125(2), pp. 158–165.

Gubbi, J., Buyya, R., Marusic, S., & Palaniswami, M. 2013. Internet of Things (IoT): a vision, architectural elements, and future directions. *Future Generation Computer Systems*, 29(7), pp. 1645–1660.

Guinard, D., & Trifa, V. 2009. Towards the web of things: web mashups for embedded devices. In: Proceedings of WWW (International World Wide Web Conferences)Workshop on Mashups, Enterprise Mashups and Lightweight Composition on the Web (MEM 2009), Madrid, Spain, April 2009, p. 15.

Gupta, K., & Silakari, S. 2011. ECC over RSA for asymmetric encryption: a review. *IJCSI International Journal of Computer Science Issues*, 8(3), pp. 370–375.

Gura, N., Patel, A., Wander, A., Eberle, H., & Shantz, S.C. 2004. Comparing elliptic curve cryptography and RSA on 8-bit CPUs. In: *Cryptographic Hardware and Embedded Systems – CHES 2004*. Springer, Berlin/Heidelberg, pp. 119–132.

Haller, S., Karnouskos, S., & Schroth, C. 2008. *The Internet of Things in an Enterprise Context*. Springer, Berlin/Heidelberg, pp. 14–28.

Hancke, G.P., Markantonakis, K., & Mayes, K.E. 2010. Security challenges for user-oriented RFID applications within the "Internet of Things." *Journal of Internet Technology*, 11(3), pp. 307–313.

Hankerson, D., Menezes, A.J., & Vanstone, S. 2006. *Guide to Elliptic Curve Cryptography*. Springer Science & Business Media.

Harmonosky, C.M., Farr, R.H., & Ni, M.C. 1997. Selective rerouting using simulated steady state system data. In: Proceedings of the 29th Conference on Winter Simulation, IEEE Computer Society, Washington, DC, December 1997, pp. 1293–1298.

Hartke, K., & Bergmann, O. 2012. Datagram Transport Layer Security in Constrained Environments. draft-hartke-core-codtls-02 (WiP), IETF, 2012. Available at http://www.ietf.org/proceedings/83/slides/slides-83-lwig-2.pdf.

Hayashi, K. 2013. Linux Worm Targeting Hidden Devices. Symantec [online], 27(11). Available at http://www.symantec.com/connect/blogs/linux-worm-targeting-hidden-devices.

Heer, T., Garcia-Morchon, O., Hummen, R., Keoh, S.L., Kumar, S.S., & Wehrle, K. 2011. Security challenges in the IP-based Internet of Things. *Wireless Personal Communications*, 61(3), pp. 527–542.

Hendler, J. 2014. Data integration for heterogenous datasets. *Big Data*, 2(4), pp. 205–215.

Ho, J.W., Wright, M., & Das, S.K. 2012. ZoneTrust: fast zone-based node compromise detection and revocation in wireless sensor networks using sequential hypothesis testing. *IEEE Transactions on Dependable and Secure Computing*, 9(4), pp. 494–511.

Hoare, C.A.R. 1978. *Communicating Sequential Processes*. Springer, New York, pp. 413–443.

Housley, R. 2009. RFC 5652-Cryptographic Message Syntax (CMS). Available at https://tools.ietf.org/html/rfc5652.

Huang, W., & Zhang, S. 2015. Research and review on novel spread spectrum communication theory. In: *International Conference on Education, Management and Computing Technology (ICEMCT-15)*. Atlantis Press.

Huang, Y.L., Cárdenas, A.A., Amin, S., Lin, Z.S., Tsai, H.Y., & Sastry, S. 2009. Understanding the physical and economic consequences of attacks on control systems. *International Journal of Critical Infrastructure Protection*, 2(3), pp. 73–83.

Hull, G. 2015. Successful failure: what Foucault can teach us about privacy self-management in a world of Facebook and big data. *Ethics and Information Technology*, 17(2), pp. 89–101.

Hwang, I., Kim, S., Kim, Y., & Seah, C.E. 2010. A survey of fault detection, isolation, and reconfiguration methods. *IEEE Transactions on Control Systems Technology*, 18(3), pp. 636–653.

IEEE Standards Association. IEEE Guide for Information Technology – System Definition – Concept of Operations (ConOps) Document, IEEE Computer Society, IEEE Std 1362-1998, March 19, 1998.

Isa, M.A.M., Hashim, H., Ab Manan, J.L., Adnan, S.F.S., & Mhmod, R. 2014. RF simulator for cryptographic protocol. In: IEEE International Conference on Control System, Computing and Engineering (ICCSCE), November 2014, pp. 518–523.

Ishaq, I., Carels, D., Teklemariam, G.K., Hoebeke, J., Abeele, F.V.D., Poorter, E.D., Moerman, I., & Demeester, P. 2013. IETF standardization in the field of the internet of things (IoT): a survey. *Journal of Sensor and Actuator Networks*, 2(2), pp. 235–287.

Jaffe, M. 2015. IoT won't work without artificial intelligence. *Wired*. Available at http://www.wired.com/insights/2014/11/iot-wont-work-without-artificial-intelligence/. Accessed on May 13, 2015.

Jennions, I.K. 2013. *Integrated Vehicle Health Management: The Technology*. Society of Automotive Engineers.

Jones, A. 2007. A framework for the management of information security risks. *BT Technology Journal*, 25(1), pp. 30–36.

Joint Publication 5-0. Joint Operation Planning, U.S. Department of Defense, August 11, 2011.

Kainth, M., Krishnan, L., Narayana, C., Virupaksha, S.G., & Tessier, R. 2015. Hardware-assisted code obfuscation for FPGA soft microprocessors. In: Proceedings of the 2015 Design, Automation & Test in Europe Conference & Exhibition, EDA Consortium, San Jose, CA, March 2015, pp. 127–132.

Karabacak, B., & Sogukpinar, I. 2005. ISRAM: information security risk analysis method. *Computers & Security*, 24(2), pp. 147–159.

Kasper, G.M. 1996. A theory of decision support system design for user calibration. *Information Systems Research*, 7(2), pp. 215–232.

Katasonov, A., Kaykova, O., Khriyenko, O., Nikitin, S., & Terziyan, V.Y. 2008. Smart semantic middleware for the Internet of Things. In: Proceedings of the 5th International Conference on Informatics in Control, Automation and Robotics, 8, pp. 169–178.

Kavun, E.B., & Yalcin, T. 2012. On the suitability of SHA-3 finalists for lightweight applications. In: The Third SHA-3 Candidate Conference, Washington, DC, March 22–23, 2012.

Keil, M., Tan, B.C., Wei, K.K., Saarinen, T., Tuunainen, V., & Wassenaar, A. 2000. A cross-cultural study on escalation of commitment behavior in software projects. *MIS Quarterly*, 24(2), pp. 299–325.

Keith, M.J., Babb, J.S., & Lowry, P.B. 2014. A longitudinal study of information privacy on mobile devices. In: IEEE 47th Hawaii International Conference on System Sciences (HICSS), January 2014, pp. 3149–3158.

Keith, M.J., Thompson, S.C., Hale, J., Lowry, P.B., & Greer, C. 2013. Information disclosure on mobile devices: re-examining privacy calculus with actual user behavior. *International Journal of Human-Computer Studies*, 71(12), pp. 1163–1173.

Keoh, S., Kumar, S., & Garcia-Morchon, O. 2013. Securing the IP-based Internet of Things with DTLS. Working Draft, LWIG Working Group, February 2013.

Kermani, M.M., Zhang, M., Raghunathan, A., & Jha, N.K. 2013. Emerging frontiers in embedded security. In: IEEE 26th International Conference on VLSI Design and 12th International Conference on Embedded Systems (VLSID), Pune, January 5–10, 2013, pp. 203–208.

Kim, S.D., Lee, J.Y., Kim, D.Y., Park, C.W., & La, H.J. 2014. Modeling BPEL-based collaborations with heterogeneous IoT devices. In: IEEE 12th International Conference on Dependable, Autonomic and Secure Computing (DASC), Dalian, August 24–27, 2014, pp. 289–294.

Knapp, E.D., & Langill, J.T. 2014. *Industrial Network Security: Securing Critical Infrastructure Networks for Smart Grid, SCADA, and Other Industrial Control Systems*. Syngress.

Knapp, E.D., & Samani, R. 2013. *Applied Cyber Security and the Smart Ggrid: Implementing Security Controls into the Modern Power Infrastructure*. Syngress.

Kocher, P., Lee, R., McGraw, G., Raghunathan, A., & Moderator-Ravi, S. 2004. Security as a new dimension in embedded system design. In: Proceedings of the 41st Annual Design Automation Conference, New York, June 2004, pp. 753–760.

Kocsis, I., Csertán, G., Pásztor, P.L., & Pataricza, A. 2008. Dependability and security metrics in controlling infrastructure. In: Second International Conference on Emerging Security Information, Systems and Technologies, Cap Esterel, August 25–31, 2008, pp. 368–374.

Kommareddy, C., Güven, T., Bhattacharjee, B., La, R.J., & Shayman, M.A. 2003. Overlay routing for path multiplicity, vol. 70, Technical Report, UMIACS-TR.

Kopetz, H. 2011. Internet of things. In: *Real-Time Systems*. Springer, pp. 307–323.

Kortuem, G., Kawsar, F., Fitton, D., & Sundramoorthy, V. 2010. Smart objects as building blocks for the internet of things. *IEEE Internet Computing*, 14(1), pp. 44–51.

Kothmayr, T., Schmitt, C., Hu, W., Brünig, M., & Carle, G. 2013. DTLS based security and two-way authentication for the Internet of Things. *Ad Hoc Networks*, 11(8), pp. 2710–2723.

Kottemann, J.E., Davis, F.D., & Remus, W.E. 1994. Computer-assisted decision making: performance, beliefs, and the illusion of control. *Organizational Behavior and Human Decision Processes*, 57(1), pp. 26–37.

Kovacshazy, T., Wacha, G., Daboczi, T., Erdos, C., & Szarvas, A. 2013. System architecture for Internet of Things with the extensive use of embedded virtualization. In: IEEE 4th International Conference on Cognitive Infocommunications (CogInfoCom), Budapest, December 2–5, 2013, pp. 549–554.

Kranz, M., Holleis, P., & Schmidt, A. 2010. Embedded interaction: interacting with the internet of things. *IEEE Internet Computing*, 14(2), pp. 46–53.

Krotofil, M., & Cárdenas, A.A. 2013. Resilience of process control systems to cyber-physical attacks. In: *Secure IT Systems*. Springer, Berlin/Heidelberg, pp. 166–182.

Krutz, R.L., & Vines, R.D. 2010. *Cloud Security: A Comprehensive Guide to Secure Cloud Computing*. Wiley Publishing.

Lam, C. 2015. Ex-aide in Medford nursing home death testifies staff ignored warning alarms for 2 hours. *Newsday*. Available at http://www.newsday.com/long-island/suffolk/medford-nursing-home-staff-ignored-warning-alarms-for-2-hours-witness-in-death-case-says-1.10496777. Accessed on June 15, 2015.

Lange, R.J. 2010. Provenance aware sensor networks for real-time data analysis. Master Thesis, University of Twente, March 14, 2010.

Langer, E.J. 1975. The illusion of control. *Journal of Personality and Social Psychology*, 32(2), p. 311.

Langer, E.J., & Roth, J. 1975. Heads I win, tails it's chance: the illusion of control as a function of the sequence of outcomes in a purely chance task. *Journal of Personality and Social Psychology*, 32(6), pp. 951–955.

Langheinrich, M. 2009. A survey of RFID privacy approaches. *Personal and Ubiquitous Computing*, 13(6), pp. 413–421.

Laprie, J.C. 1995. Dependability of computer systems: concepts, limits, improvements. In: IEEE Proceedings of the Sixth International Symposium on Software Reliability Engineering, Toulouse, October 24–27, 1995, pp. 2–11.

Leberknight, C.S., Widmeyer, G.R., & Recce, M.L. 2008. Decision support for perceived threat in the context of intrusion detection systems. In: Proceedings of the AMCIS 2008, p. 317.

Ledlie, J., & Holland, D.A. 2005. Provenance-aware sensor data storage. In: IEEE 21st International Conference on Data Engineering Workshops, April 5–8, 2005, p. 1189.

Lee, J.S., Su, Y.W., & Shen, C.C. 2007. A comparative study of wireless protocols: Bluetooth, UWB, ZigBee, and Wi-Fi. In: 33rd Annual Conference of the IEEE Industrial Electronics Society, Taipei, November 5–8, 2007, pp. 46–51.

Lee, S., Chung, B., Kim, H., Lee, Y., Park, C., & Yoon, H. 2006. Real-time analysis of intrusion detection alerts via correlation. *Computers & Security*, 25(3), pp. 169–183.

Lehtonen, M.O., Michahelles, F., & Fleisch, E. 2007. Trust and security in RFID-based product authentication systems. *IEEE Systems Journal*, 1(2), pp. 129–144.

Leventis, P., Chan, M., Chan, M., Lewis, D., Nouban, B., Powell, G., Vest, B., Wong, M., Xia, R., & Costello, J. 2003. Cyclone™: a low-cost, high-performance FPGA. In: Proceedings of the IEEE Custom Integrated Circuits Conference, November 21–24, 1999, pp. 49–52.

Lewis, J.A. 2006. Cybersecurity and critical infrastructure protection. Center for Strategic and International Studies, Washington, DC, January 2006.

Li, I., Dey, A.K., & Forlizzi, J. 2012. Using context to reveal factors that affect physical activity. *ACM Transactions on Computer-Human Interaction (TOCHI)*, 19(1), p. 7.

Li, T., Chen, S., & Ling, Y. 2013. Efficient protocols for identifying the missing tags in a large RFID system. *IEEE/ACM Transactions on Networking (TON)*, 21(6), pp. 1974–1987.

Li, X., Zhou, F., & Du, J. 2013. LDTS: a lightweight and dependable trust system for clustered wireless sensor networks. *IEEE Transactions on Information Forensics and Security*, 8(6), pp. 924–935.

Li, Z., Taylor, J., Partridge, E., Zhou, Y., Yurcik, W., Abad, C., Barlow, J.J., & Rosendale, J. 2004. *UCLog*: a unified, correlated logging architecture for intrusion detection. In: 12th International Conference on Telecommunication Systems – Modeling and Analysis (ICTSM), July 2004.

Liang, H., Huang, D., Cai, L.X., Shen, X., & Peng, D. 2011. Resource allocation for security services in mobile cloud computing. In: IEEE Conference on Computer Communications Workshops (INFOCOM WKSHPS), April 10–15, 2011, pp. 191–195.

Lim, K.H., & Benbasat, I. 2000. The effect of multimedia on perceived equivocality and perceived usefulness of information systems. *MIS Quarterly*, 24(3), pp. 449–471.

Limin, H. 2010. Embedded system for Internet of Things. *Microcontrollers & Embedded Systems*, 10, pp. 5–8.

Lin, T.H., Kinebuchi, Y., Courbot, A., Shimada, H., Morita, T., Mitake, H., Lee, C.Y., & Nakajima, T. 2011. Hardware-assisted reliability enhancement for embedded multi-core virtualization design. In: 14th IEEE International Symposium on Object/Component/Service-Oriented Real-Time Distributed Computing (ISORC), March 2011, pp. 241–249.

Liu, C., Yang, J., Zhang, Y., Chen, R., & Zeng, J. 2011. Research on immunity-based intrusion detection technology for the internet of things. In: Seventh International Conference on Natural Computation (ICNC), Vol. 1, July 26–28, 2011, pp. 212–216.

Liu, C., Zhang, Y., Cai, Z., Yang, J., & Peng, L. 2013. Artificial immunity-based security response model for the internet of things. *Journal of Computers*, 8(12), pp. 3111–3118.

Liu, D., Ning, P., & Li, R. 2005. Establishing pairwise keys in distributed sensor networks. *ACM Transactions on Information and System Security (TISSEC)*, 8(1), pp. 41–77.

Liu, P., Dai, G., & Fu, T. 2007. A web services based email extension for remote monitoring of embedded systems. In: Eighth ACIS International Conference on Software Engineering, Artificial Intelligence, Networking, and Parallel/Distributed Computing, SNPD 2007, vol. 2, pp. 412–416.

Livingston, K.M., Bada, M., Hunter, L.E., & Verspoor, K. 2013. Representing annotation compositionality and provenance for the Semantic Web. *Journal of Biomedical Semantics*, 4, p. 38.

Löffler, M., & Tschiesner, A. 2013. *The Internet of Things and the Future of Manufacturing*. McKinsey & Company.

Lopez, J., Roman, R., Agudo, I., & Fernandez-Gago, C. 2010. Trust management systems for wireless sensor networks: best practices. *Computer Communications*, 33(9), pp. 1086–1093.

Luckham, D.C. 2011. *Event Processing for Business: Organizing the Real-Time Enterprise*. John Wiley & Sons.

Luckham, D.C., & Frasca, B. 1998. Complex event processing in distributed systems. Computer Systems Laboratory Technical Report CSL-TR-98-754, Stanford University.

Luiijf, E. 2012. *Understanding Cyber Threats and Vulnerabilities*. Springer, Berlin/Heidelberg, pp. 52–67.

Lundberg, A. 2006. Leverage complex event processing to improve operational performance. *Business Intelligence Journal*, 11(1), p. 55.

Madan, B.B., Goševa-Popstojanova, K., Vaidyanathan, K., & Trivedi, K.S. 2004. A method for modeling and quantifying the security attributes of intrusion tolerant systems. *Performance Evaluation*, 56(1), pp. 167–186.

Madhura, P.M., Bilurkar, N., Jain, P., & Ranjith, J. 2015. A survey on Internet of Things: security and privacy issues. *International Journal of Innovative Technology and Research*, 3(3), pp. 2069–2074.

Malhotra, M.K., & Grover, V. 1998. An assessment of survey research in POM: from constructs to theory. *Journal of Operations Management*, 16(4), pp. 407–425.

Mármol, F.G., & Pérez, G.M. 2009. TRMSim-WSN, trust and reputation models simulator for wireless sensor networks. In: IEEE International Conference on Communications, Dresden, June 14–18, 2009, pp. 1–5.

Marquardt, N., Taylor, A.S., Villar, N., & Greenberg, S. 2010. Rethinking RFID: awareness and control for interaction with RFID systems. In: Proceedings of the SIGCHI Conference on Human Factors in Computing Systems, New York, April 2010, pp. 2307–2316.

Martins, D., & Guyennet, H. 2010. Wireless sensor network attacks and security mechanisms: a short survey. In: IEEE 13th International Conference on Network-Based Information Systems (NBiS), Takayama, September 14–16, 2010, pp. 313–320.

MathWorks. 2015. Thermal model of a house, mathworks. Available at http://www.mathworks.com/help/simulink/examples/thermal-model-of-a-house.html. Accessed on April 3, 2015.

Matrosov, A., Rodionov, E., Harley, D., & Malcho, J. 2010. Stuxnet under the microscope. Revision 1.1. ESET LLC. September 2010.

Mattern, F., & Floerkemeier, C. 2010. From the Internet of Computers to the Internet of Things. In: *From Active Data Management to Event-Based Systems and More*. Springer, Berlin/Heidelberg, pp. 242–259.

Mazzucco, M., Dyachuk, D., & Deters, R. 2010. Maximizing cloud providers' revenues via energy aware allocation policies. In: IEEE 3rd International Conference on Cloud Computing (CLOUD), Miami, FL, July 5–10, 2010, pp. 131–138.

McCumber, J. 1991. Information systems security: a comprehensive model. In: Proceedings of the 14th National Computer Security Conference, October 1991.

Meek, A. 2015. Connecting artificial intelligence with the Internet of Things. *The Guardian*. Available at http://www.theguardian.com/technology/2015/jul/24/artificial-intelligence-internet-of-things. Accessed on July 24, 2015.

Melià-Seguí, J., Pous, R., Carreras, A., Morenza-Cinos, M., Parada, R., Liaghat, Z., & De Porrata-Doria, R. 2013. Enhancing the shopping experience through RFID in an actual retail store. In: Proceedings of the 2013 ACM Conference on Pervasive and Ubiquitous Computing Adjunct Publication, New York, September 2013, pp. 1029–1036.

Melone, N.P., McGuire, T.W., Chan, L.W., & Gerwing, T.A. 1995. Effects of DSS, modeling, and exogenous factors on decision quality and confidence. In: IEEE Proceedings of the Twenty-Eighth Hawaii International Conference on System Sciences, Vol. iii, Wailea, HI, January 3–6, 1995, pp. 152–159.

Milner, R. 1980. *A Calculus of Communicating Systems*. Springer-Verlag, Berlin/New York.

Moitra, A., Barnett, B., Crapo, A., & Dill, S.J. 2009. Data provenance architecture to support information assurance in a multi-level secure environment. In: IEEE Military Communications Conference, Boston, MA, October 18–21, 2009, pp. 1–7.

Montenegro, G., Kushalnagar, N., Hui, J., & Culler, D. 2007. Transmission of IPv6 packets over IEEE 802.15. 4 networks. Internet proposed standard, RFC 4944, September 2007.

Morton, M.S.S. 1983. State of the art of research in Management Support Systems. Report no. 107, CISR working paper, Center for Information Systems Research, Sloan School of Management, Massachusetts Institute of Technology, pp. 1473–1483.

Murillo, M.J., & Slipp, J.A. 2009. Demo abstract: application of WINTeR industrial testbed to the analysis of closed-loop control systems in wireless sensor networks. In: IEEE International Conference on Information Processing in Sensor Networks, San Francisco, CA, April 13–16, 2009, pp. 409–410.

Myers, M.D., & Newman, M. 2007. The qualitative interview in IS research: examining the craft. *Information and Organization*, 17(1), pp. 2–26.

Naidu, D.S. 2002. *Optimal Control Systems*. CRC press.

National Information Assurance Partnership (NIAP). 2014. Protection Profile for Mobile Device Fundamentals, Version 2, December 2014.

National Institute of Standards and Technology (NIST). 2015. Draft framework for cyber-physical systems. Available at http://www.cpspwg.org/Portals/3/docs/CPS%20PWG%20Draft%20Framework%20for%20Cyber-Physical%20Systems%20Release%200.8%20September%202015.pdf. Accessed on September 30, 2015.

National Institute of Standards and Technology (NIST). 2015. Big data interoperability framework. Volume 4, Security and Privacy. Available at http://bigdatawg.nist.gov/_uploadfiles/NIST.SP.1500-4.pdf. Accessed on September 30, 2015.

Nedialkov, N.S., Kreinovich, V., & Starks, S.A. 2004. Interval arithmetic, affine arithmetic, taylor series methods: why, what next? *Numerical Algorithms*, 37(1–4), pp. 325–336.

Negiz, A., & Cinar, A. 1992. On the detection of multiple sensor abnormalities in multivariate processes. In: IEEE American Control Conference, Chicago, IL, June 24–26, 1992, pp. 2364–2368.

Nguyen, K.T., Laurent, M., & Oualha, N. 2015. Survey on secure communication protocols for the Internet of Things. *Ad Hoc Networks*, 32, pp. 17–31.

Nicolaou, A.I., & McKnight, D.H. 2006. Perceived information quality in data exchanges: effects on risk, trust, and intention to use. *Information Systems Research*, 17(4), pp. 332–351.

OECD. 2013. OECD privacy guidelines. Available at http://www.oecd.org/internet/ieconomy/privacy-guidelines.htm. Accessed on February 9, 2016.

O'Neill, J. 2015. Smart TV adoption – and connectivity – soars; will 4K stunt its growth? *Ooyala*. Available at http://www.ooyala.com/videomind/blog/smart-tv-adoption-%E2%80%93-and-connectivity-%E2%80%93-soars-will-4k-stunt-its-growth. Accessed on April 15, 2015.

OWSAP. Internet of Things top ten project. The open web application security project. Available at https://www.owasp.org/index.php/OWASP_Internet_of_Things_Top_Ten_Project. Accessed on July 9, 2015.

Ozvural, G., & Kurt, G.K. 2015. Advanced approaches for wireless sensor network applications and cloud analytics. In: IEEE Tenth International Conference on Intelligent Sensors, Sensor Networks and Information Processing (ISSNIP), Singapore, April 7–9, 2015, pp. 1–5.

Padmavathi, G., and Shanmugapriya, M. 2009. A survey of attacks, security mechanisms and challenges in wireless sensor networks. arXiv:0909.0576.

Pagallo, U. 2011. ISPs & Rowdy websites before the law: should we change today's safe harbour clauses? *Philosophy & Technology*, 24(4), pp. 419–436.

Page, V., Dixon, M., & Choudhury, I. 2007. Security risk mitigation for information systems. *BT Technology Journal*, 25(1), pp. 118–127.

Palen, L., & Bødker, S. 2008. Don't get emotional. In: *Affect and Emotion in Human-Computer Interaction*. Springer, Berlin/Heidelberg, pp. 12–22.

Papoulis, A., & Pillai, S.U. 2002. *Probability, Random Variables, and Stochastic Processes*. Tata McGraw-Hill Education.

Parameswaran, S., & Wolf, T. 2008. Embedded systems security – an overview. *Design Automation for Embedded Systems*, 12(3), pp. 173–183.

Park, J.S., & Chandramohan, P. 2004. Component recovery approaches for survivable distributed systems. In: 37th Hawaii International Conference on Systems Sciences (HICSS-37), Big Island, HI, January 5–8, 2004.

Park, J.S., Chandramohan, P., Devarajan, G., & Giordano, J. 2005. Trusted component sharing by runtime test and immunization for survivable distributed systems. In: *Security and Privacy in the Age of Ubiquitous Computing*. Springer, pp. 127–142.

Park, J.S., Chandramohan, P., Suresh, A.T., Giordano, J., & Kwiat, K. 2009. Component survivability at runtime for mission-critical distributed systems. *Journal of Supercomputing*, (2013), 66(3): pp. 1390–1417.

Park, J.S., Kwiat, K.A., Kamhoua, C.A., White, J., & Kim, S. 2014. Trusted Online Social Network (OSN) services with optimal data management. *Computers & Security*, 42, pp. 116–136.

Park, U., & Heidemann, J. 2008. Provenance in sensornet republishing. In: *Provenance and Annotation of Data and Processes*. Springer, Berlin/Heidelberg, pp. 280–292.

Popek, G.J., & Goldberg, R.P. 1974. Formal requirements for virtualizable third generation architectures. *Communications of the ACM*, 17(7), pp. 412–421.

Porambage, P., Kumar, P., Schmitt, C., Gurtov, A., & Ylianttila, M. 2013. Certificate-based pairwise key establishment protocol for wireless sensor networks. In: IEEE 16th International Conference on Computational Science and Engineering (CSE), Sydney, NSW, December 3–5, 2013, pp. 667–674.

Porambage, P., Schmitt, C., Kumar, P., Gurtov, A., & Ylianttila, M. 2014. Two-phase authentication protocol for wireless sensor networks in distributed IoT applications. In: IEEE Wireless Communications and Networking Conference (WCNC), Istanbul, April 6–9, 2014, pp. 2728–2733.

Prasithsangaree, P., & Krishnamurthy, P. 2004. On a framework for energy-efficient security protocols in wireless networks. *Computer Communications*, 27(17), pp. 1716–1729.

Preibusch, S. 2013. Guide to measuring privacy concern: review of survey and observational instruments. *International Journal of Human-Computer Studies*, 71(12), pp. 1133–1143.

Progress Software. 2009. Managing assurance from customer to network to service with complex event processing. *Progress Software*. Available at http://media.techtarget.com/Syndication/ENTERPRISE_APPS/ManagingAssurance_CEP.pdf. Accessed on May 1, 2015.

PUB, F. 1995. Secure hash standard. *Public Law*, 100, p. 235.

Pustejovsky, J., Littman, J., & Saurí, R. 2007. Arguments in TimeML: events and entities. *Lecture Notes in Computer Science*, 4795, p. 107.

PWNIE Express. 2015. The Internet of evil things: the rapidly emerging threat of high risk hardware. Available at http://www.internetofevilthings.com/. Accessed on April 15, 2015.

Qian, Y., Tipper, D., Krishnamurthy, P., & Joshi, J. 2010. *Information Assurance: Dependability and Security in Networked Systems*. Morgan Kaufmann.

Qian, Z., & Wang, Y. 2012. IoT technology and application. *Acta Electronica Sinica*, 40(5), pp. 1023–1028.

Qin, S.J. 2014. Process data analytics in the era of big data. *AIChE Journal*, 60(9), pp. 3092–3100.

Quinlan, J.R. 1987. Simplifying decision trees. *International Journal of Man-Machine Studies*, 27(3), pp. 221–234.

Rabaey, J.M. 2015. The human intranet: where swarms and humans meet. In: Proceedings of the 2015 Design, Automation & Test in Europe Conference & Exhibition, EDA Consortium, Grenoble, March 9–13, 2015, pp. 637–640.

Rahman, M., Carbunar, B., & Banik, M. 2013. Fit and vulnerable: attacks and defenses for a health monitoring device. arXiv:1304.5672.

Ramgovind, S., Eloff, M.M., & Smith, E. 2010. The management of security in cloud computing. In: Information Security for South Africa (ISSA), Sandton, Johannesburg, August 2–4, 2010, pp. 1–7.

Randell, B., Laprie, J.C., Kopetz, H., & Littlewood, B. (Eds.). 2013. *Predictably Dependable Computing Systems*. Springer Science & Business Media.

Rassin, E., & Muris, P. 2005. To be or not to be… indecisive: gender differences, correlations with obsessive–compulsive complaints, and behavioural manifestation. *Personality and Individual Differences*, 38(5), pp. 1175–1181.

Rassin, E., Muris, P., Franken, I., Smit, M., & Wong, M. 2007. Measuring general indecisiveness. *Journal of Psychopathology and Behavioral Assessment*, 29(1), pp. 60–67.

Raza, S., Slabbert, A., Voigt, T., & Landernas, K. 2009. Security considerations for the wireless HART protocol. In: IEEE Conference on Emerging Technologies & Factory Automation, Mallorca, September 22–25, 2009, pp. 1–8.

Razavi, B., & Wooley, B.A. 1992. Design techniques for high-speed, high-resolution comparators. *IEEE Journal of Solid-State Circuits* 27(12), pp. 1916–1926.

Reddy, A.S. 2014. Reaping the benefits of the Internet of Things. Cognizant Reports, May 2014.

Reinartz, C., Metzger, A., & Pohl, K. 2015. Model-based verification of event-driven business processes. In: Proceedings of the 9th ACM International Conference on Distributed Event-Based Systems, New York, June 2015, pp. 1–9.

Rescorla, E., & Modadugu, N. 2012. Datagram transport layer security, version 1.2.

Rimal, B.P., Jukan, A., Katsaros, D., & Goeleven, Y. 2011. Architectural requirements for cloud computing systems: an enterprise cloud approach. *Journal of Grid Computing*, 9(1), pp. 3–26.

Roman, R., Najera, P., & Lopez, J. 2011. Securing the Internet of Things. *Computer*, 44(9), pp. 51–58.

Roman, R., Zhou, J., & Lopez, J. 2013. On the features and challenges of security and privacy in distributed internet of things. *Computer Networks*, 57(10), pp. 2266–2279.

Rosa, L., Alves, P., Cruz, T., Simões, P., & Monteiro, E. 2015. A comparative study of correlation engines for security event management. In: ICCWS 2015 – The Proceedings of the 10th International Conference on Cyber Warfare and Security, Academic Conferences Limited, February 2015, p. 277.

Rouse, J. 2012. Mobile devices – the most hostile environment for security? *Network Security*, 2012(3), pp. 11–13.

Rubel, P., Ihde, M., Harp, S., & Payne, C. 2005. Generating policies for defense in depth. In: IEEE 21st Annual Computer Security Applications Conference, Tucson, AZ, December 5–9, 2005, 10p.

Rubin, H., & Rubin, I.S. (2005). *Qualitative Interviewing: The Art of Hearing Data*. Sage, Thousand Oaks, CA.

Ruj, S., & Pal, A. 2014. Analyzing cascading failures in smart grids under random and targeted attacks. In: IEEE 28th International Conference on Advanced Information Networking and Applications (AINA), Victoria, BC, May 13–16, 2014, pp. 226–233.

Russell, D., & Gangemi, G.T. 1991. *Computer Security Basics*. O'Reilly Media, Inc.

Sabahi, F., & Movaghar, A. 2008. Intrusion detection: a survey. In: IEEE 3rd International Conference on Systems and Networks Communications, Sliema, October 26–31, 2008, pp. 23–26.

Saied, Y.B., Olivereau, A., Zeghlache, D., & Laurent, M. 2014. Lightweight collaborative key establishment scheme for the Internet of Things. *Computer Networks*, 64, pp. 273–295.

Sanchez, L., Muñoz, L., Galache, J.A., Sotres, P., Santana, J.R., Gutierrez, V., Ramdhany, R., Gluhak, A., Krco, S., Theodoridis, E., & Pfisterer, D. 2014. SmartSantander: IoT experimentation over a smart city testbed. *Computer Networks*, 61, pp. 217–238.

Sanders, A.D. 2003. Teaching tip: utilizing simple hacking techniques to teach system security and hacker identification. *Journal of Information Systems Education*, 14(1), p. 5.

Sandhu, R.S., Coyne, E.J., Feinstein, H.L., & Youman, C.E. 1996. Role-based access control models. *IEEE Computer*, 29(2), pp. 38–47.

Santamarta, R. 2012. Project basecamp-attacking control logix. In: Report for 5th SCADA Security Scientific Symposium, Miami Beach, Florida, January 2012.

Schneier, B. 2014. The Internet of things is wildly insecure—and often unpatchable. *Schneier on Security*, 6. Available at http://www.wired.com/2014/01/theres-no-good-way-to-patch-the-internet-of-things-and-thats-a-huge-problem/.

Schneier, B. 2015. VW scandal could just be the beginning. *Schneier on Security*. Available at https://www.schneier.com/essays/archives/2015/09/vw_scandal_could_jus.html. Accessed on September 7, 2015.

Schoenfield, B.S. 2015. *Securing Systems: Applied Security Architecture and Threat Models*. CRC Press.

Schou, C.D., Frost, J., & Maconachy, W. 2004. Information assurance in biomedical informatics systems. *IEEE Engineering in Medicine and Biology Magazine*, 23(1), pp. 110–118.

Schumer, C. 2014. After push by Schumer, fitbit announces new privacy policies aimed at protecting personal health data. *High Beam Research*. Available at https://www.highbeam.com/doc/1G1-379551602.html. Accessed on August 10, 2014.

Schwartz, P.M. 2013. The EU-U.S. Privacy Collision: A Turn to Institutions and Procedures, 126 Harvard Law Review, 1966, pp. 1969–79.

Scott, D.S. 1982. Domains for denotational semantics. In: *Automata, Languages and Programming*. Springer, Berlin/Heidelberg, pp. 577–610.

Seba, V., Modlic, B., & Sisul, G. 2013. System model with adaptive modulation and frequency hopping in wireless networks. In: IEEE Global Information Infrastructure Symposium, Trento, October 28–31, 2013, pp. 1–3.

Shaikh, R.A., Jameel, H., d'Auriol, B.J., Lee, H., Lee, S., & Song, Y.J. 2009. Group-based trust management scheme for clustered wireless sensor networks. *IEEE Transactions on Parallel and Distributed Systems*, 20(11), pp. 1698–1712.

Shelby, Z., Hartke, K., & Bormann, C. 2014. The constrained application protocol (CoAP).

Sicari, S., Rizzardi, A., Grieco, L.A., & Coen-Porisini, A. 2015. Security, privacy and trust in Internet of Things: the road ahead. *Computer Networks*, 76, pp. 146–164.

Snediker, D.E., Murray, A.T., & Matisziw, T.C. 2008. Decision support for network disruption mitigation. *Decision Support Systems*, 44(4), pp. 954–969.

Srinivasan, A., Li, F., & Wu, J. 2008. A novel CDS-based reputation monitoring system for wireless sensor networks. In: IEEE 28th International Conference on Distributed Computing Systems Workshops, Beijing, June 17–20, 2008, pp. 364–369.

Stallings, W. 2000. *Data and Computer Communications*, 7th edition. Prentice Hall, New Jersey.

Standards for Efficient Cryptography – SEC 4. Elliptic Curve Qu-Vanstone Implicit Certificate Scheme (ECQV), Version 0.97, March 9, 2011, Certicom Research, 32 pages.

Staw, B.M., Sandelands, L.E., & Dutton, J.E. 1981. Threat rigidity effects in organizational behavior: a multilevel analysis. *Administrative Science Quarterly*, 26(4), pp. 501–524.

Steinberg, R.A., Rudd, C., Lacy, S., & Hanna, A. 2011. *ITIL Service Operation*. TSO Publications.

Strobel, D., Oswald, D., Richter, B., Schellenberg, F., & Paar, C. 2014. Microcontrollers as (in) security devices for pervasive computing applications. *Proceedings of the IEEE*, 102(8), pp. 1157–1173.

Subashini, S., & Kavitha, V. 2011. A survey on security issues in service delivery models of cloud computing. *Journal of Network and Computer Applications*, 34(1), pp. 1–11.

Suh, B., & Han, I. 2003. The IS risk analysis based on a business model. *Information & Management*, 41(2), pp. 149–158.

Sultana, S., & Bertino, E. 2013. A file provenance system. In: Proceedings of the Third ACM Conference on Data and Application Security and Privacy, New York, February 2013, pp. 153–156.

Sun, B., Xiao, Y., Li, C.C., Chen, H.H., & Yang, T.A. 2008. Security co-existence of wireless sensor networks and RFID for pervasive computing. *Computer Communications*, 31(18), pp. 4294–4303.

Sun, Y., Han, Z., & Liu, K.R. 2008. Defense of trust management vulnerabilities in distributed networks. *IEEE Communications Magazine*, 46(2), pp. 112–119.

Sztipanovits, J., Koutsoukos, X., Karsai, G., Kottenstette, N., Antsaklis, P., Gupta, V., Goodwine, B., Baras, J., & Wang, S. 2012. Toward a science of cyber–physical system integration. *Proceedings of the IEEE*, 100(1), pp. 29–44.

Takacs, J., Pollock, C.L., Guenther, J.R., Bahar, M., Napier, C., & Hunt, M.A. 2014. Validation of the Fitbit One activity monitor device during treadmill walking. *Journal of Science and Medicine in Sport*, 17(5), pp. 496–500.

Tas, B., & Tosun, A.Ş. 2011. Mobile assisted key distribution in wireless sensor networks. In: IEEE International Conference on Communications (ICC), Kyoto, June 5–9, 2011, pp. 1–6.

Teixeira, A., Pérez, D., Sandberg, H., & Johansson, K.H. 2012. Attack models and scenarios for networked control systems. In: Proceedings of the 1st international conference on High Confidence Networked Systems, New York, April 2012, pp. 55–64.

Thierer, A.D. 2015. The internet of things and wearable technology: addressing privacy and security concerns without derailing innovation. *Richmond Journal of Law and Technology*, 21(2), p. 118.

Thomas, D. 2002. *Hacker Culture*. University of Minnesota Press.

Thompson, R.S., Rantanen, E.M., & Yurcik, W. 2006. Network intrusion detection cognitive task analysis: textual and visual tool usage and recommendations. *Proceedings of the Human Factors and Ergonomics Society Annual Meeting*, 50(5), pp. 669–673.

Tiwari, A. 2015. Attacking a feedback controller. *Electronic Notes in Theoretical Computer Science*, 317, pp. 141–153.

Torrieri, D. 2015. *Principles of Spread-Spectrum Communication Systems*. Springer.

Tractinsky, N., & Meyer, J. 1999. Chartjunk or goldgraph? Effects of presentation objectives and content desirability on information presentation. *MIS Quarterly*, 23(3), pp. 397–420.

Tripwire. 2014, SOHO wireless router (In) security. Tripwire VERT Research. Available at http://www.tripwire.com/register/soho-wireless-router-insecurity/showMeta/2/. Accessed on February 25, 2014.

Tschofenig, H., & Fossati, T. 2015. TLS/DTLS Profiles for the Internet of Things. Internet-Draft draft-ietf-dice-profile-17.txt, IETF Secretariat, October 2015, pg. 1–59. Available at https://tools.ietf.org/html/draft-ietf-dice-profile-17.

Tseng, Y.W., Liao, C.Y., & Hung, T.H. 2015. An embedded system with realtime surveillance application. In: IEEE International Symposium on Next-Generation Electronics (ISNE), Taipei, May 4–6, 2015, pp. 1–4.

Tsiros, M., & Mittal, V. 2000. Regret: a model of its antecedents and consequences in consumer decision making. *Journal of Consumer Research*, 26(4), pp. 401–417.

Tufekci, Z. 2015. Volkswagen and the era of cheating software. *New York Times*, p. A35.

Tung, R., Zimetbaum, P., & Josephson, M.E. 2008. A critical appraisal of implantable cardioverter-defibrillator therapy for the prevention of sudden cardiac death. *Journal of the American College of Cardiology*, 52(14), pp. 1111–1121.

U.S. Government Publishing Office (GPO). 2015. Federal Register, vol. 80, no. 150.

Ukil, A., Sen, J., & Koilakonda, S. 2011. Embedded security for Internet of Things. In: IEEE 2nd National Conference on Emerging Trends and Applications in Computer Science (NCETACS), Shillong, March 4–5, 2011, pp. 1–6.

Underwood, M., Gruninger, M., & Obrst, L. 2015. Internet of things: toward smart networked systems and societies. The Ontology Summit 2015 Communiqué. *Applied Ontology*, 10(3), p. 4.

Unger, S., & Timmermann, D. 2015. DPWSec: devices profile for web services security. In: IEEE Tenth International Conference on Intelligent Sensors, Sensor Networks and Information Processing (ISSNIP), Singapore, April 7–9, 2015, pp. 1–6.

Vacca, J.R. 2012. *Computer and Information Security Handbook*. Newnes.

Van der Aalst, W.M. 1998. The application of Petri nets to workflow management. *Journal of Circuits, Systems, and Computers*, 8(01), pp. 21–66.

Veltri, L., Cirani, S., Busanelli, S., & Ferrari, G. 2013. A novel batch-based group key management protocol applied to the Internet of Things. *Ad Hoc Networks*, 11(8), pp. 2724–2737.

Veltri, L., Cirani, S., Ferrari, G., & Busanelli, S. 2013. Batch-based group key management with shared key derivation in the internet of things. In: IEEE 9th International Conference on Wireless Communications and Mobile Computing(IWCMC), Sardinia, July 1–5, 2013, pp. 1688–1693.

Vermesan, O., Friess, P., Guillemin, P., Gusmeroli, S., Sundmaeker, H., Bassi, A., Jubert, I.S., Mazura, M., Harrison, M., Eisenhauer, M., & Doody, P. 2011. Internet of things strategic research roadmap. Internet of Things-Global Technological and Societal Trends, pp. 9–52.

Vianello, V., Gulisano, V., Jimenez-Peris, R., Patiño-Martínez, M., Torres, R., Diaz, R., & Prieto, E. 2013. A Scalable SIEM correlation engine and its application to the olympic games IT infrastructure. In: Eighth International Conference on Availability, Reliability and Security (ARES), Regensburg, September 2–6, 2013, pp. 625–629.

Walls, J.G., Widmeyer, G.R., & El Sawy, O.A. 1992. Building an information system design theory for vigilant EIS. *Information Systems Research*, 3(1), pp. 36–59.

Wang, J., Floerkemeier, C., & Sarma, S.E. 2014. Session-based security enhancement of RFID systems for emerging open-loop applications. *Personal and Ubiquitous Computing*, 18(8), pp. 1881–1891.

Wang, L., & Ranjan, R. 2015. Processing distributed internet of things data in clouds. *IEEE Cloud Computing*, (1), pp. 76–80.

Wang, L.M., Jiang, T., & Zhu, X.Y. 2011. Updatable key management scheme with intrusion tolerance for unattended wireless sensor network. In: Global Telecommunications Conference (GLOBECOM 2011), Houston, TX, December 5–9, 2011, pp. 1–5.

Weber, R.H. 2010. Internet of Things – new security and privacy challenges. *Computer Law & Security Review*, 26(1), pp. 23–30.

Weber, R.H., & Weber, R. 2010. *Internet of Things: Legal Perspectives*, vol. 49. Springer Science & Business Media.

Webster, J., & Trevino, L.K. 1995. Rational and social theories as complementary explanations of communication media choices: two policy-capturing studies. *Academy of Management Journal*, 38(6), pp. 1544–1572.

Wortman, C.B. 1975. Some determinants of perceived control. *Journal of Personality and Social Psychology*, 31(2), p. 282.

Wu, C.H.J., & Irwin, J.D. 2013. *Introduction to Computer Networks and Cybersecurity*. CRC Press.

Wu, H. 2011. The hash function JH. Submission to NIST (Round 3), p. 6.

Xia, F., Yang, L.T., Wang, L., & Vinel, A. 2012. Internet of things. *International Journal of Communication Systems*, 25(9), p. 1101.

Xia, H.H. 1996. An analytical model for predicting path loss in urban and suburban environments. In: Seventh IEEE International Symposium on Personal, Indoor and Mobile Radio Communications, Taipei, October 15–18, 1996, vol. 1, pp. 19–23.

Xiang, W., Zexi, Z., Ying, L., & Yi, Z. 2013. A design of security module to protect program execution in embedded system. In: Green Computing and Communications (Green-Com), 2013 IEEE and Internet of Things (iThings/CPSCom), IEEE International Conference on and IEEE Cyber, Physical and Social Computing, Beijing, August 20–23, 2013, pp. 1750–1755.

Xiao, Y., Shen, X., Sun, B.O., & Cai, L. 2006. Security and privacy in RFID and applications in telemedicine. *IEEE Communications Magazine*, 44(4), pp. 64–72.

Yahav, I., Karaesmen, I., & Raschid, L. 2013. Managing on-demand computing services with heterogeneous customers. In: Proceedings of the 2013 Winter Simulation Conference: Simulation: Making Decisions in a Complex World, Washington, DC, December 8–11, 2013, pp. 5–16.

Yan, L., Zhang, Y., Yang, L.T., & Ning, H. (Eds.). 2008. *The Internet of Things: From RFID to the Next-Generation Pervasive Networked Systems*. CRC Press.

Yan, Y., Qian, Y., Sharif, H., & Tipper, D. 2013. A survey on smart grid communication infrastructures: motivations, requirements and challenges. *IEEE Communications Surveys & Tutorials*, 15(1), pp. 5–20.

Yan, Z., Zhang, P., & Vasilakos, A.V. 2014. A survey on trust management for Internet of Things. *Journal of Network and Computer Applications*, 42, pp. 120–134.

Yang, J.C., Hao, P.A.N.G., & Zhang, X. 2013. Enhanced mutual authentication model of IoT. *Journal of China Universities of Posts and Telecommunications*, 20, pp. 69–74.

Yang, W.Z., & Tan, Y.A. 2006. Buffer overflow attacks defending using a segment-based approach. In: IEEE International Conference on Computational Intelligence and Security, Guangzhou, November 3–6, 2006, pp. 1559–1562.

Yang, Y., Zhou, J., Wang, F., & Shi, C. 2014. An LPI design for secure burst communication systems. In: IEEE China Summit & International Conference on Signal and Information Processing (ChinaSIP), Xi'an, July 9–13, 2014, pp. 631–635.

Yao, Z., Kim, D., & Doh, Y. 2006. PLUS: parameterized and localized trust management scheme for sensor networks security. In: IEEE International Conference on Mobile Ad Hoc and Sensor Systems (MASS), Vancouver, BC, October 2006, pp. 437–446.

Yavagal, D.S., Lee, S.W., Ahn, G.J., & Gandhi, R.A. 2005. Common criteria requirements modeling and its uses for quality of information assurance (QoIA). In: Proceedings of the 43rd Annual Southeast Regional Conference, Vol. 2, New York, March 2005, pp. 130–135.

Yeh, M., Jin Jo, Y., Donovan, C., & Gabree, S. 2013. Human Factors Considerations in the Design and Evaluation of Flight Deck Displays and Controls. Department of Transportation in the Interest of Information Exchange, Washington.

Yoo, Y., & Alavi, M. 2001. Media and group cohesion: relative influences on social presence, task participation, and group consensus. *MIS Quarterly*, 25(3), pp. 371–390.

Yuan, Y., Wang, C., Wang, C., Zhang, B., Zhu, S., & Zhu, N. 2015. A novel algorithm for embedding dynamic virtual network request. In: IEEE 2nd International Conference on Information Science and Control Engineering (ICISCE), Shanghai, April 24–26, 2015, pp. 28–32.

Yun, M., & Yuxin, B. 2010. Research on the architecture and key technology of Internet of Things (IoT) applied on smart grid. In: International Conference on Advances in Energy Engineering (ICAEE), Beijing, June 19–20, 2010, pp. 69–72.

Zacks, J.M., & Swallow, K.M. 2007. Event segmentation. *Current Directions in Psychological Science*, 16(2), pp. 80–84.

Zawoad, S., & Hasan, R. 2015. FAIoT: towards building a forensics aware eco system for the Internet of Things. In: IEEE International Conference on Services Computing (SCC), New York, June 27–July 2, 2015, pp. 279–284.

Zhai, X., Appiah, K., Ehsan, S., Howells, G., Hu, H., Gu, D., & McDonald-Maier, K.D. 2015. A method for detecting abnormal program behavior on embedded devices. *IEEE Transactions on Information Forensics and Security*, 10(8), pp. 1692–1704.

Zhang, L., & Mitton, N. 2011. Advanced Internet of Things. In: IEEE Internet of things (iThings/CPSCom), 2011 International Conference on and 4th International Conference on Cyber, Physical and Social Computing, Dalian, October 19–22, 2011, pp. 1–8.

Zhao, J., Goble, C., Stevens, R., & Turi, D. 2008. Mining Taverna's semantic web of provenance. *Concurrency and Computation: Practice and Experience*, 20(5), pp. 463–472.

Zhou, H. 2012. *The Internet of Things in the Cloud: A Middleware Perspective*. CRC press.

Zhou, L., & Chao, H.C. 2011. Multimedia traffic security architecture for the internet of things. *IEEE Network*, 25(3), pp. 35–40.

Zhou, W., & Piramuthu, S. 2014. Security/privacy of wearable fitness tracking IoT devices. In: IEEE 9th Iberian Conference on Information Systems and Technologies (CISTI), Barcelona, June 18–21, 2014, pp. 1–5.

Zhou, W., Fei, Q., Narayan, A., Haeberlen, A., Loo, B.T., & Sherr, M. 2011. Secure network provenance. In: Proceedings of the Twenty-Third ACM Symposium on Operating Systems Principles, October 2011, pp. 295–310.

Zhu, C., Nicanfar, H., Leung, V., & Yang, L.T. 2015. An authenticated trust and reputation calculation and management system for cloud and sensor networks integration. *IEEE Transactions on Information Forensics and Security*, 10(1), pp. 118–131.

Zia, T.A. 2008. Reputation-based trust management in wireless sensor networks. In: International Conference on Intelligent Sensors, Sensor Networks and Information Processing, Sydney, NSW, December 15–18, 2008, pp. 163–166.

Zimmerman, R., & Horan, T.A. 2004. *Digital Infrastructures: Enabling Civil and Environmental Systems through Information Technology*. Psychology Press.

Zimmerman, R., & Restrepo, C.E. 2009. Information Technology (IT) and Critical Infrastructure Interdependencies for Emergency Response. In Proceedings of the 3rd ISCRAM Conference (B. Van de Walle and M. Turoff, eds.), Newark, NJ (USA), May 2006, pp. 382–386.

Zuo, Y. 2010. RFID survivability quantification and attack modeling. In: Proceedings of the Third ACM Conference on Wireless Network Security, March 2010, pp. 13–18.

INDEX

Cyber-Assurance for the Internet of Things, First Edition. Edited by Tyson T. Brooks.
© 2017 by The Institute of Electrical and Electronic Engineers, Inc. Published 2017 by John Wiley & Sons, Inc.